ROAD ATLAS JAPAN

1:250,000

HOKKAIDŌ ONLY 1:600,000

LEGEND

National Expressway

- Toll gate
- Parking area
- Service area
- Takahara 高原 — Interchange
- 20 — Distance between pins
- Kurino 栗野 — Interchange

National Highway

- Traffic information board
- 4 — National highway No.
- Pin
- 25 — Distance between pins
- Pin

Main Road

- Pin
- 25 — Distance between pins
- Pin

Toll Road

- Toll gate
- Yamada — Interchange name
- 25 — Distance between pins
- Ōmiya — Interchange name

- General road
- Ferry route
- Other major sea route
- Railway(J.R.)
- Private railway
- Prefectual boundary
- City and county boundary
- Town and Village boundary
- Kintaichi-baba金田一馬場 — Intersection name
- Closed in winter — Road information
- ORD 500 / LAR 1500 — Toll road fee { ORD···Ordinary-size vehicles / LAR···Large-size vehicles
- from Sapporo-shi: Obihiro 240Km, Hakodate 250Km — Distance from major city

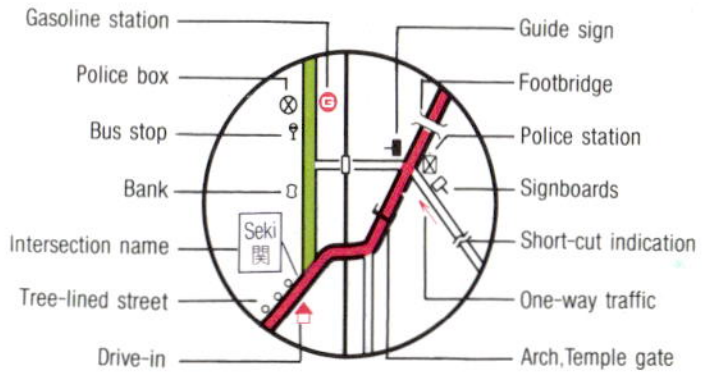

- Airport
- Port
- Factory
- Dam
- Cherry blossom viewing spot
- Plum blossom viewing spot
- Beautiful autumn scenery
- Golf course
- Skiing ground
- Swimming place
- Shrine
- Temple
- Hot springs
- Scenery viewing spot
- Place of interest

SCALE 1:600,000

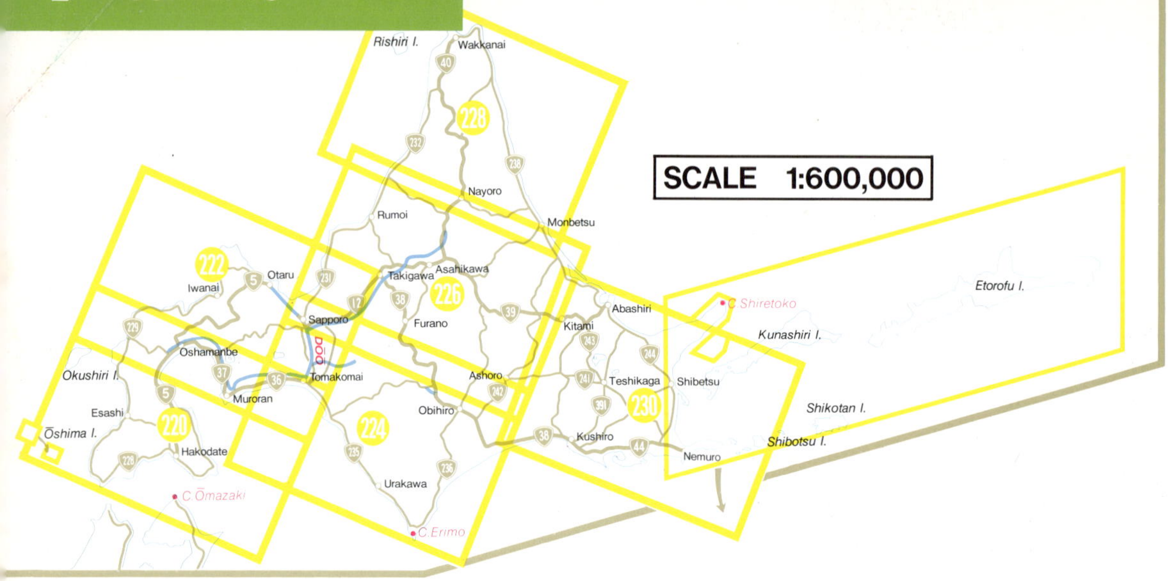

CONTENTS

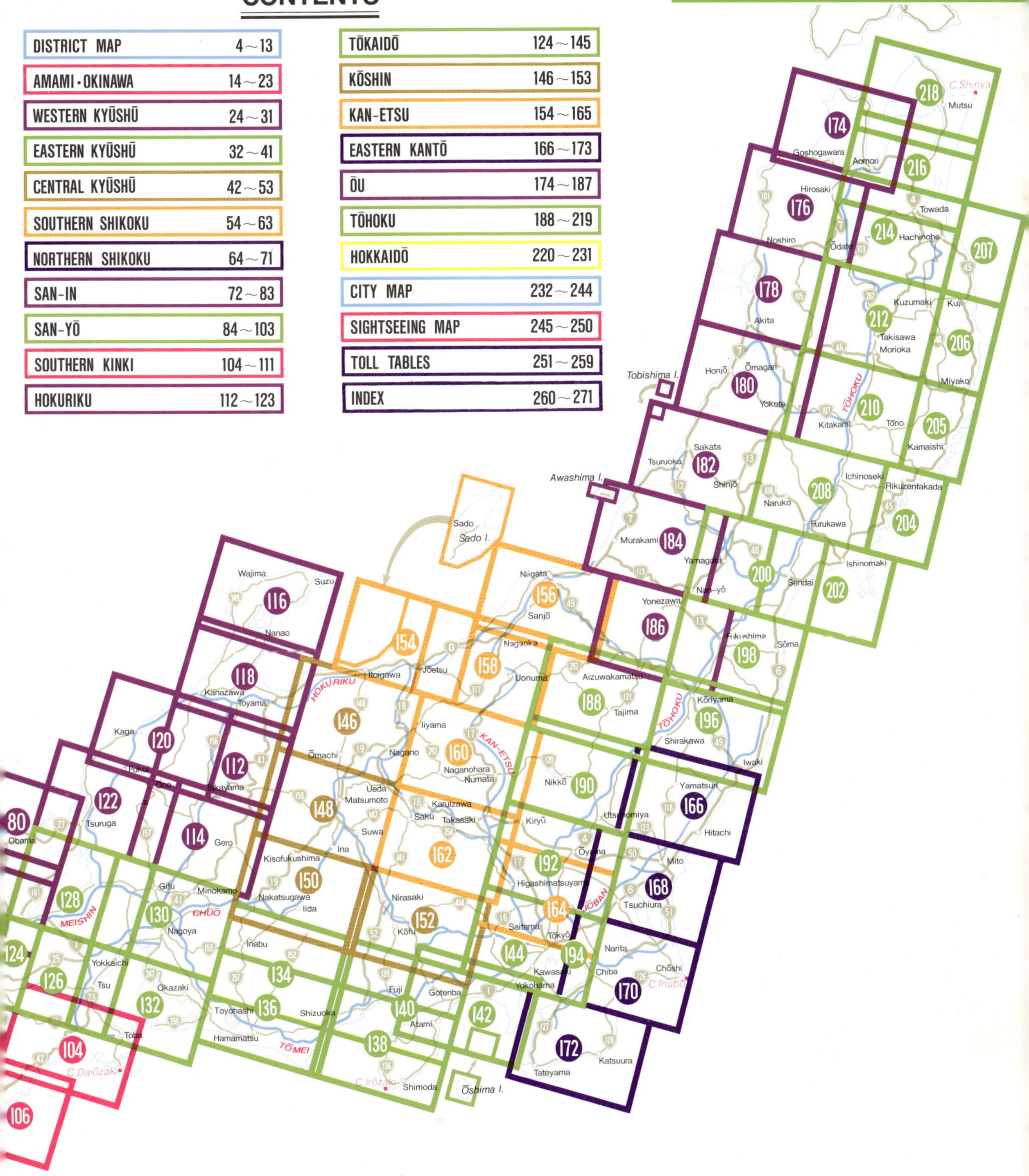

SCALE 1:250,000

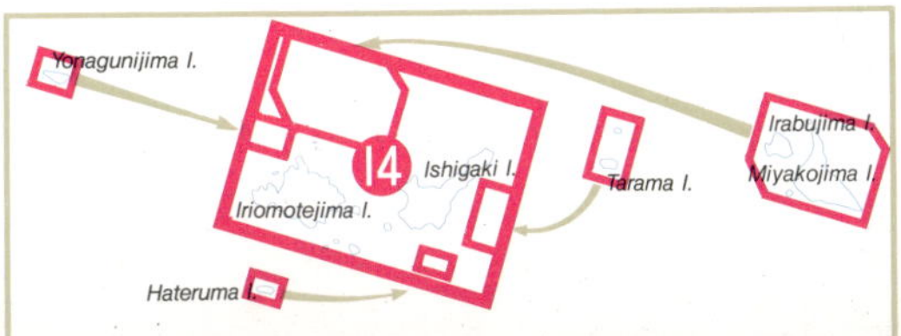

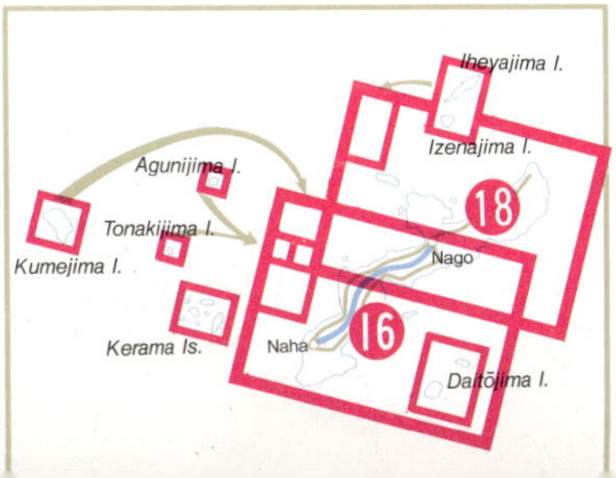

CHŪGOKU EXPRESSWAY
Kawatana
Ogori
Tokuyama-nis
HŌFU
YAMAGU
Shimonoseki
SHIMONOSEKI
Moji
ONODA
UBE
KITAKYŪSHŪ
Genkai-nada
Suō-nada
MUNAKATA
Kokura-minami
NOGATA
YUKUHASHI
Himejima I.
Iki I.
IKI
Tsushima-kaikyō
Yahata
FUKUOKA
IIZUKA
AGAWA
NAKATSU
Kunisaki Pen.
Hakata-wan
FUKUOKA
Fukuoka
Dazaifu
Yobuko
BUNGOTAKADA
KARATSU
Chikuhi Line
Nippō Line
USA
Yabakei
Usa-jingū
KITSUKI
Nijinomatsubara
Mt.Hikosan
Higashimatsuura Pen.
Mt.Sefuriyama
AMAGI
ŌITA
HIRADO
SAGA
Higashisefuri
Hayami
Saga-Yamato
Tosu Jct
Hita
ŌITA EXPRESS WAY
Beppu
Ukujima I.
Hiradoshima I.
Kitamatsuura Pen.
IMARI
KURUME
Kurume
Kusu
Yufuin
BEPPU
Takeo-Kitagata
SAGA
YAME
HITA
Amagase
SASEBO
Sasebo Line
Takeo
Hōsenji
Yufuin
YANAGAWA
Tsuetate
Handa-kogen
Kyūdai Line
ŌITA
KASHIMA
Mt.Kujūsan
Ureshino
Nankan
Kujū-kogen
Gotōrettō Is.
NAGASAKI
ŌMUTA
KYŪSHŪ EXPRESSWAY
Kikuchi
Aso
Ōmura-wan
Ariake-kai
Yamaga
KIKUCHI
Nakadōrishima I.
Nishisonogi Pen.
Ōmura
Ueki
TAKETA
Mt.Asosan
Hōhi Line
ISAHAYA
Kusasenri
Sobokatamuki
SHIMABARA
KUMAMOTO
Kumamoto
Mt.Sobosan
Nagasaki-Tarami
Mt.Unzendake
Obama
Unzen
Shimabara-wan
KUMAMOTO
Takachiho
NAGASAKI
Nagasaki
FUKUE
Tachibana wan
Shimabara Pen.
Fukuejima I.
Nagasaki Pen
UTO
Uto Pen.
Matsubase
NOBEOKA
Takachiho Line
C. Nomozaki
Hayasaki-seto
Mt.Kunimidake
YATSUSHIRO
Yatsushiro
HONDO
Kamijima I.
HYŪGA
Shimoda
Myōken-ura
Hinagu
Shimojima I.
Yatsushiro-kai
Mt.Ichifusayama
Amakusashotō Is.
Yunoura
MIYAZAKI
Amakusa-nada
MINAMATA
Hitoyoshi
USHIBUKA
HITOYOSHI
Nagashima I.
Nippō Line
SAITO
Saito
EBINO
Ebino
AKUNE
ŌKUCHI
Kurino
Kobayashi
Takabaru
Mt.Kirishimayama
MIYAZAKI
Kami-Koshikijima I.
Kyūshū Shinkansen
Miyazaki-nishi
Koshikijimarettō Is.
SATSUMASENDAI
Anraku
MIYAZAKI EXPRESSWAY
Miyazaki
Aoshima I.
Hinatayama
Kajiki
KYŪSHŪ EXPRESSWAY
KOKUBU
Miyakonojō
Shimo-Koshikijima I.
MIYAKONOJŌ
Nichinan-kaigan
Kagoshima
Sakurajima
NICHINAN
KAGOSHIMA
KAGOSHIMA
TARUMIZU
KUSHIMA
C. Nomamisaki
KASEDA
Ibusuki Makurazaki Line
Kagoshima-wan
KANOYA
Shibushi-wan
C. Toimisaki
Satsuma Pen.
Ōsumi Pen
IBUSUKI
MAKURAZAKI
Ibusuki
EAST CHINA SEA
Mt.Kaimondake
C. Satamisaki
Ōsumi-kaikyō
Kuroshima I.
Iōjima I.
NISHINOOMOTE
Ōsumishotō Is.
Tanegashima I.
Kuchino-Erabujima I.
Tanegashima-kaikyō
Mt.Miyanouradake
Yakushima I.
Tokara-kaikyō
1 : 1,800,000
0
25
50km

TOKUSHIMA
KŌCHI
EHIME
KAGOSHIMA
OKINAWA
PACIFIC OCEAN
EAST CHINA SEA
PACIFIC OCEAN
IMABARI
SHIKOKU-CHŪŌ
NIIHAMA
SAIJŌ
MATSUYAMA
IYO
ŌZU
YAWATAHAMA
SEIYO
UWAJIMA
SUKUMO
TOSASHIMIZU
SUSAKI
TOSA
KŌCHI
NANKOKU
AKI
MUROTO
ANAN
KOMATSUSHIMA
SHŪNAN
YANAI
SAIKI
SUKUMI
Matsuyama Expressway
Yosan Line
Dosan Line
Yodo Line
Tokushima Line
Mugi Line
Gantoku Line
Seto-naikai
Hiuchi-nada
Iyo-nada
Bungo-suidō
Kii-suidō
Tosa-wan
Sukumo-wan
Hyūga-nada
Yashirojima I.
Hōyoshotō Is.
Sadamisaki Pen.
C. Sadamisaki
C. Sekizaki
C. Tsurumisaki
C. Okitsuzaki
C. Ashizurimisaki
C. Murotomisaki
C. Kamodamisaki
Mt.Ishizuchisan
Mt.Dōgomori
Mt.Turugisan
Dōgo
Nibukawa
Omogōkei
Ōnogahara
Koboke
Iyadani
Ōboke
Ryūgadō
Katsurahama
Irinomatsubara
Nippō-kaigan
Fūren Cave
Onohara
Mishima-Kawanoe
Doi
Iyo-Saijō
Kawauchi
Ōtoyo
Kōchi
Ino
Ōzu
Susaki-higashi
Ōshima I.
NAZE
Kakeromajima I.
Tokunoshima I.
Amamishotō Is.
Okino-Erabujima I.
Iheyajima
Yoron I.
Ieshima I.
Motobu Pen.
NAGO
Manza Beach
Okinawashotō Is.
Okinawa I.
OKINAWA
Kumejima I.
Tokashikijima I.
NAHA
Heiwa Kinen Park
Keramarettō Is.
Irabujima I.
Miyakojima I.
HIRARA
Taramashima I.
Miyakorettō Is.
Ishigakijima I.
ISHIGAKI
Taketomijima I.
Iriomotejima I.
Haterumajima I.

Dōgo I.
Okishotō Is.
Nishinoshima I.
Nakanoshima I.
Chibūrijima I.
Kukedo
Mihonokitaura
C. Jizōzaki
Shimane Pen.
MATSUE
Miho-wan
Shinjiko Lake
Nakanoumi
Kaike
C. Hinomisaki
Izumo-taisha
IZUMO
Tamatsukuri
YONAGO
Yonago
KURAYOSHI
Mizonokuchi
Misasa
Mt.Daisen
Sekigane
Mitoya-Kisuki
San-in Line
Kisuki Line
Hakubi Line
Hiruzen-kōgen
ŌDA
SHIMANE
Mt.Sanbesan
Sanbe
OKAYAMA
Yubara
Okutsu
Yunotsu
Mt.Dōgosan
Innoshō
GŌTSU
Geibi Line
Niimi
NIIMI
Ochiai
Tatamigaura
Arifuku
HAMADA
Hamada
Dangyokei
Sanko Line
MIYOSHI
SHŌBARA
Tōjō
Taishakukyō
Asahi
Shōbara
TAKAHASHI
Kayō
Mizuho
Iwayadani
Miyoshi
Okayama
Tsuyama Line
C. Kōyamamisaki
Fukuen Line
Chiyoda
SŌJA
Kurashiki
OKAYAMA
MASUDA
HIROSHIMA
FUCHŪ
IBARA
Hayashima
Sandankyō
Kasaoka
KURASHIKI
Togouchi
Fukuyama-Higashi
Itsukaichi
SANYO EXPRESSWAY
TAMANO
C. Kawajirimisaki
Tsuwano
Hiroshima
Shiwa
Saijō
Kōchi
FUKUYAMA
Mt.Washūzan
HAGI
Ōmijima I.
CHŪGOKU EXPRESSWAY
Tomonoura
NAGATO
Nagato-Yumoto
Hatsukaichi
MIHARA
ONOMICHI
Yashima
Ōmonkyō
HIROSHIMA
Innoshima I.
Muikaichi
KURE
Kure Line
SAKAIDE
Tawarayama
YAMAGUCHI
Miyajima I.
MARUGAME
Akiyoshidō
Mine Line
ŌTAKE
Seto-naikai
Zentsūji
Hibiki-nada
YAMAGUCHI
Kano
Ōmishima I.
TAKAMATSU EXPRESSWAY
Kotohira
Kawatana
MINE
Mine
Yamaguchi
IWAKUNI
Geiyoshotō Is.
Ōshima I.
Ogōri
SHUNAN
Kurahashijima I.
Hiuchi-nada
Onohara
Sanyō Shinkansen
Sanyō Line
Hiroshima-wan
IMABARI
SHIKOKU -CHŪŌ
Shimonoseki
SHIMONOSEKI
HŌFU
YANAI
Tokuyama-nishi
Tokuyama-higashi
Kumage
Ganto Line
NIIHAMA
ONODA
UBE
Nibukawa
SAIJŌ
Mishima-Kawanoe
Moji
KITAKYUSHU
Yashirojima I.
Hōyoshotō Is.
MATSUYAMA EXPRESSWAY
Doi
Iyadani
Dōgo
Shingū
MATSUYAMA
Iyo-Saijō
Kokura-minami
Suō-nada
Kawauchi
Mt.Ishizuchisan
NOGATA
YUKUHASHI
Himejima I.
IYO
Iyo
Ōtoyo
Yahata
Omōgokei
FUKUOKA
TAGAWA
KŌCHI
IIZUKA
NAKATSU
Nippō Line
Kunisaki Pen.
EHIME
Kōchi
Ryūgadō
Hitahikosan Line
BUNGOTAKADA
Iyo-nada
Yosan Line
Ino
NANKOKU
Yabakei
USA
Usa-jingū
Ōzu
ŌZU
Ōnogahara
KŌCHI
AMAGI
Asakura
Mt.Hikosan
Hayami
Dosan Line
Katsurahama
AKI
KITSUKI
YAWATAHAMA
TOSA
Hita
ŌITA EXPRESSWAY
Kusu
Sadamisaki Pen.
SEIYO
Susaki-higashi
SUSAKI
HITA
Beppu
BEPPU
Beppu-wan
C. Sadamisaki
Yufuin
Amagase
Kyūdai Line
Yufuin
C. Sekizaki
Uwa-kai
Tosa-wan
Yodo Line
UWAJIMA
Tsuetate
Hosenji
Ōita
ŌITA
Ōita-Miyagawauchi
Handa-Kōgen
ŌITA
Mt.Kujūsan
Mt.Dōgamori
Bungo-suidō
C.Okitsuzaki
Kujū-kōgen
Usuki-magaibutsu
Kikuchi
Aso
TSUKUMI
KIKUCHI
Nippō-Kaigan
Irino-matsubara
Furen Cave
Ueki
SAIKI
Mt.Asosan
TAKETA
Hōhi Line
C. Tsurumisaki
Kusasenri
Nippō Line
SUKUMO
Kumamoto
Sobokatamuki
Sukumo-wan
KUMAMOTO
Mt.Sobosan
KUMAMOTO
Takachiho
TOSASHIMIZU
Matsubase
MIYAZAKI
C. Ashizurimisaki

JAPAN SEA
PACIFIC OCEAN
TOYAMA
ISHIKAWA
FUKUI
GIFU
SHIGA
AICHI
KYOTO
HYOGO
TOTTORI
OSAKA
NARA
MIE
WAKAYAMA
KAGAWA
TOKUSHIMA
KOMATSU
Komatsu
Gokayama
Katayamazu
Kaga
Yamashiro
Shirakawagō
HIDA
TAKAYAMA
Tōjinbō
Awara
Kanazu
Mt.Hakusan
Hida-Kiyomi
Eiheiji Temple
KATSUYAMA
Okuetsu-kōgen
FUKUI
Fukui
ŌNO
Etsumi hokusen Line
Shōkawa
Shirotori
C. Echizenmisaki
Takefu
Gero
Gujō-Hachiman
Mt.Nōgōhakusan
Minami
C. Kyōgasaki
C. Tateishimisaki
Wakasa-wan
TSURUGA
Tsuruga
HOKURIKU EXPRESSWAY
Tajima-kaigan
Kinosaki
Tango Pen.
Hamasaka
C. Nariumisaki
Amanohashidate
Mikatagoko Lakes
Sotomo
Mino
Ena
TOTTORI
Yumura
TOYOOKA
MIYAZU
MAIZURU
OBAMA
Kinomoto
Mt.Ibukiyama
TŌKAI-HOKURIKU EXPRESSWAY
GIFU
MINOKAMO
Obama-nishi
Maizuru-higashi
Nagahama
Ōgaki
Nihon Rhein
Tajimi
TAJIMI
Meiji-mura
Mt.Hyōnosan
San-in Line
AYABE
FUKUCHIYAMA
Fukuchiyama
Kosei Line
Biwako Lake
Maibara Jct
Hikone
Ichinomiya
Komaki
Kasugai
Kiyosu-higashi
NAGOYA
Nagoya
SETO
Nagoya-nishi
TŌMEI EXPRESSWAY
Toyota
Bantan Line
Kasuga
Tannan-Sasayamaguchi
Mt.Hieizan
ŌMIHACHIMAN
Tōkaidō Line
Eigenji Temple
Tsuyama
Hozukyo
KAMEOKA
KYŌTO
ŌTSU
MEISHIN EXPRESSWAY
Mt.Gozaishoyama
Yokkaichi
Kuwana
HIGASHI-MEIHAN EXPRESSWAY
CHIRYŪ
Okazaki
Sayō
Yamazaki
NISHIWAKI
Kyōto-minami
Rittō
Ōtsu
CHŪGOKU EXPRESSWAY
Fukuzaki
Kishin Line
Harima-Shingū
Fukuchiyama Line
Kameyama
TOKONAME
TAKAHAMA
HANDA
GAMAGŌRI
Toyokawa
HIMEJI
Takino-Yashiro
IKEDA
HIRAKATA
Kusatsu Line
Kansai Line
ISE EXPRESSWAY
Chita Pen.
TOYOHASHI
Sanyō Line
TAKARAZUKA
Suita Jct
IGA
Ise-wan
Mikawa-wan
Atsumi Pen.
BIZEN
AKŌ
Mt.Rokkōzan
Takarazuka
Aoyama-kōgen
Tsu
TSU
San-yō-Himeji-nishi
San-yō-Himeji-higashi
AKOGAWA
Kakogawa
San-yō shinkansen
KOBE
USJ
ŌSAKA
NARA
Hisai
C. Hazumisaki
Ieshima Is.
AKASHI
Ōsaka-wan
Ikaruga
Tenri
Meisho Line
Shōdoshima I.
Harimanada
KASHIWARA
NISHI-MEIHAN EXPRESSWAY
Murō
MATSUSAKA
Toshijima I.
Irago-suidō
C. Iragomisaki
Kankakei
TONDABAYASHI
Asuka
SAKURAI
Seiwa-Taki
ISE
Ise
TOBA
Awajishima I.
Kishiwada-Izumi
Ise Shrine
Shima Pen.
Yashima I.
TAKAMATSU
IZUMISANO
KAWACHINAGANO
Izumisano
Mt.Kongōsan
Keino-matsubara
Kaizuka
Mt.Yoshinoyama
Kashikojima
C. Daiōzaki
Kōtoku Line
Hannan
Wakayama Line
HASHIMOTO
Mt.Ōminesan
Naruto Whirlpools
SUMOTO
Takamatsu-chūō
Naruto
NARUTO
WAKAYAMA
Wakayama
Mt.Kōyasan
Mt.Ōdaigahara
TOKUSHIMA EXPRESSWAY
HANWA EXPRESSWAY
Mima
Tokushima
Kainan
Mt.Obakodake
OWASE
TOKUSHIMA
ARIDA
KOMATSUSHIMA
Kii-suidō
Tokushima Line
Totsukawa
C. Mikizaki
GOBŌ
Dorohatcho
ANAN
C. Hinomisaki
Kii Pen.
KUMANO
Kumano-nada
Mt.Tsurugisan
C. Kamodamisaki
Anan-kaigan
Mugi Line
TANABE
Shirahama
C. Setozaki
SHINGŪ
Katsuura
Kisei Line
C. Shionomisaki
C. Murotomisaki
1 : 1,800,000
0
25
50km

JAPAN SEA
C. Hajikizaki
Soto-Kaifu Coast
Uchi-Kaifu Coast
Ryotsu-wan
SADO
Sado I.
C. Sawasakibana
Sado-kaikyō
C.Rokkōzaki
Sosogikaigan
SUZU
WAJIMA
C. Saruyamazaki
Noto Pen.
Nanao-wan
Notojima I.
Notokongō
Wakura
NANAO
Nanao Line
Toyama-wan
HAKUI
HIMI
KAHOKU
TAKAOKA
HOKURIKU EXPRESSWAY
TOYAMA
Kanazawa-nishi
KANAZAWA
Fukumitsu
Komatsu
Gokayama
Katayamazu
Kaga
ISHIKAWA
Awara
Tojinbō
Shirakawagō
HIDA
Mt.Hakusan
TAKAYAMA
Hida-Kiyomi
FUKUI
Eiheiji Temple
KATSUYAMA
Okuetsu-kōgen
Echizen Coast
C. Echizenmisaki
Fukui
ŌNO
Etsumi-hokusen Line
Takefu
Kuzuryūko Lake
Shōkawa
Shirotori
Wakasa-wan
C. Tateishimisaki
FUKUI
Gujō-Hachiman
GIFU
Minami
Tsuruga
C. Nariumisaki
Mikatagoko Lakes
Sotomo
MAIZURU
OBAMA
Obama-nishi
Kinomoto
Mt.Ibukiyama
TŌKAI HOKURIKU EXPRESSWAY
GIFU
Mino
MINOKAMO
KYOTO
San-in Line
Kosei Line
Biwako Lake
Tōkaidō Line
Ōgaki
Meijimura
Mizunami
Komaki
Kasugai
SETO
OMIHACHIMAN
MEISHIN EXPRESSWAY
Nagoya-nishi
NAGOYA
Nagoya
Mt.Hieizan
Hozukyō
SHIGA
Eigenji Temple
KAMEOKA
KYOTO
ŌTSU
Yōkaichi
Kuwana
Yokkaichi
Toyota
AICHI
Kyōto-minami
Ritto
Kusatsu Line
Mt.Gozaishoyama
HIGASHI-MEIHAN EXPRESSWAY
CHIRYŪ
Otsu
IKEDA
Suita Jct
Kansai Line
TOKONANE
HANDA
TAKAHAMA
IGA
Tsu
Hisai
ISE EXPRESSWAY
TSU
Chita Pen.
GAMAGŌRI
OSAKA
Aoyama-kōgen
Ise-wan
C. Hazumisaki
Mikawa-wan
NARA
Ikaruga
Tenri
Meisho Line
Atsumi-wan
Atsumi Pen.
Matsubara
KASHIHARA
NISHI-MEIHAN EXPRESSWAY
SAKURAI
Muro
MATSUSAKA
Irako-suidō
C. Iragomisaki
Asuka
NARA
KAWACHINAGANO
ISE
Ise Shrine
Toshijima I.
TOBA
KASHIWAZAKI
Kashiwazaki
Echigo Line
Shin-etsu Line
JŌETSU
Jōetsu
TOKAMACHI
ITOIGAWA
Itoigawa
ARAI
Nakagō
Iiyama Line
Kiyotsukyō
Mt.Myokozan
Akakura
Nozawa
Myoko-kōgen
IIYAMA
Kurobe
Mt.Shiroumadake
Nojiriko Lake
Shinshū-Nakano
NAKANO
Namerikawa
Togakushi-kōgen
Happō-one
NAGANO
Shima
Kurobe Gorge
SUZAKA
Mt.Shiranesan
Mt. Tateyama
Shiga-kōgen
Manza
Midagahara
Sugadaira-kōgen
Nagano
TOYAMA
Kurobeko Lake
CHIKUMA
NAGANO EXPRESSWAY
Agatsuma
Oito Line
Togura-Kamiyamada
ŌMACHI
UEDA
Mt.Asamayama
Karuizawa
Mt. Yarigatake
Bessho
Komoro
Shin-Hotaka
Toyoshina
Utsukushigahara
Saku
Oku-Hida
Mt.Hotokadake
KOMORO
Kamikōchi
MATSUMOTO
JOSHIN-ETSU EXPRESSWAY
Matsumoto
NAGANO
SAKU
Hirayu
Mt.Norikuradake
SHIOJIRI
Mt. Tateshinayama
Norikura-kōgen
Okaya
Kirigamine
Koumi Line
Chūō Line
Tateshina
CHINO
Mt. Yatsugatake
Mt.Ontakesan
Suwa
Nobeyama-kōgen
Ina
Kobuchizawa
Nishizawa Gorge
Gero
Kiso-Koma-kōgen
Takayama Line
Mt.Komagatake
Mitake-Shōsenkyō
Komagane
Mt.Komagatake
Nirasaki
NIRASAKI
KOFU
Mt.Kitadake
Kiso
Kōfu-Shōwa
YAMANASHI
CHŪŌ EXPRESSWAY
IIDA
Kawaguchiko Lake
Iida
Nakatsugawa
Tenryūkyō
Mt.Akaishidake
Shimobe
Mt.FUJI
Mt.Minobusan
Minobu Line
Iida Line
FUJINOMIYA
Fuji
Sumatakyō
Mt.Horaijisan
SHIZUOKA
TOMEI EXPRESSWAY
Mihonomatsubara
SHINSHIRO
SHIZUOKA
Nihondaira
Tōkaidō Line
TENRYŪ
Shizuoka
SHIMADA
Toyokawa
Hamamatsu
TOYOHASHI
KAKEGAWA
Suruga-wan
Tōkaidō-Sanyō Shinkansen
OMAEZAKI
Enshū-nada
C. Omaezaki

YAMAGATA
MIYAGI
NIIGATA
FUKUSHIMA
TOCHIGI
GUNMA
IBARAKI
SAITAMA
TOKYO
CHIBA
KANAGAWA
PACIFIC OCEAN
Ojika Pen.
Kinkazan I.
Ajishima I.
Sendai-wan
Matsushima
SHIOGAMA
SENDAI
IWANUMA
KAKUDA
SOMA
HARAMACHI
IWAKI
C. Shioyazaki
Iwakikaigan
KITAIBARAKI
HITACHI
HITACHINAKA
Oarai
Kashima-nada
CHŌSHI
C. Inubōzaki
TOGANE
Kujūkurihama Coast
C. Daitōzaki
KATSUURA
KAMOGAWA
TATEYAMA
C.Nojimazaki
Bōsō Pen.
MURAKAMI
Senami
Mt.Asahidake
NAGAI
NAN-YŌ
YONEZAWA
TENDŌ
YAMAGATA
SAGAE
Sakunami
Zaō
Mt. Zaōsan
Akiu
Abukuma Rhein
Iizaka
FUKUSHIMA
NIIGATA
SHIBATA
AGANO
SANJŌ
TOCHIO
NAGAOKA
Mt.Iidesan
Tengendai
Mt.Azumasan
Ura-Bandai
KITAKATA
Mt.Bandaisan
Mt.Adatarayama
AIZUWAKAMATSU
Inawashiro Lake
Higashiyama
KŌRIYAMA
Ashinomaki
Tagokurako Lake
Ōkawa Rhein
Oku-Tadamiko Lake
Mt.Nasudake
Nasu-kōgen
SHIRAKAWA
NASUSHIOBARA
Shiobara
Oku-kuji
Fukuroda
Ozegahara
Mt.Tanigawadake
Minakami
Kinugawa
Mt.Nantaisan
Nikko
Chūzenjiko Lake
IMAICHI
NUMATA
Mt.Akagisan
KANUMA
UTSUNOMIYA
HITACHIŌTA
MAEBASHI
KIRYŪ
ASHIKAGA
OYAMA
MŌKA
KASAMA
MITO
SHIMODATE
Mt. Tsukubasan
SHIMOTSUMA
ISHIOKA
TSUCHIURA
Kasumigaura Lake
TSUKUBA
KASUKABE
TORIDE
SAWARA
Suigō
TAKASAKI
ŌTA
KUMAGAYA
KOGA
GYŌDA
CHICHIBU
Nagatoro
HANNŌ
OME
IRUMA
SAITAMA
MATSUDO
FUNABASHI
Inbanuma Lake
YOKAICHIBA
TOKYO
Tokyo Disneyresort
ICHIHARA
CHIBA
MOBARA
KAWASAKI
YOKOHAMA
KISARAZU
Tokyo-wan
YOKOSUKA
Kamakura
Enoshima
Miura Pen.
C. Kannonzaki
FUTTSU
Mt.Kanōzan
Yoro Gorge
Mt.Kiyosumiyama
Mt.Nokogiriyama
MIURA
Jōgashima I.
C. Sunosaki
Sagami-wan
Sagami-nada
ODAWARA
Hakone
Yugawara
C. Manazurumisaki
ATAMI
Atami
ITŌ
Itō
IZU
Izu Pen.
Amagi-kōgen
Atagawa
Ōshima I.
Mt.Miharayama
C. Tsumekizaki
C. Irōzaki
Mt. Tanzawayama
FUJIYOSHIDA
Yamanakako Lake
Oku-Tama
CHŪO EXPRESSWAY
TOHOKU EXPRESSWAY
BAN-ETSU EXPRESSWAY
JOBAN EXPRESSWAY
HIGASHI-KANTO EXPRESSWAY
TATEYAMA EXPRESSWAY
KAN-ETSU EXPRESSWAY
Tohoku shinkansen
Ban-etsu-sai sen Line
Ban-etsu-tōsen Line
Jōban Line
Tōhoku Line
Suigun Line
Mito Line
Narita Line
Sōbu Line
Uchibō Line
Kururi Line
Sotobō Line
Hachikō Line
Ryōmō Line
Tadami Line
Yonesaka Line
Senzan Line
Ou Line
Hakushin Line
Uetsu Line
Kashimaura
1 : 1,800,000
0 25 50km

C. Henashizaki
C. Nyūdōzaki
Oga Pe
OGA
JAPAN SEA
Tobishima I.
Sakata-minato
SAKATA
Sakata
Yunohama
TSURUOKA
345
Yudonosa
Awashima I.
Uetsu Line
7
C. Hajikizaki
Uchi-Kaifu Coast
Soto-Kaifu Coast
Senami
MURAKAMI
Ryotsu-wan
Yonesaka Line
Nakajō
SADO
Sado I.
Sado-kaikyō
NIIGATA
354
Hakushin Line
SHIBATA
NIIGATA
Niigata-chūō
Niigata-kūkō
Mt. Iidesan
AGANO
C. Sawasakihana

HOKKAIDŌ
Kameda Pen.
Mt. Esan
HAKODATE
Esashi Line
Matsumae Pen.
Tsugaru-Kaikyō
C. Ōmasaki
C. Shiriyazaki
Mt. Osoresan
Hotokegaura
Shimokita Pen.
MUTSU
C. Tappizaki
Hiratate-kaikyō
Kodomarimisaki
Tsugaru Pen.
C. Ushinokubimisaki
Mutsu-wan
C. Natsudomarizaki
Jūsanko Lakes
Tsugaru Line
Noheji-wan
Ōminato Line
Aomori-wan
GOSHOGAWARA
Aomori
AOMORI
Ogawarako Lake
Gonō Line
Mt. Iwakisan
Mt. Hakkōdasan
Tōhoku Line
MISAWA
TŌHOKU EXPRESSWAY
Kuroishi
TOWADA
HIROSAKI
Kuroishi
Oirase-Valley
Tanesashi-Kaigan
Jūniko Lakes
HACHINOHE
Hachinohe
Towadako Lake
Nangō
Hachinohe Line
HACHINOHE EXPRESSWAY
Karumai
Ōyu
NOSHIRO
Ōu Line
ŌDATE
NINOHE
Towada
KUJI
Ōtaki
KAZUNO
Ichinohe
Hanawa Line
Ashiro
Kotooka-Moritake
Mt. Moriyoshiyama
Mt. Hachimantai
Matsuo-Hachimantai
Ryūsendō
Mt. Iwatesan
Iwaizumi Line
Akita-kita
Tazawako-Kōgen
Nyūtō
AKITA
M. Komagatake
Tazawako Lake
Rikuchū-kaigan
C. Heizaki
AKITA
MORIOKA
Yamada Line
MIYAKO
Akita-minami
Akita-kūkō
Tazawako Line
Morioka
Kyōwa
AKITA EXPRESSWAY
Morioka-minami
Mt. Hayachinesan
IWATE
ŌMAGARI
Hanamaki
HONJŌ
Ōmagari
Hanamaki-minami
HANAMAKI
Yuda
KAMAISHI
YOKOTE
Kitakami Line
Yokote
TŌNO
C. Ozaki
KITAKAMI
Kitakami-nishi
ESASHI
Mt. Goyōzan
YUZAWA
Mizusawa
MIZUSAWA
OFUNATO
Chōkaizan
RIKUZENTAKATA
Hiraizumi
Ōfunato Line
Mt. Kurikomayama
Geibikei
ICHINOSEKI
KESENNUMA
Akinomiya
Ichinoseki
Onikōbe
PACIFIC OCEAN
Rikuu-saisen Line
SHINJŌ
Narugo
Rikuu-tōsen Line
Tsukidate
Tōhoku-shinkansen
Mt. Haguroyama
OBANAZAWA
Furukawa
FURUKAWA
Gassan
MIYAGI
Mt. Yudonoyama
YAMAGATA
Tōhoku Line
Senseki Line
SAGAE
Izumi
ISHINOMAKI
Sagae
TENDŌ
Sakunami
Matsushima
Ishinomaki-wan
Ojika Pen.
Kinkasan I.
Asahidake
Senzan Line
SHIOGAMA
Yamagata-kita
SENDAI
Ajishima I.
Sendai-Miyagi
Sendai-wan
KAMINOYAMA
Akiu
Zaō
Mt. Zaōsan
Ōu Line
IWANUMA
TŌHOKU EXPRESSWAY
Shiroishi
NAN-YŌ
KAKUDA
Abukuma Rhein
YONEZAWA
Iizaka
1 : 1,800,000
0
25
50km

Sōya-kaikyō
C.Sōyamisaki
C. Noshappumisaki
WAKKANAI
Sōya-wan
Mt.Rebundake
Rebuntō I.
Rishiri-suidō
Mt.Rishiridake
Rishiritō I.
Beniya-genseikaen
HAMATONBETSU
Sarobetsu-genseikaen
Sarobetsu-genya
HORONOBE
ESASHI
Sōya Line
OTOINEPPU
Teuritō I.
Yagishiritō I.
NAYORO
Sumanjaiko Lake
TOMAMAE
JAPAN SEA
SHIBETSU
Wassamu
RUMOI
Rumoi Line
Asahikawa-Takasu
ASAHIKAWA
FUKAGAWA
Fukagawa
Furano Line
Takikawa
TAKIKAWA
Ashibetsu
ASHIBETSU
SUNAGAWA
Shirogan
Mt.Tokachida
Nemuro Line
C. Shakotanmisaki
Ishikari-wan
Sasshō Line
BIBAI
Bibai
FURANO
MIKASA
Shakotan Pen.
Otaru-kaigan
YOICHI
OTARU
SASSON EXPRESSWAY
IWAMIZAWA
Iwamizawa
EBETSU
Otaru
Sapporo
Teine
SAPPORO
Ebetsu-higashi
YŪBARI
Hakodate Line
IWANAI
Jōzankei
Kitahiroshima
Sekishō Line
KUCCHAN
C. Benkeimisaki
Konbu
Mt. Yōteisan
ENIWA
Yūbari
HIDAKA
NISEKO
Chitose
CHITOSE
Chitose Line
Muroran Line
Shikotsuko Lake
Mt.Poroshiridak
C. Mottamisaki
Tomakomai-nishi
Tōyako Lake
Shiraoi
TOMAKOMAI
Oshamanbe
Abuta-Tōyako
Mt.Shōwa-shinzan
Mt.Usuzan
DOO EXPRESSWAY
OSHAMANBE
Kunnui
Noboribetsu
KITAHIYAMA
DATE
Date
Hidaka Line
Uchiura-wan
Muroran
NOBORIBETSU
Noboribetsu-Muroran
MURORAN
NIKAPPU
Okushiri-kaikyō
C.Chikyūmisaki
Okushiritō I.
Hakodate Line
MORI
Ōnuma Lake
ESASHI
Kameda Pen.
Mt.Esan
C. Esanmisaki
Esashi Line
Matsumae Pen.
HAKODATE

SEA OF OKHOTSK
PACIFIC OCEAN
HOKKAIDŌ
OKOPPE
MONBETSU
YŪBETSU
TAKINOUE
ENGARU
Saromako Lake
C. Notoromisaki
Notoroko Lake
ABASHIRI
Koshimizu-genseikaen
SHARI
Shiretoko Pen.
C. Shiretokomisaki
Shiretokogoto Lakes
Mt.Rausudake
RAUSU
Kunashiritō I.
Sekihoku Line
KAMIKAWA
KITAMI
BIHORO
RUBESHIBE
Aizankei
Sōunkyō
Daisetsuzan
Tenninkyō
Mt.Sharidake
Nemuro-kaikyō
SHIBETSU
Habomaishotō Is.
Tarakutō I.
Kawayu
Kussharoko Lake
Mashūko Lake
C. Notsukemisaki
C. Nosappumisaki
Goyōmai-kaikyō
Suishōtō I.
Shibotsutō I.
TESHIKAGA
Mt.Oakandake
Akanko Lake
Mt.Meakandake
Nukabirako Lake
Nukabira
Shikaribetsu-kohan
KAMISHIHORO
ASHORO
Ashoro
Nemuro-wan
NEMURO
Nemuro Pen.
Fūrenko Lake
C. Ochiichimisaki
Senmō Line
Nemuro Line
Hamanaka-wan
Tokachi-Shimizu
DŌTŌ EXPRESSWAY
Ikeda
Kushiro-shitsugen
Akkeshi-wan
KUSHIRO
IKEDA
OBIHIRO
URAHORO
HIROO
ERIMO
C. Erimomisaki
1 : 1,800,000
0
25
50km

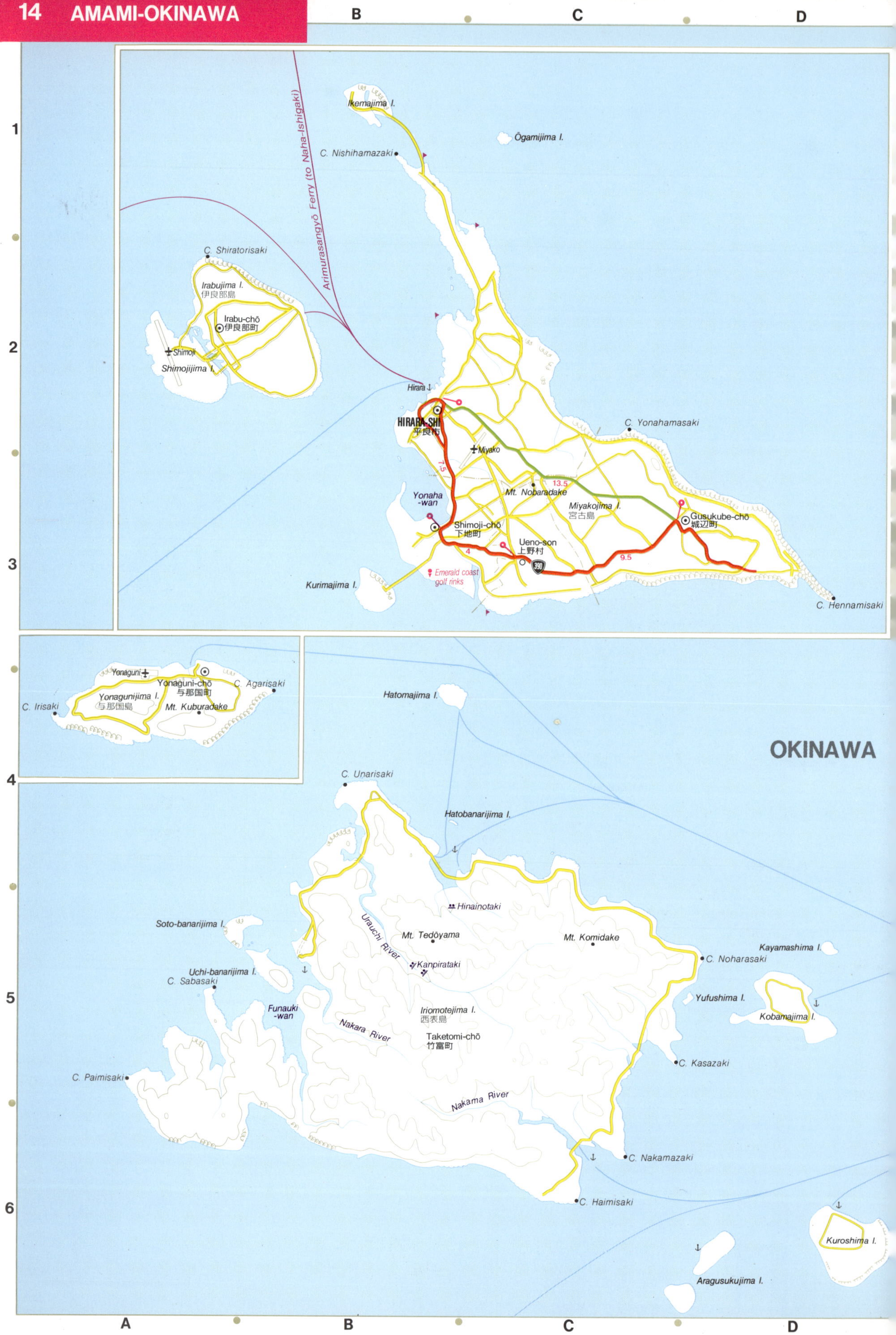
OKINAWA
Ikemajima I.
Ōgamijima I.
C. Nishihamazaki
Arimurasangyō Ferry (to Naha-Ishigaki)
C. Shiratorisaki
Irabujima I.
伊良部島
Irabu-chō
伊良部町
Shimoji
Shimojijima I.
Hirara
HIRARA-SHI
平良市
Miyako
C. Yonahamasaki
Mt. Nobaradake
Miyakojima I.
宮古島
Gusukube-chō
城辺町
Yonaha -wan
Shimoji-chō
下地町
Ueno-son
上野村
390
Emerald coast golf rinks
Kurimajima I.
C. Hennamisaki
7.5
13.5
4
9.5
Yonaguni
Yonaguni-chō
与那国町
C. Agarisaki
Yonagunijima I.
与那国島
C. Irisaki
Mt. Kuburadake
Hatomajima I.
C. Unarisaki
Hatobanarijima I.
Hinainotaki
Urauchi River
Mt. Tedōyama
Mt. Komidake
Soto-banarijima I.
Kanpirataki
Kayamashima I.
C. Noharasaki
Uchi-banarijima I.
C. Sabasaki
Yufushima I.
Kobamajima I.
Funauki -wan
Iriomotejima I.
西表島
Nakara River
Taketomi-chō
竹富町
C. Kasazaki
C. Paimisaki
Nakama River
C. Nakamazaki
C. Haimisaki
Kuroshima I.
Aragusukujima I.
A
B
C
D
1
2
3
4
5
6

E
F
G
H
1
2
3
4
5
6
Arimurasangyō Ferry (to Naha-Miyako)
C. Hirakubosaki
Mt. Arasan
C. Datefusaki
Ibaruma -wan
C. Nosokosaki
Mt. Nosokodake
C. Tamatorisaki
C. Kabiraishizaki
C. Noharasaki
Mt. Yarabudake
Yarabusaki
Mt. Omotodake
Ishigakijima I.
石垣島
Ishigakijima
Nagura-wan
Mt. Bannadake
C. Kannonzaki
Hamashima I.
ISHIGAKI-SHI
石垣市
Ishigaki
Gongendō
Miyara -wan
Taketomijima I.
竹富島
PACIFIC OCEAN
太平洋
Minnajima I.
Tarama-son
多良間村
Taramashima I.
多良間島
Tarama
C. Hamazaki
Taketomi-chō
竹富町
Haterumajima I.
波照間島
Hateruma
390

OKINAWA
EAST CHINA SEA
東シナ海
Kumejima I.
久米島
Kumejima
Kumejima-chō
久米島町
Ōhajima I.
Ōmujima I.
Kumejima Ferry (to Naha)
Irisunajima I.
Tonaki-son
渡名喜村
Tonakishima I.
Agunijima I.
Aguni
Aguni-son
粟国村
Kuroshima I.
Zamamijima I.
座間味島
Zamami-son
座間味村
C. Kitahirasezaki
Gishipujima I.
Yakabijima I.
Amuroshima I.
Kerama-kaikyō
Tokashiki-son
渡嘉敷村
Akashima I.
Gerumashima I.
Tokashikijima I.
渡嘉敷島
Hatejima I.
Nakajima I.
Kubashima I.
Kerama
Fukajishima I.
Maejima I.
Tokashiki-son
渡嘉敷村
Tokashiki-son
渡嘉敷村
Keisejima I.
Arimurasangyō Ferry (Nagoya-Ōsaka-Naha)
Oshima-un-yu Ferry Terukuni-yūsen(Kagoshima-Amami-Naha)
Kumejima Ferry (to Kumejima)
Arimurasangyō Ferry (to Miyako-Ishigaki)
Coast full of var
Onna-son
恩納村
Igei
伊芸
Yaka
屋嘉
Okinawa-kokusai
C. Zanpamisaki
残波岬
C. Maedamisaki
Ishikawa
石川
Yamado
Okinawa Royal
Kin-wan
ISHIKAWA-SHI
石川市
OKINAWA EXPRESSWAY
沖縄自動車道
Yomitan-son
読谷村
Congestion
American military base both sides
Okinawa-kita
沖縄北
GUSHIKAWA-SHI
具志川市
Hijagawa River
Kadena-chō
嘉手納町
Kadena Airport
Koza-jūjiro コザ十字路
Nago 53Km
Yonabaru 20Km
Naha 28Km
Okinawa-minami
沖縄南
OKINAWA-SHI
沖縄市
Chatan-chō
北谷町
to Koza
to Ōyama
to Nakagusuku
to Urasoe
Kitanakagusuku-son
北中城村
Futenmagū
Onishi Terrace
GINOWAN-SHI
宜野湾市
Futenma Airport
Nakagusuku
中城
Kitanakagusuku
北中城
Nakagusuku-son
中城村
to Ishikawa
Koza-jūjiro
Goya-jūjiro
to Naha
Itoman Rotary 糸満ロータリー
Nago 62Km
Yonabaru 10Km
Itoman 12Km
URASOE-SHI
浦添市
Asagawa River
Nishihara
西原
Nishihara-chō
西原町
Nishihara
Kannondo
NAHA-SHI
那覇市
Naha
那覇
Mt. Bengadake
Okinawa
Yonabarusho 与那原署前
Okinawa 20Km
Naha 10Km
Itoman 13Km
Nakagusuku-wan
Kakinohana 垣花
C. Ōminesaki
Naha
Kohagura-jūjiro 古波蔵十字路
Yonabaru-chō
与那原町
Haebaru-chō
南風原町
Higashimachi 東町
Kokuba-jūjiro 国場十字路
TOMIGUSUKU
豊見城市
C. Chinasaki
Ōzato-son
大里村
Syure
Chinen-son
知念村
C. Chinenzaki
Sashiki-chō
佐敷町
Ryukyu
to Naha
to Itoman Port
NTT
to Mabuni
Kochinda-chō
東風平町
Tamagusuku-son
玉城村
Gyokusendo(Cave)
ITOMAN-SHI
糸満市
Mt. Yaesedake
Naha
Gushikami-son
具志頭村
Southern Links
Scenic view of Pacific Ocean
Heiwa-kinen-kōen(Mem.Park)
C. Kiyansaki
喜屋武岬
C. Arasaki

18
19
E
F
G
H
1
2
3
4
5
6
NAGO-SHI
名護市
Mt. Nagodake
Nago-wan
C. Teniyazaki
Todorokinotaki
Kyoda
許田
Mt. Kushidake
Ōura-wan
Congestion
C. Henokozaki
Ginoza
宜野座
Ginoza-son
宜野座村
Kin-chō
金武町
C. Kinmisaki
Congestion in autumn
PACIFIC OCEAN
太平洋
to Nakadomari
to Kin
to Koza
to Gushikawa
Ikeijima I.
Miyagusukujima I.
Henzajima I.
Yonashiro-chō
与那城町
Hamahigajima I.
Uchibarujima I.
Minami-Uchibarujima I.
C. Katsurenzaki
Tsukenjima I.
Kudakashima I.
Kita-Daitōjima I.
北大東島
Kita-Daitō
Kitadaitō-son
北大東村
Minami-Daitōjima I.
南大東島
Minami-Daitō
Minamidaitō-son
南大東村

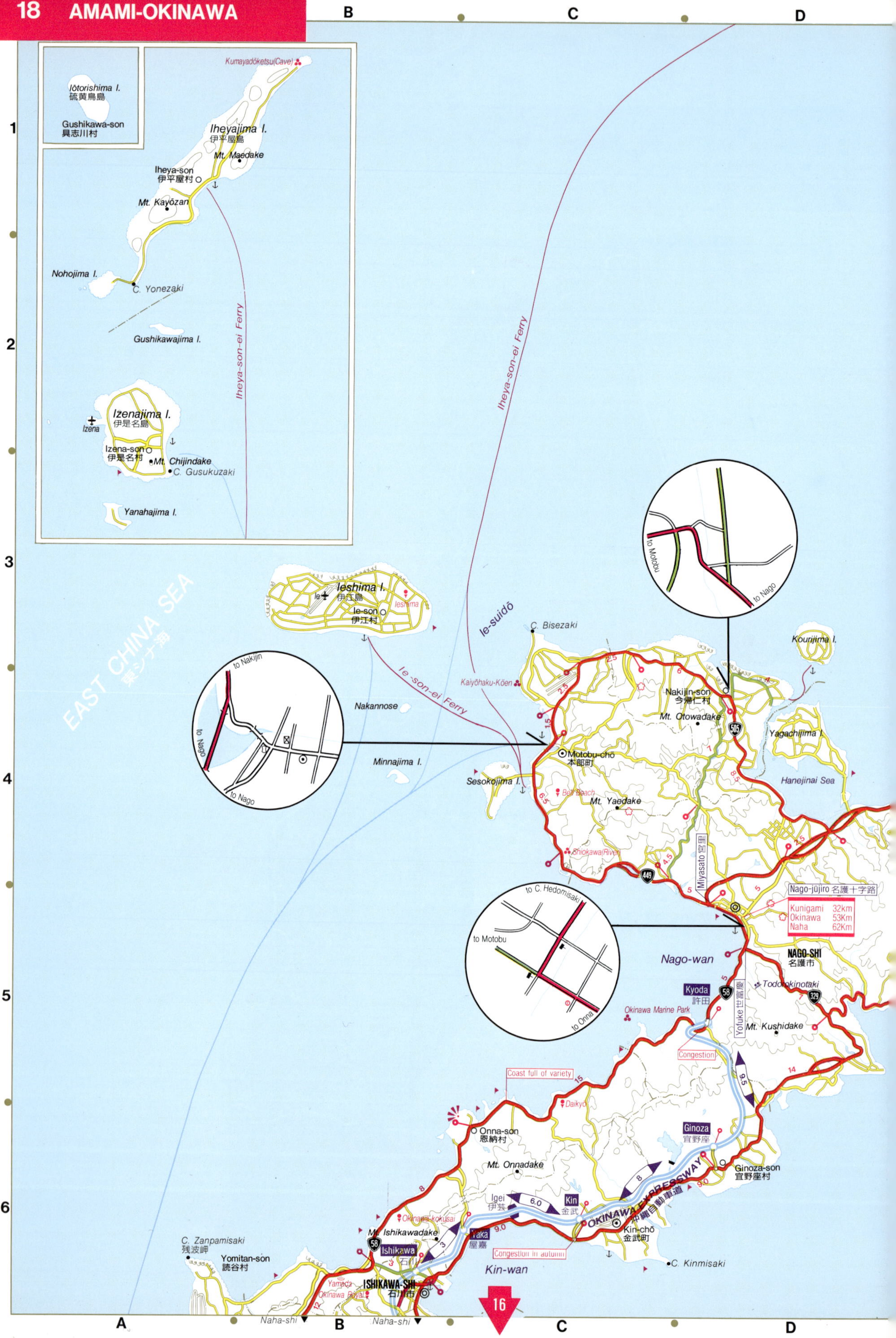
B
C
D
1
2
3
4
5
6
A
Iōtorishima I.
硫黄鳥島
Gushikawa-son
具志川村
Kumayadōketsu(Cave)
Iheyajima I.
伊平屋島
Mt. Maedake
Iheya-son
伊平屋村
Mt. Kayōzan
Nohojima I.
C. Yonezaki
Gushikawajima I.
Iheya-son-ei Ferry
Izenajima I.
伊是名島
Izena
Izena-son
伊是名村
Mt. Chijindake
C. Gusukuzaki
Yanahajima I.
EAST CHINA SEA
東シナ海
Ieshima I.
伊江島
Ie
Ie-son
伊江村
Ieshima
Ie-suidō
Ie-son-ei Ferry
to Nakijin
to Nago
to Motobu
Nakannose
Minnajima I.
C. Bisezaki
Kaiyōhaku-Kōen
Nakijin-son
今帰仁村
Mt. Otowadake
Kourijima I.
Yagachijima I.
Motobu-chō
本部町
Sesokojima I.
Bell Beach
Mt. Yaedake
Hanejinai Sea
Shiokawa(River)
Miyasato 宮里
Nago-jūjiro 名護十字路
Kunigami 32km
Okinawa 53Km
Naha 62Km
to C. Hedomisaki
to Onna
Nago-wan
NAGO-SHI
名護市
Todorokinotaki
Kyoda
許田
Yofuke 世冨慶
Okinawa Marine Park
Mt. Kushidake
Congestion
Coast full of variety
Daikyo
Onna-son
恩納村
Ginoza
宜野座
Ginoza-son
宜野座村
Mt. Onnadake
Igei
伊芸
Kin
金武
OKINAWA EXPRESSWAY
沖縄自動車道
Kin-chō
金武町
Okinawa-kokusai
Mt. Ishikawadake
Yaka
屋嘉
Ishikawa
石川
Congestion in autumn
C. Zanpamisaki
残波岬
Yomitan-son
読谷村
Kin-wan
C. Kinmisaki
Yamada
Okinawa Royal
ISHIKAWA-SHI
石川市
Naha-shi
16

E
F
G
H
1
2
3
4
5
6
Distant view of Yoron I.
C. Hedonomisaki
辺戸岬
Precipitous criff coast
Mt. Onishiyama
Mt. Nishimedake
Mt. Terukubiyama
Mt. Ibudake
C. Akamaruzaki
Kunigami-son
国頭村
Fukugawa River
Mt. Yonahadake
Ogimi-son
大宜味村
Mt. Iyudake
Mt. Tamatsujiyama
Higashi-son
東村
Mt. Tsuhayama
Fukuchi River
C. Ginansaki
Mt. Hitotsudake
C. Teniyazaki
PACIFIC OCEAN
太平洋
OKINAWA
58
331
8
20
15
13
30
9
11.5
33

EAST CHINA SEA
東シナ海
PACIFIC OCEAN
太平洋
Terukuni-yūsen·Ōshima-un-yu Ferry
(to Hanshin·Amami·Naha)
Amami-kaiun Ferry
(to Hetono·Koniya·Naze·Kikai·Kagoshima)
Ferry Kakeroma
C. Miyakozaki
C. Utsusaki
Yamato-son
大和村
C. Sonsaki
46
Ōshima I.
大島
Kawauchi River
Sumiyō River
C. Kurakibana
Mt. Eboshidake
Mt. Yuwandake
Uken-son
宇検村
Mt. Takabachiyama
Yakeuchi-wan
C. Yadonsaki
Mt. Yakukachoboshidake
5
Sumiyō-son
住用村
Mt. Takinohanayama
C. Sotsukōzaki
Mt. Togurayama
Mt. Nangōyama
Mt. Eboshidake
Mt. Kohemadake
Mt. Kanmuridake
40
C. Osaki
Mt. Eboshidake
Mt. Torigamine
Mt. Kanegawada
28
Mt. Takahachiyama
C. Atangesaki
Mt. Yuidake
Scenic view of Ōshima-str.
Mt. Kōchiyama
58
Mt. Yumishidake
Ōshima-kaikyō
Isu-wan
C. Masaki
Setouchi-chō
瀬戸内町
Mt. Kanyūyama
Yūhanare
C. Shirakisaki
Kakeromajima I.
加計呂麻島
C. Machiamisaki
Sukomohanare
C. Namikesaki
Mt. Kasakidake
C. Kasaki
C. Aojirizaki
Ukeshima-suidō
C. Kerajisaki
Yoroshima I.
Hanmyashima I.
Mt. Ōyama
Mt. Taishōsan
Ukejima I.
Kiyamashima I.
C. Yontomarisaki
Janareshima I.
A
B
C
D
1
2
3
4
5
6

E
F
G
H
1
2
3
4
5
6
KAGOSHIMA
Amami-kaiun Ferry (to Kikai·Kagoshima)
Mt. Takasakiyama
C. Kasarizaki
C. Imaizaki
C. Ayamaruzaki
Coral reef
Kasari-wan
Mt. Takadake
Kasari-chō
笠利町
Mt. Yodeyama
Mt. Ōkariyama
Amami
58
C. Bohrosezaki
Tatsugō-chō
竜郷町
Amami
C. Myōganzaki
Naze
Habu Center (Snake Zoo)
NAZE-SHI
名瀬市
Honcha Pass
Kasari 31Km
Yamato 23Km
Setouchi 57Km
Okawa River
Asato Pass
Mt. Matsunagayama
C. Tonbizaki
Amami-kaiun Ferry (to Naze)
(to Kagoshima)
Kikai
Kikai-chō
喜界町
Kikaishima I.
喜界島
C. Arakizaki
C. Kunigamimisaki
Okinoerabu
C. Tarunamisaki
Wadomari-chō
和泊町
Mt. Koshiyama
Mt. Ōyama
Shōryūdō (Cave)
Okino-Erabujima I.
沖永良部島
Suirendō (Cave)
Terukuni-yusen-Ōshima-un-yu Ferry (to Kagoshima·Amami·Naha)
C. Ichisaki
C. Sakibarasaki
C. Kanamizaki
Mt. Amagidake
Mt. Sasontsujidake
Mt. Ōgusukuyama
Tokunoshima
Mt. Makuradake
Mt. Yamatogusukusan
Amagi-chō
天城町
Mt. Minatayama
Akirigami River
Mt. Inokawadake
Tokunoshima I.
徳之島
Mt. Hagidake
Mt. Inutabudake
Tokunoshima-chō
徳之島町
C. Inutabumisaki
Isen-chō
伊仙町
Terukuni-yūsen-Ōshima-un-yu Ferry (to Kagoshima·Amami·Naha)
Terukuni-yūsen-Ōshima-un-yu Ferry (to Kagoshima·Amami·Naha)
Yoron-chō
与論町
Yoron
Yoronjima I.
与論島
C. Funchusaki
Akazakishōnyudō (Cave)
C. Chichisaki

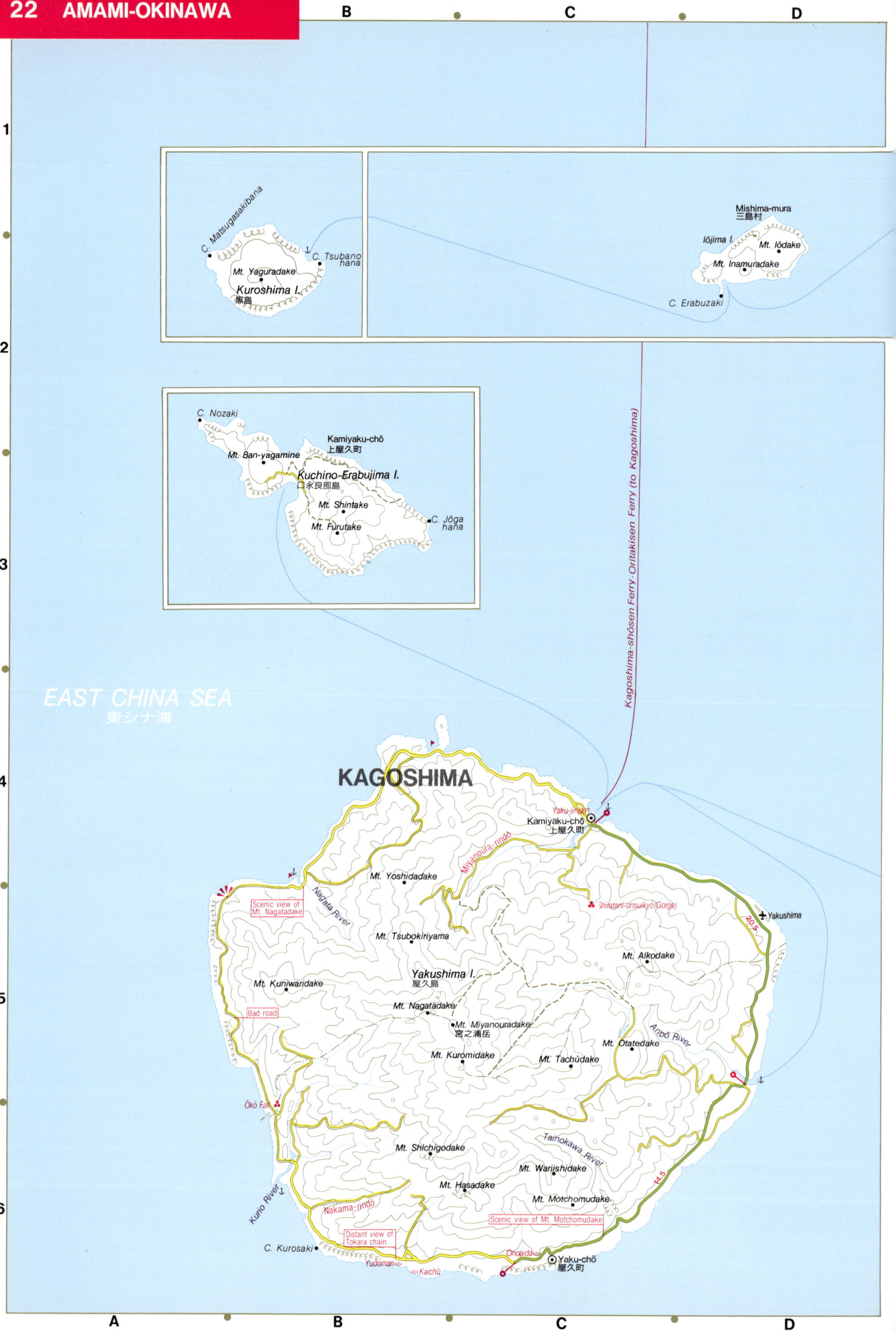
C. Matsugasakibana
C. Tsubano hana
Mt. Yaguradake
Kuroshima I.
黒島
Mishima-mura
三島村
Iōjima I.
Mt. Iōdake
Mt. Inamuradake
C. Erabuzaki
C. Nozaki
Kamiyaku-chō
上屋久町
Mt. Ban-yagamine
Kuchino-Erabujima I.
口永良部島
Mt. Shintake
Mt. Furutake
C. Jōga hana
Kagoshima-shōsen Ferry·Oritakisen Ferry (to Kagoshima)
EAST CHINA SEA
東シナ海
KAGOSHIMA
Yaku-jinja
Kamiyaku-chō
上屋久町
Miyanoura-rindō
Mt. Yoshidadake
Scenic view of Mt. Nagatadake
Nagata River
Shiratani-unsuikyō (Gorge)
Yakushima
20.5
Mt. Tsubokiriyama
Mt. Aikodake
Yakushima I.
屋久島
Mt. Kuniwaridake
Bad road
Mt. Nagatadake
Mt. Miyanouradake
宮之浦岳
Anbō River
Mt. Otatedake
Mt. Kuromidake
Mt. Tachūdake
Ōkō Fall
Mt. Shichigodake
Tainokawa River
Mt. Warijshidake
Mt. Hasadake
14.5
Kurio River
Nakama-rindō
Mt. Motchomudake
Scenic view of Mt. Motchomudake
Distant view of Tokara chain
C. Kurosaki
Yudomari
Kaichū
Onoaida
Yaku-chō
屋久町

E
F
G
H
1
2
3
4
5
6
C. Kaminomisaki
Magejima I.
NISHINOOMOTE-SHI
西之表市
Onbozaki
Takeshima I.
Kyūshū-shōsen Ferry·Kagoshima-shōsen Ferry (to Kagoshima)
Ōsumi-kaikyō
大隅海峡
C. Kishikazaki
Urada-jinja
C. Ōsaki
Hachiman-jinja
NISHINOOMOTE-SHI
西之表市
Nishinoomote
58
Kōbaki River
TANEGASHIMA-KAIKYŌ
種子島海峡
Tanegashima I.
種子島
30
Seaside road
KAGOSHIMA
Tanegashima
Nakatane-chō
中種子町
PACIFIC OCEAN
太平洋
17.5
Tanegashima
Kumano-jinja
C. Shimamazaki
58
Grand beach
Shimama River
8.5
Chikura no iwaya (Cave)
20
Minamitane-chō
南種子町
C. Ōtakezaki
Distant view of Yakushima I.
C. Kadokurazaki

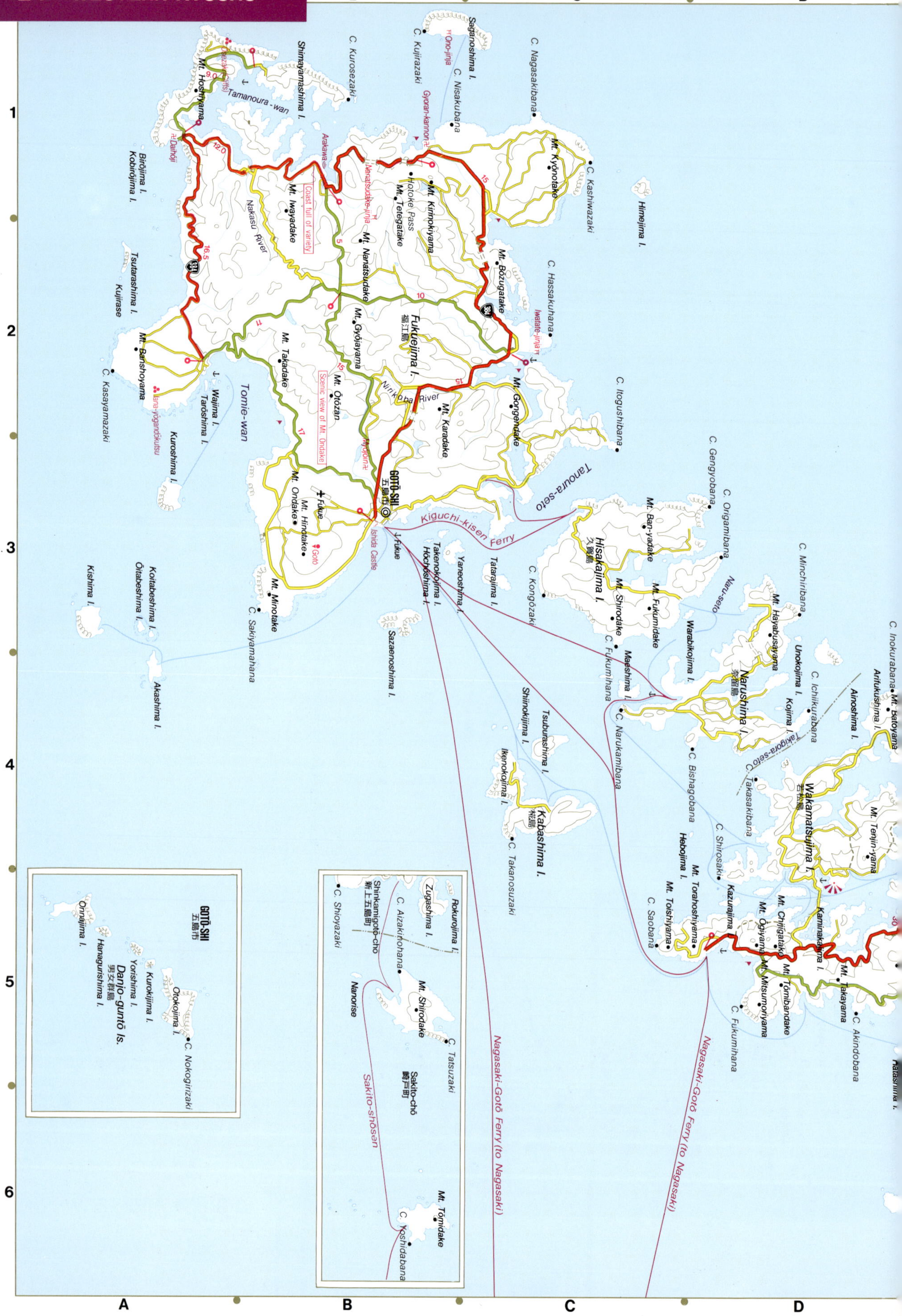

Fukuejima I.
福江島
GOTŌ-SHI
五島市
Hisakajima I.
久賀島
Narushima I.
奈留島
Wakamatsujima I.
若松島
Kabashima I.
樺島
Danjo-guntō Is.
男女群島
Shinkamigotō-chō
新上五島町
Sakito-chō
崎戸町
Tamanoura-wan
Tomie-wan
Tanoura-seto
Naru-seto
Takigoura-seto
Kiguchi-kisen Ferry
Nagasaki-Gotō Ferry (to Nagasaki)
Sakito-shōsen
Nakasu River
Ninokobashi River
Coast full of variety
Scenic view of Mt. Ondake
Ishida Castle
Fukue
Mt. Hoshiyama
Mt. Iwayadake
Mt. Kirinokiyama
Mt. Tetegatake
Mt. Nanatsudake
Mt. Gyōiayama
Mt. Takadake
Mt. Ōtozan
Mt. Ondake
Mt. Hinodake
Mt. Minotake
Mt. Banshoyama
Mt. Kyōnotake
Mt. Bōzugatake
Mt. Gongendake
Mt. Karadake
Mt. Ban-yadake
Mt. Shirodake
Mt. Fukumidake
Mt. Hayabusayama
Mt. Tenjin-yama
Mt. Torahoshiyama
Mt. Toishiyama
Mt. Chigatake
Mt. Ōgiyama
Mt. Tomibandake
Mt. Mitsumoriyama
Mt. Takayama
Mt. Batoyama
Mt. Tomidake
Hotoke Pass
Dainoji
Arakawa
Gyoran-kannon
Ono-jinja
Iwatate-jinja
Shimayamashima I.
Saganoshima I.
Birōjima I.
Kobirōjima I.
Tsutarashima I.
Kujirase
Wajima I.
Taroshima I.
Kuroshima I.
Kishima I.
Koitabeshima I.
Ōitabeshima I.
Akashima I.
Himejima I.
Takenokojima I.
Hōchoshima I.
Yaneoshima I.
Tatarajima I.
Sazaenoshima I.
Shinokojima I.
Tsuburashima I.
Ikenokojima I.
Maeshima I.
Warabikojima I.
Unokojima I.
Kojima I.
Ainoshima I.
Arifukushima I.
Hebojima I.
Kazurajima I.
Kaminakashima I.
Omagaijima I.
Hanagurishima I.
Yorishima I.
Kurokijima I.
Otokojima I.
Zugashima I.
Rokurojima I.
Nanorise
C. Kurosezaki
C. Kujirazaki
C. Nisakubana
C. Nagasakibana
C. Kashiwazaki
C. Hassakuhana
C. Itoguchibana
C. Kasayamazaki
C. Sakiyamahana
C. Gengyobana
C. Origamibana
C. Kongōzaki
C. Fukumihana
C. Narukamibana
C. Minchiribana
C. Ichikurabana
C. Inokurabana
C. Bishagobana
C. Takasakibana
C. Shirosaki
C. Takanosuzaki
C. Saobana
C. Akindobana
C. Nokogirizaki
C. Shioyazaki
C. Aizakinohana
C. Tatsuzaki
C. Yoshidabana

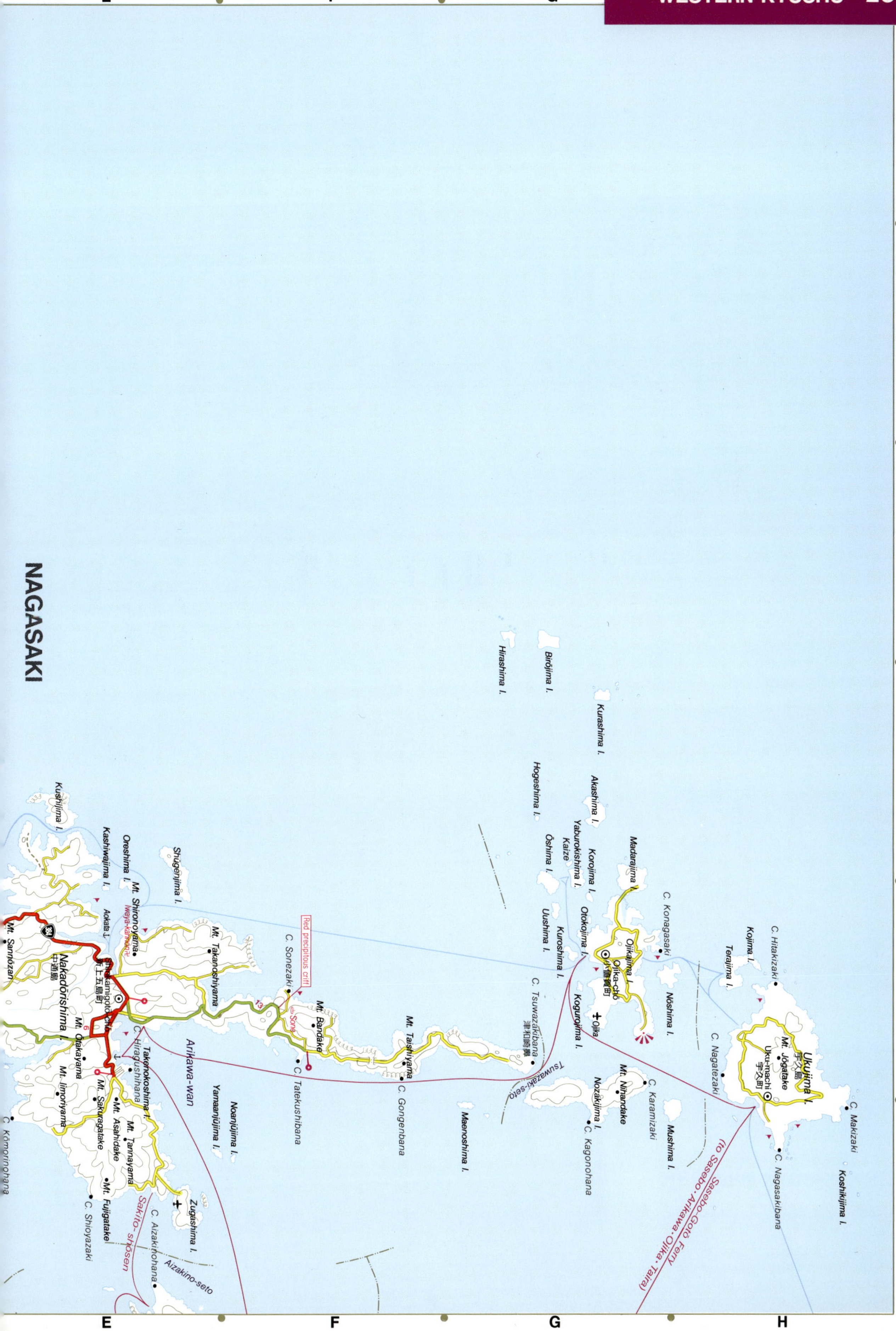
E
F
G
H
1
2
3
4
5
6
NAGASAKI
Hirashima I.
Birōjima I.
Kurashima I.
Hogeshima I.
Akashima I.
Yaburokishima I.
Kaize
Ōshima I.
Korojima I.
Madarajima I.
C. Konagasaki
Kojima I.
C. Hitakizaki
Terajima I.
Uushima I.
Kuroshima I.
Otokojima I.
Ojikajima I.
Ojika-chō
小値賀町
Ojika
Nōshima I.
C. Tsuwazakibana
津和崎鼻
Kogurojima I.
Tsuwazaki-seto
C. Nagatezaki
Ukujima I.
宇久島
Mt. Jōgatake
Uku-machi
宇久町
C. Makizaki
Koshikijima I.
C. Nagasakibana
Mt. Nihandake
C. Karamizaki
Nozakijima I.
C. Kagonohana
Mushima I.
Maenoshima I.
Sasebo-Gotō Ferry
(to Sasebo・Arikawa・Ojika・Taira)
Kushijima I.
Kashiwajima I.
Oreshima I.
Mt. Shironoyama
Iwaya-kannon
Shūgenjima I.
Aokata
Mt. Takanoshiyama
Red precipitous cliff
C. Sonezaki
Sone
Mt. Bandake
Mt. Taishiyama
C. Tatekushibana
C. Gongenbana
Mt. Sannōzan
Nakadōrishima I.
中通島
Shin-kamigotō-chō
新上五島町
Mt. Otakayama
Mt. Iimoriyama
C. Hiragushihana
Takenokoshima I.
Arikawa-wan
Yamaamijima I.
Noamijima I.
Mt. Sakuragatake
Mt. Asahidake
Mt. Tannayama
Mt. Fujigatake
C. Shioyazaki
Zugashima I.
Sakito-shōsen
C. Aizakinohana
Aizakino-seto
C. Komorinohana

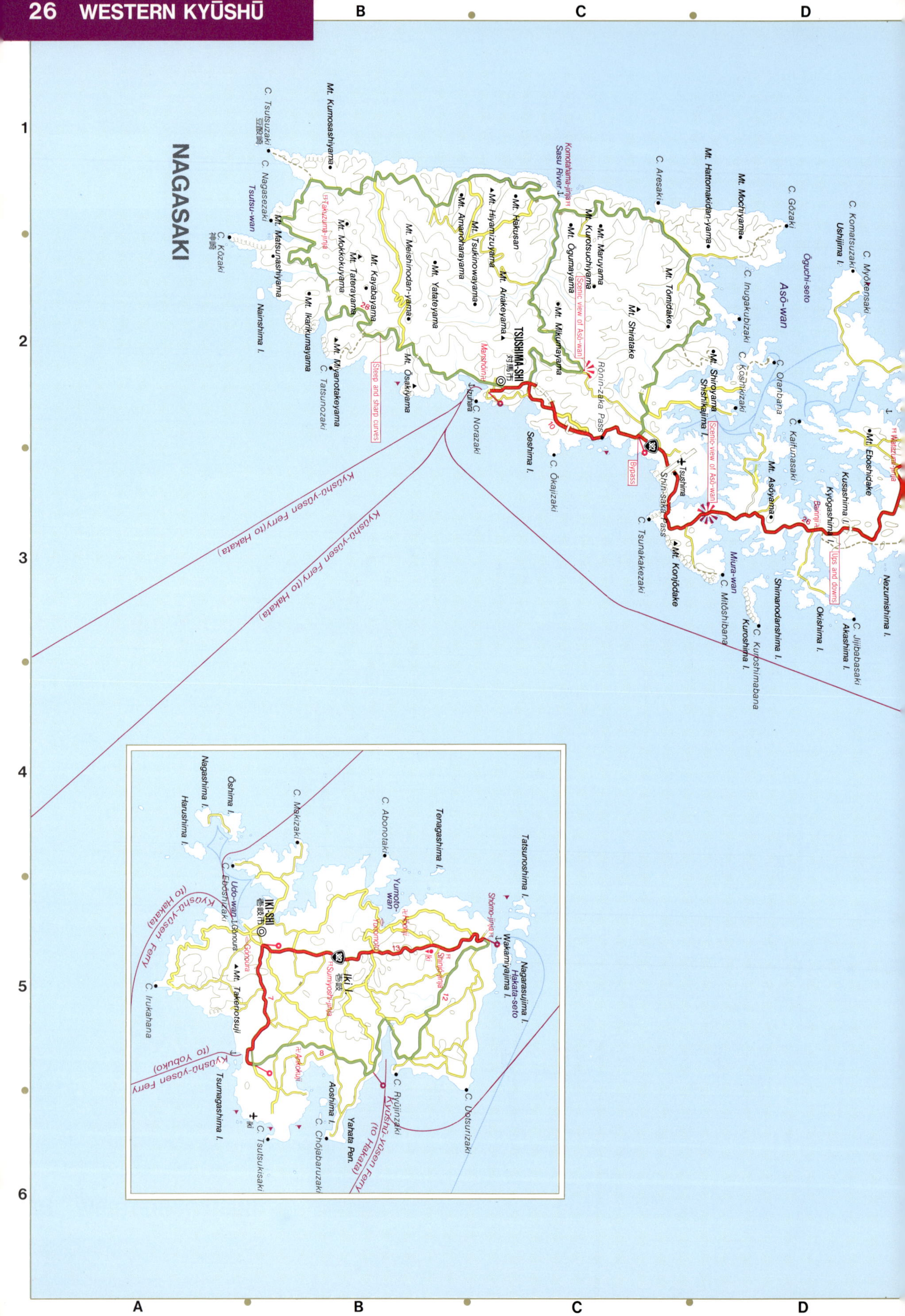

NAGASAKI
TSUSHIMA-SHI
対馬市
IKI-SHI
壱岐市
C. Tsutsuzaki
C. Nagasezaki
Tsutsu-wan
C. Kōzaki
Mt. Kumoosashiyama
Mt. Matsunashiyama
Mt. Mokkokuyama
Mt. Tateryama
Mt. Kayabayama
Mt. Ikarikumayama
Nainshima I.
Mt. Miyanotakeyama
C. Tatsunozaki
Steep and sharp curves
Mt. Meishinodan-yama
Mt. Ōsakiyama
Mt. Yatateyama
Mt. Amanoharayama
Mt. Tsukinowayama
Mt. Hiyamizuyama
Mt. Hakusan
Mt. Ariakeyama
Marushōrin
Izuhara
C. Norazaki
Seshima I.
C. Ōkajizaki
Komotahama-jinja
Sasu River
Mt. Kurotsuchiyama
Mt. Ōgumayama
Mt. Maruyama
Mt. Mikumayama
Scenic view of Asō-wan
Rōnin-zaka Pass
Mt. Shiratake
Mt. Tōmidake
C. Aresaki
Mt. Hattomakidan-yama
Mt. Mochiyama
C. Gōzaki
C. Komatsuzaki
Ushijima I.
Ōguchi-seto
Asō-wan
C. Inugakubizaki
C. Myōkenzaki
C. Koshikizaki
C. Oranbana
Mt. Shiroyama
Shishikajima I.
Bypass
Tsushima
Shin-saka Pass
Scenic view of Asō-wan
C. Kaifunasaki
Mt. Asōyama
Mt. Eboshidake
Kusashima I.
Kyōgashima I.
Bairinji
Watatsumi-jinja
C. Tsunakakezaki
Mt. Konjōdake
Miura-wan
C. Mitōshibana
Ups and downs
Shimanodanshima I.
Kuroshima I.
C. Kuroshimabana
Okishima I.
Akashima I.
C. Jijibabasaki
Nezumishima I.
Kyūshū-yūsen Ferry (to Hakata)
Kyūshū-yūsen Ferry (to Hakata)
Nagashima I.
Ōshima I.
Harushima I.
C. Makizaki
C. Abonotaki
Tenagashima I.
Tatsunoshima I.
C. Eboshizaki
Udo-wan
Gōnoura
Kyūshū-yūsen Ferry (to Hakata)
Yumoto-wan
Yunomoto
Honmi
Shōno-jinja
Wakamiyajima I.
Nagarasujima I.
Hakata-seto
Iki
Shōno-jinja
Iki I.
Sumiyoshi-jinja
Mt. Takenotsuji
C. Irukahana
Kyūshū-yūsen Ferry (to Yobuko)
Amakuji
C. Ryūjinzaki
C. Uotsurizaki
Tsumagashima I.
Aoshima I.
Yahata Pen.
C. Chōjabaruzaki
C. Tsutsukisaki
Kyūshū-yūsen Ferry (to Hakata)

E
F
G
H
1
2
3
4
5
6
TSUSHIMAKAIKYŌ-NISHI-SUIDŌ
対馬海峡西水道
(CHŌSEN-KAIKYŌ)
(朝鮮海峡)
TSUSHIMAKAIKYŌ-HIGASHI-SUIDŌ
対馬海峡東水道
Kyūshū-yūsen Ferry (to Hakata)
Tsushima I.
対馬
Kōshima I.
Enokishima I.
C. Tobisaki
Mt. Kurokumayama
Mine-wan
C. Tōnosaki
C. Inasaki
Nita-wan
Mt. Ōtakumayama
Mt. Yamadayama
Mt. Shishimouchiyama
Mt. Hanatakayama
Mt. Marukurayama
Mt. Nanahonmatsuyama
C. Saozaki
Mt. Senbyōmakiyama
Mt. Kōnokiyama
Mt. Ōkumayama
Mt. Mitake
Steep
Dō-saka Pass
Chayakuma Pass
Mt. Kajikiyama
Mt. Takanoyama
Mt. Ōboshiyama
Jizō Pass
Sugoroku-zaka Pass
C. Mushibaisaki
C. Nagasakibana
Mt. Kamiyama
C. Matsunosaki
Matsushima I.
Mt. Nanatakeyama
C. Kinzaki
Yoko-saka Pass
C. Tōnohana
Zenishima I.
Shushi-wan
C. Saginokubisaki
Shinakishima I.
Nishidomari-wan
C. Tonosaki
C. Atsuzaki
C. Sabazaki
Unishima I.
Mitsushima I.
Kujirase I.
C. Karasaki
Distant view of Korea
14
12
34
31

30
SASEBO-SHI 佐世保市
Sasebo-wan
C. Kōgozaki
C. Yorifunebana
Sasebo-Gotō Ferry (to Arikawa·Ojika)
Sakito-shōsen
Mt. Ushinotake
Mt. Iimoridake
Mt. Uwamatsudake
Huis Ten Bosch (R.A.)
Huistenbosch
Haenosaki
Saikaibashi
Saikai Pearl Line
ORD 150
LAR 400
Mt. Shiroiwadake
Mt. Kōbōdake
Hasami
Kawatana River
Kawatana-chō 川棚町
Kawatana-ekimae 川棚駅前
Kawatana
Mt. Hachiman-yama
Mt. Kokūzōzan
Mt. Takamidake
Ureshino
Ureshino-machi 嬉野町
Tea plantation
Tawarazaka Pass
Curves
Takeo-shi
Haiki
Katashima I.
C. Ushikubinohana
Nakanoshima I.
Hashinoshima I.
Saikai-chō 西海町
Mt. Kokuzōzan
Ōshima-chō 大島町
Mt. Yuridake
Nakato-seto
Terajima I.
Mt. Kamashikiyama
Yobukono-seto
大島大橋
Nanatsugama Cave
Sakito-chō 崎戸町
Kakinourashima I.
Komukae 小迎
Mt. Kazenotakamine
Saikaibashi(Bridge)
C. Myōjōnohana
Hariono-seto
Scenic view of Hariono-seto
Yokoshima I.
Ogushigo
Setojima I.
Mt. Ōsakiyama
C. Ōsaki
C. Tategaminohana
Sonogi
Egashira 江頭
Mt. Bangamiyama
Higashisonogi-chō 東彼杵町
Higashisonogi 東そのぎ
Mt. Kotohirayama
Nagashima I.
C. Horozaki
Mishima I.
Tajima I.
Takashima I.
Chiwata
Ōmura-wan 大村湾
Mt. Shiradake
Mt. Takahoyama
Mt. Gekitodake
Takenoshima I.
Seihi-chō 西彼町
Nagasaki Bio Park(Zoo)
Mt. Minedake
C. Biwanokōbana
Ōmura-wan
Matsubara
Mt. Mururoyama
Mt. Hachimakiyama
Matsushima-suidō
Kushijima I.
Ōseto-chō 大瀬戸町
Matsushima I.
Mt. Tōmidake
Yukinoura River
Mt. Kashiidake
Nitta Pass
Mt. Iimoriyama
Mt. Yakeyama
Katagami-wan
Nishisonogi Pen. 西彼杵半島
Kinkai-chō 琴海町
Usejima I.
C. Ōsezaki
Kuidetsu 杭出津
Takematsu
Suwa
Ōmura 大村
NAGASAKI
Nagasaki
Usujima I.
C. Kujimazaki
NAGASAKI
Ikeshima I.
Kuroshima I.
Futashima I.
Tatsujima I.
C. Dōzakibana
Iwamatsu
ŌMURA-SHI 大村市
Mt. Sanpōzan
Mt. Myōshōdake
Mt. Ōnodake
Maejima I.
Takashima I.
Shikashima I.
Mt. Hidake
Imamura 今村
Sumō-nada
Scenic view of East China Sea
Mt. Dōfudake
Mt. Kotooyama
Ōkusa
C. Shiraiwabana
Higashi-Sono
Mt. Kamakurayama
Tarami-chō 多良見町
Mt. Ōtake
Higuchi-Togitsu
Togitsu 時津
Togitsu-chō 時津町
Nagayo-chō 長与町
Hongawachi
Mt. Shishimidake
Ichinunme 市布
Accident-prone area
Kikitsu
Nagasaki Line
Kōuda
Nagayo
Nameshi Pass
Michinoo
C. Miezaki
長崎バイパス
Mt. Tsuyadake
Hizen-Koga
Nagasaki-Tarami 長崎多良見
Mt. Iwayasan
Mt. Tenjikudake
Mt. Hobadake
Nagasaki Bypass
ORD 410
LAR 1470
Utsutsugawa
Mt. Funaishidake
Mt. Gyōsendake
Yagamimachi 矢上町
矢上大橋
Mt. Maidake
Kawahira-dōro
ORD 200
LAR 720
Heiwa Park
Nishi-Urakami
Urakami
C. Ryūgasaki
Fuchi-jinja
NAGASAKI-SHI 長崎市
Suwa-jinja
Mt. Noroshiyama
Mt. Inasayama
Himi Pass
Nagasaki-Susukizuka 長崎芒塚
Kaminoshima
Mt. Konpiradake
Sōfukuji
ORD 100
LAR 360
Nagasaki-Gotō Ferry (to Narao·Narushima)
Nagasaki-Gotō Ferry (to Fukue)
from Nagasaki-shi
Fukuoka 160Km
Saga 100Km
Kaminoshima I.
C. Kōzakibana
Mt. Karahakkei
Nagasaki 長崎
Yagami-ōhashi (Bridge)
C. Biwazaki
C. Mabana
Iōjima I.
Mt. Ōkuboyama
Onakano-seto
Congestion in summer
Mt. Kumagamine
Nagasaki-Amakusa Ferry (to Tomioka)
Mt. Shiroyama
Mt. Hachirōdake
Mt. Kohachirōdake
Takashima I.
Mt. Teradake
Nojima I.
Nakanoshima I.
Hajima I.
Mt. Akibayama
Mt. Kumanodake
C. Ōsebana
Mt. Gongen-yama
NAGASAKI-SHI 長崎市
C. Nomozaki 野母崎
Kabashima I.
Mt. Gyōjayama
C. Kuchinohana
Scenic view of sunset
Mt. Ninotake
Mt. Gongen-yama
A
B
C
D
1
2
3
4
5
6

E
F
G
Saga-shi
31
48
46
1
2
3
4
5
H
SAGA
KUMAMOTO
Ariakekai
Shimabara-wan
Tachibana-wan
(Chijiwa-wan)
AMAKUSA-NADA
天草灘
Mt. Tōsenzan
Hizen-Kashima
Kashima River
KASHIMA-SHI
鹿島市
Hizen-Hama
Mt. Yunomineyama
Yūtoku-inari
Iwaya-kannon
Mt. Kotojidake
Hizen-Nanaura
Mt. Jōdoyama
Hizen-Iida
to Saga
Hizen
-Kashima
to Isahaya
Tara
Tara-chō
太良町
C. Kamezaki
Hiratani
Tōmeyama
Mt. Kyōgatake
Mt. Taradake
Hizen-Ōura
Mt. Gokaharadake
Todorokikyō (Gorge)
Konagai-chō
小長井町
Konagai
Takaki-chō
高来町
Yue
C. Hozaki
Ochōzu-kannon
Oe
Drive slowly
Ōmura Line
Nagasaki Line
Honmyō River
ISAHAYA SHI
諫早市
Hizen-Nagata
Higashi-Isahaya
Isahaya
Kaizumachi 貝津町
Isahaya Prefectural Sports Park
Drive-in area
Kamanohama
Nagasaki-kokusai
Funakoshimachi 小船越町
Isahayahigashi kōkōmae
Moriyama-chō
森山町
Mt. Rengeishidake
Chisan (Moriyama)
Hattendake
Congestion in spring
Aino
Aino-machi
愛野町
Aino 愛野
Aino-tenbōdai mae 愛野展望台前
Scenic view of Mt. Unzendake
Drive-in area
Iimori-chō
飯盛町
Maenoshima I.
Mukōjima I.
to Saga
to Kashima
to Nagasaki
to Obama
Ariake Ferry
Drive-in area
Saigō
Shimabara Line
Kunimi-chō
国見町
Taishō
Kobe
Mizuho-chō
瑞穂町
Azuma
Azuma-chō
吾妻町
Shimatetsu-Yue
Ariake-chō
有明町
Ōmisaki
Matsuomachi
Mie
Shimabara Pen.
島原半島
Mt. Hachimakiyama
Mt. Azumadake
Mt. Torikabutoyama
Shimabara Castle
SHIMABARA-SHI
島原市
Shimabara
Shimatetsu-Honshamae
Minami-Shimabara
Shimabara-Gaikō
Tachibana-jinja
Chijiwa-chō
千々石町
C. Tozakibana
MT. UNZENDAKE
雲仙岳
Nita-junkan-dōro
ORD 770
LAR 2140
Mt. Mayuyama
Mt. Fugendake
Mt. Heiseishinzan
仁田循環道路
Chichibugaura
Shimabara
島原
Antoku
Shimabara-Gaiko
to Unzen
to Kuchinotsu
Antoku 安徳
Isahaya 43Km
Obama 32Km
Kuchinotsu 34km
To Aino
Unzen-tozanguchi
雲仙登山口
to Kuchinotsu
to Shimabara
Mt. Takadake
Obama
小浜
Obama-chō
小浜町
Unzen
雲仙
Mt. Takaiwayama
Drive-in area
Fog
Seno-Fukae
Fukae
Fukae-chō
深江町
Drive-in area
Futsu-shinden
Futsu
Futsu-chō
布津町
Minamikushiyama-chō
南串山町
Arie-chō
有家町
Kitaarima-chō
北有馬町
Nishiarie-chō
西有家町
Kamaga
Dōzaki
Arima River
Kita-Arima
Jōkōjimae
Urata-kannon
Harajō
Harajō
C. Gondabana
Kazusa-machi
加津佐町
Scenic view of Amakusa-nada
Mt. Atagoyama
Iwato-kannon
Ana-kannon
Onsen-jinja
Kazusa
Arima-Yoshikawa
Minamiarima-chō
南有馬町
Shirahama-kaisuiyokujōmae
Higashi-Ōya
Kuchinotsu
Kuchinotsu-chō
口之津町
C. Miyazakibana
C. Sezumezaki
Shimatetsu Ferry
Gotsūiwa
Yushima I.
Nokamajima I.
KAMIAMAKUSA-SHI
上天草市
Misumi-Shimabara Ferry
Enoura
Takata-machi
高田町
Wataze
Hiraki
Nishitetsu-Wataze
Yabegawa River
Hōunji
Ariake
Higashi-Amagi
Ginsui
Higashi-Shinmachi 東新町
Suwagawa River
Ōmuta
OMUTA-SHI
大牟田市
Miike
Arao
Mitsui Greenland
ARAO-SHI
荒尾市
Kagoshima Line
Minami-Arao
Shiōji-jinja
Nagasu
Nagasu-machi
長洲町

B
C
D
1
2
3
4
5
6
A
Kofutakamijima I.
Futakamijima I.
C. Ozaki
Madarashima I.
Kaishima I.
Azuchiōshima I.
的山大島
Ōnesaka-wan
C. Ōgabana
Ōshima-mura
大島村
Azuchi -wan
C. Umanokashima
Ōshimamura Ferry
Mukushima I.
C. Aōzaki
Kuroshima I.
Hibi-suidō
Takushima I.
C. Sakisenohana
Marushima I.
Yokoshima I.
Kujirashima I.
to Tashuke-machi
NTT
to Kawachi-chō
Takashima I.
鷹島
Takashima-chō
鷹島町
Izushima I.
Aoshima I.
Takashima-kisen Ferry
Takashima Ferry
Mt. Shiratake
Tanoura
C. Nagasakibana
Usuka-wan
Hirado-seto
Ikitsuki-chō
生月町
Ikitsukishima I.
生月島
C. Tsuzaki
Mt. Jōyama
C. Nagasebana
Ōtobishi
Futajima I.
Kotobishi
ORD 100
LAR 300
Hirado-ōhashi(Bridge)
Naka-enoshima I.
HIRADO-SHI
平戸市
Hirado Castle
Tabira-chō
田平町
C. Hazusaki
Matsuura Bypass
ORD 100
LAR 360
C. Kanai
C. Nagasebana
C. Arasaki
Tatsuno-seto
生月大橋
Ikitsuki-ōhashi
ORD 600
LAR 2100
Mt. Yasumandake
Senkōji
383
Congestion in spring and summer
Drive-in area
Tabira-Hiradoguchi
Naka-Tabira
Nishi-Tabira
Higashi-Tabira
Mikuriya
Matsuura Railway
松浦バイパス
MATSUURA-SHI
松浦市
Tsukinokawa
Imabuku
Uranosaki
C. Ōsakibana
Ō-goe Pass
Mt. Uwatoko
204
Matsuura-hatsudensho-mae
Mt. Ishimoriyama
Hiradoshima I.
平戸島
Emukae-chō
江迎町
Fukui Pass
Mt. Takabotchidake
Mt. Kunimidake
Kojima I.
Emukae-Shikamachi
Maenoshima I.
Hirakojima I.
Kuzujima I.
Takaiwa
Hirado
Shisagawa River
Kuroshima I.
Nojima I.
Fukuidōketsu(Cave)
C. Ōsakibana
Fumonji
Mt. Yusozudake
C. Shiratobana
Kujūkushima I.
九十九島
Ushigashima I.
Ōshima I.
Shikamachi-chō
鹿町町
Senryūgataki
Mt. Washiodake
Yoshii-chō
吉井町
Mukuroji Pass
Hizen-Yoshii
Ōhashi-kannon
Hizen-Kōda
Tomoniiwa(Cave)
Sechibaru-chō
世知原町
Kami-ajikajima I.
Madatejima I.
Mt. Shirodake
Akajima I.
Mt. Konpiradake
Kami-Saza
Mt. Gozōdake
Eri-tōge Pass
Shimo-ajikajima I.
NAGASAKI
Saza-chō
佐々町
Saza
Sasebo
Short curver
Shimojima I.
Kosaza-chō
小佐々町
Tsukumo
Fuyukoshi Pass
Mt. Sashidake
Maeshima I.
Sharp curves
Mt. Byōbudake
Tōhakujima I.
Koura
Kashiragashima I.
C. Oihozaki
C. Bōyamahana
Nojima I.
Maeshima I.
Mt. Nagasakiyama
Enoshima I.
Masaru
Nakazato
Kaize
Hidarishi
Chōsenji
Gakijima I.
Yakejima I.
Mt. Asagodake
Tanagata
Mt. Shōkandake
from Sasebo
Fukuoka 110Km
Saga 70Km
Mt. Hamadake
Tokoijima I.
Kami-odakashima I.
Kami-Ainoura
Takashima I.
Shijiki-wan
Shimo-odakashima I.
Ainoura
C. Tateishizaki
Mt. Yumiharidake
Matsuurachō 松浦町
Mt. Shijikiyama
Takashima I.
Mt. Takadake
Naka-Sasebo
SASEBO-SHI
佐世保市
Ishima I.
C. Shijikizaki
志々伎崎
Sasebo Heavy Industries
Makishima I.
Katsurajima I.
Mt. Atagoyama
Sasebo-minato
Sasebo
Hin
to Sasebo
to Saga
to Nagasaki
Mt. Bandake
C. Mezenohana
Kuroshima I.
C. Neyanohana
Makurajima I.
C. Shichirōbana
Tagonoura 田子の浦
Hirado 45Km
Imari 22Km
Takeo 27Km
Nagasaki-shi

IKI-SUIDŌ
壱岐水道
GENKAI-NADA
玄界灘
C. En-onohana
Kakarajima I.
Ogawajima I.
Matsushima I.
Iki Ferry Yobuko (to Intsūji)
C. Hadonomisaki
Tashima-jinja
C. Dokizaki
Distant view of Ikishima I.
Nagoya Castle
Kashiwajima I.
Drive-in area
Chigasaki
C. Ōgasaki
Karatsu-wan
Higashimatsuura Pen.
東松浦半島
Scenic view of Karatsu-wan
Genkai-chō
玄海町
Ōsaki
Kariya-wan
Takenokojima I.
Ōshima I.
Takashima I.
Torishima I.
Nishi-Karatsu
Higashimachi 東町
Fukuoka 52Km
Saga 51Km
Imari 27Km
Congestion in summer
Nijino-matsubara Beautiful Beach
KARATSU-SHI
唐津市
Watada 和多田
Watada
Hamasaki
Pine trees
Karatsu chinaware sale area
Kawarabashi 河原橋
Mt. Mizunomotoyama
Irohajima I.
Fukushima-chō
福島町
Useshima I.
Matsuura River
Mt. Yūhiyama
Yamamoto
Mt. Tsubakiyama
Mt. Sanpōyama
Karatsu Line
Hon-Mutabe
Congestion in summer
Mt. Sakureizan
SAGA
Hizen-Kubo
Nishi-Ōchi
Sari
Ōchi
Saga Royal
Iwaya
Kyūragi River
Mt. Ōnodake
Mt. Jōkotake
Mt. Ōhirayama
Imari-wan
Hase
Kubara
Kusuku
Komanaki
Okawano
Ōhashi 大橋
Namise Pass
Hizen-Nagano
Mt. Daijindake
Mt. Kunimidake
IMARI-SHI
伊万里市
Karatsu 27km
Matsuura 24Km
Takeo 20Km
Mt. Bizan
Mt. Hachimandake
Sasabaru Pass
Higashi-Yamashiro
Daitsūzan
Ōzato 大里
Kami-Imari
Kanatake
Mt. Koshidake
Meotoishi
Mt. Makinoyama
Mt. Kurodake
Mt. Kurokamiyama
Mt. Tokurendake
Tosaka Pass
Takeo-Kitagata
Sōgōchōsha-iriguchi
総合庁舎入口
Nishiarita-chō
西有田町
Frozen road
Yamauchi-chō
山内町
Sasebo Line
Arita-machi
有田町
Arita
Haraake 原明
Udo-goe Pass
Kakuidake
ORD 960
LAR 3320
Mt. Makunokashira
Arita chinaware sale area
Nishi-Kyūshū-Idōshadō
Mt. Jinrokuyama
Dōshima 堂島
Saga 30Km
Imari 20Km
Haiki 27Km
TAKEO-SHI
武雄市
Takeo
Drive-in area
Mikawachi
Sasebo-kokusai
Mikawachieki-iriguchi
三川内駅入口
Hasami-chō
波佐見町
Takeo-Ureshino
Tea Plantation area
Isahaya-shi
C. Tsugamizaki
Mt. Hikosan
Shima Seaside
Mt. Koshidake
Itoshima Pen.
糸島半島
Mt. Hiyama
Keyanoōto (Scenic Rocky Coast)
芥屋大門
Mt. Tateishiyama
C. Hotokezaki
Himeshima I.
Shima-machi
志摩町
Mt. Kayayama
C. Saginokubi
Misakigaoka
MAEBARU-SHI
前原市
Chikuzen-Maebaru
Kafuri
Hatae
Raizan River
C. Haizaki
Nijō-machi
二丈町
Chikuzen-Fukae
Hashima I.
Fukuyoshi
C. Kushizaki
Drive-in area
ORD 360
LAR 1240
FUKUOKA
Scenic view of Genkai-nada
Nagano Pass
Mt. Raizan
Mt. Tonboyama
Mt. Ukidake
Mt. Haganeyama
Hatakeda はたけだ
Nanayama-mura
七山村
Kannon Pass
Mt. Kametake
Fuji-chō
富士町
Mt. Shiroishiyama
Kasegawa River
Mt. Tenzan
Mt. Hikotake
Kyūragi-Taku-dōro
ORD 200
LAR 550
Mt. Atagoyama
Kiyomizu Fall
TAKU-SHI
多久市
Ogi-machi
小城町
Yamato-chō
大和町
Higashi-Taku
Shimomachi 下町
Taku
多久
Naka-Taku
Mt. Kagamiyama
Mikazuki-chō
三日月町
Kogayama 古賀山
Mt. Futagoyama
Ushizu 牛津
NAGASAKI EXPRESSWAY
長崎自動車道
Saga Bypass
Drive-in area
Ushizu-chō
牛津町
Mt. Ōninohanayama
Kōhoku-machi
江北町
Kitagata-machi
北方町
Ōmachi-chō
大町町
Ashikari-chō
芦刈町
Kubota-chō
久保田町
Nagasaki-kaidō
Hizen-Yamaguchi
Higashibun 東分
Kamisō 上惣
Rokkaku River
Mt. Kishimayama
Hizen-Shiroishi
Shiroishi-chō
白石町
Mt. Kokuzōyama
Mt. Shiraiwayama
Hizen-Ryūō
Shiota-chō
塩田町
Ariake Sea
Kashima-shi
Nagasaki
50
29
E
F
G
H
1
2
3
4
5
6
Fukuoka-shi
Saga-shi
Saga street

B
C
D
34
Enoshima I.
Kaigata
Nankai-yūsen Ferry (to Kagoshima)
Takatoge-kogen
Kihoku-chō
輝北町
Ōsumiko Lake
Mt. Nanatake
Kagoshima-Kanoya
KAGOSHIMA-SHI
鹿児島市
Tarumizu 垂水
TARUMIZU-SHI
垂水市
Mt. Onokaradake
Mt. Takakumayama
高隈山
Mt. Hakusan
Mt. Yokodake
Mt. Ontake
Kushira River
KINKŌ-WAN
錦江湾
(KAGOSHIMA-WAN)
鹿児島湾
C. Karusahana
Sata-kaidō
佐多街道
Takasu River
Kanoya River
Kitada 北田
Kotobuki 寿
to Tarumizu
to Kushima
Terukuni-yūsen Ōshima-un-yu
Kagoshima-shi
Furue 古江
Takachiho-jinja
Mt. Ōtsukayama
Arisato 有里
Nakamyō
KANOYA-SHI
鹿屋市
Kushira-chō
串良町
C. Unosehana
Arahira-tenjin
Accident-prone area
KAGOSHIMA-SHI
鹿児島市
Kiire
Nishihara 西原
Kanoya Airport
from Kanoya-shi
Kita-Kyūshū 490Km
Kagoshima 90Km
Kimotsuki River
Yasaka-jinja
Maenohama
Kōyama-chō
高山町
Hachiman-jinja
Aira-chō
吾平町
KAGOSHIMA
Mt. Omeguriyama
Nukumi
C. Kannonzaki
Drive-in area
Satsuma-Imaizumi
Mt. Fukushidake
Takayama River
Mt. Sansuyama
Kojima I.
Miyagahama
Chiringashima I.
Kannokawa River
Ōsumi Pen.
大隅半島
Mt. Uomidake
Amami-kaiun
Ibusuki-jinja
Mt. Kiyomidake
Nigatsuden
IBUSUKI-SHI
指宿市
Katakuchi
Ōnejime-chō
大根占町
Ikedako Lake
Ibusuki
Ibusuki
指宿
Mt. Washiodake
Ogawa River
Nejime-chō
根占町
Kaimon-chō
開聞町
Unagiike Lake
Yamakawa
Hirakiki-jinja
C. Konpirahana
Ogawa Gorge
Mt. Araseyama
Mt. Tsujinotake
Yamagawa-chō
山川町
Tashiro-chō
田代町
Mt. Rokurōyakatadake
Makurazaki-shi
Kaimon
Higashi-Kaimon
Satsuma-Kawashiri
Ōyama
Nishi-Ōyama
Narikawa 成川
Ibusuki
Kyūshū-Shōsen
Mt. Kaimondake
開聞岳
Kawashiri
Mt. Tsujidake
Kaimon
C. Kaimonzaki
Nagasakibana Parking Garden
Nagasakibana
Scenic view of Mt. Kaimondake
C. Nagasakibana
長崎鼻
Sata-kaidō
佐多街道
Sata-chō
佐多町
C. Tachimezaki
C. Akasezaki
to Sata chō
to Sakamoto
C. Hayasaki
佐多岬ロードパーク
Satamisaki Road Park
Birōjima I.
ORD 1000
LAR 4000
Southern edge of Kyūshū
C. Satamisaki
佐多岬
1
2
3
4
5
6
43
A
B
C
D

E
F
G
H
1
2
3
4
5
6
35
Mt. Chitoriyama
Nichinan Line
Nango-chō
南郷町
Ōshima I.
C. Kurasakibana
Hyūga-Ōtsuka
Toname 外行
Mt. Kasagidake
Mt. Kameizan
Ariake-chō
有明町
Shibushi-chō
志布志町
kushima-ekimae 串間駅前
Nichinanshi 29Km
Toimisaki 24Km
Kanoya 42Km
Hyūga-Kitakata
MIYAZAKI
Tsukishima I.
Ōsumi-Natsui
Shibushi
Kushima
KUSHIMA-SHI
串間市
Torishima I.
Kōjima I.
Anraku River
C. Dagurizaki
Uemachi 上町
Hishida River
Fukushima-Takamatsu
Fukushima-Imamachi
Fukushima River
Mt. Takahatayama
Ōsaki-chō
大崎町
Birōjima I.
Bindarejima I.
Sanmoji 三文字
Tabaru River
C. Nagatazaki
Shibushi-wan
C. Arasaki
C. Toimisaki
都井岬
Scenic view of Pacific ocean
Kimotsuki River
Blue Highway Line (to Ōsaka)
Mt. Kunimiyama
C. Hidesaki
Uchinoura-wan
C. Hizaki
Uchinoura-chō
内之浦町
Mt. Hoyoshidake
Drive-in area
C. Tozaki

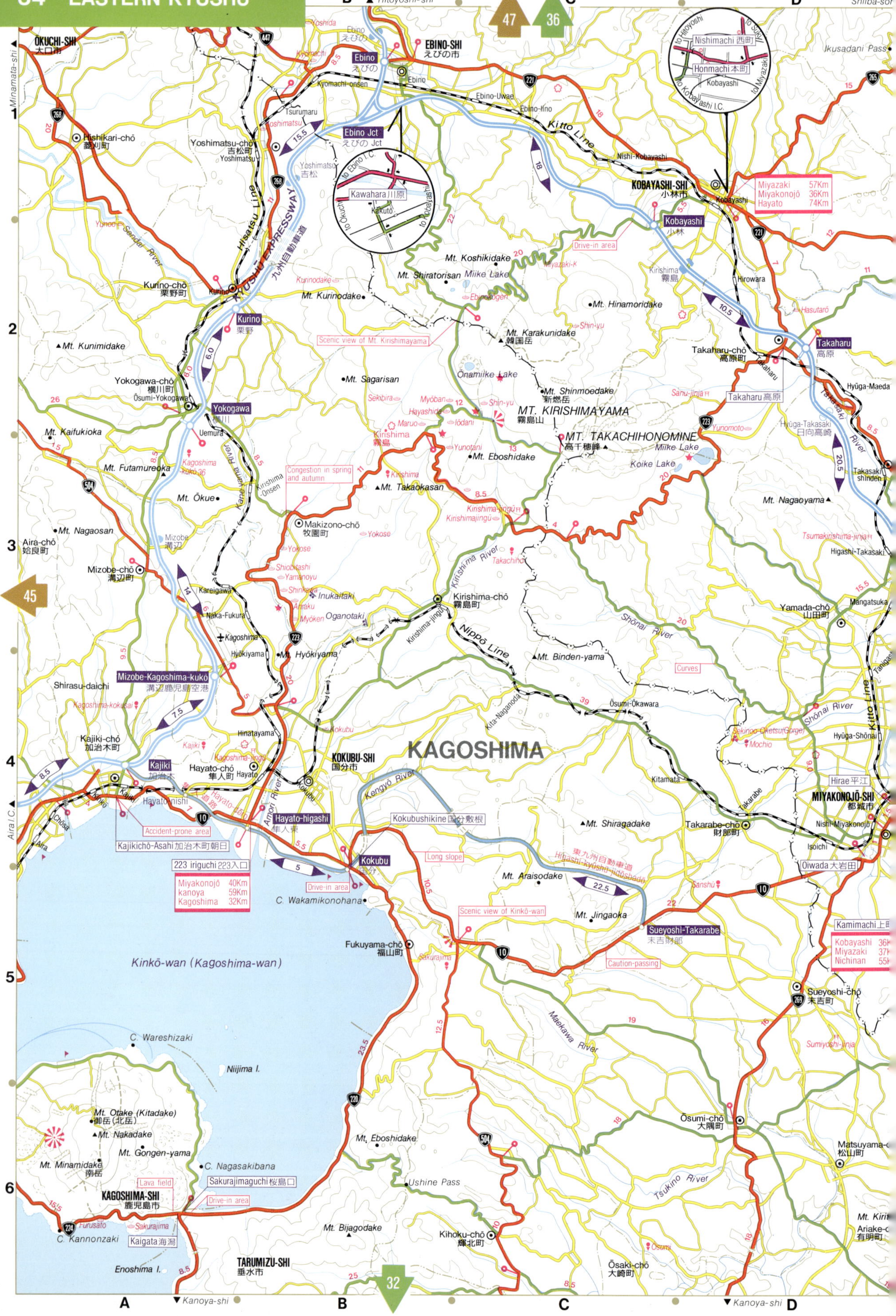

B
Hitoyoshi-shi
47
36
C
D
Shiiba-son
ŌKUCHI-SHI 大口市
Minamata-shi
EBINO-SHI えびの市
Ebino えびの
Yoshida
Kyomachi-onsen
Ebino-Uwae
Ebino-Iino
Kitto Line
Nishi-Kobayashi
Ikusadani Pass
Nishimachi 西町
Honmachi 本町
Kobayashi
to Hitoyoshi
to Miyazaki
to Kobayashi I.C.
to Suki
Tsurumaru
Yoshimatsu
Ebino Jct えびの Jct
Hishikari-chō 菱刈町
Yoshimatsu-chō 吉松町
Yoshimatsu 吉松
Kawahara 川原
to Ebino I.C.
to Ōkuchi
to Kobayashi
Kakutō
KOBAYASHI-SHI 小林市
Kobayashi 小林
Miyazaki 57Km
Miyakonojō 36Km
Hayato 74Km
Yunoo
Sendai River
Hisatsu Line
KYUSHU EXPRESSWAY 九州自動車道
Drive-in area
Miyazaki-K
Mt. Koshikidake
Mt. Shiratorisan
Miike Lake
Ebinokōgen
Kirishima 霧島
Hirowara
Kurino-chō 栗野町
Kurino 栗野
Kurinodake
Mt. Kurinodake
Mt. Hinamoridake
Shin-yu
Hasutarō
Mt. Karakunidake 韓国岳
Scenic view of Mt. Kirishimayama
Mt. Kunimidake
Takaharu-chō 高原町
Takaharu 高原
Ōnamiike Lake
Mt. Sagarisan
Yokogawa-chō 横川町
Ōsumi-Yokogawa
Yokogawa 横川
Uemura
Mt. Shinmoedake 新燃岳
Sanu-jinja
Hyūga-Maeda
Sekibira
Myōban
Hayashida
MT. KIRISHIMAYAMA 霧島山
Maruo
Iōdani
Mt. Kaifukioka
Hyūga-Takasaki 日向高崎
Takasaki River
Yunomoto
MT. TAKACHIHONOMINE 高千穂峰
Miike Lake
Koike Lake
Yunotani
Mt. Eboshidake
Kagoshima-kūkō 36
Kirishima-Onsen
Kareigawa River
Congestion in spring and autumn
Mt. Futamureoka
Mt. Takaokasan
Takasaki shinden
Mt. Nagaoyama
Mt. Ōkue
Kirishima-jingū
Kirishimajingū
Makizono-chō 牧園町
Yokose
Mt. Nagaosan
Mizobe 溝辺
Aira-chō 始良町
Tsumakirishima-jinja
Higashi-Takasaki
Mizobe-chō 溝辺町
Shiobitashi
Yamanoyu
Shinkawa
Inukaitaki
Anraku
Myōken
Oganotaki
Takachiho
Kirishima River
Kirishima-chō 霧島町
Kirishima-jingū
45
Kareigawa
Naka-Fukura
Kagoshima
Nippō Line
Shōnai River
Yamada-chō 山田町
Mangatsuka
Hyōkiyama
Mt. Hyōkiyama
Mt. Binden-yama
Mizobe-Kagoshima-kūkō 溝辺鹿児島空港
Curves
Shirasu-daichi
Kagoshima-kokusai
Ōsumi-Ōkawara
Kita-Naganoda
Hinatayama
Kokubu
Shōnai River
Sekinoo-Oketsu(Gorge)
Mochio
Hyūga-Shōnai
Kitto Line
Kajiki-chō 加治木町
Kajiki
Kagoshima-jingū
KAGOSHIMA
Kajiki 加治木
Hayato-chō 隼人町
Hayato
KOKUBU-SHI 国分市
Kengyō River
Hirae 平江
Kitamata
Takarabe
MIYAKONOJŌ-SHI 都城市
Chōsa
Hayatonishi
Hayato-Kaidō
Amori River
Hayato-higashi 隼人東
Kokubushikine 国分敷根
Aira I.C.
Aira
Accident-prone area
Kajikichō-Asahi 加治木町朝日
Mt. Shiragadake
Takarabe-chō 財部町
Nishi-Miyakonojō
Isoichi
Oiwada 大岩田
Long slope
Higashi-kyūshū-jidōshadō 東九州自動車道
223 iriguchi 223入口
Miyakonojō 40Km
kanoya 59Km
Kagoshima 32Km
Kokubu 国分
Drive-in area
Mt. Araisodake
Sanshū
C. Wakamikonohana
Scenic view of Kinkō-wan
Mt. Jingaoka
Sueyoshi-Takarabe 末吉財部
Kamimachi 上町
Kobayashi 36
Miyazaki 37
Nichinan 55
Fukuyama-chō 福山町
Sakurajima
Caution-passing
Kinkō-wan (Kagoshima-wan)
Sueyoshi-chō 末吉町
Maekawa River
C. Wareshizaki
Sumiyoshi-jinja
Niijima I.
Mt. Otake (Kitadake) 御岳(北岳)
Mt. Nakadake
Mt. Gongen-yama
Ōsumi-chō 大隅町
Mt. Eboshidake
C. Nagasakibana
Matsuyama-chō 松山町
Mt. Minamidake 南岳
Lava field
Sakurajimaguchi 桜島口
Ushine Pass
Tsukino River
KAGOSHIMA-SHI 鹿児島市
Drive-in area
Furusato
Sakurajima
Kaigata 海潟
C. Kannonzaki
Mt. Bijagodake
Kihoku-chō 輝北町
Ōsumi
Mt. Kiri
Ariake-chō 有明町
Enoshima I.
TARUMIZU-SHI 垂水市
Ōsaki-chō 大崎町
32
A
Kanoya-shi
B
C
Kanoya-shi
D
1
2
3
4
5
6

E
F
G
H
1
2
3
4
5
6
37
33
Onoko Lake
Mt. Shakagatake
Ayagawa Gorge
Mt. Nakumayama
Suki-son
須木村
Nasaki Pass
Ayakita River
SAITO-SHI
西都市
Hitotsuse River
Shintomi-chō
新富町
Miyazaki-kokusai
Sadowara-chō
佐土原町
Sadowara
Miyazaki GC
Aya-chō
綾町
Kunitomi-chō
国富町
Hyūga-Sumiyoshi
Honjo River
Phoenix
Nojiri-chō
野尻町
Phoenix-kōgen
Takaoka Bypass
Hōji
Hōji 芳士
Seagaia Ocean Dome
Iwase Dam
Nojiriko Lake
Takaoka-chō
高岡町
Miyazaki Oyodogawa
Ikime 生目
Miyazaki-nishi
宮崎西
Hitotsuba-dōro
ORD 370
LAR 1260
Miyazaki-jingū
Miyazaki-jingu
Drive-in area
Yunotani
Tachibana 橋
Hitotsuba-jinja
Miyazaki
from Miyazakishi
Kita-Kyūshū 380Km
Kagoshima 130Km
Mt. Takaoyama
Ikime-jinja
MIYAZAKI-SHI
宮崎市
MIYAZAKI
Nakamura 中村
Minami-Miyazaki
Ōyodo River
Mt. Iwahoneyama
Gendōchō 源藤町
Tayoshi
Takazaki-chō
高崎町
Mt. Kunimiyama
Kand
Miyazaki
宮崎
Miyazaki
Miyazaki-kūkō
Mt. Keragatsuka
Kiyotake
清武
Kiyotake
清武
Miyazaki CC
Minamikata
Miyazaki-minami Bypass
Hyūga-Kutsukake
Kiyotake
Kiyotake-chō
清武町
Aoshima Public
Mt. Aoidake
Nippō Line
Tano-chō
田野町
Tano
Kiyotake River
Prefectual Sports Park
Miyazaki Univ.
Kibana
Aoidake
Miyazaki-kokusaikūkō
MIYAZAKI EXPRESSWAY
宮崎自動車道
Tano
田野
Mt. Arahirayama
Sosanji
Rainbow Sportsland
Children's Garden(P.G.)
Aoshima I.
Takajō-chō
高城町
Aoshima
Aoshima Island
(Scenic Rocky Coast)
青島
Yamanokuchi
山之口
Oryūzako
C. Tozakibana
Yamanokuchi
Ōtono-goe Pass
Scenic view of elevated coast
Horikiri Pass
堀切峠
Miyakonojō
都城
Yamanokuchi-chō
山之口町
Mt. Wanitsukayama
Uchiumi
Mochibaru
Mt. Yukigamine
Drive-in area
Kouchiumi
Miyakonojō
Mimata
Mimata-chō
三股町
Mt. Yanagidake
Ibii
Nichinan Line
Saboten-en(Cactus Garden)
to Miyazaki
Nishi Miyakonojō
to Kagoshima
to Ōsumi
Mt. Komatsuyama
Kitagō
Kitagō-chō
北郷町
Kitagō
Udo-jingū
鵜戸神宮
Drive-in area
C. Udozaki
Uchinoda
Mt. Inugajōyama
Mt. Onigajōyama
Obi Castle
Obi
Sakatani River
Mt. Osuzuyama
NICHINAN-SHI
日南市
Nichinan
HYŪGA-NADA
日向灘
Miyatayama
Hirose River
Kasugacho 春日町
Mt. Gozaishodake
Ōyodo River
Shibushi-kaidō
Aburatsu
Aburatsu
Miyazaki 54Km
Miyakonojō 55Km
Kanoya 72Km
Mt. Kakyūsan
C. Izaki
Shibushi-chō
志布志町
Ōdotsu
Nanatsuiwa I.
Mt. Takigahirayama
Nangō River
Kobashima I.
Yowara-jinja
Taninokuchi
Ōshima I.
Yowara
Nangō
Nangō-ekimae 南郷駅前
Nangō-chō
南郷町
Kushima-shi

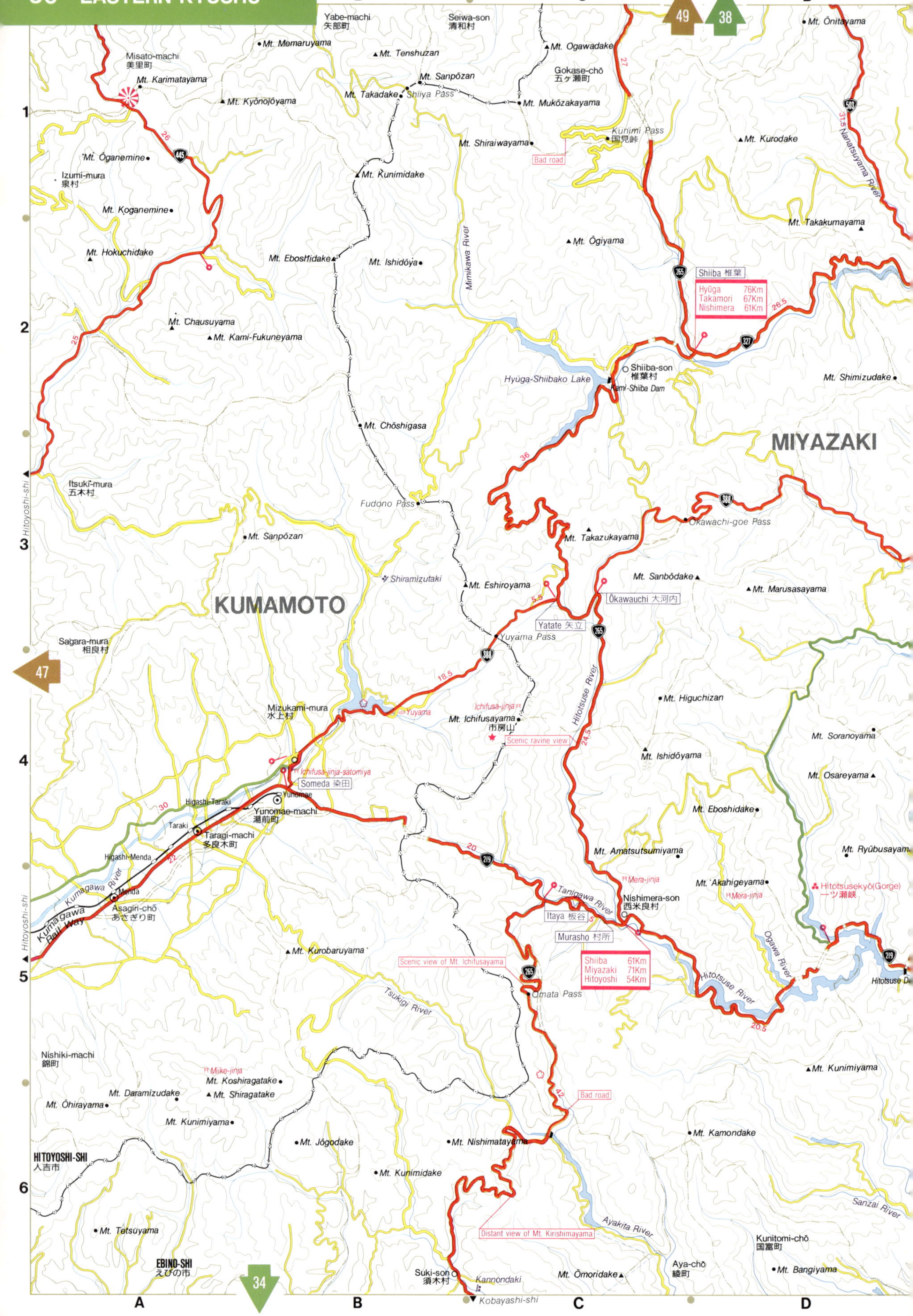

B
C
D
49
38
Yabe-machi
矢部町
Seiwa-son
清和村
Mt. Ōnitayama
Misato-machi
美里町
Mt. Memaruyama
Mt. Tenshuzan
Mt. Ogawadake
Gokase-chō
五ヶ瀬町
Mt. Karimatayama
Mt. Sanpōzan
Mt. Takadake
Shiiya Pass
Mt. Mukōzakayama
Mt. Kyōnojōyama
1
Kunimi Pass
国見峠
Mt. Shiraiwayama
Bad road
Mt. Kurodake
Nanatsuyama River
Mt. Ōganemine
Izumi-mura
泉村
Mt. Kunimidake
Mt. Koganemine
Mt. Takakumayama
Mt. Ōgiyama
Mt. Hokuchidake
Mt. Eboshidake
Mt. Ishidōya
Mimikawa River
Shiiba 椎葉
Hyūga 76Km
Takamori 67Km
Nishimera 61Km
2
Mt. Chausuyama
Mt. Kami-Fukuneyama
Shiiba-son
椎葉村
Hyūga-Shiibako Lake
Kami-Shiiba Dam
Mt. Shimizudake
Mt. Chōshigasa
MIYAZAKI
Itsuki-mura
五木村
Hitoyoshi-shi
Fudono Pass
Ōkawachi-goe Pass
Mt. Takazukayama
3
Mt. Sanpōzan
Mt. Sanbōdake
Mt. Marusasayama
Shiramizutaki
Mt. Eshiroyama
KUMAMOTO
Ōkawauchi 大河内
Yatate 矢立
Yuyama Pass
Sagara-mura
相良村
47
Hitotsuse River
Mt. Higuchizan
Ichifusa-jinja
Mizukami-mura
水上村
Yuyama
Mt. Ichifusayama
市房山
Scenic ravine view
Mt. Soranoyama
4
Mt. Ishidōyama
Ichifusa-jinja-satomiya
Someda 染田
Mt. Osareyama
Higashi-Taraki
Yunomae
Yunomae-machi
湯前町
Taraki
Taragi-machi
多良木町
Mt. Eboshidake
Higashi-Menda
Mt. Amatsutsumiyama
Mt. Ryūbusayama
Kumagawa River
Menda
Mera-jinja
Mt. Akahigeyama
Hitotsusekyō(Gorge)
一ツ瀬峡
Mera-jinja
Taniqawa River
Nishimera-son
西米良村
Kuma gawa Rail Way
Asagiri-chō
あさぎり町
Itaya 板谷
Murasho 村所
Hitoyoshi-shi
Mt. Kurobaruyama
Shiiba 61Km
Miyazaki 71Km
Hitoyoshi 54Km
Ogawa River
5
Scenic view of Mt. Ichifusayama
Hitotsuse D
Ōmata Pass
Hitotsuse River
Tsukigi River
Nishiki-machi
錦町
Mt. Kunimiyama
Miike-jinja
Mt. Koshiragatake
Mt. Daramizudake
Mt. Shiragatake
Bad road
Mt. Ōhirayama
Mt. Kunimiyama
Mt. Kamondake
HITOYOSHI-SHI
人吉市
Mt. Jōgodake
Mt. Nishimatayama
Mt. Kunimidake
6
Sanzai River
Mt. Tetsuyama
Distant view of Mt. Kirishimayama
Ayakita River
Kunitomi-chō
国富町
EBINO-SHI
えびの市
Suki-son
須木村
Kannondaki
Mt. Ōmoridake
Aya-chō
綾町
Mt. Bangiyama
34
Kobayashi-shi
A
B
C
D

E
F
G
H
1
2
3
4
5
6
39
35
Takachiho-chō
Hinokage-chō
日之影町
Makimine
Kamegasaki
Hayahino
Takachiho Railway
Mukabaki-jinja
from Nobeoka-shi
Kita-Kyūshū 290Km
Kagoshima 220Km
Nishi-Nobeoka
Nobeoka
Drive-in area
Mukabaki
Asahi Chemical Industry
NOBEOKA-SHI
延岡市
Minami-Nobeoka
Nobeoka Bypass
C. Hiuchizaki
火打崎
Gionmachi
祇園町
Kawarazaki
川原崎
to Takachiho
to Hyūga
Mt. Mayumidake
Kamizaki
Soki
Hakiai
Hyūga-Okamoto
Hosomi
Kitakata-chō
北方町
Kawasuru
Mt. Hayahinomine
Gokase River
Miwa-jinja
Kitakata
Mt. Eboshidake
Nobeoka-minami-dōro
ORD 250
LAR 900
Asahigaoka
C. Kurakakehana
Totoro
Morotsuka-son
諸塚村
Yoshino-jinja
Zenchōji
Kitagō-son
北郷村
Mt. Komaseyama
Mt. Karamatsuyama
Mt. Tōmiyama
Isuzu River
Kadogawa
Kadogawa-wan
Mt. Togirino
Zasshodokoro Pass
Kadogawa-chō
門川町
Otojima I.
Birōjima I.
Marin Express (to Kaizuka·Kawasaki)
to Nobeoka
to Ferry port
Hyūgashi
to Shiiba
to Miyazaki
Oserinotaki
Saigō-son
西郷村
HYŪGA-SHI
日向市
Hyūgashi
Hosojima
Tobishima I.
Myōkokuji
Mt. Komenoyama
Kannondaki
Mt. Togariyama
Mt. Tateyama
Mt. Nagatayama
Zaikōji
Ōmagari 大曲
Nobeoka 22Km
Shiiba 76Km
Miyazaki 67Km
Mikado-jinja
Mt. Chinjinsan
Tōgō-chō
東郷町
Drive-in area
Nangō-son
南郷村
Mt. Kashiyama
Yamage 山陰
Mt. Takamoriyama
Kokuragahama-dōro
ORD 100
LAR 370
Minami-Hyūga
Tsuboya River
Mt. Kumayama
Togawa River
Kamae Pass
Mt. Seirinzan
Mimikawa River
Ishinami River
Mimitsu
Mimitsu
Drive-in area
Mt. Takatsukayama
Mt. Osuzuyama
尾鈴山
Camelia trees
Mt. Hatakurayama
Higashi-Tsuno
Mt. Tsuekiyama
Fudōdaki
Tsuno-jinja
Tsuno-chō
都農町
Mandarin sale area
Tsuno
Nanuki River
HYŪGA-NADA
日向灘
Nippō Line
Mt. Hiehatayama
Mera-kaidō
Kawaminami-chō
川南町
Kawaminami
Kijō-chō
木城町
Omura River
Hitotsuse River
Takanabe daishi
Nakazuru 中鶴
Takanabe-chō
高鍋町
Takanabe
to Hitoyoshi
to Takanabe
to Takaoka
to Miyazaki
Saitobaru Old Mound Group
Zaronbai
SAITO-SHI
西都市
Hothouse area
Niitabaru Airport
Saito
西都
Shintomi-chō
新富町
Hyūga-Shintomi

A
B
C
D
1
2
3
4
5
6
Ōita-shi
Mt. Waitasan
Kokonoe-machi
九重町
Handa Plateau
飯田高原
やまなみハイウェー
Yutsubo
Chōjaharu
Ōtake
Hizenyu
Mt. Kuroiwayama
Kannojigoku
Sujiyu
Mt. Hitomeyama
Scenic view of Mt. Aso
Mt. Hijidake
Mt. Mimatayama
Mt. Kurotake
Mt. Daisenzan
Hokkein
Mt. Ryōshidake
Mt. Kujūsan
Kujū Plateau
久住高原
Kujū-kōgen Road Park
久住高原ロードパーク
ORD 500
LAR 2000
Oguni-machi
Senomoto Plateau
瀬ノ本高原
Akagawa
Yamanami Highway
Shonai-chō
庄内町
Mt. Hanamureyama
Naoiri-machi
直入町
Nagayu
Shichirida
Serigawa River
Nippō
Uso-jinja
Mt. Shōjidake
Mt. Hongūsan
Mt. Gozagatake
Mt. Yoroidake
Jinkakuji
Inukai-machi
犬飼町
Mt. Kamegadake
Kujū-machi
久住町
Kujū-jinja
Mt. Kibaruyama
Asaji-machi
朝地町
Asaji
Asaji 朝地
Ōno-machi
大野町
Akane River
Higo-kaidō
Mt. Yayama
Chitose-mura
千歳村
Ōno River
Sugao
Mt. Daisangoyama
Ubuyama-mura
産山村
TAKETA-SHI
竹田市
Hira 平
Taketa
Oka Castle
Inaba River
Tamarai River
Drive-in area
Aso-Yamanami
Ogata
Ogata-machi
緒方町
Bungo-Kiyokawa
Kiyokawa-mura
清川村
Miemachi
Mie-machi
三重町
Mt. Honjōsan
Tamarai
Mt. Kofuji
Aso-machi
Namino
Takimizu
Hōhi Line
Bungo-Ogi
Namino-son
波野村
Ogi-machi
荻町
Naminogahara
Mt. Ogidake
Okutake River
Mikuni Pass
Ondake-jinja
Inazumi-syonyudo(Cave)
Mt. Karasudake
Mt. Inazumiyama
Umezugoe Pass
Mt. Kashiwayama
Mt. Shiroyama
Yurugi-jinja
KUMAMOTO
Mt. Koshikidake
Mt. Yurugisan
Takamori-machi
高森町
Mt. Katamukiyama
Mt. Sobosan
祖母山
Obiragoe Pass
Mt. Hontaniyama
Sugiga-goe Pass
Mt. Kosobosan
Mt. Shinhyakushōyama
Mt. Tenjinbaruyama
to Takamori
Takachiho
高千穂
to Amanoiwato
to Yabe
to Nobeoka
Takamori-machi
Mt. Otonoyama
Mt. Goyōdake
Mt. Natsukisan
Mt. Kuwabaruyama
Shimono-hachimangū
Mt. Syōsanjiyama
Amanoiwato-jinja
Mt. Ōkueyama
大崩山
MIYAZAKI
Soyō-machi
蘇陽町
Takachiho-chō
高千穂町
Takachiho-jinja
Amanoiwato
Mt. Tsuriganeyama
Houri River
Scenic ravine view
Nanaori Cave
Takachihokyō(Gorge)
高千穂峡
Hinokage River
Tsunanose River
Mt. Oninomeyama
Tsubana Pass
津花峠
Nobeoka 50Km
Takamori 33Km
Uto 85Km
Fukasumi
Mt. Kunimiyama
Gokase-chō
五ヶ瀬町
Takachiho Railway
Gokase River
Kagemachi
Mt. Kuroiwayama
Tsugenotaki Cave
Mt. Tansukedake
Mt. Yahazudake
Mt. Hieizan
Hinokage-chō
日之影町
Hinokage-onsen
Mt. Akatogishiyama
Mt. Takajōyama
Mt. Morozukayama
Mt. Gion-yama
Iiboshi Pass
Hyūga-kaidō
Mt. Mukabakiyama
Mt. Yurugidake
Gomi
Kitakata-chō
北方町
Mukabaki-jinja
Mt. Ōnitayama
Morozuka-son
諸塚村
Makimine

40
49
36
37

Ōita-shi
E
F
G
H
41
1
2
3
4
5
6
Tsukumijima I.
Usuki-wan
Kumasaki
USUKI-SHI
臼杵市
Usuki Castle
Usuki
臼杵
Ōita (Yoshino)
Ōita (Tsukigata)
Usuki
C. Kusuyahana
Hodoshima I.
Tsukumi Pass
C. Kannonzaki
Tsukumi-wan
Inukai 犬飼
Ōita 24Km
Saiki 39Km
Ichinomiya 64Km
Hōhi Line
Usuki River
Oaza-Fukura 大字福良
Mt. Chinnanzan
Mt. Takeyama
Usuki Wall Relief Buddhist Image
臼杵磨崖仏
Onoda Cement
Tsukumi
津久見
TSUKUMI-SHI
津久見市
Inukai-machi
犬飼町
Mt. Karasudakeyama
Mt. Himedake
Hijiro
Tsuigoe Pass
津井越
Mt. Takahirayama
C. Kamadozaki
蒲戸崎
Kamiura-machi
上浦町
Nozugawa River
Shimotsuo 下津尾
Mt. Gobangadake
Mt. Hikodake
Azamui
Kariu Cave
Kariu
Hikojima I.
Fūren Cave
風連鍾乳洞
Hyūga-kaidō 日向街道
Shakuma-jinja
Ōnyūjima I.
Saiki-wan
Sukumo-Saeki Ferry (to Sukumo)
Kyūshi Ferry (to Yawatahama)
Kaizaki
Katashiroshima I.
Nakanotani Pass
Takegashima I.
Takateshima I.
Komashima I.
Mt. Tsubakiyama
Saiki
Banjō River
Yashima I.
ŌITA
Mt. Tategashiroyama
Mt. Kanmuridake
Banjō 番匠
Yayoi-machi
弥生町
Goshoshan
Oteku 大手区
SAIKI-SHI
佐伯市
Kamioka
Yokagil
Honjō-mura
本匠村
Mt. Samagatake
from Saiki-shi
Fukuoka 190Km
Kagoshima 310Km
C. Shirasaki
Ōshima I.
Motonoma-kaikyō
Mt. Haidateyama
Banjō River
Onagara Cave
Mt. Nadayama
Tsurumi-machi
鶴見町
Mt. Beikazan
Naomi
Nippō Line
C. Tsurumisaki
鶴御崎
Yonouzu-mura
米水津村
Yokoshima I.
Mt. Motogoshiyama
C. Oshidenohana
Naokawa
Naokawa-son
直川村
Hatanami Bypass
Katada River
C. Marubaenohana
Chiguroshima I.
Okikuroshima I.
Mt. Sakaridake
Fukiwara Pass
Miakari Pass
Mt. Kakurayama
Ume-machi
宇目町
Mt. Imashiroyama
C. Ryūgūbana
C. Senzakihana
Shigeoka
Todoroki Pass
Mt. Nakanomine
Ushigami-goe Pass
Mt. Bateruyama
Kamae-chō
蒲江町
Mt. Hokoyama
Mt. Sebirayama
C. Inumodoribana
Mt. Itadoyama
Sōtaro
Mt. Kuroiwayama
Yakatajima I.
C. Nagoyazaki
Mt. Tsushimahatayama
C. Udozaki
Mt. Tōmiyama
Mt. Jingamine
Furuegoe Pass
Mt. Dakeyama
Mt. Iizukayama
Ichitana
Ogawa River
Fukashima I.
Kitaura-chō
北浦町
Mt. Tōmiyama
Mt. Moriyama
Mt. Kagamiyama
C. Tomasuzaki
Kitagawa-chō
北川町
Kitagawa
Takashima I.
HYŪGA-NADA
日向灘
Shimaurató I.
Hyūga-Nagai
Mt. Enodake
Nippō Line
Kitagawa River
Nobeoka
Urashiro Bypass
Kita-Nobeoka
NOBEOKA-SHI
延岡市
Nobeoka-shi

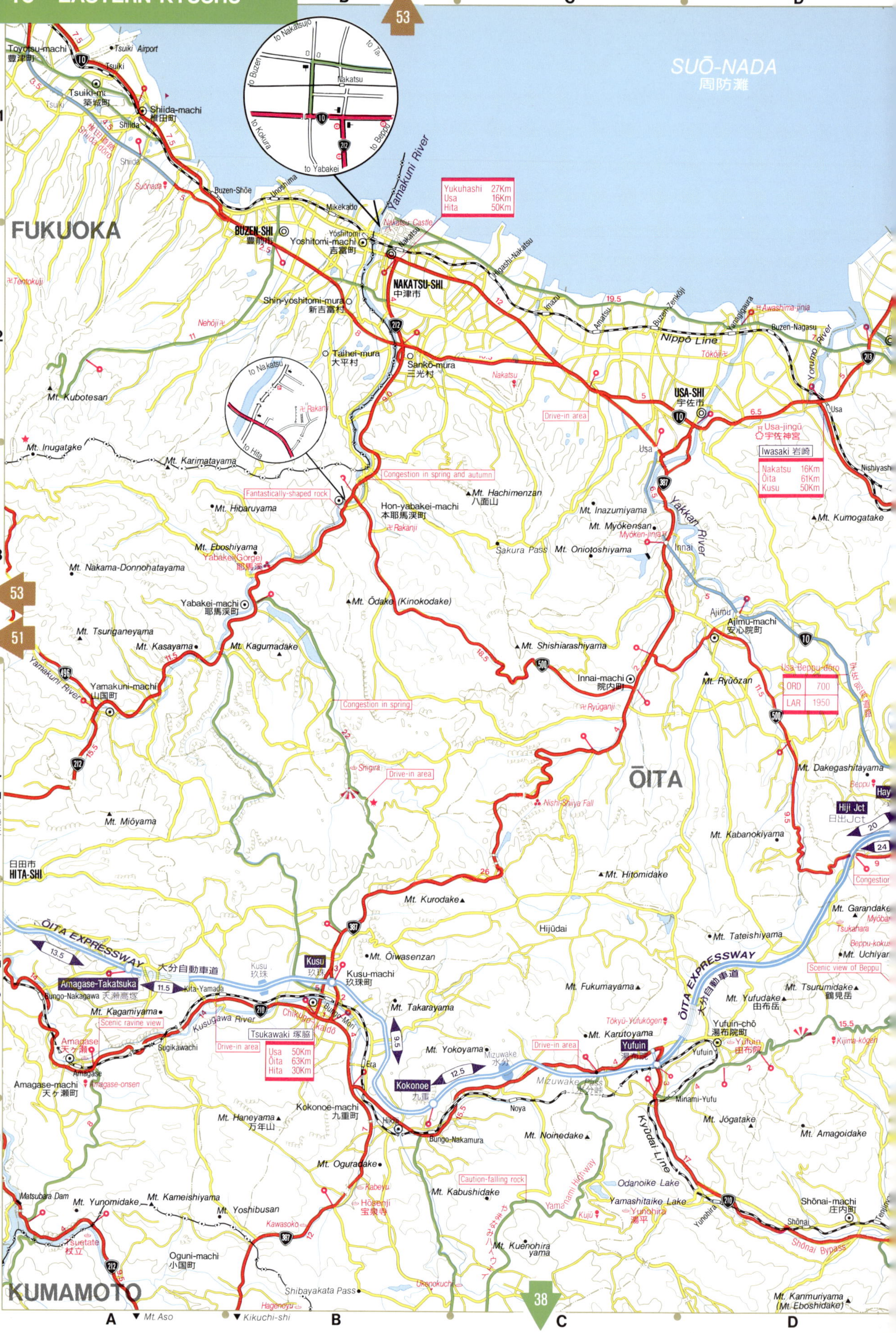

SUŌ-NADA
周防灘
FUKUOKA
ŌITA
KUMAMOTO
Toyotsu-machi 豊津町
Tsuiki Airport
Shiida-machi 椎田町
BUZEN-SHI 豊前市
Yoshitomi-machi 吉富町
NAKATSU-SHI 中津市
Shin-yoshitomi-mura 新吉富村
Taihei-mura 大平村
Sankō-mura 三光村
USA-SHI 宇佐市
Usa-jingū 宇佐神宮
Yukuhashi 27Km
Usa 16Km
Hita 50Km
Iwasaki 岩崎
Nakatsu 16Km
Ōita 61Km
Kusu 50Km
Nippō Line
Yamakuni River
Yakkan River
Nakatsu Castle
Congestion in spring and autumn
Fantastically-shaped rock
Hon-yabakei-machi 本耶馬渓町
Mt. Hachimenzan 八面山
Yabakei(Gorge) 耶馬溪
Yabakei-machi 耶馬渓町
Yamakuni-machi 山国町
Ajimu-machi 安心院町
Innai-machi 院内町
Usa-Beppu-dōro
ORD 700
LAR 1950
Congestion in spring
Drive-in area
Nishi-Shiiya Fall
Hiji Jct 日出Jct
Congestion
Scenic view of Beppu
ŌITA EXPRESSWAY 大分自動車道
Amagase-Takatsuka
Kusu 玖珠
Kusu-machi 玖珠町
Tsukawaki 塚脇
Usa 50Km
Ōita 63Km
Hita 30Km
Scenic ravine view
Amagase 天ヶ瀬
Amagase-machi 天ヶ瀬町
Kokonoe 九重
Kokonoe-machi 九重町
Yufuin 湯布院
Yufuin-chō 湯布院町
Caution-falling rock
Yamanami Highway
Kyūdai Line
Shōnai-machi 庄内町
Shōnai Bypass
Hōsenji 宝泉寺
Tsuetate 杖立
Oguni-machi 小国町
Shibayakata Pass
Hita-shi
日田市 HITA-SHI
Mt. Aso
Kikuchi-shi
Mt. Kanmuriyama (Mt. Eboshidake)

53
51
38

E
F
G
H
1
2
3
4
5
6
Himeshima-mura
姫島村
Himeshima I.
姫島
C. Hashiragadakebana
Mt. Yahazudake
Himeshimamura Ferry
Kunimi-cho
国見町
C. Kamezaki
C. Gongenzaki
Drive-in area
C. Biwazaki
C. Nagasakihana
C. Sumiyoshizaki
C. Osaki
Betsugū-hachimansha
Kunimi-cho
国見町
C. Konpirahana
Kakaji-cho
香々地町
Kitsuki-enkaidō
Mt. Kurokiyama
Mt. Sendōdake
Reisenji
Matama-machi
真玉町
Mt. Inomureyama
Monjusenji
Inubana Pass
大暮峠
Mt. Imiyama
Mudōji
MT. FUTAGOSAN
両子山
Mt. Ōdakeyama
Tennenji
Futagoji
Mt. Yayama
Tabuka River
Kunisaki-machi
国東町
NGOTAKADA-SHI
豊後高田市
Kunisaki Pen.
国東半島
C. Kurotsuzaki
Saikōji
Hōdaiji
Musashi-machi
武蔵町
Shōonji
Sharp curves
Ōta-mura
大田村
Mt. Ogiyama
Buzen-kaidō
Chishanoki Pass
Aki-machi
安岐町
Ōita
Tateishi
Mt. Tabarusan
(Mt. Nokogiriyama)
Jōgatani Pass
Hatagata Pass
Akigawa River
Ōmurayama
Yamaga-machi
山香町
Naka-Yamaga
Drive-in area
Ōita-kūkō-dōro
大分空港道路
Aki
Kitsuki
Wakamiya-hachimansha
KITSUKI-SHI
杵築市
Kitsuki
Drive-in area
Yasaka River
C. Usuishibana
Akamatsu Pass
Mt. Toyadake
Mt. Shiroyama
Hiji-machi
日出町
Mt. Bizōdake
C. Kanukibana
Bungo-Toyooka
Hori 堀
Hiji
to Kokura
Beppu
to Yamanami Highway
to Ōita
C. Ukusobana
Beppu-wan
別府湾
Shibaseki
Kamegawa
Chinoikejigoku
Kannawa
Kamegawa
Beppu-kankō Ferry (to Ōsaka)
Diamond Ferry (to Kōbe)
BEPPU-WAN
別府湾
Uwajima-un-yu Ferry (to Yawatahama·Misaki)
Beppu-daigaku
Bōzugoku
Beppu
別府
Beppu-Hachiyu
別府八湯
BEPPU-SHI
別府市
Beppu
from Ōita-shi
Kita-Kyushu 130Km
Kagoshima 375Km
Kokudō-Kyūshi Ferry (to Misaki)
Kankaiji
Cable
Rakutenchi
Ōnogawa-Ōhashi
ORD 100
LAR 360
C. Sekizaki
関崎
Shōwa Denkō
Nippon Steel
to Beppu
to Sagan-oseki
to Takeda
Ōita
to Nobeoka
Mt. Takasakiyama
Mt. Takasakiyama Natural Park (Zoo)
ŌITA-SHI
大分市
Ōita Castle
Sumitomo Chemical
大野川大橋
Saganoseki
Kōzaki
Tsutashima I.
Nippō Line
Ōno River
Otozu River
Tsurusaki
Beppu-nittō
Shiraki
Fuji Spinning
Yusuhara-hachimangū
Aoshima-jinja
Ōita
大分
Minami-Ōita
Ōita River
Furuichi
Kaku
ORD 150
LAR 570
Takio
Ōita Sunnyhill
Hasama-machi
挟間町
Bungo-Kokubu
Ōita-Mitsuyoshi
大分光吉
Ōita-Mera
大分米良
HIGASHI-KYŪSHŪ EXPRESSWAY
東九州自動車道
Ōita-Miyagawauchi
大分宮河内
Mt. Mominokiyama
C. Kushigahana
Onigase
Mukaibaru
Ōita-chūō
Ōita-Fujimi
Mt. Kojōyama
Gosen Pass
Sashū
Kuroshima I.
Hōhi Line
Sasamuta-jinja
Ōita-Tōkyū
Kurokui Pass
Rokkasako
Tsukano
Mt. Ryōzen
Naka-Handa
Mt. Kurokuisan
Shitanoe
64
39
Saiki-shi
Usuki-shi

B
C
D
44
1
2
3
4
5
6
A
Ichiki-chō
市来町
Mandarin sale area
Yunomoto
Higashiichiki-chō
東市来町
C. Tozakihana
Higashi-Ichiki
Kagoshima Line
Kagoshima sea side
Koyamada 小山田
Tokushige-jinja
Ijūin
Minami-Kyūshū
Ijūin-chō
伊集院町
Kyūshū-Shinkansen
南九州自動車道
Kaminokawa River
Mt. Jōyama
Matsumoto
Mt. Mukaiesan
Hiyoshi-chō
日吉町
Kami-Ijūin
Kagoshima-nis
Yamad
Kutajima I.
Drive-in area
Taniyama
Izuku Pass
Mt. Takamine
Satsumako Lake
Mt. Gongengao
Fukiage-chō
吹上町
Satsuma Pen.
薩摩半島
Fukiage
Kinkō
Ibusuki Skyline
ORD 930
LAR 3310
Suzuyama
Caution-landslides
Fukiagehama
Mt. Kinpōsan
Mt. Kumagatake
Kawana
Manose River
Kinpō-chō
金峰町
C. Kozakibana
Mt. Nakadake
Tatebajima I.
Kodoko Pass
C. Nomamisaki
野間岬
Nomaike Lake
Takaya-jinja
KASEDA-SHI
加世田市
Scenic view of Sakurajima I.
Kasasa-chō
笠沙町
Mt. Karasuyama
Takeda-jinja
Mt. Tagamidake
Chira
Noma-jinja
Mt. Hahagatake
Kawanabe-chō
川辺町
Chiran-chō
知覧町
Mt. Nakadake
Ōura-chō
大浦町
Mt. Chōyasan
長屋山
Fumoto River
Fog
Okiakimejima I.
Mt. Kuratayama
Mt. Isomadake
磯間岳
Mt. Jinnoo
C. Karanosaki
Mt. Imadake
Kami-Bepp
Mineo Pass
Mt. Shimoyamadake
下山岳
Bōnotsu-chō
坊津町
C. Ajirobana
Mt. Onnaidake
Mt. Kurumadake
Mt. Sonomidake
270 gō iriguchi 270号入口
Minakata-jinja
MAKURAZAKI-SHI
枕崎市
Bonit restaurant area
C. Minegasaki
Makurazaki
Bōnotsu
Satsuma-Tashiki
Satsuma-Shioya
Matsugaura
Ei-Ōkawa
Mizunarikawa
Ishikaki
Mimitori Pass
耳取峠
Ibusuki Makurazaki Line
C. Bōnomisaki
坊ノ岬
C. Yamatategami
C. Ōsakibana
Sendai 74Km
kagoshima 50Km
Ibusuki 48Km
Nishi-Ei
Ei-chō
頴娃町

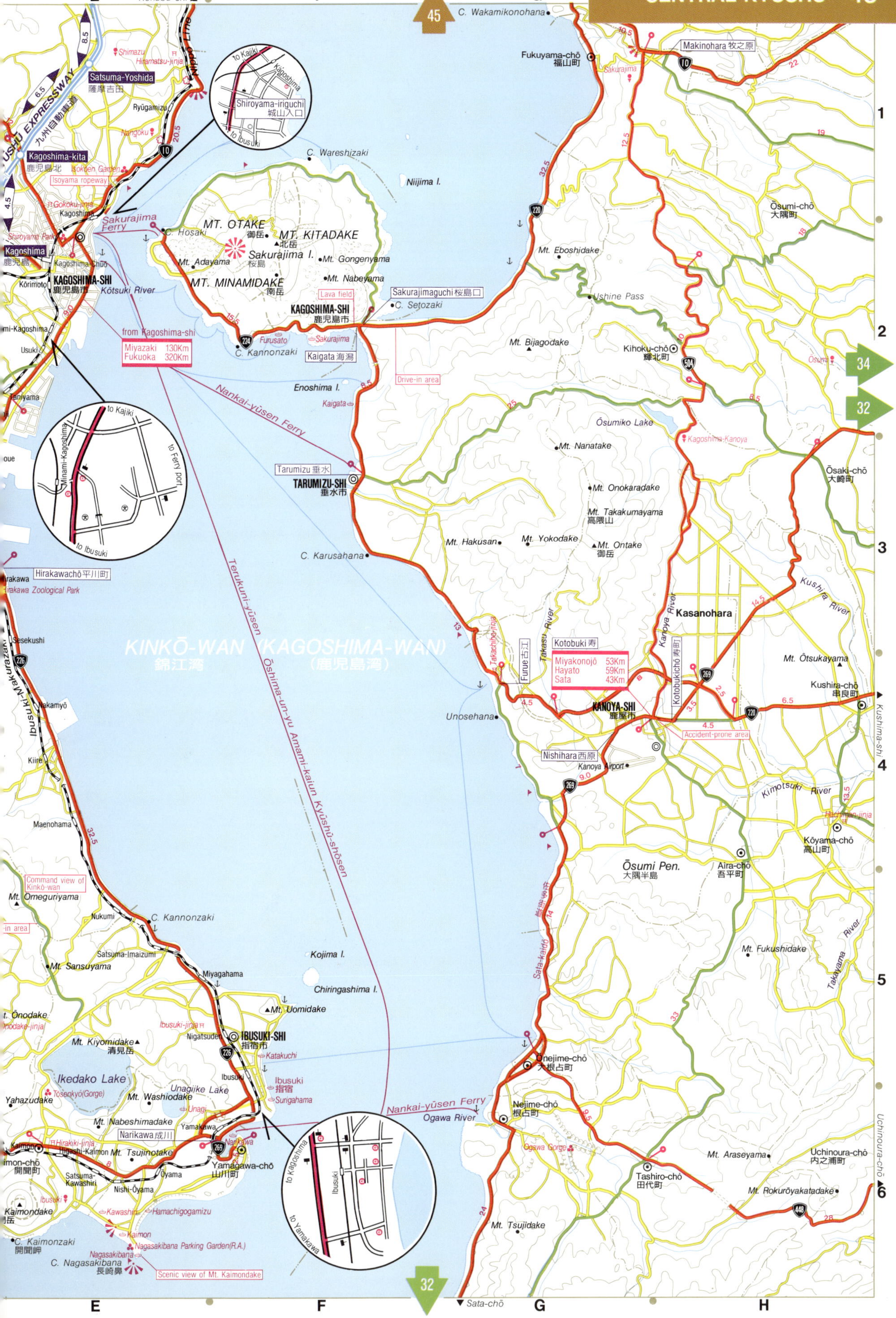

45
32
34
32
Kokubu-shi
C. Wakamikonohana
Fukuyama-chō
福山町
Makinohara 牧之原
Sakurajima
Satsuma-Yoshida
薩摩吉田
Shimazu
Hiramatsu-jinja
Ryūgamizu
Nangoku
KYŪSHŪ EXPRESSWAY
九州自動車道
Kagoshima-kita
鹿児島北
Isoken Garden
Isoyama ropeway
Gokoku-jinja
Kagoshima
Shiroyama Park
Kagoshima
鹿児島
Kagoshima-Chūō
KAGOSHIMA-SHI
鹿児島市
Kōtsuki River
Kōrimoto
Minami-Kagoshima
Usuki
Taniyama
Shiroyama-iriguchi
城山入口
to Kajiki
to Ibusuki
to Ferry port
Sakurajima Ferry
C. Hosaki
MT. OTAKE
御岳
MT. KITADAKE
北岳
Sakurajima I.
桜島
Mt. Adayama
Mt. Gongenyama
Mt. Nabeyama
MT. MINAMIDAKE
南岳
Lava field
C. Wareshizaki
Niijima I.
Sakurajimaguchi 桜島口
C. Setozaki
KAGOSHIMA-SHI
鹿児島市
Furusato
Sakurajima
C. Kannonzaki
Kaigata 海潟
from Kagoshima-shi
Miyazaki 130Km
Fukuoka 320Km
Drive-in area
Enoshima I.
Kaigata
Nankai-yūsen Ferry
Tarumizu 垂水
TARUMIZU-SHI
垂水市
C. Karusahana
Mt. Eboshidake
Ushine Pass
Mt. Bijagodake
Kihoku-chō
輝北町
Ōsumi-chō
大隅町
Ōsumi
Ōsumiko Lake
Kagoshima-Kanoya
Mt. Nanatake
Mt. Onokaradake
Mt. Takakumayama
高隈山
Mt. Hakusan
Mt. Yokodake
Mt. Ontake
御岳
Ōsaki-chō
大崎町
Hirakawachō 平川町
Hirakawa Zoological Park
Sesekushi
Ibusuki-Makurazaki
Nakamyō
Kiire
KINKŌ-WAN (KAGOSHIMA-WAN)
錦江湾 (鹿児島湾)
Terukuni-yūsen Ōshima-un-yu Amami-kaiun Kyūshū-shōsen
Takachiho-jinja
Furue 古江
Takasu River
Kotobuki 寿
Miyakonojō 53Km
Hayato 59Km
Sata 43Km
Kanoya River
Kasanohara
Kotobukichō 寿町
Kushira River
Mt. Ōtsukayama
Kushira-chō
串良町
Kushima-shi
KANOYA-SHI
鹿屋市
Accident-prone area
Unosehana
Nishihara 西原
Kanoya Airport
Kimotsuki River
Hachiman-jinja
Kōyama-chō
高山町
Maenohama
Ōsumi Pen.
大隅半島
Aira-chō
吾平町
Command view of Kinkō-wan
Mt. Omeguriyama
C. Kannonzaki
Nukumi
Satsuma-Imaizumi
Mt. Sansuyama
Kojima I.
Chiringashima I.
Miyagahama
Mt. Uomidake
Sata-kaidō
Mt. Fukushidake
Takayama River
Mt. Ōnodake
Ōnodake-jinja
Ibusuki-jinja
Nigatsuden
IBUSUKI-SHI
指宿市
Katakuchi
Mt. Kiyomidake
清見岳
Ibusuki
Ibusuki
指宿
Surigahama
Onejime-chō
大根占町
Ikedako Lake
Tōsenkyō (Gorge)
Unagiike Lake
Mt. Washiodake
Yahazudake
Unagi
Mt. Nabeshimadake
Yamakawa
Narikawa 成川
Narikawa
Hirakiki-jinja
Kaimon
Higashi-Kaimon
Mt. Tsujinotake
Yamagawa-chō
山川町
Kaimon-chō
開聞町
Satsuma-Kawashiri
Ōyama
Nishi-Ōyama
Ibusuki
Kaimondake
Kawashiri
Hamachigogamizu
Kaimon
Nagasakibana Parking Garden (R.A.)
C. Kaimonzaki
開聞岬
C. Nagasakibana
長崎鼻
Nagasakibana
Scenic view of Mt. Kaimondake
to Kagoshima
to Yamakawa
Nankai-yūsen Ferry
Ogawa River
Nejime-chō
根占町
Ogawa Gorge
Tashiro-chō
田代町
Mt. Araseyama
Uchinoura-chō
内之浦町
Uchinoura-chō
Mt. Rokuroyakatadake
Mt. Tsujidake
Sata-chō

46
Nagashima-chō
Izumi street
Izumi
IZUMI-SHI
出水市
Nishi-Izumi
C. Banshonohana
Noda-chō
野田町
Takaono-chō
高尾野町
Origuchi
Nodagō
Takaono
Kuwajima I.
Ōshima I.
Nagashima-iriguchi 長島入口
Akune
C. Kuratsunohana
AKUNE-SHI
阿久根市
Mt. Tōyadake
C. Akasakibana
Caution-landslides
Ushinohama
Mt. Shibisan
Miyanojō-chō
宮之城町
Kyūshū-Shinkansen
Tarumi River
Satsuma-Ōkawa
Nishikata
Yunomoto
Mt. Majiridake
Satsuma-Taki
Mt. Kasayama
Futagojima I.
Nojima I.
Chikashima I.
Hisatsu Orange Rail Way
C. Nishizaki
Mt. Tōmiyama
C. Tonosaki
Sendai River
Sendai
Kusamichi
Kami-Sendai
Nitta-jinja
C. Tōsengatomo
Mt. Ōkuradake
Kami-Koshikijima I.
上甑島
Mt. Tōmekiyama
Mt. Nekodake
267 iriguchi 267入口
Minamata 66Km
Ōkuchi 57Km
Kagoshima 52Km
SATSUMASENDAI-SHI
薩摩川内市
Mt. Kasayama
Mt. Yanagisan
Urauchi-wan
Nakakoshiki-wan
Nakajima I.
C. Kayamutazaki
C. Tengubana
Kumanojō
Mt. Maruyama
Mt. Higasayama
Ichihino
Suwa-jinja
Mt. Benzaitensan
Mt. Hebaiyama
C. Yazaki
Naka- Koshikijima I.
中甑島
C. Umanorizaki
Kobanchaya
Mt. Higashidake
Mt. Kanmuridake
C. Hashimazaki
Kagoshima Line
Imuta-seto
Okinoshima I.
Mt. Hitategaoka
C. Hirasezaki
Kushikino-ekimae 串木野駅前
KUSHIKINO-SHI
串木野市
Kushikino
Mt. Yadake
C. Kumagasebana
Drive slowly
Koshikijima rettō Is.
SATSUMASENDAI-SHI
薩摩川内市
Ichiki-chō
市来町
Minato River
Ichiki
Mt. Shigehirasan
270gō iriguchi 270号入口
Yunomoto
Ichiki
C. Tozakihana
Higashiichiki-chō
東市来町
Mt. Odayama
Sharp curves
Mt. Odake
Higashi-Ichiki
Kagoshima sea side
Tokushige-jinja
Minami-Kyūshū
Shimo-Koshikijima I.
下甑島
Ijūin-chō
伊集院町
Ijūin
Kamino River
Mt. Jōyama
Mt. Aoshiodake
C. Sebizaki
Mt. Taniyama
Mt. Mukaiesan
Hiyoshi-chō
日吉町
Mt. Katsuyama
C. Hayasaki
C. Tsuguchibana
Kutajima I.
Fukiage-chō
吹上町
C. Tsurikakezaki
Makurazaki-shi
A
B
C
D
1
2
3
4
5
6

E
F
G
H
Minamata-shi
Hitoyoshi-shi
47
43
34
Makurazaki-shi
Tarumizu-shi
Miyazaki-shi
Kobayashi I.C.
Takeharu-chō
Kōriyama-hachimanjinja
Hitoyoshi 36Km
Minamata 32Km
Kagoshima 73Km
ŌKUCHI-SHI
大口市
Shirakigawachi
Shiraki-jinja
Hishikari-chō
菱刈町
Sendai River
Soji Fall
Tsuruta-damuko Lake
Tsuruta Dam
Yunoo
Tsuruda-chō
鶴田町
Miyanojō
Tsuruta
Anagawa River
Satsuma-chō
薩摩町
Miyanojō-chō
宮之城町
Accident-prone area
Torai 虎居
Mt. Kunimidake
Mt. Aradake
Mt. Eboshidake
KAGOSHIMA
Kubuki River
Mt. Nagaosan
Mt. Tōmigajō
Mt. Katashirosan
Mt. Akashi
Mt. Funamidake
Mt. Sengandake
Imuta
Gamō
Mt. Magurodake
Kamō-chō
蒲生町
Mt. Ryūgayama
Mt. Yaeyama
Iriki Pass
入来峠
Mt. Takamine
Mt. Hanaoyama
Mt. Miegatake
Mt. Akakue
Shimazu
Hiramatsu-jinja
Mt. Muregaoka
Koyamada 小山田
Satsuma-Yoshida
薩摩吉田
Caution-Falling rock
Kogashira
Nangoku
Kagoshima-kita
鹿児島北
Iso Garden
Isoyama ropeway
Gokoku-jinja
Minami-Kyūshū-jidōshadō
南九州自動車道
Kagoshima
鹿児島
Kagoshima-nishi
Shiroyama Park
Kagoshima-Chūō
Kōrimoto
Yamada
KAGOSHIMA-SHI
鹿児島市
Minami-Kagoshima
Usuki
Ibusuki Skyline
ORD 930
LAR 3310
Kōtsuki River
from Kagoshima-shi
Miyazaki 130Km
Fukuoka 320Km
Sakurajima Ferry
Yoshida
Kyōmachi
Tsurumaru
Yoshimatsu
Yoshimatsu-chō
吉松町
Hisatsu Line
Kurino-chō
栗野町
Kurino
栗野
Yokogawa-chō
横川町
Ōsumi-Yokogawa
Yokogawa
横川
Uemura
Kagoshima-kūkō 36
Kareigawa
Naka-Fukura
Mizobe
溝辺
Mizobe-chō
溝辺町
KYŪSHŪ EXPRESSWAY
九州自動車道
Kagoshima
Hyōkiyama
Mizobe-Kagoshima-kūkō
溝辺鹿児島空港
Shirasudaichi
シラス台地
Kagoshima-kokusai
Kajiki-chō
加治木町
Kajikichō-Kida 加治木町木田
Kajiki
加治木
Sakurajima
桜島
Aira
姶良
Aira-chō
姶良町
Chōsa
Beppu River
Accident-prone area
Kajikichō-Asahi
加治木町朝日
Hayato-nishi
Hayato-dōro
Shigetomi
Nippō Line
Scenic view of Sakurajima
C. Ōsakigahana
Ryūgamizu
Kinkō-wan (Kagoshima-wan)
C. Wareshizaki
Niijima I.
Sakurajima I.
桜島
Mt. Otake
御岳
Mt. Nakadake
Mt. Gongenyama
Mt. Atagoyama
Mt. Minamidake
Mt. Nabeyama
C. Hosaki
Yunodaira
KAGOSHIMA-SHI
鹿児島市
C. Setozaki
Sakurajimaguchi 桜島口
C. Kannonzaki
to Makizono
Kokubu
Hayato
to Kirishima
to Kagoshima
to Miyakonojō
to Hayato-dōro
Amori River
EBINO-SHI
えびの市
Ebino
えびの
Sendai River
Ebino-Uwae
Ebino-Iino
MIYAZAKI EXPRESSWAY
宮崎自動車道
Ebino Jct
えびの Jct
Yoshimatsu
吉松
MIYAZAKI
Mt. Iimorisan
Shiratori
Mt. Koshikidake
Mt. Shiratorisan
Miike Lake
Ebino-kōgen
Kurinodake
Mt. Kurinodake
KOBAYASHI-SHI
小林市
Mt. Karakunidake
韓国岳
Scenic view of Mt. Kirishima
Kirishima Skyline
Mt. Kirishimayama
霧島山
Onamiike Lake
Mt. Shinmoedake
新燃岳
Mt. Sagarisan
Kirishima
霧島
Sekibira
Myoban
Hayashida
Shin-yu
Maruo
Iōdani
Yunotani
Mt. Eboshidake
Kirishima
Mt. Takaokasan
Kirishima-Onsen
Congestion in spring and autumn
Kaneyama River
Kirishima-jingū
Kirishima
Takachiho
Makizono-chō
牧園町
Yokose
Shiobitashi
Yamanoyu
Shinkawa
Inukaitaki
Anraku
Myōken
Oganotaki
Kirishima-chō
霧島町
Kirishimajingū
Nippō Line
Mt. Bindenyama
Kita-Naganoda
Hinatayama
Kokubu
Kajiki
Kagoshima-jingū
Hayato-chō
隼人町
KOKUBU-SHI
国分市
Hayato
Hayato-higashi
隼人東
223iriguchi 223入口
Kobayashi 74Km
Miyakonojō 40Km
Kagoshima 32Km
Kokubushikine 国分敷根
Long slope
Kokubu
国分
Mt. Araisodake
C. Wakamikonohana
Drive-in area
Scenic view of Kinkō-wan
Fukuyama-chō
福山町
Sakurajima
Ōsumi-chō
大隅町
Mt. Eboshidake
Ushine Pass
TARUMIZU-SHI
垂水市
Mt. Bijagodake
Kihoku-chō
輝北町

29
48
44
A
B
C
D
1
2
3
4
5
6
Obama-chō
Shimabara-shi
Minamiarima-chō
南有馬町
Kuchinotsu-chō
口之津町
C. Sezumezaki
Yushima I.
AMAKUSA-NADA
天草灘
SHIMABARA-WAN
島原湾
Gotsūiwa
Hayasaki-seto
Shimatetsu Ferry
Nagasaki-Amakusa Ferry (to Mogi)
Tsūjijima I.
Kamejima I.
C. Nagasakibana
Mt. Tenjinyama
C. Shikizakimisaki
Tomioka-wan
Reihoku-machi
苓北町
Itsuwa-machi
五和町
Hoshōji
Takamokujima
Hiaij
Takeshima I.
Kuroshima I.
Ikeshimano-s
Ariake-machi
有明町
Amakusa
to Matsushima
to Ushibuka
to Sumoto
Mt. Oidake
Amakusa-kamishima I.
天草上島
Mt. Hashiradake
Hirose River
Hondo
HONDO-SHI
本渡市
Amakusa-shimoshima I.
天草下島
Amakusa-Shimoshima-ōdan-dōro
大草下島横断道路
ORD 410
LAR 1470
Mt. Dōmeizan
Himeura-jin
Mt. Tenjiku
Hondo-seto
Mt. Kuradake
Mt. Nenjudake
Shimoda
Mt. Bōshidake
Chōbegoe Pass
Sumoto-machi
栖本町
Kuratake-machi
倉岳町
Busshōzan-Enshōji
Kuratake-jinja
Goshikijima I.
Mt. Gongen-yama
Sumoto River
Kami-chizukajima I.
Shimo-chizukajima I.
Myōkengaura
(Scenic Rocky Coast)
Mt. Binnomizuyama
Mt. Kadoyama
Hirasejima I.
Mt. Atagoyama
Mt. Yahazudake
Ōmiyaji River
C. Tōnosaki
Mt. Jūsannoyama
Mt. Kusubarutōge
Mt. Nabewarizan
Amakusa-machi
天草町
Yokoshima I.
Hyōtanjima I.
Datekujima I.
Kusumorijima I.
Shōkyōji
Kaichōji
Shinwa-machi
新和町
Yokourajima I.
Mt. Gyōnindake
Nangoku-kaiun Ferry·Sanwa-shōsen Ferry
Nangoku-kaiun Ferry
Mt. Araodake
Mt. Yahazudake
Mt. Kashiradake
Makishima I.
Maeshima I.
Mt. Byōbuzan
C. Arakuchi
Tensōzan-Sōenji
Kawaura-machi
河浦町
Kuroshima I.
Goshoura-machi
御所浦町
Takeshima I.
Goshourajima I.
御所浦島
Ōhirajima I.
Mt. Gotsūyama
Mt. Hashiradake
C. Takenosaki
Mt. Kajikidake
Amakusa Ferry
C. Ejimabana
Mt. Ishigamiyama
Shishijima I.
獅子島
Mt. Shichirōyama
Yawatano-seto
to Kagoshima
Minamata
to Ōkuchi
Mt. Rokurōjiyama
Ubushima I.
C. Dōzakibana
Mt. Takatoriyama
C. Kushizaki
Fukami-wan
C. Otegazaki
Mt. Tōmidake
C. Onikizaki
Akashima I.
Shourajima I.
Mt. Gongenyama
C. Nagasebana
C. Hayasaki
Nagashima-kaikyō
Akashima I.
Ikarajima I.
MINAMATA-SHI
水俣市
Kuwashima I.
Kutama-ura
C. Katsuzaki
Azuma-chō
東町
Minamata
C. Tsurusaki
Amakusa-Kagoshima-kokudō Ferry
Ōshima I.
USHIBUKA-SHI
牛深市
Kuroshima I.
C. Ōsaki
Nagashima I.
長島
Kamoise I.
Ushijima I.
Mt. Gyōnindake
Gezushima I.
Hōgashima I.
C. Sabanokuchibana
Nagashima-chō
長島町
Futagojima I.
Tsukinoshima I.
Mt. Yadake
Fukuro
Katsurajima I.
Ishikiribana I.
Katashima I.
Komenotsu River
C. Nagasakibana
C. Izumizaki
Kuro-seto
Komenotsu
Mt. Yahazudake
Mt. Kasayama
C. Ōsaki
AKUNE-SHI
阿久根市
IZUMI-SHI
出水市
Izumi
Nishi-Izumi
Hirose 広瀬
Takaono-chō
高尾野町
Akune-shi
Miyanojō

KUMAMOTO
MIYAZAKI
KAGOSHIMA
UKI-SHI
宇城市
KAMIAMAKUSA-SHI
上天草市
YATSUSHIRO-SHI
八代市
HITOYOSHI-SHI
人吉市
ŌKUCHI-SHI
大口市
EBINO-SHI
えびの市
YATSUSHIRO-KAI
八代海
(Shiranui-kai)
Uto-shi
Kumamoto-shi
Ōkuchi-shi
Ebino-shi
Mt. Hidake
Tobasejima I.
Gokyō-iriguchi 五橋入口
Ōyanoshima I.
大矢野島
Yagyūjima I.
Senzokuzōzojima I.
Ōshima I.
C. Kamiwatonohana
Sejima I.
Mitsujima I.
Matsushima Ferry
C. Shimowatonohana
Umatake 馬建
Mt. Konpirayama
Ōtsukushima I.
Otsuijima I.
Kumagawa River
C. Uryūmisaki
C. Biwanokubi
Ryūhoku-machi
竜北町
Kagami-machi
鏡町
Miyahara-machi
宮原町
Senchō-machi
千丁町
Shin-Yatsushiro
Kagoshima Line
Yatsushiro
八代
Yatsushiro Jct
八代Jct
Hagihara 萩原
Uto 26Km
Hitoyoshi 53Km
Minamata 57Km
Sendan 栴壇
Matsui-jinja
Higo-Kōda
Yatsushiro-minami
Dam
Mt. Hachiryūzan
Sakamoto-mura
坂本村
Sakamoto
坂本
Hinagu
日奈久
Hinagu-Onsen
Higo-Futami
Kami-Tanoura
Akamatsutarō Pass
赤松太郎峠
Torigoe Pass
鳥越
Hisatsu Orange Rail Way
Narrow road
Haki
Kamase
Setoishi
Kaiji
Hisatsu Line
Higo-Tanoura
Mt. Kasayama
KYŪSHŪ EXPRESSWAY
九州自動車道
Yoshio
Uminoura
Ashikita-machi
芦北町
Sashiki
Sashiki River
Kyūshū-Shinkansen
Shiroishi
Kumanoza-jinja
Steep and sharp curves
Mt. Gongen-yama
Kyusendō(Cave)
Congestion
Takazawa(Cave)
Mt. Akiharaiyama
Mt. Somanohanayama
Mt. Shiraiwayama
Mt. Maruoyama
Mt. Kagamiyama
Mt. Terudake
Yunoura
Caution-falling rock
Tsunagitarō Pass
Tsunagi-machi
津奈木町
Mt. Toraishiyama
Mt. Kagamiyama
Kumagawa Rhein
球磨川ライン
Kuma-mura
球磨村
Hitoyoshi-kaidō
Mt. Takaoyama
Kojō 古城
Yatsushiro 57Km
Ōkuchi 32Km
Sendai 47Km
Shin-Minamata
Mt. Ōzekiyama
Mt. Kunimiyama
Kaname Fall
Hitoyoshi
Sagarahan -Ganyōji
Nishiaidakami 西間上
from Hitoyoshi-shi
Fukuoka 200Km
Kagoshima 110Km
Minamata River
Yunotsuru-hanataki(Fall)
Yunotsuru
Mt. Onidake
Mt. Miyanooyama
Kyūshichi Pass
Mt. Tsuoyama
Mt. Hagedake
Mt. Manegahira
Mt. Takakumasan
Kōriyama-hachiman-jinja
Yatake
Yatake-kōgen
Mt. Yatakesan
Mt. Hyakkanyama
Horikiri Pass
Masaki
UKI-SHI
宇城市
Ogawa
Misato-machi
美里町
Mt. Hakusan
Hikawa River
Tōyō-mura
東陽村
Mt. Yayamadake
Izumi-mura
泉村
Miyahara
宮原
Mt. Ropponsugiyama
Mt. Hiraishiyama
Ōtorigoe Pass
Mt. Shiragayama
Itsuki River
Ogawa River
Itsuki-mura
五木村
Mt. Yatsuharudake
Mt. Nokeeboshiyama
Mt. Takadake
Kawabe River
Yamae
山江
Yamae-mura
山江村
Sagara-mura
相良村
Asagiri-chō
あさぎり町
Hitoyoshi
Kuma
Kinoe
Maegawa River
Kumagawa Rail Way
Nishiki-machi
錦町
Ōkoba
Hisatsu Line
E
F
G
H
1
2
3
4
5
6
36
45

B
C
D
A
1
2
3
4
5
6
50
29
FUKUOKA
Yamato-machi 大和町
Nishitetsu-Nakashima
Minami-Setaka
Yamakawa-machi 山川町
Yamakawa 山川
Tachibana-machi 立花町
Yabe-m 矢部村
Nebiki Pass
Mt. Kyūrokusan
Enoura
Takata-machi 高田町
Hiraki
Wataze
Nose 濃施
Yabetani Pass
Sarukake Pass
Oguri Pass
Mt. Nishidake
Arahira Pass
Yabegawa River
Nishitetsu-Watase
Yoshino
Hōunji
Ariake
Nankan 南関
Mt. Mitsuoyama
Aira-kannon
Higashi-Amagi
Mikawa-machi 三加和町
Hatsushima I.
Mitsui Tōatsu Chemicals
Ginsui
Mt. Nijōsan
Hirayama
Fukakura Pass
Mt. Yurugidake
Iwano River
Uchida River
Shin-Sakaemachi
Higashi-Shinmachi 東新町
Nankan-machi 南関町
Nichirinji
Fukkoji
Suwagawa River
Ōmuta
ŌMUTA-SHI 大牟田市
Shiranui
Mt. Miikeyama
Shinmachi 新町
Kumairi
YAMAGA-SHI 山鹿市
Yamaga
Chūō-dōri 中央通り
Miike
Naka-Kyūshū
Tamana 玉名
Oguni 45Km
Kurume 60Km
Kumamoto 25Km
Arao
Mitsui Greenland
Mitsui Green Land(R.A.)
Kikusui
Kikusui 菊水
ARAO-SHI 荒尾市
Mt. Shōdaisan
Mt. Menoyama
Fukuoka-kaidō
Miyabaru
Shichijō-machi 七城町
Kōfukuji
Hiraiima
Minami-Arao
Miike-kaidō
Kikusui-machi 菊水町
Ueki
Mt. Hidake
Tamana
Mt. Kunimiyama
Shiōji-jinja
Nagasu
Tamana 玉名
TAMANA-SHI 玉名市
Shimono-kannondō
Nagasu-machi 長洲町
Ueki 植木
Shisui-machi 泗水町
Ariake Ferry (to Taira)
Ōnoshima
Taimei-machi 岱明町
Higokoku
Konoha
Tabaruzaka Pass
Ueki-machi 植木町
Nishigōshi-machi 西合志町
Gyokutō-machi 玉東町
Mouno 舞尾
Tabaruzaka
Kita-Kumamoto 北熊本
Kōshi-machi 合志町
Congestion
Miyoshi
Kikuchi River
Ueki
Kuroishi
Yokoshima-machi 横島町
Suya
Tensui-machi 天水町
Ōama
Nishisato
Horikawa
Hōhi Line
Musashizuka
Yuge
Kumamoto 熊本
Mt. Kumanodake
Yamamuro 山室
Tōjin River
Kawachi
Sōjō-daigaku-mae
Ikeda
Tatsutaguchi
Kami-Kumamoto
Uchikoshi
Honmyōji
Iwadō-kannon
Reigandō(cave)
Mt. Kinpōzan
Kumamoto Castle
Fujisaki-hachimangū
Kumamoto-higashi Bypass
Mie
SHIMABARA-SHI 島原市
Kunimi-chō
KUMAMOTO-SHI 熊本市
Suizenji
Shin-Suizenji
Suizenji Garden
Mashiki-Kumamoto kūkō 益城熊本空港
Shimabara
Shimatetsu-houshamae
Kumamoto
Minami-Shimabara
Kumamoto
Shirakawa River
Minami-Kumamoto
Heisei
from Kumamoto-shi
Fukuoka 110Km
Kagoshima 220Km
Ocean Arrow Kyūshū-Shōsen Ferry
Shimabara
Tsukumojima I.
SHIMABARA-WAN 島原湾
Obama-chō
Antoku
Kashima-machi 嘉島町
KYŪSHŪ EXPRESSWAY 九州自動車道
Kawashiri
Daijizenji
Kagoshima Line
Misumi-Shimabara Ferry
Fukae-chō 深江町
Mifune 御船
Midori River
Jōnan-machi 城南町
Tomiai-machi 富合町
Kōtokuji
Midorikawa 緑川
Drive-slowly
Sumiyoshi-jinja
Sumiyoshi
Congestion in summer
C. Ōsakibana
Futsu-chō 布津町
Kuchinotsu-chō
Uto
Accident-prone area
Higo-Nagahama
Midorikawa
UTO-SHI 宇土市
Kumamoto 14Km
Misumi 29Km
Yashiro 26Km
Atsumaru Lake
Kumamoto-minami (Otome)
Ouda
Mt. Ōtake
Matsubase
Matsubase 松橋
Congestion in summer
Akase
Akase
Ishiuchi Dam
Uto Pen. 宇土半島
Misumi Line
UKI-SHI 宇城市
Misato-machi 美里町
Misumi-seto
Mt. Misumidake
Kanaketa
Einoo-jinja
Ōno River
Kagoshima-kaidō
Congestion
Mt. Hidake
Hataura
Misumi
Mt. Jōyama
KAMIAMAKUSA-SHI 上天草市
Misumi
Oniishima I.
Terashima I.
Ryūhoku-machi 竜北町
Ogawa
Yatsushiro I.C.

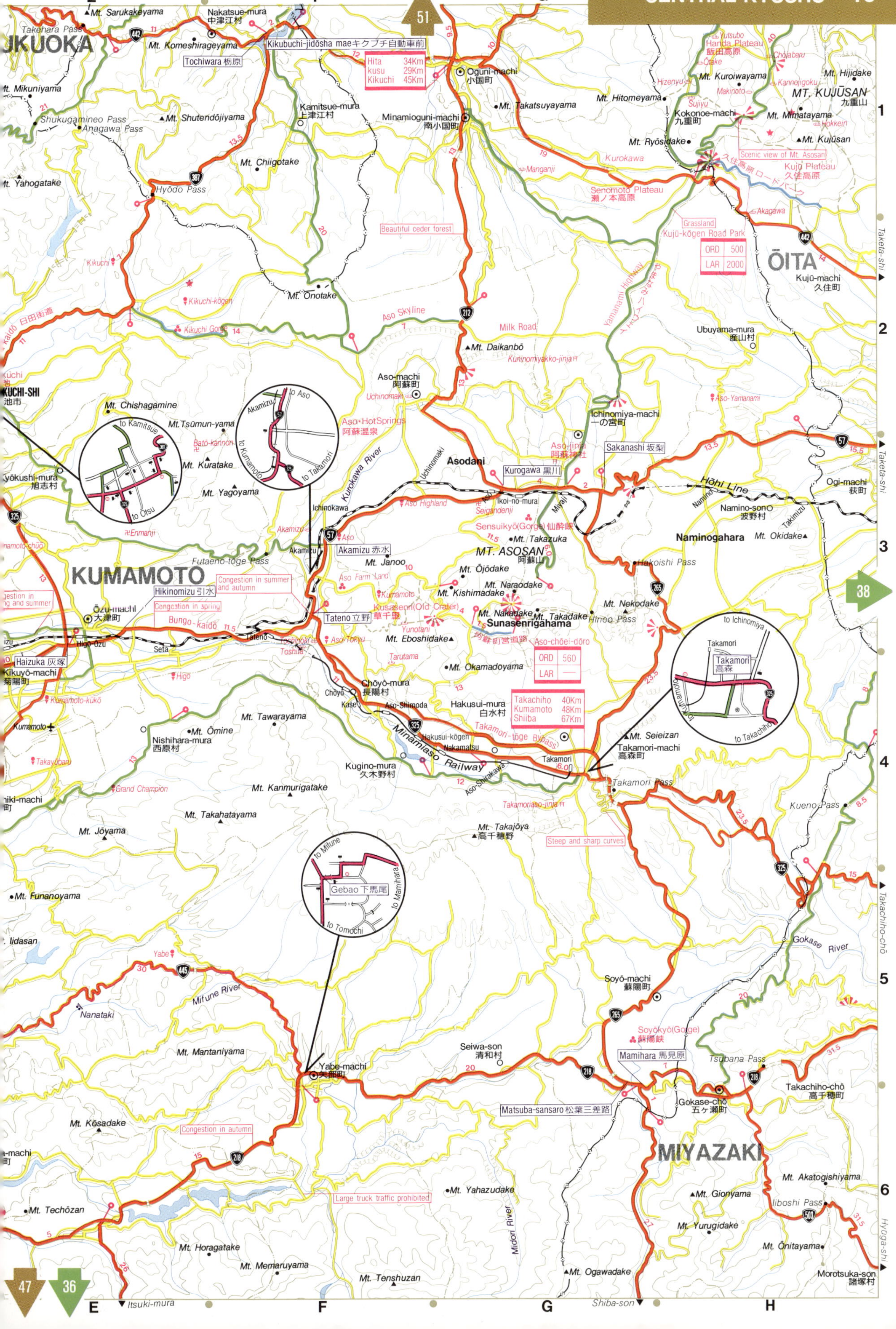
FUKUOKA
KUMAMOTO
ŌITA
MIYAZAKI
Mt. Sarukakeyama
Takehara Pass
Nakatsue-mura 中津江村
Mt. Komeshiragеyama
Tochiwara 栃原
Kikubuchi-jidōsha mae キクブチ自動車前
Hita 34Km
kusu 29Km
Kikuchi 45Km
Oguni-machi 小国町
Minamioguni-machi 南小国町
Kamitsue-mura 上津江村
Mt. Mikuniyama
Shukugamineo Pass
Anagawa Pass
Mt. Shutendōjiyama
Mt. Takatsuyayama
Mt. Hitomeyama
Mt. Chiigotake
Mt. Yahogatake
Hyōdo Pass
Manganji
Kurokawa
Senomoto Plateau 瀬ノ本高原
Beautiful ceder forest
Kikuchi
Kikuchi-kōgen
Kikuchi Gorge
Mt. Onotake
Aso Skyline
Milk Road
Mt. Daikanbō
Kuninomiyakko-jinja
Yamanami Highway
Handa Plateau 飯田高原
Yutsubo
Chōjabaru
Ōtake
Hizenyu
Mt. Kuroiwayama
Makinoto
Kannojigoku
Mt. Hijidake
MT. KUJŪSAN 九重山
Sujiyu
Kokonoe-machi 九重町
Mt. Mimatayama
Hokkein
Mt. Kujūsan
Mt. Ryōsidake
Scenic view of Mt. Asosan
Kujū Plateau 久住高原
久住高原ロードパーク
Akagawa
Grassland
Kujū-kōgen Road Park
ORD 500
LAR 2000
Kujū-machi 久住町
Ubuyama-mura 産山村
Aso-Yamanami
Aso-machi 阿蘇町
Uchinomaki
Aso HotSprings 阿蘇温泉
Mt. Chishagamine
Mt. Tsūmun-yama
Batō-kannon
Mt. Kuratake
Mt. Yagoyama
Kyōkushi-mura 旭志村
Enmanji
to Kamitsue
to Ōtsu
to Aso
Akamizu
to Kumamoto
to Takamori
Kurokawa River
Uchinomaki
Asodani
Kurogawa 黒川
Aso-jinja 阿蘇神社
Ichinomiya-machi 一の宮町
Sakanashi 坂梨
Hōhi Line
Ogi-machi 荻町
Namino-son 波野村
Naminogahara
Mt. Okidake
Ichinokawa
Aso Highland
Ikoi-no-mura
Seigandenji
Sensuikyō(Gorge) 仙酔峡
Mt. Takazuka
MT. ASOSAN 阿蘇山
Akamizu 赤水
Mt. Janoo
Futaeno-tōge Pass
Hakoishi Pass
Mt. Ōjōdake
Mt. Naraodake
Mt. Kishimadake
Mt. Nekodake
Mt. Nakadake
Mt. Takadake
Sunasenrigahama
Hinoo Pass
Aso Farm Land
Kumamoto
Kusasenri(Old Crater) 草千里
Yunotani
Congestion in summer and autumn
Hikinomizu 引水
Congestion in spring
Bungo-kaidō
Ōzu-machi 大津町
Tateno 立野
Aso-Tokyu
Mt. Eboshidake
Aso-chōei-dōro 阿蘇町営道路
ORD 560
LAR —
Higo-Ōzu
Seta
Tochinoki
Toshita
Tarutama
Mt. Okamadoyama
Haizuka 灰塚
Kikuyō-machi 菊陽町
Higo
Kumamoto-kūkō
Chōyō-mura 長陽村
Chōyō
Kase
Aso-Shimoda
Hakusui-mura 白水村
Takachiho 40Km
Kumamoto 48Km
Shiiba 67Km
Takamori-tōge Bypass
Hakusui-kōgen
Nakamatsu
Minamiaso Railway
Takamori
Aso-Shirakawa
Mt. Tawarayama
Nishihara-mura 西原村
Mt. Ōmine
Kugino-mura 久木野村
Takayubaru
Grand Champion
Mt. Kanmurigatake
Mt. Takahatayama
Mt. Jōyama
Takamoriaso-jinja
Mt. Takajōya 高千穂野
Steep and sharp curves
to Ichinomiya
Takamori 高森
to Takachiho
to Kumamoto
Mt. Seieizan
Takamori-machi 高森町
Takamori Pass
Kueno Pass
Mt. Funanoyama
to Mifune
Gebao 下馬尾
to Mamihara
to Tomochi
Iidasan
Yabe
Mifune River
Nanataki
Mt. Mantaniyama
Yabe-machi 矢部町
Seiwa-son 清和村
Soyō-machi 蘇陽町
Soyōkyō(Gorge) 蘇陽峡
Mamihara 馬見原
Tsubana Pass
Takachiho-chō 高千穂町
Gokase River
Gokase-chō 五ケ瀬町
Matsuba-sansaro 松葉三差路
Mt. Kōsadake
Congestion in autumn
Large truck traffic prohibited
Mt. Yahazudake
Mt. Akatogishiyama
Mt. Gionyama
Iiboshi Pass
Mt. Techōzan
Midori River
Mt. Yurugidake
Mt. Horagatake
Mt. Ōnitayama
Mt. Memaruyama
Mt. Tenshuzan
Mt. Ogawadake
Morotsuka-son 諸塚村
Itsuki-mura
Shiba-son
Taketa-shi
Takachiho-chō
Hyūga-shi
E F G H
1 2 3 4 5 6
51 38 47 36

52
31
48
A
B
C
D
1
2
3
4
5
6
Koga-shi
Takata-machi
Yamaga-shi
Karatsu-shi
Takeo-shi
Kashima-shi
FUKUOKA
SAGA
KUMAMOTO
Shikanoshima I.
Drive-in area
Saitozaki seaside
Scenic view of Genkai-nada
Kyūshū-yūsen (to Gonoura-Izuhara-Ashibe Hitakatsu)
C. Yarasaki
Hakata-wan
Nokonoshima I.
C. Hamasaki
Congestion in summer
Imazu-wan
Muromi River
Wakiyamaguchi 脇山口
Matsushima 5 松島五
Tatara River
Kashii
Kashiigū 香椎宮
Hisayama
Hisayama-machi 久山町
Inunaki Pass
Wakamiya-machi 若宮町
Neko Pass
Mt. Hokotateyama
Yagiyama Pass
IIZUKA-SHI 飯塚市
Fukuoka 福岡
Higashi-ku 東区
Hakata
Kasuya-machi 粕屋町
Sasaguri-machi 篠栗町
RKB Satsuki(Ryūō)
Caution-fallingrock
Honami-machi 穂波町
Mt. Wakasugiyama
Chūō-ku 中央区
Nishitetsu-Fukuoka
Hakata-ku 博多区
Shime-machi 志免町
Sue-machi 須恵町
Nishi-ku 西区
Arae 荒江
Sawara-ku 早良区
Jōnan-ku 城南区
Minami-ku 南区
Umi-machi 宇美町
Mt. Toishiyama
ORD 520
LAR 1890
Yagiyama Bypass
Chikuho-machi 筑穂町
Keisen-machi 桂川町
Sasaguri Line
Chikuhō Line
Mt. Kōsozan
Mt. Kanōdake
Mt. Sangunzan
Mt. Hōmanzan
Mt. Haseyama
Mt. Yayamadake
Usui-machi 碓井町
Dazaifu
DAZAIFU-SHI 太宰府市
Mt. Odakeyama
Hinata Pass
Aburayama-kannon
Mt. Aburayama
MAEBARU-SHI 前原市
Mt. Nishiyama
Chikushigaoka
From Fukuoka-shi
Kita-Kyūshū 65Km
Nagasaki 170Km
KASUGA-SHI 春日市
Mizuki 水城
Kanzeonji
Tenmangū 太宰府
Congestion in spring
Drive-in area
Mt. Ōnejiyama
Hiyamizu Pass
Shirasaka Pass
Hatchōgoe Pass
Mt. Togamidake
Nakagawa-machi 那珂川町
Kogasagi Pass
Seven Million
ŌNOJŌ-SHI 大野城市
Chikushino 筑紫野
Mt. Ushikubiyama
Hiyamizu-dōro
ORD 420
LAR 1440
Mitsuse Pass
Mt. Kanayama
CHIKUSHINO-SHI 筑紫野市
Chikushi 筑紫
Yasu-machi 夜須町
Mt. Kiyama
Itaya Pass
Mt. Ichinotake
Mt. Seburiyama 脊振山
Mitsuse-mura 三瀬村
Kiyama-chō 基山町
Mt. Gongen-yama
Tosu-chikushino-dōro
ORD 150
LAR 520
Nagayoshi 永吉
Tosu Jct
Tenjin Ōmuta Line
Miwa-machi 三輪町
Mt. Shiroyama
Amagi Railway
AMAGI-SHI 甘木市
Ōuchi Pass
Sakamoto Pass
to Fukuoka
to Saga
Tosu 鳥栖
OGŌRI-SHI 小郡市
Chikugo-Ogōri 筑後小郡
Amagi 甘木
Tachiarai-machi 大刀洗町
Sefuri-mura 脊振村
Nakabaru-chō 中原町
Higashiseburi-son 東脊振村
TOSU-SHI 鳥栖市
Higashimachi 東町
Chikushino Bypass
Nishitetsu Amagi Line
Kitano-machi 北野町
Tanushimaru-machi 田主丸町
NAGASAKI EXPRESSWAY
Higashisefuri
Yamato-chō 大和町
Fukuoka 40Km
Saga 25Km
Kumamoto 69Km
Kyūdai Line
Saga-Yamato 佐賀大和
Tate 田手
Kyōwamachi 協和町
Mitagawa-chō 三田川町
Kamimine-chō 上峰町
Kitashigeyasu-chō 北茂安町
Chikugogawa Riverside
Higashi machi 東町
Kurume
Kanzaki-machi 神埼町
KURUME-SHI 久留米市
Kōra-taisha
Mt. Hosshinzan
Mt. Kōrasan
Drive-in area
Nagasaki Line
Accident-prone area
Mine-chō 三根町
to Fukuoka
Tōrichō 10 通町10
Higashi machi 東町
to Ōmuta
Takagi 高木
SAGA-SHI 佐賀市
Chiyoda-chō 千代田町
Mizuma-machi 三潴町
Kagoshima Line
KYŪSHŪ EXPRESSWAY
Hirokawa 広川
Jōyō-machi 上陽町
Mt. Morinotsukayama
Hoshino River
Sagu Castle
Jōjima-machi 城島町
Hirokawa-machi 広川町
Mt. Takamine
Fukuoka 59Km
Kurume 25Km
Yanagawa 18Km
morodomi-chō 諸富町
Ōki-machi 大木町
CHIKUGO-SHI 筑後市
Yame
YAME-SHI 八女市
Nōso 納楚
Ōkawa-shi 大川市
Yamanoi 山の井
Kurogi-machi 黒木町
Yabegawa River
Higashiyoka-chō 東与賀町
Kawasoe-machi 川副町
Tachibana-machi 立花町
YANAGAWA-SHI 柳川市
Mitsuhashi-machi 三橋町
Mt. Himegozedake
Mt. Tobikatayama
Shimonoshō 下庄
Setaka-machi 瀬高町
Kiyomizudera
Kahoku-machi 鹿北町
Yamakawa-machi 山川町
Yamato-machi 大和町
Minami-Setaka
Chikugo River
Hayatsue River
Okinohata River
ARIAKE-KAI 有明海

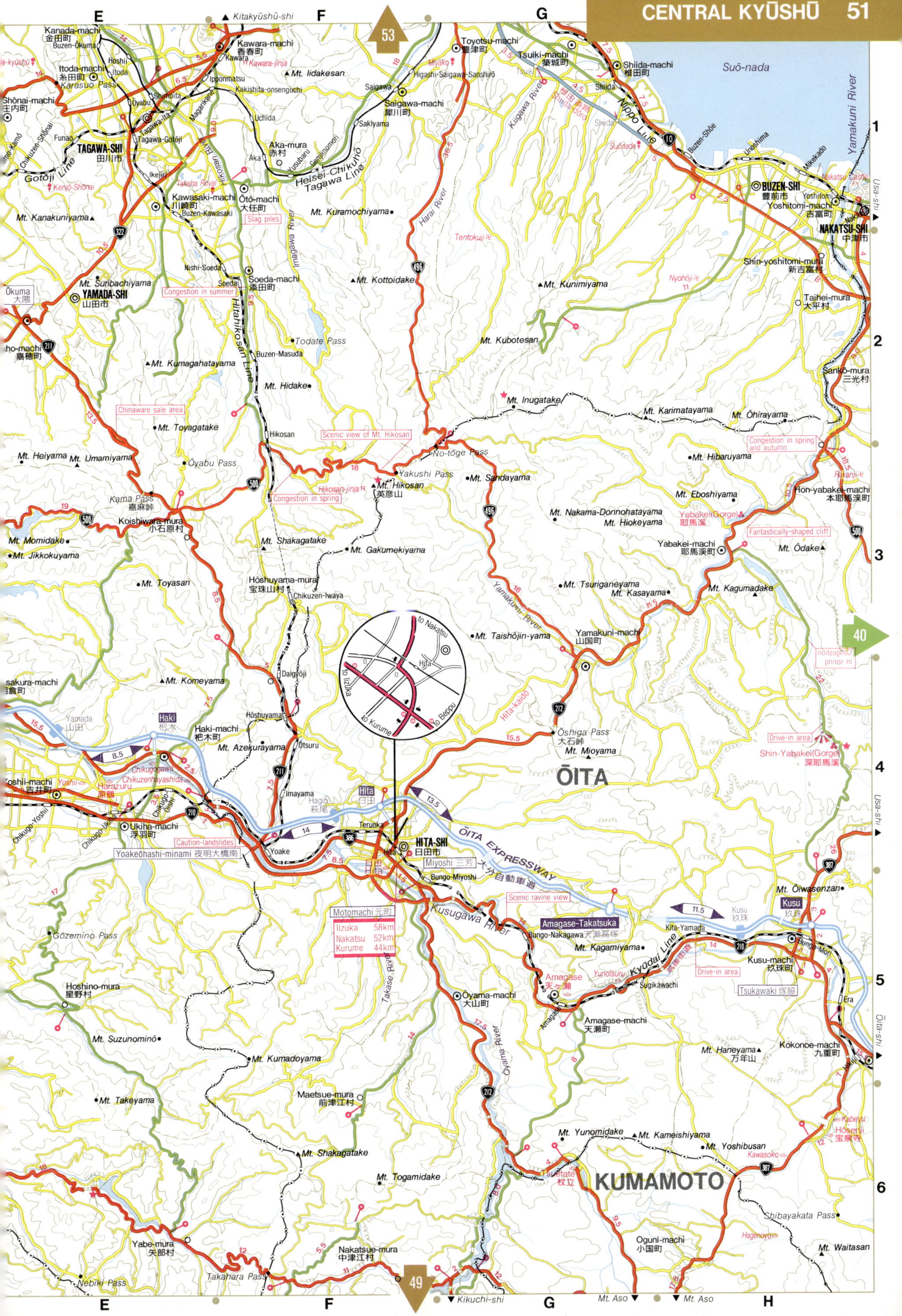
Kitakyūshū-shi
53
Kanada-machi
金田町
Kawara-machi
香春町
Toyotsu-machi
豊津町
Tsuiki-machi
築城町
Shiida-machi
椎田町
Suō-nada
Yamakuni River
Itoda-machi
糸田町
Karasuo Pass
Mt. Iidakesan
Saigawa-machi
犀川町
Shōnai-machi
庄内町
TAGAWA-SHI
田川市
Gotōji Line
Aka-mura
赤村
Heisei-Chikuhō Tagawa Line
Nippō Line
BUZEN-SHI
豊前市
Yoshitomi-machi
吉富町
NAKATSU-SHI
中津市
Kawasaki-machi
川崎町
Ōtō-machi
大任町
Slag piles
Mt. Kuramochiyama
Mt. Kanakuniyama
Harai River
Tentokuji
Shin-yoshitomi-mura
新吉富村
Soeda-machi
添田町
Mt. Kottoidake
Mt. Kunimiyama
Nyohōji
Taihei-mura
大平村
Mt. Suribachiyama
YAMADA-SHI
山田市
Congestion in summer
Ōkuma
大隈
Todate Pass
Mt. Kubotesan
Kaho-machi
嘉穂町
Mt. Kumagahatayama
Buzen-Masuda
Mt. Hidake
Sankō-mura
三光村
Mt. Inugatake
Mt. Karimatayama
Mt. Ōhirayama
Chinaware sale area
Mt. Toyagatake
Hikosan
Scenic view of Mt. Hikosan
Congestion in spring and autumn
No-tōge Pass
Mt. Heiyama
Mt. Umamiyama
Ōyabu Pass
Yakushi Pass
Mt. Sandayama
Mt. Hibaruyama
Rakanji
Kama Pass
嘉麻峠
Hikosan-jinja
Mt. Hikosan
英彦山
Congestion in spring
Mt. Eboshiyama
Hon-yabakei-machi
本耶馬渓町
Koishiwara-mura
小石原村
Mt. Nakama-Donnohatayama
Mt. Hiokeyama
Yabakei(Gorge)
耶馬渓
Mt. Momidake
Mt. Jikkokuyama
Mt. Shakagatake
Mt. Gakumekiyama
Fantastically-shaped cliff
Yabakei-machi
耶馬渓町
Mt. Ōdake
Mt. Toyasan
Hōshuyama-mura
宝珠山村
Chikuzen-Iwaya
Mt. Tsuriganeyama
Mt. Kasayama
Mt. Kagumadake
Mt. Taishōjin-yama
Yamakuni-machi
山国町
40
Asakura-machi
朝倉町
Mt. Komeyama
Daigyōji
to Nakatsu
Hita
to Iizuka
to Kurume
to Beppu
Hita-kaidō
Haki
Haki-machi
杷木町
Mt. Azekurayama
Ōtsuru
Ōshiga Pass
大石峠
Mt. Mioyama
Drive-in area
Shin-Yabakei(Gorge)
深耶馬渓
ŌITA
Yoshii-machi
吉井町
Harazuru
Imayama
Hita
日田
Ukiha-machi
浮羽町
Caution-landslides
Yoakeōhashi-minami 夜明大橋南
Yoake
HITA-SHI
日田市
Miyoshi 三芳
Bungo-Miyoshi
ŌITA EXPRESSWAY
大分自動車道
Mt. Ōiwasenzan
Kusu
Motomachi 元町
Iizuka 58km
Nakatsu 52km
Kurume 44km
Kusugawa River
Scenic ravine view
Amagase-Takatsuka
Bungo-Nakagawa
Kita-Yamada
Mt. Kagamiyama
Kusu-machi
玖珠町
Gozemino Pass
Takase River
Amagase
天ヶ瀬
Yunotsuru
Kyūdai Line
Sugikawachi
Drive-in area
Tsukawaki 塚脇
Hoshino-mura
星野村
Ōyama-machi
大山町
Amagase-machi
天瀬町
Mt. Suzunominō
Ōyama River
Mt. Haneyama
万年山
Kokonoe-machi
九重町
Mt. Kumadoyama
Maetsue-mura
前津江村
Mt. Takeyama
Mt. Yunomidake
Mt. Kameishiyama
Mt. Yoshibusan
Kabeyu
Hōsenji
宝泉寺
Mt. Shakagatake
Kawasoko
Mt. Togamidake
Tsuetate
杖立
KUMAMOTO
Shibayakata Pass
Yabe-mura
矢部村
Oguni-machi
小国町
Nakatsue-mura
中津江村
Mt. Waitasan
Nebiki Pass
Takahara Pass
49
Kikuchi-shi
Mt. Aso
Usa-shi
Ōita-shi
E
F
G
H
1
2
3
4
5
6

B
C
D
1
2
3
4
5
6
A
GENKAI-NADA
玄界灘
C. Kanzakibana
Ōshima I.
C. Kashirobana
Jinoshima I.
Mt. Mitake
Ōshima-mura
大島村
Ōshimamura Ferry
C. Kanenomisaki
Katsushima I.
C. Kusazaki
Tsurikawa River
Satsukimatsubara
Mt. Yukawayama
Tarumi Pass
Okagaki-machi
岡垣町
Mt. Kōdaijiyama
Munakata-taisha
宗像大社
Mt. Todayama
Fujihara 富地原
Kagoshima Line
MUNAKATA-SHI
宗像市
C. Sonenohana
Shingū-machi
新宮町
Ainoshima I.
FUKUTSU-SHI
福津市
Saigō River
Mt. Konomiyama
Akagi Pass
Misaka Pass
Wakamiya
若宮
Wakamiya-machi
若宮町
Koga
古賀
KOGA-SHI
古賀市
C. Isozakihana
Congestion in summer
Shingū-machi
新宮町
Mt. Nishiyama
Miyata-machi
宮田町
San-yō-Shinkansen
Mt. Inunakiyama
FUKUOKA
Inunaki Pass
Neko Pass
Mt. Hokotateyama
Shin-Iizuka 新飯塚
Kita-Kyūshū 45Km
Fukuoka 33Km
Tosu 28Km
IIZUKA-SHI
飯塚市
Yagiyama Pass
Katashima 3 片島三
Shikanoshima I.
Scenic view of Genkai-nada
Drive-in area
Saitozaki Seaside
Kashii Line
Saitozaki
Kyūshū-yūsen
Tatara River
Matsushima 5 松島五
Hakata-wan
Hisayama-machi
久山町
Fukuoka
福岡
C. Yarasaki
Nokonoshima I.
Wakiyamaguchi
脇山口
Arae 荒江
Higashi-ku
東区
Kasuya-machi
粕屋町
Sasaguri Line
Sasaguri-machi
篠栗町
Caution-falling rock
Honami-machi
穂波町
C. Hamazaki
Congestion in summer
Chūō-ku
中央区
Hakata-ku
博多区
Shime-machi
志免町
Mt. Wakasugiyama
Inatsuki-machi
稲築町
Chikuhi Line
Nishi-ku
西区
Sawara-ku
早良区
FUKUOKA-SHI
福岡市
Sue-machi
須恵町
Mt. Toishiyama
ORD 520
LAR 1890
Yagiyama Bypass
Keisen-machi
桂川町
Chikuho-machi
筑穂町
Jōnan-ku
城南区
Minami-ku
南区
Umi-machi
宇美町
Mt. Sangunzan
Usui-machi
碓井町
Mt. Kanōdake
Mt. Yayamadake
Mt. Haseyama
Mt. Hōmanzan
Komenoyama Pass
Dazaifu
太宰府
Hinata Pass
KASUGA-SHI
春日市
DAZAIFU-SHI
太宰府市
Mt. Odakeyama
Drive-in area
MAEBARU-SHI
前原市
Mt. Aburayama
Mizuki 水城
Mt. Ōnejiyama
from Fukuoka-shi
Kita-Kyūshū 65Km
Nagasaki 170Km
Congestion in spring
Hiyamizu Pass
Mt. Nishiyama
Nakagawa-machi
那珂川町
ŌNOJŌ-SHI
大野城市
Shirasaka Pass
Hatchō-goe Pass
ORD 250
LAR 870
Kogasaki Pass
Tosu-Chikushino-dōro
Hiyamizu-dōro
ORD 420
LAR 1440
Mitsuse Tunnel
Mitsuse Pass
ORD 150
LAR 520
Chikushino
筑紫野
Mt. Kanayama
Yasu-machi
夜須町
AMAGI-SHI
甘木市
CHIKUSHINO-SHI
筑紫野市
50
Saga-shi
Mitagawa-chō
Tosu I.C.
Amagi-shi
Amagi-shi
C. Tōminohana
Dōzantō I.
Onga River
Ashiya-machi
芦屋町
Ashiya Airport
Mizumaki-machi
水巻町
Onga-chō
遠賀町
NAKAMA-SHI
中間市
Kurate-machi
鞍手町
Mt. Rokugatake
Kotake-machi
小竹町
Chikuhō Line

YAMAGUCHI
SUŌ-NADA
周防灘
ŌITA
KITAKYŪSHŪ-SHI
北九州市
Hiroshima 230Km
Fukuoka 65Km
SHIMONOSEKI-SHI
下関市
YUKUHASHI-SHI
行橋市
TAGAWA-SHI
田川市
BUZEN-SHI
豊前市
NAKATSU-SHI
中津市
ONODA-SHI
小野田市
YAMADA-SHI
山田市
KYŪSHŪ EXPRESSWAY
九州自動車道
Kokura-higashi
Kokura-minami
Shimonoseki
Mojikō
Moji
Shin-Moji
Kanmon Tunnel
Hinoyama Parkway
Hikojima-dōro
Wakato-ōhashi(Bridge)
ORD 400
LAR 2030
ORD 310
LAR 1100
ORD 200
LAR 550
ORD 150
LAR 520
Kanpu Ferry (to Pusan)
Kansai-kisen Ferry (to Matsuyama)
Meimon taiyō Ferry (to Ōsaka)
Hankyu Ferry (to Kōbe, Izumiōtsu)
Ocean-tōkyū Ferry (to Tokushima-Tōkyō)
Yukuhashishi-Gyōji 行橋市行事
Kita-Kyūshū 22Km
Tagawa 17Km
Nakatsu 27Km
Buzenshi-Higashiyahata
豊前市東八幡
Tsutsui 筒井
Chinzeibashi
鎮西橋
Sanbashidōri
桟橋通
to Kitakyūshū-Toshi-kōsoku
Hiraodai Plateau
平尾台
Sharp curves
Drive slowly
Slag piles
Congestion in summer
Chinaware sale area
Congestion in spring
Scenic view of Mt. Hikosan
Congestion in spring and autumn
Mt. Hikosan
Mt. Inugatake
Mt. Kunimiyama
Mt. Kubotesan
Mt. Nukisan
Mt. Ryūgahana
Mt. Adachiyama
Mt. Tobigasuyama
Mt. Sarakurayama
Mt. Kongōyama
Mt. Shakudake
Mt. Fukuchiyama
Mt. Ushikiriyama
Mt. Shōjigatake
Mt. Iidakesan
Mt. Funaoyama
Mt. Kanakuniyama
Mt. Suribachiyama
Mt. Kumagahatayama
Mt. Toyagatake
Mt. Umamiyama
Mt. Momidake
Mt. Shakagatake
Mt. Gakumekiyama
Mt. Sandayama
Mt. Kottoidake
Mt. Kuramochiyama
Mt. Hidake
Mt. Koyagatake
Mt. Karimatayama
Mt. Ōhirayama
Mt. Hibaruyama
Mt. Eboshiyama
Mt. Ōdake (Kinokodake)
Mt. Nozokiyama
Mt. Takajōyama
Kibe Pass
Ajimi Pass
Todate Pass
Ōyabu Pass
Kama Pass
Yakushi Pass
No-tōge Pass
Hashima I.
Mashima I.
Kōnoshima I.
Takenokojima I.
Mutsurejima I.
Umashima I.
Aijima I.
Kanjushima I.
Manjushima I.
C. Hezaki
C. Motoyamamisaki
Yabakei(Gorge)
耶馬溪
Nippō Line
Hitahikosan Line
Heisei-Chikuhō Tagawa Line
Onoda Line
Kakuhō Line
Kanmon-kaikyō
Tsuiki Airport
Katsuyama-machi
勝山町
Kanda-machi
苅田町
Toyotsu-machi
豊津町
Tsuiki-machi
築城町
Shiida-machi
椎田町
Saigawa-machi
犀川町
Kawara-machi
香春町
Soeda-machi
添田町
Ōtō-machi
大任町
Kawasaki-machi
川崎町
Yoshitomi-machi
吉富町
Shin-yoshitomi-mura
新吉富村
Taihei-mura
大平村
Sankō-mura
三光村
Hon-yabakei-machi
本耶馬渓町
Yabakei-machi
耶馬渓町
Koishiwara-mura
小石原村
Hita-shi
Ōita-shi
Ube-shi
Ogōri I.C.
Sanyō-chō

UWAJIMA-SHI
宇和島市
Ōzu-shi
Kita-Uwajima
Uwajima
Uwajima Castle
Warei-motomachi 和霊元町
Sakaemachi Rotary 栄町ロータリー
Ōzu 48Km
Kubokawa 100Km
Sukumo 77Km
Mt. Takatsukiyama
Nametoko Gorge
MT. ONIGAJŌYAMA
鬼ヶ城山
Mt. Gongen-yama
Drive-in area
Kuroson-rindō
Kuroson River
Iwamatsu River
Nojima I.
Kashima I.
Uwajima-wan
Kushima I.
Takashima I.
Toshima I.
Bubushino-seto
Biwagashima I.
Okinoshima I.
C. Ryūōbana
Tōdoshima I.
Chigirishima I.
Hiburishima I.
Kuroshima I.
Mt. Gongen-yama
Hayaisono-seto
Tsushima-chō
津島町
Iwamatsu-eigyōsho mae 岩松営業所前
Mt. Otonashiyama
Mt. Daikokuyama
Oitsukamijima I.
Nedokoshima I.
Takegashima I.
EHIME
Funakoshi-unga
C. Hotokezaki
Drive-in area
Mt. Sasayama
Sasayama-jinja
Scenic view of C. Yuranohana
Mt. Kannondake
C. Yurahana
Mt. Kannonmori
BUNGO-SUIDŌ
Mt. Shiraishiyama
Nishiumi-dōro
ORD 420
LAR 1470
Uchiumi
Drive-in area
Sōzugawa River
Kanjizaiji
Ainan-chō
愛南町
西海道路
Kashima I.
Yokoshima I.
Koyokoshima I.
Ojishima I.
Mt. Gongen-yama
Congestion
Sukumo-Saeki Ferry (to Saeki)
Ategijima I.
C. Kurosakibana
Kirishima I.
C. Kōmomisaki
Nojishima I.
to Uwajima
to Nishiumi
to Sukumo
Sukumo-wan
C. Shirahana
Mt. Ōhorayama
Ugurushima I.
C. Tsutomezaki
Daidō obsavation platform
Odokaigan(Beach)
Futanamijima I.
C. Asabaezaki
SUKUMO-SHI
宿毛市
Kōjima I.
Birōtō I.
Himeshima I.
Sannosejima I.
Mt. Imoseyama
Okinoshima I.
C. Kushigahana

65
56
E
F
G
H
1
2
3
4
5
6
KŌCHI
TOSA-WAN
土佐湾
Yoshinobu
Matsumaru
atsuno-chō
野町
Matsuchi
Yoshino River
Jizō Pass
Hage
Nishigatō
Ekawasaki
Nishitosa-mura
西土佐村
Meguro River
Tōkawa
Tōwa-son
十和村
Toza-Shōwa
Steep and Sharp curves
Yodo Line
Yusuhara River
Taishō-chō
大正町
Tosa-Taishō
Mt. Takanosuyama
Mt. Dōgamori
堂ヶ森
Kubokawa-chō
窪川町
Kubokawa
Kubokawachō-Higashimachi
窪川町東町
Wakai
Niida River
Mt. Gozaishonomine
Katasaka Pass
Steep and Sharp curves
Utsuigawa
Ienigawa
Saga
Toriuchiba Pass
Kaina
Tosa Kuroshio Railway
Mt. Hotokegamori
Iyoki
Tosa-Saga
Saga-chō
佐賀町
Scenic view of C. Ashizurimisaki
Saga-kōen
Tosa-Shirahama
Tosa Utopia
Umino-Ou-mukae
Tosa-Kami-Kawaguchi
Ariigawa
Ukibuchi
Irino-matsubara(Beautiful Beach)
Kamo-jinja
Ōgata-chō
大方町
Tosa-Irino
C. Inomisaki
Mt. Ishimijiyama
Nishi-Ōgata
Iwata River
Mt. Gōkiyama
Mt. Hokegamori
Mt. Hachigamori
Mt. Nabegamori
Myōjōgamori
Matsuda River
Yasunami
Accident-prome area
Mt. Daitōzan
Mt. Takamoriyama
NAKAMURA-SHI
中村市
Nakamura
Kotsuka
Drive-in area
Kunimi
Fuwa Hachimangū
Sukumoshi-Sukumo 宿毛市宿毛
Uwajima 77Km
Nakamura 23Km
Tosa-Shimizu 59Km
Nakamurashi-Fuba
中村市不破
Kubokawa 48km
Sukumo 23Km
Tosa-Shimizu 38Km
Sukumoshi-Hirata 宿毛市平田
Enkōji
Arioka
Drive-in area
Mt. Honjōyama
JMO-SHI
宿毛市
kumo
to Uwajima
to Ashizuri
Mt. Araseyama
Mt. Kaigamori
Hirano-kaigan
Ashizuri
Shimanto River
to Kōchi
Nakamura
to Sukumo
Uyama 右山
to Tosashimizu
Izuta Pass
Mt. Tsuzurayama
Mihara-mura
三原村
Mt. Nakahatayama
C. Arisaki
Mt. Kumamori
Mt. Imanoyama
Ōtsuki-chō
大月町
Drive-in area
Ōki-kaigan
Mt. Takatoriyama
Mt. Kurinmori
Tatsukushi (Scenic Rocky Coast)
TOSASHIMIZU-SHI
土佐清水市
C. Kubotsusaki
from Tosashimizu
Matsuyama 230Km
Kōchi 160Km
Ashizuri Sunny Road
足摺サニーロード
Narrow road
C. Kanaezaki
C. Chihiromisaki
to Tatsukushi
C. Ourasaki
Ashizuri Skyline
Scenic view of Pacific ocean
Fog in spring
Ashizuri Pen.
Tunnel of camellia
Kongōfukuji
Precipitous criff coast
C. Ashizurimisaki
足摺岬

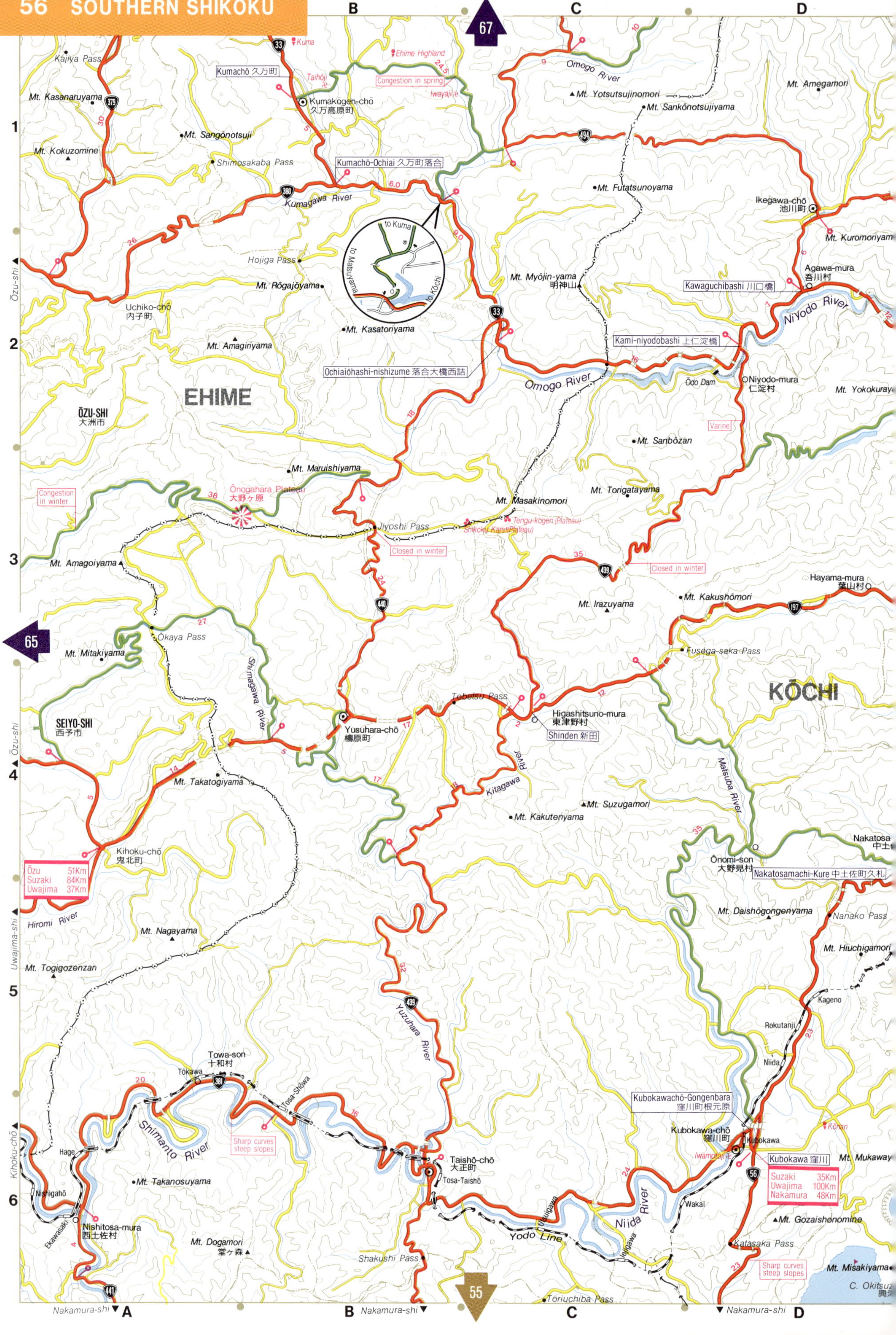

B
C
D
67
65
55
1
2
3
4
5
6
A
B
C
D
Kajiya Pass
Kuma
Ehime Highland
Kumachō 久万町
Taihōji
Congestion in spring
Iwayaji
Kumakōgen-chō 久万高原町
Mt. Kasanaruyama
Mt. Sangōnotsuji
Mt. Kokuzomine
Shimosakaba Pass
Kumachō-Ochiai 久万町落合
Kumagawa River
Omogo River
Mt. Yotsutsujinomori
Mt. Sankōnotsujiyama
Mt. Amegamori
Mt. Futatsunoyama
Ikegawa-chō 池川町
Mt. Kuromoriyama
Agawa-mura 吾川村
to Kuma
to Matsuyama
to Kōchi
Hojiga Pass
Mt. Rōgajōyama
Uchiko-chō 内子町
Ōzu-shi
Mt. Kasatoriyama
Mt. Myōjin-yama 明神山
Kawaguchibashi 川口橋
Niyodo River
Mt. Amagiriyama
Kami-niyodobashi 上仁淀橋
Ochiaiōhashi-nishizume 落合大橋西詰
Omogo River
Ōdo Dam
Niyodo-mura 仁淀村
Mt. Yokokuraya
EHIME
ŌZU-SHI 大洲市
Varine
Mt. Sanbōzan
Mt. Maruishiyama
Congestion in winter
Ōnogahara Plateau 大野ヶ原
Mt. Torigatayama
Mt. Masakinomori
Jiyoshi Pass
Tengu-kōgen (Plateau)
Shikoku Karst (Plateau)
Closed in winter
Closed in winter
Mt. Amagoiyama
Mt. Irazuyama
Mt. Kakushōmori
Hayama-mura 葉山村
Ōkaya Pass
Mt. Mitakiyama
Shimagawa River
Fusega-saka Pass
KŌCHI
Tobetsu Pass
Higashitsuno-mura 東津野村
Shinden 新田
SEIYO-SHI 西予市
Yusuhara-chō 檮原町
Ōzu-shi
Mt. Takatogiyama
Kitagawa River
Matsuba River
Mt. Suzugamori
Mt. Kakutenyama
Kihoku-chō 鬼北町
Nakatosa 中土
Ōnomi-son 大野見村
Nakatosamachi-Kure 中土佐町久礼
Ōzu 51Km
Suzaki 84Km
Uwajima 37Km
Hiromi River
Uwajima-shi
Mt. Daishōgongenyama
Nanako Pass
Mt. Nagayama
Mt. Hiuchigamori
Mt. Togigozenzan
Yuzuhara River
Kageno
Rokutanji
Towa-son 十和村
Tōkawa
Tosa-Shōwa
Niida
Kubokawachō-Gongenbara 窪川町根元原
Sharp curves steep slopes
Shimanto River
Hage
Kihoku-chō
Kubokawa-chō 窪川町
Kubokawa
Kōnan
Taishō-chō 大正町
Iwamotoji
Kubokawa 窪川
Suzaki 35Km
Uwajima 100Km
Nakamura 48Km
Mt. Mukaiyama
Nishigahō
Mt. Takanosuyama
Tosa-Taishō
Uchigawa
Niida River
Wakai
Nishitosa-mura 西土佐村
Ekawasaki
Mt. Dogamori 堂ヶ森
Yodo Line
Mt. Gozaishonomine
Katasaka Pass
Shakushi Pass
Sharp curves steep slopes
Mt. Misakiyama
C. Okitsu
Nakamura-shi
Nakamura-shi
Toriuchiba Pass
Nakamura-shi

E
F
G
H
1
2
3
4
5
6
Saijō-shi
Ōtoyo-chō
68
58
Mt. Jingamori
Tosa-chō
土佐町
Mt. Kuishiyama
Closed in winter
Ananaigawa -chosuichi Lake
Nebiki Pass
Mt. Takashirikiyama
Mt. Koshikigadai
Mt. Sekkōzan
Mt. Hosoyabuyama
KŌCHI EXPRESSWAY
高知自動車道
Pacific
Kaminaka-chō
Takaiwa 高岩
Mt. Gozaishoyama
Mt. Takabagamori
Nankoku
南国
Shōbudō(Cave)
Mt. Nishinomineyama
Tosa-Yamada
Yamada-nishi-machi
Kōchi
Kosaka Pass
7.5
Shiino Pass
Engyōji
Kōchi
高知
Ōsaka-goe Pass
Kokubunji
Tosa-Nagaoka
Tosayamada-chō
Mt. Kōnomori
Tosa-jinja
Zenrakuji
Kokubu River
Gomen
10.5
Azono
Tosa-Ikku
NANKOKU-SHI
南国市
Gomen-machi
Tateba
Matsuyama-kaidō
Niyodogawabashi -higashizume
仁淀川橋東詰
Ino
伊野
Asakura-jinja
Kōchi Castle
Asahi
Kōchi
Nunoshida
Tosa-Ōtsu
Nankoku-dōro
Aki-shi
Sugimoto-jinja
Asakura
KŌCHI-SHI
高知市
Godaisan Park
Chikurinji
Watermelon sale area
Mt. Hachifushiyama
Hotoke Pass
Nishikiyama
Ino
Kōchi-Ryōma
Kōchi-chō
越知町
Hidaka-mura
日高村
Hakawa
Ino-chō
いの町
Kōchi-Katsurahama-dōro
Kōchi
Kusaka
Okabana
Mt. Washioyama
Tosa-Kamo
9.1
Urado-wan
from Kōchi-shi
Takamatsu 150Km
Matsuyama 130Km
Nishi-Sakawa
Mt. Saragamine
Sakawachō-Kamigō 佐川町上郷
Kiyotakiji
Tosa
土佐
TOSA-SHI
土佐市
Sakawa
Sakawa-chō
佐川町
Mt. Ōhiramine
Sekkeiji
Katsurahama
Haruno-chō
春野町
Erinono
Tanemaji
Tosashi-Takaokahonmachi
土佐市高岡本町
Mt. Takamori
Scenic view of Pacific Ocean
Togano
Mt. Yokoseyama
Pinetree boulerard
14.8
Mt. Kokūzōsan
Mt. Chausuyama
Mt. Kuroiwayama
Niyodo River
Mt. Katsugamori
Mt. Bandagamori
Asakura
to Kōchi
to Matsuyama
to Nakamura
Asō
Yokonamisanri
Mt. Utsugayama
C. Shironohana
Susaki -chūgakkō-mae
須崎中学校前
Uranouchi-wan
Drive-in area
Seiryūji
Kōchi 38Km
Kubokawa 35Km
Hiyoshi 84Km
Susaki-higashi
須崎東
PL Yakō
Onogō
Ōma
Otonashi-jinja
SUSAKI-SHI
須崎市
Susaki
Fog in spring
to Susaki
to Kōchi
C. Kōzaki
Tosa-Shinjō
Susaki-wan
to Usa
TOSA-WAN
土佐湾
Susaki
Nomi-wan
Dosan Line
Awa
Tojima I.
Nakanoshima I.
Drive-in area
Kure
Kure-wan
C. Ōtsuzaki
C. Yatabezaki
C. Kanmurisaki

B
C
D
69
A
B
C
D
1
2
3
4
5
6
57
Closed in winter
Ananaigawa-chosuichi Lake
Ananaigawa Dam
Shigetō
Mt. Kuishiyama
Mt. Takashikisan
KŌCHI EXPRESSWAY
高知自動車道
Shingai
to Takamatsu
to Kōchi
to Muroto
Pacific
Mt. Hosoyabuyama
Nankokushi-Ryoseki
南国市領石
Nankoku
南国
Nankokushi-Yahata 南国市八幡
Mt. Nishinomineyama
from Kōchi
Takamatsu 150Km
Matsuyama 130Km
Kōchi
高知
Osakagoe Pass
Engyōji
Tosa-jinja
Zenrakuji
Nangoku
Tosa-Yamada
Yamadanishimachi
Dosan Line
Tosayamada-chō
土佐山田町
Tosa-Nagaoka
Nankokushi-Ōdōri
南国市大通
Gomen
Gomen-machi
Tateba
NANKOKU-SHI
南国市
Mt. Kōnomori
Kōchi Castle
Kōchishi-Hongūchō
高知市本宮町
KŌCHI-SHI
高知市
Asahi
Azōno
Nunoshida
Kokubu River
Nankoku-dōro
Watermelon sale area
Godaisan Park
Chikurinji
Mt. Hachifushiyama
Accident-prone area
Kōchi-Ryōma
Noichi
Yoshikawa
Yoshikawa-mura
吉川村
Monobe River
Akaoka
Akaoka-chō
赤岡町
Mt. Washioyama
Kōchi
Urado-wan
Kōchi Katsurahama-dōro
Zenshibuji
Urado-ōhashi
浦戸大橋
ORD 260
LAR 940
Haruno-chō
春野町
Sekkeiji
Katsurahama(Beautiful Beach)
桂浜
C. Ryūōmisaki
Tanemaji
Pine trees
Sakawa-chō
Yumeno
Mt. Akatsukayama
Birafu-jinja
Kahoku-chō
香北町
Mt. Shimizugamori
Ryūgadō (Cave)
竜河洞
Congestion in spring and autumn
Mt. Kikurakuyama
Steep
Noichichō-Higashimachi
野市町東町
Noichi-chō
野市町
Kagami-chō
香我美町
Akaokachō-Ipponmatsu 赤岡町一本松
Kagami
Yasu-chō
夜須町
Yasu
Mt. Ōmineyama
C. Teimisaki
Nishibun
Wajiki
Akano
Geisei-mura
芸西村
Mt. Koigamori
Mt. Kumaōyama
KŌCHI
Mt. Mitsujigamori
Tosa Kuroshio Railway
Anapai
Kyūjō-mae
Aki
AKI-SHI
安芸市
Hothouse area
Aki River
Ioki
Shimoyama
Mt. Unpenjisan
Unpenji
Ikedachō-Hakuchi 池田町白地
Ikeda-chō
池田町
Hashikura
Tsukuda
Miyoshi-chō
三好町
Tsuji
Ikawa-chō
井川町
Tokushima-shi
Awa-Ikeda
Rengeji
Kotohira 28Km
Kawanoe 33Km
Kōchi 87Km
Ikawachō-Nishiikawa
井川町西井川
Hakuchi
Minawa
Iyaguchi
TOKUSHIMA
Awa-Kawaguchi
Yamashiro-chō
山城町
Mt. Shiozukamine
Koboke
Ōboke Koboke(Gorge)
大歩危 小歩危
Iyakei
Iyakei(Gorge)
祖谷渓
Mt. Nakatsusan
TOSA-WAN
土佐湾
Drive-in area
Mt. Kanbō
Nishiiyayama-son
西祖谷山村
Iyagawa River
Mt. Sanbōjiyama
Ōboke
Yamashirochō-Kamimyō 山城町上名
Yoshino River
Mt. Nokanoikeyama
Higashiiyayama-son
東祖谷山村
Tachikawa
立川
Tosa-Iwahara
Burakuji-yakushidō
Jōfukuji
Toyonaga
Ōtoyomachi-Takazu
大豊町高須
Ōtaguchi
Tosa-Anapai
Ōtoyo
大豊
Ōsugi
Ōtoyo-chō
大豊町
Accident-prone area
Mt. Kōnoitasan
Mt. Kajigamori
Mt. Tsutatateyama
KŌCHI
KŌCHI EXPRESSWAY
高知自動車道
Kaminaka-chō
Kahoku-chō
香北町
Tosa-Kitagawa
Mt. Shigenomori
Inosawa
Monobe-mura
物部村
Mt. Myōjindake
Kakumodani
Mt. Gozaishosan
Kōchi-shi
Kōchi-shi

60
E
F
G
H
1
2
3
4
5
6
TOKUSHIMA
Mt. Hōzōyama
Mt. Asetaniyama
Mt. Hiegoyayama
Mt. Hindenmaru
Mt. Ōtoyama
Mt. Tengumori
Mt. Setoyama
Mt. Nishigamine
Mt. Kamedaniyama
Yanase-chosuichi Lake
Yanase Dam
Mt. Yatsusugimori
Kumano-jinja
Umaji-mura
馬路村
Konjinji
Deep ravine
Mt. Kanegaryūmori
Fukkoshino-tōge Pass
Mt. Suzugamine
Kaifu River
193
Mugi-chō
牟岐町
Mugi
55
Scenic view of coastline
Sabase
Mugi Line
Tosahama-kaidō
Asakawa
C. Ajirosaki
Mugichō-Nakamura 牟岐町中村
Kainan-chō
海南町
Awa-Kainan
Shihōhara 四方原
Anan 70Km
Kaminaka 48Km
Muroto 57Km
Kaifu-chō
海部町
Kaifu
Nasa-wan
Shishikui
Drive-in area
Shishikui-chō
宍喰町
Kannoura
Takegashima I.
Kuzushima I.
Tōyō-chō
東洋町
C. Matsushitagahana
Shirōgane Pass
493
Toyōchō-None 東洋町野根
None River
Yasuda River
Kōnomine-jinja
Mt. Noneyama
Shōzoku Pass
Mt. Kosakayama
Seaside road
Yasudachō-Yasuda 安田町安田
Yasuda
Kitagawa-mura
北川村
安田町
Tano-chō
田野町
Nahari
Nahari-chō
奈半利町
Nahari River
Mt. Ōsumiyama
C. Hanemisaki
Mt. Kasagiyama
Drive-in area
Higashinokawa River
Caution-side wind
Kongōchōji
Steep
Murotomisakichō-Mitsu 室戸岬町三津
C. Gyōdōmisaki
MUROTO-SHI
室戸市
Shinshōji
Mt. Otareyama
Murotoshi-Ukitsu 室戸市浮津
Muroto Skyline
Hatsumisakiji
C. Murotozaki
Murotoshi-Sakamoto 室戸市坂本
室戸岬
Ōsaka-Kōchi tokkyū Ferry (to Ōsaka)

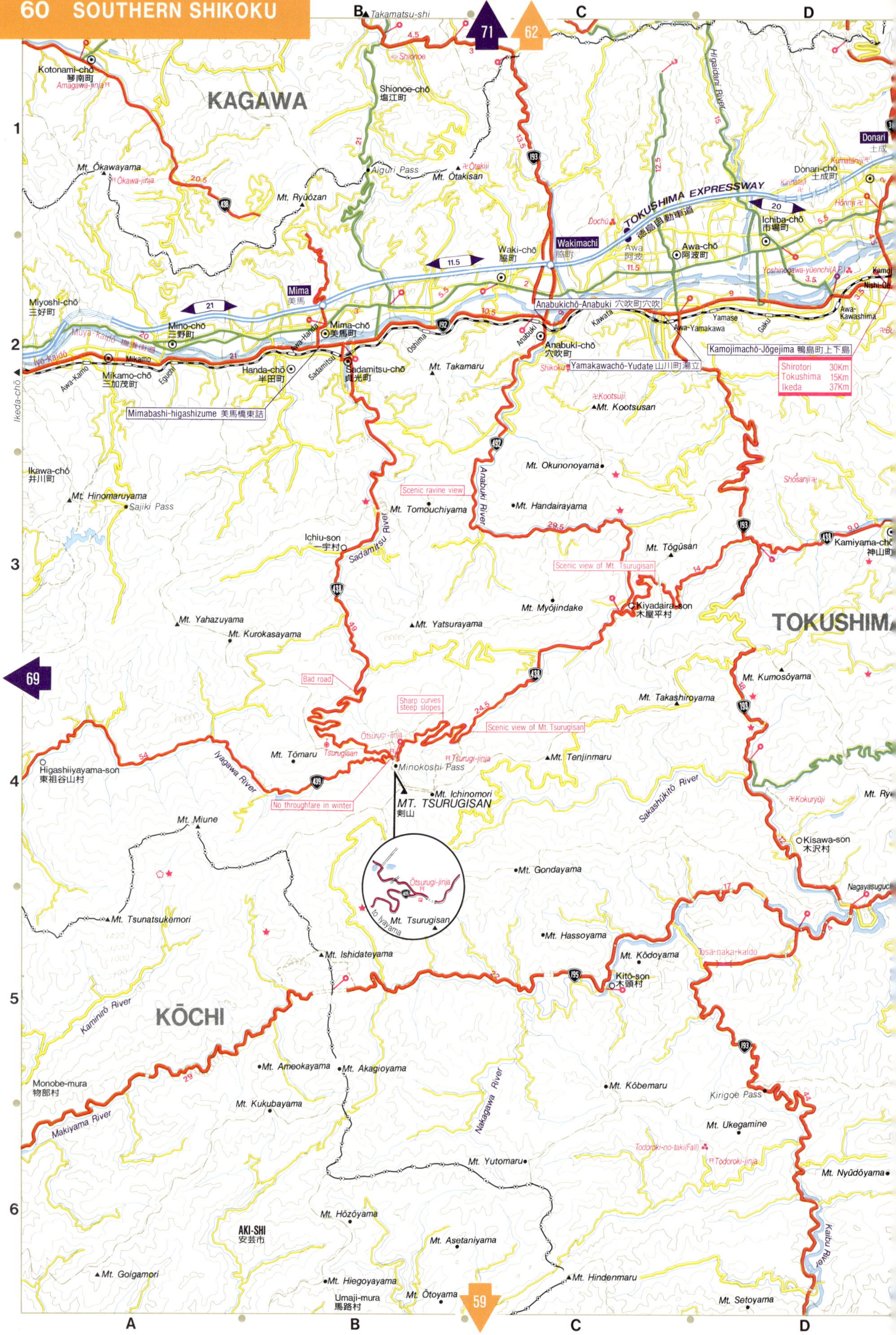

KAGAWA
TOKUSHIMA
KŌCHI
Takamatsu-shi
71
62
69
59
Kotonami-chō
琴南町
Amagawa-jinja
Shionoe
Shionoe-chō
塩江町
Mt. Ōkawayama
Ōkawa-jinja
Aiguri Pass
Ōtakiji
Mt. Ōtakisan
Mt. Ryūōzan
Higaidani River
Donari
土成
Donari-chō
土成町
Kumataniji
Kirihataji
Hōrinji
TOKUSHIMA EXPRESSWAY
徳島自動車道
Dochū
Ichiba-chō
市場町
Wakimachi
脇町
Waki-chō
脇町
Awa
阿波
Awa-chō
阿波町
Yoshinogawa-yuenchi(A.P.)
Kamojima
Nishi-Oe
Mima
美馬
Miyoshi-chō
三好町
Mino-chō
三野町
Muya-kaidō
撫養街道
Iyo-kaidō
Mikamo
Mima-chō
美馬町
Anabukichō-Anabuki 穴吹町穴吹
Kawata
Yamase
Gakū
Awa-Kawashima
Awa-Yamakawa
Awa-Kamo
Mikamo-chō
三加茂町
Eguchi
Handa-chō
半田町
Sadamitsu
Sadamitsu-chō
貞光町
Oshima
Mt. Takamaru
Anabuki
Anabuki-chō
穴吹町
Shikoku
Yamakawachō-Yudate 山川町湯立
Kamojimachō-Jōgejima 鴨島町上下島
Shirotori 30Km
Tokushima 15Km
Ikeda 37Km
Ikeda-chō
Mimabashi-higashizume 美馬橋東詰
Kootsuji
Mt. Kootsusan
Ikawa-chō
井川町
Mt. Hinomaruyama
Sajiki Pass
Mt. Okunonoyama
Shōsanji
Scenic ravine view
Mt. Tomouchiyama
Anabuki River
Mt. Handairayama
Ichiu-son
一宇村
Sadamitsu River
Mt. Tōgūsan
Kamiyama-chō
神山町
Scenic view of Mt. Tsurugisan
Mt. Myōjindake
Kiyadaira-son
木屋平村
Mt. Yahazuyama
Mt. Kurokasayama
Mt. Yatsurayama
Mt. Kumosōyama
Bad road
Mt. Takashiroyama
Sharp curves
steep slopes
Scenic view of Mt. Tsurugisan
Ōtsurugi-jinja
Tsurugisan
Mt. Tōmaru
Tsurugi-jinja
Mt. Tenjinmaru
Higashiiyayama-son
東祖谷山村
Iyagawa River
Minokoshi Pass
Mt. Ichinomori
MT. TSURUGISAN
剣山
No throughfare in winter
Sakashūkitō River
Kokuryūji
Mt. Ry
Mt. Miune
Kisawa-son
木沢村
Mt. Gondayama
Nagayasuguchi
Ōtsurugi-jinja
to Iyayama
Mt. Tsurugisan
Mt. Tsunatsukemori
Mt. Hassoyama
Mt. Ishidateyama
Mt. Kōdoyama
Tosa-naka-kaidō
Kitō-son
木頭村
Kaminiro River
Mt. Ameokayama
Mt. Akagioyama
Monobe-mura
物部村
Mt. Kukubayama
Mt. Kōbemaru
Kirigoe Pass
Makiyama River
Nakagawa River
Mt. Ukegamine
Todoroki-no-taki(Fall)
Todoroki-jinja
Mt. Yutomaru
Mt. Nyūdōyama
Mt. Hōzōyama
AKI-SHI
安芸市
Mt. Asetaniyama
Kaifu River
Mt. Goigamori
Mt. Hiegoyayama
Mt. Hindenmaru
Umaji-mura
馬路村
Mt. Ōtoyama
Mt. Setoyama
A
B
C
D
1
2
3
4
5
6

62
63
NARUTO-SHI
鳴門市
Muya
Utatsu-goe Pass
Ōasahiko-jinja
Kotoku Line
Ryōzenji
Gokurakuji
Daisenji
Konsenji
Bandō
Dainichiji
Kamiita
上板
Itano-chō
板野町
Awa-Kawabata
Awa-Ōtani
Ikenotani
Tatsumichi
Yoshinogawa Bypass
Awaji-kaidō
Kyū-Yoshino River
Matsushige-chō
松茂町
Tokushima
Itano
Jizōji
Aizumi-chō
藍住町
Kitajima-chō
北島町
Shōzui
Tōhō Rayon
Yoshinari
Kamiita-chō
上板町
Aizumi
藍住
Jūrakuji
Anrakuji
Bekku-hachiman-jinja
Imagiri River
Tokushima
徳島
Kuramotochō 3 chōme 蔵本町三丁目
Ishii-chō
石井町
Ushinoshima
Tokushima Line
Idoji
Sako
TOKUSHIMA-SHI
徳島市
Yoshino River
Nankai Ferry(to Wakayama)
Shimoura
Ishii
Kō
Kasuga-jinja
Bizan Park
Dōgakuji
Kan-onji
Iyo-kaidō
Ishiichō-ishii 石井町石井
Akuichō 2 chōme 鮎喰町二丁目
INOGAWA-SHI
Kokubunji
Jōrakuji
Jizōin
Tokushima
Akui River
Nikenya
Bunkanomori
Shinhamahonchō 2 chōme 新浜本町二丁目
Kii-suidō
Tokushima Forest
Ocean-tōkyū Ferry(to Tōkyō-Shin-Moji)
Kenjiji
Mt. Nishiryūōsan
Mt. Higashiryūōsan
Minami-komatsushimachō 南小松島町
Jizōbashi
Hinomine-jinja
from Tokushima-shi
Takamatsu 80Km
Kōchi 200Km
C. Wadanohana
KOMATSUSHIMA-SHI
小松島市
Komatsushima
Komatsushima-wan
Jōrokuji
Sanagouchi-son
佐那河内村
Onzanji
Awa-Akaishi
to Tokushima
to Sanagouchi
Minami-Komatsushima
to Anan
Tatsue
Tatsueji
Nyoirinji
Mt. Nakatsumineyama
Hanoura-chō
羽ノ浦町
Hanoura
Nakagawa-chō
那賀川町
Nishibara
Awa-Nakashima
Nakagawa River
Tokuenji
Jiganji
Anan Bypass
Katsuura-chō
勝浦町
Oji Paper
Awashima-jinja
Katsuura River
Kakurinji
Ananshi-Tomiokachō 阿南市富岡町
Anan
ANAN-SHI
阿南市
Nakatsushima I.
Eboshijima I.
Marushima I.
Tokushima 25Km
Kaminaka 58Km
Kainan 65Km
Minobayashi
Ananshi-Minobayashichō
阿南市見能林町
Awa-Tachibana
to Kuwano
to Tokushima
to Hiwasa·Muroto
Tsunomine-jinja
Tsunomine Skyline
ORD 600
LAR 2400
katsu-chō
上勝町
Tairyūji
Tairyūji Ropeway
Mt. Tairyūjisan
Kuwano
Nagashima I.
Tachibanachō-Ōura 橘町大浦
Takashima I.
Urumejima I.
Nonoshima I.
Kokatsushima I.
Wajiki-chō
鷲敷町
Byōdōji
Aratano
Maikojima I.
Tanagojima I.
Ishima I.
Maejima I.
C. Kamodamisaki
蒲生田岬
Fukuichō-Ōnishi 福井町大西
Kaminaka-chō
那賀町
Aioi-chō
相生町
Awa-Fukui
Izari Pass
Mt. Gozeyama
Mt. Myōjinyama
Yukisaka Pass
Jorōiwa
C. Kanokubimisaki
Yuki
Yuki-chō
由岐町
Kiki
Drive-in area
Mt. Ōkageyama
Hiwasa-chō
日和佐町
ANAN COAST
阿南海岸
Kitagawachi
Hiwasa River
Yakuōji
Hiwasa
Mt. Dōgiriyama
Yamagawachi
Mugi Line
to Tokushima
Kita-Kawachi
Yakuōji
Hiwasa
to Mugi
Hegawa
Sharp curves steep slopes
Clift
PACIFIC OCEAN
太平洋
Pass
Mugi
Mugi-chō
牟岐町
Scenic shore view
Mugichō-Nakamura 牟岐町中村
Tosahama-kaidō
Tokuzenyama
Ōshima I.
ishikui-cho

B
C
D
100
OKAYAMA
SETOUCHI-SHI
瀬戸内市
Kongōchōji
Nezumishima I.
Kamiikadashō I.
Maejima I.
Aoshima I.
Kishima I.
C. Sakakenohana
Kuroshima I.
1
Olive Line (to Hinase)
Shōdoshima-kyūkō Ferry (to Himeji)
Bōzejima I.
Kuroshima I.
Kashima I.
Ōyakeshima I.
Takashima I.
Komatsujima I.
Katsurajima I.
Ōtsufurashima I.
Nagashima I.
Mitsugashirajima I.
Matsushima I.
to Kankakei
to Tonoshōko
C. Kanagasaki
Kojima I.
Chiburishima I.
Okinoshima I.
2
Kazurashima I.
C. Murosaki
Mt. Kensoyama
Shōdoshima
Shōdoshima Skyline
Mt. Hoshigajōyama
Kankakei (Valley)
寒霞渓
Shōdoshima I.
Uchinomi-chō
内海町
Scenic view of Harima-nada
HARIMA-NADA
播磨灘
Tonoshō-chō
土庄町
Mt. Ōmiyama
Ikeda-chō
池田町
Olive growing area
Tachibana Pass
Yoshima I.
Ikeda-wan
Uchinomi-wan
Mt. Goishiyama
C. Kurosaki
Kokusai Ferry (to Takamatsu)
Blue Line (to Takamatsu)
Kansai-Kisen
Kansai-kisen
Kazenokojima I.
C. Ōkadobana
71
3
Mt. Shirahamayama
Fukubeshima I.
C. Shakagahana
Inageshima I.
to Kankakei
to Tonoshō
Takashima I.
Aji-chō
庵治町
Mt. Gokenzan
Takamatsu-shi
C. Kogushimisaki
Kabe River
C. Umagabana
Shido
Mure-chō
牟礼町
Shioya
Shido-wan
4
SANUKI-SHI
さぬき市
Yashima
Sanuki
Shido-kaidō
Shido
Takamatsu-jidōshadō
Sanuki-Miki
Ōvangetown
Tsuda-Samukawa
Sanuki-Tsuda
Tsuruwa
Tsuda-higashi
Mt. Amatakiyama
Miki-chō
三木町
Nagaō
Ōuchichō-Machida
大内町町田
Nibu
Shakuōji
Minato 湊
Takamatsu 35Km
Kamojima 30Km
Tokushima 47Km
Sanbonmatsu
HIGASHIKAGAWA-SHI
東かがわ市
Sanuki-Shirotori
Mt. Dakeyama
5
Shirotori-Ōchi
Hiketa
Hiketachō-sakamoto 引田町坂元
Naruto
Kusaka Pass
Mt. Kasagamine
Mizushi-jinja
Mt. Dantokusan
Hoshigoe Pass
Awa-kaidō
阿波街道
Mt. Yahazuyama
Ōsakagoe Pass
Chestnut picking area
Ōkubojī
Mt. Ōasayama
Utrtsugoe Pass
Ōasahiko-jinja
Naruto Line
Daisenji
Itano-chō
板野町
Kōtoku Line
Gokurakuji
6
Ichiba-chō
市場町
Higashi River
Gosho
Konsenji
Ikenotani
Kamiita
上板
Dainichiji
Waki-chō
脇町
Donari
土成
Gosho
Jizōji
TOKUSHIMA EXPRESSWAY
徳島自動車道
Aizumi-chō
藍住町
Matsushige-chō
松茂町
Kitajima-chō
北島町
Tōhō Rayon
Shōzui
Yoshinari
Kumataniji
Jūrakuji
Anrakuji
Kamiita-chō
上板町
TOKUSHIMA
Kirihataji
Aizumi
藍住
60
61
Anabuki-chō
A
B
C
D

E
F
G
H
101
110
61
1
2
3
4
5
6
HYŌGO
AKASHI-SHI
明石市
KŌBE-SHI
神戸市
Maiko
Tarumi
Akashi-Awaji Ferry
Akashi-kaikyō
Scenic view of Awajishima I.
Akashi-kaikyō-ōhashi (Bridge)
Iwaya 岩屋
Awaji-chō
淡路町
Mt. Kagaribayama
Loquat picking area
Ōiso
Hokudan-chō
北淡町
Higashiura
Higashiura-chō
東浦町
Kuruma 久留麻
Hokudan
Scenic view of marguerite
Mt. Isenomori
Mt. Myōken-yama
Awaji
Tōzanji
Mt. Mayasan
Ichinomiya-chō
一宮町
C. Eisaki
Drive slowly
Izanagi-jingu
ŌSAKA-WAN
大阪湾
Nankai-Awaji Line
Tsuna-ichimiya
Tsuna-chō
津名町
Shizuki 志筑
Mt. Ryūhōjiyama
Side roads ahead
Goshiki-chō
五色町
C. Hotokezaki
Awajishima I.
ORD 6050
LAR 17550
Senkōji
Goshikihama (Beautiful Beach)
Drive-in area
Shioya 塩屋
Keino-matsubara (Beautiful Beach)
Sumoto
SUMOTO-SHI
洲本市
Mikumayama Park
Sumoto
C. Karikomisaki
Kobe-Awaji-Naruto-jidoshado
神戸淡路鳴門自動車道
Shikoku-kaido 四国街道
Ayuya
Sumoto
Seidan-Mihara
MINAMIAWAJI-SHI
南あわじ市
Tomogashima-suidō
Tomogashima I.
Kadano-seto
Jinoshima I.
Okinoshima I.
Mt. Kashiwarayama
Katakasuga-jima
C. Taguchizaki
C. Oishinohana
Yahata 八幡
Kokuga 国衙
Don't look off when narcissuses in bloom
WAKAYAMA
WAKAYAMA-SHI
和歌山市
Awajishima -minami
C. Magosaki 大鳴戸橋
Naruto Whirlpools
鳴門のうず潮
Tobishima I.
Naruto-kaikyō
Mt. Yuzuruhasan
Scenic view of Nushima
Wakame sale area
from Naruto
Takamatsu 65Km
Kōchi 180Km
C. Chiozaki
Muyachō 撫養町
Nushima I.
Kyū-Yoshino River
to Takamatsu
Naruto
to Itano
to Tokushima
to Iwaya
to Fukura
to Yura

B C D
1
2
3
4
5
6
A B C D

IYO-NADA
伊予灘
EHIME
MATSUYAMA EXPRESSWAY
松山自動車道
Yosan Line
Yodo Line
ŌZU-SHI
大洲市
YAWATAHAMA-SHI
八幡浜市
SEIYO-SHI
西予市
UWAJIMA-SHI
宇和島市
Uchiko-chō
内子町
Nakayama-chō
中山町
Futami-chō
双海町
Ikata-chō
伊方町
Honai-chō
保内町
Yoshida-chō
吉田町
Mima-chō
三間町
Kihoku-chō
鬼北町
Matsuno-chō
松野町
Nishitosa-mura
西土佐村
Uchikobashi 内子橋
Uchiko-Ikazaki
内子五十崎
Ōzu-Kitatada
大洲北只
Kami-Matsuba 上松葉
Unomachi 卯之町
Seiyo-Uwa
西予宇和
Wareimotomachi
和霊元町
Matsuyama 50Km
Yawatahama 20Km
Uwajima 48Km
Matsuyama 81Km
Ōzu 20Km
Misaki 46Km
Matsuyama 100Km
Kōchi 120Km
from Uwajima
Congestion in winter
Mandarin sale area
Drive-in area
Uwajima-wan
Hiroi River
Hijikawa River
Kawabe River
Inou River
Yoshino River
Asagiriko Lake
Kanogawa Dam
Nametoko Gorge
Mt. Gozaishozan
Mt. Gozaishoyama
Mt. Onosan
Mt. Hachigamori
Mt. Takamoriyama
Mt. Kokuzomine
Mt. Shinnōzan
Mt. Ushinomine
Mt. Kamakurayama
Mt. Tsubokamiyama
Mt. Saitōyama
Mt. Amagoiyama
Mt. Kurakakeyama
Mt. Kōsanjiyama
Mt. Kannōjiyama
Mt. Kitayama
Mt. Higashiuyama
Mt. Kannanzan
Mt. Tomisuyama
Mt. Nebutoyama
Mt. Takeyama
Mt. Ryūōzan
Mt. Dōshoyama
Mt. Izumigamori
Mt. Makinoyama
Mt. Kumagamine
Mt. Togigozensan
Ishigami Pass
Gozega Pass
Taimatsu Pass
Hanaga Pass
Sakuraga-tōge Pass
Chinnoa Pass
Jizō Pass
Kajiya Pass
C. Muemisaki
C. Ōsakibana
C. Tadanamihana
C. Ryūōbana
Ōshima I.
Kashima I.
Tojima I.
Tōdoshima I.
Kuroshima I.
Kushima I.
Bubushino-seto
Hokezu-wan
Matsuyama-shi
Susaki-shi
Taishō-chō
Tsushima-chō
to Ozu
to Matsuyama
to Uwajima
to Misaki
to Uwa
to Sukumo
Yawatahama
E F G H
1 2 3 4 5 6
66 56 54

B
C
D
92
91
89
65
1
2
3
4
5
6
A
ETAJIMA-SHI
江田島市
KURE-SHI
呉市
Hiro
Nigata
安芸灘大橋
Ozegawa River
Inokojima I.
Atetajima I.
Iwakuni
IWAKUNI-SHI
岩国市
Iwakuni Airport
Nishi-Nōmijima I.
西能美島
Mitsugojima I.
Ondo-Ohashi
Ondono-seto
Ondo-chō
音戸町
Hironishiokawa River
Shimo-Kamagarijim
下蒲刈島
HIROSHIMA
Shimoguroshima I.
Kamiguroshima I.
Nasakejima I.
Ōgurokamishima I.
Mt. Kushinoune
Higashi-Nōmijima I.
東能美島
C. Oyayasumibana
Kurahashijima I.
倉橋島
Uwagi Pass
Kurahashi-chō
倉橋町
Katsuragahama-jinja
Sasakojima I.
C. Nagakushinohana
Kure-Matsuyama Ferry
Matsuyama-Hiroshima Kokaku Ferry
AKI-NADA
安芸灘
Hodakajima I.
Funegaiiwa
Teshima I.
Kuroshima I.
Kashima I.
Hashiwajima I.
Kobashirajima I.
Yokoshima I.
Hayamajima I.
Kotachibajima I.
Ōtachibashima I.
Isekojima I.
Hashirajima I.
Maejima I.
Kuroshima I.
Nagarekojima I.
C. Kazakiribana
Fukushima I.
Kurakakejima I.
Nagashima I.
Fukurashima I.
Tsuwajishima I.
Nuwajima I.
Mt. Tainoyama
Nakajima I.
中島
Bōyo-kisen (Yanai-Mitsuhama)
Kashirajima I.
YAMAGUCHI
Nasakejima I.
Heyano-seto
Sekido-kaikyō
Muzukijima I.
C. Ōsakibana
Ukishima I.
Mitsushima I.
Moroshima I.
Takashima I.
C. Akasaki
Mt. Ōmisan
Mt. Tainomine
Yashirojima I.
屋代島
Tobisejima I.
Otokojima I.
Futagamijima I.
Yokoshima I.
Tsurishima-kaiky
Katashima I.
Mt. Inuboeya
Mt. Kanōzan
Mt. Dakesan
Wagashima I.
Suōōshima-chō
周防大島町
Sasashima I.
Mt. Takatoyama
Gogoshim
興居島
Tsurushima I.
Mt. Kofuji
C. Agesaki
Tatsushima I.
Okikamurojima I.
Yurijima I.
Bōyo-kisen (Yanai-Mitsuhama)
Kakezushima I.
Ōminasejima I.
YANAI-SHI
柳井市
C. Sakarizaki
Hegurijima I.
Kominasejima I.
IYO-NADA
伊予灘
Kansai-kisen (to Kokura)
Aoshima I.
Muk
Kōnoka
Futami-chō
双海町

E
F
G
H
92
93
68
56
1
2
3
4
5
6
Kurushima I.
Ōsakikamijima I.
大崎上島
Ōmishima I.
大三島
Mt. Yakushisan
Ōmishima～Hakatashima
Shimanami-Kaidō
ORD 1550
LAR 4550
Omishimabashi (Bridge)
Hakatashinma I.
伯方島
Tsubashima I.
C. Kanagasaki
Hakatashima
Mijikashima I.
Hakata-Ōshima-Ōhashi (Bridge)
Funaori-seto
Ushima I.
Kashiwajima I.
Komatsujima I.
Ōmatsushima I.
Kamagari-chō
蒲刈町
Kami-Kamagarijima I.
上蒲刈島
Kashiwajima I.
Okamurajima I.
Ōgejima I.
Koejima I.
Toyoshima I.
Toyohama-chō
豊浜町
Yutaka-machi
豊町
Ōsakishimojima I.
大崎下島
Chū-Shikoku Ferry
Ōshima I.
大島
Ōshima-Kita
Tsushima I.
Shimanami-Kaidō
ORD 1850
LAR 5500
Yokoshima I.
Okubishima I.
C. Ōsuminohana
大角鼻
Kansai-kisen
Oshima I.
Mushijima I.
Ōshima-minami
Nakadoshima I.
Nagoma Pass
Kajishima I.
C. Kajitorinohana
Umashima I.
Kurushima-seto
Hashihama Park
Kurushima-kaikyō
to Matsuyama
Hashi hama
to Imabari
Imabari
to Nibukawa
to Komatsu
Namikata
Hashihama
Imabari-Kita
Mt. Chikamiyama
Itsuki-nada
Aijima I.
Ōnishi
Enmeiji
Nankōbō
Imabari Castle
IMABARI-SHI
今治市
Imabari
Taisanji
Ōnishichō-Miyawaki
大西町宮脇
Higishima I.
Koajima I.
Iyo-Kameoka
Iyo-Tomita
Kikumachō 菊間町
Eifukuji
Imabari Bypass
Kokubunji
Karakohama Park(A.P)
Kikuma
Scenic view of Setonaikai
Drive-in area
Matsuyama Seaside
San-yūji
Heichijima I.
Iyo-Sakurai
Imabarishi-Sakurai 今治市桜井
Diamond Ferry
Asanami
Mt. Takahagiyama
Ōura
Hōjō
Imabari-Yunoura
Shell gathering
Nibukawa
鈍川
Mt. Kasamatsuyama
Tateiwa River
Sunset Hills
Kashima-jinja
Sayano Pass
Ogutsunajima I.
Iyo-Hōjō
Kunitsuhikonomikoto-jinja
Dōgo CC
Sōja River
Imabari
Scenic view of Mt.Ishizuchisan
Hōjō Bypass
Okudōgo
Mt. Ryūmon-yama
Iyo-Miyoshi
Tōyo-dōro
ORD 310
LAR 1150
Yanagihara
Mt. Kitasanpōgamori
Mt. Takanawasan
Mt. Goyōgamori
Awai
Narahara-jinja
Mt. Narabarasan
Nyūgawa
Tōyo
Kōyōdai
Yosan Line
Tōyo-Tanbara
東予道路
Tamanoe
Elleair(Matsuyama)
Horie-wan
Horie
Gongen
Kōryūji
Mt. Higashisanpōgamori
Iyo-Komatsu
Iyo-Himi
Hōjuji
Mt. Meotoyama
Ishizuchiyama
石鎚山
Kisshōji
Enmyōji
Horieeki-kōsaten 堀江駅交差点
Mt. Fumisan
Fumiji
Ayanobe-jinja
Ishizuchi-jinja Kuchinomiya
Taisanji
Iyo-Wake
Drive in area
Mt. Katsuokayama
Bad road
Nakayama River
Iyo-Komatsu
いよ小松
15.5
Takahama
Jizō-saka Pass
Dōgo GC
Mado-tōge Pass
Kurose Pass
Okudōgo
奥道後
Ishide River
SAIJŌ-SHI
西条市
Mitsu
Mitsuhama
Dōgo
道後
from Matsuyama-shi
Takamatsu 160Km
Kōchi 130Km
EHIME
Kinuyama
Ishiteji
Matsuyamashi
Matsuyama Castle
MATSUYAMA EXPRESSWAY
松山自動車道
Caution-falling rock
Matsuyama
MATSUYAMA-SHI
松山市
Matsuyama-higashi
Kurase River
Hantaji
Iyo Railway
Kita-Kume
Mt. Shiomiyama
Jōdoji
Mt. Omokiyama
Iyotsuhikonomikoto-jinja
Iyo Yokokawara Line
Sakurasanri
桜三里
Kamata
Ichitsubo
Hirai
Shigenobu River
Mt. Sangamori
Yokogawara
Ushibuchi
Matsuyama GC
Matsuyama
松山
Sairinji
Masaki-chō
松前町
Kita-Iyo
Iyo-jinja
Kawauchi
川内
Mt. Shiogamori
Ishizuchi-jinja
MT. ISHIZUCHISAN
石鎚山
Iyo-Yokota
Tobechō-Takōda
砥部町高尾田
TŌON-SHI
東温市
Closed in winter
Mt. Aotakiyama
Mt. Ninomori
Torinoki
Iyo-nada
伊予灘
Matsuyama-kokusai
Shiraitaki
Karakai Fall
Mt. Omogōyama
IYO-SHI
伊予市
Yasakaji
Jōruriji
Mt. Mitakeyama
Kuromori Pass
Tobe-chō
砥部町
Tobechō-senzoku 砥部町千足
Mt. Godaigamori
Iyo
伊予
Mt. Yagamisan
Osogoe Pass
Kutani River
Iuchi Pass
Mt. Ishizumiyama
Omogokei(Gorge)
面河渓
Mt. Tsutsujōsan
Scenic view of Matsuyama plain
Ishizuchi Skyline
Iyo-Ōhira
Tobegawa River
Kuma
Mt. Saragamine
Misaka Pass
Congestion in summer and autumn
Sharps curves
Kumakōgen-chō
久万高原町
Matsuyama Royal
Mt. Hajikamiyama
Kuma

70
67
57
Takaikamishima I.
Uoshima I.
Kamijima-chō
上島町
Enoshima I.
Hyōtanjima I.
Marukamijima I.
Miyakubo-chō
宮窪町
Kajishima I.
Myōjinshima I.
Shisakashima I.
四阪島
Minoshima I.
HIUCHI-NADA
燧灘
Kan-onji
to Zentsūji
Matashima I.
Shikoku Orange Ferry (Tōyo-Ōsaka)
Ōshima I.
C. Hotokezaki
Miyoshima I.
Sumitomo Chemical
Sumitomo Metal Mining
Niihama
Kokuryō River
Murogawa River
Takamatsu 100Km
Kōchi 120Km
from Niihama
Tōyo-dōro
ORD 310
LAR 1150
Kuraray
Takihama
NIIHAMA-SHI
新居浜市
Yosan Line
Sekigawa
Sekigawa River
Iyo-Doi
Akaboshi
Iyo-Sangawa
MATSUYAMA EXPRESSWAY
松山自動車道
Mishima-Kawanoe
三島川之江
Fuji Spinning
Kawanoe
Toyohama 11Km
Ikeda 26Km
Saijō 41Km
Iyo-Mishima
Doi
土居
Irino
入野
SHIKOKUCHŪŌ-SHI
四国中央市
Mt. Suihamine
Kinshako Lake
Sankawa
SAIJŌ-SHI
西条市
東予道路
Takinomiya
Nakahagi
Niihama
新居浜
Mandarin sale area
Iyo-Saijō
いよ西条
Oshishinji
Besshi
Ishizuchiyama
Yunotani
Kisshōji
Zenjiji
Kawanoe 41Km
Matsuyama 51Km
Kōchi 110Km
EHIME
Mt. Akaboshiyama
Mt. Kumatakayama
Mt. Tsujigamine
Mt. Futatsudake
Mt. Hanezuruyama
Mt. Nishiakaishiyama
Mt. Higashiakaishiyama
Mt. Sazareoyama
Mt. Amazutsumiyama
Mt. Tamatoriyama
Mt. Kuromoriyama
Mt. Mitsumoriyama
Mt. Sasagamine
Mt. Ōgiyama
Mt. Ōzareyama
Mt. Kanmuriyama
Closed in Winter
Mt. Inokawayama
Mt. Sōtenzan
Mt. Shiragayama
Mt. Ōgoyayama
Mt. Kamegamori
瓶ヶ森
Mt. Iyofuji
Mt. Mitakiyama
Mt. Kamojirō
Large truck traffic prohibited
Closed in winter
Gravel road
Yoshino River
Ōkawa-mura
大川村
Mt. Nōtaniyama
Mt. Iwatsutsujiyama
岩躑躅山
Sameuara Dam
Mt. Iwaguroyama
Mt. Inamurayama
Setogawa River
Motoyama-chō
本山町
Mt. Tsutsujōsan
Ino-chō
いの町
Tosa-chō
土佐町
Mt. Taiyama
Ishizuchi Skyline
Ōmori River
Mt. Jingamori
NANKOKU-SHI
南国市
Ikegawa-chō
池川町
Mt. Kuishiyama
Closed in winter
Mt. Amegamori
Mt. Koshikigadai
Mt. Takashirikiyama
Ino-chō

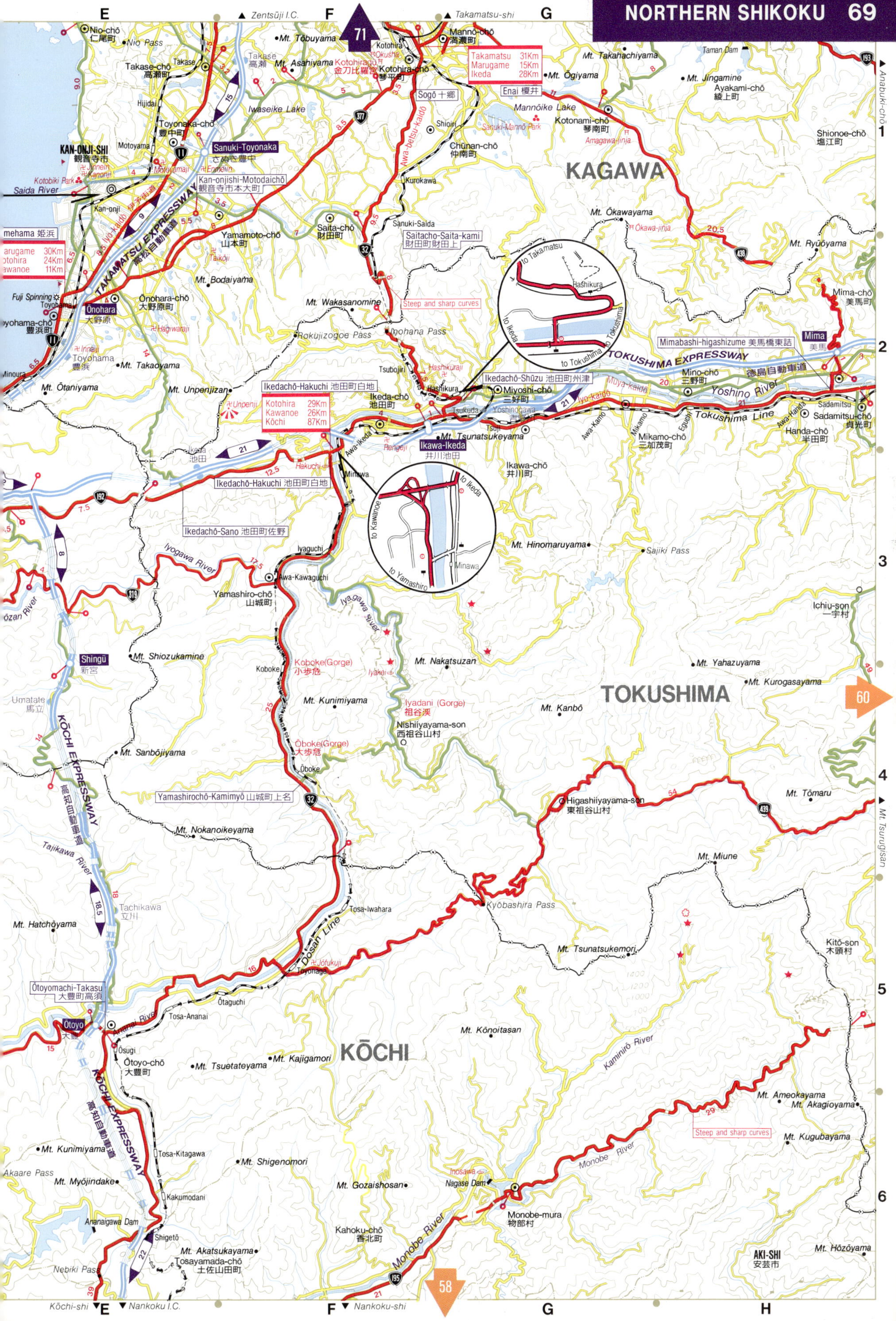
E
F
G
H
1
2
3
4
5
6
Zentsūji I.C.
Takamatsu-shi
Anabuki-chō
Mt. Tsurugisan
Kōchi-shi
Nankoku I.C.
Nankoku-shi
71
60
58
KAGAWA
TOKUSHIMA
KŌCHI
Nio-chō
仁尾町
Nio Pass
Mt. Tobuyama
Mannō-chō
満濃町
Takase-chō
高瀬町
Takase
高瀬
Mt. Asahiyama
Kotohira
Kotohiragū
金刀比羅宮
Kotohira-chō
琴平町
Takamatsu 31Km
Marugame 15Km
Ikeda 28Km
Mt. Ōgiyama
Mt. Takahachiyama
Taman Dam
Mt. Jingamine
Ayakami-chō
綾上町
Enai 榎井
Sogō 十郷
Iwaseike Lake
Mannōike Lake
Sanuki-Mannō Park
Kotonami-chō
琴南町
Amagawa-jinja
Shionoe-chō
塩江町
Hijidai
Toyonaka-chō
豊中町
Shioiri
KAN-ONJI-SHI
観音寺市
Motoyama
Sanuki-Toyonaka
さぬき豊中
Chūnan-chō
仲南町
Awa-betsu-kaidō
Jinnein
Kan-onji
Motoyamaji
Enmein
Kotobiki Park
Kan-onjishi-Motodaichō
観音寺市本大町
Kurokawa
Saida River
Kan-onji
TAKAMATSU EXPRESSWAY
高松自動車道
Iyo-kaidō
Mt. Ōkawayama
Ōkawa-jinja
mehama 姫浜
arugame 30Km
otohira 24Km
awanoe 11Km
Yamamoto-chō
山本町
Saita-chō
財田町
Sanuki-Saida
Saitacho-Saita-kami
財田町財田上
Mt. Ryūōyama
Taikōji
Mt. Bodaiyama
Fuji Spinning
Toyohama
Ōnohara
大野原
Ōnohara-chō
大野原町
Mt. Wakasanomine
Steep and sharp curves
Mima-chō
美馬町
yohama-chō
豊浜町
Hagiwaraji
Rokujizogoe Pass
Inohana Pass
to Takamatsu
Hashikura
to Ikeda
to Tokushima
Mimabashi-higashizume 美馬橋東詰
Mima
美馬
Innaji
Toyohama
豊浜
Mt. Takaoyama
Tsubojiri
Hashikuraji
TOKUSHIMA EXPRESSWAY
徳島自動車道
Minoura
Mt. Ōtaniyama
Mt. Unpenjizan
Unpenji
Ikedachō-Hakuchi 池田町白地
Ikedachō-Shūzu 池田町州津
Miyoshi-chō
三好町
Mino-chō
三野町
Muya-kaidō
Yoshino River
Kotohira 29Km
Kawanoe 26Km
Kōchi 87Km
Ikeda-chō
池田町
Tsukuda
Yoshinogawa
Iyo-kaidō
Sadamitsu
Sadamitsu-chō
貞光町
Tokushima Line
Awa-Handa
Ikeda
池田
Rengeji
Ikawa-Ikeda
井川池田
Mt. Tsunatsukeyama
Tsuji
Awa-Kamo
Mikamo
Eguchi
Mikamo-chō
三加茂町
Handa-chō
半田町
Awa-Ikeda
Hakuchi
Ikedachō-Hakuchi 池田町白地
Minawa
Ikawa-chō
井川町
to Kawanoe
to Yamashiro
Ikedachō-Sano 池田町佐野
Iyaguchi
Mt. Hinomaruyama
Sajiki Pass
Iyogawa River
Awa-Kawaguchi
Yamashiro-chō
山城町
Iyagawa River
Ichiu-son
一宇村
Shingū
新宮
Mt. Shiozukamine
Koboke
Koboke(Gorge)
小歩危
Iyakei
Mt. Nakatsuzan
Mt. Yahazuyama
Mt. Kurogasayama
Umatate
馬立
Mt. Kunimiyama
Iyadani (Gorge)
祖谷渓
Mt. Kanbō
Nishiiyayama-son
西祖谷山村
KŌCHI EXPRESSWAY
高知自動車道
Mt. Sanbōjiyama
Ōboke(Gorge)
大歩危
Ōboke
Yamashirochō-Kamimyō 山城町上名
Higashiiyayama-son
東祖谷山村
Mt. Tōmaru
Mt. Nokanoikeyama
Tajikawa River
Mt. Miune
Kyōbashira Pass
Tosa-Iwahara
Tachikawa
立川
Mt. Hatchōyama
Dosan Line
Mt. Tsunatsukemori
Kitō-son
木頭村
Jōfukuji
Toyonaga
Ōtoyomachi-Takasu
大豊町高須
Ōtaguchi
Otoyo
大豊
Anani River
Tosa-Ananai
Ōsugi
Ōtoyo-chō
大豊町
Mt. Kōnoitasan
Kaminiro River
Mt. Tsuetateyama
Mt. Kajigamori
Mt. Ameokayama
Mt. Akagioyama
Steep and sharp curves
Mt. Kugubayama
Mt. Kunimiyama
Tosa-Kitagawa
Mt. Shigenomori
Monobe River
Akaare Pass
Mt. Myōjindake
Inosawa
Nagase Dam
Mt. Gozaishosan
Kakumodani
Ananaigawa Dam
Monobe-mura
物部村
Shigetō
Kahoku-chō
香北町
Mt. Akatsukayama
Tosayamada-chō
土佐山田町
Monobe River
AKI-SHI
安芸市
Mt. Hōzōyama
Nebiki Pass

A
B
C
D
1
2
3
4
5
6
98
93
68
Takahashi-shi
OKAYAMA
HIROSHIMA
Miwa
Narrow road-Drive slowly
Yamano
Mt. Kyōnoueyama
Odagawa River
Mt. Umanoriyama
Mt. Kasagiyama
Mt. Tenjin-yama
Mt. Jaendake
Yoshii-chō
芳井町
Bisei-chō
美星町
Narrow road
Onigadake
Mt. Masakiyama
Kibi
Mt. Kōyama
Mt. Jubūzan
Yakage
Yakage-chō
矢掛町
Mabi-chō
真備町
Odagawa River
Mt. Yatakayama
Senjuin
Drive-in
Shōkakuin
IBARA-SHI
井原市
Ibara
Kōzanji
Ichibata Railway
Tamashima
玉島
Tomi Pass
Funao-chō
船穂町
Mt. Abesan
Kasaoka
Yoshōzan
Mt. Ryūōzan
Kibitsu-jinja
Nakano 中野
Fukuyama (Kannabe)
Takagi
Shinichi
Kami-Tode
Goryō
Kannabe-chō
神辺町
Kannabe
Fukuen Line
Yudamura
Michinoue
Kamogata
鴨方
Mt. Myōkenzan
Michikuchi
道口
Shin-Kurashiki
Konkō-chō
金光町
Konkō
Okayama Kasumibashi
Sangyō-dōro
産業道路
Entsūji
Kasaoka
笠岡
Mt. Ishizuchiyama
SAN-YŌ EXPRESSWAY
山陽自動車道
Mermaid-Fukuyama
Fukuyama (Nakatsuhara)
Kamogata-chō
鴨方町
Kamogata
Satoshō-chō
里庄町
Satoshō
Congestion in summer
Mizutama Bridge Line
ORD 300
LAR 1080
Takahashi River
Mt. Takamasuyama
Yokoo
Mt. Zaōzan
Fukuyama-higashi
福山東
KASAOKA-SHI
笠岡市
Kasaoka
San-yō Line
Nishinohama
西ノ浜
Fukuyama
福山
Bingo-Honjō
Fukuyama Castle
Caution-Bump into the rear
Higashi-Fukuyama
Daimon
Myōjinchō 明神町
Side roads ahead
Yorishima-chō
寄島町
Yorishima I.
Matsunaga-Hongō
Matsunaga
Bingo-Akasaka
FUKUYAMA-SHI
福山市
Myōōin
Fukuyama
Fuchū-wakare 府中分れ
Tōjō 63Km
Kurashiki 45Km
Onomichi 23Km
Mt. Ōsayama
Mt. Mitakeyama
C. Ōsabana
Narrow road
Kōnoshima I.
神島
Kamimizushima
Shimomizushima I.
Mizushima-nada
Fukuyama-nishi I.C.
Matsunaga
Mt. Ryūōzan
Mt. Hikoyama
C. Misaki
Sashideshima I.
Myōchishima I.
Inatsumijima I.
Takashima I.
Kodakashima I.
Imazuchō-Taishō
今津町大正
Ashida River
Fukuyama-Tadotsu Ferry
C. Takanogoehana
C. Hajikamihana
Teshima I.
One-lane in the street
Congestion in summer
Shiraishijima I.
C. Nunokoshi
Numakuma-chō
沼隈町
Numakuma-jinja
Ankokuji
Sensuijima I.
Tomonoura(Scenic Bay)
鞆ノ浦
Kajikoshima I.
Kitagishima I.
Koteshima I.
Hiroshima
広島
Momoshima I.
Bojino-seto
Yanoshima I.
Tajima I.
田島
Abuto-kannon
Abuto-seto
Scenic view of Tomo
Mt. Takayama
Kajiyashima I.
Hakamajima I.
Hashirijima I.
Manabeshima I.
Sanagishima I.
Kojima I.
Yokoshima I.
Ōbishima I.
Ategijima I.
Ujishima I.
Takamishima I.
Mushima I.
Awashima I.
Shishishima I.
C. Hakozaki
Kamegasajima I.
C. Takadanibana
Takuma-wan
C. Furumisaki
Mt. Shiundeyama
Takase River
Yosan Line
Toyoshima I.
Takuma
Takuma
Maruyamashima I.
Takumagoe Pass
Takuma-chō
詫間町
Kamo-jinja
Mino-chō
三野町
Tsutajima I.
Nio-chō
仁尾町
Nio Pass
HIUCHI-NADA
燧灘
Takaikamijima I.
Uoshima I.
Enoshima I.
Takase
Hijidai
Marukamijima I.

E
F
G
H
1
2
3
4
5
6
99
62
69
Tsuyama-shi
Okayama-Sōja
Okayama
SŌJA-SHI
総社市
Kibi Line
San-yō Shinkansen
San-yō Line
OKAYAMA-SHI
岡山市
Kurata 倉田
Aoe 青江
from Okayama-Shi
Ōsaka 170Km
Hiroshima 170Km
Kurashiki
Hayashima
KURASHIKI-SHI
倉敷市
Okayama 20Km
Sōja 11Km
Fukuyama 45Km
Akō Line
SETOUCHI-SHI
瀬戸内市
Yoshii River
Asahi River
Sasagase River
Kojima-wan
Kōnan Airport
Maeshima I.
C. Sakakenohana
Kuroshima I.
C. Yonezaki
Inunoshima I.
Okinotsuzumijima I.
Jitakenokojima I.
Okino-takenokojima I.
C. Dainyūsaki
Todate Pass
Ryōbi Ferry
Shikoku Ferry
C. Kaburazaki
Uno Line
Mt. Jūzenjiyama
Hatagoshima I.
Ushigakubijima I.
C. Tojiribana
C. Murosaki
Shōdoshima Ferry
Shōdoshima I.
C. Miyazaki
Tonoshō-chō
土庄町
Mt. Ōmiyama
Odejima I.
TAMANO-SHI
玉野市
Uno
Mt. Tenguyama
Nagao Pass
Scenic view of Shikoku
Mt. Konpirasan
Mt. Senzuizan
Mt. Kamogatsujiyama
Mt. Fukuminamiyama
Mizushima-rinkai Railway
Kazurajima I.
Mt. Ryūōzan
Kojima
Mt. Shintozan
Katsurajima I.
Naoshima-chō
直島町
Mt. Jizōyama
Naoshima I.
Kōjinshima I.
C. Inumodoribana
to Okayama
Rupu-bashi-minami
ループ橋南
to Kojima
C. Reidasaki
C. Kurosaki
Shikoku Ferry
Kansai Ferry
Kokusai Ferry (to Ikeda)
Tatebashima I.
Mt. Washuzan (Scenic View Point)
Congestion in summer
Scenic view of setouchi
Seto-chūō-jidōshadō
ORD 4100
LAR 12150
Matsushima I.
Kamashima I.
Hitsuishijima I.
Murokijima I.
Iwaguroshima I.
Ferry
Mt. Washūzan
鷲羽山
Scenic view of Kozuchi and Ōzuchi
Kabutojima I.
Yoroijima I.
Inageshima I.
Ōtakejima I.
Ōshima I.
Yashima Driveway
ORD 610
LAR 2450
Megijima I.
Takashima I.
Aji-chō
庵治町
C. Fukubehana
Mt. Takamubōyama
Hasashima I.
Oyoshima I.
Yoshima I.
Honjima I.
Honjima-kisen
C. Ōsakinohana
Tarumi-wan
Steep slope
Ikushima-wan
Mt. Kōnomine
C. Shinzainohana
Takamatsu-Sakaide-dōro
ORD 260
LAR 940
Shiratori 35Km
Marugame 29Km
Kotohira 31Km
Mt. Gokenzan
Koseishima I.
Mt. Ogoshiyama
Seishima I.
Seto-ōhashi Line
Ayagawa River
Kotō River
Mt. Kushinoyama
Amidagoe Pass
Mt. Katsugayama
Mt. Meyama
Yashima-nishimachi
屋島西町
Takamatsuchō 高松町
Mure-chō
牟礼町
Shido-wan
Marugame
to Matsuyama
to Takamatsu
Takamatsu 29Km
Kotohira 14Km
Toyohama 30Km
SAKAIDE-SHI
坂出市
Nishinoshō 西庄
TAKAMATSU-SHI
高松市
Ritsurin Garden
栗林公園
Kōtoku Line
Yosan Line
Congestion in autumn
SANUKI-SHI
さぬき市
Naruto-shi
Utazu-chō
宇多津町
Sakaide
Mt. Kaneyama
Mt. Fukuroyama
Kokubunji-chō
国分寺町
Chokushichō
勅使町
Takamatsu-nishi
高松西
Takamatsu-chūō
高松中央
Shidochō-shido 志度町志度
MARUGAME-SHI
丸亀市
Kawatsu 川津
Mt. Kiyama
Mt. Sanukifuji
Tadotsu-chō
多度津町
Hanzan-chō
飯山町
Ryōnan-chō
綾南町
Mt. Hinoyama
Takamatsu Kotohira Railway
KAGAWA
Mt. Uwasayama
Miki-chō
三木町
Congestion in summer
Zentsūji
ZENTSŪJI-SHI
善通寺市
Okada-shimo 岡田下
Enai 榎井
Ayauta-chō
綾歌町
Mt. Kurakakeyama
Kōnan-chō
香南町
Kagawa-chō
香川町
Mt. Dakeyama
TAKAMATSU EXPRESSWAY
Dosan Line
Takamatsu 31Km
Marugame 14Km
Toyohama 34Km
to Zentsūji
Kotohira
to Takamatsu
to Kōchi
Ayakami-chō
綾上町
Mt. Takamoriyama
Mt. Tōbuyama
Mt. Ōsayama
Takasechō-Katsuoka
高瀬町勝岡
Mt. Asahiyama
Mannō-chō
満濃町
Chūnanchō-Sogō
仲南町十郷
Mt. Ōgiyama
Mt. Takahachiyama
Taman Dam
Shionoe-chō
塩江町
Kotohira-cho
琴平町
Mt. Jingamine
Kamegoeike Lake
Takase-chō
高瀬町
Mt. Ryūōzan
Mannōike Lake
Kotonami-chō
琴南町
Chūnan-chō
仲南町
Sanuki-Toyonaka I.C.
Toyohama-chō

Okinoshima I.
Shiroshima I.
Oki-Shirashima-kaigan (Scenic Rocky Coast)
C. Kumisaki
C. Noritanohana
Mt. Ōmineyama
Mt. Dakesan
Dakesan-jinja
Nakamura River
C. Sakiyamamisaki
Fuse Coast (Scenic Rocky Coast)
C. Misaki
Omosu River
Mt. Koshikibarayama
Mizuwakasu-jinja
Mt. Takaoyama
Mt. Tokihariyama
Mt. Daimanjisan
大満寺山
Mt. Ōmine
Dōgo I.
島後
Mt. Yokooyama
Dankyōdaki
Yabigawa River
Kokubunji
Oki
Okinoshima-chō
隠岐の島町
C. Nagumisaki
Tamawakasunomikoto-jinja
Saigō
Mt. Kinpōzan
Mt. Iinoyama
Mt. Koguwakoyama
Okishōtō Is.
隠岐諸島
C. Shirosaki
Shijikijima I.
Kamishima I.
Oki-kisen ryokaku Ferry
C. Takasakibana
Mt. Takasakiyama
Kanmurijima I.
Ōmorijima I.
Komorishima I.
Nishinoshima I.
西ノ島
Oki-Kuniga-kaigan (Scenic Rocky Coast)
Beppu-wan
Suwa-wan
Ama-chō
海士町
Matsushima I.
Yurahime-jinja
Nishinoshima-chō
西ノ島町
Mt. Atodoyama
Oki-jinja
Mt. Takuhiyama
Nakanoshima I.
中ノ島
Takuhi-jinja
C. Chichiimisaki
Hiigoshima I.
Dōzen I.
島前
Ōkatsurashima I.
C. Kuroshimabana
Akanada-seto
(to Shichirui·Sakaiminato)
Chibusekiheki (Scenic Rocky Coast)
知夫赤壁
Chiburijima I.
知夫里島
Chibu-mura
知夫村
Shimazushima I.
Kamishima I.
C. Saigasaki
Asashima I.
Kohakajima I.
Ōkagajima I.
to Matsue
Hamada
to Yamaguchi
to Kake
Tsunozu
Uyagawa
C. Ōsakibana
Hashi
Gōtsu-nishi
Kushiro
Uyakawa River
Arifuku
Congestion in summer
Shimokō
Hamada-higashi
Mt. Honmyō
Tadaji
Hamada
浜田
Shimokō River
HAMADA EXPRESSWAY
浜田自動車道
Hamadashi-Kyōmachi 浜田市京町
Umajima I.
from Hamada-shi
Hiroshima 120Km
Kita-Kyūshū 240Km
Yanajima I.
HAMADA-SHI
浜田市
Kanagi
金城
C. Akajimabana
Hamada
Mt. Sankaizan
Atsuta-kōsaten 熱田交差点
Sufu
Nishi-Hamada
Hamada River
Kanagi-chō
金城町
Hamada
Mt. Karakurayama
Takashima I.
Scenic view of Japan sea
Mt. Kumogiyama
Orii
Drive-in area
Mt. Taimasan
San-in Line
Misumi River
Mihomisumi
Mt. Isariyama
Hazagawa River
Misumi
Yasaka-mura
弥栄村
Misumi-chō
三隅町
Okami
Araiso
Ōtsubo Pass
sharp curves
Kamate
Masuda-shi
Bōji Pas

90

E
F
G
H
1
2
3
4
5
6
JAPAN SEA
日本海
to Izumo
to Gōtsu
Ōdashi
to Mt. Sanbesan
Izumo-shi
Miyoshi-shi
74
94
91
Oda
Taki-chō
多伎町
Tagi
San-in Line
Hane
Kute
Daini-chūgakkōmae 第二中学校前
Shinji 48Km
Gōtsu 39Km
Miyoshi 86Km
Mt. Iimoriyama
Mt. Takamaruyama
Ōdashi
ŌDA-SHI
大田市
Mochida
Shizuma
Isotake
Kongō
Shizuma River
Mt. Taisen-yama
Sanbe River
Mt. Mitsugoyama
Kando River
Congestion
Koyahara
Mononobe-jinja
Kobayashi
Radium
MT. SANBESAN
三瓶山
Pine trees
Mt. Tsurufuriyama
Ukinunonoike Lake
Sanbe
三瓶
Sharp curves
Yugakae
Nima
Nima 仁万
Nima-chō
仁摩町
Yuzako
Maji
Ginzan River
Mt. Takayama
Yusato
Yunotsu
温泉津
Yunotsu-machi
温泉津町
Mt. Sen-yama
Iwami-Fukumitsu
Fukumitsu 福光
Watazu 渡津
Ōda 39Km
Hamada 22Km
Asa 92Km
Mt. Ōetakayama
大江高山
Mt. Mitsugoyama
Kuromatsu
Misato-chō
美郷町
Kasubuchi
Chihara
Hamahara
Sawadani
Akatsuka
Asari
Mt. Murogamiyama
Tsuchigawa River
San-in-dō 山陰道
Minamiyama
Iwami-Yanaze
Gōgawa River
Mt. Toyagamaruyama
Mt. Aosugigajōyama
Onbara
Mt. Iwamiyama
Ushio
Sojiki River
Mt. Nishiyama
Kawamoto
Take
Gōtsuhonmachi
Chigane
Kawahira
Iwami-Kawamoto
Kirohara
Kawamoto-machi
川本町
Iwami-Matsubara
Kawado
Mt. Kannamijiyama
Shikaga
Inbara
Mt. Tōkeiyama
Uoginatani
Sankō Line
Tazu
Iwami-Kawagoe
Mt. Obeshiyama
Iwami-Tsuga
Mt. Shinzōjiyama
Yatogawa River
Dangyokei
Dangyokei(Gorge)
断魚溪
SHIMANE
Senjokei(Gorge)
Mimata River
Ōtoshi Pass
Mt. Kyōtaroyama
Mt. Kanmuriyama
Mt. Tanoharakanmuriyama
Mt. Matsubarayama
Mizugoe Pass
Mimata
Nishime Pass
Izuha River
Uzui
Ikawashi
Asahi
旭
Mt. Bōrokuyama
Ōnan-chō
邑南町
Mt. Yojirōyama
Kuchiba
Gōbira
Asahi-chō
旭町
Mt. Harayama
Mt. Futatsuyama
Togauchi Pass
Mt. Hanzōyama
Ichigi River
Mt. Ōharayama
Nagase River
Mizuho
瑞穂
Mt. Maruseyama
Misaka Pass
Asahi-tengustone
Mt. Inubushiyama
Mt. Ungetsuzan
Kitao Pass
Mt. Tenguishiyama
Mt. Asayama
阿佐山
Kanbikizan
Mt. Kanbikizan
Mt. Tōjiroyama
Kuriya Pass
Mt. Kumagaiyama
Mt. Kanmuriyama
Mt. Tatamiyama
Kanbikiyama
寒曳山
Mt. Kijinomeyama
Ōasa-chō
大朝町
HIROSHIMA
AKITAKATA-SHI
安芸高田市
Geihoku-chō
芸北町
Ōasa
大朝
Mt. Bunzōyama
Iketa River
Chiyoda-chō

B
C
D
1
2
3
4
5
6
JAPAN SEA
日本海
Uppurui-wan
C. Hinomisaki
日御碕
Hinomisaki-jinja
Fukushōji
Mitsu Pass
Mt. Ofunayama
Ichibata-yakushi
Koyukan-shin-eki
Nunoza
HIRATA-SHI
平田市
Hiratashi
Kōkokuji
Gakuenji
Mt. Tabuseyama
Mt. Hanadakayama
Manpukuji
Congestion
Mt. Misen
Izumo-taisha
出雲大社
Accident prone area
Kawato
Hikawa-chō
斐川町
Izumotaishamae
Taisha-machi
大社町
Taisha
Yōkan
Shiyakusho mae 市役所前
San-in Line
Naoe
Yunokawa
IZUMO-SHI
出雲市
Izumo
Shiroeda 白枝
Izumoshi
to Hirata
to Taisha
To Matsue
Kando River
Kandōji
Mt. Bukkyōyama
Kōmyōji
Jinzaiko Lake
Maki-fudōson
Nishi-Izumo
Koryō-chō
湖陵町
Izumo-Jinzai
Mt. Takaseyama
Asayama-hachimangū
Kōnan
Kōnan-wakare 江南別れ
Drive-in area
Mt. Ōbukuroyama
Tachikue-yakushi
Tachikue
Tachikuekyō(Gorge)
立久恵峡
Izumo-taisha
Oda
Oda
Tagi
Taki-chō
多伎町
Mt. Ōin-yama
Mt. Kuroyama
Sada-chō
佐田町
SHIMANE
Entsuji
Mitoya River
Mt. Mitsugoyama
Susa-jinja
Hane
C. Kasagahana
Daini-chūgakkō-mae 第二中学校前
Shinji 48Km
Gōtsu 39Km
Miyoshi 86Km
Mt. Iimoriyama
Ōdashi
Shizuma
Mt. Takamaruyama
Mt. Toyagamaru
Ryūzugataki(Fall)
Isotake
Mochida
Kongō
ŌDA-SHI
大田市
Mt. Taisen-yama
Sanbe River
Mt. Tochiyama
Mt. Ondakasan
Mt. Manjusan
Hatagawa River
Mononobe-jinja
Kobayashi
Koyahara
Nima
Yuzako
Nima-chō
仁摩町
Raziumu
Tonbara-dōro
Yaedaki(Fall)
MT. SANBESAN
三瓶山
Pine trees
Mt. Nodayama
Mt. Tsurufuriyama
Ukinunonoike Lake
Mt. Jin-yama
Scenic view of Mt. Sanbesan
Gōtsu-shi
Shizuma River
Sanbe
三瓶
Sharp curves
Mt. Okinogōyama
Mt. Sen-yama
Tonbara 頓原
Mt. Ōyorogiyama
Chihara
Tonbara
Tonbara River
Kasubuchi
Misato-chō
美郷町
Hamahara
Sawadani
Iinan-chō
飯南町
Mt. Ōetakayama
大江高山
73
94
A
B
Miyoshi-shi
C
Miyoshi-shi
D

E
F
G
H
1
2
3
4
5
6
Nanatsuana
Kakishima I.
Oki-kisen ryokaku Ferry
(to Saigō·Uragō)
(to Saigō·Uragō)
Kushima I.
Miho-no-kitaura
(Scenic Rocky Coast)
Kukedo(Scenic Rocky Coast)
潜戸
Katsurajima I.
Mt. Tsumesakayama
Chikumi-wan
Katae-wan
Shichirui-wan
C. Jizōzaki
地蔵崎
Mt. Takaoyama
Mt. Inariyama
Miho-jinja
Shimane-chō
島根町
Mt. Takashibiyama
Mihonoseki-chō
美保関町
Mt. Shiragayama
Oki-kisen
Ferry
Mt. Tadayama
Scenic view of Nakaumi
Sakai
境水道大橋
Scenic view of
Yumigahama and Mt. Daisen
Kojima I.
Mt. Misakayama
Sakaiminato
Mt. Ōhirasan
Mitaraidaki
Kezōji
SAKAIMINATO-SHI
境港市
Aganomichi
to Mihonoseki
to Matsue
suidō-ōhashi
to Yonago
Kashima-chō
鹿島町
Congestion in spring and autumn
Amariko
Takamatsu-chō
Eshima I.
Miho-wan
Mt. Asahiyama
Takadao Pass
Mt. Shin-yama
Daikonjima I.
大根島
Yatsuka-chō
八束町
Nakahama
Sada-jinja
Shimane Pen.
島根半島
Ōshinozu
Miho(Yonago)
Misakaguchi
Sakai Line
Kōkaidō-mae 公会堂前
Matsue
MATSUE-SHI
松江市
Mt. Dakesan
Wadahama
Sakaiminato 16Km
Hawai 54Km
Matsue 31Km
Takanomiya
Ichibata Railway
Asahigaoka
Mt. Wakurasan
C. Onzakibana
Matsue Castle
Tenrin-ji
Matsue
Matsue-shinjiko
Pine trees
Yumigahama
Yumigahama
Shimane
Nakanoumi Lake
Iugawa River
from Matsue
Ōsaka 360Km
Hiroshima 180Km
Kawasakiguchi
Shinjiko Lake
Nogi
Aioichō 相生町
Higashi-Matsue
YONAGO-SHI
米子市
Yonago-mizudori Park
Gotō
Yonago
Bakuromachi
Yodoe-chō
Tamayu
Tamatsukuri
Onsen
Adakaya 出雲郷
Honmachi 本町
Matsue-Tamatsukuri
松江玉造
宍道湖
Shinjiko
San-in-dō 山陰道
Kamosu-jinja
Higashiizumo
Iya
San-in Line
Arashima
Yasugi
Yasugi
Higashiizumo-chō
東出雲町
Kōfu-chō
Shinji-chō
宍道町
Kimachi
Mt. Kasenzan
YASUGI-SHI
安来市
Yonago-nishi
Tamayu-chō
玉湯町
Tamatsukuri
玉造
Iinashi River
Nokō-jinja
Kiyomizudera
山陰道
Kimachi
Yakumo-mura
八雲村
Unjuji
Shinji
Tamatsukuri-onsen
Mt. Hoshigamiyama
Matsue 17Km
Ōda 48Km
Bingo-Ochiai 89Km
Mt. Kyōragisan
ORD 650
LAR 1800
Shinji
宍道
Mt. Karayama
Saginoyu
Minami-Shinji
Shinji 宍道
Mt. Ōhirayama
Saino-toge Pass
Kumano-jinja
Yakumo
Mt. Dokushōsan
San-indō
Jōanji
Mt. Takanomine
Suga-jinja
Mt. Ōtsujiyama
Nanbu-chō
南部町
Kamonaka
Mt. Tenguyama
Hataya
Akagawa River
Izumo-Daitō
Ushio
SHIMANE
Hakuta River
Kashō Dam
76
Minami-Daitō
Mitoya-Kisuki
Kisuki 三刀屋木次
Rengeji
UNNAN-SHI
雲南市
Hinobori
Kawai Pass
Kisuki Line
Shimokuno
akaseyama
Mt. Takairiyama
Mt. Sangunsan
Mt. Iwabuseyama
Gorin Pass
Kubisu Pass
Izumo-Yashiro
Yumura
Mt. Jōyama
Mt. Tamaminesan
Nichinanko Lake
Ōsuge Pass
Hino-chō
Mt. Yōgaisan
Kamedake
Izumo-Minari
Nita-chō
仁多町
Shimoyokota River
Kamisuge
Shōyama
Sekkakei (Gorge)
Izumo-Yokota
Yokota-chō
横田町
Onino-Shitaburui(Gorge)
Nichinan-chō
日南町
Ōtani Pass
Mt. Sentsūzan
Yakawa
TOTTORI
Ōmaki River
Tatsunokoma Pass
Mt. Kirinzan
Hakubi Line
Mt. Madoyama
Mt. Tainosuyama
Mt. Takahatayama
Congestion in winter
Mt. Inazumiyama
Mt. Myōkenzan
Izumo-Sakane
Tawarabara-goe Pass
Ikenohara
Miinohara
Miinohara
Shingō
Ōnuki Pass
Mt. Sarumasayama
Mt. Mikuniyama
Mt. Dōgoyama
道後山
Takano-chō
高野町
Mt. Azumayama
Mt. Eboshiyama
Dōgoyama
HIROSHIMA
Mt. Hibayama
比婆山
OKAYAMA
Mt. Mikuniyama
95
ara-shi
Shōbara-shi
Shōbara-shi
E
F
G
H

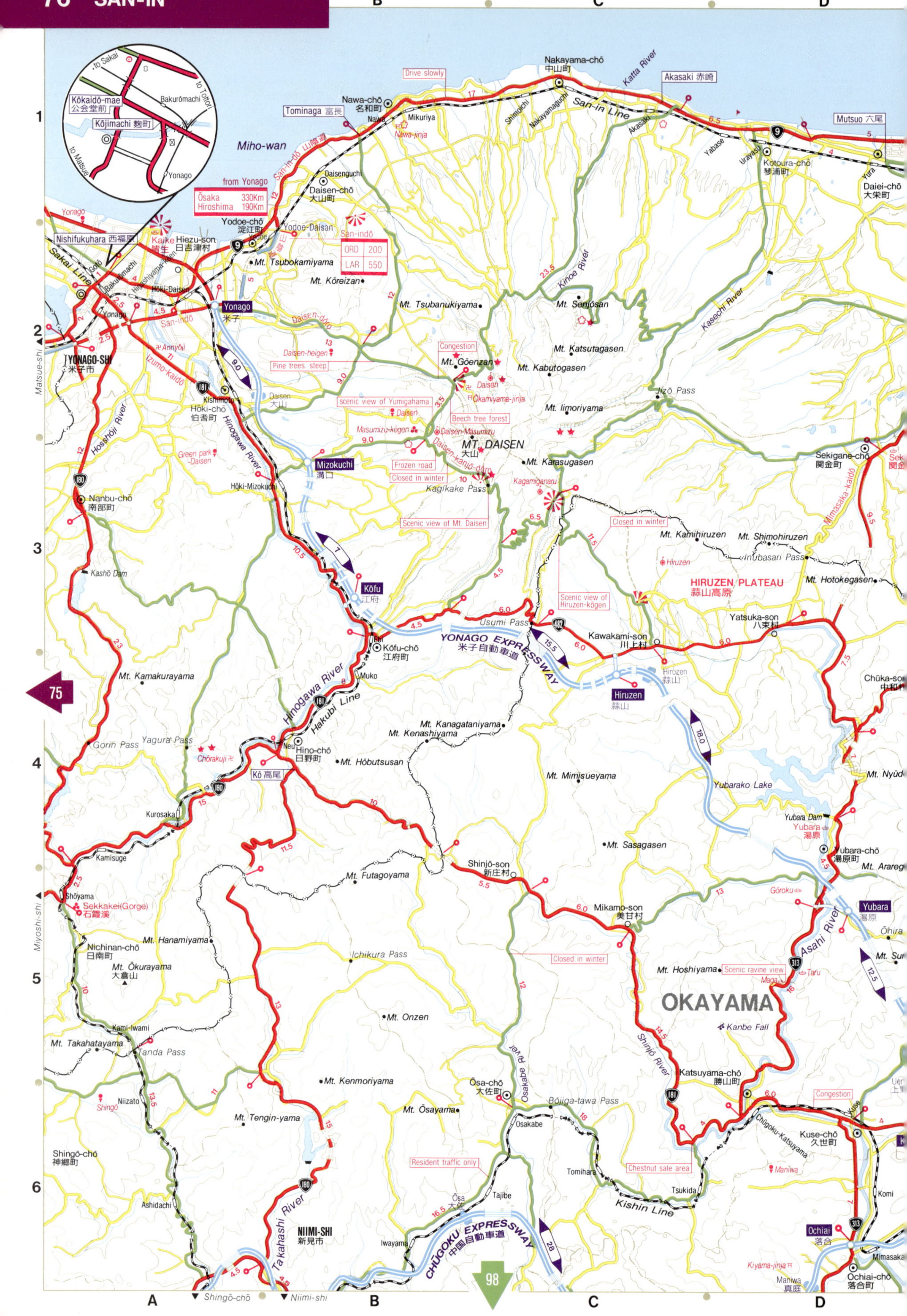
Miho-wan
from Yonago
Ōsaka 330Km
Hiroshima 190Km
Kōkaidō-mae 公会堂前
Kōjimachi 麹町
Bakurōmachi
to Sakai
to Tottori
to Matsue
Yonago
Nakayama-chō 中山町
Katta River
Akasaki 赤崎
Drive slowly
Nawa-chō 名和町
Tominaga 富長
Mikuriya
Nawa-jinja
San-in Line
Mutsuo 六尾
Kotoura-chō 琴浦町
Daiei-chō 大栄町
Daisenguchi
Daisen-chō 大山町
Yodoe-chō 淀江町
Yodoe-Daisen
San-indō
ORD 200
LAR 550
Nishifukuhara 西福原
Kaike 皆生
Hiezu-son 日吉津村
Mt. Tsubokamiyama
Mt. Kōreizan
Sakai Line
Yonago 米子
YONAGO-SHI 米子市
Daisen-dōro
Daisen-heigen
Pine trees, steep
Mt. Tsubanukiyama
Mt. Senjōsan
Kinoe River
Kasechi River
Congestion
Mt. Gōenzan
Mt. Katsutagasen
Mt. Kabutogasen
Jizō Pass
Annyōji
Izumo-kaidō
Kishimoto
Hōki-chō 伯耆町
Daisen 大山
scenic view of Yumigahama
Ōkamiyama-jinja
Beech tree forest
Mt. Iimoriyama
Masumizu-kōgen
Daisen-Masumizu
MT. DAISEN
Hosshōji River
Hinogawa River
Green park -Daisen
Mizokuchi 溝口
Frozen road
Closed in winter
Daisen-kanjō-dōro
Mt. Karasugasen
Sekigane-chō 関金町
Hōki-Mizokuchi
Kagikake Pass
Kagamiganaru
Nanbu-chō 南部町
Scenic view of Mt. Daisen
Closed in winter
Mt. Kamihiruzen
Mt. Shimohiruzen
Inubasari Pass
Mimasaka-kaidō
Kashō Dam
Hiruzen
HIRUZEN PLATEAU 蒜山高原
Mt. Hotokegasen
Kōfu 江府
Scenic view of Hiruzen-kōgen
Usumi Pass
Yatsuka-son 八束村
Kawakami-son 川上村
Kōfu-chō 江府町
YONAGO EXPRESSWAY 米子自動車道
Hiruzen 蒜山
Chūka-son
Mt. Kamakurayama
Muko
Hakubi Line
Mt. Kanagataniyama
Mt. Kenashiyama
Gorin Pass
Yagura Pass
Chōrakuji
Neu
Hino-chō 日野町
Kō 高尾
Mt. Hōbutsusan
Mt. Mimisueyama
Yubarako Lake
Mt. Nyūdō
Kurosaka
Yubara Dam
Yubara 湯原
Mt. Sasagasen
Yubara-chō 湯原町
Kamisuge
Shinjō-son 新庄村
Mt. Futagoyama
Mt. Arareg
Shōyama
Sekkakei(Gorge) 石霞渓
Mikamo-son 美甘村
Gōroku
Yubara 湯原
Nichinan-chō 日南町
Mt. Hanamiyama
Ichikura Pass
Closed in winter
Asahi River
Ōhira
Mt. Ōkurayama 大倉山
Mt. Hoshiyama
Scenic ravine view
Maga
Taru
OKAYAMA
Mt. Onzen
Kami-Iwami
Mt. Takahatayama
Tanda Pass
Kanbe Fall
Shinjō River
Osakabe River
Mt. Kenmoriyama
Ōsa-chō 大佐町
Katsuyama-chō 勝山町
Congestion
Niizato
Shingō
Bōjiga-tawa Pass
Mt. Ōsayama
Mt. Tengin-yama
Osakabe
Chūgoku-Katsuyama
Kuse-chō 久世町
Shingō-chō 神郷町
Resident traffic only
Chestnut sale area
Tomihara
Tsukida
Maniwa
Komi
Ashidachi
Tajibe
Kishin Line
Ōsa 大佐
Takahashi River
NIIMI-SHI 新見市
Iwayama
CHŪGOKU EXPRESSWAY 中国自動車道
Ochiai 落合
Mimasaka
Kiyama-jinja
Ochiai-chō 落合町
Maniwa 真庭
Matsue-shi
Miyoshi-shi
Shingō-chō
Niimi-shi
75
98

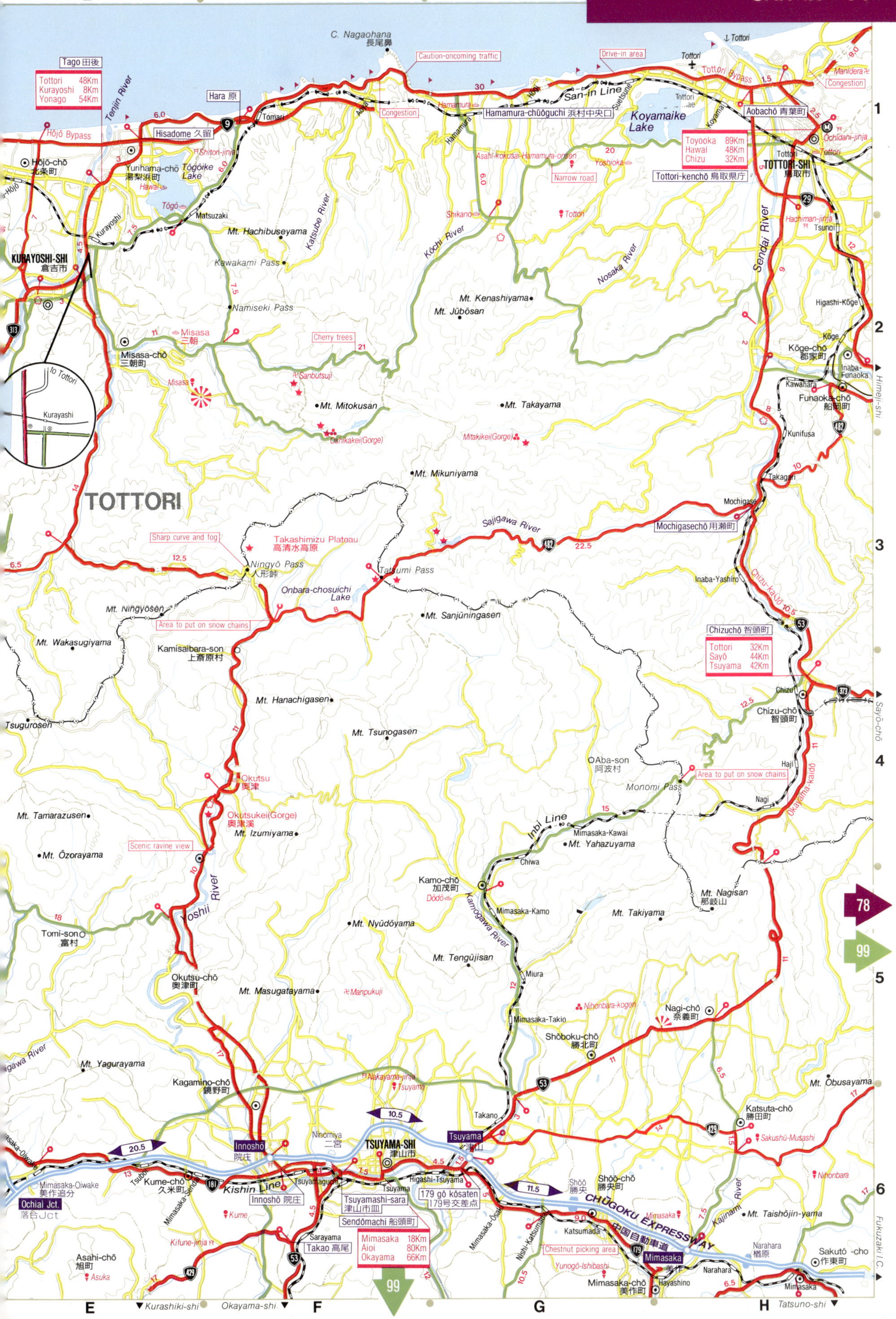

TOTTORI
TOTTORI-SHI 鳥取市
KURAYOSHI-SHI 倉吉市
TSUYAMA-SHI 津山市
Tago 田後
Tottori 48Km
Kurayoshi 8Km
Yonago 54Km
Hara 原
Hisadome 久留
Hamamura-chūōguchi 浜村中央口
Aobachō 青葉町
Toyooka 89Km
Hawai 48Km
Chizu 32Km
Tottori-kenchō 鳥取県庁
Mochigasechō 用瀬町
Chizuchō 智頭町
Tottori 32Km
Sayō 44Km
Tsuyama 42Km
Innoshō 院庄
Tsuyamashi-sara 津山市皿
179 gō kōsaten 179号交差点
Sendōmachi 船頭町
Mimasaka 18Km
Aioi 80Km
Okayama 66Km
Takao 高尾
Ochiai Jct. 落合Jct
Mimasaka
Tsuyama
Caution-oncoming traffic
Drive-in area
Congestion
Narrow road
Cherry trees
Sharp curve and fog
Area to put on snow chains
Scenic ravine view
Chestnut picking area
C. Nagaohana 長尾鼻
Koyamaike Lake
Tōgōike Lake
San-in Line
Inbi Line
Kishin Line
CHŪGOKU EXPRESSWAY 中国自動車道
Hōjō Bypass
Tottori Bypass
Hōjō-chō 北条町
Yurihama-chō 湯梨浜町
Misasa-chō 三朝町
Misasa 三朝
Kamisaibara-son 上斎原村
Okutsu 奥津
Okutsukei(Gorge) 奥津渓
Okutsu-chō 奥津町
Kagamino-chō 鏡野町
Tomi-son 富村
Kume-chō 久米町
Mimasaka-Oiwake 美作追分
Asahi-chō 旭町
Kamo-chō 加茂町
Aba-son 阿波村
Nagi-chō 奈義町
Shōboku-chō 勝北町
Shōō-chō 勝央町
Katsuta-chō 勝田町
Mimasaka-chō 美作町
Sakutō-cho 作東町
Kōge-chō 郡家町
Funaoka-chō 船岡町
Chizu-chō 智頭町
Takashimizu Plateau 高清水高原
Ningyō Pass 人形峠
Onbara-chosuichi Lake
Tatsumi Pass
Monomi Pass
Kawakami Pass
Namiseki Pass
Mt. Hachibuseyama
Mt. Kenashiyama
Mt. Jūbōsan
Mt. Mitokusan
Mt. Takayama
Mt. Mikuniyama
Mt. Ningyōsen
Mt. Wakasugiyama
Mt. Sanjūningasen
Mt. Hanachigasen
Mt. Tsunogasen
Mt. Tamarazusen
Mt. Ōzorayama
Mt. Izumiyama
Mt. Yahazuyama
Mt. Nagisan 那岐山
Mt. Takiyama
Mt. Nyūdōyama
Mt. Tengūjisan
Mt. Masugatayama
Mt. Yagurayama
Mt. Obusayama
Mt. Taishōjin-yama
Tenjin River
Katsube River
Kōchi River
Nosaka River
Sendai River
Sajigawa River
Yoshii River
Kamogawa River
Kajinami River
Chizu-kaidō
Okayama-kaidō
Sanbutsuji
Oshikakei(Gorge)
Mitakikei(Gorge)
Manpukuji
Nihonbara-kogen
Sakushū-Musashi
Nihonbara
Nakayama-jinja
Tsuyama
Kume
Kifune-jinja
Asuka
Yunogō-Ishibashi
Hawai
Tōgō
Shitori-jinja
Asahi-kokusai-Hamamura-onsen
Yoshioka
Shikano
Hachiman-jinja
Ochidani-jinja
Manidera
Dōdō
Himeji-shi
Sayō-chō
Kurashiki-shi
Okayama-shi
Tatsuno-shi
Fukuzaki I.C.
to Tottori
Kurayashi
78
99

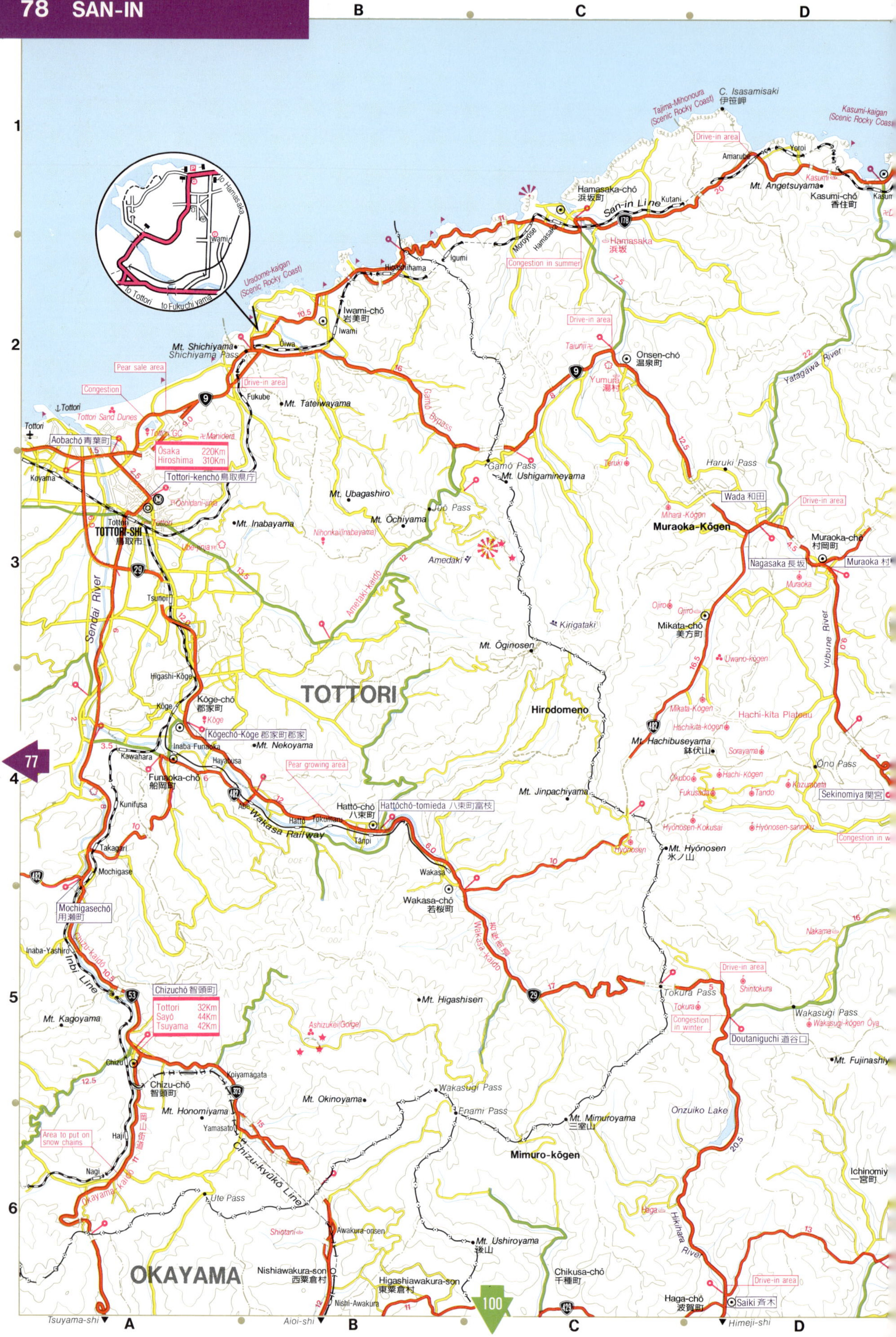

B
C
D
1
2
3
4
5
6
A
C. Isasamisaki 伊笹岬
Tajima-Mihonoura (Scenic Rocky Coast)
Kasumi-kaigan (Scenic Rocky Coast)
Drive-in area
Yoroi
Amarube
Kasumi
Mt. Angetsuyama
Kasumi-chō 香住町
Hamasaka-chō 浜坂町
Kutani
San-in Line
Moroyose
Hamasaka
Hamasaka 浜坂
Congestion in summer
Igumi
Higashihama
Uradome-kaigan (Scenic Rocky Coast)
to Hamasaka
Iwami
to Tottori
to Fukuchiyama
Iwami-chō 岩美町
Iwami
Ōiwa
Mt. Shichiyama
Shichiyama Pass
Pear sale area
Congestion
Drive-in area
Fukube
Mt. Tateiwayama
Gamō Bypass
Tottori
Tottori Sand Dunes
Tottori GC
Manidera
Aobachō 青葉町
Ōsaka 220Km
Hiroshima 310Km
Koyama
Tottori-kenchō 鳥取県庁
Ochidani-jinja
Tottori
TOTTORI-SHI 鳥取市
Mt. Inabayama
Mt. Ubagashiro
Mt. Ōchiyama
Jūō Pass
Gamō Pass
Mt. Ushigamineyama
Nihonkai(Inabayama)
Ube-jinja
Amedaki
Ameitaki-kaidō
Drive-in area
Taiunji
Onsen-chō 温泉町
Yumura 湯村
Teruki
Haruki Pass
Wada 和田
Mihara-Kōgen
Muraoka-Kōgen
Drive-in area
Muraoka-chō 村岡町
Nagasaka 長坂
Muraoka 村
Muraoka
Yatagawa River
Ojiro
Ojiro
Mikata-chō 美方町
Uwano-kōgen
Yubune River
Kirigataki
Mt. Ōginosen
Tsunoi
Sendai River
Higashi-Kōge
Kōge-chō 郡家町
Kōge
Kōge
Kōgechō-Kōge 郡家町郡家
TOTTORI
Hirodomeno
Mikata-Kōgen
Hachikita-kōgen
Hachi-kita Plateau
Mt. Hachibuseyama 鉢伏山
Sorayama
Ōno Pass
Hachi-Kōgen
Ōkubo
Fukusada
Tando
Kazurabata
Sekinomiya 関宮
Hyōnosen-Kokusai
Hyōnosen-sanroku
Congestion in w
Inaba Funaoka
Mt. Nekoyama
Kawahara
Hayabusa
Pear growing area
Funaoka-chō 船岡町
Kunifusa
Abe
Wakasa Railway
Hattō
Tokumaru
Hattō-chō 八東町
Hattōchō-tomieda 八東町富枝
Tanpi
Mt. Jinpachiyama
Hyōnosen
Mt. Hyōnosen 氷ノ山
Takagari
Mochigase
Mochigasechō 用瀬町
Wakasa
Wakasa-chō 若桜町
Wakasa-kaidō
Inaba-Yashiro
Chizu-kaidō
Inbi Line
Chizuchō 智頭町
Tottori 32Km
Sayō 44Km
Tsuyama 42Km
Mt. Kagoyama
Mt. Higashisen
Tokura Pass
Tokura
Congestion in winter
Drive-in area
Shintokura
Doutaniguchi 道谷口
Wakasugi Pass
Wakasugi-kōgen Ōya
Nakama
Mt. Fujinashiyama
Ashizukei(Gorge)
Chizu
Chizu-chō 智頭町
Koiyamagata
Mt. Honomiyama
Yamasato
Mt. Okinoyama
Wakasugi Pass
Enami Pass
Mt. Mimuroyama 三室山
Mimuro-kōgen
Onzuiko Lake
Area to put on snow chains
Haji
Nagi
Okayama-kaidō
Chizu-kyūkō Line
Ute Pass
Shiotani
Awakura-onsen
Mt. Ushiroyama 後山
Haga
Hikihara River
Ichinomiya 一宮町
OKAYAMA
Nishiawakura-son 西粟倉村
Higashiawakura-son 東粟倉村
Nishi-Awakura
Chikusa-chō 千種町
Haga-chō 波賀町
Drive-in area
Saiki 斉木
Tsuyama-shi
Aioi-shi
Himeji-shi

77
100

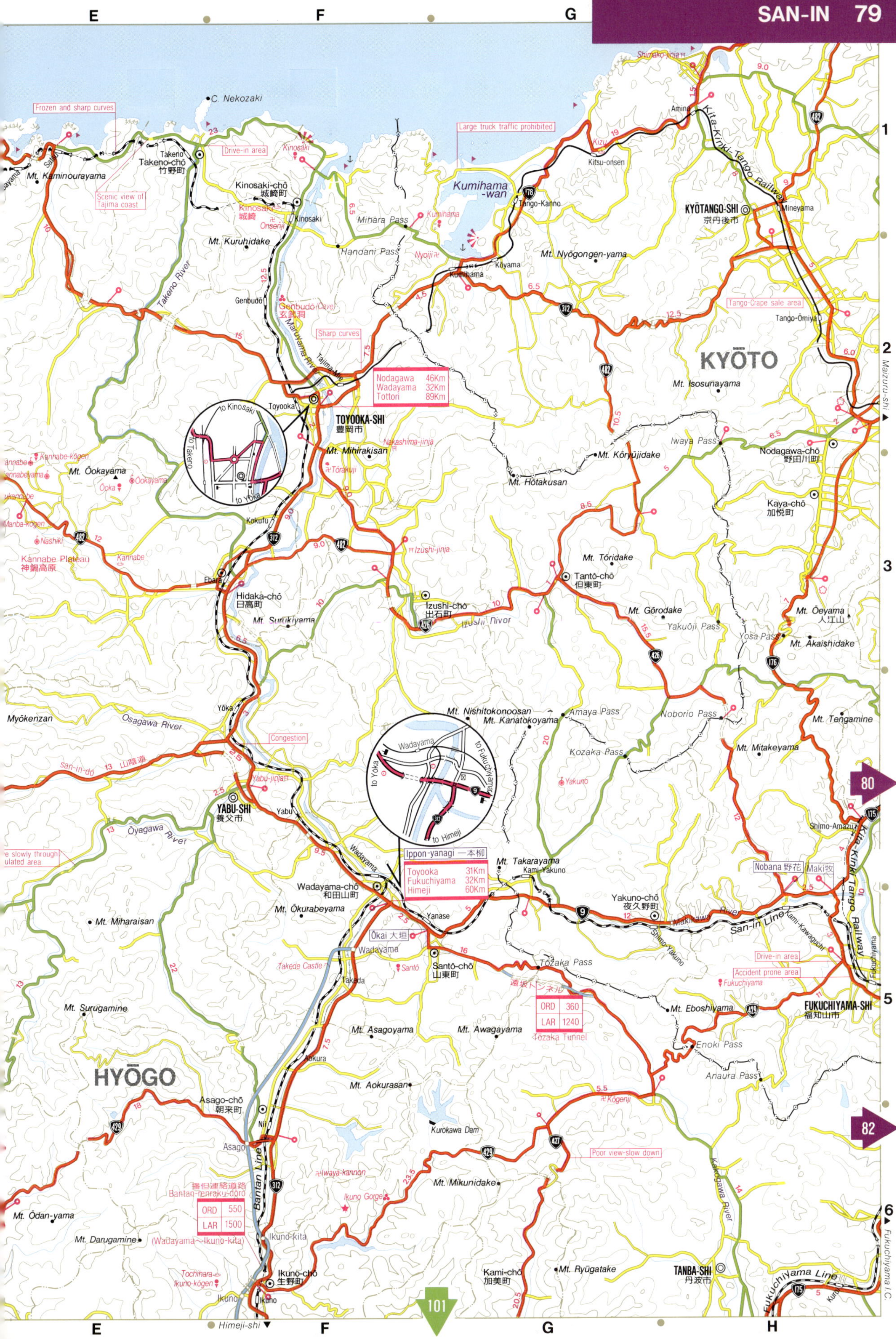
E
F
G
H
1
2
3
5
6
KYŌTO
HYŌGO
C. Nekozaki
Frozen and sharp curves
Drive-in area
Large truck traffic prohibited
Shimako-jinja
Amino
Kita-Kinki-Tango Railway
Kizu
Kitsu-onsen
Takeno
Takeno-chō
竹野町
Mt. Kaminourayama
Scenic view of Tajima coast
Kinosaki
Kinosaki-chō
城崎町
城崎
Onsenji
Kumihama-wan
Tango-Kanno
KYŌTANGO-SHI
京丹後市
Mineyama
Mihara Pass
Kumihama
Handani Pass
Nyoiji
Mt. Kuruhidake
Kōyama
Mt. Nyōgongen-yama
Genbudō
Genbudō Cave
玄武洞
Takeno River
Maruyama River
Tango-Crape sale area
Tango-Ōmiya
Sharp curves
Tajima-Mie
Nodagawa 46Km
Wadayama 32Km
Tottori 89Km
Mt. Isosunayama
Maizuru-shi
to Kinosaki
to Takeno
to Yōka
Toyooka
TOYOOKA-SHI
豊岡市
Mt. Mihirakisan
Nakashima-jinja
Tōrakuji
Iwaya Pass
Nodagawa-chō
野田川町
Mt. Kōryūjidake
Mt. Hōtakusan
Kannabe-kōgen
Mt. Ōokayama
Ōoka
Manba-kōgen
Nashiki
Kannabe Plateau
神鍋高原
Kannabe
Kaya-chō
加悦町
Kokufu
Izushi-jinja
Mt. Tōridake
Tantō-chō
但東町
Ebara
Hidaka-chō
日高町
Izushi-chō
出石町
Izushi River
Mt. Surukiyama
Mt. Gōrodake
Yakuōji Pass
Mt. Ōeyama
大江山
Yosa Pass
Mt. Akaishidake
Yōka
Myōkenzan
Osagawa River
Mt. Nishitokonoosan
Mt. Kanatokoyama
Amaya Pass
Noborio Pass
Mt. Tengamine
Congestion
San-in-dō
山陰道
Kozaka Pass
Mt. Mitakeyama
Yakuno
Yabu-jinja
YABU-SHI
養父市
Yabu
Ōyagawa River
Wadayama
to Fukuchiyama
to Himeji
Shimo-Amazu
Ippon-yanagi 一本柳
Toyooka 31Km
Fukuchiyama 32Km
Himeji 60Km
Mt. Takarayama
Kami-Yakuno
Nobana 野花
Maki 牧
Wadayama-chō
和田山町
Mt. Ōkurabeyama
Yanase
Yakuno-chō
夜久野町
Makikawa River
San-in Line
Shimo-Yakuno
Kami-Kawaguchi
Kita-Kinki Tango Railway
Mt. Miharaisan
Ōkai 大垣
Takeda Castle
Santō
Santō-chō
山東町
Tōzaka Pass
Drive-in area
Accident prone area
Fukuchiyama
遠坂トンネル
ORD 360
LAR 1240
Tōzaka Tunnel
Mt. Eboshiyama
FUKUCHIYAMA-SHI
福知山市
Mt. Surugamine
Takeda
Mt. Asagoyama
Mt. Awagayama
Enoki Pass
Aokura
Anaura Pass
Mt. Aokurasan
Kōgenji
Asago-chō
朝来町
Nii
Kurokawa Dam
Asago
Bantan Line
Poor view-slow down
播但連絡道路
Bantan-renraku-dōro
ORD 550
LAR 1500
(Wadayama~Ikuno-kita)
Iwaya-kannon
Ikuno Gorge
Mt. Mikunidake
Kakogawa River
Mt. Ōdan-yama
Mt. Darugamine
Ikuno-kita
Tochihara Ikuno-kōgen
Ikuno-chō
生野町
Ikuno
Kami-chō
加美町
Mt. Ryūgatake
TANBA-SHI
丹波市
Fukuchiyama Line
Fukuchiyama I.C.
Himeji-shi
80
82
101

A
B
C
D
1
2
3
4
5
6
C. Kyōgasaki
経ヶ岬
178
Caution-Monkeys
Scenic view of Japan sea
Ugawa River
Takeno River
Mt. Ichigaoyama
Ikari Pass
Congestion in summer
482
Mt. Taikoyama
C. Araizaki
Koshima I.
Kanmurijima I.
Tango Pen.
丹後半島
Ine-chō
伊根町
Amino
Mt. Kongōdōjiyama
KYŌTANGO-SHI
京丹後市
Mineyama
Miyazu
Shin-Nihonkai Ferry (to Otaru)
312
Seaside road
Nariaiji
C. Kurosaki
Miyazu-wan
Kasamatsu Park
Kono-jinja
Tango-crape sale area
Tango-Ōmiya
Iwataki-chō
岩滝町
Amanohashidate(Beautiful Beach)
天橋立
Ōuchi Pass
Chionji
Monjū
Amanohashidate
C. Nariumisaki
成生岬
Kejima
Umatatejima
C. Shōmen
C. Bakuchimisaki
Mt. Isosuna yama
Maizuru 45Km
Fukuchiyama 44Km
Toyooka 47Km
Drive-in area
Iwatakiguchi
Nodagawa
Kunda
Nodagawa-chō
野田川町
Iwaya Pass
MIYAZU-SHI
宮津市
Miyamura
Kita-Kinnki-Tango Railway
Drive-in area
Mihama Pass
C. Kanegamisaki
Yurahama
Maizuru
Miyazu-Amanohashidate
Tango-Yura
Tango-Kanzaki
Shiokumi Pass
Mt. Aobayama
Kaya-chō
加悦町
79
Mt. Yuragatake
Mt. Akaiwayama
Toshima I.
Maizuru-wan
Maizuru-higashi
Otoshima I.
Matsuoji
Matsuno-Odera
Kitsusaka Pass
Taki Pass
Bukō Pass
Ōeyama
Shinonome
MAIZURU-SHI
舞鶴市
Kongōin
Alpine drive course
Karakawa
Maizuru-nishi
Higashi-Maizuru
Ōte-kōsaten
大手交差点
Mt. Ōeyama
大江山
Kita-Kinki Tango Railway
Accident-prone area
Maizuru-higashi
舞鶴東
Closed in winter
Yakuōji Pass
Yosa Pass
Mt. Akaishidake
Shisho
from Maizuru
Ōsaka 130Km
Kanazawa 220Km
Izushi-chō
176
Kōtai-jinja
Maizuru-Ōe
Oeyamaguchi-naiku
Miyazu-Kaidō
宮津街道
Nishi-Maizuru
Mt. Yōrōyama
Mt. Tengamine
to Higashi Maizuru
to Miyazu
to Ayabe
Nishi-Maizuru
Closed in winter
Noborio Pass
Futamata
175
Kyōto-Jūkan Jidōshadō
Magura
Maizuru Line
Toyoukedai-jinja
Mt. Mitakeyama
Ōe-chō
大江町
Ōe-kōkō-mae
Ōe
Maizuru-nishi
舞鶴西
Mt. Misen-yama
Mt. Kimioyama
Kōmyōji
426
Gujō
Ayabe
綾部
Shimo-Amazu
Ayabe Jct
綾部JCT
Umezako
Kanbayashi River
Nobana 野花
Maki 牧
Kami-Kawaguchi
Maki
Makikawa River
to Miyazu
Fukuchiyama
to Kyoto
to Tottori
Ankokuji
Ayabe
綾部
Ayabe-Ankokuji
Fuchigaki
FUKUCHIYAMA-SHI
福知山市
Drive-in area
Congestion in summer
Ayabe
Wadayama-chō
Yuragawa River
Accident-prone area
KYŌTO
Fukuchiyama
San-in Line
Takatsu
AYABE-SHI
綾部市
Higashiyama 東山
Mt. Chōrōgatake
Fukuchiyama
福知山
Accident-prone area
429
27
Tanba Rhein
Yamaga
Maizuru 47Km
Wadayama 33Km
Ikeda 99Km
Hazegawa River
MAIZURU WAKASA EXPRESSWAY
舞鶴若狭自動車道
Shichiyama Pass
Tachiki
Anaura Pass
Shiotsu Pass
173
Aseri
Wachi-chō
和知町
Mt. Mitokeyama
Tanba-Takeda
82
Mizuho-chō
Kyōto-shi

E
F
G
H
1
2
3
4
5
6
WAKASA-WAN
若狭湾
C. Mongasaki
C. Tsunegamisaki
常神岬
Ongamijima I.
Mikatagoko Rainbow Line
ORD 1020
LAR 4070
三方五湖
レインボーライン
C. Kurosaki
Higashi-Mihama
Tokushōji
Mihama
Obama Line
Mihama-chō
美浜町
Mimikawa River
Hirugako Lake
Ryūtakuji
Mikatagoko Lakes(P.G.)
三方五湖
Kogashima
Suigetsuko Lake
Kiyama
Sugako Lake
Ubejima I.
C. Kurosaki
Mikatako Lake
Radon
Sotomo (Scenic Rocky Coast)
蘇洞門
Mt. Kusuyagatake
C. Nokogirizaki
C. Matsugasaki
Mikata
Mikata-chō
三方町
Mt. Kumodaniyama
122
128
Fujii
Tomura
Hagadera
Obama-wan
Ōtoba
Obama Castle
OBAMA-SHI
小浜市
Obama
Higashi-Obama
Mt. Sanjūsangen-yama
Mt. Sanjūdake
Wakasa-Takahama
Wakasa-Wada
Aoto-irie
Mitsumatsu
Sakichi-jinja
Tango-kaidō 丹後街道
Seihama
Kokubunji
Tadadera
Wakasa-Arita
Kurami Pass
Wakasa-Hongō
Ōi-chō
大飯町
Kato
Obama-nishi
小浜西
Wakasahime-jinja
Myōrakuji
Mantokuji
Shin-Hirano
Takahama-chō
高浜町
Drive-in area
Enshōji
Wakasahiko-jinja
Jingūji
Myōtsūji
Kaminaka
Miyake 三宅
Wakasa
Saburi River
Mt. Hanseizan
Kaminaka-chō
上中町
Ōi-Takahama
大飯高浜
Ishiyamazaka Pass
FUKUI
Kōchi
Misaka Pass
Ishida River
Minami River
Natashō-mura
名田庄村
Mt. Hyakurigatake
Mt. Tōkinzan
Horikoshi Pass
Mt. Yatsugamine
Mt. Mikunidake
TAKASHIMA-SHI
高島市
Kutsuki
Mt. Amidayama
Mt. Shiraoyama
Yuragawa River
Mt. Mikunidake
Mt. Jayagamine
Adogawa River
Kamogawa River
Tanano River
SHIGA
Congestion in summer
Miyama-chō
美山町
Sasari
Closed in winter
Mt. Bunagatake
Hirasan
Katsukawa-myōōin
Kita-Komatsu
83
Kyōto-shi
Ōtsu-shi

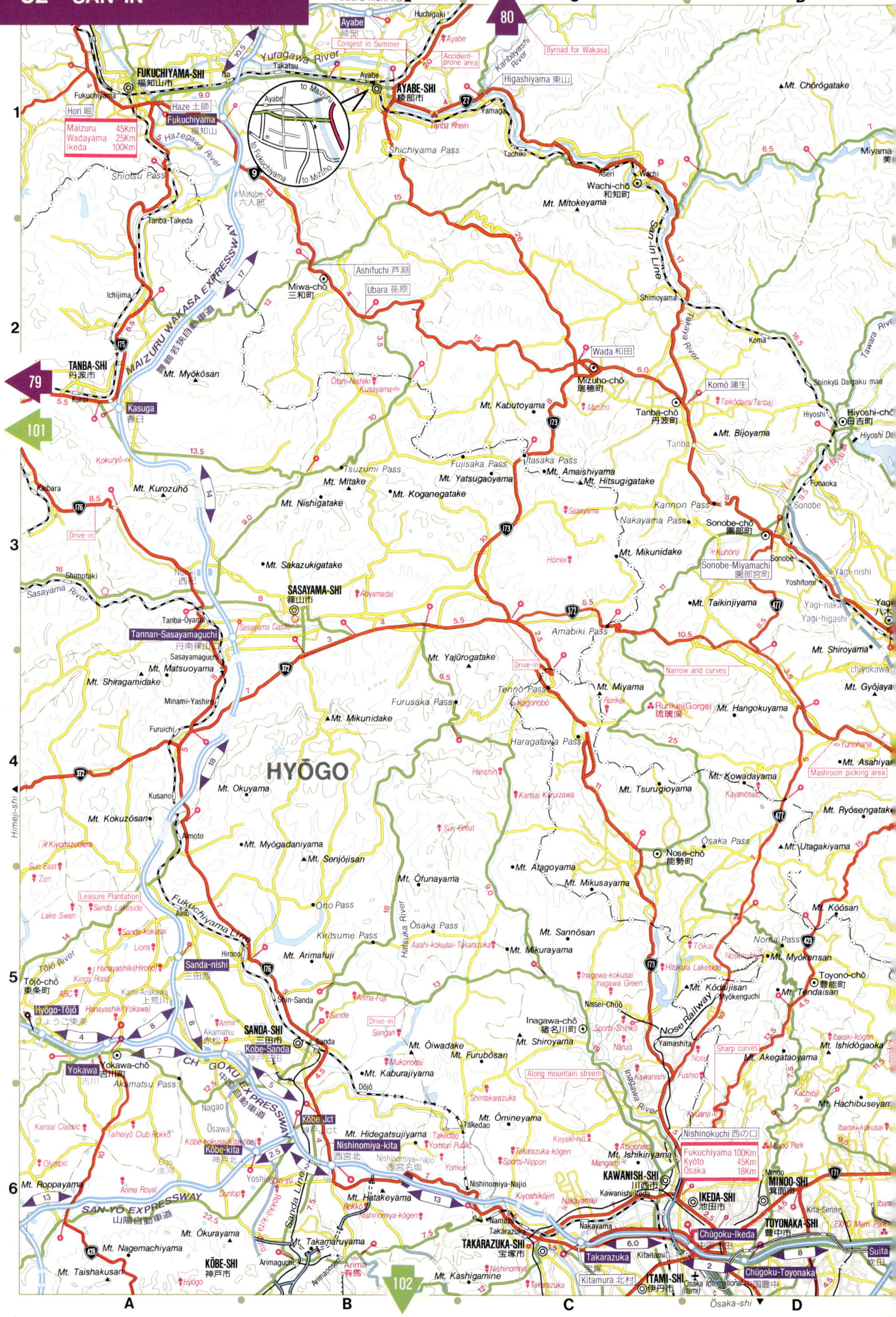

A
B
C
D
1
2
3
4
5
6
80
79
101
102
Maizuru-nishi I.C
Ayabe
綾部
Huchigaki
Congest in Summer
Accident-prone area
Byroad for Wakasa
Kanbayashi River
Yuragawa River
Takatsu
FUKUCHIYAMA-SHI
福知山市
AYABE-SHI
綾部市
Higashiyama 東山
Fukuchiyama
Haze 土師
Hori 堀
Fukuchiyama
福知山
Maizuru 45Km
Wadayama 25Km
Ikeda 100Km
Hazegawa River
Tanba Rhein
Yamaga
to Maizuru
to Fukuchiyama
to Mizuho
Shichiyama Pass
Tachiki
Mt. Chōrōgatake
Shiotsu Pass
Mutobe
六人部
Tanba-Takeda
Aseri
Wachi
Wachi-chō
和知町
Mt. Mitokeyama
Miyama
San-in Line
MAIZURU WAKASA EXPRESSWAY
舞鶴若狭自動車道
Ashifuchi 芦淵
Ubara 莵原
Miwa-chō
三和町
Ichijima
Shimoyama
Takaya River
Koma
Tawara River
TANBA-SHI
丹波市
Mt. Myōkōsan
Kuroi
Kasuga
春日
Ōtani-Nishiki
Kusayama
Wada 和田
Mizuho-chō
瑞穂町
Komō 蒲生
Taikōdaira(Tanba)
Shinkyū Daigaku mae
Hiyoshi
Hiyoshi-chō
日吉町
Mt. Kabutoyama
Mizuho
Tanba-chō
丹波町
Mt. Bijoyama
Tanba
Kokuryō
Tsuzumi Pass
Fujisaka Pass
Itasaka Pass
Mt. Amaishiyama
Mt. Hitsugigatake
Mt. Mitake
Mt. Yatsugaoyama
Mt. Kurozuhō
Mt. Nishigatake
Mt. Koganegatake
Kaibara
Kannon Pass
Funaoka
Sonobe
Sasayama
Nakayama Pass
Sonobe-chō
園部町
Drive-in
Mt. Mikunidake
Kuhōnji
Sonobe-Miyamachi
園部宮町
Shimotaki
Mt. Sakazukigatake
Hōmei
Yagi-nishi
Sasayama River
Nishiki
西紀
SASAYAMA-SHI
篠山市
Aoyamadai
Yoshitomi
Mt. Taikinjiyama
Yagi-naka
Yagi-higashi
Tanba-Ōyama
Tannan-Sasayamaguchi
丹南篠山口
Sasayama Castle
Amabiki Pass
Sasayamaguchi
Mt. Matsuoyama
Mt. Shiragamidake
Mt. Yajūrogatake
Narrow and curves
Mt. Shiroyama
Minami-Yashiro
Tennō Pass
Kagonobō
Mt. Miyama
Rurikei(Gorge) 琉璃渓
Mt. Gyōjaya
Furusaka Pass
Mt. Hangokuyama
Mt. Mikunidake
Furuichi
Haragatawa Pass
Yunohana
Mt. Asahiyama
HYŌGO
Hanshin
Mushroom picking area
Kusano
Mt. Okuyama
Kansai Karuizawa
Mt. Kowadayama
Mt. Tsurugioyama
Kayanosato
Mt. Ryōsengatake
Himeji-shi
Mt. Kokuzōsan
Sun Great
Amoto
Kiyomizudera
Mt. Myōgadaniyama
Mt. Senjōjisan
Nose-chō
能勢町
Ōsaka Pass
Mt. Utagakiyama
Sun East
Zen
Mt. Ōfunayama
Mt. Atagoyama
Mt. Mikusayama
Leisure Plantation
Sanda Lakeside
Lake Swan
Fukuchiyama Line
Aino
Ono Pass
Hatsuka River
Mt. Kōosan
Sanda-kokusai
Kiritsume Pass
Ōsaka Pass
Mt. Sannōsan
Noma Pass
Lions
Mt. Arimafuji
Asahi-kokusai-Takarazuka
Mt. Mikurayama
Tōkai
Mt. Myōkensan
Hanayashiki(Hirono)
Hirono
Sanda-nishi
三田西
Hitokura Lake
Tōjō River
Tōjō-chō
東条町
Kings Road
Toyono-chō
豊能町
Kami-Arakawa
上荒川
Inagawa-kokusai
Inagawa Green
Mt. Kōdaijisan
Myōkenguchi
Mt. Tendaisan
ABC
Hanayashiki(Yokawa)
Shin-Sanda
Arima-Fuji
Nissei-Chūō
Nose Railway
Hyōgo-Tōjō
ひょうご東条
Sanda
Arima
Akamatsu
赤松
SANDA-SHI
三田市
Kobe-Sanda
Drive-in
Sengari
Inagawa-chō
猪名川町
Mt. Shiroyama
Sports-Shinkō
Sharp curves
Ibaraki-kōgen
Mt. Ishidōgaoka
Yokawa-chō
Yokawa
吉川町
Mt. Ōiwadake
Mt. Furubōsan
Narui
Yamashita
Nose
Mt. Akegataoyama
Akamatsu Pass
CHŪGOKU EXPRESSWAY
中国自動車道
Mukonodai
Mt. Kaburajiyama
Along mountain stream
Kawanishi
Fushio
Inagawa River
Dōjō
Nagao
Shintakarazuka
Kachioji
Mt. Hachibuseyama
Kyūanji
Kansai Classic
Ōsawa
Kōbe Jct
Mt. Ōmineyama
Takedao
Nishinokuchi 西の口
Ibaraki-kokusai
Taiheiyō Club Rokkō
Kōbe-kokusai(Kitakōbe)
Kōbe-kita
神戸北
Mt. Hidegatsujiyama
Nishinomiya-kita
西宮北
Takedao
Yomiuri Public
Keyaki-hill
Atagohara
Mt. Ishikiriyama
Fukuchiyama 100Km
Kyōto 45Km
Ōsaka 18Km
Minoo Park
Olympic
Ogo
淡河
Nishinomiya-najio
西宮名塩
Takarazuka-kōgen
Sports-Nippon
Yomiuri
Mangami
KAWANISHI-SHI
川西市
Mino
MINOO-SHI
箕面市
Mt. Roppayama
Arima Royal
Yoshio
Shin-yū
Mt. Hatakeyama
Nishinomiya-Najio
Kiyoshikōjin
Nakayamadera
Kawanishi-Ikeda
IKEDA-SHI
池田市
Rokkō
Nishinomiya-kōgen
Dunlop
Sanda Line
Rokkō-Kita
SAN-YŌ EXPRESSWAY
山陽自動車道
Mt. Ōkurayama
Namaze
Takarazuka
Nakayama
Chūgoku-Ikeda
中国池田
TOYONAKA-SHI
豊中市
Kita-Senri
EXPO Mem. Park
Suita
吹田
Mt. Nagemachiyama
Mt. Takamaruyama
Arimaguchi
Arimaonsen
Arima
有馬
TAKARAZUKA-SHI
宝塚市
Nishinomiya
Takarazuka
宝塚
Kitamura 北村
Kitaitami
Chūgoku-Toyonaka
中国豊中
KŌBE-SHI
神戸市
Mt. Taishakusan
Hyōgo
Mt. Kashigamine
ITAMI-SHI
伊丹市
Ōsaka International (Itami)
Ōsaka-shi

KYŌTO
SHIGA
ŌSAKA
BIWAKO LAKE
琵琶湖
81
103
128
126
Mt. Shiraoyama
Yuragawa River
Mt. Mikunidake
Mt. Jatanigamine
TAKASHIMA-SHI
高島市
Mt. Takeyama
Ōmi-Takashima
Scenic view of lake
Congestion in summer
Kutsuki-saka Pass
Closed in winter
Mt. Bunagatake
Kita-Komatsu
Ōmi-maiko(Beautiful Beach)
近江舞子
Mt. Daihizan
Mt. Hirasan
Hara Pass
Blwako Valley
Mt. Hōraisan
Shiga-chō
志賀町
Mt. Gongen-yama
Mt. Ryōsenzan
Trout farm
Tochū Tunnel
ORD 150
LAR 570
途中トンネル
Tochūgoe Pass
Scenic view of Hirasan
Keihoku-chō
京北町
Mt. Meshimoriyama
Mt. Kurooyama
Mt. Kurooyama
Congestion in summer
Hanase Pass
Seryō Pass
Momoi Pass
Frozen and sharp curves
Japan cedar
Kurio Pass
Ōi River
Chitoseyama
Mt. Hangokutakayama
Mt. Kibuneyama
Mt. Kuramayama
Kurama
Okuhiei Driveway
ORD 1500
LAR 6000
Imakatada
今堅田
Biwako-ōhashi
ORD 200
LAR 710
Katata
Mt. Ryūōgatake
Mt. Mitsuzukoyama
Japan cedar
Mt. Minouragatake
Mt. Hyōtankuzureyama
from Kyōto-shi
Nagoya 160Km
Ōsaka 45Km
Congestion in spring and autumn
Hieizan Driveway
ORD 820
LAR 3260
Mt. Hieizan
Mt. Mitsuishidake
ORD 830
LAR 2930
Kosei-dōro
Mt. Saburōgatake
Mt. Mineyama
Mt. Sawayama
Hara Pass
Kino
Sakamoto
Kita-ku
北区
Takaragaike
Enryakuji
延暦寺
MORIYAMA-SHI
守山市
Moriyama
Mikyōsaka Pass
Congestion in spring and autumn
Arashiyama-Takao Parkway
ORD 1150
LAR 4650
Mt. Ushimatsuyama
Mt. Daimonjiyama
Kinkakuji
金閣寺
Karasaki
Ōmi-ōhashi
ORD 150
LAR 570
Bad road
Hozugawa River
KAMEOKA-SHI
亀岡市
Kameoka
Umahori
Arashiyama
嵐山
Mt. Arashiyama
Sakyō-ku
左京区
Ginkakuji
銀閣寺
Mt. Nyoigadake
Kamigyō-ku
上京区
Ukyō-ku
右京区
Nakagyō-ku
中京区
Nijō
Karasuma-Gojō 烏丸五条
Shimogyō-ku
下京区
Kyōto
Kiyomizudera
清水寺
ŌTSU-SHI
大津市
Ōtsu
大津
Zeze
KUSATSU-SHI
草津市
RITTŌ-SHI
栗東市
Rittō
Congestion
Nishikyō-ku
西京区
Katsurarikyū
桂離宮
Minami-ku
南区
Higashiyama-ku
東山区
Yamashina-ku
山科区
Kyōto-higashi
Seta 瀬田
Kusatsu-tanakami
Mt. Keikanzan
Kyōto-Tanba-dōro
ORD 1000
LAR 2800
Keihan-kokudōguchi
京阪国道口
Fushimi-inari
伏見稲荷
Imazu 50Km
Hikone 55Km
Kyōto 13Km
Seta-nishi
瀬田西
Seta-higashi
瀬田東
Ishiyamadera
石山寺
Mt. Oshioyama
Mt. Kuroedake
MUKŌ-SHI
向日市
Kyōto-minami
Keiji Bypass
ORD 930
LAR 3350
Mt. Ponpon-yama
NAGAOKAKYŌ-SHI
長岡京市
Ōtesuji
大手筋
Fushimi-ku
伏見区
Mt. Daigoyama
Mt. Hakamagoshiyama
Mt. Sasamagatake
Mt. Taishinyama
Ōyamazaki-chō
大山崎町
Alongside Yodogawa River
Mt. Kisen-yama
Mt. Hanatatenomine
Shimamoto-chō
島本町
Kumiyama-chō
久御山町
Ōkubo 大久保
Byōdōin
平等院
UJI-SHI
宇治市
Mt. Inoseyama
Zenjōji Pass
Mt. Abuyama
MEISHIN EXPRESSWAY
YAWATA-SHI
八幡市
Shimo-Nara
下奈良
Mt. Ōminesan
KŌKA-SHI
甲賀市
Hatchōnawate
八丁畷
Ujitawara-chō
宇治田原町
Urajiro Pass
TAKATSUKI-SHI
高槻市
ORD 600
LAR 1850
Scenic view of Ujigawa Rhein
JŌYŌ-SHI
城陽市
Ibaraki
茨木
Yamashiro-ōhashi-higashizume 山城大橋東詰
Mt. Gorinzan
Mt. Jūbuzan
HIRAKATA-SHI
枚方市
Ikenomiya-Kita 池之宮北
IBARAKI-SHI
茨木市
Mt. Takaoyama
Mt. Ōyakiyama
Mt. Kannabiyama
KYŌTANABE-SHI
京田辺市
Mt. Mitsugatake
Amanogawa
天の川
KATANO-SHI
交野市
Ide-chō
井手町
Wazuka-chō
和束町
Mt. Mikamiyama
Settsu-kita
摂津北
Settsu-minami I.C.
Ōsaka-shi
Nara-shi
Hikone-shi
E
F
G
H
1
2
3
4
5
6

JAPAN SEA
日本海
C. Kawajirimisaki
川尻岬
Ōshima I.
Hatakejima I.
Ryūgū-no-shiofuki
C. Washiishihana
Yuyajima I.
Mt. Amagoidake
Tenagajima I.
Nagato-Furuichi
Yuya-wan
Hitomaru
Heki-chō
日置町
Tsunoshima I.
Amaga-seto
C. Honbahana
Igami
Yuya-chō
油谷町
Hatojima I.
San-in Line
Nagato-Awano
Mt. Kumanodake
Mt. Ōfujiyama
Futagojima I.
Agawa
Awano River
Kabeshima I.
Kottoi 特牛
Mt. Tenjōgadake
Jariga Pass
Kottoi
Mt. Ichiigatake
C. Kandamisaki
神田岬
Hohoku-chō
豊北町
Tawarayama
Takibe
YAMAGUCHI
Caution-falling stones
Tsubashiki
Ichinomata
Mt. Tsuesakayama
Nagato-Futami
Araki
Ukahongō
C. Ōsakimisaki
Mt. Kurusonzan
Ōkawachi
Kuruson-kannon
Yutama
Toyota-chō
豊田町
Lake Swan(Mine)
Jinjōji
Kawatanagoe Pass
Mt. Gezan
Kiba Pass
Gezan
Menjima I.
Onjima I.
Kogushi
Koyagawa River
Mt. Toyogadake
Kawadanaonsen
Toyoura-chō
豊浦町
C. Kannonsaki
Shimonoseki
Kawatana
Kuroimura
Kikugawa-chō
菊川町
Yamaguchi (Kanmon Kikukawa)
Yamaguchi New Zealand Village
Yutani
Futaoijima I.
C. Toyanohana
Shimonoseki Jct
C. Kanegasaki
Umegatō
Mt. Onigajō
Drive-in
Mizushima I.
Ozuki
小月
Habuguchi Pass
Yoshimi

86

E
F
G
H
1
2
3
4
5
6
Susa-chō
Tsuwano-chō
Tokuji I.C.
San-yō-chō
Ube-shi
Hōfu-shi
Hōfu-shi
90
87
87
Utashima I.
Himeshima I.
Utagō
Noshima I.
C. Modoromisaki
Varied shore line
Kiyo
Hitsushima I.
Aishima I.
Saega Pass
Mt. Mitsugatake
Abu-chō
阿武町
Nago
Ogashima I.
Megashima I.
Oshima I.
Ōshima I.
C. Hizaki
Hishima I.
San-in Line
Nagato-Ōi
Hashima I.
C. Toragasaki
Pine trees boulevard
Kushima I.
Koshigahama
Mutsumi-mura
むつみ村
Omotomachi 御許町
Susa 41Km
Nagato 28Km
Yamaguchi 45Km
Sabashima I.
Mt. Tōjinyama
Fukue-son
福栄村
C. Kurosaki
HAGI
萩
HAGI-SHI
萩市
Higashi-Hagi
Tōkōji
Shōin-jinja
Kasuga-jinja
Tamae
Hagi
Kanetani-jinja
Ryūzōji
Mt. Amagoeyama
to Masuda
to Shimonoseki
to Shūhōdō, Yamaguchi
Ōmijima I.(Scenic Rocky Coast)
C. Imamisaki
Ōmishima I.
Shizuga-ura
Senzaki-wan
Ōmiko Lake
Sasajima I.
Sanmi
Ebisujima I.
Kōjima I.
Kiwado
Fukagawa -wan
Senzaki
Nagatoshi
Mt. Chausuyama
Nanmyōji
Zōmeki River
Abugawa River
Abugawa Dam
NAGATO-SHI
長門市
Nagato-Misumi
Misumi-chō
三隅町
Myōhōji
Yumen
Misumi River
Misumichō-Munetō
三隅町宗頭
Hagi-dōro
ORD 150
LAR 560
Kawakami-son
川上村
Shōmyōichi 正明市
Hagi 28Km
Mine 29Km
Shimonoseki 81Km
Congestion in spring and autumn
Mt. Tetsuwariyama
Asahi-son
旭村
Yunose
Nagato-Yumoto
Nagato-Yumoto
長門湯本
Mt. Gongenyama
Ōhira Pass
Frozen road
Chōmonkyō(Gorge)
長門峡
Shibuki
Fukagawa River
Mt. Katsuragiyama
Mt. Kujiragatake
Mt. Nomarudake
Drive-in
Chōmonkyō
Curves-Drive slowly
Hibari Pass
Sasanami River
Mt. Nyoidake
Akiyoshidai Safari Land
Ōgatōge Pass
Mt. Hanaoyama
Kidoyama 木戸山
Shinome
Mt. Monomi -dake
Mt. Dōgatake
Hinataze Pass
Caution-falling stones
Akiyoshidai(Plateau)
秋吉台
Mine
Mt. Ondake
Mt. Ryūmon -dake
Kido Pass
Yamaguchi(Nagato-Toyodako)
Mt. Datsuyayama
Mt. Kidoyama
Mine Line
Ōfuku
Mt. Karitobiyama
Congestion in spring and autumn
Mt. Yabitsuyama
Yamaguchi Line
Akiyoshido
Akiyoshidō(Cave)
秋芳洞
Mitō-chō
美東町
Mt. Higashihōbenzan
Orimoto 折本
Niho
to Ogōri
Shūhō-chō
秋芳町
Mt. Nishihōbenzan
from Yamaguchi-shi
Hiroshima 140Km
Kita-Kyūshū 90Km
Niho-iriguchi
仁保入口
Shigeyasu
Mt.Amagoyama
Mt. Emineyama
Runkoji
YAMAGUCHI-SHI
山口市
Kami-Yamaguchi
Miyano
Yamaguchi (Yamaguchi-sensuibara)
Kunigyō 国行
Yamaguchi 41Km
Nagato 30Km
Ōzuki 25Km
MINE-SHI
美祢市
Mine
美祢
Yūda
Yamaguchi
Furukuma -jinja
Yuda
Mt. Sobagayama
Mt. Hinodake
Yudaonsen
Minami-Ōmine
Suzumigi Pass
Mitō
美東
Nihongi Pass
Mt. Hotakiyama
Yabara
Yamaguchi
山口
Yamaguchi Bypass
Ouchi-Miyano Bypass
Mt. Sakurayama
CHŪGOKU EXPRESSWAY
中国自動車道
Ōta River
Otoshi
Shirōgahara
Asagawa River
Isa
伊佐
Nihotsu
Yuda
湯田
Tokiwa Royal
Ogōri
小郡
SAN-YŌ EXPRESSWAY
山陽自動車道
Atsu
Kotō River
Kamigō
Mine-nishi
美祢西
Mt. Hiraharadake
Ogōri-chō
小郡町
Suō-Shimogō
Yamaguchi-minami
山口南
HŌFU-SHI
防府市
Shin-Yamaguchi
UBE-SHI
宇部市
Yunotō
San-yō-chō
山陽町
Onoko Lake
Yotsutsuji
Tentokuji
to Ōmishima I.
Nagatoshi
to Hagi
to Shimonoseki
to Yumoto

B
C
D
84
53
Nagato-shi
Tagawa-shi
Kabeshima I.
Kottoi
Kottoi 特牛
Awano Pass
C. Kandamisaki
神田岬
Hōhoku-chō
豊北町
Takibe
Tsubashiki
Mt. Tsuesakayama
Caution landslides
Nagato-Futami
Ukahongō
C. Ōsakimisaki
Okawachi
Yutama
San-in Line
Mejima I.
Ojima I.
Kogushi
Kawatanaonsen
Toyoura-chō
豊浦町
Kawatana
C. Kannonzaki
Shimonoseki
Kuroimura
C. Toyanohana
Umegatō
Mt. Onigajōyama
Drive-in
C. Ajironohana
Kamoshima I.
Yoshimi
Mt. Ryūōzan
Fukue
Pine trees
Yasuoka
Hikoshima-dōro
ORD 310
LAR 1100
Mutsurejima I.
Umashima I.
Kanesakishima I.
Nagato 81Km
Ozuki 21Km
Kita-Kyūshū 15Km
彦島道路
Kyūshū-yūsen Ferry (to Hitakatsu)
Kanpu Ferry (to Pusan)
SHIMONOSEKI-SHI
下関市
Shimonoseki
Kanmon-kaikyō
Yuya-chō
油谷町
Mt. Tenjōgadake
Jariga Pass
Mt. Ichiigatake
Tawarayama
Ichinomata
Araki
Mt. Kurusonzan
Kuruson-kannon
Kawatanagoe Pass
Kiba Pass
Mt. Gesan
Jinjōji
Toyota-chō
豊田町
Kikugawa-chō
菊川町
Yamaguchi Kanmonkikukawa
Yamaguchi New Zealand Village
Ozuki-kōsaten 小月交差点
Mine 25Km
Ogōri 44Km
Shimonoseki 21Km
Ozuki
小月
Shimonoseki Jct
下関Jct
Habuguchi Pass
San-yo Shinkansen
Ōji
王司
Mt. Shiōjisan
Chōfu
Innai-kōsaten 印内交差点
Shin-Shimonoseki
Ayaragi
Kōsanji
Hatabu
Shimonoseki
下関
Mojikō
門司港
Hinoyama Parkway
ORD 400
LAR 2030
C. Hesaki
Kanmon Tunnel
ORD 200
LAR 550
Moji-ku
門司区
Kasuga
Moji
門司
Kaburajima I.
Dairi
Chinzeibetsuin
Shin-Moji
新門司
Kishi
吉志
Tomino
Kokurakita-ku
小倉北区
Adachi
Fukujuzenji
Mt. Adachiyama
Myōken-jinja
Mt. Tobigasuyama
KYŪSHŪ EXPRESSWAY
九州自動車道
Minami-kokura
Murasakigawa
Kokura Castle
Yahata I.C.
Kokuraminami-ku
小倉南区
Ishida
Kokura-higashi
小倉東
Kitakyūshū
Shimo-Sone
Mashima I.
Hajima I.
KITAKYŪSHŪ-SHI
北九州市
FUKUOKA
Kokura-minami
Shii
Kusami
Nippō Line
Kōnoshima I.
Ocean
Nagato-Yumoto
Daineiji
Taineiji Pass
Shibuki
NAGATO-SHI
長門市
Curves-Drive slowly
Mt. Gongen-yama
Ōhira Pass
Mt. Nyoidake
Ōga Pass
Mt. Hanaoyama
Drive-in
Mt. Dōgatake
Caution landslides
Mine
Sekichūkei(Gorge)
Yamaguchi(Nagato-Toyodako)
Toyodako Lake
Kiyagawa Dam
Mt. Karitobiyama
Ofuku
Akiyoshidai(Plateau)
秋吉台
Mine Line
YAMAGUCHI
Congestion in spring and autumn
Kunigyō 国行
Nagato 30Km
Yamaguchi 41Km
Ozuki 25Km
Koyagawa River
Lake Swan
Gezan
Shigeyasu
Shuhō-chō
秋芳町
Mt. Amagoiyama
Mt. Toyogadake
Minami-Ōmine
MINE-SHI
美祢市
Mine
美祢
Suzumigi Pass
Mt. Sakurayama
Mt. Hinodake
Shirōgahara
CHŪGOKU EXPRESSWAY
中国自動車道
Mine-nishi
美祢西
Isa
伊佐
Atsu
Yunotō
President CC San-yō
San-yō-chō
山陽町
Exclusive road of Ubekōsan
Kōtōgawa Dam
Ubeshi-Kurumaji 宇部市車地
Sanyōchō-Asa 山陽町厚狭
Okanosaka-kōsaten 岡ノ坂交差点
Asa
Chōfu
Sanyō-kokusai
Sanyō Green
Habu
Dango Pass
談合峠
Kamiichi上市
Suōnada
周防灘
Asagawa River
Onoda
小野田
Funaki
Kotō
Jiseiji
Mt. Shimofuridake
SAN-YŌ EXPRESSWAY
山陽自動車道
Ube
宇部
ONODA-SHI
小野田市
Mede
Minami-Nakagawa
Minamionoda
Iwahana
Onoda Cement
Onodakō
Arita River
Onoda Line
Tsumazaki
Nagato-Nagasawa
Suzumeda
Kōtō River
Ubeshinkawa
UBE-SHI
宇部市
Tokiwako Lake
Kotoshiba
Ube Industries
Shinkawa
Tokiwa Park
Hamagōchi
Nagato-Motoyama
Willow trees
Ubemisaki
Kusae
C. Motoyamamisaki
Matsuyamachō 1 chōme
松山町一丁目
Yamaguchi-Ube
C. Ubemisaki
宇部岬
Yoshida River
San-yō Line
to Nagato
Ozuki I.C
to Shimonoseki
to Hōfu
Ozuki

Hagi-shi
HAGI-SHI
萩市
Mt. Kujiragatake
Katsuragiyama
Hibari Pass
Mt. Nomarudake
Chōmonkyō(Gorge)
長門峡
Drive-in
Watarigawa
Chōmon-kyō
to Masuda
Chōmon-kyō
Shinome
to Yamaguchi
Mt. Tsuzuradake
Taishōdō(Cave)
Asahi-son
旭村
Sasanami River
San-in-dō
Shinome
Mt. Monomidake
Ōharako Lake
Mt. Higuregatake
Mt. Takabachiyama
Hinataze Pass
Notani Pass
Sabagawa River
Mt. Ondake
Mt. Gongenyama
Mt. Ryūmondake
Mt. Datsuyayama
Kido Pass
Mt. Ishigadake
Kidoyama 木戸山
Mt. Kidoyama
Yamaguchi Line
Mt. Yabitsuyama
Mitō-chō
美東町
Mt. Higashihōbenzan
Okuyuda
Orimoto 折本
Niho
Mt. Nishihōbenzan
from Yamaguchi-shi
Hiroshima 140Km
Kita-Kyūshū 90Km
Matsukara Pass
Mt. Kurusonzan
Tokuji
徳地
Tokuji-chō
徳地町
Mt. Shiraishiyama
CHŪGOKU EXPRESSWAY
中国自動車道
Ō-dao Pass
Miyano
Niho-iriguchi
仁保入口
Nioroshi Pass
荷卸峠
Mt. Yōgaidake
Sengokudake
Mt. Emineyama
YAMAGUCHI-SHI
山口市
Kami-Yamaguchi
Yamaguchi
Yamaguchi (Yamaguchi-sensuibara)
Niorshitōge
荷卸峠
Mt. Madagatake
Izumo-jinja
Shūtō-chō
Yuda
Yudaonsen
Mt. Sobagayama
Mitō
美東
Mt. Hotakiyama
Nihongi Pass
Yahara
Yamaguchi
山口
Ōta River
Drive-in
Ōtoshi
Yamaguchi Bypass
Yuda
湯田
Nihotsu
Tokiwa Royal
Ogōri
小郡
Kamigō
Mt. Hiraharadake
Yamaguchi 12Km
Ube 28Km
Ozuki 44Km
Suō-Shimogō
Ogōri-chō
小郡町
Yamaguchi-minami
山口南
No-dao Pass
Kakinoki Pass
Tokuyama-kokusai
Mt. Shikumagatake
Mt. Yahazugatake
Drive-in area
Yuno
SAN-YŌ EXPRESSWAY
山陽自動車道
Ukitakai 沖高井
Tentokuji
Hōfu-higashi
防府東
Mt. Ōhirayama
Tokuyama-higashi I.C.
Yotsutsuji
Mt. Takakoyama
Kami-Kagawa
Hōfu-nishi
防府西
San-yo Shinkansen
Tonomi
Tsubaki Pass
椿峠
Heta
Fukugawa
SHŪNAN-SHI
周南市
Kagawa
Drive-in area
Hōfu-tenmangū
Sanyō-dō
Yamaguchi
富海
Tokuyama-nishi
徳山西
Fukamizo
Mt. Ōmiyama
Daitō
Sabagawa
山陽道
HŌFU-SHI
防府市
Hōfu
Sanyō Line
YAMAGUCHI
Hachiōji 八王子
Tokuyama 28Km
Yamaguchi 17Km
Ogōri 25Km
Congestion in summer
Tonomi 富海
Hon-Yura
Suō-Sayama
Fushino River
Sabagawa River
Mitajiri
Ōtsushima I.
Kurokamishima I.
Iwakura
Aio-chō
秋穂町
Ube
Ajisu-chō
阿知須町
Ajisu
Ōmi-wan
Mt. Nishikiyama
Itsutsujima I.
Yamaguchi-Ube dōro
ORD 360
LAR 1310
Mukōshima I.
Tokuyama-wan
Kiwa
C. Akaishihana
C. Tazunohana
Umashima I.
C. Kanagamisaki
Sukumojima I.
Sujima I.
C. Mitsuishihana
Maruo
C. Maruozaki
Takeshima I.
Ube Line
Okijima I.
Hirajima I.
Noshima I.
to Yamaguchi
Ogōri I.C
Kamigō
Suō Shimogō
to Shimonoseki
to Hiroshima
Shin-Yamaguchi
SUŌ-NADA
周防灘
Suōnada Ferry
(to Tokuyama·Takedazu·Mitsuhama)
Kansai-kisen (to Matsuyama)
Meimontaiyō Ferry (to Ōsaka)
Hankyū Ferry(to Kōbe, Izumiōtsu)
E
F
G
H
1
2
3
4
5
6
85
90
88

90
91
87
64

YAMAGUCHI
SUŌ-NADA
周防灘
CHŪGOKU EXPRESSWAY
中国自動車道
SAN-YO EXPRESSWAY
山陽自動車道
Kano
鹿野
Tokuji-chō
徳地町
Mt. Sengokudake
Kinpō Pass
Mt. Kinpōsan
Kōdōko Lake
Tokuyama
Mt. Midoriyama
Sugano Dam
Nishiki-chō
錦町
Kawayama
Nishikigawa Railway
Mikawa-chō
美川町
Naguwa
Mukuno
Miwa-chō
美和町
Miwa
Yasakako Lake
Iwakunishi-kuina 岩国市杭名
Iwakuni
Nishiki River
Kita-Gōchi
Minami-Gōchi
Mishō
Shin-Iwa
Shuuchi-Kasakami
Yukaba
Kugachō-Uwaichi 玖珂町上市
Hashirano
Mt. Monomidake
Mt. Rengeyama
Mt. Genkuroyama
Shūtō-chō
周東町
Kuga-chō
玖珂町
Kuga
Hataki Pass
Kinmeiji
Kuga
玖珂
Suō-Takamori
Drive-in
Yonekawa
Gantoku Line
Shūtōchō-nishi-Nagano 周東町西長野
Mt. Eboshigatake
Tokuyama-kokusai
Mt. Shikumagadake
Sugiga-tōge Pass
Nakasu
Kumagechō-Hara
熊毛町原
Hōfu-shi
Yamaguchi I.C.
Tokuyama-nishi I.C.
Heta
SHŪNAN-SHI
周南市
Shin-nan-yō
Hiroshima 100Km
Kita-Kyūshū 130Km
Tokuyama-higashi
徳山東
Tsuji 辻
Tokuyama
Kudamatsu
下松
Hanaoka-inari
Suō-Hanaoka
Suō-Kubo
Shūnan
Katsuma
Yobitsuru
Takamizu
Kumage
熊毛
Mitsuo
Suetake-naka 末武中
KUDAMATSU-SHI
下松市
Kudamatsu
Mt. Eboshidake
Ōuchi Pass
Himurodake
Nishinoshima I.
Nakanoshima I.
Yokoshima I.
Senjima I.
Kawazujima I.
Tokuyama-Kudamatsu
Kushigahama
Kurokamishima I.
Kabashima I.
Tokuyama-wan
Ōzushima I.
大津島
Nisshin Steel
Mt. Taikazan
Suōnada Ferry (to Takedazu)
Kasado-wan
Mt. Hachigōyama
Nijigahama
Mishima
Shimata
San-yō Line
Hikari
Iwata
Mt. Iwakisan
Iwakisan-jinja
Mt. Ōhirayama
Yanaishi-higashi-Okiwari
柳井市東沖割
YANAI-SHI
柳井市
Yanai
Mt. Kotoishiyama
Ōbatake-chō
大畠町
Yanaiminato
Sukumojima I.
C. Mitsuishihana
C. Kanagamisaki
Furushima I.
HIKARI-SHI
光市
Shimadaichi 島田市
Shimada River
Tonaka 戸仲
Mt. Senbōyama
Tabuse
Tabuse-chō
田布施町
Mt. Akagoyama
Hirao-chō
平生町
Kasadoshima I.
C. Hiburimisaki
Kominasejima I.
Ōminasejima I.
Kasasajima
Karasujima I.
C. Kajitorimisaki
Umashima I.
Haneshima I.
Sagōshima I.
Ojima I.
Ushima I.
Drive-in
Mt. Ōzasan
Mt. Kamisakariyama
C. Chibasa
Kaminoseki-chō
上関町
Yokoshima I.
Koiwaijima I.
Iwaijima I.
祝島
C. Eboshibana
Amatajima I.
Uwajima I.
Yashima I.
八島
to Kano
to Hōfu
to Iwakuni
Tokuyama
to Takamori
Yanai
to Tokuyama

HIROSHIMA
Miyajima I.
宮島
Ōtake
Kuba
Midorigawa-bashi みどり川橋
ŌTAKE-SHI
大竹市
Waki-chō
和木町
Marifu 麻里布
Hiroshima 44Km
Yanai 35Km
Tokuyama 54Km
IWAKUNI-SHI
岩国市
Iwakuni
Nishi-Iwakuni
Imazu River
Iwakuni Airport
Monzen River
Himekojima I.
Atatajima I.
Inokojima I.
Kogurokamishima I.
Nishi-Nōmijima I.
西能美島
Etajima-wan
ETAJIMA-SHI
江田島市
Setonaikai-kisen
Kure
KURE-SHI
呉市
Yotsu-dōro
四ッ道路
Kameyama-hachiman-jinja
Hiro 広
Aki-Aga
Kure Line
Hironishiōkawa River
Ondono-seto
Mitsugojima I.
Ondo-chō
音戸町
Ondo-Ōhashi(Bridge)
Congestion in summer
Drive in
Kure-Matsuyama Ferry (to Horie)
Hiroshima-Matsuyama-Ryokaku Ferry
(Ujina-Kure-Mitsuhama)
Ōgurokamishima I.
Mt. Kushinoune
Okinoshima I.
Higashi-Nōmijima I.
東能美島
Konasakejima I.
Nasakejima I.
Kurahashijima I.
倉橋島
Uwagi Pass
Katsurahama-jinja
Kurahashi-chō
倉橋町
C. Nagakushinohana
Sasakojima I.
Nagashima I.
C. Oyayasumibana
to Tokuyama
to Hiroshima
Kintaikyo Bridge
Nishi-Iwakuni
Fujū
Tsuzu
Scenic view Setouchi
Hodakajima I.
Funegaiiwa
Teshima I.
Kuroshima I.
Kashima I.
AKI-NADA
安芸灘
IWAKUNI-SHI
岩国市
Hashiwajima I.
Yokoshima I.
Hayamajima I.
Kotachibajima I.
Yuu-chō
由宇町
Yuu
Drive-in
Kobashirajima I.
Ōtachibashima I.
Isekojima I.
Hashirajima I.
Zenitsuboyama
Maejima I.
Kōjiro
Kuroshima I.
Fukushima I.
Kurakakejima I.
Nagashima I.
Nagarekojima I.
C. Kazakiribana
Mt. Tainoyama
Hachiman-jinja
Fukurashima I.
Tsuwajishima I.
Nuwajima I.
Heyano-seto
Nakajima I.
中島
Orange Line (to Mitsuhama)
Obatake-seto
Heburijima I.
Kashirajima I.
C. Jōnohana
MATSUYAMA-SHI
松山市
Ōshima-ōhashi
C. Ōsakibana
Ukishima I.
Mitsushima I.
Nasakejima I.
Moroshima I.
C. Setogahana
C. Akasaki
Yashirojima I.
屋代島
Suōōshima-chō
周防大島町
Tobisejima I.
Otokojima I.
Mt. Ōmisan
Mt. Tainomine
Futagamijima I.
Yokoshima I.
Mt. Chōkaizan
Mt. Kanōzan
Mt. Takeyama
Wagashima I.
Katashima I.
Koichijima I.
Sasashima I.
Tsurushima I.
C. Agesaki
Tatsushima I.
C. Hōshizaki
Kami-Ninaishima I.
Shimo-Ninaijima I.
Okikamurojima I.
Yurijima I.
Kakezujima I.
Ōminasejima I.
Mt. Nagamiyama
Hegurijima I.
平郡島
YANAI-SHI
柳井市
C. Sakarizaki
Kominaseshima I.
Aoshima I.
EHIME
92
91
66
65
E
F
G
H
1
2
3
4
5
6

B
C
D
72
1
2
3
4
5
6
A
85
87
88
Hagi-shi
Yamaguchi-shi
Tokuji I.C.
Iwakuni-shi
to Hagi
to Hamada
to Kake
to Yamaguchi
Masuda
Scenic view of Japan Sea
Masudashi-hakayoshida
益田市中吉田
Hamada 43Km
Susa 27Km
Nichihara 23Km
Okami
Misumi-chō
三隅町
Kamate
San-in-dō 山陰道
Mt. Eboshiyama
Iwami-Tsuda
Mt. Hirefuriyama
Masuda River
Sendō River
Taikian Ikōji
Kakimoto-jinja
San-in Line
Iwami
MASUDA-SHI
益田市
Takatsu River
Tada
Ōtani
Honmatage
Yamashima I.
C. Kōyamamisaki
高山岬
Mt. Kōyama
Todakohama
Iihoura
Tamagawa-chō
田万川町
Esaki
Tenjinjima I.
Susawan
Susa-chō
須佐町
Susa
Nakazu 中津
Masuda 27Km
Hagi 41Km
Atō 41Km
Tamagawa River
Hikimi-hōmen-iriguchi
匹見方面入口
Iwami-Yokota
SHIMANE
Mt. Shirasuyama
Utagō
Mt. Inunakiyama
Higashi-Aohara
Mt. Akaishiyama
Aohara
Nichihara-chō
日原町
Iwakuni-hōmen-iriguchi 岩国方面入口
Masuda 23Km
Iwakuni 86Km
Atō 22Km
Mt. Mitsugoyama
Nichihara
Mt. Iraoyama
Mt. Sugōtayama
Mt. Gongen-yama
Tsuwano River
Yoshiga River
Mt. Tsubamegatake
Kamiutsudani Pass
Mt. Azōjiyama
Tsuwano
TSUWANO
津和野
Tsuwano Castle
Tsuwano-chō
津和野町
Aonoyama
Mt. Ōshikayama
Mt. Aonoyama
Mutsumi-mura
むつみ村
Mt. Tokusagamine
Yamaguchi Line
Kakinoki-mura
柿木村
Mt. Yajūroyama
Drive slowly
Funahirayama
Mt. Taishōzan
Fukukawa River
Mt. Kogorōyama
Tokusa
Atō-chō
阿東町
Tokusanaka-Kamiichi-nishi 徳佐中上市西
Nichihara 22Km
Yamaguchi 32Km
Tokuyama 51Km
Mt. Tsukiyama
Zōmeki River
Nabekura
Mt. Ōkuragatake
Mt. Suzunoōtaniyama
Mt. Mottagatake
Ikumo River
Mt. Kurojishiyama
Jifuku
Nodō Pass
Hotoke Pass
Muikaichi
六日市
Asakura
朝倉
Yunose
Nagusa
Mitani
Mitani 三谷
Muikaichi-machi
六日市町
Chōmonkyō(Gorge)
長門峡
Wataригawa
Mt. Iigadake
Mt. Adamigatake
Bōjiga Pass
Usagawa River
Closed in winter
Komine Pass
Mt. Heikegatake
Mt. Tsuzuradake
YAMAGUCHI
Yoneyama Pass
Mt. Jōshōzan
Chōmonkyō
Drive-in
Ōharako Lake
Mt. Higuregatake
SHŪNAN-SHI
周南市
Mt. Mizunoosan
Mt. Monomidake
Shinome
Mt. Takabachiyama
Notani Pass
Sabagawa River
Nishikichō
Deai 出合
Nishiki River
Yanaze
Mt. Bafungatake
Nishiki-chō
錦町
Mikawa-chō
美川町
Tokuji-chō
徳地町
Mt. Ishigadake
Kan-yō
Kano
鹿野
Kawayama
Nishikigawa Railway

HIROSHIMA
Yasaka-mura
弥栄村
Ōtsubo Pass
Mt. Ōsayama
Bōji Pass
Ōsayama
Sharp curves
Takiyama River
Ōgure River
Ōasa-chō
大朝町
Ōasa
大朝
Mt. Hinoyama
Mt. Yauneyama
Kitsuka Pass
Mt. Kakezuyama
Congestion in winter
Geihoku-chō
芸北町
Shiiya Pass
Shijihara River
Mt. Garyūzan
Ōsa River
Hijiriko Lake
Mt. Takadake
Shinnyū Pass
Mt. Shinnyūzan
Mt. Ōhōkisan
Toyohira-chō
豊平町
Yamazaki sansaro
山崎三差路
to Hamada
to Togouchi
to Kabe
Mt. Kasugayama
Mt. Iwakurayama
Mochinoki Pass
Sandankyō(Gorge)
三段峡
to Kake
to Sandankyō
to Togouchi I.C.
to Tsutsuga
Mt. Toishigōsan
Hikimi River
Hikimikyō(Gorge)
匹見峡
Mt. Osorakanzan
Osorakan
Large truck traffic prohibited
Mt. Ōmarumine
Mt. Unamiyama
Chiyoda-chō
Hamada 56Km
Masuda 83Km
Hiroshima 51Km
Curves
Minosumi 箕角
Akiōta-chō
安芸太田町
Togouchi
戸河内
Asa
安佐
Hiroshima-Kita Jct
広島北 Jct
Hiroshima-kita
広島北
Congestion in summer
Closed in winter
Mt. Jippōsan
Tsutsuga
筒賀
Mt. Tenjōsan
Tateiwa-chosuichi Lake
Deep ravine
Minochi River
Mt. Tatoiwayama
Pine trees
CHŪGOKU EXPRESSWAY
中国自動車道
HIROSHIMA EXPRESSWAY
広島自動車道
Ōta River
Asakita-ku
安佐北区
Asa Zoo
Hagiwara Pass
Kuchi
久地
Yunoyama
Yuki-chō
湯来町
Toyama
Hiroshima-seifūshinto
広島西風新都
Mt. Kanmuriyama
Yoshiwa
吉和
Ushiobara
Yuki
Mt. Tōgōsan
Bairin
Shichi-Kenjaya
Midori
Numata
沼田
Ōmachi
Hiroshima
広島
Furuichibashi
Narrow curves
Mt. Mukaiyama
Hiroshima Jct
広島 Jct
Shimo-Gion
Itsukaichi
五日市
Asaminami-ku
安佐南区
Aki-Nagatsuka
Hesaka
Mitaki
Yokogawa
Mt. Ōminesan
Mt. Onigajōyama
Kusatsu-Numata dōro
ORD 150
LAR 570
SAN-YŌ EXPRESSWAY
山陽自動車道
Geinan
Nishi-Hiroshima
Hiroshima Castle
Heiwa-kinen-kōen (Mem.Park)
Kaita-chō
HIROSHIMA-SHI
広島市
Higashi-ku
東区
Rakan
Rakan Gorge
Iwakura
Chestnut growing area
Miyajima
Nishi-Hiroshima Bypass
Shin-Inokuchi
Itsukaichi
Hiroshima-nishi
Naka-ku
中区
Mazda
Numayama Pass
Mt. Rakanzan
Akaishi Pass
Hatsukaichi
Saeki-ku
佐伯区
Yahata River
Mitsubishi Heavy Industries
Closed in winter
Hiroshima-Saeki
Hayatani-jinja
HATSUKAICHI-SHI
廿日市市
Hiroshima Railway
Kanawajima I.
Congestion in spring
Hatsukaichi
廿日市
Jigozen
Hiroshima-wan
Grape growing area
Mt. Mikuradake
Ozegawa River
Hiroshima Natalie(A.P.)
from Hiroshima
Ōsaka 350Km
Kita-Kyūshū 230Km
Hiroshima-Matsuyama Ferry
- Ryokaku Ferry (to Matsuyama)
Drive-in
Ajina
Hiroden-Miyajimaguchi
Miyajimaguchi
C. Hijirizaki
Bentenjima I.
Mt. Akikofuji
Tōgejima I.
Ninoshima I.
Drive-in
San-yō Line
Itsukushima-jinja
厳島神社
Miyajima-chō
宮島町
Ōzu-seto
Hongō-son
本郷村
Ōno
Mt. Kyōgoyayama
Ōnoura
Ōno-chō
大野町
Ōno-seto
Enoshima I.
Unshōji Pass
Drive slowly
Mt. Misen
Ōnasabishima I.
Itsukushima-kaikyō
Edajima I.
江田島
Scenic ravine view
Mt. Takahachiyama
Miyahama
Itsukushima I.
(Miyajima I.)
Nasami-seto
Mt. Furutakayama
Miwa-chō
美和町
Kuba
Ōtake
ŌTAKE-SHI
大竹市
Nishi-Nōmijima I.
西能美島
Etajima-wan
Kogurokamishima I.
ETAJIMA-SHI
江田島市
Iwakuni-shi
E
F
G
H
1
2
3
4
5
6
73
88
89
92
94

A
B
C
D
1
2
3
4
5
6
94
91
66
67
Miyoshi I.C.
Miyoshi-shi
Togouchi I.C.
Miyajimaguchi
HIROSHIMA
HAMADA EXPRESSWAY
浜田自動車道
CHŪGOKU EXPRESSWAY
中国自動車道
SAN-YŌ EXPRESSWAY
山陽自動車道
Shijihara River
Mt. Heikenoshiroyama
Hongō
本郷
Takada
高田
Mt. Tsuzurayama
Innai Pass
Mt. Takagoyayama
Kami-Kawatachi
Drive slowly
MIYOSHI-SHI
三次市
Mt. Onigajōyama
Takamiya-wakare 高宮分れ
Kōtachi
Madouri Pass
Kōrinbō
Toyohira-chō
豊平町
Chiyoda-chō
千代田町
Chiyoda
千代田
Yachiyoko Lake
AKITAKATA-SHI
安芸高田市
Yoshidaguchi
Mt. Sarumameyama
Haji Dam
Enokawa River
Chūgoku
Mt. Ōzuchiyama
Katsuta sansaro 勝田三差路
Mt. Dōtokoyama
Yachiyo
Mt. Hirauneyama
Mt. Unamiyama
Mukaihara
Mt. Akashibayama
Myōjin Pass
明神峠
Asa
安佐
Ibaraichi
Mt. Dōtokoyama
Geibi Line
Mt. Takanosuyama
Mt. Tenjin
Hiroshima-kita Jct
広島北 Jct
Gōtsu 92Km
Kake 24Km
Hiroshima 27Km
Congestion in summer
Hiroshima-kita
広島北
Fukuōji
Shiwaguchi
Toyosaka-chō
豊栄町
Mt. Itanabeyama
Kami-Mita
Asakita-ku
安佐北区
Fukutomi-chō
福富町
Kabeshishomae 可部支所前
Mt. Shirakiyama
Naka-Mita
Misasa River
Kabe
Asa Zoo
Hagiwara Pass
Ōta River
Shirakiyama
Mt. Adayama
Nakashima
Mt. Abusan
Kami-Yagi
Shimo-Fukawa
Mt. Gokuzōyama
Bairin
Hiroshima-chuō
Naka-Fukawa
Karuga
Mt. Takahachiyama
Astram Line
Kumura
Miyajima-Shiwa
Asahi
Shichikenjaya
Kami-Fukawa
Midori
Aki-Yaguchi
Hiroshima
Higashi-Hiroshima
Nyūno
Furuichishisho-iriguchi
古市支所入口
Ōmachi
広島
Enoyama Pass
Shiwa
志和
Saijō
西条
Numata
沼田
Asaminami-ku
安佐南区
Furuichibashi
Hiroshima-higashi
広島東
Hachihonmatsu
Nishi-Takaya
Shimo-Gion
Hesaka
San-yō Line
Kamo
Kodani
小谷
from Hiroshima-shi
Ōsaka 330Km
Kita-Kyūshū 230Km
Aki-Nagatsuka
Mt. Gosasouyama
Seno
Frozen road
Hachihonmatsuchō-Minogoshi 八本松町見之越
HIGASHIHIROSHIMA-SHI
東広島市
Miyoshi 59Km
Mihara 38Km
Hiroshima 36Km
ORD 250
LAR 920
Senogawa
Mt. Mizumaruyama
Mitaki
Yokogawa
Higashi-ku
東区
Nishi-Hiroshima
Drive-in
Saijōchō-Shimominaga
西条町下三永
San-yō-dō 山陽道
Hiroshima Castle
Heiwa Kinen-Kōen (Mem. park)
Aki-Fuchū-dōro
Nakano-higashi
Yaga
Fuchū-chō
府中町
Hiroshima(Hachihonmatsu)
Hiroshima(Saijō)
Nishi-ku
西区
Tenjingawa
Aki-Nakano
Kogoe Pass
Aki-ku
安芸区
Higashi-Hiroshima
Hesaka Pass
Hiroshima-tōei
HIROSHIMA-SHI
広島市
Mukainada
Minami-ku
南区
San-yō Shinkansen
Hiroshima-nishi
Mitsubishi Heavy Industries
Kaitaichi
Kaita-chō
海田町
Senogawa River
Mazda
Taishōmachi
大正町
Accident-prone area
Kumano-wakare 熊野分れ
Mt. Odayama
Kanashi Pass
Kurose River
to Saijō
Takehara
to Kure
Hiroshima
Kanawajima I.
Yano
Saka
Saka-chō
坂町
Saka-minami
Kumano-chō
熊野町
広島熊野道路
Kurose-chō
黒瀬町
Hiroshima-kokusai
Akitsu-chō
安芸津町
Akitsu
Mt. Akikofuji
Tōgejima I.
Mizushiri
Hiroshima-Matsuyama Ferry
Ninoshima I.
Koyaura
Gōbara
Akitsuchō-Sakakiba
安芸津町榊原
Kazahaya
Mitsu-wan
Ryūōjima I.
Ōzu-Seto
Kure Port Pia
Tennō-nishi
Tennō-higashi
Hiroshima-Kure-dōro
ORD 900
LAR 2500
Akitsu Ferry
Ainoshima I.
Kure Line
Yasuura
Yasuura-chō
安浦町
Yasuurachō-yakubamae
安浦町役場前
Ōshibashima I.
Etajima I.
江田島
Tennō
Mt. Haigamine
Yotsu-dōro 四ッ道路
広島呉道路
Mt. Norosan
Mt. Zendanayama
Hiroshima 29Km
Higashi-Hiroshima 34Km
Mihara 72Km
Mitsuguchi-wan
Kashiwajima I.
Koshibajima I.
Nagashima I.
Tsukugashima I.
Ōsogashima
Karugahama
Mt. Furutakayama
Yoshiura
Kure
KURE-SHI
呉市
Kure
to Mt. Norosan
to Mihara
Etajima-wan
Kawaraishi
Ōurumejima I.
Kameyama-hachiman-jinja
Hiro 広
Drive-in
Aki-Kawajiri
Nishi-Nōmijima I.
西能美島
Aki-Aga
Shin-Hiro
Hiro
Kashiwajima I.
Ōsakikamijima
大崎上島
ETAJIMA-SHI
江田島市
Ondono-seto
Kure-Matsuyama Ferry
Nigata
安芸灘大橋
C. Inumodorigahana
Menekojima I.
Ōmatsushima I.
Aki-Kawajiri
to Kure
Heraji
Congestion in summer
Kamagari-chō
蒲刈町
Mitsugojima I.
Ondo-chō
音戸町

Miyoshi-shi
Bingo-Yasuda
Kisa
Side road ahead
Kajita
Kōnu
Mt. Kōboyama
Jōge
Mt. Okadayama
Jinsekikōgen-chō
神石高原町
Odagawa River
Curves
Mt. Tōshiyama
Yano
Bingo-Yano
Narrow road -Drive slowly
Mt. Ojikayama
Mt. Mejikayama
Fukuen Line
Mt. Takeyama
Mt. Kyōnoueyama
Bingo-Mikawa
Mt. Takayama
Mt. Tenjinyama
Mt. Jaendake
Sera Plaza mae
世羅プラザ前
Sera-chō
世羅町
Kawasa
Nakahata
Shayo Center mae
車両センター前
FUCHŪ-SHI
府中市
Kibitsu-jinja
Fuchū
Ukai
Takagi
Shin-Ichi
Kami-Tode
Onomichi(Uneyama)
Mt. Uneyama
Shimo-Kawabe
Ashida River
Fukuyama street
Daiwa-chō
大和町
Onomichi
Fukuyama (Nakatsuhara)
Kui-chō
久井町
Winding slopes
Mitsugi-chō
御調町
Mt. Takamasuyama
FUKUYAMA-SHI
福山市
SAN-YŌ EXPRESSWAY
山陽自動車道
Fukuyama
福山
Hakuryūko
Kui
Hongō
Matsunaga
Bingo-Honjō
Kōchi-chō
河内町
Takasaka
高坂
Yahata
八幡
Onomichi(Uzushio)
Myōōin
Onomichi
尾道
Fukuyama-nishi
福山西
Bingo-Akasaka
Nutagawa River
Mihara-kui
三原久井
Buttsūji
Mitsugi-hachimangū
Mihara
to Hiroshima
to Onomichi
Imazuchō-Taishō 今津町大正
Matsunaga
Mt. Ryūōzan
Caution-Bump into the rear
ONOMICHI-SHI
尾道市
Shin-Onomichi
Onomichi Bypass
Higashi-Ohomichi
Caution
Shimanami-Kaidō
Hiroshima
Scenic view of Numata River
Hongō
本郷
Onomichi 12Km
Higashi-Hiroshima 38Km
Kure 72Km
Fukuyama 23Km
Mihara 12Km
Miyoshi 70Km
ORD 1300
LAR 3700
Saikokuji
Senkōji
Jōdoji
Hongō-chō
本郷町
Shinjōchō 新庄町
Keisatsu-iriguchi
警察入口
Onomichi-ōhashi(Bridge)
Hitachi Shipbuilding & Engineering
Rakuonji
Hongō-ōhashi 本郷大橋
Mitsubishi Heavy Industries
Mt. Hachigamine
San-yō Line
Mukaishima-chō
向島町
Numakuma-chō
沼隈町
Sports Shinkō Takehara
MIHARA-SHI
三原市
Onomichi-Itozaki
Kujirashima I.
Kajima I.
Momoshima I.
Bōjino-seto
TAKEHARA-SHI
竹原市
Sunami
Seaside course
Mt. Takamiyama
Tajima I.
Abuto-seto
Hososhima I.
Innoshima-ōhashi(Bridge)
Kosagishima I.
Kohososhima I.
Scenic view of Setouchi
Mt. Takayama
Yokoshima I.
Mekari-seto
Sagishima I.
Innoshima-kita
Konrenji
Ōnori
Tadanoumi
Takehara
Aki-Nagahama
Aki-Saizaki
Ategijima I.
Abashima I.
Mihara-seto
Innoshima I.
因島
Kamogawa River
Kōneshima I.
Kogunojima I.
Okunojima
Chū-Shikoku Ferry
Chigirishima I.
Karashima I.
Ōkunoshima I.
C. Tottorimisaki
Setoda-chō
瀬戸田町
Kōjōji
Kōsanji
Ikuchijima-kita
Innoshima-minami
INNOSHIMA-SHI
因島市
Sakumijima I.
Matsushima I.
Ikuchijima I.
生口島
Mt. Miyama
Taruhashijima I.
Kōmyōbō
Shindenjima I.
Ikinashima I.
Yugeshima I.
C. Kagamizaki
Mt. Kannonyama
Ōsakikamijima-chō
大崎上島町
Ikuchijima-minami
Kamijima-chō
上島町
Koyokojima I.
IMABARI-SHI
今治市
Ōmishima
Shimanami-Kaidō
Ōyamazumi-jinja
ORD 1550
LAR 4550
Ōyokojima I.
Mt. Washigatōyama
Akahonejima I.
Hanaguri-seto
Kamiura
Hakatashima I.
伯方島
Sashima I.
Sasageshima I.
Ōmishima I.
大三島
Ōmishimabashi(Bridge)
Tsubashima I.
C. Kanagasaki
Enmyōji
EHIME
Mt. Yakushisan
Kashiwajima I.
Hakatashima
Mijikashima I.
Koejima I.
to Fukuyama
to Hiroshima
Senkōji
Onomichi
95
96
67
68
E
F
G
H
1
2
3
4
5
6

B
C
Izumo-shi
Shinji-chō
D
74
73
91
92
1
2
3
4
5
6
A
Itsukaichi I.C.
Hiroshima-shi
Gotsu-shi
Asahi I.C.
Kake-chō
Togouchi I.C.
SHIMANE
Mt. Ōetakayama
Sanin-do 25
Sojiki River
Minamiyama
Misato-chō
美郷町
Kasubuchi
Chihara
Hamahara
Sawadani
Akatsuka
Gōkawa River
Iwami-Yanaze
Mt. Aosugigajōyama
Onbara
Sankō Line
Take
Mt. Iwamiyama
Kawamoto
Iwami-Kawamoto
Kirohara
Kawamoto-machi
川本町
Mt. Toyagamaruyama
Ushio
Mt. Jūmanyama
Iwami-Matsubara
Tonbara 頓原
Kijima 来島
Mt. Kotobikiyama
Mt. Ōyorogiyama
Akana River
Iinan-chō
飯南町
Mt. Funayama
Fudaga Pass
Mt. Kannamijiyama
Shikaga
Inbara
Iwami-Kawagoe
Mt. Obeshiyama
Mt. Tōkeiyama
Uokindani
Iwami-Tsuga
Mt. Shinzōjiyama
Frozen road
Mt. Menkameyama
Kutsugahara
Dangyokei
Dangyokei(Gorge)
断魚渓
Mt. Kanmuriyama
Ōtoshi Pass
Mt. Tanoharakanmuriyama
Mt. Azuma
Mt. Kanmuriyama
Kannose River
Nishime Pass
Ōnan-chō
邑南町
Uzui
Ikawashi
Kuchiba
Izuha River
Mizugoe Pass
Mt. Yojirōyama
Gōbira
Mt. Futatsuyama
Mt. Harayama
Mt. Hanzōyama
Sakugiguchi
Togauchi Pass
Mt. Ōharayama
Nagase River
Mizuho
瑞穂
Kōyodo
Congestion in spring
Ozekiohashi-kita 尾関大橋北
MIYOSHI
三次市
Misaka Pass
Mt. Inubushiyama
Enokawa River
Shikiji
Nobuki
Tokorogi
Funasa
Nagatani
Awaya
Miyoshi
Nishi-Miyoshi
Kanbikizan
Mt. Kanbikiyama
Kanbikiyama
寒曳山
Mt. Tōjiroyama
Kuriya Pass
Mt. Kumagaiyama
from Miyoshi-shi
Ōsaka 350Km
Hiroshima 70Km
Mt. Kijinomeyama
Ōasa-chō
大朝町
Iketa River
Ōasa
大朝
Mt. Bunzōyama
Gōnokawa
江の川
Apple and Cherry growing
Mt. Ōshioyama
Shiwachi
Mt. Hinoyama
HAMADA EXPRESSWAY
浜田自動車道
Mt. Heikenoshiroyama
Kami-Kawatachi
Takada
高田
Drive slowly
Takamiya-wakare 高宮分れ
Mt. Onigajōyama
Shiijihara River
Shiiya Pass
Hongō
本郷
Innai Pass
Mt. Takagoyayama
Kōtachi
Chiyoda-chō
千代田町
Mt. Tsuzurayama
Kōrinbō
Madōri Pass
Toyohira-chō
豊平町
Chiyoda Jct
千代田Jct
Chiyoda
千代田
Yachiyoko Lake
AKITAKATA-SHI
安芸高田市
Yoshidaguchi
Mt. Sarumameyama
Haji Dam
Enokawa River
CHŪGOKU EXPRESSWAY
中国自動車道
Mt. Ōzuchiyama
Katsuta-sansaro 勝田三差路
Geibi Line
Mt. Dōtokoyama
Yachiyo
Mt. Hirauneyama
Mt. Unamiyama
Mukaihara
Myōjin Pass
Kaikenzan
Mt. Akashibayama
Asa
安佐
Mt. Dōtokoyama
Ibaraichi
Mt. Tenjin
Hiroshima-kita Jct
広島北 Jct
Mt. Takanosuyama
Gōtsu 92Km
Kake 24Km
Hiroshima 27Km
Fukuōji
Hiroshima-kita
広島北
Shiwaguchi
Toyosaka-chō
豊栄町
Mt. Itanabeyama
184
54
261
375
433

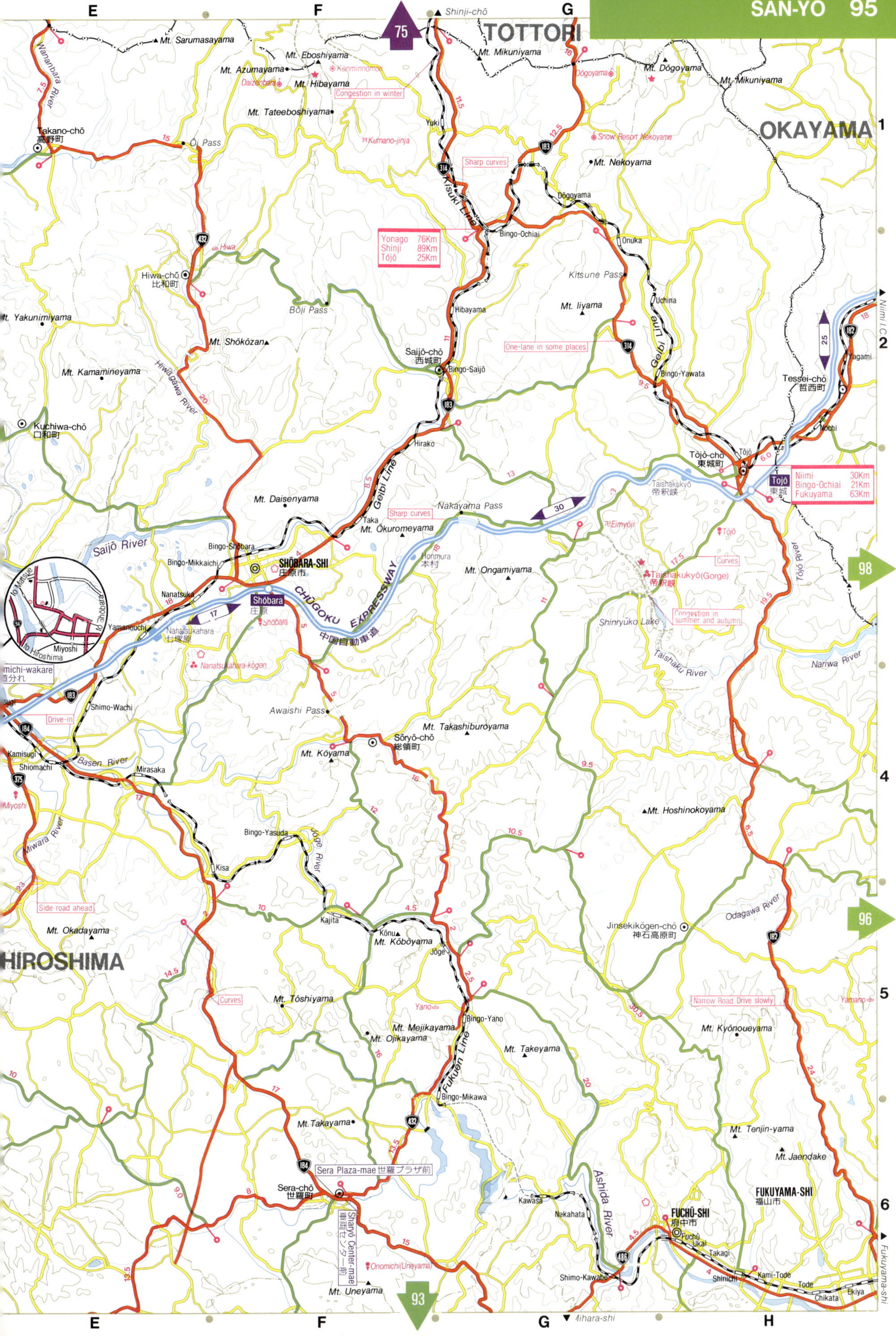
E
F
G
H
75
Shinji-chō
TOTTORI
OKAYAMA
HIROSHIMA
1
2
4
5
6
98
96
93
Mt. Sarumasayama
Nanahara River
Mt. Eboshiyama
Mt. Azumayama
Kenminnomori
Daizenbara
Mt. Hibayama
Congestion in winter
Mt. Tateeboshiyama
Mt. Mikuniyama
Dōgoyama
Mt. Dōgoyama
Mt. Mikuniyama
Takano-chō
高野町
Ōji Pass
Kumano-jinja
Yuki
Snow Resort Nekoyama
Sharp curves
Mt. Nekoyama
Kisuki Line
Dōgoyama
Hiwa
Yonago 76Km
Shinji 89Km
Tōjō 25Km
Bingo-Ochiai
Onuka
Hiwa-chō
比和町
Kitsune Pass
Bōji Pass
Hibayama
Mt. Iiyama
Uchina
Niimi I.C.
Mt. Yakunimiyama
Mt. Shōkōzan
Saijō-chō
西城町
Bingo-Saijō
One-lane in some places
Geibi Line
Mt. Kamamineyama
Hiwagawa River
Bingo-Yawata
Tessei-chō
哲西町
Yagami
Kuchiwa-chō
口和町
Hirako
Nochi
Tōjō-chō
東城町
Tōjō
Niimi 30Km
Bingo-Ochiai 21Km
Fukuyama 63Km
Tōjō
東城
Taishakukyō
帝釈峡
Mt. Daisenyama
Nakayama Pass
Sharp curves
Taka
Mt. Ōkuromeyama
Eimyōji
Tōjō
Saijō River
Bingo-Shōbara
Bingo-Mikkaichi
SHŌBARA-SHI
庄原市
Honmura
本村
Mt. Ongamiyama
Taishakukyō(Gorge)
帝釈峡
Curves
Tōjō River
Nanatsuka
Shōbara
庄原
CHŪGOKU EXPRESSWAY
中国自動車道
Congestion in summer and autumn
Shinryūko Lake
to Matsue
to Shōbara
to Hiroshima
Miyoshi
Yamanouchi
Nanatsukahara
七塚原
Shōbara
Nanatsukahara-kōgen
Taishaku River
Nariwa River
omichi-wakare
道分れ
Shimo-Wachi
Drive-in
Awaishi Pass
Mt. Takashiburoyama
Sōryō-chō
総領町
Kamisugi
Shiomachi
Basen River
Mt. Kōyama
Mirasaka
Miyoshi
Mt. Hoshinokoyama
Bingo-Yasuda
Jōge River
Miwara River
Kisa
Side road ahead
Kajita
Kōnu
Mt. Kōboyama
Jōge
Odagawa River
Jinsekikōgen-chō
神石高原町
Mt. Okadayama
Curves
Mt. Tōshiyama
Yano
Bingo-Yano
Narrow Road Drive slowly
Yamano
Mt. Mejikayama
Mt. Ojikayama
Mt. Kyōnoueyama
Mt. Takeyama
Fukuen Line
Bingo-Mikawa
Mt. Takayama
Mt. Tenjin-yama
Mt. Jaendake
Sera Plaza-mae 世羅プラザ前
Sera-chō
世羅町
Shanyō Center-mae
車両センター前
Kawasa
Nakahata
Ashida River
FUCHŪ-SHI
府中市
Fuchū
Ukai
Takagi
FUKUYAMA-SHI
福山市
Fukuyama-shi
Onomichi(Uneyama)
Mt. Uneyama
Shimo-Kawabe
Shinichi
Kami-Tode
Tode
Ekiya
Chikata
Mihara-shi

98
68
93
OKAYAMA
HIROSHIMA
Jinsekikōgen-chō
神石高原町
Narrow road-Drive slowly
Mt. Kyōnoueyama
Miwa
Yamano
Odagawa River
Yamanokyō Gorge
Mt. Umanoriyama
Mt. Kasagiyama
Yoshii-chō
芳井町
Bisei-chō
美星町
Narrow road
Onigadake
Takahashi-shi
Mt. Masakiyama
Kibi
Mt. Kōyama
Mt. Jubūzan
Yakage
Yakage-chō
矢掛町
Mabi-chō
真備町
Odagawa River
Mt. Yatakayama
Mt. Tenjin-yama
Mt. Jaendake
Senjuin
Ibara
Drive-in
Shōkakuin
IBARA-SHI
井原市
Ibara
Ibara Railway
Kōzanji
Tamashima
玉島
Tomi Pass
Funao
Mt. Abesan
Kasaoka
Yoshōzan
Kibitsu-jinja
Nakano 中野
Fukuyama (Kannabe)
Takagi
Shinichi
Kami-Tode
Tode
Chikata
Ekiya
Manguro
Michinoue
Yudamura
Fukuen Line
Kannabe-chō
神辺町
Kannabe
Mt. Ryūōzan
Mt. Myōkenzan
Kamogata
鴨方
Michiguchi
道口
Shin-Kurashiki
Konkō-chō
金光町
Konkō
Okayama
Entsūji
Sangyō-dōro
産業道路
Shinosaka
篠坂
SAN-YŌ EXPRESSWAY
山陽自動車道
Kasaoka
笠岡
Mt. Ishizuchiyama
Mermaid-Fukuyama
Fukuyama (Nakatsuhara)
Yokoo
Kamogata-chō
鴨方町
Kamogata
水玉ブリッジライン
Congestion in summer
Takahashi River
Mt. Takamasuyama
Mt. Zaozan
Fukuyama-higashi
福山東
KASAOKA-SHI
笠岡市
Kasaoka
Satoshō-chō
里庄町
Satoshō
Mizutama Bridge Line
ORD 300
LAR 1080
Fukuyama
福山
Matsunaga-Hongō
Bingo-Honjō
Caution-Bump into the rear
Fukuyama Castle
Daimon
Higashi-Fukuyama
Myōjinchō 明神町
Nishinohama
西ノ浜
San-yō Line
Side roads ahead
Matsunaga
Fukuyama
FUKUYAMA-SHI
福山市
Bingo-Akasaka
Fuchū-wakare 府中分れ
Tōjō 63Km
Kurashiki 45Km
Onomichi 23Km
Myōōin
Fukuyama
Yorishima-chō
寄島町
Mt. Ōsayama
Yorishima I.
Kamimizushima I.
Mt. Mitakeyama
C. Ōsabana
Shimomizushima I.
Kōnoshima I.
神島
Narrow road
Mizushima-nada
Fukuyama-nishi I.C.
Matsunaga
Mt. Ryūōzan
Imazuchō-Taishō
今津町大正
Mt. Hikoyama
C. Misaki
Sashideshima I.
Fukuyama
Myōchishima I.
Inatsumijima I.
Takashima I.
Ashida River
Kodakashima I.
Fukuyama-Tadotsu Ferry
C. Takanogoehana
One-lane in the street
Congestion in summer
Shiraishijima I.
C. Hajikamihana
Numakuma-chō
沼隈町
Numakuma-jinja
Ankokuji
Sensuijima I.
Tomonoura(Scenic Bay)
鞆ノ浦
Kajikoshima I.
C. Nunokoshi
Kitagishima I.
Teshima I.
Koteshima I.
Hiroshima
広島
Momoshima I.
Bojino-seto
Yanoshima I.
Tajima I.
田島
Abuto-kannon
Abuto-seto
Mt. Takayama
Scenic view of Tomo
Kajiyashima I.
Hakamajima I.
Hashirijima I.
Manabeshima I.
Yokoshima I.
Ōbishima I.
Sanagishima I.
Kojima I.
Ategijima I.
Ujishima I.
Mushima I.
Takamishima I.
Awashima I.
Shishishima I.
C. Hakozaki
Kamegasajima I.
C. Takadanibana
C. Furumisaki
Mt. Shiundeyama
Takuma-wan
Takase River
Toyoshima I.
Yosan
Takuma
Maruyamashima I.
Takumagoe Pass
Takuma-chō
詫間町
Kamo-jinja
Mino-chō
三野町
HIUCHI-NADA
燧灘
Takaikamijima I.
Tsutajima I.
Nio-chō
仁尾町
Nio Pass
Uoshima I.
Enoshima I.
Hijidai
Marukamijima I.
A
B
C
D
1
2
3
4
5
6

Tsuyama-shi
99
Okayama-Sōja
岡山総社
Okayama
岡山
SŌJA-SHI
総社市
Kibi Line
Sanyō Shinkansen
San-yō Line
OKAYAMA-SHI
岡山市
from Okayama-Shi
Ōsaka 170Km
Hiroshima 170Km
Kurata 倉田
Aoe 青江
Akō Line
SETOUCHI-SHI
瀬戸内市
Yoshii River
Asahi River
Sasagase River
Kurashiki
倉敷
Hayashima
早島
KURASHIKI-SHI
倉敷市
Hayashima-chō
早島町
Kojima-wan
Okayama Airport
Drive-in
Okayama 20Km
Sōja 11Km
Fukuyama 45Km
Kurashiki River
Mizushima-rinkai Railway
Nadasaki-chō
灘崎町
Uno Line
Utōgi 宇藤木
Mt. Jūzenjiyama
Tōdate Pass
Ryōbi Ferry
Shikoku Ferry
Shōdoshima Ferry
Shōdoshima I.
Tonoshō-chō
土庄町
TAMANO-SHI
玉野市
Uno
Nagao Pass
Scenic view of Shikoku
Mt. Shintozan
Naoshima-chō
直島町
Rupu-bashi-minami
ループ橋南
to Okayama
to Kojima
Congestion in summer
Mt. Washūzan
(Scenic View Point)
Mt. Washūzan
鷲羽山
Ferry
to Kojima
Scenic view of setouchi
Seto-chūō-jidōshadō
ORD 4100
LAR 12150
Scenic view of Kozuchi and Ōzuchi
Shikoku Ferry
Kansai Ferry
Kokusai Ferry
(to Ikeda)
62
Yashima Driveway
ORD 610
LAR 2450
Seto-ōhashi Line
Honjima-kisen
Steep slope
Takamatsu-Sakaide-dōro
ORD 260
LAR 940
Shiratori 35Km
Marugame 29Km
Kotohira 31Km
Kotō River
Yashima-nishimachi
屋島西町
Takamatsuchō 高松町
Marugame
to Matsuyama
to Takamatsu
Takamatsu 29Km
Kotohira 14Km
Toyohama 30Km
SAKAIDE-SHI
坂出市
Nishinoshō 西庄
Sakaide
坂出
Utazu-chō
宇多津町
TAKAMATSU-SHI
高松市
Ritsurin Garden
栗林公園
Kōtoku Line
Yosan Line
Chokushichō
勅使町
Takamatsu-nishi
高松西
Takamatsu-chūō
高松中央
Congestion in autumn
SANUKI-SHI
さぬき市
MARUGAME-SHI
丸亀市
Kawatsu 川津
KAGAWA
Mt. Uwasayama
Miki-chō
三木町
Tadotsu-chō
多度津町
Congestion in summer
Zentsūji
善通寺
ZENTSŪJI-SHI
善通寺市
Okada-shimo 岡田下
Enai 榎井
Takamatsu-Kotohira Railway
Ayauta-chō
綾歌町
Ryōnan-chō
綾南町
Kōnan-chō
香南町
Kagawa-chō
香川町
Takamatsu 31Km
Marugame 14Km
Toyohama 34Km
to Zentsūji
to Kōchi
Drive in
TAKAMATSU EXPRESSWAY
Dosan Line
Ayakami-chō
綾上町
Shionoe-chō
塩江町
Takasechō-Katsuoka
高瀬町勝岡
Mannō-chō
満濃町
Chūnanchō-Sogō
仲南町十郷
Kotohira-chō
琴平町
Takase
高瀬
Takase-chō
高瀬町
Chūnan-chō
仲南町
Kotonami-chō
琴南町
69
Sanuki-Toyonaka I.C.
Toyohama-chō
Naruto-shi
E
F
G
H
1
2
3
4
5
6

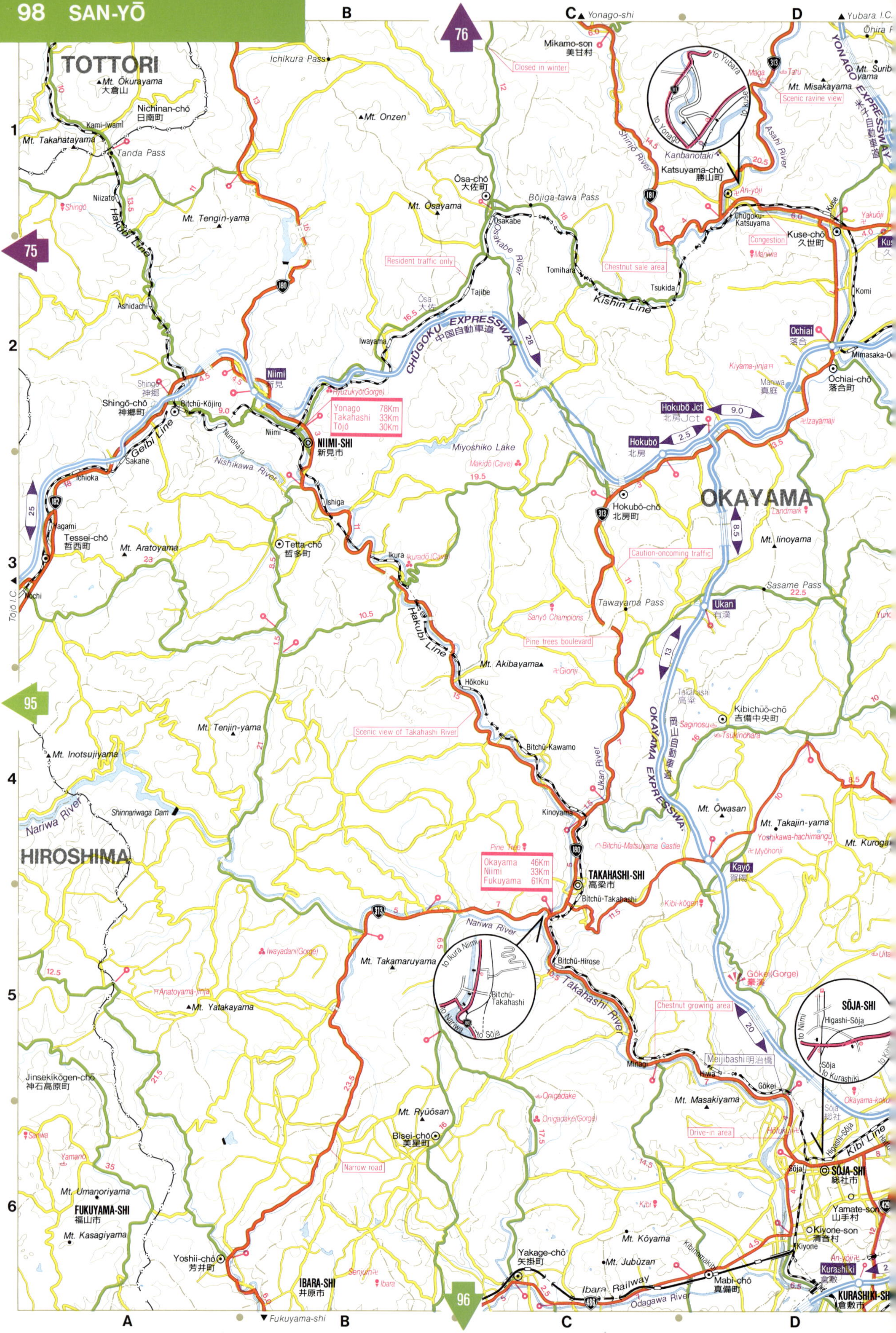

TOTTORI
HIROSHIMA
OKAYAMA
Mt. Ōkurayama 大倉山
Nichinan-chō 日南町
Kami-iwami
Mt. Takahatayama
Tanda Pass
Niizato
Shingō
Hakubi Line
Mt. Tengin-yama
Ichikura Pass
Mt. Onzen
Mt. Ōsayama
Ōsa-chō 大佐町
Bōjiga-tawa Pass
Osakabe
Osakabe River
Tomihara
Tsukida
Kishin Line
Mikamo-son 美甘村
Closed in winter
Yonago-shi
Yubara I.C.
Ōhira
Mt. Surib
Mt. Misakayama
Maga
Tatu
Scenic ravine view
YONAGO EXPRESSWAY 米子自動車道
to Yubara
to Kuse
to Yonago
Kanbanotaki
Shinjō River
Asahi River
Katsuyama-chō 勝山町
An-yōji
Chūgoku-Katsuyama
Congestion
Kuse
Kuse-chō 久世町
Yakuōji
Manwa
Chestnut sale area
Resident traffic only
Ōsa 大佐
Tajibe
Iwayama
Ashidachi
CHŪGOKU EXPRESSWAY 中国自動車道
Komi
Ochiai 落合
Mimasaka-O
Ochiai-chō 落合町
Kiyama-jinja
Maniwa 真庭
Hokubō Jct 北房Jct
Hokubō 北房
Izayamaji
Shingō 神郷
Shingō-chō 神郷町
Bitchū-Kōjiro
Niimi 新見
Hyuzukyō(Gorge)
Yonago 78Km
Takahashi 33Km
Tōjō 30Km
Niimi
NIIMI-SHI 新見市
Numohara
Nishikawa River
Geibi Line
Sakane
Ichioka
Miyoshiko Lake
Makidō(Cave)
Hokubō-chō 北房町
Landmark
Mt. Iinoyama
Yagami
Tessei-chō 哲西町
Mt. Aratoyama
Tetta-chō 哲多町
Ishiga
Ikura
Ikuradō(Cave)
Caution-oncoming traffic
Tawayama Pass
Sasame Pass
Ukan 有漢
Tōjō I.C.
Nochi
Sanyō Champions
Pine trees boulevard
Hakubi Line
Mt. Akibayama
Gionji
Hōkoku
Takahashi 高梁
Kibichūō-chō 吉備中央町
Saginosu
Tsukinohara
Yuno
Scenic view of Takahashi River
Bitchū-Kawamo
Ukan River
OKAYAMA EXPRESSWAY 岡山自動車道
Mt. Tenjin-yama
Mt. Inotsujiyama
Shinnariwaga Dam
Nariwa River
Kinoyama
Mt. Ōwasan
Mt. Takajin-yama
Yoshikawa-hachimangū
Myōhōji
Mt. Kurogar
Pine Tree
Okayama 46Km
Niimi 33Km
Fukuyama 61Km
Bitchū-Matsuyama Castle
TAKAHASHI-SHI 高梁市
Bitchū-Takahashi
Kayō 賀陽
Kibi-kōgen
Nariwa River
Iwayadani(Gorge)
Mt. Takamaruyama
to Ikura Niimi
Bitchū-Takahashi
to Nariwa
to Sōja
Bitchū-Hirose
Takahashi River
Gōkei(Gorge) 豪渓
Uta
Anatoyama-jinja
Mt. Yatakayama
Chestnut growing area
SŌJA-SHI
Higashi-Sōja
to Niimi
Sōja
to Kurashiki
Meijibashi 明治橋
Minagi
Hiwa
Gōkei
Jinsekikōgen-chō 神石高原町
Mt. Masakiyama
Okayama-koku
Onigadake
Onigadake(Gorge)
Sōja 総社
Mt. Ryūōsan
Bisei-chō 美星町
Drive-in area
Hofukuji
Higashi-Sōja
Kibi Line
Sanwa
Yamano
Narrow road
Sōja
SŌJA-SHI 総社市
Mt. Umanoriyama
FUKUYAMA-SHI 福山市
Mt. Kasagiyama
Kibi
Mt. Kōyama
Yamate-son 山手村
Kiyone-son 清音村
Kiyone
Yoshii-chō 芳井町
Yakage-chō 矢掛町
Mt. Jubūzan
Kibinomakibi
An-yōji
Kurashiki 倉敷
KURASHIKI-SHI 倉敷市
Senjumji
Ibara
IBARA-SHI 井原市
Ibara Railway
Odagawa River
Mabi-chō 真備町
Fukuyama-shi
A
B
C
D
1
2
3
4
5
6
75
76
95
96

E
F
G
H
1
2
3
4
5
6
77
100
97
Okutsu-Onsen
Tomi-son 富村
Okutsu-chō 奥津町
Yoshii River
Mt. Yagurayama
Kagamino-chō 鏡野町
Innoshō 院庄
Mimasaka-Oiwake
Mimasaka-Sendai
Sakura-jinja
Tsubo
Kume-chō 久米町
Kume
Mimasaka-Oiwake 美作追分
Ochiai Jct. 落合Jct
Kifune-jinja
Asuka
Mt. Masugatayama
Mt. Tengūjisan
Mt. Yamagatasen
Mimasaka-Takio
Shōboku-chō 勝北町
Nihonbara Plateau
Nagi-chō 奈義町
Inbi Line
Kamagawa River
Nakayama-jinja
Tsuyama
Chizu 42Km
Kurayoshi 72Km
Okayama 66Km
Takano
Tsuyama 津山
Ninomiya 二宮
Tsuyamaguchi
Tsuyama Castle
179gō-kōsaten 179号交差点
Sendōmachi 船頭町
Tsuyamaguchi Sara 津山口皿
Tsuyama
TSUYAMA-SHI 津山市
Sarayama
to Kurayoshi
Innoshō I.C.
Innoshō
to Okayama
Mt. Obusayama
Kajinami River
Katsuta-chō 勝田町
Musashi
Nihonbara
Shōō 勝央
Shōō-chō 勝央町
Mimasaka-Osa
Nishi-Katsumada
Katsumada
Mt. Taishōjin-yama
Mimasaka
美作
Mimasaka
Narahara 楢原
Narahara
Mimasaka-Emi
Sakutō-chō 作東町
Kishin Line
Hayashino
Mimasaka-chō 美作町
Chestnut growing area
Yunogō-Ishibashi
Mt. Takahinoyama
Yunogō 湯郷
Mushroom picking area
Mimasaka-Doi
Sayō I.C.
Yunogō
Poor view-slowdown
Asahi-chō 旭町
Chestnut picking area
Mt. Futakamiyama
Kamenokō
Chūō-chō 中央町
Sports-shinko-Tsuyama
Obara
Tanjōji
Tanjōji
Yanahara-chō 柵原町
Honzanji
Mt. Kōnomine
Aida-Hikari
Aida-chō 英田町
Asahigawako Lake
Wada-jinja
Komori
Asahikawa-daiichi Dam
Mt. Hongūzan
Yuge
Kumenan-chō 久米南町
Munakata-jinja
Yoshii-chō 吉井町
Chōfukuji
Bukkyōji
Taizanji
Tsuyama Line
Kōme
Hataganaru Pass
Takebe-chō 建部町
Fukuwatari
Yūmen
Sanyō Drive-in area
Mt. Myōken-yama
Bizen
Kibi-Kōgen
Yoshii River
Peach Hill
Ukan River
Takebe
Great-Okayama
Akasaka
Saeki-chō 佐伯町
Mt. Torigoeyama
Inba-Kaidō 因幡街道
Okayama-Mitsu
Saeki Pass
Wake-jinja
Yoshinaga-chō 吉永町
Yoshinaga
Akasaka-chō 赤坂町
Ida-goe Pass
Mitsu-chō 御津町
Kanagawa
Mt. Honjin-yama
Katsu Pass
Shortcut for Chūgokudō
Kumayama-chō 熊山町
Hikogi Pass
Wake-chō 和気町
Kyū-Shizutani-gakkō (Historic Site)
Mt. Myōjin-yama
Okayama-kinryō
Nonokuchi
Okayama
Kumayama
Wake 和気
to Wake
Bizen-Katakami
to Aioi
to Ushimado
Inbe-higashi 伊部東
Mimasaka 43Km
Aioi 38Km
Okayama 37Km
Bizen 備前
San-yō-chō 山陽町
Mantomi
Mt. Kanayama
Makiyama
Asahi River
San-yō 山陽
San-yō Line
Seto-chō 瀬戸町
Seto
Inbe
Nishi-Katakami
Bizen-Katakami
BIZEN-SHI 備前市
Aioi-shi
Nodani
Tomada
La Rainbow
Okayama-momonoseto
Higashi-Hirajima 東平島
Kagato
Yokoshima I.
Hinase-chō 日生町
Myōkyōji
Okayama-Sōja 岡山総社
Kibi Line
Monzen 門前
Bitchū-Takamatsu
Kibi 吉備
Okayama 岡山
Tamagashi
Bizen-Hara
Osafune
Osafune
Kōshima I.
San-yō Shinkansen
San-yō-dō 山陽道
Bizen-Ichinomiya
Hōkaiin
Takashima
Higashi-Okayama
SETOUCHI-SHI 瀬戸内市
Miwa-jinja
Saino-toge Pass
Dannoshima I.
Nagashima I.
Kishima I.
Kibitsu
Kibitsuhiko-jinja
Kibitsu-jinja
Bizen-Mikado
Daianji
Okayama
Kōrakuen (Garden)
Okayama Castle
Ōdara
Saidaiji
Akō Line
Oku
Saidaiji 西大寺
Yokeiji
Odomi
SAN-YŌ EXPRESSWAY 山陽自動車道
Uno Line
OKAYAMA-SHI 岡山市
Munetada-jinja
Ōsaka 170Km
Hiroshima 170Km
Niwase
Bizen-Nishiichi
Izumida 泉田
Kurata 倉田
C. Kaburazaki
Kongōchōji
Nakashō
Hayashima I.C.
Tamano-shi

B
C
D
78
Tottori-shi
Nishi-Awakura
Higashiawakura-son
東粟倉村
Mt. Hinakurasan
Chikusa-chō
千種町
Saiki 斉木
Haga-chō
波賀町
Bodaiji
Mt. Takaterumine
Nagi-chō
奈義町
Ōhara-chō
大原町
Ōhara
Chigusa
Inaba-kaidō
Mikata River
Mt. Funakoshiyama
Azumibashi 安積橋
Ichinomiya-chō
一宮町
Mt. Kuroosan
Higashi-Ichiba 東市場
Miyamoto-Musashi
Sayogawa River
Mt. Takiyama
Mt. Obusayama
Yoshino River
Ruriji
Iwa-jinja
Kajinami River
Tsuyama-shi
Ishii
Drive-in area
Katsuta-chō
勝田町
Chizu-Kyūkō Line
Sakushū-Musashi
Nihonbara
Mt. Taishōjinyama
Hirafuku
19.5
Ibogawa
揖保川
Sayō
佐用
Narahara
楢原
Sakutō-chō
作東町
Kōzuki
上月
Sayō-chō
佐用町
Chizu 44Km
Mimasaka 27Km
Aioi 35Km
Yamasaki-chō
山崎町
Narahara
Mimasaka-Emi
20
Mushroom picking area
Sayo
Kōzuki-chō
上月町
Nankō-chō
南光町
Yamasaki
山崎
Yasutomi-chō
安富町
Yasutomi
安富
Mimasaka-Doi
Harima-Tokusa
Mikazuki-chō
三日月町
Kōzuki
Mikazuki
20.5
Yunogō
Anji-minami 安志
Kuzaki
Kuzaki
Nishi-Kurisu
Hayashida River
OKAYAMA
Senbon
Kishin Line
Tsunogame Pass
Harima-Shingū
播磨新宮
Scenic view of Chikusa-River
Harima-Shingū
Shingū-chō
新宮町
Ōzutsumi Pass
Mt. Hattojiyama
Kōnohara-Enshin
Narrow pass
to Okayama
to Himeji
Aioi
to Akō
Mt. Shirahatayama
Mt. Minōsan
Minasaka Fall
Kurai River
Kokenawa
Yamabushi Pass
99
Aoki Isao
Higashi-Hashisaki
Sanyō-Himeji-nishi
山陽姫路西
Shira
白鷺
Tatsuno Castle
Kamigōri-chō
上郡町
TATSUNO-SHI
龍野市
6.5
Kamigōri
Tsubaki Pass
Hon-Tatsuno
Ōichi
Shikisai 飾西
Aioi(Kobe-Aioi)
Futatsugi Pass
Tatsuno
龍野
Taishi-Tatsuno
Bypass
Aoyama
Orochi 落池
Namazu Pass
鯰峠
Irino 入野
Himeji 18Km
Sayō 35Km
Bizen 38Km
Ikaruga 鵤
Harima-Shizenkōgen
-Funasaka
Akō-Kokusai
Ibogawa-chō
揖保川町
Taishi-kita
太子北
Mt. Ishidōmaruyama
Une
San-yō Line
Tatsuno-nishi
龍野西
Taishi-chō
太子町
Taishi-higashi
太子東
Wake-jinja
Yoshinaga-chō
吉永町
Higashi-une 東有年
Unehara 有年原
Tatsuno
Aboshi
Yoshinaga
14.5
Aioi
Mitsuishi
AIOI-SHI
相生市
Kyū-Shizutani-gakkō
(Historic Site)
San-yō Shinkansen
Nishi-Aioi
Congestion in spring and summer
Sanden Aboshi Line
Mt. Myōjinyama
SAN-YŌ EXPRESSWAY
山陽自動車道
Plum grove
Mitsu-chō
御津町
10.5
Fukuishi
福石
Hosaka Pass
Mt. Kuroganeyama
Sanyō-Aboshi
Akō Line
Aioi-wan
Bizen
備前
10.5
Akō
赤穂
Sakoshi
Kamo-jinja
Ibogawa River
Akō
Banshū-Akō
Sumitomo Cement
C. Kamasaki
Kimishima I.
Bizen-Katakami
Nishi-Katakami
Ōishi-jinja
AKŌ-SHI
赤穂市
Chinokaranijima I.
Tenwa
Katsurashima I.
Nakanokaranijima I.
BIZEN-SHI
備前市
Iri
Hinase-chō
日生町
Sōgo
Bizen-Fukukawa
Akō Castle
Sharp curves
Okayama-shi
Hinase
Orange picking area
C. Maobana
C. Misaki
Scenic view of Ieshima I.
Kakuishima I.
Chikusa River
Shōdoshima-kyūkō Ferry (to Fukuda)
HARIMA-NADA
播磨灘
Soshima I.
Kōshima I.
Kashirajima I.
鹿久居島
Tsurushima I.
C. Tatezaki
Ōtabushima I.
C. Osaki
Uwajima I.
Futonjima I.
Nagashima I.
Ieshima-chō
家島町
Ieshima I.
家島
Tangajima I.
男鹿島
Kishima I.
Nishinoshima I.
西島
Yanoshima I.
C. Ōsaki
C. Mikurisensaki
Bōzejima I.
Kuroshima I.
Kashima I.
Ōyakeshima I.
C. Kaburazaki
Kanakojima I.
Komatsujima I.
Takashima I.
62
A
B
C
D

79
63
102
HYŌGO
Wadayama-chō
Ikuno Pass
生野峠
Mt. Sengamine
Mt. Sasagamine
Mt. Hakusan
TANBA-SHI
丹波市
Kaibara
Congestion in summer
Drive-in
Bantan Line
Kanzaki-kita
ORD 710
LAR 1070
Bantan-renraku-dōro
(Ikuno-kita~Fukusaki)
Hōrakuji
Awaga
Narrow pass
Kami-chō
加美町
Sugihara River
Mt. Myōkensan
Onojiri Pass
Fukuchiyama Line
Sekiganji
Kugemura
Sasayama River
Funamachiguchi
Ochigawa River
Ōkawachi-chō
大河内町
Teramae
Kanzaki-minami
Kanzaki-chō
神崎町
Mt. Kasagatayama
Kasagatadera
Kaya-jinja
Niino
Naka-chō
中町
Funasaka Pass
Kurodashō-chō
黒田庄町
Kurodashō
Tsurui
Drive-in
Ichikawa-kita
Mt. Nagusayama
Nagusataki
Yachiyo-chō
八千代町
Nishiwaki
Mt. Saikōjisan
SASAYAMA-SHI
篠山市
Mt. Myōjinyama
Birdy cup
Ichikawa-chō
市川町
Ichikawa-minami
Amaji
NISHIWAKI-SHI
西脇市
Hie
Pine Lake
Shimotoda 下戸田
Golden Valley
Yumesaki-chō
夢前町
Shin-Nishiwaki
Nomura
Mt. Ōkurayama
CHŪGOKU EXPRESSWAY
中国自動車道
Fukusaki
Fukusaki-chō
福崎町
Kasai
加西
West Ones
Sun East
Zen
Kiyomizu Sports Garden
Yashiro
Sanda Lakeside
Lake Swan
Tōjōko Lake
Authent
Kasai
加西
Taki
Takino
Takino-chō
滝野町
Aoi
Yashiro-chō
社町
Drive-in area
Yumesaki River
Mizoguchi
KASAI-SHI
加西市
Kasai Inter
Hōjōmachi
Takino-Yashiro
滝野社
Yashirochō
Chōkōji
Tōjōko
Sun Royal
Kings Road
Green Ace
Yokawa-chō
吉川町
Asahi-kokusai-Himeji
Banshū-Tōyō
Sports Shinko Kasai
Fukusaki~San-yō-Himeji-higashi
Bantan renraku-dōro
Yamazono
Yashiro 社
Fukuchiyama 47Km
Himeji 28Km
Akashi 34Km
Tōjō-chō
東条町
ABC
Kuresaka Pass
Kōdera-chō
香寺町
Kōro
Funatsu
Harima-Yokota
ORD 260
LAR 410
Osa
Drive-in
Aonogahara
Green Ace
Yokawa
吉川
Shoshazan-Enkyōji
Shoshazan
Hiroshi
Hōjō Railway
Harima-Shimosato
Kawainishi
Tōjō River
Hyōgo-Tōjō
ひょうご東条
Nibuno
Tobori
Hofu
Hokkeguchi
Side road ahead
Asahi-kokusai-Tōjō
Tobori
Himeji Central Park (R.A.)
Tahara
Ono Grand
Minagi
Abiki
Jōdoji
Kansai Classic
Nozato
Kakogawa-kita
加古川北
Ao
ONO-SHI
小野市
Century Miki
Minou River
Mikiyokawa
Mt. Ishigamiyama
Olympic
Gomachi 元町
San-yō-Himeji-higashi
山陽姫路東
Ōsaka 98Km
Hiroshima 260Km
Shiroyama
Ono
Ōnotōyō
Himeji Castle
Kyōguchi
Mt. Takayama
Kashima-jinja
Gongenko
権現湖
Onomachi
Century Yoshikawa
Miki-Ono
三木小野
Kashiyama
Masters
Miki Jct
三木JCT
Rotary
Himeji
Hanada
Ichiba
Kakogawa
Harima
Cherry hills
Miki Seven Hundred
Miki
Kayama
HIMEJI-SHI
姫路市
Mt. Jinjusan
Shioo-Bessho Jct
Shikama
Takasago-kita Ramp 高砂北ランプ
Kakogawa-nishi Ramp 加古川西ランプ
Honmachi 本町
Miki Railway
Kunikane
Ishino
Bessho
Miki
MIKI-SHI
三木市
Kamitetsu Ao Line
Miki-higashi
三木東
Mt. Tanjōsan
Himeji-higashi
Bessho
Drive way
Sone
Kakogawa Line
Kanno
Yakujin
Leasure plantation
Hironogolfjō-mae
Hirono
Rokkō-kokusai-kita
Ichikawa River
Yaka
Takasago-nishi
Hoden
Hioka
Kakogawa Ramp 加古川ランプ
Higashi-Hirono
Mt. Shibureyama
Rokkō-kokusai
Clamming
Iho
TAKASAGO-SHI
高砂市
Kakogawa
KAKOGAWA-SHI
加古川市
Inami-chō
稲美町
Mt. Okkosan
Oshibedani
Kakurinji
Kakogawa Bypass
Takasago-jinja
Higashi-Kakogawa
San-yō Line
Higashi-Harima
Akashi
Mt. Takatsukayama
Kōbe-nishi
神戸西
Kōbe Steel
Kakogawa River
Akashi-nishi
Tsuchiyama
Akashi River
Dai-Kōbe
Kōbe-kokusai (Nishi-Kōbe)
Harima-chō
播磨町
Ōkubo
Daini-Shinmei-dōro
ORD 300
LAR 1060
Nishi-ku
西区
Uozumi
Okubo
Tamatsu
第二神明道路
Mt. Yokooyama
Nishi-Akashi
Suma-ku
須磨区
Suma
Sumadera
San-yō Shinkansen
Tarumi-ku
垂水区
Suzurichō 硯町
Akashi Castle
Okuradani
Akashi
Asagiri
Drive-in
Takamaru
Sumaura Park
to Miki
Akashi
to Kōbe
to Himeji
to Takasago
Ferry
Kōbe 23Km
Yashiro 34Km
Himeji 36Km
AKASHI-SHI
明石市
Maiko
Shioya
Tarumi
Akashi-kaikyō
Akashi-kaikyō-ōhashi (Bridge)
Kōbe street
E
F
G
H
1
2
3
4
5
6

HYŌGO
ŌSAKA
ŌSAKA-WAN
大阪湾
SASAYAMA-SHI
篠山市
SANDA-SHI
三田市
KAWANISHI-SHI
川西市
IKEDA-SHI
池田市
MINOO-SHI
箕面市
TAKARAZUKA-SHI
宝塚市
ITAMI-SHI
伊丹市
TOYONAKA-SHI
豊中市
SUITA-SHI
吹田市
ASHIYA-SHI
芦屋市
NISHINOMIYA-SHI
西宮市
AMAGASAKI-SHI
尼崎市
KŌBE-SHI
神戸市
ŌSAKA-SHI
大阪市
SAKAI-SHI
堺市
TAKAISHI-SHI
高石市
Nose-chō
能勢町
Toyono-chō
豊能町
Inagawa-chō
猪名川町
Tōjō-chō
東条町
Yokawa-chō
吉川町
CHŪGOKU EXPRESSWAY
中国自動車道
SAN-YO EXPRESSWAY
山陽自動車道
MAIZURU WAKASA EXPWY
舞鶴若狭自動車道
Hankyū Kōbe Line
Tōkaidō Line
Arima Line
Hanwa Line
Nankai Kōya Line
Mt. Shiragamidake
Mt. Mikunidake
Mt. Okuyama
Mt. Kokuzōsan
Mt. Senjōjisan
Mt. Ōfunayama
Mt. Atagoyama
Mt. Mikurayama
Mt. Miyama
Mt. Hangokuyama
Mt. Tsurugioyama
Mt. Kowadayama
Mt. Gyōjayama
Mt. Asahiyama
Mt. Ryōsengatake
Mt. Kōosan
Mt. Myōkensan
Mt. Tendaisan
Mt. Ishidōgao
Mt. Ōiwadake
Mt. Nagemachiyama
Mt. Taishakusan
Mt. Kongōdōjiyama
Mt. Rokkōsan
Mt. Kabutoyama
Mt. Nagasakayama
Mt. Mayasan
Tennō Pass
Nishi-tōge Pass
Halagatawa Pass
Ōsaka Pass
Ono Pass
Kiritsume Pass
Sanbon Pass
Noma Pass
Komi Pass
Hiyodorigoe Pass
Ōsaka Pass
Tōjōko Lake
Hatsuka River
Hazukawa River
Inagawa River
Minoo River
Mukogawa River
Kanzaki River
Ajigawa River
Yamato River
Ogo River
Tōjō River
Hyōgo-Tōjō
Yokawa
Kōbe-Sanda
Sanda-nishi
Kōbe Jct
Kōbe-kita
Nishinomiya-kita
Miki Jct
Kōbe-nishi
Nishinomiya
Takarazuka
Chūgoku-Ikeda
Chūgoku-Toyonaka
Amagasaki
Toyonaka
Suita
Sakai
Sakai Jct
Nishinomiya Inter
西宮インター
Nishinokuchi
西の口
Kitamura 北村
Ōsaka International (Itami)
Rokkō Island
Port Island
C. Wadamisaki
Universal Studios Japan
ユニバーサル・スタジオ・ジャパン
Ōsaka-Kōchi tokkyū Ferry(to Kōchi)
Rokkō-Kita-dōro
ORD 400
LAR 1510
Shin-Kōbe Tunnel
ORD 600
LAR 2200
Nishi-Kōbe-dōro
ORD 200
LAR 730
Daini-Shinmei-dōro
ORD 300
LAR 1060
Harbor Highway
ORD 200
LAR 200
Congestion in autumn
ORD 250
LAR 900
Dōyu Driveway
ORD 800
LAR 3200
Namihaya-Ōhashi
ORD 100
LAR 360
Nagoya 210Km
Hiroshima 350Km
Ōhama-Kita machi 大浜北町
Ōsaka 17Km
Kawachi-Nagano 17Km
Izumi-Otsu 11Km
Kitajima 北島
Congestion
Leisure Plantation
Iris garden
Drive in area
Along mountain torrent
Congestion in spring and summer
Frozen road
Narrow and curves
Mashroom picking area
Sharp curve
to Nose
to Takarazuka
to Ōsaka
to Nanba
to Sakai
Suminoe
住之江
Wakayama-shi
A
B
C
D
1
2
3
4
5
6
82
101
63
110

E
F
G
H
83
111
126
1
2
3
4
5
6
Biwako Lake
KYŌTO-SHI 京都市
KAMEOKA-SHI 亀岡市
Mt. Ushimatsuyama
Mt. Atagoyama
Mikyōsaka Pass
Kita-ku 北区
Kamigyō-ku 上京区
Sakyō-ku 左京区
Nakagyō-ku 中京区
Ukyō-ku 右京区
Shimogyō-ku 下京区
Higashiyama-ku 東山区
Nishikyō-ku 西京区
Minami-ku 南区
Fushimi-ku 伏見区
Yamashina-ku 山科区
MORIYAMA-SHI 守山市
KUSATSU-SHI 草津市
ŌTSU-SHI 大津市
RITTŌ-SHI 栗東市
Ōmi-ōhashi
ORD 150
LAR 570
ORD 1150
LAR 4650
ORD 1000
LAR 2800
ORD 930
LAR 3350
Nagoya 160Km
Ōsaka 45Km
Karasuma-Gojō 烏丸五条
Keihankokudōguchi 京阪国道口
Kyōto-minami 京都南
Kyōto-higashi 京都東
Seta-higashi 瀬田東
Kusatsu-tanakami 草津田上
Seta-nishi
Mt. Senzudake
Keiji Bypass
Mt. Hakamagoshiyama
SHIGA
Mt. Daishinyama
Mt. Inoseyama
MUKŌ-SHI 向日市
NAGAOKAKYŌ-SHI 長岡京市
Ōyamazaki-chō 大山崎町
Shimamoto-chō 島本町
Ōtesuji 大手筋
Ōyamazaki 大山崎
Kumiyama-chō 久御山町
Ōkubo 大久保
Shimo-Nara 下奈良
UJI-SHI 宇治市
Mt. Kisenyama
Mt. Ōminesan
Zenjōji Pass
YAWATA-SHI 八幡市
JŌYŌ-SHI 城陽市
Ujitawara-chō 宇治田原町
Urajiro Pass
Mt. Jūbuzan
KYŌTO
MEISHIN EXPRESSWAY
TAKATSUKI-SHI 高槻市
IBARAKI-SHI 茨木市
HIRAKATA-SHI 枚方市
Deyashiki-minami 出屋敷南
Yamashiro-ōhashi-higashizume 山城大橋東詰
Ikenomiya-kita 池之宮北
Amanogawa 天の川
Nakaburi 中振
KYŌTANABE-SHI 京田辺市
Ide-chō 井手町
Mt. Ōyakiyama
Mt. Mitsugatake
Wazuka-chō 和束町
KATANO-SHI 交野市
SETTSU-SHI 摂津市
Settsu-kita 摂津北
ORD 700
LAR 1950
Mt. Mikamiyama
Mt. Yuyasan
Minamiyamashiro-mura 南山城村
Seika-chō 精華町
Kasagi-chō 笠置町
Takayama Dam
NEYAGAWA-SHI 寝屋川市
SHIJŌNAWATE-SHI 四條畷市
Yamashiro-chō 山城町
Kamo-chō 加茂町
Kamikoma 4 上狛四
Kizu 木津
Kizu-chō 木津町
Higashi-Nakano 東中野
KADOMA-SHI 門真市
DAITŌ-SHI 大東市
Daitō-Tsurumi 大東鶴見
Higashiōsaka-kita 東大阪北
Ueno 46Km
Tsu 93Km
Kashihara 19Km
ORD 800
LAR 2300
IKOMA-SHI 生駒市
HIGASHIŌSAKA-SHI 東大阪市
Mt. Ikomayama 生駒山
Kuragari Pass
NARA-SHI 奈良市
ORD 1720
LAR 5130
Nara-Okuyama Driveway
Mt. Kōnosan
YAMATOKŌRIYAMA-SHI 大和郡山市
ORD 1300
LAR 5200
NARA
Mt. Shiroyama
Kintetsu Nara Line
Higashiōsaka-minami 東大阪南
YAO-SHI 八尾市
Heguri-chō 平群町
Ikaruga-chō 斑鳩町
Andō-chō 安堵町
Yokota 横田
Kōriyama
Tenri
TENRI-SHI 天理市
Tsuge-mura 都祁村
Sangō-chō 三郷町
Andō 安堂
Nara 30Km
Ōsaka 19Km
Kashihara 22Km
KASHIWARA-SHI 柏原市
Ōji-chō 王寺町
Hōryuji 法隆寺
Kawanishi-chō 川西町
Kaho 嘉穂
Miyake-chō 三宅町
NISHI-MEIHAN EXPRESSWAY
FUJIIDERA-SHI 藤井寺市
HABIKINO-SHI 羽曳野市
KASHIBA-SHI 香芝市
Kanmaki-chō 上牧町
Kawai-chō 河合町
Kōryō-chō 広陵町
Tawaramoto-chō 田原本町
Mt. Ryūōyama
Mt. Kaigahirayama
Mt. Tenjinsan
Mt. Miwasan
Murō-mura 室生村
Kōzui Pass
Taishi-chō 太子町
YAMATOTAKADA-SHI 大和高田市
KASHIHARA-SHI 橿原市
SAKURAI-SHI 桜井市
Haibara-chō 榛原町
Kintetsu Minami Osaka Line
Sakura Pass
Hasegawa River
Kizugawa River
Yodogawa River
Katsura River
Ujigawa River

B
C
D
Hisai I.C
126
127
103
111
107
Matsusaka
to Ise
Shorenji
Akameguchi
NABARI-SHI
名張市
IGA-SHI
伊賀市
Nunobiki Pass
Ise-Takehara
Kintetsu Ōsaka Line
Murō Royal
Leasure vineyard
Akame
Sanbonmatsu
Murōguchi-Ono
Murō-mura
室生村
Mt. Nagasakayama
Enjun
Akame Waterfalls
赤目四十八滝
Shōrenji River
Caution-Monkeys
Nabari River
Sakura Pass
Mt. Amagatake
Misugi-mura
美杉村
Meishō Line
Ise-Kamakura
Iseyashi
Misugi
Kumozu River
Hatemata River
Mt. Higeyama
Hossaka Pass
Ibutaji
Mt. Hossakayama
Hosono Pass
Mt. Amagoiyama
Hitsu
Hitsu Pass
Sakurai-shi
Murōji
室生寺
Mt. Kunimiyama
Mt. Kurosoyama
Mt. Ōborayama
Ise-Okitsu
Kitabatake-jinja
Mt. Sumizukayama
Soni-mura
曽爾村
Mt. Kogosan
伊勢本街道
Mt. Takasunomine
Mt. Shiraisan
Fudōin
Isehon-kaidō
Togasaka Pass
Mitsue-mura
御杖村
Seiwa-mura
勢和
Mt. Tsubonegatake
Mt. Karasudake
Sakura Pass
Mt. Miuneyama
Kushida River
Mt. Takamiyama
Takami Pass
Ise-kaidō
伊勢街道
Mt. Takahachiyama
Wakayama-kaidō
和歌山街道
Closed in winter
Caution-Bump into the rear
Misedani
Higashiyoshino-mura
東吉野村
Ōdai-chō
大台町
Mt. Kunimiyama
Okukahadakyō
Miyagawa-mura
宮川村
Takihara
Mt. Sengenyama
Ōmiya-chō
大宮町
Mt. Mayoidake
Ōuchiyama River
Aso
NARA
Mt. Ryūzuyama
Mt. Yoshinoyama
Kawakami-mura
川上村
Mt. Shirakurayama
Mt. Ikegoyayama
Kisei-chō
紀勢町
Mt. Gyōjasan
Ise-Kashiwazaki
Kowa Pass
古和峠
Mt. Shirahigedake
Kongōji
Miyakawa Dam
Mt. Kunimiyama
Mt. Ōkōchiyama
Ōuchiyama
Ōuchiyama-mura
大内山村
Mt. Yagamine
Yoshino River
Mt. Komoriyama
Mt. Uchisan
Drive-in area
Nishiki Pass
Mt. Takenotaoyama
Narrow and sharp curves
Mt. Senchiyogamine
Accident-prone area
Nisaka Pass
Mt. Obagamine
Obamine Pass
Ōdaigahara Driveway
大台ヶ原ドライブウェイ
Higashi-Kumano-kaidō
Mt. Himekoshiyama
Zasaike Lake
Fudōtaki
Mt. Ōkōchiyama
Arikuji
Ōsugi Gorge
Senhirodaki
Kii-Nagashima
Tomoedaki
Hikarutaki
Fudōtaki
Mitsutaki
MT. ŌDAIGAHARA
大台ヶ原
Mt. Kyōgamine
Kiinagashima-chō
紀伊長島町
Takanoshima I.
Komejima I.
Futagoshima I.
Akabane River
Mt. Hinodegatake
Nishinotaki
Ogimoridaki
Koesukijima I.
Ōesukijima I.
Mimianajima I.
Kodochi River
Ōdaigahara
大台ヶ原
Maruyamajima I.
Akanoshima I.
Minose
Suzushima I.
Ōshima I.
Kisei Line
Funatsu
Funatsu River
Ōtanuma Lake
Sabarujima I.
Kamikitayama-mura
上北山村
Dorohatchō
Mt. Tochiyama
Mt. Takamaruyama
Shiraishiko Lake
Aiga
Miyama-chō
海山町
Mt. Binshiyama
Mt. Hiyoriyama
C. Edohana
Sakamoto Dam
Sakabachō 坂場町
Nagoya 170Km
Ōsaka 340Km
OWASE-SHI
尾鷲市
Owase
Suzumejima I.
C. Binasohana
Terashima I.
Owase-wan
Sabarujima I.
Kumano-shi
A
B
D

E
F
G
H
1
2
3
4
5
6
132
127
132
Tsu-shi
Central Glass
Kaminoshō
Harai River
Matsusaka
松阪
Matsusaka Park
Miyamachi 宮町
MATSUSAKA-SHI
松阪市
Higashi-Matsusaka
Tsu 17Km
Ise 20Km
Kumano 120Km
Meiwa-chō
明和町
Tokuwa
Kushida
Koishiro
Saikū
Kintetsu Yamada Line
Kisei Line
Myōjō
Akeno Airport
Akeno
ISE EXPRESSWAY
Matsusaka
Taki
Sangū Line
Obata-chō
小俣町
Miyagawa
Omata
Misono-mura
御薗村
Miyagawa River
Hōsenji
Taki-chō
多気町
Ōka
Tokida
Tamaru
Miyamachi
Iseshi
Ise-jingū-gegū
伊勢神宮外宮
Futami-kaidō-iriguchi 二見街道入口
Sana
Taki
多気
Tamaki-chō
玉城町
Matsusaka 20km
Toba 14km
Nansei 21km
Ise-nishi
伊勢西
Niu-taisha
Seiwa-Taki
勢和多気
Tamaki
玉城
Mt. Sengenyama
Mt. Kuzukayama
Tochihara
Ise-jingū-naigū
伊勢神宮内宮
Scenic sunrise view of Mt. Asamagatake
Mt. Kamijiyama
Mt. Maeyama
Mt. Shūrei
Watarai-chō
度会町
MIE
Iseshi
Ise I.C
to Futami
to Matsusaka
to Toba
Futami-no-ura(Rocks)
Futami-chō
二見町
Futaminoura
Ise-sengokujidaimbia
伊勢二見鳥羽ライン
ISE-SHI
伊勢市
Ise
伊勢
Asama
Isuzugaoka
Ise-Toba-Futami Line
ORD 200
LAR 600
Mt. Asamagatake
Ikenoura
Matsushita
Ushijima I.
Tōshijima I.
C. Kōzakimisaki
Ise-wan Ferry (to Irago)
C.Shirasaki
TOBA-SHI
鳥羽市
Toba
Sakatejima I.
Mt. Ōyama
Sugashima I.
Pearl Island(Pearl Museum)
Nakanogō
Shima-Akazaki
伊勢志摩スカイライン
Ise-Shima Skyline
ORD 1220
LAR 4900
Mt. Maruyama
Funatsu
Ōura-wan
Ōmurajima I.
Kamo
Matsuo
Shiraki
Kintetsu-Shima Line
Gochi Pass
五知峠
Shōfukuji
Mt. Aomineyama
Mt. Sengenyama
C. Yoroizaki
パールロード
Toba
Kajiya Pass
Mt. Ushikusayama
Tsurugi Pass
Mt. Shishigatake
Mt. Nanahoradake
Kutsukake
Shima-Isobe
Shima Spain Village
Matoya-wan
C. Anorizaki
安乗崎
Iseno-ura
Anagawa
Mt. Ryūsenzan
Nansei-chō
南勢町
Nanukajima I.
SHIMA-SHI
志摩市
Ugata
Gokasho-wan
Mt. Yokoyama
Kashikojima
Hamajima
Congestion in summer
C. Jōnosaki
Nomizaka Pass
Miura Pass
Caution-weak road shoulder
Kashikojima
Kashikojima
Nemunosato(S.C.)
Tendōjima I.
Mt. Takayama
Aiharajima I.
C. Tomarinohana
Nantō-chō
南島町
Mt. Tsubonegadaki
Seafood sale area
Ago-wan
Daiōjima I.
C. Daiōzaki
大王崎
C. Gozamisaki
御座岬
Nie-wan
Nayano-ura
Bentenjima I.
Kokata Pass
小方峠
Kamizaki-wan
C. Shidonohana
Fukaya-suidō
C. Mugisaki
Mieshima I.
Tenjinyama
Houza-ura
C. Jōnohana
Kojima I.
Ōshima I.
C. Kakezaki
Hekonoshima I.
E
F
G
H

B
C
D
111
Mt. Yoshinoyama
Kawarahi River
Asahi River
Biggest suspension bridge in Japan
Mt. Shakagatake
釈迦ヶ岳
Kamikitayama-mura
上北山村
Mt. Kotōgeyama
Mt. Tenguyama
Sakamoto Dam
Mt. Obakodake
伯母子岳
Mt. Tenjikuyama
Takigawa River
Sasanotaki
Mt. Nehandake
Mt. Okusatayama
Ikehara Dam
Kazaya Dam
Mt. Hosuoyama
Mt. Nakahachinin-yama
Kanno River
NARA
Sharp curves
Shimokitayama-mura
下北山村
Mt. Gyōsendake
Tosenji
Ashinose River
Higashi-Kumano-Kaidō
東熊野街道
Mt. Gakematayama
Totsukawa-mura
十津川村
Mt. Ōmoriyama
Mt. Kasasuteyama
WAKAYAMA
Ushimawashi-goe Pass
Closed in winter
Mt. Tenjōzen
Nishikawa River
Totsukawa River
Nanayasunotaki
Mt. Dagueyama
Mt. Onoyama
Mt. Amedaniyama
Nanairo Dam
Mt. Maruoyama
Mt. Nishinomine
北山村
Kuzugawa River
Mt. Tenjinmaruyama
Mt. Higureyama
Totsukawa
十津川
Kitayama River
Hikiushi-goe Pass
Kamiyu River
Mt. Tamakisan
Tamaki-jinja
Mitsutaki
Mt. Wadamori
Futatsuno Dam
Mt. Andoyama
Mt. Ōhiratayama
Dorohatchō(Gorge)
瀞八丁
Mt. Nagaoyama
Mt. Tsuenomine
Fudatate Pass
Mt. Kashiomoriyama
Kiwa-chō
紀和町
Mt. Shirokurayama
Mt. Hyakuzenmoriyama
Mt. Nishinomineyama
Mt. Senjōsan
Seijun
Mt. Takachirayama
Yunokuchi
Mt. Ichizokuyama
Fuden Pass
Shirahama-Onsen
Gojō 110Km
Shingū 35Km
Tanabe 69Km
Mt. Ōseyama
Mikoshi Pass
Hongū-chō
本宮町
Mt. Takaoyama
Kobiro Pass
Mt. Yōgaimoriyama
Kumanohongū-taisha
熊野本宮大社
Drive-in area
Kōshiya
Yunomine
Torohatchō jet-boat boarding
Kii-Ichigi
Kumano-Kaidō 熊野街道
Mt. Ōchiyama
Mt. Asamayama
Mt. Ōkamidawayama
Yomura River
Kawayu
Mihama-chō
御浜町
Kumanogawa-chō
熊野川町
Atawa
Mt. Nyohōsan
Hikigawa River
to Totsugawa
Yunomine
Akagi River
Mt. Zakōyama
Oroshi River
Mt. Nodakehōshi
Ōtō River
Open-air hot spring
Meototaki
Ayukaeridaki
Kisei Line
Mt. Dakeyama
to Asso
to Singū
Mt. Ōeboshiyama
Ōsugidaki
Mt. Kashiyama
Mt. Shiramiyama
Kiho-chō
紀宝町
Yasukawa River
Ōtō-mura
大塔村
Ainodani River
Narukawa 成川
SHINGŪ-SHI
新宮市
Udono
Kumanohayatama-taisha
Udono-mura
鵜殿村
Mt. Hōshiyama
Mt. Ōtōyama
Mt. Ōkurahatayama
Shingū
Mt. Ashigōyama
Hashimoto 橋本
from Shingū-shi
Nagoya 230Km
Ōsaka 280Km
Mt. Nyūdoyama
Mt. Ōkumotoriyama
Ōkumotori-goe Pass
Kumano Kaidō
to Asahi
to Kumano
Mt. Eboshiyama
Mt. Takaoyama
WAKAYAMA
Mt. Mineyama
Mt. Nachisan
Miwasaki
Suzushima I.
Nachidaki(Fall)
那智滝
to Kusimoto
Kii-Sano
Kushima I.
Seigantoji
Kumanonachitaisha
Mt. Hibanomori
那智山スカイライン
Ukui
Akajima I.
Mt. Shōgun-yama
Mt. Daishiyama
Kozagawa River
Nachisan Skyline
Amidaji
Nachikatsuura
ORD 400
LAR 1600
Nachi-ekimae 那智駅前
Fudarakusanji
Katsuura Public
C. Komagasaki
Nachi
Kii-Tenma
Bentenjima I.
Katsuura
勝浦
Mt. Kasagiyama
Mt. Toyakurayama
Kii-Katsuura
Nachikatsuura-chō
那智勝浦町
Nakajima I.
Yamanarijima I.
Mt. Takayama
Tsurushima I.
Yukawa
Katsuojima I.
Kogawa River
Yukawa
Moriura 森浦
Yunohana
C. Tōmyōzaki
Taiji
Taiji-chō
太地町
Samoto River
Ōtō River
Mt. Toyanomoriyama
C. Kajitorizaki
Shimosato
109
A
B
C
D

E
F
G
104
MIE
Mt. Tochiyama
Mt. Takamaruyama
Aiga
Miyama-chō
海山町
Mt. Hiyoriyama
Mt. Binshiyama
Mataguchi River
425
Sakabachō 坂場町
Owase
OWASE-SHI
尾鷲市
Owase-wan
Suzumejima I.
C. Binasohana
Sabarujima I.
Tōgashima I.
Ōsoneura
Kumano-Kaidō 熊野街道
Mt. Yakiyama
Mt. Takamineyama
Bad road
Mt. Itadakiyama
C. Kukizaki
九木崎
Yanoko Pass
Kisei Line
Takashiroyama
Mikisato
Mt. Hoiroyama
Mt. Taninoyama
Mt. Igataniyama
311
Mt. Gejoyama
Ōmata River
C.Mikisaki
三木崎
Kata
Mt. Ryūmonzan
Hatchō Pass
Nigishima
Mt. Daijamine
C. Tategasaki
Kosaka Pass
Atashika
Odomari
Hadasu
KUMANO-SHI
熊野市
Matsusaka 120Km
Kashihara 130Km
Shingū 26Km
Kumanoshi
Onigajō (Scenic Rocky Coast)
Arii
42
to Matsusaka
Kumanoshi
to Miki I.
to Narairokyo
to Shingū
KUMANO-NADA
熊野灘
1
2
3
4
5
6
E
F
G
H

A
B
C
D
1
2
3
4
5
6
110
Mt. Shigeyama
Arishima I.
Yura-chō
由良町
Mt. Yakushidaniyama
Mt. Koyama
Mt. Inugatakeyama
Miyama-mura
美山村
Kashiwa Pass
Hidaka-chō
日高町
Kii-Uchihara
Kawabe
Yuasa-Gobō-dōro
Mt. Seireizan
Mt. Yahazudake
Dōjōji
Sougawa River
Nakaiso
Komatsubara-nishi 小松原西
Kawabe-chō
川辺町
Mt. Wasayama
Hotokenokushi Pass
Mt. Nishiyama
Gobō
Mt. Shiroyama
Ryūjin-mura
竜神村
Miham-chō
美浜町
GOBŌ-SHI
御坊市
Gobō
御坊
Wasa
Mt. Mazumayama
Mt. Sanrigamine
Kainan 49Km
Ryūjin 57Km
Tanabe 33Km
Nishi-Gobō
Gobō-minami
御坊南
Sasa Pass
笹峠
Kōya 68Km
Gobō 57Km
Tanabe 33Km
C. Hinomisaki
日ノ御崎
Hidaka River
Hidaka
Kita-Shioya 北塩屋
Kisei Line
Mt. Gyōjayama
Kinan
Mt. Kuroiwayama
Inahara
Toragamine Pass
Mt. Toragamine
Hakoya Pass
C. Kabegozaki
Mt. Takashiroyama
Mt. Akamatsuyama
Greenhill Wakayama
Kumano-kaidō
熊野街道
Inami
印南
Inami-chō
印南町
WAKAYAMA
Mt. Mioyama
Drive-in
Kido Pass
Nakahechi-chō
中辺路
Kirime River
Kirime
Mt. Noroshiyama
Mt. Ryūjinsan
Kogome Pass
Mt. Makiyama
C. Kirimezaki
Mt. Takadayama
Hayagawa River
Mt. Takaoyama
Iwashiro
Minabe
みなべ
Nanryūsen-iriguch 南竜線入口
Minabe
C. Metsuzaki
Minabe-chō
みなべ町
Asso-kaidō
朝来街道
to Ryūjin
Koizumi-kita 小泉北
Kashima I.
Haya
Gobō 33Km
Hongū 69Km
Shingū 93Km
Mt. Ōmoriyama
Kii-Tanabe
to Shirahama
Motoshima I.
C. Ōhana
Tōkei-jinja
TANABE-SHI
田辺市
Kii-Shinjō
Mt. Takahatayama
Ōtō-mura
大塔村
Tanabe-wan
Mt. Mugikomori
Kashima I.
Hatakejima I.
Asso
C. Banshonozaki
Shisōjima I.
Fujishima I.
Kamitonda-chō
上富田町
Shirahama
白浜
Shirahama Beach
from Shirahama
Ōsaka 180Km
Nagoya 340Km
Shirahama-chō
白浜町
Adventure World (Safari Park)
Yubinbashi 郵便橋
C. Setozaki
瀬戸崎
Shirahama
Mt. Jōnomoriyama
Scenic view of Pacific Ocean
Nanki-Shirahama
Minami Shirahama Dōro
to Tanabe
Kii-Tonda
Tondabashi 富田橋
to Shirahama
Tonda River
Sōdōji
Mt. Shiozuyama
Mt. Mimaiyama
Kyū-Kumano-kaidō
旧熊野街道
Kii-Tanabe
Tsubaki
Mt. Yoneyama
to Shingū
Tsubaki
Hikigawa River
Mt. Takaseyama
C. Ichiezaki
Kii-Hiki
Hikigawa-chō
日置川町
Hiki-Ōhashi 日置大橋
C. Atagisaki
Susami
すさみ
Susami
C. Wabukasaki

Kōya-chō
E
F
G
H
106
111
Gojō-shi
NARA
MIE
Ryūjin
龍神街道
Ushimawashigoe Pass
Mt. Ushimawashiyama
Closed in winter
Mt. Tenjōzen
Mt. Maruoyama
Totsukawa River
Mt. Onoyama
Mt. Dagueyama
Mt. Amedaniyama
Mt. Nishinomine
Kitayama-mura
北山村
Kitayama River
Totsukawa
十津川
Hikiushigoe Pass
Kamiyu River
Mt. Tamakisan
Ōkuboyama
Mt. Wadamori
Mt. Andoyama
Futatsuno Dam
Mt. Ōhiratayama
Dorohatchō(Gorge)
瀞八丁
Niuno River
Mt. Kashiomoriyama
Mt. Hyakuzenmoriyama
Mt. Tsuenomine
Kiwa-chō
紀和町
Mt. Shirokurayama
Kumano-shi
Mt. Kasatōyama
Mt. Senjosan
Seijun
Yunokuchi
Mt. Ichizokuyama
Fūden Pass
Drive-in
Gojō 110Km
Shingū 35Km
Tanabe 69Km
Mt. Fujineyama
Mt. Ōseyama
Mikoshi Pass
Kumanohongū-taisha
熊野本宮大社
Mt. Takaoyama
Kobiro Pass
Mt. Yogaimoriyama
Hongū-chō
本宮町
Yunomine
Mt. Takahoshiyama
Mt. Ōtōyama
Mt. Ōkamidawayama
Mt. Ōhorayama
Mt. Ōchiyama
Kumano-kaidō
熊野街道
Yomura River
Kawayu
Open-air hot spring
Mt. Nyōhōsan
Kumanogawa-chō
熊野川町
Shingū (Kumano) River
Mt. Akushirōyama
Ōtō River
Akagi River
Mt. Zakōzan
Mt. Masakiyama
Mt. Nodakehōshi
Meototaki
Ayukaeridaki
Mt. Nishinomine
Mt. Dakeyama
Ōsugidaki
Ōtō Gorge
Mt. Kashiyama
Mt. Shiramiyama
Yasukawa River
Mt. Fudontonomine
Mt. Hansarei
Mt. Hōshiyama
Mt. Ōtōyama
大塔山
Mt. Ōkurahatayama
Mt. Ashigōyama
Mt. Ōkumotoriyama
Ōkumotorigoe Pass
大雲取越
SHINGŪ-SHI
新宮市
Hashimoto 橋本
Mt. Nyūdōyama
Mt. Handamine
Mt. Takaoyama
Mt. Eboshiyama
Mt. Mineyama
Mt. Nachisan
那智山
Mt. Hikarigamine
Mt. Kongōnomine
Mt. Mizugaitoyama
Nachidaki(Fall)
那智滝
Seigantoji
Kumanonachitaisha
那智山スカイライン
Kii-Sano
Ūgui
Shōgun River
Maeno River
Mt. Daishiyama
Mt. Hibanomori
Nachisan Skyline
ORD 400
LAR 1600
Amidaji
Nachikatsuura
Fudarakusanji
Katsuura Public
Mt. Shōgunyama
Hirai River
C. Shirasuhana
C. Komagasaki
Kii-Tenma
Nachi-ekimae 那智駅前
Mt. Kasagiyama
Mt. Toyakurayama
Kogawa River
Mt. Takaoyama
Nachikatsuura-chō
那智勝浦町
Katsuura
勝浦
Kii-Katsuura
Nakajima I.
Tsurushima I.
Yukawa
Zenjinomoriyama
Mt. Jūzenyama
Yunohana
古座街道
Koza-kaidō
Samoto River
Mt. Toyanomoriyama
C. Tōmyōzaki
燈明崎
Taiji-chō
太地町
Shimosato
Moriura 森浦
C. Kajitorizaki
梶取崎
Shishime Pass
Mt. Horayama
Mt. Takamine
Mt. Hachirōyama
Ōta River
Koto-no-taki (Fall)
Susami River
Mt. Iyayama
Kii-Uragami
Tamanoura
C. Miminohana
耳ノ鼻
C. Fukuranomonzaki
Kokashi Pass
Kozagawa River
Kozagawa-chō
古座川町
Kii-Tahara
Kumano-kaidō
Mt. Shimizuyama
Mt. Nishinomineyama
Mt. Kasaneyama
Koza-chō
古座町
Koza
C. Moritosaki
Mirozu
Esumi
Wabuka 和深
Rokurō Pass
Kumano-kaidō
Inokuroshima I.
熊野街道
Karekinada-kaigan
Scenic Rocky Coast
C. Misaki
Tako
Kisei Line
Kii-Hime
Hakojima I.
C. Esuzaki
Yokojima I.
Sōjima I.
Tahami
Kii-Arita
Drive-in
Hashikui-iwa(Scenic Rocky Coast)
C. Toshimazaki
Drive-in
Muryōji
Kushimoto
Kushimoto-chō
串本町
Katsuojima I.
C. Kashinozaki
樫野崎
Ōshima I.
to Tanabe
to Katsuura
to C. Shionomisaki
Shionomisaki-nishi-iriguchi 潮岬西入口
Tsuyajima I.
C. Suezaki
C. Izumozaki
C. Shionomisaki
潮岬
1
2
3
4
5
6

102
108
63
ŌSAKA
ŌSAKA-WAN
大阪湾
WAKAYAMA
Sakai 11Km
Kawachi-Nagano 21Km
Wakayama 46Km
IZUMIŌTSU-SHI
泉大津市
Ōsaka street
KISHIWADA-SHI
岸和田市
IZUMI-SHI
和泉市
KAIZUKA-SHI
貝塚市
IZUMISANO-SHI
泉佐野市
SENNAN-SHI
泉南市
Kansai International Airport
HANNAN-SHI
阪南市
Tajiri-chō
田尻町
Kumatori-chō
熊取町
Kishiwada-Izumi
岸和田和泉
Izumisano Jct
泉佐野Jct
Izumisano
Kaizuka
Kaminogō
Hannan
Sennan
HANWA EXPRESSWAY
KANSAI KŪKŌ EXPRESSWAY
Hanwa Line
Nankai Line
Kūkō-renraku Railway
Nankai-Awaji Line(to Tsuna)
Kogigawa River
Mt. Kōnoyama
Mt. Iwaoyama
Mt. Mikuniyama
Mt. Ōishigamine
Mt. Katsurakisan
Nabetani Pass
Mt. Mitsumineyama
Mt. Yotsuishiyama
Kazefuki Pass
Onoyama Pass
Mt. Manaitaishiyama
Mt. Fudatateyama
Mt. Higashiyama
Mt. Kabutoyama
Mt. Hachimakiyama
Kyōshi Pass
C. Kurosaki
C. Kannonzaki
C. Myōjinzaki
Kadano-seto
Misaki-chō
岬町
Tannowa 淡輪
Tottori 鳥取
Tarui 樽井
Nankai Kada Line
Kinokawa-kakō-ōhashi
紀ノ川河口大橋
ORD 100
LAR 350
from wakayama-Shi
Ōsaka 70Km
Nagoya 440Km
WAKAYAMA-SHI
和歌山市
Wakayama
Kinokawa River
Wakayama Line
Nankai Kishigawa Line
Mt. Shirogamine
Scenic view of Kinokawa River
Iwade-chō
岩出町
Bizen 備前
Miya 宮
Uchita-chō
打田町
Kokawa 粉河
Kokawa-chō
粉河町
Naga-chō
那賀町
Anabushi 穴伏
Katsuragi
かつらぎ
Momoyama-chō
桃山町
Kishigawa-chō
貴志川町
Mt. Ryūmonzan
Mt. Iimoriyama
Mt. Karasumine
Ichi Pass
Kurokawa Pass
Tomobuchi River
Mt. Atagoyama
Zakuro River
Kishigawa River
Mt. Ameyama
Nankai Ferry (to Tokushima)
Ōshima I.
Futagojima I.
Kimiidera
紀三井寺
KAINAN-SHI
海南市
Kainan
Kainan-higashi
海南東
Wakayama 11Km
Kōya 59Km
Gobō 49Km
to Kamekawa
to Wakayama
to Hannan I.C
to Shirahama
Kainan I.C
Nokami-chō
野上町
Mt. Maruyama
Shigano River
Misato-chō
美里町
Mt. Onjiyama
Mt. Ichimineyama
Mt. Kurosawayama
Mt. Tobigasuyama
Mt. Kumaoderayama
Mt. Kagamiishiyama
Mandarin Picking area
Shimotsu-chō
下津町
Jinoshima I.
Okinoshima I.
Kisei Line
Mt. Myōjin-yama
Drive-in area
Kainan-Yuasa-dōro
ORD 930
LAR 3350
Mt. Ōishigamine
Mt. Dōnarumiyama
Mt. Senpōzan
Mt. Tokoyama
Mt. Amayama
Hanazono-mura
花園村
Arita River
Mt. Ryūgosan
Shimizu-chō
清水町
Mt. Toishiyama
Arida River
ARIDA-SHI
有田市
Koemi 古江見
Kibi-chō
吉備町
Kanaya-chō
金屋町
Mt. Kuroishiyama
Yukawa River
Mt. Mizugahogyōyama
Mt. Wakayabu
Mt. Shiraiyama
Mt. Ishidōyama
Mt. Jōgamoriyama
C. Kirisaki
Kenashijima I.
Karimojima I.
Hirogawa-chō
広川町
Yuasa-chō
湯浅町
Mt. Sanbonmatsumine
Takashima I.
C. Nabaenohana
Kuroshima I.
Mt. Shiramayama
Hattomaki Pass
Mt. Kushigayamine
Hōji Pass
C. Chigasaki
ORD 600
LAR 1700
Mt. Takakora
C. Shirosaki
Monzen 門前
Yura-chō
由良町
Mt. Chōjagamine
Nakatsu-mura
中津村
Miyama-mura
美山村
Hirokawa-minami
Mt. Teng
Mt. Mizugahogyōyama

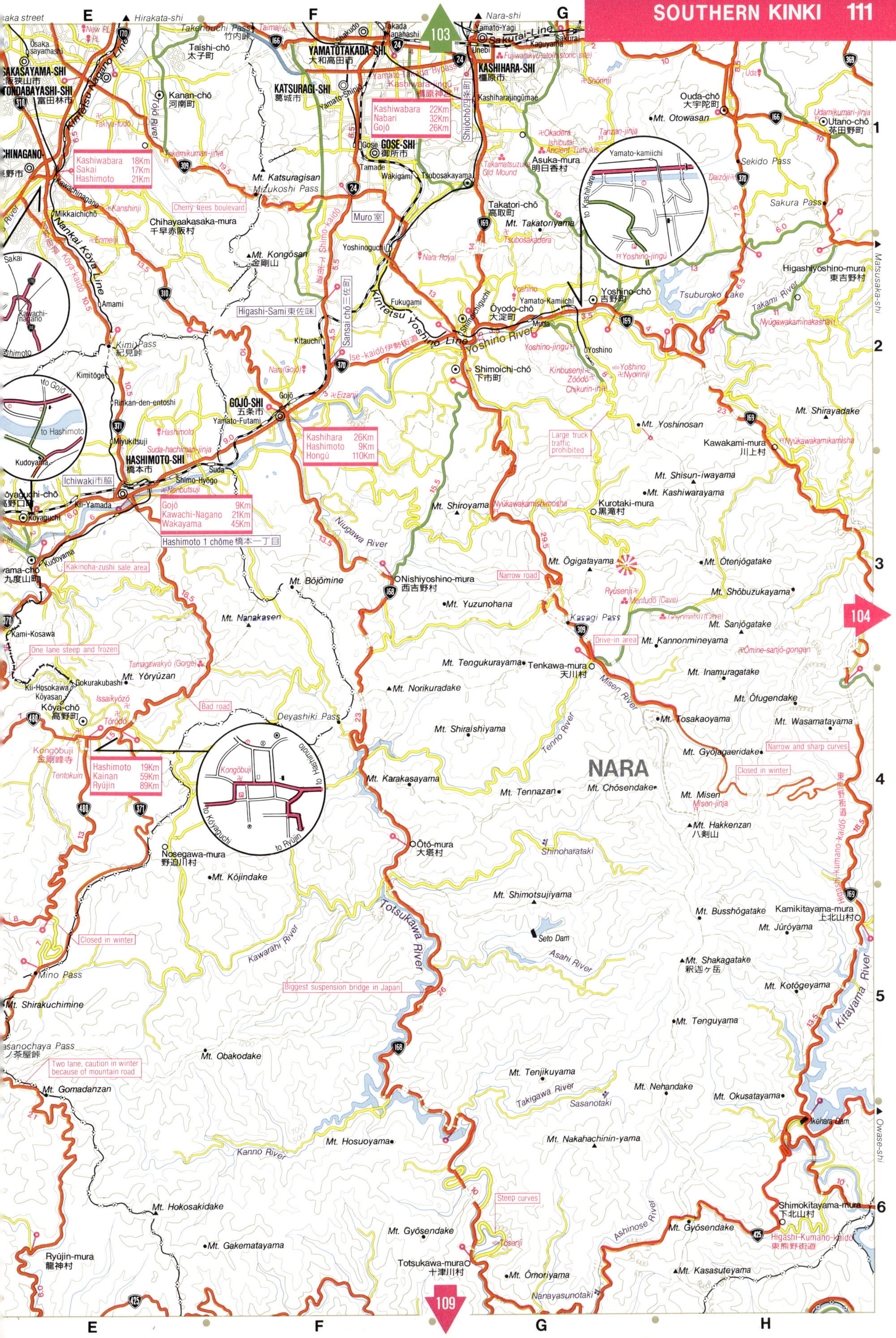
E
F
G
H
1
2
3
4
5
6
103
104
109
Hirakata-shi
Nara-shi
Matsusaka-shi
Owase-shi
Sakurai-Line
Takenouchi Pass
竹内峠
Taishi-chō
太子町
YAMATOTAKADA-SHI
大和高田市
KASHIHARA-SHI
橿原市
KATSURAGI-SHI
葛城市
SAKASAYAMA-SHI
TONDABAYASHI-SHI
富田林市
Kanan-chō
河南町
Kashiwabara 22Km
Nabari 32Km
Gojō 26Km
GOSE-SHI
御所市
Ouda-chō
大宇陀町
Mt. Otowasan
Utano-chō
菟田野町
Kashiwabara 18Km
Sakai 17Km
Hashimoto 21Km
Mt. Katsuragisan
Mizukoshi Pass
Asuka-mura
明日香村
Sekido Pass
Sakura Pass
Yamato-kamiichi
Yoshino-jingū
Cherry trees boulevard
Chihayaakasaka-mura
千早赤阪村
Muro 室
Takatori-chō
高取町
Mt. Takatoriyama
Mt. Kongōsan
金剛山
Yoshinoguchi
Nara Royal
Higashiyoshino-mura
東吉野村
Nankai Kōya Line
Kintetsu Yoshino Line
Higashi-Sami 東佐味
Fukugami
Yoshino-chō
吉野町
Ōyodo-chō
大淀町
Tsuburoko Lake
Takami River
Yoshino River
Kimi Pass
紀見峠
Ise-kaidō 伊勢街道
Sansai chō 三佐田
Shimoichi-chō
下市町
Yoshino
Kinbusenji
Mt. Shirayadake
GOJŌ-SHI
五条市
Mt. Yoshinosan
Kawakami-mura
川上村
Large truck traffic prohibited
Kashihara 26Km
Hashimoto 9Km
Hongū 110Km
HASHIMOTO-SHI
橋本市
Mt. Shisun-iwayama
Mt. Kashiwarayama
Ichiwaki 市脇
Mt. Shiroyama
Kurotaki-mura
黒滝村
Gojō 9Km
Kawachi-Nagano 21Km
Wakayama 45Km
Hashimoto 1 chōme 橋本一丁目
Niugawa River
Mt. Ōgigatayama
Mt. Ōtenjōgatake
Kakinoha-zushi sale area
Nishiyoshino-mura
西吉野村
Narrow road
Mt. Bōjōmine
Mt. Shōbuzukayama
Mt. Yuzunohana
Mt. Nanakasen
Kasagi Pass
Mt. Sanjōgatake
Kami-Kosawa
One lane steep and frozen
Drive-in area
Mt. Kannonmineyama
Ōmine-sanjō-gongen
Mt. Tengukurayama
Tenkawa-mura
天川村
Mt. Yōryūzan
Mt. Inamuragatake
Mt. Norikuradake
Kōya-chō
高野町
Bad road
Deyashiki Pass
Misen River
Mt. Ōfugendake
Mt. Shiraishiyama
Mt. Tosakaoyama
Mt. Wasamatayama
Kongōbuji
金剛峰寺
Tenno River
Mt. Gyōjagaeridake
Narrow and sharp curves
Closed in winter
Hashimoto 19Km
Kainan 59Km
Ryūjin 89Km
NARA
Mt. Karakasayama
Mt. Tennazan
Mt. Chōsendake
Mt. Misen
Mt. Hakkenzan
八剣山
Ōtō-mura
大塔村
Nosegawa-mura
野迫川村
Shinoharataki
Mt. Kōjindake
Mt. Shimotsujiyama
Mt. Busshōgatake
Kamikitayama-mura
上北山村
Mt. Jūrōyama
Seto Dam
Closed in winter
Totsukawa River
Kawarabi River
Asahi River
Mt. Shakagatake
釈迦ヶ岳
Kitayama River
Mino Pass
Biggest suspension bridge in Japan
Mt. Kotōgeyama
Mt. Shirakuchimine
Mt. Tenguyama
Two lane, caution in winter because of mountain road
Mt. Obakodake
Mt. Tenjikuyama
Mt. Nehandake
Mt. Gomadanzan
Takigawa River
Sasanotaki
Mt. Okusatayama
Ikehara Dam
Mt. Nakahachinin-yama
Mt. Hosuoyama
Kanno River
Steep curves
Mt. Hokosakidake
Shimokitayama-mura
下北山村
Ashinose River
Mt. Gyōsendake
Mt. Gyōsendake
Higashi-Kumano-kaidō
東熊野街道
Mt. Gakematayama
Ryūjin-mura
龍神村
Totsukawa-mura
十津川村
Mt. Ōmoriyama
Mt. Kasasutеyama
Nanayasunotaki

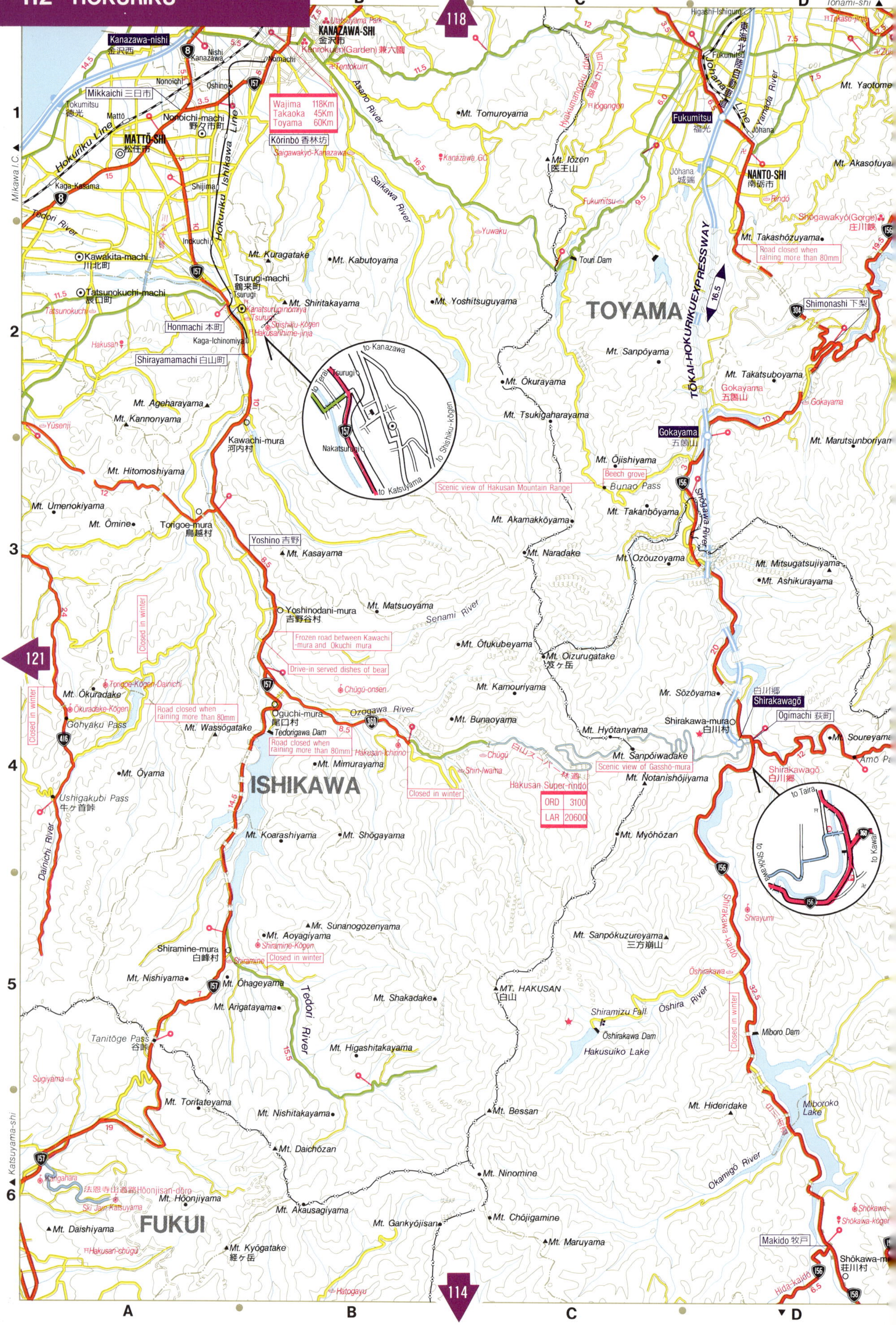
118
121
114
TOYAMA
ISHIKAWA
FUKUI
KANAZAWA-SHI 金沢市
Kenrokuen(Garden) 兼六園
Kanazawa-nishi 金沢西
Mikkaichi 三日市
MATTŌ-SHI 松任市
Nonoichi-machi 野々市町
Hokuriku Line
Hokuriku Ishikawa Line
Wajima 118Km
Takaoka 45Km
Toyama 60Km
Kōrinbō 香林坊
Asano River
Saikawa River
Tedori River
Kawakita-machi 川北町
Tatsunokuchi-machi 辰口町
Tsurugi-machi 鶴来町
Honmachi 本町
Shirayamamachi 白山町
Kaga-Ichinomiya
Mt. Kuragatake
Mt. Kabutoyama
Mt. Shiritakayama
Mt. Yoshitsuguyama
Mt. Tomuroyama
Mt. Iōzen 医王山
Fukumitsu 福光
NANTO-SHI 南砺市
Jōhana 城端
TŌKAI-HOKURIKU EXPRESSWAY
Mt. Yaotome
Mt. Akasofuyama
Mt. Takashōzuyama
Road closed when raining more than 80mm
Shimonashi 下梨
Mt. Sanpōyama
Mt. Takatsuboyama
Gokayama 五箇山
Mt. Ōkurayama
Mt. Tsukigaharayama
Mt. Ōjishiyama
Beech grove
Bunao Pass
Scenic view of Hakusan Mountain Range
Mt. Takanbōyama
Mt. Akamakkōyama
Mt. Naradake
Mt. Ozōuzoyama
Mt. Mitsugatsujiyama
Mt. Ashikurayama
Mt. Marutsunboriyama
Mt. Ageharayama
Mt. Kannonyama
Kawachi-mura 河内村
Mt. Hitomoshiyama
Mt. Umenokiyama
Mt. Ōmine
Torigoe-mura 鳥越村
Yoshino 吉野
Mt. Kasayama
Yoshinodani-mura 吉野谷村
Mt. Matsuoyama
Senami River
Frozen road between Kawachi-mura and Okuchi mura
Drive-in served dishes of bear
Closed in winter
Mt. Ōkuradake
Gohyaku Pass
Mt. Wassōgatake
Oguchi-mura 尾口村
Tedorigawa Dam
Ozogawa River
Mt. Ōfukubeyama
Mt. Oizurugatake 笈ヶ岳
Mt. Kamouriyama
Mt. Bunaoyama
Mt. Hyōtanyama
Mr. Sōzōyama
Shirakawa-mura 白川村
Shirakawagō 白川郷
Ogimachi 荻町
Mt. Soureyama
Mt. Sanpōiwadake
Scenic view of Gasshō-mura
Hakusan Super-rindō
ORD 3100
LAR 20600
Mt. Notanishōjiyama
Mt. Mimurayama
Mt. Ōyama
Ushigakubi Pass 牛ヶ首峠
Dainichi River
Mt. Koarashiyama
Mt. Shōgayama
Mt. Myōhōzan
Mt. Sunanogozenyama
Mt. Aoyagiyama
Shiramine-mura 白峰村
Mt. Sanpōkuzureyama 三方崩山
Mt. Nishiyama
Mt. Ōhageyama
Mt. Arigatayama
Mt. Shakadake
MT. HAKUSAN 白山
Shiramizu Fall
Ōshirakawa Dam
Ōshira River
Hakusuiko Lake
Shirakawa-kaidō
Miboro Dam
Tanitōge Pass 谷峠
Mt. Higashitakayama
Mt. Toritateyama
Mt. Nishitakayama
Mt. Bessan
Mt. Hideridake
Miboroko Lake
Mt. Daichōzan
Mt. Ninomine
Okamigō River
Hōonjisan-dōro
Mt. Hōonjiyama
Mt. Akausagiyama
Mt. Daishiyama
Mt. Chōjigamine
Mt. Gankyōjisan
Mt. Kyōgatake 経ヶ岳
Mt. Maruyama
Makido 牧戸
Shōkawa-mura 荘川村
Hida-kaidō
to Kanazawa
to Katsuyama
to Shishiku-kōgen
to Taira
to Shōkawa
to Kawai

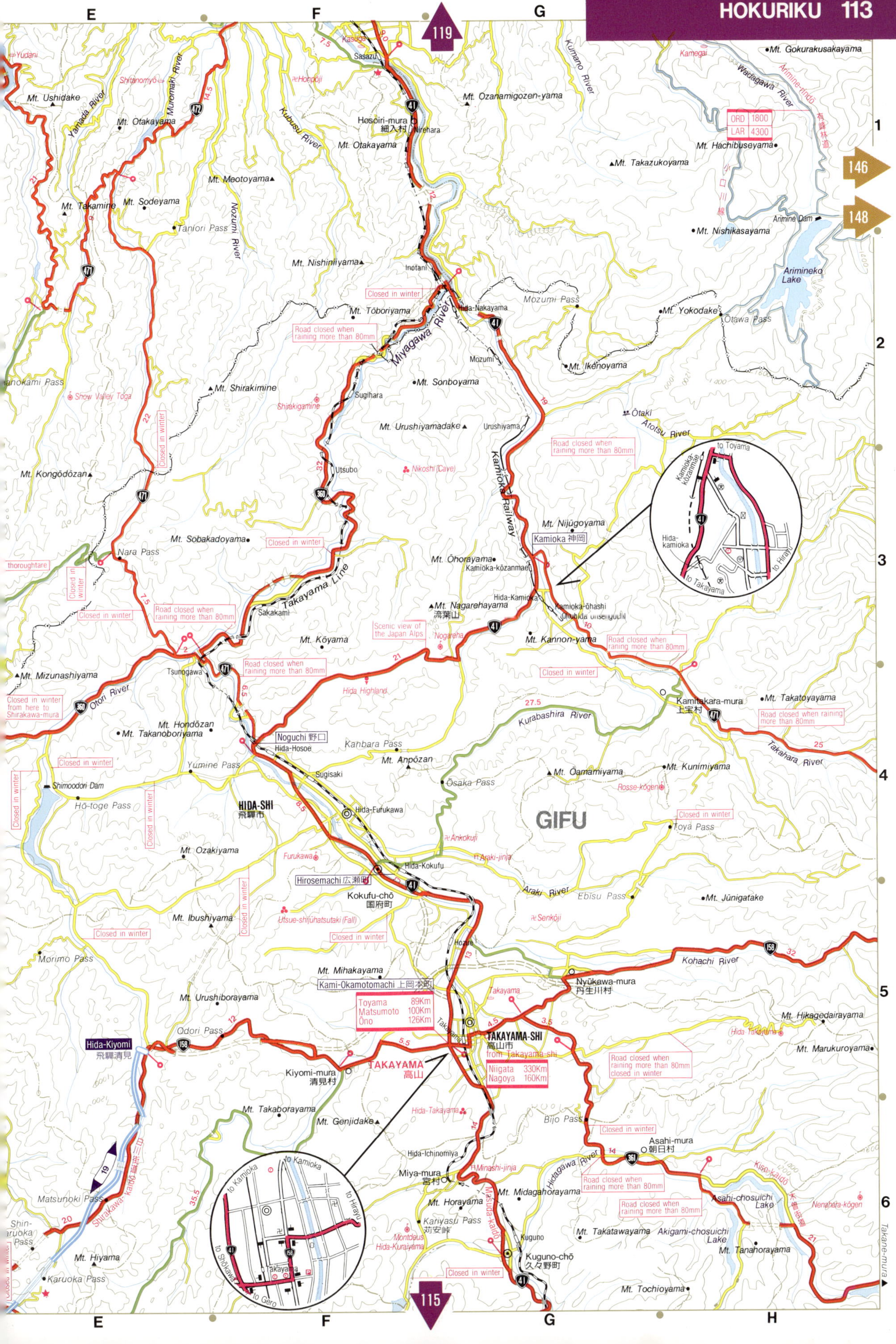
E
F
G
H
119
115
146
148
1
2
3
4
5
6
Mt. Gokurakusakayama
Mt. Ozanamigozen-yama
Mt. Ushidake
Mt. Otakayama
Hosoiri-mura
細入村
Nirehara
Mt. Otakayama
Mt. Hachibuseyama
Mt. Takazukoyama
Mt. Meotoyama
Mt. Takamine
Mt. Sodeyama
Taniori Pass
Mt. Nishikasayama
Arimine Dam
Arimineko Lake
Mt. Nishiniiyama
Inotani
Closed in winter
Mt. Toboriyama
Hida-Nakayama
Mozumi Pass
Mt. Yokodake
Otawa Pass
Road closed when raining more than 80mm
Miyagawa River
Mozumi
Mt. Ikenoyama
Mt. Sonboyama
Sugihara
Mt. Shirakimine
Show Valley Toga
Shirakigamine
Mt. Urushiyamadake
Urushiyama
Ōtaki
Atotsu River
Road closed when raining more than 80mm
Mt. Kongōdōzan
Utsubo
Nikoshi (Cave)
Kamioka Railway
to Toyama
Kamioka-kōzanmae
Hida-kamioka
to Takayama
to Hiraiyu
Mt. Nijūgoyama
Mt. Sobakadoyama
Closed in winter
Kamioka 神岡
Nara Pass
thoroughtare
Closed in winter
Mt. Ōhorayama
Kamioka-kōzanmae
Takayama Line
Hida-Kamioka
Mt. Nagarehayama
流葉山
Kamioka-ōhashi
Road closed when raining more than 80mm
Closed in winter
Sakakami
Scenic view of the Japan Alps
Nogareha
Mt. Kōyama
Mt. Kannon-yama
Road closed when raining more than 80mm
Mt. Mizunashiyama
Tsunogawa
Road closed when raining more than 80mm
Closed in winter
Closed in winter from here to Shirakawa-mura
Otori River
Hida Highland
Kamitakara-mura
上宝村
Mt. Takatoyayama
Road closed when raining more than 80mm
Kurabashira River
Mt. Hondōzan
Mt. Takanoboriyama
Noguchi 野口
Hida-Hosoe
Kanbara Pass
Mt. Anpōzan
Takahara River
Closed in winter
Yumine Pass
Sugisaki
Mt. Ōamamiyama
Mt. Kunimiyama
Shimoodori Dam
Ōsaka Pass
Rosse-kōgen
Closed in winter
Hō-toge Pass
Closed in winter
HIDA-SHI
飛騨市
Hida-Furukawa
GIFU
Closed in winter
Toya Pass
Mt. Ozakiyama
Ankokuji
Furukawa
Araki-jinja
Hida-Kokufu
Hirosemachi 広瀬町
Kokufu-chō
国府町
Araki River
Ebisu Pass
Mt. Jūnigatake
Mt. Ibushiyama
Closed in winter
Utsue-shijūhatsutaki (Fall)
Closed in winter
Senkōji
Closed in winter
Hozue
Morimo Pass
Mt. Mihakayama
Kohachi River
Kami-Okamotomachi 上岡本町
Nyūkawa-mura
丹生川村
Mt. Urushiborayama
Toyama 89Km
Matsumoto 100Km
Ōno 126Km
Takayama
Mt. Hikagedairayama
Odori Pass
Hida-Kiyomi
飛騨清見
TAKAYAMA-SHI
高山市
from Takayama-shi
Hida Takayama
Mt. Marukuroyama
Kiyomi-mura
清見村
TAKAYAMA
高山
Niigata 330Km
Nagoya 160Km
Road closed when raining more than 80mm closed in winter
Mt. Takaborayama
Hida-Takayama
Mt. Genjidake
Bijo Pass
Closed in winter
Asahi-mura
朝日村
Hida-Ichinomiya
Hidagawa River
Kiso-kaidō
木曽街道
to Kamioka
to Kamioka
to Hiraiyu
Miya-mura
宮村
Minashi-jinja
Road closed when raining more than 80mm
Mt. Midagahorayama
Road closed when raining more than 80mm
Asahi-chosuichi Lake
Nenohara-kōgen
Matsunoki Pass
Shirakawa-kaidō
Mt. Horayama
Kariyasu Pass
苅安峠
Masuda-kaidō
Shin-Karuoka Pass
Montdeus Hida-Kuraiyama
Kuguno
Mt. Takatawayama
Akigami-chosuichi Lake
Mt. Tanahorayama
Takane-mura
Mt. Hiyama
to Shōkawa
to Gero
Kuguno-chō
久々野町
Karuoka Pass
Closed in winter
Mt. Tochioyama
Yudani
Shitanomyo
Honpoji
Kasuga
Sasazu
Kamegai
Wadagawa River
Arimine-rindō
ORD 1800
LAR 4300
Kumano River
Yamada River
Muromaki River
Kubusu River
Nozumi River
Ishitanomyo
anokami Pass

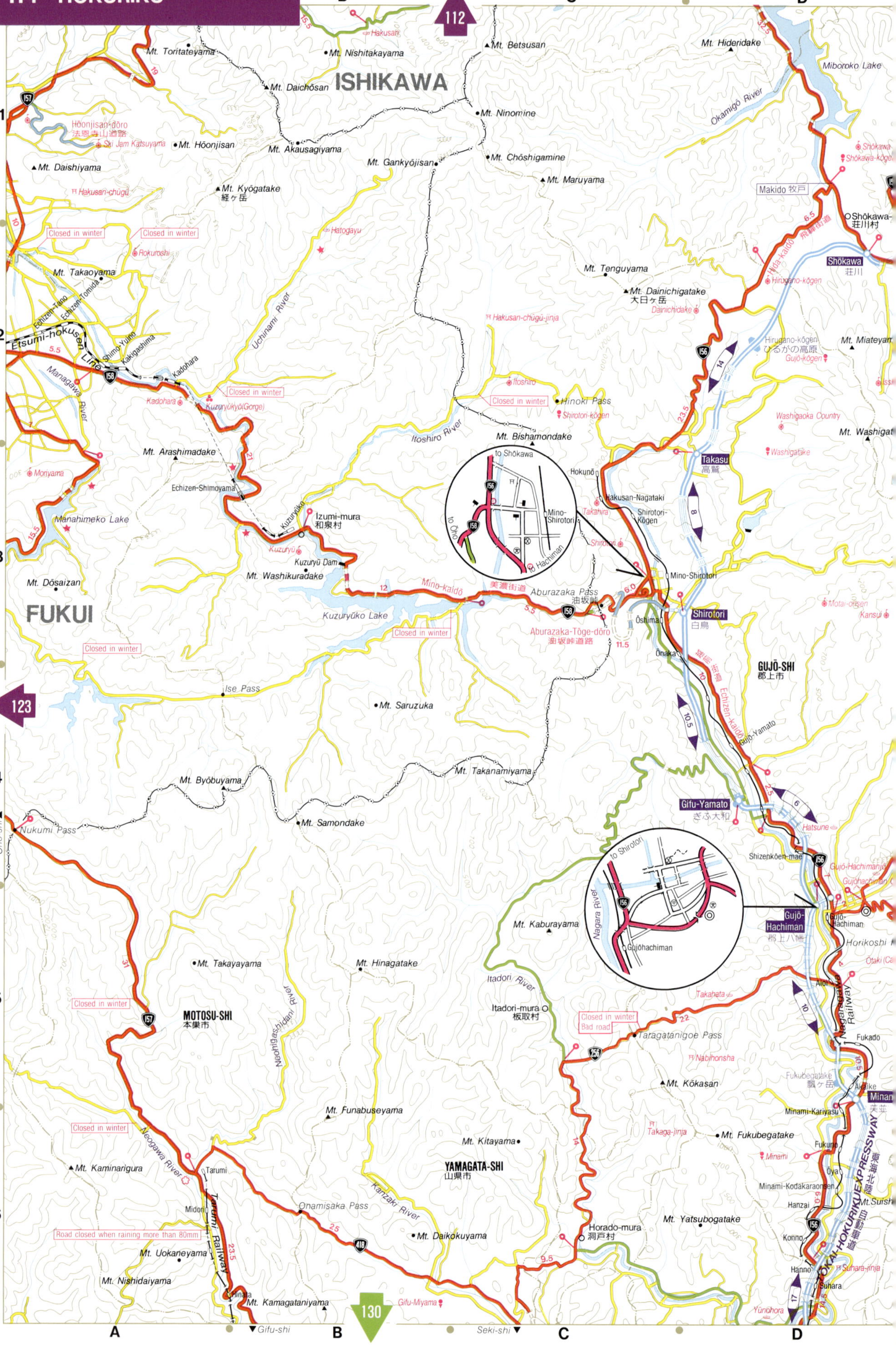
B
C
D
112
1
2
3
4
5
6
123
130
A
B
C
D
ISHIKAWA
FUKUI
Mt. Toritateyama
Mt. Nishitakayama
Hakusan
Mt. Betsusan
Mt. Hideridake
Miboroko Lake
Okamigō River
Mt. Daichōsan
Mt. Ninomine
Hōonjisan-dōro
法恩寺山道路
Ski Jam Katsuyama
Mt. Hōonjisan
Mt. Akausagiyama
Mt. Gankyōjisan
Mt. Chōshigamine
Shōkawa
Shōkawa-kōgen
Mt. Daishiyama
Hakusan-chūgū
Mt. Kyōgatake
経ヶ岳
Mt. Maruyama
Makido 牧戸
Shōkawa-
荘川村
Closed in winter
Closed in winter
Rokuroshi
Hatogayu
Shōkawa
荘川
Hida-kaidō
飛騨街道
Mt. Takaoyama
Mt. Tenguyama
Mt. Dainichigatake
大日ヶ岳
Dainichidake
Hirugano-kōgen
Echizen-Tano
Echizen-Tomida
Uchinami River
Hakusan-chūgū-jinja
Hirugano-kōgen
ひるがの高原
Gujō-kōgen
Mt. Miateyama
Etsumi-hokusen Line
Shimo-Yuino
Kakigashima
Kadohara
Managawa River
Closed in winter
Kadohara
Kuzuryūkyō(Gorge)
Itoshiro
Closed in winter
Hinoki Pass
Shirotori-kōgen
Washigaoka Country
Mt. Washigatake
Itoshiro River
Mt. Bishamondake
Washigatake
Takasu
高鷲
Mt. Arashimadake
Moriyama
Echizen-Shimoyama
Kuzuryūkyō
Izumi-mura
和泉村
to Shōkawa
to Ōno
Mino-Shirotori
Hachiman
Hokunō
Hakusan-Nagataki
Shirotori-Kōgen
Takahira
Shirotori
Manahimeko Lake
Kuzuryū
Kuzuryū Dam
Mt. Washikuradake
Mino-Shirotori
Mt. Dōsaizan
Mino-kaidō
美濃街道
Aburazaka Pass
油坂峠
Kuzuryūko Lake
Ōshima
Shirotori
白鳥
Motai-onsen
Kansui
Aburazaka-Tōge-dōro
油坂峠道路
Closed in winter
Closed in winter
Ōnaka
GUJŌ-SHI
郡上市
Echizen-kaidō
越前街道
Ise Pass
Mt. Saruzuka
Gujō-Yamato
Mt. Byōbuyama
Mt. Takanamiyama
Gifu-Yamato
ぎふ大和
Hatsune
Nukumi Pass
Ōno-shi
Mt. Samondake
Shizenkōen-mae
Gujō-Hachiman
to Shirotori
Nagara River
Gujōhachiman
Gujō-Hachiman
郡上八幡
Gujō-Hachiman
Horikoshi
Ōtaki
Mt. Kaburayama
Mt. Takayayama
Mt. Hinagatake
Closed in winter
Itadori River
Aioi
Nagaragawa Railway
Takahata
MOTOSU-SHI
本巣市
Neohigashidani River
Itadori-mura
板取村
Closed in winter
Bad road
Taragatanigoe Pass
Fukado
Nabihonsha
Fukubegatake
瓢ヶ岳
Mt. Kōkasan
Akaike
Mt. Funabuseyama
Closed in winter
Minami-Kariyasu
Takaga-jinja
Mt. Fukubegatake
Mt. Kitayama
YAMAGATA-SHI
山県市
Fukuno
Neogawa River
Mt. Kaminarigura
Minami
Tarumi
Ōya
TŌKAI-HOKURIKU EXPRESSWAY
東海北陸自動車道
Minami-Kodakaraonsen
Midori
Tarumi Railway
Onamisaka Pass
Kanzaki River
Hanzai
Road closed when raining more than 80mm
Horado-mura
洞戸村
Mt. Yatsubogatake
Mt. Daikokuyama
Mt. Uokaneyama
Konno
Hanno
Suhara-jinja
Mt. Nishidaiyama
Hinata
Mt. Kamagataniyama
Gifu-Miyama
Suhara
Yunohora
Gifu-shi
Seki-shi

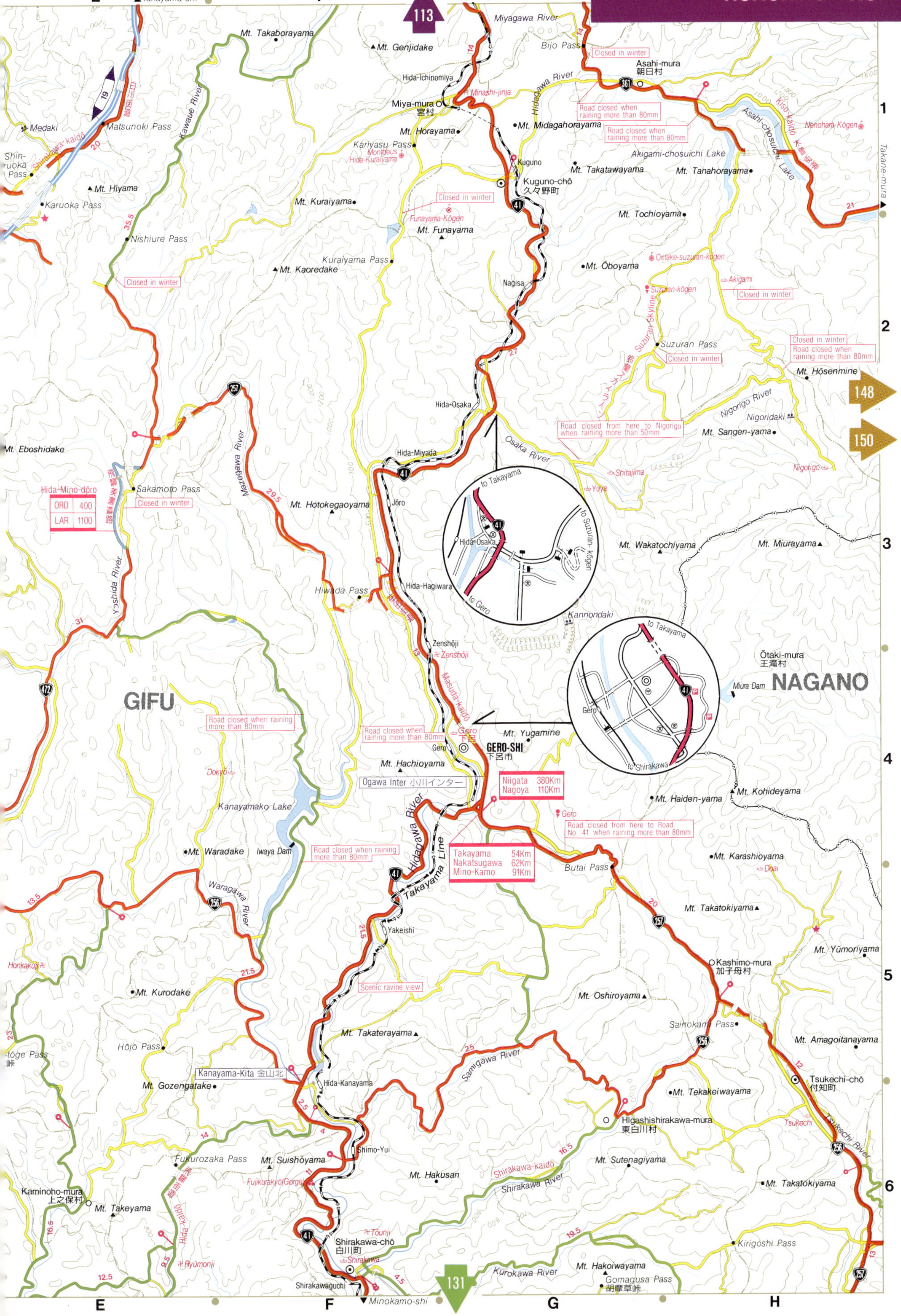
E
F
G
H
Takayama-shi
113
148
150
131
Minokamo-shi
Takane-mura
Mt. Takaborayama
Mt. Genjidake
Miyagawa River
Bijo Pass
Closed in winter
Asahi-mura
朝日村
361
Hida-Ichinomiya
Minashi-jinja
Hidagawa River
Miya-mura
宮村
Road closed when raining more than 80mm
Mt. Midagahorayama
Kiso-kaidō
Nenohara-Kōgen
Asahi-chosuichi Lake
Akigami-chosuichi Lake
Mt. Horayama
Kariyasu Pass
Montdeus Hida-Kuraiyama
Kuguno
Kuguno-chō
久々野町
Mt. Takatawayama
Mt. Tanahorayama
Medaki
Matsunoki Pass
Shin-ruoka Pass
Shirakawa-kaidō
Kawaue River
Mt. Hiyama
Karuoka Pass
Mt. Kuraiyama
Closed in winter
Funayama-Kōgen
Mt. Funayama
Mt. Tochioyama
Nishiure Pass
Kuraiyama Pass
Mt. Kaoredake
Mt. Ōboyama
Ontake-suzuran-kōgen
Nagisa
Akigami
Closed in winter
Suzuran-kōgen
Closed in winter
Suzuran Skyline
Suzuran Pass
Closed in winter
Closed in winter
Road closed when raining more than 80mm
Mt. Hōsenmine
Hida-Osaka
Nigorigo River
Nigoridaki
Road closed from here to Nigorigo when raining more than 50mm
Mt. Sangen-yama
Mt. Eboshidake
Osaka River
Hida-Miyada
Nigorigo
Shitajima
Yuya
Hida-Mino-dōro
ORD 400
LAR 1100
Sakamoto Pass
Closed in winter
Mazegawa River
Mt. Hotokegaoyama
Jōro
to Takayama
to Suzuran-kōgen
Hida-Osaka
to Gero
Mt. Wakatochiyama
Mt. Miurayama
Yoshida River
Hiwada Pass
Hida-Hagiwara
Kannondaki
to Takayama
Zenshōji
Zenshōji
Ōtaki-mura
王滝村
Masuda-kaidō
Miura Dam
NAGANO
GIFU
Road closed when raining more than 80mm
Road closed when raining more than 80mm
Gero
下呂
Gero
GERO-SHI
下呂市
Mt. Yugamine
to Shirakawa
Dokyō
Mt. Hachioyama
Ogawa Inter 小川インター
Niigata 380Km
Nagoya 110Km
Mt. Haiden-yama
Mt. Kohideyama
Kanayamako Lake
Hidagawa River
Gero
Road closed from here to Road No. 41 when raining more than 80mm
Mt. Waradake
Iwaya Dam
Road closed when raining more than 80mm
Takayama Line
Takayama 54Km
Nakatsugawa 62Km
Mino-Kamo 91Km
Butai Pass
Mt. Karashioyama
Doai
Waragawa River
Mt. Takatokiyama
Yakeishi
Honkakuji
Mt. Yūmoriyama
Kashimo-mura
加子母村
Mt. Kurodake
Scenic ravine view
Mt. Oshiroyama
Sainokami Pass
Mt. Amagoitanayama
Mt. Takaterayama
Hōjō Pass
Samigawa River
-tōge Pass
峠
Tsukechi-chō
付知町
Kanayama-Kita 金山北
Mt. Gozengatake
Hida-Kanayama
Mt. Tekakeiwayama
Higashishirakawa-mura
東白川村
Tsukechi
Tsukechi River
Shimo-Yui
Fukurozaka Pass
Mt. Suishōyama
Mt. Sutenagiyama
Mt. Hakusan
Shirakawa-kaidō
Shirakawa River
Fujikurakyō Gorge
Kaminoho-mura
上之保村
Mt. Takeyama
Hida-kaidō
Mt. Takatokiyama
Tōunji
Shirakawa-chō
白川町
Kirigoshi Pass
Ryūmonji
Shirakawa
Kurokawa River
Mt. Hakoiwayama
Gomagusa Pass
胡摩草峠
Shirakawaguchi
1
2
3
4
5
6

B
C
D
1
2
3
4
5
6
A
B
C
D
to Hekurajima
to Osawa
to Sosogi
to Monzen
Fugeshimachi 鳳至町
Wajima River
Nanao 58Km
Takaoka 101Km
Kanazawa 118Km
Road closed when raining more than 80mm
Shiryone-senmaida (terraced Paddy-field)
Nebuta
C. Zōzōbana
WAJIMA-SHI
輪島市
C. Segamisaki
C. Atakemisaki
Mt. Takasuyama
Mt. Hachibuseyama
Sharp curves
Mt. Sanjayama
Mt. Kikachiyama
C. Ōnagasaki
Mt. Banbayama
C. Michigahana
Minazuki-wan
C. Kosaki
Caution falling stones
Mt. Takanosuyama
Mt. Saruyama
Honkō 本江
Mt. Itanotanzan
C.Saruyamazaki
猿山岬
Mt. Tsubonoyama
ISHIKAWA
to Wajima
to Anamizu
to Togi
Sōjiji
Motoichi 本市
Mt. Takatsukayama
Mt. Kiharadake
Noto
Sōjiji
總持寺
Monzen-machi
門前町
Road closed when raining more than 80mm
Mt. Ōmaruyama
Nakai 中居
Nakai
Bira
Kawas
川尻
Caution-hightwaves
Kanami
Mt. Kuwatsukayama
Anamizu-machi
穴水町
Anamizu
C. Sekinohana
Mt. Takatsumeyama
Koshinohara
Aoshima I.
to Monzen
to Tomasu
Kawashima
川島
to Kawachi
Anamizu
to Nanao
Mt. Besshōdake
Scenic view of sea
Mt. Kazafukidake
Noto-dōro
ORD 1180
LAR 4210
Noto-Kashima
Mt. Takatsukayama
Besshōdake
Caution-falling stones
Scenic view of sea
C. Yoshigaurahana
Noto Nanao Line
C. Amasaki
Nishigishi
Mitsugakuchi seto
C. Takaiwamisaki
Togigawa River
Togi-machi
富来町
Mt. Mushigamine
Yokota
Notojima I.
能登島
Ryōkemachi 領家町
Caution-falling stones
Urukami 生神
Hamada 浜田
Mt. Yomurazukaya
Drive-in
Urugami
Nichiyo River
Noto-Nakajima
Notokongō
(Scenic Rocky Coast)
Noto-Nakajima
C. Miyaz
Wakura
和倉
C. Byōbuzaki
Mt. Takatsuboriyama
Shirahama 白浜
Kasashiho
Wakuraonsen
Mt. Henjōdake
Tatsuruhama
Tokuda-Ōtsu
Tatsuruhama
田鶴浜
田鶴浜道路
Tatsuruhama-dōro
Takada
Nanao
Akaura
Kawaramachi 川原町
Mt. Akakurayama
Wajima 58Km
Takaoka 43Km
Kanazawa 65Km
Nanao
NANAO-SHI
七尾市
Noto
Shikanosato
Horimatsu 堀松
118
Nishiyama I.C.

E
F
G
H
1
2
3
4
5
6
C. Shakuzaki
C. Rokkôzaki
禄剛崎
C. Kongôzaki
Yoshigaura
C. Suzumisaki
珠洲岬
C. Sôzaki
Suzu-jinja
Scenic view of sea
C. Wanizaki
C. Ôsaki
Ôtani 大谷
Cation-hign waves
Ôtani Pass
C. Tsubazaki
Mt. Nekogatake
Scenic view of sea
Sosogikaigan
(Scenic Rocky Coast)
Mt. Matsugaseyama
Machino River
C. Shirasaki
Sosogi 曽々木
Mitsugohama
Wakayama River
Hattarô Pass
八田郎峠
Mt. Hôryûzan
SUZU-SHI
珠洲市
Suzu-Iida
Iida
Suzu
Shôin
Takojima
C. Nagatezaki
Azuma 吾妻
Uedo
Funakoya Pass
船木谷峠
Satomachi 里町
Mt. Maidanigozen-yama
Suzu-Ukai
Ukai
Ukai River
Minami-Kuromaru
Scenic view of
Mitsukejima I.
to Sosogi
Suzu
to Wajima
to Ushitsu
Ushima
Koiji
Koiji
Yanagida-mura
柳田村
Matsunami
Uchiura-machi
内浦町
C. Akasaki
Strawberty
farm
Kuri
-Kawashiri
C. Jôgasaki
C. Miyazaki
Mt. Somatayama
Shiromaru
Noto-machi
能都町
Ushitsu
Ushitsu daini 宇出津第二
Tsukumo-wan-Ogi
Tsukumo-wan
Mt. Manaitagurayama
Uohitsu daiichi 宇山津第一
Tategayachi Pass
Hane
Ogi
C. Mifunezaki
Jômon-Mawaki
Fujinami
Yakiyama
Hanami
Caution-high waves
Yanami
Shichimi
Soyama Pass
Ukawa
C. Ogurasaki
Yamada River
Ukawa 鵜川
Furukimi
Myôsenji
Noto Noto Line
Maenami
Okinami
Kabuto
Sodezaki
Oguchi seto
C. Taurabana
Koguchi seto
C. Kannonzaki
Yugawa
Akasaki
Mt. Ikakeyama
Caution-
falling stones
Scenic view of Tateyama Mountain Range
Caution-high waves
from Nanao
Niigata 320Km
Nagoya 310Km

116
Monzen-machi
Anamizu-machi
Noto-Nakajima
Nanaosei-wan
Wakura
Notojima-ōhashi (Bridge)
C. Byōbuzaki
Nanaonan-wan
Wakura-onsen
Notokongō (Scenic Rocky Coast)
Mt. Takatsubonyama
Mt. Henjōdake
Shirahama 白浜
Kasashiho
Noto Nanao Line
Tokuda-Ōtsu
Takada
Tatsuruhama-dōro
Tatsuruhama 田鶴浜
Mt. Akakurayama
Kawaramachi 川原町
NANAO-SHI
七尾市
Nanao
Wajima 58Km
Takaoka 43Km
Kanazawa 65Km
Noto
Shikanosato
Horimatsu 堀松
Shika-machi
志賀町
Nishiyama
Bentenjima I.
Takahamachō 高浜町
Mt. Jōyama
Tokuda
Toriya-machi
鳥屋町
Noto-Ninomiya
Uwadanayada
Yoshikawa
Kashima-machi
鹿島町
Shakushiga-toge Pass
Rokusei-machi
鹿西町
Kashima Bypass
Mt. Bijōsan
Notobe
Mt. Sekidōzan
Arayama Pass
Myōjōji
Tokinodai
Kanemaru
Keta-jinja
Nanao Line
Ouchigata Lake
Harayama Pass
Eikōji
Mt. Goishigamine
Yanaida
Yanaidamachi 柳田町
Nanao-kaidō
Aogawa River
Hakui River
HAKUI-SHI
羽咋市
Hakui
Iinoyama 飯山
Senrihama
Chūōmachi 中央町
Minami-Hakui
Shio-machi
志雄町
Saiwaichō 幸町
Oshimizumachi-Shuku 押水町宿
Shikinami
Himishi 氷見市
Chirihama
Imahama
Shingū
Oshimizu-machi
押水町
Hōdatsu
Shimotako 下田子
Oshimizu Bypass
Noto-dōro
ORD 1180
LAR 4210
Mt. Gorinzan
Menden
Mt. Sanpōmine
Mt. Hōdatsusan
Nashinoki Pass
Kenritsu-Kangodai
Mt. Sanzenbōyama
Takaoka-kita
ISHIKAWA
Takamatsu
Nanao 43km
Toyama 27km
Kanazawa 45km
Yokoyama
Hokuriku Green Hill
Hanao
Kanazawa CC
Takaoka
Kyōzu Pass
Mt. Maruyama
Mt. Mikuniyama
Saimyōji
Shirao
Unoke
KAHOKU-SHI
かほく市
Nishi-Takaoka
Mt. Inabayama
Fukuoka-machi
福岡町
Uchihisumi-kita 内日角北
Nose
Oyabe Bypass
Fukuoka
Hokuriku Line
Hon-Tsubata
Kurami
Kurikara
Frozen road
OYABE-SHI
小矢部市
Tsubata
Tsubata-machi
津幡町
Naka-Tsubata
Mt. Tonamiyama
Hachimangū
Fudōji
Kurikara Pass
倶利伽羅峠
Oyabe River
Aburaden
Obama-jinja
Kahokugata Lake
Asada 浅田
Ōta 太田
Oyabe-higashi
TONAMI-SHI
砺波市
Uchinada-machi
内灘町
Uchinada
Hokurikudō
Oyabe
小矢部
Oyabe-Tonami Jct
Kanazawa links
Kanazawa
Hokuriku Line
Asanogawa Line
Imamachi 今町
Uchiyama Pass
Kitama
Morimoto
Oyabegawa
Higashi-Nojiri
Tonami
Kanazawa-higashi
金沢東
Morimoto 森本
Fudōji
不動寺
Senbadaira
Gold win
Takagi
Mitsukuchi
Saikawa River
Ōnominato-jinja
Kanazawa-Morimoto
金沢森本
Kannon
Tōkai-Hokuriku Ex Pressway
Jōhana Line
Kami-Moroe
Higashi-Kanazawa
Takakubo
Fukuno
Frozen road
Yudani
Kanazawa
Utatsuyama Park
Kawaida
NANTO-SHI
南砺市
Higashi-Ishiguro
Kanazawa-nishi
金沢西
Korinbō 香林坊
Kenrokuen (Garden)
Takase-jinja
KANAZAWA-SHI
金沢市
Wajima 118km
Takaoka 45km
Toyama 60km
Zuisenji
Fukumitsu
112
Mikawa I.C.
Fukumitsu I.C.

E
F
G
H
117
113
146
1
2
3
4
5
6
TOYAMA-WAN
富山湾
TOYAMA
Yukawa
Akasaki
Mt. Ikakeyama
Caution-falling stones
Caution-high waves
Caution-falling stones
Caution-high waves
to Anamizu
to Himi
Nanao
to Hakui
to Kanazawa
to Himi
to Fushiki
to Toyama
to Oyabe
to Tonami
Takaoka
Toyama
to Toyamakō
Toyamaguchi
to Uozu
to Tonami
Fujikoshi
to Tateyama
to Ōyama
from Toyama-shi
Niigata 240Km
Nagoya 250Km
Shimao
Himi Line
Scenic view of sea
Amaharashi
Kokutaiji
Etchū-Kokubu
Shōgawa River
Futakamiyama
Fushiki
SHINMINATO-SHI
新湊市
Fushiki-Toyama
Koshinokata
Manyō Line
Sumitomo Chemical
TAKAOKA-SHI
高岡市
Nōmachi
Etchū-Nakagawa
Etchū-Daimon
Ōshima-machi
大島町
Takaoka
Daimon-machi
大門町
Futatsuka
Shimo-mura
下村
Hokurikudō
Kureha
Taikōyama
Kosugi
小杉
Kosugi-machi
小杉町
Nishi-Toyama
Mt. Jōyama
Toyama-nishi
富山西
HOKURIKU EXPRESSWAY
北陸自動車道
Mt. Takatsumineyama
Takaoka
Kureha
呉羽
Kosugi
Kureha
Takaoka
高岡
Kakuganji
Yoshitani 吉谷
Yasukawa 安川
Jōrakuji
Yamada River
Takayama Line
Idagawa River
Chisato
Hayahoshi
Fuchū-machi
婦中町
Toyama
富山
Saishōji
Terao
Yumenodaira
Yamada-mura
山田村
Yamada
Etchū-Yatsuo
Yatsuo-machi
八尾町
Higashi-Yatsuo
Takakuma
Yatsuo
Saishōji
Kasuga
Sasazu
Ōsawano-machi
大沢野町
Toyama
Tōyakuji
Honpōji
Shitanomyō
Takayama-shi
TOYAMA-SHI
富山市
Toyama Castle
Fujikoshi
Nachi-Fujikoshi
Itoigawa 78Km
Kanazawa 60Km
Takayama 89Km
Nagaregsugi
流杉
Kosugi
Nunoichi
Toyama Kamidaki Line
Saikōji
Jinzū River
Iwasehama
Shōwa Denkō
Chiharazaki 千原崎
Hasumachi
Higashi-Toyama
Kinsenji 金泉寺
Etchū-Nakajima
Toyamakō Line
Mizuhashi
Jōganji River
Road closed when wave's more than 4m
Etchū-Ebara
Etchū-Sangō
Funahashi-mura
船橋村
Chigozuka
Namerikawa
Toyama Bypass
Nishi-Kazumi
Naka-Kazumi
Shin-Miyakawa
Kamiichi
Kamiichi-machi
上市町
Tateyama
立山
Gohyakkoku
Tateyama-machi
立山町
Toyama Tateyama Line
Myōkōji
Yunomiko
Ryūsenji
Caution-falling stones Melting snow
Caution-falling stones Melting snow
Ōiwa-fudō
Kamagafuchi
Shimoda 下田
Tateyama
Daisenji
Iwakuraji
Oyama-jinja
Ōyama-machi
大山町
Drive-in
Yokoe
Ashikuraji
Chigasa
Arimineguchi
Hongū
Gokurakuzaka
Mt. Gokurakusakayama
Wadagawa River
Kumano River
ORD 1800
LAR 4300
to Gohyakkoku
to Tateyamaeki
to Ōyama
Tateyama
ORD
LAR 35280
Tateyama-dōro
Bijodaira(P.G.)
美女平
Tateyama
Bijodaira
Kurobe River
Itoigawa-shi
Asahi I.C.
Nishi-Nyūzen
Ikuji
YKK
C. Ikujihana
Niiharu-jinja
Ikuji
Kutsukake 沓掛
Hokuriku Line
Dentetsu-Kurobe
Kurobe
黒部
Ōgyū 荻生
KUROBE-SHI
黒部市
Dentetsu-Ishida
Katakai River
Kyōden
Fusegawa River
UOZU-SHI
魚津市
Uozu
Uozu-kokusai
Uozu
魚津
Ōtani
Nishi-Uozu
Sanga 三ヶ
Higashi-Namerikawa
Etchū-Nakamura
Caution-falling stones
Kannon
Kitayama
Namerikawa
NAMERIKAWA-SHI
滑川市
Toyamachihō Railway
Arisoumi
有磯海
Hayatsuki River
Namerikawa
滑川
Saikōji
Caution-falling stones
Mt. Shirakurayama
Mt. Shiritakayama
fu-shi

ISHIKAWA
FUKUI
HOKURIKU EXPRESSWAY 北陸自動車道
Komatsu 小松
KOMATSU-SHI 小松市
Neagari-machi 根上町
Kyōmachi 京町
Kita-Asai 北浅井
Ataka 安宅
Katayamazu 片山津
Amagozen 尼御前
C. Amagozenmisaki
C. Kasanomisaki
Kaga-hyakumangoku-jidaimura (R.A.)
Shibayamagata Lake
Kibagata Lake
Awazu 粟津
Kaga-onsen
KAGA-SHI 加賀市
Kaga 加賀
Daishōji
Daishōji River
Kurose 黒瀬
Kanazawa 43Km
Fukui 37Km
Ōno 63Km
Yamashiro 山代
Kawaminamimachi 河南町
Mt. Funamidake
Ushinoya Pass 牛ノ谷峠
Kitagatako Lake
Yamanaka 山中
Yamanaka-machi 山中町
Mt. Kariyasuyama
Kanazu 金津
Tōjinbō(Scenic Rocky Coast) 東尋坊
Ojima I.
Funatsu 舟津
Kakuzen 覚善
Mikuni-minato
Mikuni-chō 三国町
Nakamoto 中元
AWARA-SHI あわら市
Awara-onsen
Echizen-Mikuni-Awara Line
Mt. Tsurugigatake
Mt. Fujishagatake
Ōuchi Pass 大内峠
Onagatani 女形谷
Ippondennaka 一本田中
Sakai-chō 坂井町
Maruoka-chō 丸岡町
Maruoka 丸岡
Kuzuryū River
Yanagihara 柳原
from Fukui-shi
Nagoya 170Km
Ōsaka 220Km
Scenic view of sea
Mt. Takasuyama
Harue-chō 春江町
Hokuriku Line
Matsuoka-chō 松岡町
Narukabashi 鳴鹿橋
Higashi-Furuichi 東古市
Echizen-Katsuyama-Eiheiji Line
Eiheiji-chō 永平寺町
Fukui-kita 福井北
Kaga 37Km
Ōno 33Km
Tsuruga 58Km
FUKUI-SHI 福井市
Nishigata 西方
Fukui 福井
Mt. Kunimidake
Ōmi 大味
Mt. Konpirayama
Koshino-mura 越廼村
Shimizu-chō 清水町
Mt. Yoshinogatake
Ōtani-Saka Pass 大谷坂
Kamishihi-mura 上志比村
Mt. Daibutsujiyama
Mt. Kyōgatake
Mt. Mizunashiya
Mt. Washigatake
Closed in winter
Echizen-chō
to Komatsu
to Tsubata
to Kaga
to Kanazu
to C. Echizenmisaki
to Fukui
Maruoka I.C.
122
123

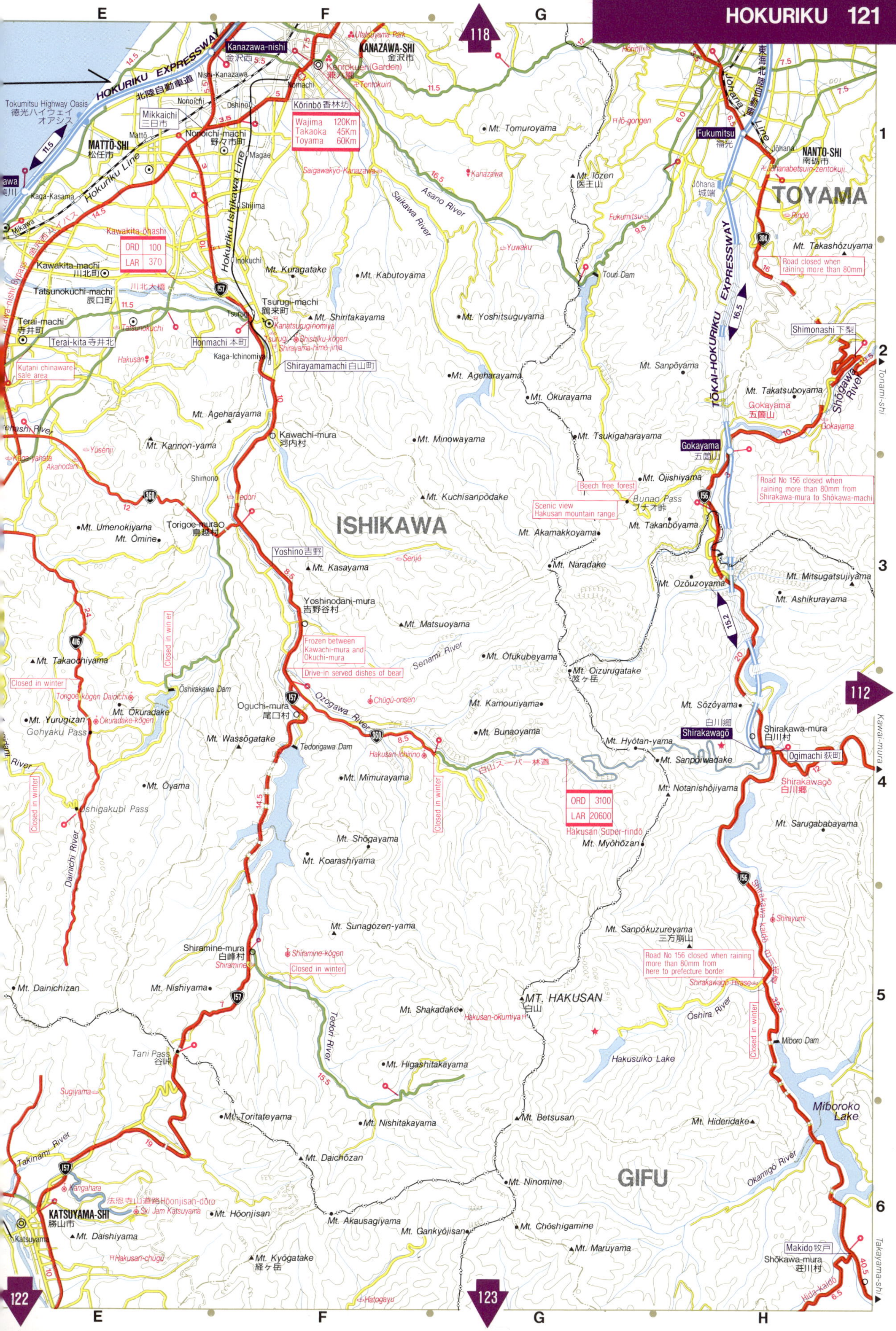
E
F
G
H
118
1
2
3
4
5
6
112
122
123
HOKURIKU EXPRESSWAY
北陸自動車道
Kanazawa-nishi
金沢西
KANAZAWA-SHI
金沢市
Utatsuyama Park
Kenrokuen (Garden)
兼六園
Tentokuin
Nomachi
Nishi-Kanazawa
Nonoichi
Oshino
Tokumitsu Highway Oasis
徳光ハイウェイオアシス
Mikkaichi
三日市
MATTŌ-SHI
松任市
Mattō
Nonoichi-machi
野々市町
Magae
Kōrinbō 香林坊
Wajima 120Km
Takaoka 45Km
Toyama 60Km
Saigawakyō-Kanazawa
Kaga-Kasama
Hokuriku Line
Mikawa
Shijima
Hokuriku Ishikawa Line
Kawakita-ōhashi
ORD 100
LAR 370
Inokuchi
Kawakita-machi
川北町
Tatsunokuchi-machi
辰口町
川北大橋
Terai-machi
寺井町
Tatsunokuchi
Terai-kita 寺井北
Honmachi 本町
Tsurugi-machi
鶴来町
Tsurugi
Kanatsurugi-nomiya
Shishiku-kōgen
Shirayama-hime-jinja
Kaga-Ichinomiya
Kutani chinaware sale area
Hakusan
Shirayamamachi 白山町
Mt. Kuragatake
Mt. Kabutoyama
Mt. Shiritakayama
Mt. Yoshitsuguyama
Mt. Ageharayama
Mt. Tomuroyama
Iō-gongen
Hōrinji
Kanazawa
Asano River
Saikawa River
Yuwaku
Mt. Iōzen
医王山
Fukumitsu
Touri Dam
Fukumitsu
福光
Jōhana
城端
Jōhana Line
東海北陸自動車道
NANTO-SHI
南砺市
Jōhanabetsuin-zentokuji
TOYAMA
Rindō
Mt. Takashōzuyama
Road closed when raining more than 80mm
TŌKAI-HOKURIKU EXPRESSWAY
Shimonashi 下梨
Tonami-shi
Mt. Sanpōyama
Mt. Takatsuboyama
Gokayama
五箇山
Shōgawa River
Gokayama
五箇山
Mt. Ōkurayama
Mt. Tsukigaharayama
Mt. Ōjishiyama
Beech free forest
Bunao Pass
ブナオ峠
Road No 156 closed when raining more than 80mm from Shirakawa-mura to Shōkawa-machi
Mt. Ageharayama
Kawachi-mura
河内村
Mt. Minowayama
Mt. Kannon-yama
Yūsenji
Kaga-yahata
Akahodani
Shimono
Tedori
Mt. Kuchisanpōdake
ISHIKAWA
Scenic view Hakusan mountain range
Mt. Akamakkoyama
Mt. Takanbōyama
Mt. Umenokiyama
Mt. Ōmine
Torigoe-mura
鳥越村
Yoshino 吉野
Senjō
Mt. Kasayama
Mt. Naradake
Mt. Ozōuzoyama
Mt. Mitsugatsujiyama
Mt. Ashikurayama
Yoshinodani-mura
吉野谷村
Mt. Matsuoyama
Mt. Takaochiyama
Closed in winter
Frozen between Kawachi-mura and Okuchi-mura
Drive-in served dishes of bear
Sename River
Mt. Ōfukubeyama
Mt. Oizurugatake
笈ヶ岳
Closed in winter
Torigoe-kōgen Daichichi
Ōshirakawa Dam
Mt. Ōkuradake
Ōkuradake-kōgen
Mt. Yurugizan
Gohyaku Pass
Oguchi-mura
尾口村
Ozogawa River
Chūgū-onsen
Mt. Kamouriyama
Mt. Sōzōyama
Mt. Bunaoyama
白川郷
Shirakawagō
Shirakawa-mura
白川村
Ogimachi 荻町
Kawai-mura
Mt. Wassōgatake
Tedorigawa Dam
Hakusan-Ichirino
白山スーパー林道
Mt. Hyōtan-yama
Mt. Sanpōiwadake
River
Mt. Ōyama
Mt. Mimurayama
ORD 3100
LAR 20600
Hakusan Super-rindō
Mt. Notanishōjiyama
Shirakawagō
白川郷
Closed in winter
Ushigakubi Pass
Closed in winter
Dainichi River
Mt. Shōgayama
Mt. Koarashiyama
Mt. Myōhōzan
Mt. Sarugababayama
Shirakawa-kaidō
Shirayumi
Mt. Sunagozen-yama
Mt. Sanpōkuzureyama
三方崩山
Shiramine-mura
白峰村
Shiramine
Shiramine-kōgen
Closed in winter
Road No 156 closed when raining more than 80mm from here to prefecture border
Shirakawagō-Hirase
Mt. Dainichizan
Mt. Nishiyama
Tedori River
MT. HAKUSAN
白山
Mt. Shakadake
Hakusan-okumiya
Ōshira River
Closed in winter
Miboro Dam
Tani Pass
谷峠
Hakusuiko Lake
Mt. Higashitakayama
Sugiyama
Miboroko Lake
Mt. Toritateyama
Mt. Nishitakayama
Mt. Betsusan
Mt. Hideridake
Takinami River
Mt. Daichōzan
GIFU
Okamigō River
Kangahara
Mt. Ninomine
法恩寺山道路 Hōonjisan-dōro
Ski Jam Katsuyama
KATSUYAMA-SHI
勝山市
Katsuyama
Mt. Hōonjisan
Mt. Akausagiyama
Mt. Gankyōjisan
Mt. Chōshigamine
Mt. Daishiyama
Mt. Maruyama
Makido 牧戸
Shōkawa-mura
荘川村
Takayama-shi
Mt. Kyōgatake
経ヶ岳
Hakusan-chūgū
Hatogayu
Hida-kaidō

B
C
D
Mikuni-chō
Kaga-shi
1
2
3
4
5
6
A
WAKASA-WAN
若狭湾
Shin-Nihonkai Ferry (to Tomakomai, Akita, Niigata)
to Harue
Echizen Line
Fukuiguchi
to Awara
to Shimizu
Fukui
to Sabae
to Ōno
FUKUI-SHI
福井市
Fukui
福井
Mt. Konpirayama
Koshino-mura
越廼村
Hōnji
Mt. Takaoyama
Closed in winter
Mt. Torigatake
Shimizu-chō
清水町
Amadani
Bushūgaike Lake
Mt. Ochisan
Mt. Rokushozan
Mt. Otsusakayama
C. Echizenmisaki
越前岬
Tamagawa 玉川
Tamagawa
Drive-in area
Umeura 梅浦
Ota-chō
織田町
Tsurugi-jinja
Tenno River
Asahi-chō
朝日町
SABAE-SHI
鯖江市
Nishi-Sabae 西鯖江
Nishi-Sabae
Sabae
鯖江
to Echizenmisaki
to Ota
to Kōno
Echizen-chō
越前町
Mt. Shiroyama
Miyazaki-mura
宮崎村
ECHIZEN COAST
越前海岸
Mt. Wakasudake
Mt. Onigatake
TAKEFU-SHI
武生市
Ōmushi-jinja
Komatsu 小松
Takase 高瀬
Myōhōji 妙法寺
Kasuga-jinja
Takefu
Yokoichi
横市
Takefu
武生
Komeno 米ノ
C. Kareizaki
Yoshinose River
Ōshio
Hachiman-jinja
Mt. Yarasudake
Minamiechizen-chō
南越前町
Mt. Iwataniyama
Nanjō
南条
Okunoin
Closed in winter
Mt. Honokeyama
Imajō
今庄
Yunoo
Mt. Somayama
Mt. Nabekurayama
Mt. Hinosan
Kuratani River
Hinokawa River
Shizukawa River
Asōzu River
Hirgashihonganji-betsuin
Asuwayama Park
Daiwa Spinning
Mt. Hachiman-yama
Hanandō
Bell mae
Rokujō
Asuwa
Imaichi 今市
Suginokidai
Asōzu
Ōdoro 大土呂
Mt. Monjusan
Kita-Sabae
北鯖江
Shinmei
Shimoshinjō
Kuninaka-jinja
Imadate-chō
今立町
Ōtaki-jinja
Iehisa
Fukui Bypass
Fukui Fukutake Line
Echizen Mikuni-Awara Line
Daianji
Nakatsuno
Morita
Oiwakegu
Fukui-eki-mae-Nishi-Fukui
Echizen-Hanando
Fukui
from Tsurugashi
Nagoya 110Km
Ōsaka 170Km
Kōnokaigan-dōro
ORD 890
LAR 3100
C. Tateishimisaki
立石岬
Sakurabashi-minami 桜橋南
C. Okazaki
C. Mongasaki
C. Myōjinsaki
Mizushima I.
Tsuruga-wan
Scenic view of sea
Crab saleared Drive-in
C. Washizaki
Mt. Saihōgatake
Jōgū-jinja
Scenic view of sea
C. Kozaki
Shirogane 白銀
Fukui 58Km
Ōno 88Km
Gifu 115Km
Tsuruga-kaidō
Mt. Tabatakeyama
Minami-Imajō
Imajō
Suizu
杉津
Mt. Hachibuseyama
Kinome Pass
Closed in winter
Closed in winter
HOKURIKU EXPRESSWAY
Hokuriku Line
Tochinoki Pass
栃ノ木峠
Mt. Kamitaniyama
Hokkoku-kaidō
Mt. Daikokuyama
Tsubakisaka Pass
椿坂峠
Mt. Anzōyama
Takatoki River
SHIGA
Yogo-chō
余呉町
Mt. Yokoyamadake
Mt. Shintaniyama
Mt. Nanazugatake
Tone
刀根
Hayase
Hiruga
Rainbow Line
Hirugako Lake
Kugushiko Lake
to Fukui
to Maibara
Tsuruga
81
C. Tsunekamimisaki
常神岬
Onkamijima I.
Congestion in spring and summer
Mikatagoko Lakes
三方五湖
Hirugako Lake
Kugushiko Lake
Mikatagoko Rainbow Line
三方五湖 レインボーライン
ORD 1020
LAR 4070
Ryūtakuji
Uwase-jinja
Suigetsuko Lake
Kogashima
Sugako Lake
C. Kurosaki
Ubejima I.
Kiyama
Mihama-chō
美浜町
Mihama
Tango-kaidō
Hōshunji
Tokushōji
Higashi-Mihama
Mt. Hatagoyama
C. Kurosaki
Seki Pass
Obama Line
Awano
Nishi-Tsuruga
Saifukuji
Kehinomatsubara (Beautiful Beach)
Tsuruga
TSURUGA-SHI
敦賀市
Kanayama Bypass
Kehi-jingū
Tsuruga
敦賀
Tsuruga-tunnel
Hikida 疋田
Tsuruga-kokusai
Shin-Hikida
Mt. Nosakadake
Kinomoto I.C.
81
128

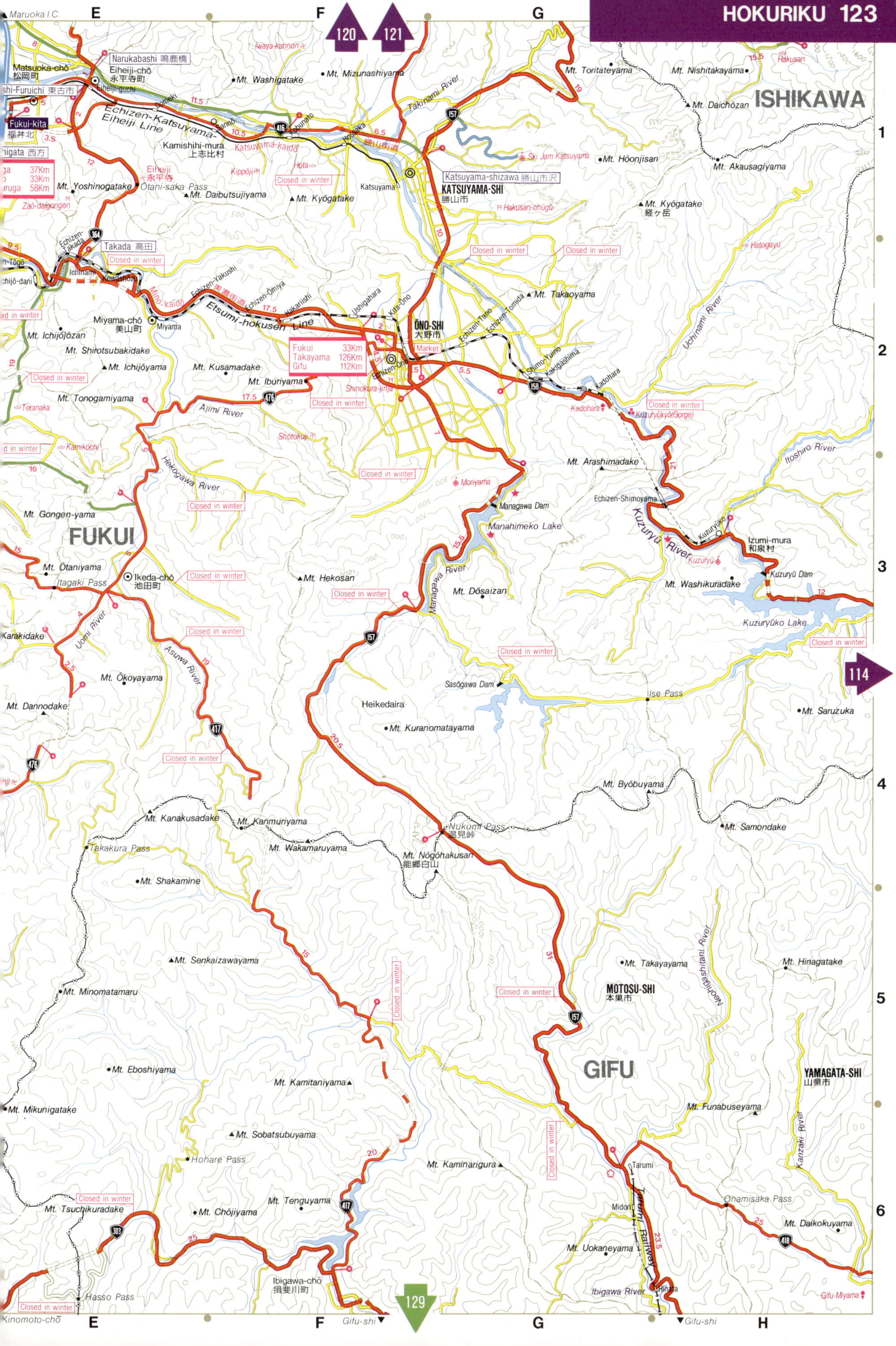

E
F
G
H
120
121
114
129
1
2
3
4
5
6
Maruoka I.C.
Matsuoka-chō
松岡町
Narukabashi 鳴鹿橋
Eiheiji-chō
永平寺町
Eiheiji-guchi
Fukui-kita
福井北
Echizen-Katsuyama-Eiheiji Line
Kamishihi-mura
上志比村
Katsuyama-kaidō
勝山街道
Eiheiji
永平寺
Ōtani-saka Pass
Mt. Yoshinogatake
Zaō-daigongen
Mt. Daibutsujiyama
Mt. Kyōgatake
Kippōji
Hota
Closed in winter
Mt. Washigatake
Mt. Mizunashiyama
Iwaya-kannon
Takinami River
Katsuyama
Katsuyama-shizawa 勝山市沢
KATSUYAMA-SHI
勝山市
Ski Jam Katsuyama
Hakusan-chūgū
Mt. Toritateyama
Mt. Nishitakayama
Hakusan
Mt. Daichōzan
ISHIKAWA
Mt. Hōonjisan
Mt. Akausagiyama
Mt. Kyōgatake
経ヶ岳
Hatogayu
Takada 高田
Echizen-Takada
Ichinami
Kowashōzu
Mino-kaidō
美濃街道
Echizen-Yakushi
Echizen-Ōmiya
Etsumi-hokusen Line
Hakarishi
Ushigahara
Kita-Ōno
Miyama-chō
美山町
Miyama
Mt. Ichijōjōzan
Mt. Shirotsubakidake
Mt. Ichijōyama
Mt. Kusamadake
Mt. Tonogamiyama
Mt. Iburiyama
Teranaka
Kamikōchi
Ajimi River
Shōtokuji
Fukui 33Km
Takayama 126Km
Gifu 112Km
ŌNO-SHI
大野市
Market
Echizen-Ōno
Shinokura-jinja
Echizen-Tano
Echizen-Tomida
Mt. Takaoyama
Shimo-Yuino
Kakigashima
Kadohara
Kuzuryūkyō(Gorge)
Uchinami River
Itoshiro River
Mt. Arashimadake
Moriyama
Managawa Dam
Manahimeko Lake
Echizen-Shimoyama
Kuzuryūko
Izumi-mura
和泉村
Kuzuryū River
Kuzuryū Dam
Mt. Washikuradake
Kuzuryūko Lake
Hekogawa River
Mt. Gongen-yama
FUKUI
Mt. Ōtaniyama
Itagaki Pass
Ikeda-chō
池田町
Uomi River
Karakidake
Mt. Ōkoyayama
Asuwa River
Mt. Dannodake
Mt. Hekosan
Managawa River
Mt. Dōsaizan
Sasōgawa Dam
Ise Pass
Mt. Saruzuka
Heikedaira
Mt. Kuranomatayama
Mt. Byōbuyama
Mt. Kanakusadake
Mt. Kanmuriyama
Nukumi Pass
温見峠
Mt. Samondake
Takakura Pass
Mt. Wakamaruyama
Mt. Nōgōhakusan
能郷白山
Mt. Shakamine
Mt. Senkaizawayama
Mt. Minomatamaru
Mt. Takayayama
Mt. Hinagatake
MOTOSU-SHI
本巣市
Neohigashitani River
Mt. Eboshiyama
GIFU
YAMAGATA-SHI
山県市
Mt. Kamitaniyama
Mt. Mikunigatake
Mt. Funabuseyama
Kanzaki River
Mt. Sobatsubuyama
Hohare Pass
Mt. Kaminarigura
Tarumi
Tarumi Railway
Midori
Mt. Tsuchikuradake
Mt. Chōjiyama
Mt. Tenguyama
Onamisaka Pass
Mt. Daikokuyama
Mt. Uokaneyama
Ibigawa-chō
揖斐川町
Ibigawa River
Hinata
Hasso Pass
Gifu-Miyama
Kinomoto-chō
Gifu-shi

HYŌGO
ŌSAKA
ŌSAKA-WAN
大阪湾
SASAYAMA-SHI
篠山市
MAIZURU WAKASA EXPWY
舞鶴若狭自動車道
Mt. Shiragamidake
Mt. Mikunidake
Mt. Okuyama
Mt. Kokuzōsan
Mt. Senjōjisan
Mt. Ōfunayama
Mt. Atagoyama
Mt. Mikurayama
Mt. Miyama
Mt. Hangokuyama
Rurikei(Gorge)
Mt. Tsurugioyama
Mt. Kowadayama
Mt. Gyōjayama
Mt. Asahiyama
Mt. Ryōsengatake
Nose-chō
能勢町
Ōusaka Pass
Tennō Pass
Haraigatawa Pass
Nishi-tōge Pass
Sanbon Pass
Ono Pass
Kiritsume Pass
Ōsaka Pass
Noma Pass
Mt. Myōkensan
Mt. Tendaisan
Toyono-chō
豊能町
Mt. Ishidōgatake
Tōjōko Lake
Tōjō River
Tōjō-chō
東条町
Hyōgo-Tōjō
ひょうご東条
Sanda-nishi
三田西
SANDA-SHI
三田市
Yokawa
吉川
Yokawa-chō
吉川町
Kōbe-Sanda
神戸三田
Kōbe Jct
神戸Jct
Nishinomiya-kita
西宮北
Kōbe-kita
神戸北
Miki Jct
三木Jct
SAN-YŌ EXPRESSWAY
山陽自動車道
CHŪGOKU EXPRESSWAY
中国自動車道
Inagawa-chō
猪名川町
Mt. Ōiwadake
Hatsuka River
Hazukawa River
Inagawa River
Minoo River
KAWANISHI-SHI
川西市
IKEDA-SHI
池田市
MINOO-SHI
箕面市
Chūgoku-Ikeda
中国池田
Chūgoku-Toyonaka
中国豊中
TAKARAZUKA-SHI
宝塚市
Takarazuka
ITAMI-SHI
伊丹市
TOYONAKA-SHI
豊中市
SUITA-SHI
吹田市
Ōsaka International (Itami)
Mt. Nagemachiyama
Mt. Taishakusan
Mt. Kongōdōjiyama
Mt. Rokkōsan
六甲山
Mt. Kabutoyama
Mt. Nagasakayama
Mt. Mayasan
Arima-onsen
有馬
Arima Line
Rokkō-Kita-dōro
Nishinomiya-kita-dōro
Dōyū Driveway
Shin-Kōbe Tunnel
Kōbe-nishi
神戸西
Nishi-Kōbe-dōro
Kita-ku
北区
Hankyū Kōbe Line
Tōkaidō Line
Nishinomiya Inter
西宮インター
Nishinomiya
Amagasaki
尼崎
ASHIYA-SHI
芦屋市
NISHINOMIYA-SHI
西宮市
AMAGASAKI-SHI
尼崎市
KŌBE-SHI
神戸市
Chūō-ku
中央区
Hyōgo-ku
兵庫区
Nagata-ku
長田区
Suma-ku
須磨区
Nada-ku
灘区
Higashinada-ku
東灘区
Harbor Highway
Rokkō Island
Port Island
C. Wadamisaki
Mukogawa River
Kanzaki River
Ajigawa River
Yamato River
Universal Studios Japan
ユニバーサル・スタジオ・ジャパン
Konohana-ku
此花区
Fukushima-ku
福島区
ŌSAKA-SHI
大阪市
Nishi-ku
西区
Minato-ku
港区
Taishō-ku
大正区
Naniwa-ku
浪速区
Nishinari-ku
西成区
Suminoe-ku
住之江区
Sumiyoshi-ku
住吉区
Nishiyodogawa-ku
西淀川区
Yodogawa-ku
淀川区
SAKAI-SHI
堺市
TAKAISHI-SHI
高石市
Sakai Jct
Sakai
Nagoya 210Km
Hiroshima 350Km
Kitajima
北島
Ōhama-Kita machi
大浜北町
Ōsaka 17Km
Kawachi-Nagano 17Km
Izumi-Ōtsu 11Km
Hanwa Line
Nankai Kōya Line
Kansai-kisen (to Beppu·Matsuyama)
Shikoku Orange Ferry(to Tōyo)
Ōsaka-Kōchi tokkyū Ferry(to Kōchi)
to Nanba
to Sakai
Suminoe
住之江
to Nose
to Takarazuka
to Ōsaka
ORD 400 LAR 1510
ORD 250 LAR 900
ORD 800 LAR 3200
ORD 600 LAR 2200
ORD 200 LAR 730
ORD 200 LAR 300
ORD 300 LAR 1060
ORD 100 LAR 360
Congestion
Leisure Plantation
Iris garden
Drive in area
Along mountain torrent
Congestion in autumn
Frozen road
Narrow and curves
Mashroom picking area
Sharp curve
Wakayama-shi
Yashiro-chō
82
101
63
110
A
B
C
D
1
2
3
4
5
6

E
F
G
H
83
111
126
1
2
3
4
5
6
KYŌTO-SHI 京都市
KAMEOKA-SHI 亀岡市
Biwako Lake
MORIYAMA-SHI 守山市
ŌTSU-SHI 大津市
KUSATSU-SHI 草津市
RITTŌ-SHI 栗東市
SHIGA
KYŌTO
NARA
MEISHIN EXPRESSWAY 名神高速道路
NISHI-MEIHAN EXPRESSWAY 西名阪自動車道
San-in Line
Tōkaidō Line
Keihan Line
Kintetsu Kyōto Line
Nara Line
Kansai Line
Kintetsu Nara Line
Kintetsu Kashihara Line
Katamachi Line
Kizugawa River
Yodogawa River
Ujigawa River
Katsura River
Hozugawa River
Hasegawa River
MUKŌ-SHI 向日市
NAGAOKAKYŌ-SHI 長岡京市
UJI-SHI 宇治市
JŌYŌ-SHI 城陽市
YAWATA-SHI 八幡市
TAKATSUKI-SHI 高槻市
IBARAKI-SHI 茨木市
HIRAKATA-SHI 枚方市
KATANO-SHI 交野市
NEYAGAWA-SHI 寝屋川市
SHIJŌNAWATE-SHI 四條畷市
KADOMA-SHI 門真市
DAITŌ-SHI 大東市
HIGASHIŌSAKA-SHI 東大阪市
YAO-SHI 八尾市
KASHIWARA-SHI 柏原市
FUJIIDERA-SHI 藤井寺市
HABIKINO-SHI 羽曳野市
IKOMA-SHI 生駒市
NARA-SHI 奈良市
YAMATOKŌRIYAMA-SHI 大和郡山市
TENRI-SHI 天理市
KASHIBA-SHI 香芝市
YAMATOTAKADA-SHI 大和高田市
KASHIHARA-SHI 橿原市
SAKURAI-SHI 桜井市
KYŌTANABE-SHI 京田辺市
SETTSU-SHI 摂津市
Seika-chō 精華町
Kizu 木津
Kamo-chō 加茂町
Kasagi-chō 笠置町
Wazuka-chō 和束町
Ujitawara-chō 宇治田原町
Ide-chō 井手町
Oyamazaki-chō 大山崎町
Kumiyama-chō 久御山町
Heguri-chō 平群町
Ikaruga-chō 斑鳩町
Sangō-chō 三郷町
Ōji-chō 王寺町
Kawai-chō 河合町
Kanmaki-chō 上牧町
Kōryō-chō 広陵町
Tawaramoto-chō 田原本町
Miyake-chō 三宅町
Kawanishi-chō 川西町
Ando-chō 安堵町
Tsuge-mura 都祁村
Minamiyamashiro-mura 南山城村
Taishi-chō 太子町
Haibara-chō 榛原町
Kyōto-minami 京都南
Ōyamazaki 大山崎
Seta 瀬田
Seta-higashi 瀬田東
Seta-nishi 瀬田西
Kusatsu-tanakami 草津田上
Kyōto-higashi 京都東
Ōtsu 大津
Rittō
Ibaraki
Settsu-kita
Kadoma
Daitō-Tsurumi
Higashiōsaka-kita
Higashiōsaka-minami
Yao
Matsubara
Fujiidera
Mihara-kita
Mihara-minami
Kashiwara
Kashiba
Hōryūji
Kōriyama
Tenri
ORD 1150 LAR 4650
ORD 1000 LAR 2800
ORD 150 LAR 570
ORD 930 LAR 3350
ORD 700 LAR 1950
ORD 800 LAR 2300
ORD 1720 LAR 5130
ORD 1300 LAR 5200
from kyōto shi
Nagoya 160Km
Ōsaka 45Km
Ueno 46Km
Tsu 93Km
Kashihara 19Km
Nara 30Km
Ōsaka 19Km
Kashihara 22Km
Accident prone area
Congestion
Congestion in spring
Congestion in spring and autumn
Drive-in area
Vehicles prohibited
Side roads ahead
Tea sale area
Tea plantation area
Scenic view of Nara basin
Scenic view of Ujigawa river
Sumiyama artisan village
Along Yodogawa River
Nara-Okuyama Driveway
Shigikoma Skyline
Mt. Atagoyama
Mt. Ushimatsuyama
Mt. Hakamagoshiyama
Mt. Daishinyama
Mt. Inoseyama
Mt. Kisenyama
Mt. Ōminesan
Mt. Jūbuzan
Mt. Ōyakiyama
Mt. Mitsugatake
Mt. Mikamiyama
Mt. Yuyasan
Mt. Ikomayama
Mt. Shiroyama
Mt. Kōnosan
Mt. Ryūōyama
Mt. Kaigahirayama
Mt. Tenjinsan
Mt. Miwasan
Zenjōji Pass
Uchiro Pass
Kōzui Pass
Kuragari Pass
Oinosaka Pass
Mikyōsaka Pass
Sakura Pass
Obama-shi
Iga-shi
Nabari-shi

128
125
111
104
SHIGA
KYŌTO
NARA
Biwako Lake
KYŌTO-SHI
京都市
ŌTSU-SHI
大津市
KUSATSU-SHI
草津市
RITTŌ-SHI
栗東市
KONAN-SHI
湖南市
KŌKA-SHI
甲賀市
UJI-SHI
宇治市
IGA-SHI
伊賀市
NARA-SHI
奈良市
TENRI-SHI
天理市
NABARI-SHI
名張市
SAKURAI-SHI
桜井市
KASHIHARA-SHI
橿原市
Ōmi-ōhashi-dōro
ORD 150
LAR 570
Imazu 50Km
Kusatsu 10Km
Kyōto 13Km
Keiji Bypass
ORD 930
LAR 3350
Hikone 48Km
Minakuchi 22Km
Ōtsu 10Km
Hikone 41Km
Kameyama 31Km
Kusatsu 22Km
Hino-Minakuchi Green
ORD 200
LAR 730
Kameyama 35Km
Nabari 16Km
Nara 44Km
Kyōto 37Km
Ōsaka 37Km
Kashihara 19Km
ORD 1720
LAR 5130
Nara-Okuyama Driveway
Ueno 16Km
Tsu 43Km
Kashihara 31Km
MEISHIN EXPRESSWAY
Tōkaidō-Sanyō-Shinkansen
Tōkaidō Line
Kusatsu Line
Shigaraki-kōgen Railway
Kansai Line
Kintetsu Ōsaka Line
Nara Line
Sakurai Line
Iga Line
Kizugawa River
Ujigawa River
Igagawa River
Nabari River
Hattori River
Kawakami River
Mt. Daishin-yama
Mt. Inoseyama
Mt. Iwaosan
Mt. Sasagadake
Mt. Jūbuzan
Mt. Mitsugatake
Mt. Kōnosan
Mt. Shiroyama
Mt. Ryūōyama
Mt. Kaigahirayama
Mt. Tenjinsan
Mt. Kunimiyama
Mt. Kurosoyama
Mt. Amagatake
Mt. Ōborayama
Sakura Pass
Otoki Pass
Ima Pass
Kōzui Pass
Scenic view of Ujigawa Rhein
Scenic view of Nara basin
Tea sale area
Tea plantation
Chinaware shopping area
Grape picking area
Caution-Monkeys
Bus priority area
Side roads ahead
Limited traffic in poor weather con
Akame Waterfalls
赤目四十八滝
Hikone-shi
Ryūō I.C.
Hikone-shi
Haibara-chō
Kyōto Street
Kyoto-minami I.C.
Shiōnawate-shi

E
F
G
H
1
2
3
4
5
6
129
130
132
104
105
MIE
ISE-WAN
伊勢湾
HIGASHI-MEIHAN EXPRESSWAY
東名阪自動車道
ISE EXPRESSWAY
伊勢自動車道
Yokkaichi-higashi
四日市東
Asahi-chō
朝日町
Wahgan-Nagashima
湾岸長島
Kawagoe-chō
川越町
Wangan-Kuwana
湾岸桑名
Mie-Kawagoe
みえ川越
Mt. Ryūzan
Saimyōji
Mt. Gozaishodake
御在所岳
Gozaisho
Mt. Watamukiyama
Yunoyama
湯の山
Komono-chō
菰野町
Yunoyama Line
Asake-keikoku (Gorge)
Closed in winter
Buhei Pass
Suzuka Skyline
鈴鹿スカイライン
Yokkaichi
四日市
Kasumigaura
Tomidahama
Nagoya 42Km
Kameyama 20Km
Tsu 30Km
Suehirochō 末広町
Chūbu 中部
YOKKAICHI-SHI
四日市市
Mt. Nyūdōgatake
Tsubaki-ōkami-yashiro
Closed in winter
Matsuo River
Mt. Sengatake
Minami-Tsuchiyama 南土山
Oiwake 追分
Suzuka River
Utsube River
Unemechō 妥女町
Kusu-chō
楠町
Suzuka
鈴鹿
Tamura-jinja
Tōkaidō
東海道
Drive-in area
Suzuka Pass
鈴鹿峠
One-way traffic
Mt. Takahatayama
Mt. Myōjōgatake
Mt. Nasugaharayama
Kansai Line
Kasado
加佐登
SUZUKA-SHI
鈴鹿市
Ise-Wakamatsu
KAMEYAMA-SHI
亀山市
Kameyama
亀山
Seki
関
Kuga
Minami-Zaike
Mukai
Accident-prone area
Accident-prone area
Yokkaichi 21Km
Tsu 20Km
Ueno 35Km
Suzuka Circuit
Shimonoshō
Geinō-chō
芸濃町
Geinō
芸濃
Kisei Line
Ise Railway
Kintetsu Nagoya Line
Shiroko
Kawage-chō
河芸町
Igagoe Pass
Mt. Kyōgamine
Anō-chō
安濃町
Anōgawa River
Shiratsuka 白塚
Mt. Kasatoriyama
Misato-mura
美里村
Iga-kaidō
Nagano River
TSU-SHI
津市
Akogigaura
Nagoya 65Km
Ōsaka 120Km
Nishi-Akogi
西阿漕
HISAI-SHI
久居市
Hisai
久居
to Tsu
to Nabari
to Matsusaka
Limited traffic in poor weather conditions
Sakakibaraonsenguchi
Kintetsu Ōsaka Line
Kumozu River
Ichishi-chō
一志町
Ichishi-Ureshino
一志嬉野
Hakusan-chō
白山町
Karasu-chō
香良洲町
Ureshino
嬉野
Kozu 小津
Meishō Line
MATSUSAKA-SHI
松阪市
Miyamachi 宮町
Matsusaka
松阪
Tsu 17Km
Ise 20Km
Kumano 120Km
Mt. Kannondake
Hossaka Pass
Mt. Higeyama
Mt. Hossakayama
Mt. Amagoiyama
Hosono Pass
Hatemata River
Sakanai River
Kushida River
Kintetsu Yamada Line
Meiwa-chō
明和町
Miyagawa River
Obata-chō
小俣町
Misono-mura
御薗村
Mt. Shiraisan
Taki-chō
to Nagoya

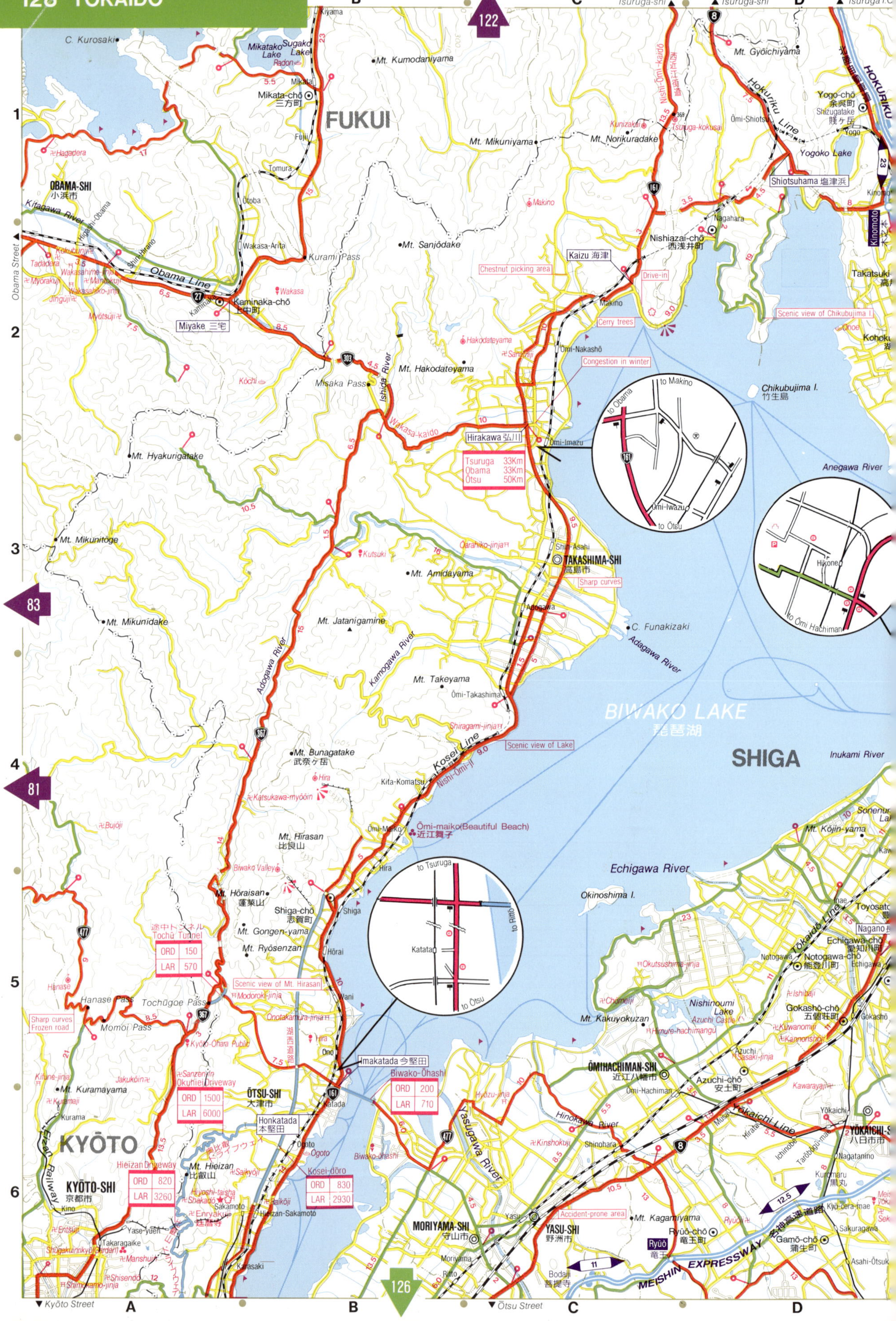
122
126
83
81
FUKUI
SHIGA
KYŌTO
BIWAKO LAKE
琵琶湖
Tsuruga-shi
Tsuruga I.C
C. Kurosaki
Mikatako Lake
Sugako Lake
Mikata-chō
三方町
Mt. Kumodaniyama
Mt. Gyōichiyama
Yogo-chō
余呉町
Yogoko Lake
HOKURIKU
Hokuriku Line
Ōmi-Shiotsu
Shiotsuhama 塩津浜
Kinomoto
Mt. Mikuniyama
Mt. Norikuradake
Nishi-Ōmi-kaidō
Kunizakai
Tsuruga-kokusai
OBAMA-SHI
小浜市
Hagadera
Kitagawa River
Obama Line
Obama Street
Tadadera
Myōrakuji
Mantokuji
Jinguji
Myōtsūji
Kaminaka-chō
上中町
Miyake 三宅
Kumami Pass
Wakasa
Mt. Sanjōdake
Makino
Nishiazai-chō
西浅井町
Nagahara
Kaizu 海津
Chestnut picking area
Drive-in
Cerry trees
Scenic view of Chikubujima I.
Takatsuki
Hakodateyama
Mt. Hakodateyama
Misaka Pass
Ishida River
Kōchi
Wakasa-kaido
Ōmi-Nakashō
Congestion in winter
Chikubujima I.
竹生島
Hirakawa 弘川
Ōmi-Imazu
Tsuruga 33Km
Obama 33Km
Ōtsu 50Km
to Makino
to Obama
Ōmi-Iwazu
to Ōtsu
Anegawa River
Hikone
to Ōmi Hachiman
Mt. Hyakurigatake
Mt. Mikunitoge
Mt. Mikunidake
Kutsuki
Oarahiko-jinja
Mt. Amidayama
Shin-Asahi
TAKASHIMA-SHI
高島市
Sharp curves
Adogawa
C. Funakizaki
Adagawa River
Mt. Jatanigamine
Kamogawa River
Adogawa River
Mt. Takeyama
Ōmi-Takashima
Shiragami-jinja
Scenic view of Lake
Mt. Bunagatake
武奈ヶ岳
Kosei Line
Nishi-Ōmi-ji
Kita-Komatsu
Hira
Katsukawa-myōōin
Inukami River
Bujōji
Mt. Hirasan
比良山
Ōmi-Maiko
Ōmi-maiko(Beautiful Beach)
近江舞子
Mt. Kōjin-yama
Biwako Valley
Mt. Hōraisan
蓬莱山
Shiga-chō
志賀町
Shiga
Mt. Gongen-yama
Mt. Ryōsenzan
Hōrai
Echigawa River
Okinoshima I.
to Tsuruga
Katata
to Ritto
to Ōtsu
Toyosato
Nagano
Echigawa-chō
Notogawa
Notogawa-chō
能登川町
Tōkaidō Line
途中トンネル
Tochū Tunnel
ORD 150
LAR 570
Scenic view of Mt. Hirasan
Modoroki-jinja
Wani
Okutsushima-jinja
Chōmeiji
Nishinoumi Lake
Azuchi Castle
Gokashō-chō
五個荘町
Ishibaji
Kuwanomiji
Kannonshōji
Hanase
Hanase Pass
Tochūgoe Pass
Momoi Pass
Sharp curves Frozen road
Onotakamura-jinja
Mt. Kakuyokuzan
Himure-hachimangū
Imakatada 今堅田
Biwako-Ōhashi
ORD 200
LAR 710
ŌMIHACHIMAN-SHI
近江八幡市
Azuchi-chō
安土町
Sasaki-jinja
Kawarayaji
Kitune-jinja
Mt. Kuramayama
Jakukōin
Sanzen-in
Ohara
Ōkuhiei Driveway
ORD 1500
LAR 6000
ŌTSU-SHI
大津市
Katada
Honkatada
本堅田
Yasugawa River
Hyōzu-jinja
Hinokawa River
Ōmi-Hachiman
Yōkaichi Line
Yōkaichi
YŌKAICHI-SHI
八日市市
Kurama
Eizan Railway
KYŌTO-SHI
京都市
Hieizan Driveway
ORD 820
LAR 3260
Mt. Hieizan
比叡山
Saikyōji
Hiyoshi-taisha
Shakadō
Enryakuji
延暦寺
Ogoto
Kosei-dōro
ORD 830
LAR 2930
Biwako-ohashi
Kinshokuji
Shinohara
Accident-prone area
Mt. Kagamiyama
Ryūō-chō
竜王町
Nagatanino
Kuromaru
Kyō-cera-mae
Gamō-chō
蒲生町
Sakuragawa
Asahi-Ōtsuka
Kino
Entsūji
Shūgakuinrikyū (Imperial Garden)
Takaragaike
Yase-yuen
Manshuin
Shisendō
Shimogamo-jinja
Sakamoto
Hieizan-Sakamoto
Karasaki
MORIYAMA-SHI
守山市
Moriyama
Ritto
Yasu
YASU-SHI
野洲市
Bodaiji
菩提寺
Ryūō
MEISHIN EXPRESSWAY
Kyōto Street
Ōtsu Street

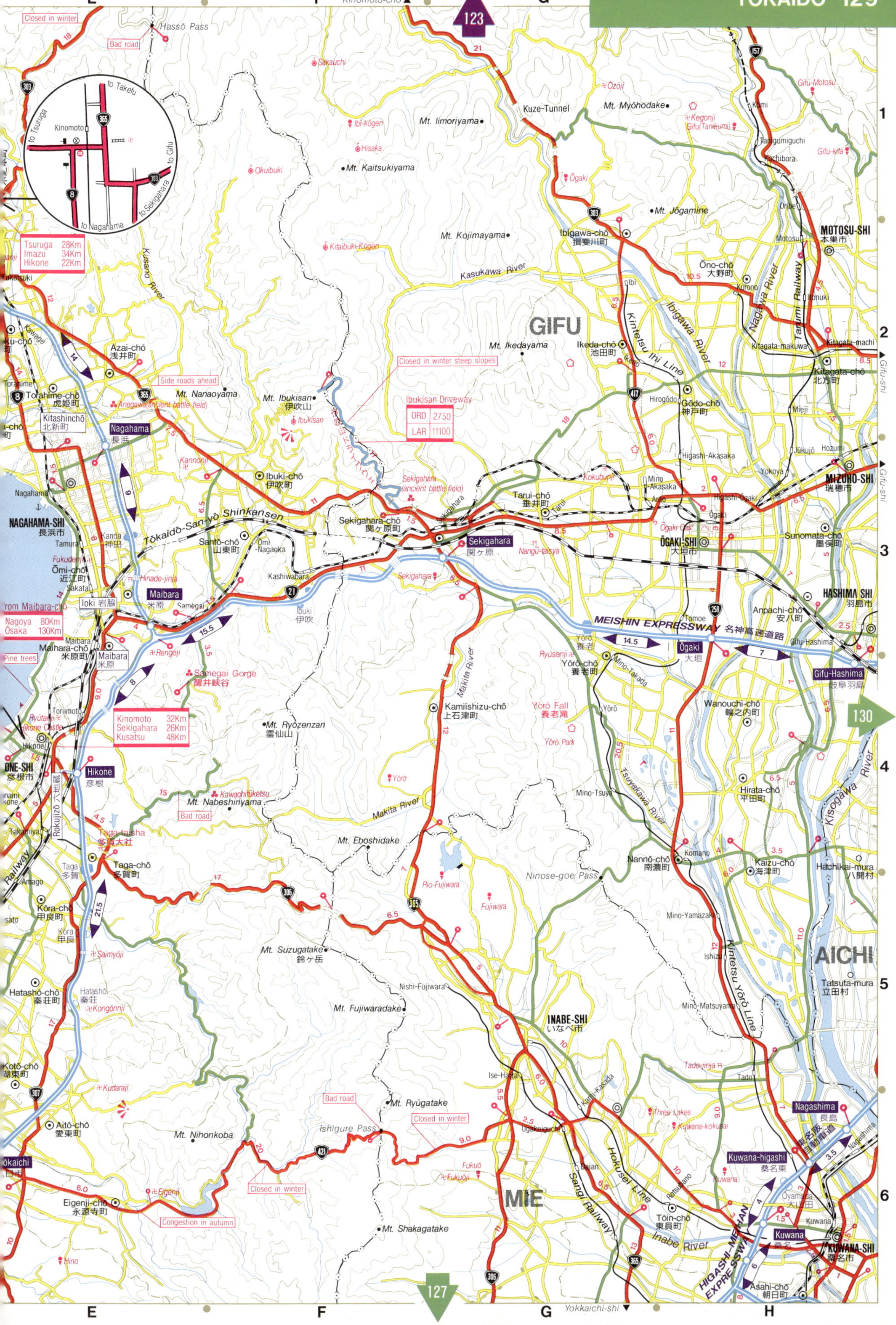
E
F
G
H
123
127
130
Kinomoto-chō
Yokkaichi-shi
Gifu-shi
1
2
3
4
5
6
GIFU
AICHI
MIE
Closed in winter
Bad road
Hassō Pass
to Takefu
to Tsuruga
Kinomoto
to Gifu
to Sekigahara
to Nagahama
Tsuruga 28Km
Imazu 34Km
Hikone 22Km
Kuze-Tunnel
Mt. Myōhodake
Mt. Iimoriyama
Mt. Kaitsukiyama
Mt. Kojimayama
Mt. Jōgamine
Ibigawa-chō 揖斐川町
MOTOSU-SHI 本巣市
Ōno-chō 大野町
Kasukawa River
Ibigawa River
Nagara River
Tarumi Railway
Kintetsu Ibi Line
Mt. Ikedayama
Ikeda-chō 池田町
Kitagata-chō 北方町
Gōdo-chō 神戸町
Closed in winter steep slopes
Ibukisan Driveway
ORD 2750
LAR 11100
Mt. Ibukisan 伊吹山
Mt. Nanaoyama
Side roads ahead
Azai-chō 浅井町
Torahime-chō 虎姫町
Kitashinchō 北新町
Nagahama 長浜
NAGAHAMA-SHI 長浜市
Ibuki-chō 伊吹町
Tōkaidō-San'yō Shinkansen
Santō-chō 山東町
Sekigahara-chō 関ケ原町
Sekigahara 関ケ原
Tarui-chō 垂井町
ŌGAKI-SHI 大垣市
MIZUHO-SHI 瑞穂市
Sunomata-chō 墨俣町
HASHIMA SHI 羽島市
Anpachi-chō 安八町
Ōmi-chō 近江町
Maibara 米原
Maihara-chō 米原町
Nagoya 80Km
Ōsaka 130Km
MEISHIN EXPRESSWAY 名神高速道路
Ōgaki 大垣
Gifu-Hashima 岐阜羽島
Yōrō-chō 養老町
Yōrō Fall 養老滝
Samegai Gorge 醒井峡谷
Kinomoto 32Km
Sekigahara 26Km
Kusatsu 48Km
Mt. Ryōzenzan 霊仙山
Kamiishizu-chō 上石津町
Makita River
Hikone 彦根
HIKONE-SHI 彦根市
Wanouchi-chō 輪之内町
Hirata-chō 平田町
Kisogawa River
Mt. Nabeshiriyama
Taga-taisha 多賀大社
Taga-chō 多賀町
Mt. Eboshidake
Ninose-goe Pass
Nannō-chō 南濃町
Kaizu-chō 海津町
Hachikai-mura 八開村
Kōra-chō 甲良町
Mt. Suzugatake 鈴ヶ岳
Mt. Fujiwaradake
Hatashō-chō 秦荘町
Tatsuta-mura 立田村
INABE-SHI いなべ市
Kintetsu Yōrō Line
Kotō-chō 湖東町
Mt. Ryūgatake
Ishigure Pass
Aitō-chō 愛東町
Mt. Nihonkoba
Nagashima 長島
Kuwana-higashi 桑名東
Hokusei Line
Sangi Railway
Eigenji-chō 永源寺町
Congestion in autumn
Mt. Shakagatake
Tōin-chō 東員町
Inabe River
Kuwana 桑名
KUWANA-SHI 桑名市
HIGASHI-MEIHAN EXPRESSWAY
Asahi-chō 朝日町

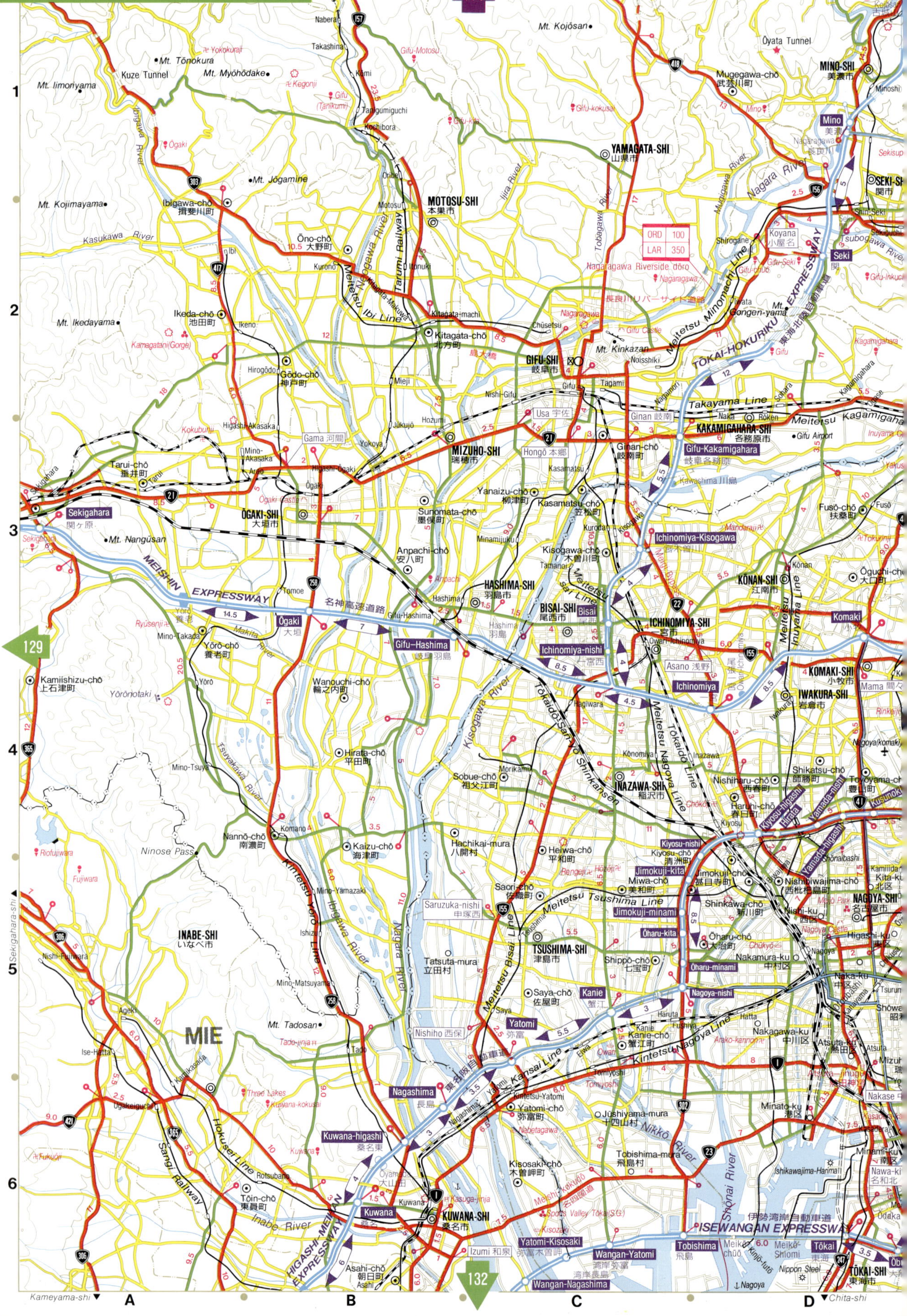
114
129
132
MIE
MOTOSU-SHI 本巣市
YAMAGATA-SHI 山県市
MINO-SHI 美濃市
SEKI-SHI 関市
GIFU-SHI 岐阜市
KAKAMIGAHARA-SHI 各務原市
MIZUHO-SHI 瑞穂市
ŌGAKI-SHI 大垣市
HASHIMA-SHI 羽島市
BISAI-SHI 尾西市
ICHINOMIYA-SHI 一宮市
KŌNAN-SHI 江南市
KOMAKI-SHI 小牧市
IWAKURA-SHI 岩倉市
INAZAWA-SHI 稲沢市
TSUSHIMA-SHI 津島市
NAGOYA-SHI 名古屋市
INABE-SHI いなべ市
KUWANA-SHI 桑名市
TŌKAI-SHI 東海市
MEISHIN EXPRESSWAY
名神高速道路
TŌKAI-HOKURIKU EXPRESSWAY
東海北陸自動車道
ISEWANGAN EXPRESSWAY
伊勢湾岸自動車道
HIGASHI-MEIHAN EXPRESSWAY
Nagara River
Ibigawa River
Kisogawa River
Shōnai River
Nikkō River
Tōkaidō Shinkansen
Tōkaidō Line
Meitetsu Nagoya Line
Kintetsu Nagoya Line
Kansai Line
Sangi Railway
Hokusei Line
Tarumi Railway
Takayama Line
Sekigahara
Ōgaki
Gifu-Hashima
Ichinomiya-Kisogawa
Ichinomiya-nishi
Ichinomiya
Komaki
Kuwana
Kuwana-higashi
Nagashima
Yatomi
Kanie
Wangan-Yatomi
Wangan-Nagashima
Tobishima
Tōkai
Mt. Kinkazan
Mt. Tadosan
Ninose Pass
Kameyama-shi
Chita-shi
Sekigahara-shi
Kameyama-shi ▼ A B C D ▼ Chita-shi

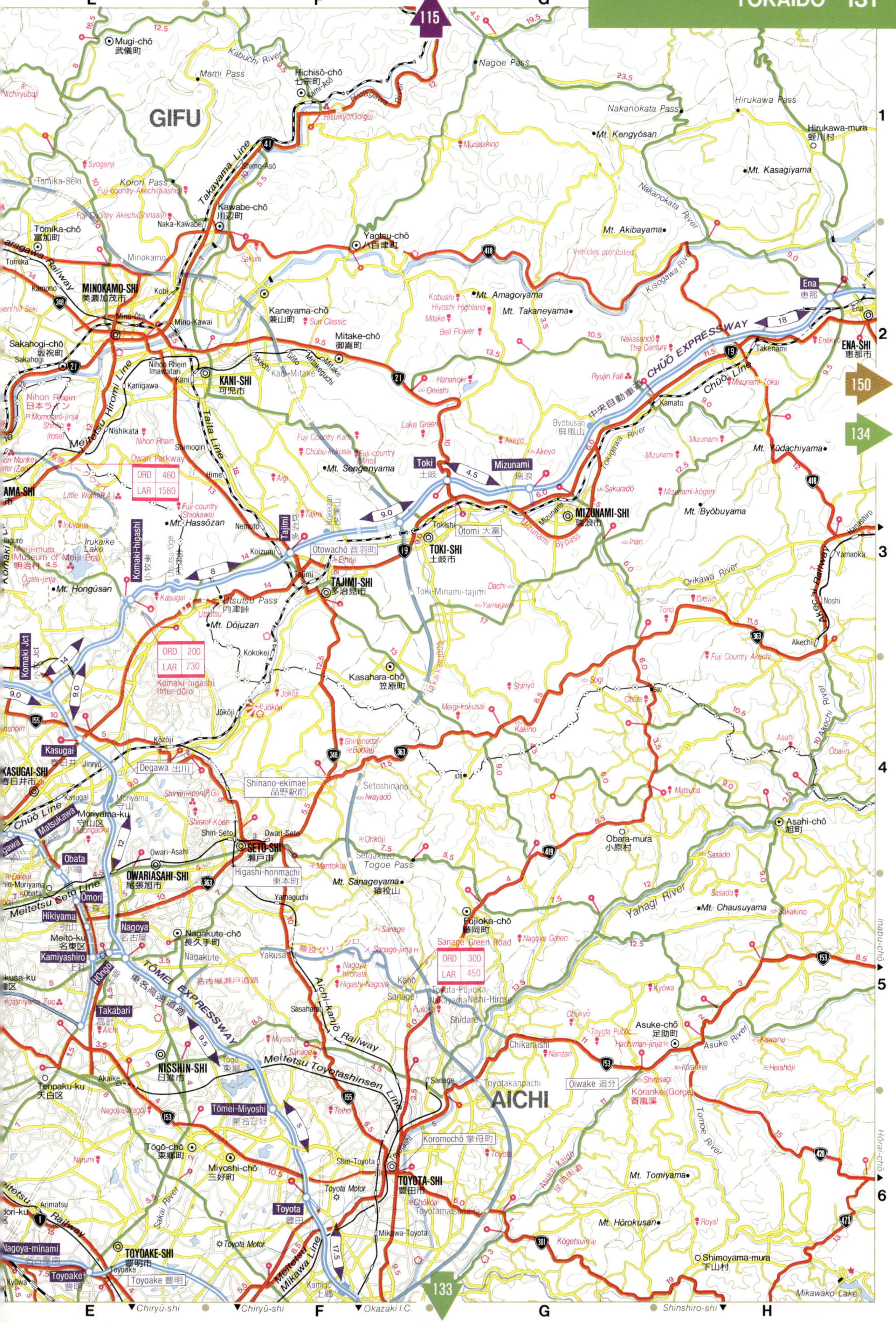
GIFU
AICHI
Mugi-chō 武儀町
Hichisō-chō 七宗町
Kabuchi River
Mami Pass
Nagoe Pass
Nakanokata Pass
Hirukawa Pass
Mt. Kengyōsan
Hirukawa-mura 蛭川村
Mt. Kasagiyama
Nakanokata River
Mt. Akibayama
Takayama Line
Shimo-Asō
Kawabe-chō 川辺町
Naka-Kawabe
Tomika-chō 富加町
Tomika-Seki
Korori Pass
Minokamo
MINOKAMO-SHI 美濃加茂市
Mino-Ōta
Mino-Kawai
Yaotsu-chō 八百津町
Kaneyama-chō 兼山町
Mitake-chō 御嵩町
Mt. Amagoiyama
Mt. Takaneyama
Sakahogi-chō 坂祝町
Sakahogi
Nihon Rhein 日本ライン
KANI-SHI 可児市
Kani
Taita Line
Meitetsu Hiromi Line
Nishikata
Kanigawa
Shimogiri
Owari Parkway
Mt. Sengenyama
Toki 土岐
Mizunami 瑞浪
Byōbusan 屏風山
Mt. Yūdachiyama
Mt. Byōbuyama
MIZUNAMI-SHI 瑞浪市
Mizunami Bypass
Toki River
Ena 恵那
ENA-SHI 恵那市
Takenami
Chūō Line
CHŪŌ EXPRESSWAY
中央自動車道
Kamato
Mizunami-Tōkai
150
134
115
Mt. Hassōzan
Mt. Hongūsan
Irukaike Lake
Komaki-higashi 小牧東
Komaki Jct
Tajimi
Otowachō 音羽町
Ōtomi 大富
TOKI-SHI 土岐市
Tokishi
Toki-Minami-tajimi
TAJIMI-SHI 多治見市
Utsutsu Pass 内津峠
Mt. Dōjuzan
Kokokei
Kasahara-chō 笠原町
Orikawa River
Akechi Railway
Yamaoka
Noshi
Akechi
Obara-mura 小原村
Asahi-chō 旭町
Yahagi River
Mt. Chausuyama
Akechi River
Jōkōji
Kōzōji
Kasugai
KASUGAI-SHI 春日井市
Degawa 出川
Shinano-ekimae 品野駅前
Setoshinano
SETO-SHI 瀬戸市
Owari-Seto
Shin-Seto
Higashi-honmachi 東本町
Moriyama-ku 守山区
Matsukawa
Chūō Line
Obata
Owari-Asahi
OWARIASAHI-SHI 尾張旭市
Ōmori
Meitetsu Seto Line
Hikiyama
Nagoya 名古屋
Meitō-ku 名東区
Kamiyashiro
Hongō
Takabari
Nagakute-chō 長久手町
Nagakute
TOMEI EXPRESSWAY
東名高速道路
Setoakazu
Togoe Pass
Mt. Sanageyama 猿投山
Yamaguchi
Yakusa
Aichi-kanjō Railway
Fujioka-chō 藤岡町
Sanage Green Road
Sanage
Toyota-Fujioka
Nakayama
Nishi-Hirose
Shidare
Chikaraishi
Asuke-chō 足助町
Asuke River
Kōrankei (Gorge) 香嵐渓
Oiwake 追分
Toyotakaneochi
Tomoe River
Mt. Tomiyama
Mt. Hōrokusan
Shimoyama-mura 下山村
Mikawako Lake
NISSHIN-SHI 日進市
Tenpaku-ku 天白区
Meitetsu Toyotashinsen Line
Tōmei-Miyoshi
Tōgō-chō 東郷町
Miyoshi-chō 三好町
Shin-Toyota
TOYOTA-SHI 豊田市
Koromochō 挙母町
Toyota
Toyota Motor
Mikawa-Toyota
TOYOAKE-SHI 豊明市
Toyoake 豊明
Nagoya-minami
Meitetsu Mikawa Line
Sakai River
Arimatsu
133
Chiryū-shi
Okazaki I.C.
Shinshiro-shi
ORD 460
LAR 1580
ORD 200
LAR 730
ORD 300
LAR 450
E
F
G
H
1
2
3
4
5
6

130
127
105
MIE
ISE-WAN
伊勢湾
Yokkaichi Jct
四日市Jct
Yokkaichi-higashi
四日市東
Asahi
朝日
Wangan-Nagashima
湾岸長島
Wangan-Yatomi
湾岸弥富
Yatomi-Kisosaki
弥富木曽岬
Kisogawa River
Nagashima
Nagashima Spa Land(A.P.)
Mie-Kawagoe
Wangan-Kuwana
Ibigawa River
Asahi-chō
朝日町
Kawagoe-chō
川越町
Sangi Railway
Komono-chō
菰野町
Yunoyamaonsen
Komono
Gozaisho
御在所
Sakabe
Tsuzumigaura
Tomida
Tomidahama
Hamada 浜田
HIGASHI-MEIHAN EXPRESSWAY
東名阪自動車道
Yokkaichi
四日市
Mitaki River
Yunoyama Line
Ise-Kawashima
Yokkaichi Central
Chūbu 中部
Nagoya 42Km
Kameyama 20Km
Tsu 30Km
YOKKAICHI-SHI
四日市市
Kintetsu-Yokkaichi
Yokkaichi
Hinaga
Nishi-Hino
Oiwake 追分
Minami-Yokkaichi
Suzuka River
Utsube River
Utsube
Suzuka
鈴鹿
Kita-Kusu
Kusu-chō
楠町
Kawarada
Kojinyama-kannonji
Kasato-jinja
Ishiyakushiji
Kansai Line
Kawano
Kasato
SUZUKA-SHI
鈴鹿市
Nagoya Line
Hiratacho
Suzuka Line
Suzuka
Idagawa
Ise-Wakamatsu
Kitatamagaki-chō 北玉垣町
Tamagaki
Suzuka Circuit
Suzuka Circuit Ino
Ino-jinja
Tokuda
Ise Railway
Ise-kaidō
Shiroko
Shimonoshō
Nakaseko
Ise-Ueno
Kisei Line
Kawage-chō
河芸町
Toyotsuueno
Kawage
Senshūji
Ishinden
Higashi-Ishinden
Kurima 栗真
Anōgawa River
Tsu
津
ISE EXPRESSWAY
伊勢自動車道
TSU-SHI
津市
Akogigaura
Tsushinmachi
Akogi
Yūki-jinja
Nishi-Akogi
西阿漕
Tsu-Matsuzaka
Hisai
久居
HISAI-SHI
久居市
Takachaya
Karasu-chō
香良洲町
Kumozu River
Ise-Nakagawa
Rokken
Kotsu 小津
Gōngenmae
Isenakahara
Ureshino
嬉野
Matsusaka
松阪
Kaminoshō
MATSUSAKA-SHI
松阪市
Miyamachi 宮町
Higashi-Matsusaka
Kushida River
Harai River
Sakanai River
Kushida
Koishiro
Tokuwa
Meiwa-chō
明和町
Tsu 17Km
Ise 20Km
Kumano 120Km
Kintetsu Yamada Line
Akeno Airport
Myōjō
Taki
Ise
Obata
Obata-chō
小俣町
Miyagawa
Miyagawa River
Isuzu River
Misono-mura
御薗村
Futaminoura
Futami-chō
二見町
Ushijima I.
Tōshijima I.
答志島
C. Kanzakimisaki
Oka
Seiwa-Taki I.C
Ōdai-chō
Ise-shi
Toba-shi
Geinō-chō
Iga-shi
Shūrakuen
Nippon Steel
Nagoya
TŌKAI-SHI
東海市
Ōtagawa
Daido Steel
Yokosukachō 横須賀町
CHITA-SHI
知多市
Asakura
Minami-Kagiya
Meitetsu Tokoname Line
Meitetsu Kōwa Line
Jiunji
Hachiman-jinja
Aichi-yōsui River
Agui
Tōun-in
Agui-chō
阿久比町
Ōnomachi
Chita-ōdan-dōro
ORD 200
LAR 730
Handa-chūō
Sumiyoshichō
知多横断道路
Tokoname
TOKONAME-SHI
常滑市
Rinkū
中部国際空港連絡道
Centrair-higashi
Meitetsu Kūkō Line
Handa
Aoyama
Higashi-Narawa
Central Japan International Airport
Taketoyo
Taketoyo-chō
武豊町
Fuki
Higashi-kosugaya
東小鈴谷
Chita
Chita Pen.
知多半島
Mihama
Kaminoma
Futto
Minami Chita-dōro
ORD 400
LAR 1100
Minami-Chita Beach Land(R.A.)
Meitetsu Chitashinsen Line
Noma
Mihama-chō
美浜町
C. Nomasaki
Minami-Chita
Minami-Aichi (Mihama)
Utsumi
Minami-Chita Green Valley(S.G.)
Iwaya
Minamichita-chō
南知多町
Nakasu-jima
Taiheiyō Ferry (to Sendai-Tomakomai)
Arimurasangyō Ferry (to Ōsaka-Naha)

AICHI
Toyoake
Toyoake Inter 豊明インター
Toyota-minami
Toyota-higashi
Toyota Auto Body
Toyota Motor
Toyota I.C.
131
ŌBU-SHI 大府市
Negichō 楝宜町
Miyanokoshi 宮腰
CHIRYŪ-SHI 知立市
KARIYA-SHI 刈谷市
ANJŌ-SHI 安城市
OKAZAKI-SHI 岡崎市
Ōsaka 240Km
Tōkyō 320Km
Okazaki 岡崎
Hatchō 八帖
Aichi-Kanjō Railway
Tōkaidō 東海道
Meitetsu Nagoya Line
Meitetsu Nishio Line
Tōkaidō San-Yō-Shinkansen
TŌMEI EXPRESSWAY
TAKAHAMA-SHI 高浜市
HEKINAN-SHI 碧南市
Wakamatsuchō 若松町
HANDA-SHI 半田市
NISHIO-SHI 西尾市
Kōta-chō 幸田町
Mikawa-wan Skyline
ORD 520
LAR 2100
ORD 250
LAR 930
ORD 450
Otowa-Gamagōri 音羽蒲郡
Otowa-chō 音羽町
Nukata-chō 額田町
Hagisaka Pass
Somasaka Pass
Otogawa River
Fukōzu-jinno 深溝神野
GAMAGŌRI-SHI 蒲郡市
Mikawa-wan Orange Road
ORD 250
LAR 930
TOYOKAWA-SHI 豊川市
Meitetsu Toyokawa Line
Iida Line
Mito-chō 御津町
Kozakai-chō 小坂井町
Miyashita 宮下
ORD 100
LAR 360
Kozakai Bypass
136
Sanganesan Skyline
ORD 410
LAR 1680
Mt. Sanganesan
Meitetsu Gamagōri Line
Kira-chō 吉良町
Isshiki-chō 一色町
Hazu-chō 幡豆町
Maeshima I.
Ōshima I.
Kojima I.
Kajishima I.
Sarugashima I.
C. Gozenzaki
Toyokawa River
ORD 200
LAR 730
Toyokawahashi
TOYOHASHI-SHI 豊橋市
Toyohashi Railway
Toyohashi Bypass
C. Ōsuzaki
Himeshima I.
to Gamagōri
to Kira
Katahara
Yahagi River
Yahagifuru River
Chita-wan
Mikawa-wan
Sakushima I. 佐久島
Himagashima I.
C. Hazumisaki 羽豆岬
Shinojima I.
Nojima I.
Mt. Zaōsan
TAHARA-SHI 田原市
Tahara Bypass
Ashigaike Lake
Atsumi Pen. 渥美半島
Atsumi-chō 渥美町
Higashi-akazawa 東赤沢
Hamamatsu-shi
Tōkyō 340km
Nagoya 90km
Irako Seaside
Atsumi Flower Center(flower garden)
C. Iragomisaki 伊良湖岬
Meitetsu Ferry
Ise-wan Ferry (to Toba)
Kamijima I. 神島
Taiheiyō Ferry(to Sendai)
E
F
G
H
1
2
3
4
5
6

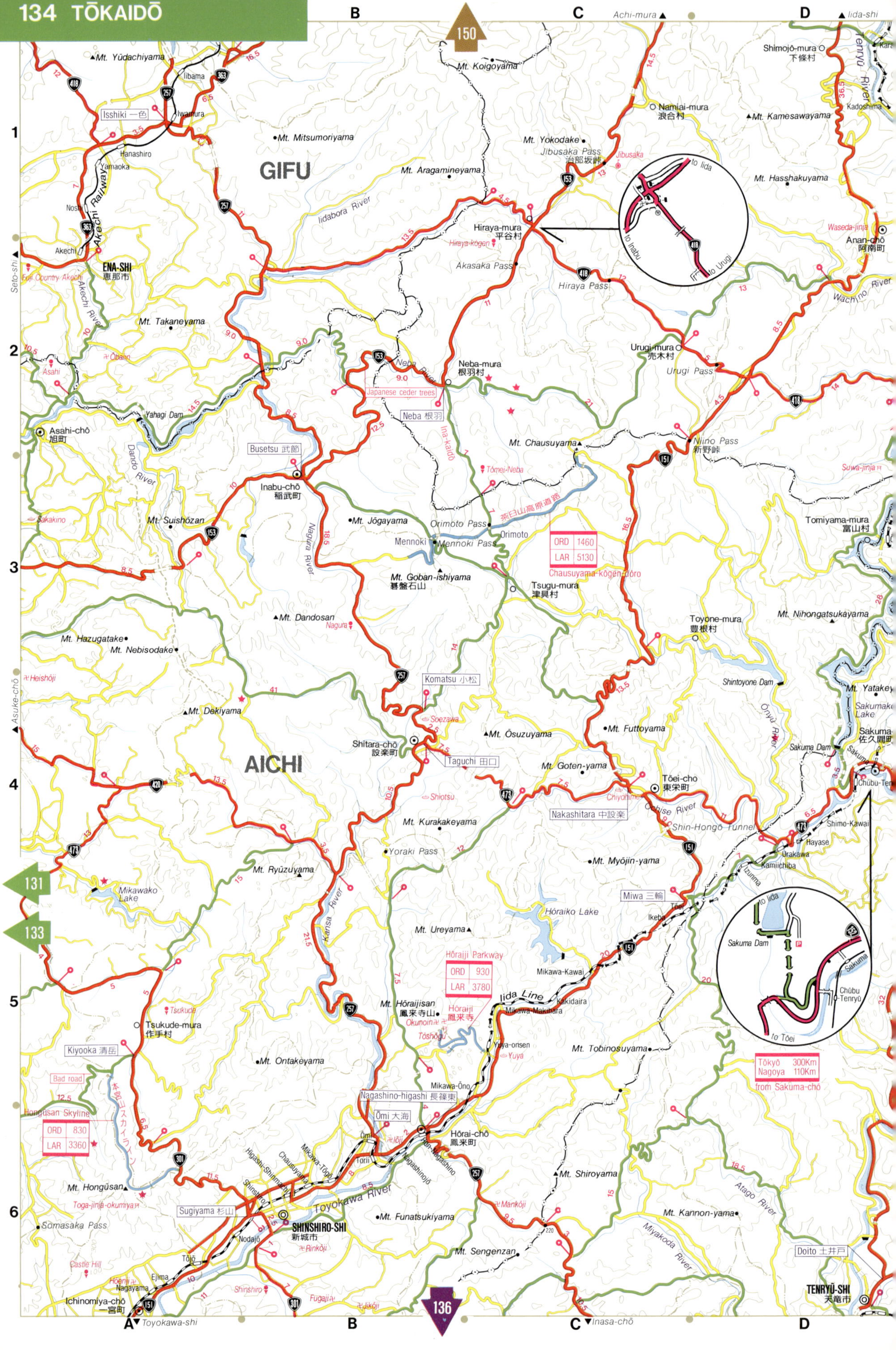
B
C
D
A
150
136
131
133
1
2
3
4
5
6
Achi-mura
Iida-shi
Seto-shi
Asuke-chō
Toyokawa-shi
Inasa-chō
GIFU
AICHI
Mt. Yūdachiyama
Ibama
Isshiki 一色
Iwamura
Hanashiro
Yamaoka
Akechi Railway
Nosu
Akechi
ENA-SHI
恵那市
Fuji Country Akechi
Akechi River
Mt. Mitsumoriyama
Mt. Koigoyama
Mt. Aragamineyama
Iidabora River
Mt. Yokodake
Jibusaka Pass
治部坂峠
Jibusaka
Namiai-mura
浪合村
Shimojō-mura
下條村
Tenryū River
Kadoshima
Mt. Kamesawayama
Mt. Hasshakuyama
to Iida
to Inabu
to Urugi
Hiraya-mura
平谷村
Hiraya-kōgen
Akasaka Pass
Hiraya Pass
Waseda-jinja
Anan-chō
阿南町
Wachino River
Mt. Takaneyama
Ōbaira
Asahi
Yahagi Dam
Asahi-chō
旭町
Dando River
Japanese ceder trees
Neba River
Neba-mura
根羽村
Neba 根羽
Ina-kaidō
Urugi-mura
売木村
Urugi Pass
Niino Pass
新野峠
Mt. Chausuyama
Busetsu 武節
Inabu-chō
稲武町
Tōmei-Neba
Suwa-jinja
茶臼山高原道路
Sakakino
Mt. Suishōzan
Mt. Jōgayama
Nagura River
Orimoto Pass
Orimoto
Mennoki
Mennoki Pass
ORD 1460
LAR 5130
Chausuyama-kōgen-dōro
Tomiyama-mura
富山村
Mt. Goban-ishiyama
碁盤石山
Tsugu-mura
津具村
Mt. Dandosan
Nagura
Toyone-mura
豊根村
Mt. Nihongatsukayama
Mt. Hazugatake
Mt. Nebisodake
Heishōji
Komatsu 小松
Shintoyone Dam
Ōnyū River
Mt. Yatakey
Sakumako Lake
Mt. Dekiyama
Soezawa
Mt. Ōsuzuyama
Mt. Futtoyama
Shitara-chō
設楽町
Taguchi 田口
Sakuma Dam
Sakuma
佐久間町
Mt. Goten-yama
Tōei-chō
東栄町
Chūbu-Tenryū
Shiotsu
Chiyohime
Nakashitara 中設楽
Ōchise River
Shin-Hongō Tunnel
Shimo-Kawai
Hayase
Urakawa
Kamiichiba
Izumma
Mt. Kurakakeyama
Yoraki Pass
Mt. Myōjin-yama
Mt. Ryūzuyama
Mikawako Lake
Kansa River
Miwa 三輪
Tōei
Ikeba
Hōraiko Lake
Mt. Ureyama
Hōraiji Parkway
ORD 930
LAR 3780
Mikawa-Kawai
Sakuma Dam
Chūbu-Tenryū
to Tōei
Tsukude
Tsukude-mura
作手村
Mt. Hōraijisan
鳳来寺山
Hōraiji
鳳来寺
Okunoin
Tōshōgū
Iida Line
Kakidaira
Mikawa-Makihara
Yuya-onsen
Yuya
Mt. Tobinosuyama
Kiyooka 清岳
Mt. Ontakeyama
Tōkyō 300Km
Nagoya 110Km
from Sakuma-chō
Bad road
Hongūsan Skyline
ORD 830
LAR 3360
本宮山スカイライン
Mikawa-Ōno
Nagashino-higashi 長篠東
Ōmi 大海
Ōmi
Iōji
Torii
Hōrai-chō
鳳来町
Higashi-Shinmachi
Chausuyama
Mikawa-Tōgō
Nagashinojō
Hon-Nagashino
Mt. Shiroyama
Atago River
Mt. Hongūsan
Toga-jinja-okumiya
Sugiyama 杉山
Shinshiro
Toyokawa River
SHINSHIRO-SHI
新城市
Rinkōji
Mt. Funatsukiyama
Mankōji
Mt. Kannon-yama
Miyakoda River
Somasaka Pass
Nodajō
Tōjō
Castle Hill
Hōenji
Mt. Sengenzan
Doito 土井戸
Ejima
Nagayama
Shinshiro
Ichinomiya-chō
一宮町
Fugaji
Jikōji
TENRYŪ-SHI
天竜市

E
F
G
H
1
2
3
4
5
6
151
137
140
Jizō Pass
Mt. Miikeyama
Kami-mura
上村
Yasuoka-mura
泰阜村
Kamimura River
Tōyama River
Mt. Yahazuyama
Mt. Kamigōchidake
Mt. Aonagiyama
Mt. Kagikakeyama
NAGANO
Mt. Hatanagiyama
Mt. Tekaridake
Nukuta
Mt. Ikeguchidake
Minamishinano-mura
南信濃村
Mt. Tougurayama
Shiteguri
Iida Line
Hatanagi-daiichi Dam
Akiha-kaidō
Mt. Shinanomata
Mt. Shirokurayama
Mt. Nakanooneyama
Bottom of ravine route
Tenryū-mura
天竜村
Hiraoka
Ōigawa River
Mt. Ōnesawayama
Mt. Kumabuseyama
Mt. Kurosawayama
Mt. Sasayama
Mt. Daimugenzan
Mt. Morozawayama
Aokuzure Pass
Mt. Kannon-yama
Mt. Narayoyama
Ikawako Lake
Shinshū-kaidō
Precipitous cliff route
Sumata River
Mt. Kangyōmine
Ikawa
Mt. Asahidake
Ikawa Dam
Setsusokyō
Omori
Kanzō
Mt. Kurobōshidake
Misakubo Dam
Misakubo River
Sumatakyō(Gorge)
Sumatakyō
寸又峡
Sessokyō-onsen
Fujimi Pass
Misakubo-chō
水窪町
Misakubo
to Sumatakyō
Senzu
to Shizuoka
to Tenryū
Ikawa Line
Hiranda
Nagashima Dam
Abt Ichishiro
Okuizumi
Okuōji-Kojō
Mt. Nanatsumine
Mt. Jōkōjiyama
Mukaichiba
Mt. Ōdake
Mt. Ōborayama
Yamazumi Pass
Yamazumi-jinja
Kawane-Koyama
Mt. Tenguishiyama
Shironishi
Domoto
Two-lane
Mt. Sobatsubuyama
Sawama
Aizuki
Honkawane-chō
本川根町
Kawane-Ryōgoku
Chishazan-jinja
Mt. Ōfudayama
Ōi-jinja
Ketagawa River
Mt. Kyōmaruyama
Aobe
Sakidaira
Yakushidō
Mt. Ryūtōsan
Suruga-Tokuyama
Road closed when raining more than 100mm
Mt. Tossakiyama
Ōibashi-minamihashi 大井橋南端
SHIZUOKA
Mt. Shirahasan
Mt. Musōrenzan
Chimanji
Tanokuchi
Tenryū River
Nakakawane-chō
中川根町
Sugikawa River
Shimizuchūshajō-mae
清水駐車場前
Ravine route narrow road
Sezawa 瀬沢
Shimoizumi
Kaikōin
Ōigawa Railway
Warashina River
Kumakiri River
Sasama River
Mt. Akihasan
秋葉山
Shiogō
Akiba-jinja
Jina
Mt. Takaneyama
Shizuoka-shi
Haruno-chō
春野町
Shinguike Lake
Nishimata Pass
Hirao 平尾
Kawane-onsen-Sasamado
Nukuri
Kawane-chō
川根町
Ieyama
Mt. Bodaizan
Satogawa River
Asahina River
Kōmyōyama
Japanese ceder trees
Ōwada
Mt. Komohariyama
Mt. Hakkōzan
Mt. Eboshigatayama
Okabe-chō
岡部町
Fujieda Bypass
ORD 400
LAR 1400
Fukuyō
Mt. Takayama
藤枝バイパス
Jizō Pass
Kamio
Hōhata
Yabuta
Yaizu
焼津
Tentokuji
FUJIEDA-SHI
藤枝市
Yainaba
Fujieda
Tōkōji
Shimada-shi

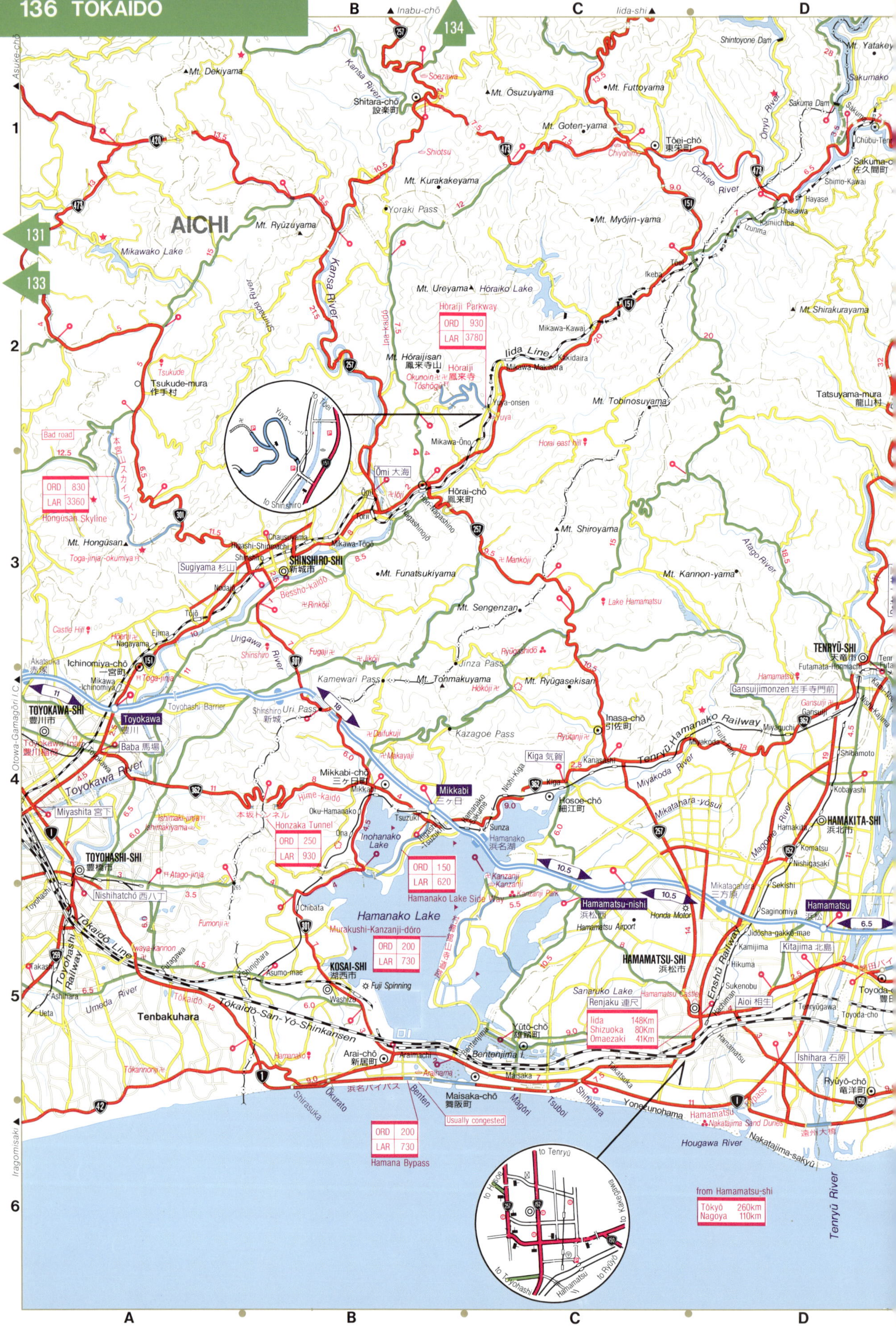

A
B
C
D
1
2
3
4
5
6
134
131
133
AICHI
Inabu-chō
Iida-shi
Asuke-chō
Otowa-Gamagōri I.C.
Iragomisaki
Mt. Dekiyama
Soezawa
Shitara-chō
設楽町
Kansa River
Mt. Ōsuzuyama
Mt. Futtoyama
Shintoyone Dam
Mt. Yatakey
Sakumako
Sakuma Dam
Ōnyū River
Mt. Goten-yama
Tōei-chō
東栄町
Chiyohime
Shiotsu
Mt. Kurakakeyama
Ōchise River
Sakuma-c
佐久間町
Shimo-Kawai
Hayase
Urakawa
Kamiichiba
Izunma
Yoraki Pass
Mt. Myōjin-yama
Mt. Ryūzuyama
Mikawako Lake
Shimada River
Ikeba
Tōei
Mt. Ureyama
Hōraiko Lake
Hōraiji Parkway
ORD 930
LAR 3780
Mikawa-Kawai
Mt. Shirakurayama
Iida Line
Kakidaira
Mikawa-Makihara
Mt. Hōraijisan
鳳来寺山
Hōraiji
鳳来寺
Okunoin
Tōshōgū
Tsukude
Tsukude-mura
作手村
Yuya-onsen
Yuya
Mt. Tobinosuyama
Tatsuyama-mura
龍山村
to Tōei
to Shinshiro
Bad road
12.5
ORD 830
LAR 3360
Hongūsan Skyline
本宮山スカイライン
Mikawa-Ōno
Horai east hill
Ōmi 大海
Hōrai-chō
鳳来町
Ōmi
Iōji
Tōri
Hon-Nagashino
Nagashinojō
Mt. Hongūsan
Toga-jinja-okumiya
Chausuyama
Higashi-Shinmachi
Mikawa-Tōgō
Mt. Shiroyama
Atago River
Sugiyama 杉山
Shinshiro
SHINSHIRO-SHI
新城市
Mt. Funatsukiyama
Mankōji
Mt. Kannon-yama
Nodaiō
Bessho-kaidō
Rinkōji
Mt. Sengenzan
Lake Hamamatsu
Tōjō
Castle Hill
Hōenji
Nagayama
Ejima
Urigawa River
Shinshiro
Fugaji
Jikōji
Ryūgashidō
Jinza Pass
TENRYŪ-SHI
天竜市
Futamata-Honmachi
Akatsuka
赤塚
Ichinomiya-chō
一宮町
Mikawa-Ichinomiya
Toga-jinja
Kamewari Pass
Mt. Tonmakuyama
Hōkōji
Mt. Ryūgasekisan
Hamamatsu
Gansuijimonzen 岩手寺門前
Toyohashi Barrier
TOYOKAWA-SHI
豊川市
Toyokawa
豊川
Shinshiro Uri Pass
新城
Daifukuji
Kazagoe Pass
Inasa-chō
引佐町
Ryūtanji
Tenryū-Hamanako Railway
Gansuiji
Miyaguchi
Toyokawa-inari
豊川稲荷
Baba 馬場
Makayaji
Kiga 気賀
Kanasashi
Miyakoda
Shibamoto
Toyokawa River
Mikkabi-chō
三ヶ日町
Mikkabi
Hime-kaidō
Nishi-Kiga
Kiga
Hosoe-chō
細江町
Miyakoda River
Kobayashi
Miyashita 宮下
Ishimaki-jinja
Ishimakiyama
本坂トンネル
Honzaka Tunnel
ORD 250
LAR 930
Oku-Hamanako
Tsuzuki
Mikkabi
三ヶ日
Hamanako Sakume
Sunza
Hamanako
浜名湖
Mikatahara-yōsui
Magome River
HAMAKITA-SHI
浜北市
Hamakita
Inohanako Lake
Ona
ORD 150
LAR 620
Komatsu
Nishigasaki
TOYOHASHI-SHI
豊橋市
Atago-jinja
Kanzanji
Kanzanji Park
Mikatagahara
三方原
Sekishi
Nishihatchō 西八丁
Hamanako Lake Side Way
Hamamatsu-nishi
浜松西
Honda Motor
Saginomiya
Hamamatsu
浜松
Chibata
Hamanako Lake
Hamamatsu Airport
Jidōsha-gakkō-mae
Fumonji
Murakushi-Kanzanji-dōro
ORD 200
LAR 730
Kamijima
Kitajima 北島
Iwaya-kannon
Tōkaidō Line
Toyohashi Railway
Futagawa
Shinjohara
KOSAI-SHI
湖西市
HAMAMATSU-SHI
浜松市
Hikuma
Takashi
Asumo-mae
Fuji Spinning
Enshū Railway
Sukenobu
Toyoda-c
Ashihara
Umeda River
Sanaruko Lake
Hamamatsu Castle
Aioi 相生
Tenryūgawa
Toyoda-chō
Ueta
Tenbakuhara
Tōkaidō
Tōkaidō-San-Yō-Shinkansen
Washizu
Renjaku 連尺
Iida 148Km
Shizuoka 80Km
Omaezaki 41Km
Yūtō-chō
雄踏町
Hachiman
Hamanako
Arai-chō
新居町
Araimachi
Bentenjima I.
Ishihara 石原
Tōkannon
Araihama
Maisaka
Takatsuka
Ryūyō-chō
竜洋町
浜名バイパス
Benten
Maisaka-chō
舞阪町
Magōri
Tsuboi
Shinohara
Yonezunohama
Hamamatsu
Nakatajima Sand Dunes
Bypass
Shirasuka
Ōkurato
Usually congested
遠州大橋
Hougawa River
Nakatajima-sakyū
ORD 200
LAR 730
Hamana Bypass
to Tenryū
to Hosoe
to Kakegawa
to Toyohashi
Hamamatsu
to Ryūyō
from Hamamatsu-shi
Tōkyō 260km
Nagoya 110km
Tenryū River

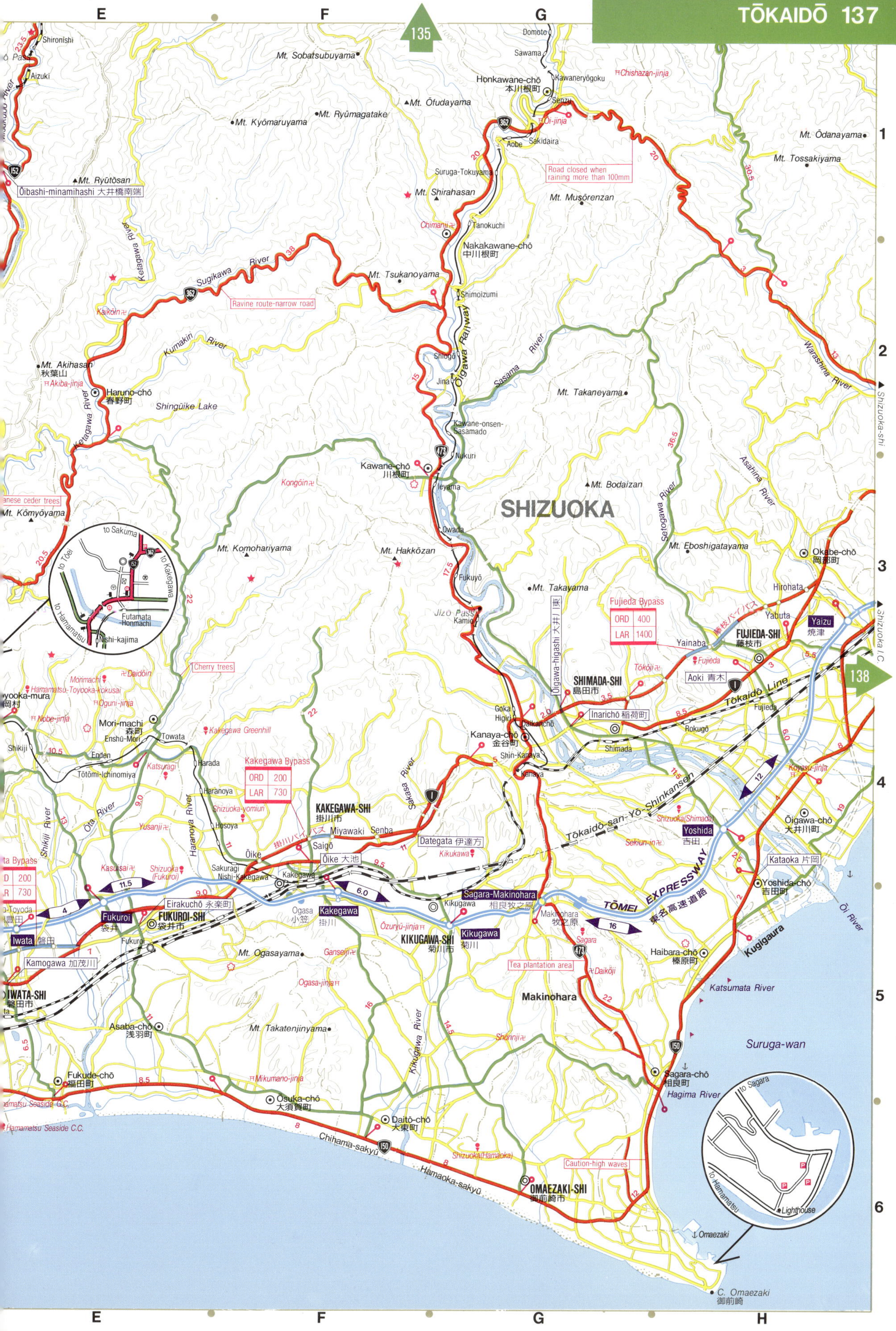

E
F
G
H
135
138
1
2
3
4
5
6
Mt. Sobatsubuyama
Mt. Ōfudayama
Mt. Kyōmaruyama
Mt. Ryūmagatake
Shironishi
Aizuki
Mt. Ryūtōsan
Ōibashi-minamihashi 大井橋南端
Domoto
Sawama
Honkawane-chō
本川根町
Kawaneryōgoku
Chishazan-jinja
Senzu
Ōi-jinja
Aobe
Sakidaira
Road closed when raining more than 100mm
Mt. Ōdanayama
Mt. Tossakiyama
Suruga-Tokuyama
Mt. Shirahasan
Mt. Musōrenzan
Chimanji
Tanokuchi
Nakakawane-chō
中川根町
Ketagawa River
Sugikawa River
Mt. Tsukanoyama
Shimoizumi
Ravine route-narrow road
Kaikōin
Kumakiri River
Ōigawa Railway
Sasama River
Warashina River
Mt. Akihasan
秋葉山
Akiba-jinja
Haruno-chō
春野町
Shingūike Lake
Shiogō
Jina
Mt. Takaneyama
Shizuoka-shi
Kawane-onsen-Sasamado
Nukuri
Kawane-chō
川根町
Ieyama
Kongōin
Mt. Bodaizan
Asahina River
SHIZUOKA
Setogawa River
Mt. Kōmyōyama
Owada
Mt. Komohariyama
Mt. Hakkōzan
Fukuyō
Mt. Eboshigatayama
Okabe-chō
岡部町
to Sakuma
to Tōei
to Kakegawa
to Hamamatsu
Futamata Honmachi
Nishi-kajima
Mt. Takayama
Ōigawa-higashi 大井川東
Jizō Pass
Kamio
Fujieda Bypass
ORD 400
LAR 1400
Hirohata
Yabuta
Yaizu
焼津
Shizuoka I.C.
Yainaba
FUJIEDA-SHI
藤枝市
Fujieda
Tōkōji
Aoki 青木
Cherry trees
Daidōin
Morimachi
Hamamatsu-Toyooka-kokusai
Oguni-jinja
Nobe-jinja
Mori-machi
森町
Enshū-Mori
Towata
Kakegawa Greenhill
SHIMADA-SHI
島田市
Tōkaidō Line
Inarichō 稲荷町
Goka
Higiri
Daikancho
Kanaya-chō
金谷町
Shimada
Rokugō
Shikiji
Enden
Tōtōmi-Ichinomiya
Katsuragi
Harada
Kakegawa Bypass
ORD 200
LAR 730
Sakasa River
Shin-Kanaya
Kanaya
Koyasu-jinja
Haranoya
Haranoya River
Ōta River
Shikiji River
Yusanji
Shizuoka-yomiuri
Hosoya
KAKEGAWA-SHI
掛川市
Miyawaki
Senba
Saigō
Ōike
Ōike 大池
Datagata 伊達方
Kikukawa
Tōkaidō-san-Yō-Shinkansen
Shizuoka(Shimada)
Yoshida
吉田
Sekiun-in
Ōigawa-chō
大井川町
Kataoka 片岡
Kasuisai
Shizuoka (Fukuroi)
Sakuragi
Nishi-Kakegawa
Kakegawa
11.5
Eirakuchō 永楽町
Fukuroi
袋井
FUKUROI-SHI
袋井市
Ogasa
小笠
掛川
6.0
Kikugawa
Sagara-Makinohara
相良牧之原
TŌMEI EXPRESSWAY
東名高速道路
Yoshida-chō
吉田町
Ōi River
Iwata
磐田
Kamogawa 加茂川
Fukuroi
Mt. Ogasayama
Ganseiji
Ōzuryū-jinja
KIKUGAWA-SHI
菊川市
Kikugawa
菊川
Makinohara
牧之原
16
Sagara
Haibara-chō
榛原町
Kugigaura
Tea plantation area
Daikōji
Katsumata River
IWATA-SHI
磐田市
Ogasa-jinja
Makinohara
Asaba-chō
浅羽町
Mt. Takatenjinyama
Kikugawa River
Shōnnji
Suruga-wan
Fukude-chō
福田町
Mikumano-jinja
Sagara-chō
相良町
Hagima River
to Sagara
Hamamatsu Seaside G.C.
Osuka-chō
大須賀町
Daitō-chō
大東町
Chihama-sakyū
Shizuoka(Hamaoka)
Hamaoka-sakyū
Caution-high waves
OMAEZAKI-SHI
御前崎市
to Hamamatsu
Lighthouse
Omaezaki
C. Omaezaki
御前崎

A
B
C
D
1
2
3
4
5
6
140
137
Fuji I.C.
Fujikawa
Numazu Byp.
Yoshiwara
Tagonoura
Higashi-Tagonoura
Mt. Hamaishidake
Rinkōji
26.5
Shin-Kanbara
Yui-chō
由比町
Kanbara-chō
蒲原町
Kanbara
Fujikawa River
Okitsu River
Warabino
Mt. Ōdanayama
Mt. Monjudake
Hozumi-jinja
Yoshiwara
SHIZUOKA
Hirayama
Kitanumagami
Shimizu
清水
Shinkansen
Okitsu
Okitsunakachō 興津中町
TŌMEI EXPRESSWAY
Tōkaidō San-yō
Hongōchō 本郷町
Shimizu
C. Masaki
Miho Land(R.A.)
Miho-no-matsubara
Miho-jinja
Shizuoka Railway
Kusanagi
Kusanagi-jinja
Ryūgeji
Hitachi
Seishin Bypass
Tōkeiin
Rinzaiji
Asama-jinja
Warashina River
SHIZUOKA-SHI
静岡市
Higashi-Shizuoka
Nihondaira
日本平
Nihondaira
Mt. Kunōzan
Tōshōgū
東照宮
Shōwamachi 昭和町
Togepposaiokuji
Tokuganji
Shizuoka
Toro-iseki (historic site)
東名高速道路
Abekawa
Shizuoka
静岡
Strawberry picking from Jan.through May
Suruga-wan Ferry
Fujieda-shi
Mochimune
Abekawa River
Mt. Takakusayama
Nihonzaka
日本坂
Yaizu
Tōkaidō Line
Okuzure-kaigan
Yaizu
Setogawa River
Yaizu
YAIZU-SHI
焼津市
Honkyoku mae 本局前
Jōdoji
Tochiyama River
SURUGA-WAN
駿河湾
Techno-Super Liner Kibō
to Heda
to Matsuzaki
to Shuzenji
Koibito-misaki(V.P.)
C. Koganezaki
Tagoshima I.
Ukima
Tensōdō
Kikkōiwa
to Toi
to Kumomi
to Shimoda
to Shimoda
Statues along road
C. Hagiyazaki
Kumomi
C. Hagachizaki
波勝岬

E F G

1 2 3 4 5 6

E F G H

B
152
C
D
1
2
3
4
5
6
135
138
A
B
C
D
Mt. Minobusan
Kuonji 久遠寺
Minobu
Mt. Shichimenzan 七面山
YAMANASHI
Shionosawa
Minobu-chō 身延町
Minobu
Kai-Ōshima
Minobu Line
Nanbu Bypass
Mt. Goten-yama
Umegashima
Mt. Shishinzan
Utsubuna
Sanogawa River
Yorihata
Mt. Jūmaisan
Mt. Shinoiyama
Ide
Nanbu-chō 南部町
Tōshima
Inako
Green Park(S.G.)
Asagiri Kōgen
Asagiri Jamboly
Tanukiko Lake
Mt. Tenshigatake
Odakyū-nishi-Fuji
The National
Kamiide IC 上井出インター
Shiraito Falls
Shiraito-no-taki(Falls) 白糸の滝
Omoteguchi-tozandō
Fuji Skyline
Closed in win
Komitake-jinja
MT. FUJI 富士山
Mt. Hōeizan 宝永山
Daisekiji
Mt. Anmoyama
Kitayama IC 北山インター
Shibakawa River
Mt. Hakusuizan
Honmonji
Fuji-Chisan
Sengen-taisya
FUJINOMIYA-SHI 富士宮市
Kuonji
Nishi-Fuji-dōro
ORD 200
LAR 730
Minamifuji
Nishi-Fujinomiya
An-yōji
Shibakawa-chō 芝川町
Shibakawa
Fujinomiya
Numakubo
Fujine
Daifuji
Fuji Royal
Iriyamase
Fuji 富士
River Fuji
Fugaku
Fujimigaoka
Fujimi Pass
Mt. Mizukiyama
Nakagouchi River
Mt. Mafujiyama
Fujigawa 富士川
Fujikawa-chō 富士川町
Tatebori
FUJI-SHI 富士市
Gakunan Railway
Gakunan-Enoo
Yunoki
Fuji
Shin-Fuji
Fujikawa
Yoshiwara
Numazu Bypass
Tagonoura
Higashi-Tagonoura
Night (Pm22:00~Am6:00)
Large truck traffic prohibited
Kanbara-chō 蒲原町
Shin-Kanbara
Aoshima 青島
Kōfu 65Km
Gotenba 44Km
Numazu 19Km
Rinkoji
Kanbara
Yui-chō 由比町
Yui
Yui 由比
Fujikawa River
Okitsu River
SHIZUOKA
Mt. Ōdanayama
Mt. Monjudake
to Numazu IC
to Gotenba
Ōoka
to Mishima
Numazu
Yahata 八幡
to Fuji
to Mito
Tōkaidō-San-Yō Shinkansen
Tōkaidō Line
Shimizu 清水
Okitsu
Okitsunakachō 興津中町
Hongōchō 本郷町
Ryōzenji
Shimizu
C. Masaki
Shimizu
Miho Land(R.A.)
Seishin Bypass
Shizuoka Railway
Miho-jinja
Kusanagi-jinja
Ryūgeji
Hitachi
SURUGA-WAN 駿河湾
Dōkeiin
SHIZUOKA-SHI 静岡市
Rinzaiji
Sengen-jinja
Sunpu Castle
Warashina River
Shōwachō 昭和町
Fuji 38Km
Hamamatsu 80Km
Omaezaki 43Km
Higashi-Shizuoka
Nihondaira 日本平
Nihondaira
Mt. Kunōzan
Tōshōgū
Shizuoka
Tokugan
Toro-iseki (historic site)
Suruga-wan Ferry
Shizuoka 静岡
Abekawa
Mochimune
Abekawa River
Hirono 広野
Nihonzaka 日本坂
Okuzure-kaigan
Yaizu
Yaizu 焼津
Yaizu
YAIZU-SHI 焼津市
to Umegashima
Shin-Shizuoka
to Shimizu
to Senzu
Shizuoka
Shizuoka 静岡
to Shimada
TOMEI EXPRESSWAY 東名高速道路
Koibito-misaki(V.P.)

YAMANASHI
KANAGAWA
Kawaguchiko I.C.
Mikuni Pass
Myōjin Pass
Asahigaoka 旭ケ丘
Kagosaka Pass
籠坂峠
東富士五湖道路
Higashi Fujigoko-dōro
ORD 1040
LAR 3780
Mt. Kofuji
Subashiri
Higashiguchi-tozando
Oyama-chō
小山町
Mt. Ōnoyama
Yamakita-machi
山北町
Matsuda-machi
松田町
HADANO-SHI
秦野市
Odakyū Odawara Line
Hadano-Nakai
秦野中井
Ōi-Matsuda
大井松田
Kaisei-machi
開成町
Ōi-machi
大井町
Nakai-machi
中井町
Gumizawa ぐみ沢
Kōfu 77Km
Numazu 25Km
Odawara 32Km
GOTENBA-SHI
御殿場市
Gotenba
御殿場
Gotemba Line
Ashigara Pass
Mt. Yaguradake
MINAMIASHIGARA-SHI
南足柄市
Daiyūzan Line
Hagiwara-kita 萩原北
Mt. Kintokiyama
金時山
ORD 500
LAR 2000
Minami-Fuji Evergreen Line
南富士エバーグリーンライン
Minami-Gotenba
Hakone-shindō
ORD 250
LAR 700
ODAWARA-SHI
小田原市
Odawara-Higashi
Seishō Bypass
ORD 450
LAR 1250
Odawara Castle
Sakawa River
Mt. Myōjōgadake
Miyanoshita 宮の下
Nagao Pass
長尾峠
ORD 350
LAR 1430
Komakado
駒門
Mt. Echizendake
Hakone Tozan Railway
Honchō 本町
Gotenba 36Km
Atsugi 34Km
Yokohama 53Km
MT. HAKONEYAMA
箱根山
Ashinoko Lake
HAKONE
箱根
Hakone-machi
箱根町
Kojiri Pass
湖尻峠
Mt. Ihaidake
Susono
裾野
Iwanami
Ashinoko Skyline
ORD 600
LAR 2200
Mt. Ashitakayama
愛鷹山
Nebukawa
Manazuru-dōro
ORD 310
LAR 1100
Mt. Hoshigayama
ORD 700
LAR 2900
Hakone TurnPike
Hakone Pass
箱根峠
Mt. Taikanzan
SUSONO-SHI
裾野市
Manatsuru-machi
真鶴町
C. Manazurumisaki
真鶴岬
Yugawara-machi
湯河原町
Yugawara Parkway
UHU 470
LAR 1900
TŌMEI EXPRESSWAY
東名高速道路
Numazu
沼津
Nagaizumi-chō
長泉町
MISHIMA-SHI
三島市
Jikkoku Pass
十国峠
Atami Beach Line
ORD 250
LAR 960
Tōkaidō-San-yō Shinkansen
Tōkaidō Line
Atami Pass
熱海峠
Yahata 八幡
Futsukamachi 二日町
Kannami-chō
函南町
NUMAZU-SHI
沼津市
Shimizu-chō
清水町
ATAMI-SHI
熱海市
Itō Line
Kanogawa River
Izu-chūōdōro
ORD 200
LAR 730
伊豆中央道
Izu-Hakone Railway
Nirayama-chō
韮山町
Yamabushi Pass
Izutaga
Hatsushima I.
SAGAMI WAN
相模湾
from Numazu-shi
Tōkyō 130Km
Nagoya 240Km
Enoura-wan
C. Ōsezaki
大瀬崎
C. Wakamatsuzaki
Izunagaoka-chō
伊豆長岡町
Ōhito-chō
大仁町
ORD 960
LAR 3870
Kameishi Pass
亀石峠
Mifuku Inter 三福インター
ORD 200
LAR 550
Shuzenji-dōro
修善寺道路
Mt. Sukumoyama
Usami
Heta Pass
戸田峠
Heta-mura
戸田村
IZU-SHI
伊豆市
Shuzenji
修善寺
ITŌ-SHI
伊東市
C. Kawanazaki
川奈崎
Mt. Darumayama
達磨山
Ippekiko Lake
Deguchi 出口
Naka-Izu Bypass
ORD 360
LAR 1250
Izukyū Railway
Toi Pass
土肥峠
Mt. Ōmuroyama
大室山
Yugashima
湯ケ島
C. Nichirenzaki
Mt. Tōgasayama
Nishina Pass
Toren Fall
Matsuzaki-chō
Higashiizu-chō
153
143
139

YAMANASHI
KANAGAWA
SHIZUOKA
FUJIYOSHIDA-SHI 富士吉田市
Oshino-mura 忍野村
Yamanakako Lake
Yamanakako-mura 山中湖村
Mt. Mikuniyama
Mikuni Pass 三国峠
Myōjin Pass 明神峠
Asahigaoka 旭ヶ丘
Kagosaka Pass 籠坂峠
Mt. Torinomuneyama
Mt. Shakushiyama
Mt. Mishōtaiyama
Mt. Azegamaruyama
Mt. Komotsuriyama
Mt. Ishiwariyama
Mt. Gongenyama
Tanzawako Lake
Mt. Hirugatake
Mt. Tanzawayama 丹沢山
Mt. Tōgatake 塔ヶ岳
Mt. Mitsumineyama
Mt. Ōyama 大山
Yabitsu Pass ヤビツ峠
Nakatsu River
TOMEI EXPRESSWAY
Ōi-Matsuda 大井松田
to Atsugi
to Gotenba
to Odawara
Matsuda
Shin-Matsuda
HADANO-SHI 秦野市
Hadano-Naka 秦野中井
Yamakita-machi 山北町
Matsuda-machi 松田町
Kaisei-machi 開成町
Sōryō 惣領
Ōi-machi 大井町
Nakai-machi 中井町
Ninomiya-machi 二宮町
MINAMIASHIGARA-SHI 南足柄市
Izu-Hakone-Daiyūzan
Gotenba Line
Odawara-Atsugi-dōro
ORD 350
LAR 950
Gumisawa-kami ぐみ沢上
Gumisawa ぐみ沢
Kōfu 77km
Odawara 32km
Numazu 25km
GOTENBA-SHI 御殿場市
Gotenba 御殿場
Minami-Gotenba
Hagiwara-kita 萩原北
Mt. Kintokiyama 金時山
Mt. Myōjingatake
Mt. Myōjōgatake
Mt. Yaguradake
Mt. Daigatake
Nagao Pass 長尾峠
Miyanoshita 宮の下
Hakone-shindō
ORD 250
LAR 700
ODAWARA-SHI 小田原市
Odawara Honchō 本町
Seishō Bypass
ORD 450
LAR 1250
Yokohama 53km
Atsugi 34km
Gotenba 36km
Honchō 本町
to Matsuda
to Hiratsuka
to Yumoto
Mt. Hakoneyama
HAKONE 箱根
Hakone-machi 箱根町
Ashinoko Lake
Hakone Pass
Kojiri Pass 湖尻峠
Hakone Skyline
ORD 350
LAR 1430
Ashinoko Skyline
ORD 600
LAR 2200
Mt. Kurakakeyama
Hakone Turnpike
ORD 700
LAR 2900
Manazuru-dōro
ORD 310
LAR 1100
Manazuru-machi 真鶴町
C. Manazurumisaki 真鶴岬
Yugawara Parkway
ORD 470
LAR 1900
Yugawara-machi 湯河原町
Jukkoku Pass 十国峠
Beach Line
ORD 250
LAR 960
Atami 熱海
ATAMI-SHI 熱海市
Odawara 25km
Numazu 32km
Shimoda 69km
Mt. Echizendake
Mt Ihaidake
Mt. Ashitakayama
Susono 裾野
SUSONO-SHI 裾野市
Numazu 沼津
Nagaizumi-chō 長泉町
MISHIMA-SHI 三島市
Shinkansen
Sanmaibashi-chō 三枚橋町
Futsuka-machi 二日町
Gotenba 25km
Odawara 45km
Shimoda 119km
NUMAZU-SHI 沼津市
Shimizu-chō 清水町
Kannami-chō 函南町
Kanogawa River
SURUGA-WAN 駿河湾
C. Ōkubonohana
Izu-chūōdō
ORD 200
LAR 730
Nirayama-chō 韮山町
Izu-Hakone Line
Izunagaoka-chō 伊豆長岡町
Ōhito-chō 大仁町
Shuzenji-dōro
ORD 200
LAR 550
IZU-SHI 伊豆市
Shuzenji 修善寺
C. Wakamatsuzaki
Mt. Katsuragiyama
Mt. Sanagiyama
Yamabushi Pass 山伏峠
Izu Skyline
ORD 960
LAR 3870
Mt. Sukumoyama
Hatsushima I.
Itō Line
ITŌ-SHI 伊東市
C. Shiofukizaki
Higashiizu-chō

E
F
G
H
1
2
3
4
5
6
144
172
Kaneda 金田
Tōkyō 53km
Hachiōji 27km
Yokohama 31km
Kiyokawa-mura
Mizuhiki 水引
ATSUGI-SHI 厚木市
Atsugi 厚木
Hon-Atsugi
EBINA-SHI 海老名市
Ebina
ZAMA-SHI 座間市
Zama
Sōbudaishita
Sōbudaimae
Nissan Motor
Sagamihara-shi
Yokohama-Machida
YAMATO-SHI 大和市
Hodogaya
Sōtetsu Line
Mitsukyō
Asahi-ku 旭区
Seya-ku 瀬谷区
Atsugi Airport
AYASE-SHI 綾瀬市
Izumi-ku 泉区
TOMEI EXPRESSWAY
東名高速道路
Odakyū Odawara Line
Sinkansen
Isuzu Motors
Shōnandai
Mutsuai-Nichidai-mae
Nihon Univ.(Agr)
Odakyū Enoshima Line
Samukawa-machi 寒川町
Samukawa-jinja
Three Hundred
Shōnan
新湘南バイパス
Kagawa
Kita-chigasaki
CHIGASAKI-SHI 茅ヶ崎市
Chigasaki
FUJISAWA-SHI 藤沢市
HIRATSUKA-SHI 平塚市
Hiratsuka
Shindo 真土
Odawara-Atsugi Dōro
Yachiyo-chō 八千代町
Sagami River
Shōnan Seaside
Tōkaidō Line
Ōiso-machi 大磯町
Ōiso 大磯
Ōiso Long Beach(R.A.)
Takahamadai 高浜台
Tōkyō 60km
Nagoya 300km
ORD 350
LAR 950
ORD 400
LAR 1510
ORD '00
LAR 550
ORD 1200
LAR 3350
ORD 200
LAR 700
ORD 100
LAR 300
ORD 300
LAR 850
ORD 100
LAR 520
Totsuka-ku 戸塚区
Totsuka
Hitachi
Yokohama-shindō
Hodogaya-ku 保土ヶ谷区
Minami-Makigahara
Ryokuentoshi
Kōnan-ku 港南区
Isogo-ku 磯子区
Minami-ku 南区
Nishi-ku 西区
Naka-ku 中区
Kanagawa Univ.
Higashi-Kanagawa
Nissan Motor
Shōwa Denko
JFE
Tōkyō 33km
Hachiōji 40km
Yokosuka 33km
YOKOHAMA-SHI 横浜市
Yamashita Park
Ishikawachō
Yamate
Mitsubishi Heavy Industries
Negishi
Tōkyō Gas
Ishikawajima-Harima
Sugita
Shin-Sugita
TŌKYŌ-WAN 東京湾
Sakae-ku 栄区
Yokohama-Yokosuka-dōro
Negishi Line
Kaskio River
Ōfuna
Kamakura Public
Kenchōji
Tsurugaoka-hachimangū
Kita-Kamakura
KAMAKURA-SHI 鎌倉市
KAMAKURA 鎌倉
Kamakura
Kanazawa-ku 金沢区
Kanazawa-Shizen-kōen
Tōkyū Car Manufacturing
Kanazawahakkei
Sumitomo Heavy Industries
Kantō Gakuin Univ.
Oppama
Namiki
Nōkendai
Fujisawa
Tatsunokuchi
Kataseenoshima
Koshigoe
Enoshima 江の島
Shichirigahama
Inamuragasaki
Enoden Line
Hase
Jimmuji
Higashi-Zushi
Yokosuka Line
ZUSHI-SHI 逗子市
Zushi
Zuyō-shindō
Nagae 長柄
Hayama-machi 葉山町
Shōnan Kokusai-mura
Hayama Kokusai
C. Chōgasaki
Nagaura-wan
Yokosuka-wan
Dainikaiho I.
本町山中道路
Honcho-yamanaka-dōro
Sarushima I.
YOKOSUKA-SHI 横須賀市
Miharu-chō 3 三春町三
Taura
Kinugasa
Shin-Ōtsu
C. Kannonzaki
Defense Academy
Uraga
Kita-kurihama
Kurihama
Sawara
Miura-jūkan-dōro
Odawa-wan
Miura Pen. 三浦半島
Y.R.P.Nobi
Tsukuihama
Keikyū Line
Miurakaigan
Misakiguchi
C. Arasaki
SAGAMI-WAN 相模湾
Koajiro-wan
Hikihashi 引橋
Mt. Gandōyama
C. Amasaki
C. Tsurugizaki
MIURA-SHI 三浦市
Jōgashima 城ヶ島
城ヶ島大橋
C. Nagatsurozaki
Jōgashima I.
C. Abōzaki
Jōgashima-Ōhashi
to Fujisawa
to Asahina Pass
to Enoshima
Kamakura
to Zushi
Hinode 日の出
C. Chigasaki
Ōshima
Ōshima-machi 大島町
Mt. Miharayama 三原山
Ōshima I. 大島

SAITAMA
TŌKYŌ
KANAGAWA
KAN-ETSU EXPRESSWAY
CHŪŌ EXPRESSWAY
TŌMEI EXPRESSWAY
SAKADO-SHI 坂戸市
TSURUGASHIMA-SHI 鶴ヶ島市
KAWAGOE-SHI 川越市
AGEO-SHI 上尾市
HIDAKA-SHI 日高市
HANNŌ-SHI 飯能市
SAYAMA-SHI 狭山市
IRUMA-SHI 入間市
KAMIFUKUOKA-SHI 上福岡市
FUJIMI-SHI 富士見市
SHIKI-SHI 志木市
TOKOROZAWA-SHI 所沢市
NIIZA-SHI 新座市
ASAKA-SHI 朝霞市
WAKŌ-SHI 和光市
KIYOSE-SHI 清瀬市
ŌME-SHI 青梅市
HAMURA-SHI 羽村市
FUSSA-SHI 福生市
MUSASHIMURAYAMA-SHI 武蔵村山市
HIGASHIYAMATO-SHI 東大和市
HIGASHIMURAYAMA-SHI 東村山市
HIGASHIKURUME-SHI 東久留米市
NISHITŌKYŌ-SHI 西東京市
AKIRUNO-SHI あきる野市
KODAIRA-SHI 小平市
KOKUBUNJI-SHI 国分寺市
TACHIKAWA-SHI 立川市
AKISHIMA-SHI 昭島市
MUSASHINO-SHI 武蔵野市
KOGANEI-SHI 小金井市
KUNITACHI-SHI 国立市
MITAKA-SHI 三鷹市
HACHIŌJI-SHI 八王子市
FUCHŪ-SHI 府中市
HINO-SHI 日野市
CHŌFU-SHI 調布市
KOMAE-SHI 狛江市
TAMA-SHI 多摩市
INAGI-SHI 稲城市
SAGAMIHARA-SHI 相模原市
MACHIDA-SHI 町田市
ZAMA-SHI 座間市
YAMATO-SHI 大和市
ATSUGI-SHI 厚木市
EBINA-SHI 海老名市
AYASE-SHI 綾瀬市
Yokota Airport
Iruma Airport
Sagami River
Tama River
Arakawa River
Iruma River
Sagamiko-machi
Tsukui-machi 津久井町
Shiroyama-machi 城山町
Aikawa-machi 愛川町
Kiyokawa-mura 清川村
Hinode-machi 日の出町
Mizuho-machi 瑞穂町
Moroyama-machi 毛呂山町
Ogose-machi 越生町
Kawajima-machi 川島町
Miyoshi-machi 三芳町
Ōi-machi 大井町
Sayamako Lake
Tamako Lake
Tsukuiko Lake
Mt. Takaosan 高尾山
Mt. Ōyama 大山
Tsurugashima
Tsurugashima Jct
Kawagoe
Tokorozawa
Toda-higashi
Toda-nishi
Wakō-kita
Wakō
Ōizumi
Nerima
Takaido
Chōfu
Inagi
Kunitachi-Fuchū
Hachiōji
Sagamiko-higashi
Tōmei-Kawasaki
Yokohama-Aoba
Yokohama-Machida
Tōkyō
ORD 200
LAR 730
ORD 250
LAR 940
163
153
192
142
143
A
B
C
D
1
2
3
4
5
6

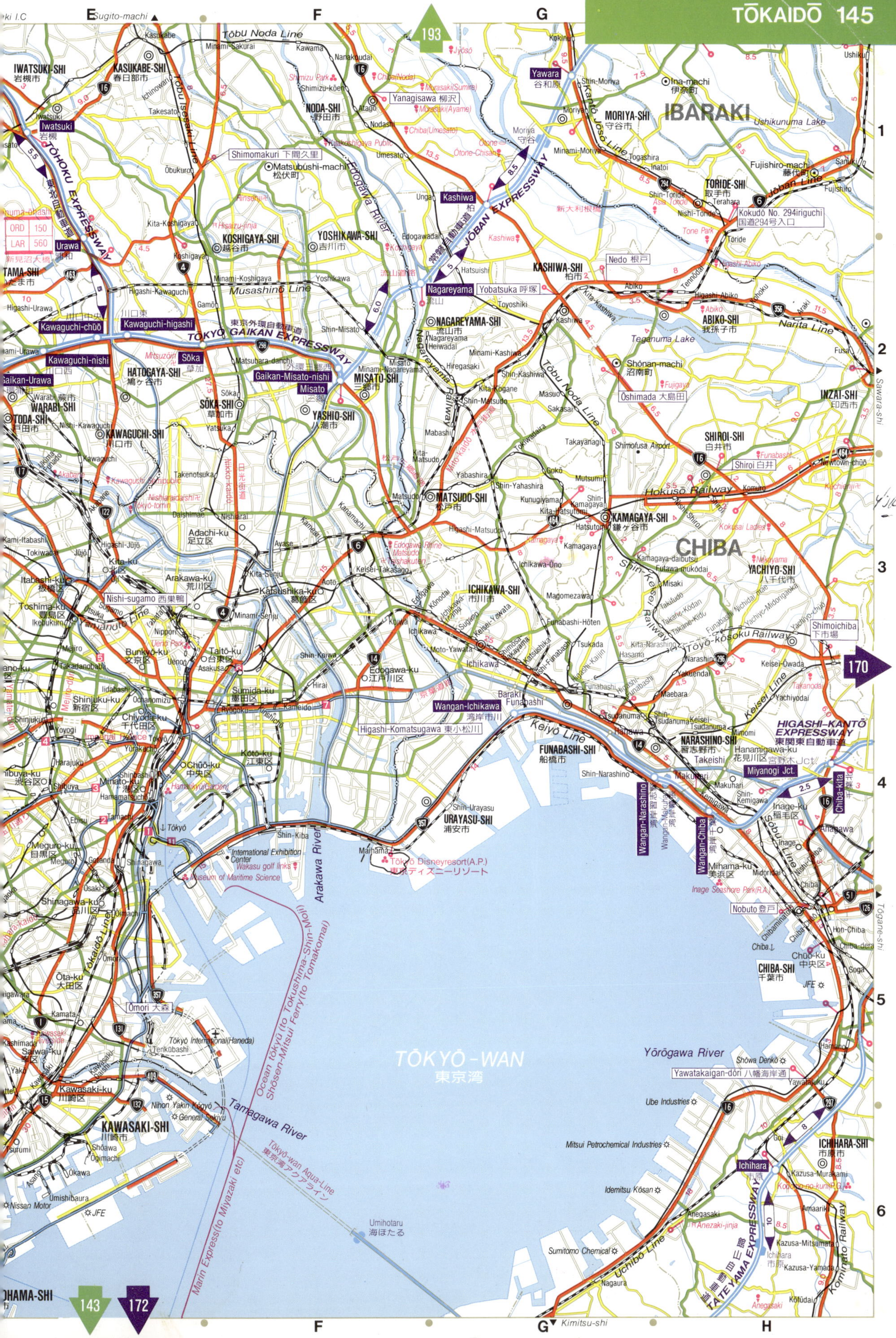

E
F
G
H
1
2
3
4
5
6
193
170
143
172
IBARAKI
CHIBA
TŌKYŌ-WAN
東京湾
IWATSUKI-SHI
岩槻市
KASUKABE-SHI
春日部市
NODA-SHI
野田市
MORIYA-SHI
守谷市
TORIDE-SHI
取手市
KOSHIGAYA-SHI
越谷市
YOSHIKAWA-SHI
吉川市
KASHIWA-SHI
柏市
ABIKO-SHI
我孫子市
NAGAREYAMA-SHI
流山市
MISATO-SHI
三郷市
HATOGAYA-SHI
鳩ヶ谷市
SŌKA-SHI
草加市
YASHIO-SHI
八潮市
WARABI-SHI
蕨市
TODA-SHI
戸田市
KAWAGUCHI-SHI
川口市
INZAI-SHI
印西市
SHIROI-SHI
白井市
MATSUDO-SHI
松戸市
KAMAGAYA-SHI
鎌ヶ谷市
YACHIYO-SHI
八千代市
ICHIKAWA-SHI
市川市
NARASHINO-SHI
習志野市
FUNABASHI-SHI
船橋市
URAYASU-SHI
浦安市
CHIBA-SHI
千葉市
ICHIHARA-SHI
市原市
KAWASAKI-SHI
川崎市
TAMA-SHI
たま市
TŌHOKU EXPRESSWAY
JŌBAN EXPRESSWAY
TŌKYŌ GAIKAN EXPRESSWAY
HIGASHI-KANTŌ EXPRESSWAY
東関東自動車道
TATEYAMA EXPRESSWAY
Tōbu Noda Line
Tōbu Isesaki Line
Musashino Line
Jōban Line
Narita Line
Hokusō Railway
Shin-Keisei Railway
Tōyō-kōsoku Railway
Keisei Line
Keiyō Line
Sōbu Line
Uchibō Line
Kominato Railway
Yamanote Line
Tōkaidō Line
Edogawa River
Arakawa River
Tamagawa River
Yōrōgawa River
Ushikunuma Lake
Teganuma Lake
Adachi-ku
足立区
Arakawa-ku
荒川区
Katsushika-ku
葛飾区
Edogawa-ku
江戸川区
Kita-ku
北区
Itabashi-ku
板橋区
Toshima-ku
豊島区
Bunkyō-ku
文京区
Taitō-ku
台東区
Sumida-ku
墨田区
Kōtō-ku
江東区
Chūō-ku
中央区
Chiyoda-ku
千代田区
Shinjuku-ku
新宿区
Shibuya-ku
渋谷区
Minato-ku
港区
Meguro-ku
目黒区
Shinagawa-ku
品川区
Ōta-ku
大田区
Saiwai-ku
Kawasaki-ku
川崎区
Mihama-ku
美浜区
Hanamigawa-ku
花見川区
Inage-ku
稲毛区
Chūō-ku
中央区
Tōkyō Disneyresort(A.P.)
東京ディズニーリゾート
Tōkyō International(Haneda)
Tōkyō-wan Aqua-Line
東京湾アクアライン
Umihotaru
海ほたる
Ocean Tōkyū (to Tokushima-Shin-Moji)
Shōsen-Mitsui Ferry(to Tomakomai)
Marin Express(to Miyazaki etc)
Museum of Maritime Science
International Exhibition Center
Wakasu golf links
Shimoichiba
下市場
Kokudō No. 294iriguchi
国道294号入口
Yawatakaigan-dōri 八幡海岸通
Ōmori 大森
Nishi-sugamo 西巣鴨
Higashi-Komatsugawa 東小松川
Shimomakuri 下間久里
Yanagisawa 柳沢
Nedo 根戸
Yobatsuka 呼塚
Ōshimada 大島田
Shiroi 白井
Nobuto 登戸
Miyanogi Jct.
Shimofusa Airport
Kawaguchi-chūō
Kawaguchi-higashi
Kawaguchi-nishi
Gaikan-Misato-nishi
Gaikan-Urawa
Wangan-Ichikawa
Wangan-Narashino
Wangan-Chiba
Chiba-kita
Ichihara
Nagareyama
Kashiwa
Yawara
Iwatsuki
Urawa
Sōka
Misato
Showa Denkō
Ube Industries
Mitsui Petrochemical Industries
Idemitsu Kōsan
Sumitomo Chemical
JFE
Nissan Motor
Nihon Yakin Kōgyō
General Sekiyu
Sugito-machi
Kimitsu-shi
Sawara-shi
Tōgane-shi

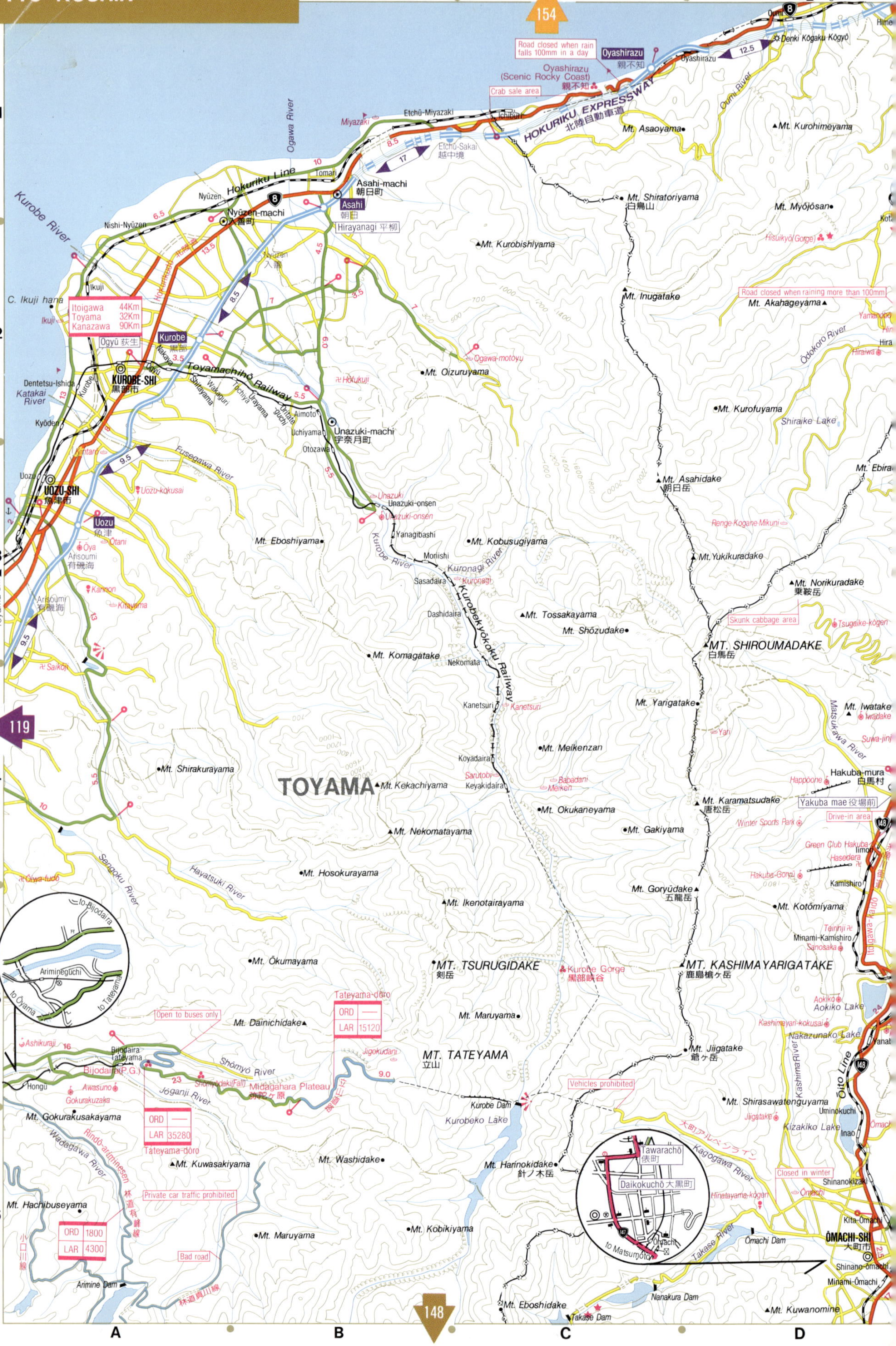

A
B
C
D
1
2
3
4
5
6
154
119
148
Itoigawa-shi
Toyama-shi
Road closed when rain falls 100mm in a day
Oyashirazu
親不知
Oyashirazu (Scenic Rocky Coast)
親不知
Crab sale area
HOKURIKU EXPRESSWAY
北陸自動車道
Denki Kōgaku Kōgyō
12.5
Ōmi River
Mt. Asaoyama
Mt. Kurohimeyama
Ichiburi
Etchū-Sakai
越中境
Etchū-Miyazaki
Miyazaki
Ogawa River
17
8.5
10
Tomari
Asahi-machi
朝日町
Asahi
朝日
Hirayanagi 平柳
Hokuriku Line
Nyūzen
Nyūzen-machi
入善町
Nishi-Nyūzen
Kurobe River
6.5
13.5
Mt. Shiratoriyama
白鳥山
Mt. Myōjōsan
Hisuikyō (Gorge)
Mt. Kurobishiyama
Mt. Inugatake
Road closed when raining more than 100mm
Mt. Akahageyama
Ikuji
C. Ikuji hana
Itoigawa 44Km
Toyama 32Km
Kanazawa 90Km
Kurobe
黒部
Ogyū 荻生
Ōdokoro River
Ogawa-motoyu
Mt. Oizuruyama
Hōfukuji
Dentetsu-Ishida
KUROBE-SHI
黒部市
Katakai River
Toyamachihō Railway
Mt. Kurofuyama
Shiraike Lake
Kyōden
Unazuki-machi
宇奈月町
Uchiyama
Otozawa
Aimoto
Fusegawa River
Kintarō
Mt. Ebira
Uozu-kokusai
Uozu
UOZU-SHI
魚津市
Unazuki
Unazuki-onsen
Mt. Asahidake
朝日岳
Renge-Kogane-Mikuni
Yanagibashi
Mt. Eboshiyama
Mt. Kobusugiyama
Ōya
Otani
Arisoumi
有磯海
Moriishi
Kuronagi River
Kurobe River
Mt. Yukikuradake
Sasadaira
Kuronagi
Kurobekyōkoku Railway
Mt. Norikuradake
乗鞍岳
Kannon
Kitayama
Dashidaira
Mt. Tossakayama
Skunk cabbage area
Tsugaike-kōgen
Mt. Shōzudake
MT. SHIROUMADAKE
白馬岳
Saikōji
Mt. Komagatake
Nekomata
Kanetsuri
Mt. Yarigatake
Mt. Iwatake
Iwadake
Matsukawa River
Yari
Suwa-jinja
Mt. Meikenzan
Koyadaira
Hakuba-mura
白馬村
Happōone
TOYAMA
Mt. Kekachiyama
Sarutobi
Keyakidaira
Babadani
Meiken
Mt. Shirakurayama
Mt. Karamatsudake
唐松岳
Yakuba mae 役場前
Drive-in area
Mt. Okukaneyama
Winter Sports Park
Mt. Nekomatayama
Mt. Gakiyama
Green Club Hakuba
Hasedera
Hakuba-Gorqū
Kamishiro
Ōiwa-fudō
Sengoku River
Hayatsuki River
Mt. Hosokurayama
Mt. Goryūdake
五龍岳
Mt. Kotomiyama
Mt. Ikenotairayama
Minami-Kamishiro
Sanosaka
Itoigawa-kaidō
to Bijodaira
Ariminegūchi
to Ōyama
to Tateyama
Mt. Ōkumayama
MT. TSURUGIDAKE
剣岳
Kurobe Gorge
黒部峡谷
MT. KASHIMAYARIGATAKE
鹿島槍ヶ岳
Aokiko
Aokiko Lake
Tateyama-dōro
ORD —
LAR 15120
Open to buses only
Mt. Dainichidake
Mt. Maruyama
Kashimayari-kokusai
Nakazunako Lake
Ashikuraji
Bijodaira
Tateyama
Jigokudani
MT. TATEYAMA
立山
Mt. Jiigatake
爺ヶ岳
Kashima River
Ōito Line
Hongū
Bijodaira (P.G.)
Shōmyō River
Shōmyōdaki (Fall)
9.0
Awasuno
Gokurakuzaka
Jōganji River
Midagahara Plateau
弥陀ヶ原
Vehicles prohibited
Kurobe Dam
Kurobeko Lake
Mt. Shirasawatenguyama
Jigatake
Uminokuchi
Mt. Gokurakusakayama
ORD —
LAR 35280
Tateyama-dōro
Tawarachō
俵町
Daikokuchō 大黒町
Kagogawa River
Kizakiko Lake
Inao
Wadagawa River
Rindō-ariminesen
Mt. Kuwasakiyama
Mt. Washidake
Mt. Harinokidake
針ノ木岳
Closed in winter
Shinanokizaki
Private car traffic prohibited
Hinatayama-kōgen
Ōmachi
Mt. Hachibuseyama
ORD 1800
LAR 4300
林道有峰線
Mt. Maruyama
Mt. Kobikiyama
to Matsumoto
Ōmachi
Takase River
Ōmachi Dam
Kita-Ōmachi
ŌMACHI-SHI
大町市
Bad road
Shinano-Ōmachi
Minami-Ōmachi
Arimine Dam
小口川線
林道真川線
Mt. Eboshidake
Nanakura Dam
Takase Dam
Mt. Kuwanomine

E
F
G
H
1
2
3
4
5
6
154
155
149
160
NIIGATA
NAGANO
ARAI-SHI
新井市
JŌETSU-SHI
上越市
Nakagō
Himegawara 姫川原
Nihongi
Mt. Awadachiyama
Mt. Hanareyama
Sasakura
Kubiki-Ōno
Umikawa River
Mt. Funaurayama
Mt. Eboshidake
Undaiji
Mt. Komagatake
駒ヶ岳
Kajiyamamotoyu
Mt. Nokogiriyama
Itoigawa Seaside Valley
Kajiyamashinyu
Mt. Yakeyama
Mt. Hiuchiyama
火打山
Himekawa Gorge
Mt. Amakazariyama
雨飾山
Mt. Tenguharayama
to Jōetsu
to Nagano
Myōkō-kōgen
Katakai River
Iiyama-kaidō
Myōkō-mura
妙高村
Myōkō
妙高
Sekikawa River
Mt. Furutōyama
Myōkō Pine Valley
Shinanodaira
MT. MYŌKŌZAN
Mt. Akakurayama
Tsubame
Seki
Akakura
Shin-Akakura
Ikenodaira
Ikenotaira
Myōkōkōgen-machi
妙高高原町
Myōkō-kokusai
Myōkōkōgen
Mt. Ōhiramine
Road closed when raining more than 100mm
Uzuha Pass
Mt. Manaitayama
Otari-onsen
Otari
Arsuyu
Otomiyama Pass
乙見山峠
Mt. Matsuoyama
Alpine flora area
Nojiri-kita-iriguchi 野尻北入口
Madarao-Tokyu
Madarao-kōgen
Iiyama-kokusai
Iiyama
Mt. Madaraoyama
Kita-Otari
Mt. Jizōyama
Mizusawa River
Nojiriko Lake
Toyota-mura
豊田村
Madarao-kōgen Wakui
Kurohime-kōgen
Kurohime-Nojiriko
黒姫野尻湖
Toyota-Iiyama
豊田飯山
Hachisu
Nakatsuchi
Mt. Takazumayama
Mt. Otozumayama
Mt. Sadoyama
Mt. Kurohimeyama
黒姫山
Shinano-machi
信濃町
Buno
Mt. Okunishiyama
Closed in winter
Kurohime
Furuma
Shiga-Nakano-dōro
ORD 100
LAR 100
Madarao-kōgen
Kudarise
Oku-susobana-shizen-en
Furuike Lake
Torii River
Mt. Nabeyama
Shin-etsu Line
Iiyama Line
Otari-mura
小谷村
Cortina
Minami-Otari
Mt. Togakushiyama
戸隠山
Togakushi-okusha
Skunk cabbage area
Samizu-mura
三水村
Kaesa
Hakuba-Norikura
Chikuni
Mt. Higashiyama
Mt. Nishidake
Mt. Menōyama
Togakushi
Togakushi-chūsha
Closed in winter
Mt. Iizunayama
飯綱山
Iizuna Resort
Iizuna-kōgen
Mure-jinja
Mure-mura
牟礼村
Nagano-kokusai
Tategahana
Shinano-Asano
Shinshū-Nakano
信州中野
Hakuba-Ōike
Mt. Iwatoyama
Mt. Happōyama
Togakushi-kōgen
Togakushi-hōkōsha
Congestion in summer
Iizuna-kōgen
Asano 浅野
Himekawa River
Mt. Hitoyoyama
Scenic view of buckwheat bloom in summer
Iizuna
Oike Lake
Sakanaka Pass
Obuse-machi
小布施町
Nakano-Moriue
Hakubashiojima
Mt. Karayama
Susobana River
Nagano
Apple sale area
Toyono
Obuse
Tsusumi
Ganshōin
Obuse Highway Oasis
Road closed when raining more than 100mm
Karida-hachiman
Sansai
Yanagihara-kita
柳原北
Kita-Suzaka
Mt. Arakurayama
Kusugawa River
Naoetsu 80Km
Takasaki 120Km
Matsumoto 75Km
Mt. Ōmineyama
Apple Line
Chikuma River
Nagano Railway
Yokoyama-chūō
横山中央
Ōhora-kōgen
Susobana
Zenkōji
Zenkōjishita
Kita-Nagano
Suzaka
Mt. Sobatsubuyama
Nakagosho 中御所
Higashi-wada 東和田
Nishiowaribe 西尾張部
SUZAKA-SHI
須坂市
Tōkyō 220Km
Nagoya 260Km
NAGANO-SHI
長野市
Suzaka-Nagano-higashi
須坂長野東
Nakamachi 中町
to Matsumoto
to Obuse
to Ueda
Ogawa-mura
小川村
Amori
Kami-senda 上千田
Inoue
Saigawa River
Wakachi
Nuruyu
Araki 荒木
Vehicles prohibited
Kawanakajima
Gorin ohashi
Shinano-Kawada
Rendaiji
Dojiri River
Daianji
Nakajō-mura
中条村
Renkōji
Nakaoyama
白馬長野道路
Hakuba-Nagano-dōro
Sasadaira 笹平
Koiwadake
Nagano Shinkansen
Kanaiyama
JOSHIN-ETSU EXPRESSWAY
上信越自動車道
Hoshina-Kannon
Hoshina
to Nakano
Nakamachi 中町
to Sugadaira
Seni
ORD 200
LAR 550
Kawanakajima ancient battle field
Shinonoi
Matsushiro
松代
Nagano
長野
Miasa-mura
美麻村
Shinshūshin-machi
信州新町
Chōshōji
Kawanakajima
Matsushiro
Mt. Kimyōsan
Mt. Kumakuboyama
Nakamachi 中町
Kōshoku
Iwano
Zōzan-jinja
Kaizenji
Kōchi
Mt. Kokūzōyama
Hasedera
Inariyama
Kōshoku Jct
更埴 Jct
CHIKUMA-SHI
千曲市
Sairakuji
Sugadaira Green
Closed in winter
Mt. Chōjayama
Daikokuchō 大黒町
Itoigawa 75Km
Nagano 48Km
Matsumoto 35Km
Fudō
NAGANO EXPRESSWAY
Inariyama
Yashiro
Kuisezawa 杭瀬沢
Scenic view of apricot blossom in April
Mt. Hokiyadake
Sugadaira-kōgen
Sugadaira Plateau
Azumaya
Nishi-kaidō
Mt. Takagariyama
Tagotonotsuki (Terraced Paddy-field)
Obasute
Jizō Pass
Mt. Ōmatsuyama
Yasaka-mura
八坂村
Kanakuma
Ōhita
Togura
Shintokura
Kamiyamada
Mt. Hijiriyama
Sarugababa Pass
Chikuma-kōgen
Hijiri-kōgen
Furusaka
Mt. Daidōsan
Matsumoto-shi
Ueda-shi

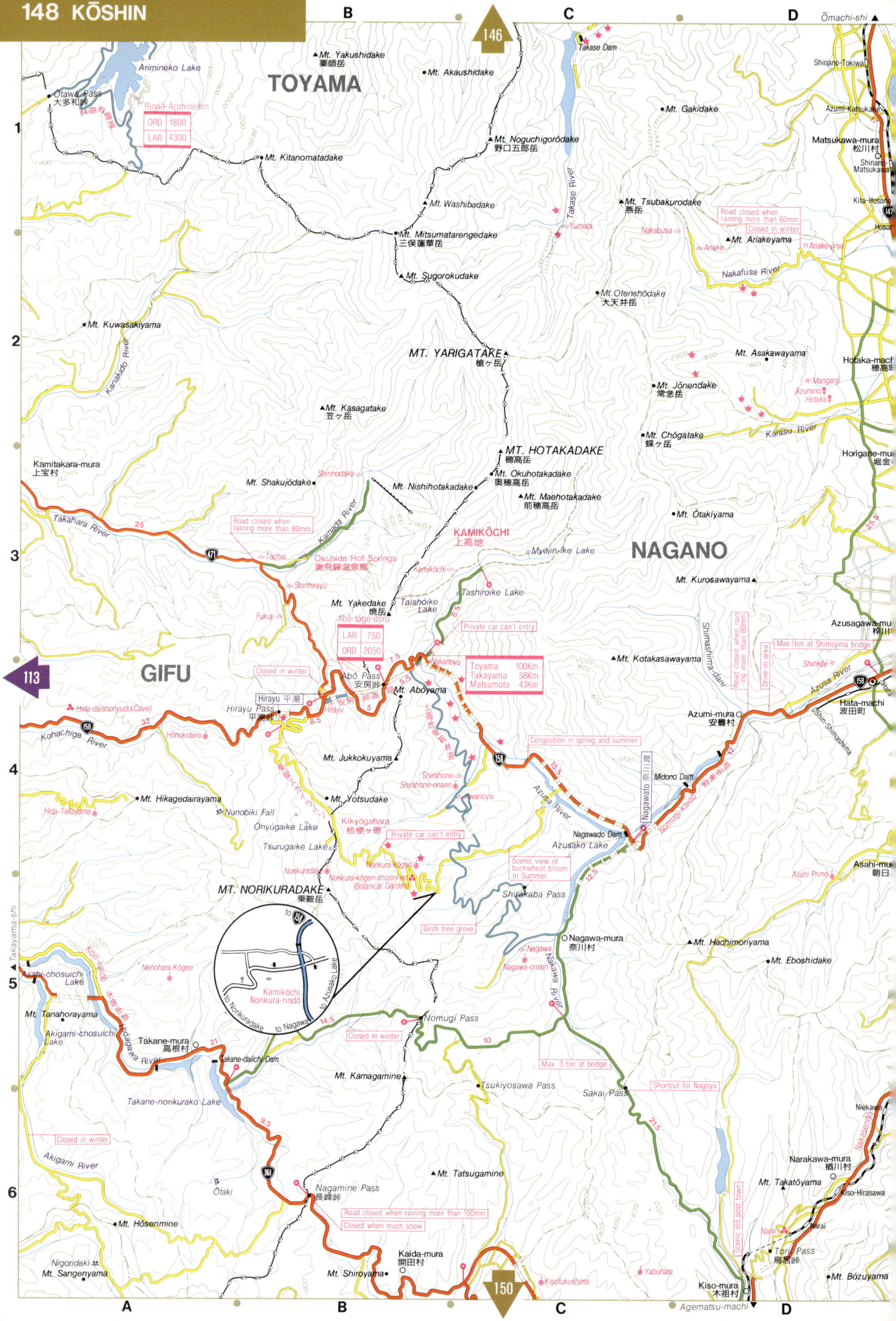

B
C
D
146
Ōmachi-shi
Mt. Yakushidake
薬師岳
Arimineko Lake
TOYAMA
Mt. Akaushidake
Takase Dam
Shinano-Tokiwa
Otawa Pass
大多和峠
Rindō-Ariminesen
林道有峰線
ORD 1800
LAR 4300
Mt. Gakidake
Azumi-Kutsukake
Mt. Noguchigorōdake
野口五郎岳
Matsukawa-mura
松川村
Shinano-Matsukawa
Mt. Kitanomatadake
Takase River
Mt. Tsubakurodake
燕岳
Kita-Hosono
Mt. Washibadake
Road closed when raining more than 60mm
Closed in winter
Yumata
Nakabusa
Mt. Mitsumatarengedake
三俣蓮華岳
Mt. Ariakeyama
Ariake
Ariake-jinja
Nakafusa River
Mt. Sugorokudake
Mt. Otenshōdake
大天井岳
Mt. Kuwasakiyama
Kanakido River
MT. YARIGATAKE
槍ヶ岳
Mt. Asakawayama
Hotaka-machi
穂高町
Mt. Jōnendake
常念岳
Manganji
Azumino Hotaka
Mt. Kasagatake
笠ヶ岳
Mt. Chōgatake
蝶ヶ岳
Karasu River
Kamitakara-mura
上宝村
MT. HOTAKADAKE
穂高岳
Horigane-mura
堀金村
Shinhodaka
Mt. Okuhotakadake
奥穂高岳
Mt. Shakujōdake
Mt. Nishihotakadake
Mt. Maehotakadake
前穂高岳
Mt. Ōtakiyama
Takahara River
Road closed when raining more than 80mm
Kamada River
KAMIKŌCHI
上高地
Myōjin-ike Lake
NAGANO
Tochio
Okuhida Hot Springs
奥飛騨温泉郷
Kamikōchi
Mt. Kurosawayama
Shinhirayu
Tashiroike Lake
Mt. Yakedake
焼岳
Taishōike Lake
Abō-tōge-doro
LAR 750
ORD 2050
Fukuji
Private car can't entry
Shimashima-dani
Azusagawa-mura
梓川村
Max.1ton at Shimojima bridge
Road closed when rain -ing more than 80mm
Drive-in area
113
GIFU
Closed in winter
Nakanoyu
Toyama 100Km
Takayama 58Km
Matsumoto 43Km
Mt. Kotakasawayama
Shinkōji
Azusa River
Abō Pass
安房峠
Mt. Abōyama
Hirayu 平湯
Hirayu Pass
平湯峠
Hirayu
Hida-daishōnyudo(Cave)
Hata-machi
波田町
Azumi-mura
安曇村
Shin-Shimashima
Kohachiga River
Hōnokidaira
Congestion in spring and summer
Mt. Jukkokuyama
Nagawato 奈川渡
Midono Dam
Nomugi-kaidō
野麦街道
Shirahone
Shirahone-onsen
Mt. Hikagedairayama
Mt. Yotsudake
Awanoyu
Azusa River
Hida-Takayama
Nunobiki Fall
Ōnyūgaike Lake
Kikyōgahara
桔梗ヶ原
Nagawado Dam
Azusako Lake
Private car can't entry
Tsurugaike Lake
Norikuradake
Norikura-kōgen
Norikura-kōgen-shizen-en (Botanical Garden)
Scenic view of buckwheat bloom in Summer
Asahi-mura
朝日
Asahi Prime
MT. NORIKURADAKE
乗鞍岳
Shirakaba Pass
Takayama-shi
Birch tree grove
Nagawa-mura
奈川村
Mt. Hachimoriyama
Kiso-kaidō
Nenohara-Kōgen
Nagawa
Nagawa-onsen
Mt. Eboshidake
Asahi-chosuichi Lake
Kamikōchi Norikura-rindō
to Norikuradake
to Nagawa
to Azusako Lake
Nakawa River
Mt. Tanahorayama
木曽街道
Nomugi Pass
Akigami-chosuichi Lake
Closed in winter
Takane-mura
高根村
Hidagawa River
Takane-daiichi Dam
Max. 3 ton at bridge
Mt. Kamagamine
Tsukiyosawa Pass
Sakai Pass
Shortcut for Nagoya
Takane-norikurako Lake
Niekawa
Closed in winter
Nakasendō
Akigami River
Narakawa-mura
楢川村
Mt. Tatsugamine
Mt. Takatōyama
Ōtaki
Nagamine Pass
長峰峠
Kiso-Hirasawa
Road closed when raining more than 100mm
Closed when much snow
Mt. Hōsenmine
Narai
Scenic old post town
Torii Pass
鳥居峠
Nigoridaki
Mt. Sangenyama
Kaida-mura
開田村
Mt. Shiroyama
Yabuhara
Kisofukushima
Kiso-mura
木祖村
Mt. Bōzuyama
150
A
B
C
D
Agematsu-machi
1
2
3
4
5
6

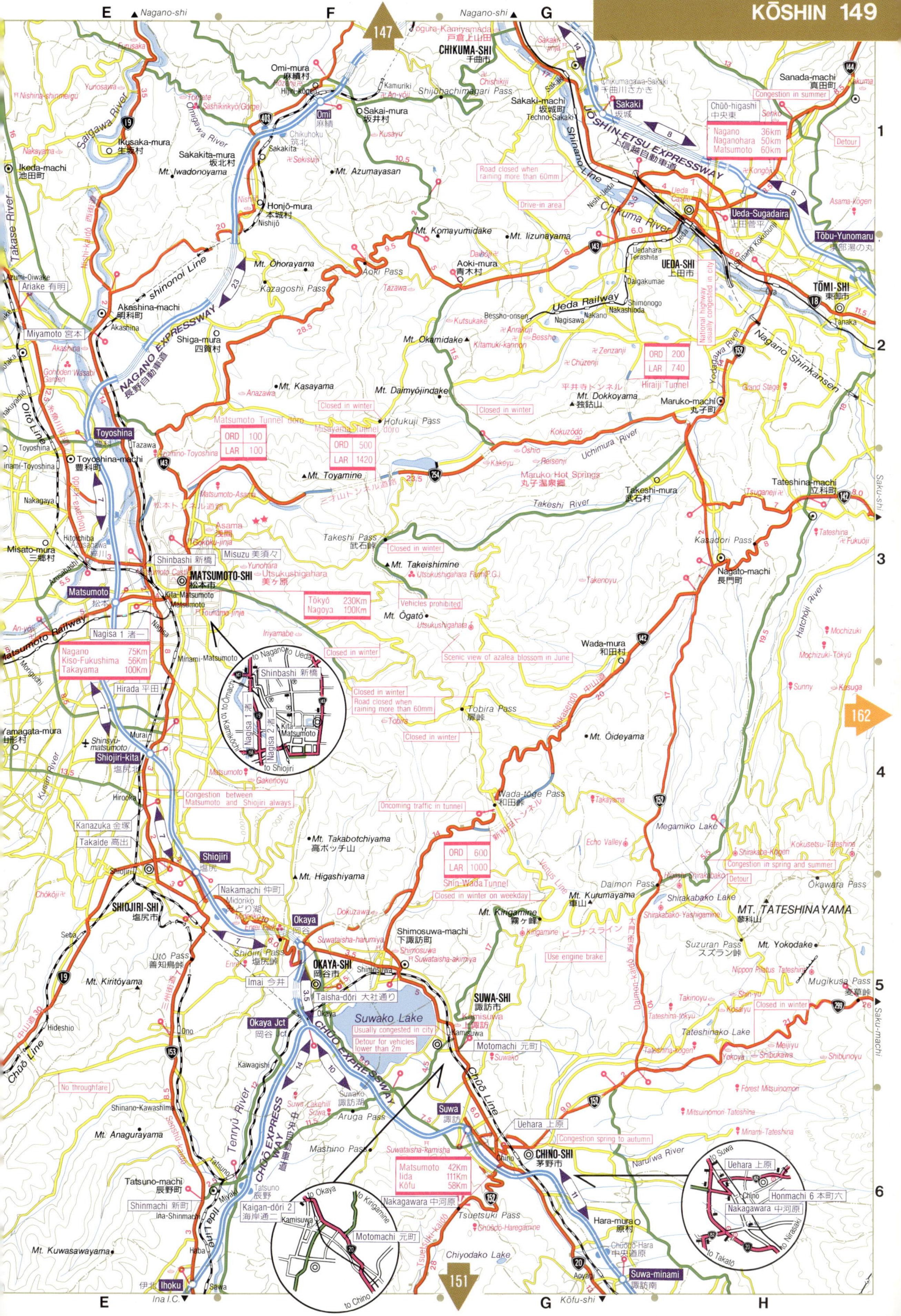
Nagano-shi
147
Togura-Kamiyamada 戸倉上山田
CHIKUMA-SHI 千曲市
Omi-mura 麻績村
Sakai-mura 坂井村
Sakaki-machi 坂城町
Sakaki
Chikumagawa-Sakaki 千曲川さかき
Sanada-machi 真田町
Congestion in summer
Chūō-higashi 中央東
Nagano 36Km
Naganohara 50Km
Matsumoto 60Km
Detour
JŌSHIN-ETSU EXPRESSWAY 上信越自動車道
Road closed when raining more than 60mm
Drive-in area
Ueda-Sugadaira
Tōbu-Yunomaru
TŌMI-SHI 東御市
UEDA-SHI 上田市
Ueda Railway
Chikuma River
Shinano Line
Ikusaka-mura 生坂村
Sakakita-mura 坂北村
Mt. Iwadonoyama
Mt. Azumayasan
Ikeda-machi 池田町
Honjō-mura 本城村
Mt. Komayumidake
Mt. Iizunayama
Aoki-mura 青木村
Aoki Pass
Mt. Ōhorayama
Kazagoshi Pass
shinonoi Line
Akashina-machi 明科町
Shiga-mura 四賀村
NAGANO EXPRESSWAY 長野自動車道
Ariake 有明
Miyamoto 宮本
Mt. Okamidake
Mt. Kasayama
Mt. Daimyōjindake
Closed in winter
ORD 200
LAR 740
Hiraiji Tunnel
Maruko-machi 丸子町
Mt. Dokkoyama
Nagano Shinkansen
Toyoshina
Toyoshina-machi 豊科町
Hofukuji Pass
Matsumoto Tunnel
ORD 100
LAR 100
ORD 500
LAR 1420
Mt. Toyamine
Maruko Hot Springs 丸子温泉郷
Uchimura River
Takeshi River
Takeshi-mura 武石村
Tateshina-machi 立科町
Takeshi Pass
Mt. Takeishimine
Kasadori Pass
Nagato-machi 長門町
Shinbashi 新橋
Misuzu 美須々
MATSUMOTO-SHI 松本市
Utsukushigahara 美ヶ原
Matsumoto
Tōkyō 230Km
Nagoya 190Km
Vehicles prohibited
Mt. Ōgatō
Nagisa 1 渚一
Nagano 75Km
Kiso-Fukushima 56Km
Takayama 100Km
Hirada 平田
Matsumoto Railway
Scenic view of azalea blossom in June
Wada-mura 和田村
Road closed when raining more than 60mm
Tobira Pass
Mt. Ōideyama
Yamagata-mura 山形村
Shiojiri-kita
Congestion between Matsumoto and Shiojiri always
Oncoming traffic in tunnel
Wada-tōge Pass 和田峠
Kanazuka 金塚
Takaide 高出
Mt. Takabotchiyama 高ボッチ山
ORD 600
LAR 1000
Shin-Wada Tunnel
Closed in winter on weekday
Megamiko Lake
Shirakaba-Kōgen
Congestion in spring and summer
Ōkawara Pass
Shiojiri
Mt. Higashiyama
Nakamachi 仲町
SHIOJIRI-SHI 塩尻市
Okaya
Shimosuwa-machi 下諏訪町
Mt. Kirigamine 霧ヶ峰
Daimon Pass
Mt. Kurumayama 車山
Shirakabako Lake
MT. TATESHINAYAMA 蓼科山
Use engine brake
Suzuran Pass スズラン峠
Mt. Yokodake
Utō Pass 善知鳥峠
Mt. Kiritōyama
Imai 今井
OKAYA-SHI 岡谷市
Taisha-dōri 大社通り
Suwako Lake
Usually congested in city
Detour for vehicles lower than 2m
SUWA-SHI 諏訪市
Motomachi 元町
Mugikusa Pass 麦草峠
Closed in winter
Tateshinako Lake
Okaya Jct
CHŪŌ EXPRESSWAY
Chūō Line
No throughfare
Mt. Anagurayama
Tenryū River
Suwa
Uehara 上原
Congestion spring to autumn
CHINO-SHI 茅野市
Naruiwa River
Matsumoto 42Km
Iida 111Km
Kōfu 58Km
Nakagawara 中河原
Tsuetsuki Pass
Honmachi 6 本町六
Tatsuno-machi 辰野町
Shinmachi 新町
Kaigan-dōri 2 海岸通二
Mt. Kuwasawayama
Chiyodako Lake
Hara-mura 原村
Suwa-minami
Ihoku
151
162
Ina I.C.
Kōfu-shi
Saku-shi
Saku-machi

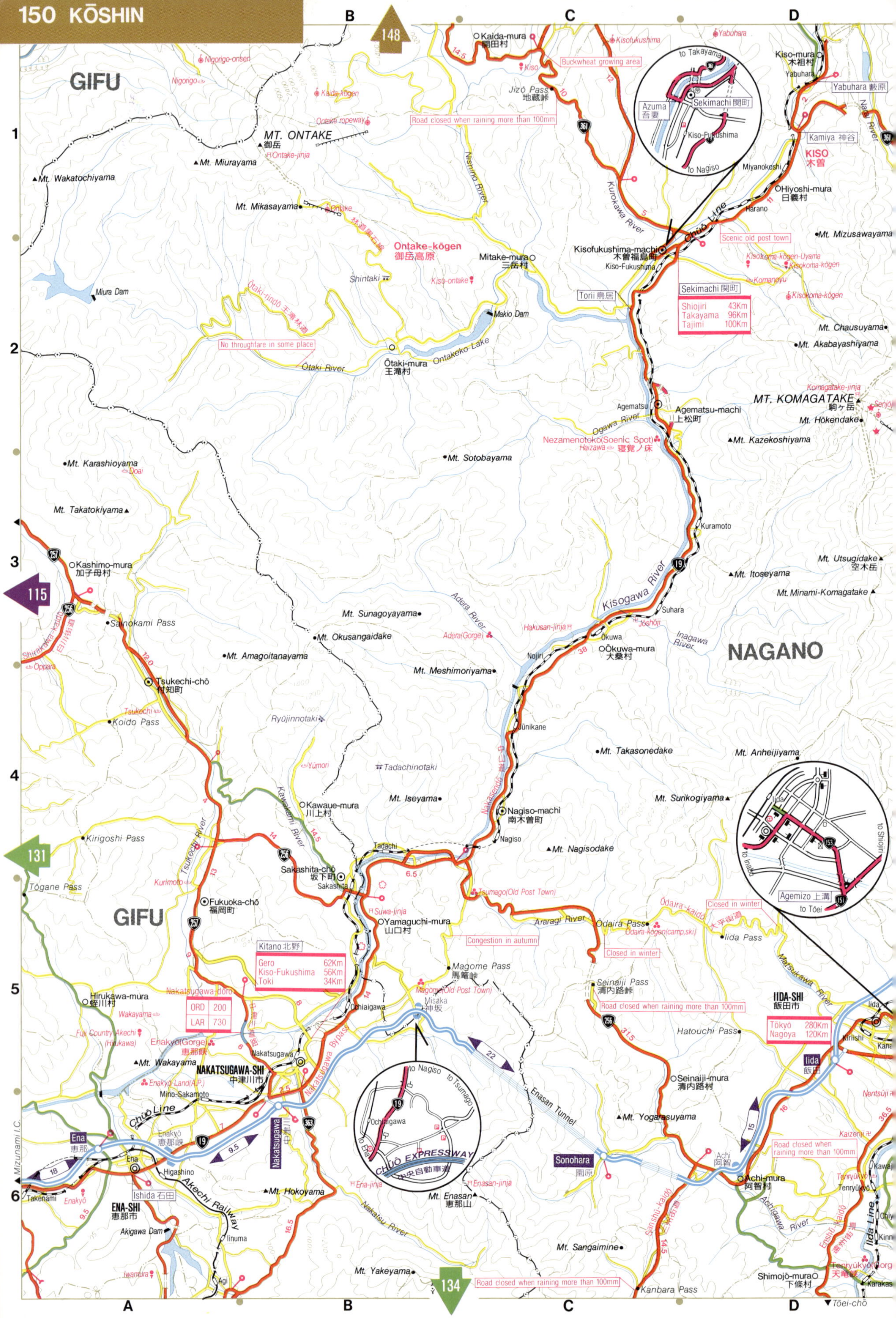

148
134
115
131
GIFU
NAGANO
MT. ONTAKE
御岳
Ontake-jinja
Mt. Miurayama
Mt. Wakatochiyama
Mt. Mikasayama
Ontake
Ontake-kōgen
御岳高原
Ontake ropeway
Kaida-kōgen
Nigorigo-onsen
Nigorigo
Kaida-mura
開田村
Kiso
Buckwheat growing area
Kisofukushima
Yabuhara
Jizō Pass
地蔵峠
Road closed when raining more than 100mm
Nishino River
Kurokawa River
Miura Dam
Shintaki
Kiso-ontake
Mitake-mura
三岳村
Makio Dam
Ōtaki-mura
王滝村
Ontakeko Lake
Ōtaki River
No throughfare in some place
Kisofukushima-machi
木曽福島町
Kiso-Fukushima
Torii 鳥居
Chūō Line
Sekimachi 関町
Shiojiri 43Km
Takayama 96Km
Tajimi 100Km
Azuma 吾妻
Kiso-Fukushima
to Takayama
to Nagiso
Kiso-mura
木祖村
Yabuhara 藪原
Kamiya 神谷
KISO
木曽
Miyanokoshi
Hiyoshi-mura
日義村
Harano
Narai River
Scenic old post town
Mt. Mizusawayama
Kisokoma-kōgen-Uyama
Kisokoma-kōgen
Komanoyu
Mt. Chausuyama
Mt. Akabayashiyama
Komagatake-jinja
MT. KOMAGATAKE
駒ヶ岳
Mt. Hōkendake
Senjōjiki
Mt. Kazekoshiyama
Agematsu
Agematsu-machi
上松町
Ogawa River
Nezamenotoko(Soenic Spot)
Haizawa
寝覚ノ床
Mt. Sotobayama
Mt. Karashioyama
Doai
Mt. Takatokiyama
Kuramoto
Mt. Utsugidake
空木岳
Mt. Itoseyama
Mt. Minami-Komagatake
Kashimo-mura
加子母村
Sainokami Pass
Shirakawa-kaidō
白川街道
Oppara
Mt. Sunagoyayama
Adera River
Adera(Gorge)
Hakusan-jinja
Kisogawa River
Suhara
Jōshōji
Ōkuwa
Ōkuwa-mura
大桑村
Inagawa River
Nojiri
Mt. Okusangaidake
Mt. Amagoitanayama
Mt. Meshimoriyama
Tsukechi-chō
付知町
Tsukechi
Koido Pass
Ryūjinnotaki
Jūnikane
Mt. Takasonedake
Mt. Anheijiyama
Yumori
Tadachinotaki
Nakasendō
Kawaue-mura
川上村
Kawakami River
Mt. Iseyama
Nagiso-machi
南木曽町
Nagiso
Mt. Surikogiyama
Mt. Nagisodake
Kirigoshi Pass
Tsukechi River
Tadachi
Sakashita-chō
坂下町
Sakashita
Kurimoto
Tōgane Pass
Fukuoka-chō
福岡町
GIFU
Suwa-jinja
Yamaguchi-mura
山口村
Tsumago(Old Post Town)
Araragi River
Ōdaira Pass
Ōdaira-kaidō
Ōdaira-kōgen(camp,ski)
Closed in winter
Iida Pass
Kitano 北野
Gero 62Km
Kiso-Fukushima 56Km
Toki 34Km
Congestion in autumn
Magome Pass
馬籠峠
Closed in winter
Seinaiji Pass
清内路峠
Road closed when raining more than 100mm
Matsukawa River
Iida
Agemizo 上溝
to Tōei
to Shiojiri
to Inada
IIDA-SHI
飯田市
Tōkyō 280Km
Nagoya 120Km
Hirukawa-mura
蛭川村
Nakatsugawa-dōro
ORD 200
LAR 730
Wakayama
Fuji Country Akechi (Hirukawa)
Enakyō(Gorge)
恵那峡
Magome(Old Post Town)
Ochiaigawa
Misaka
神坂
Nakatsugawa
Mt. Wakayama
NAKATSUGAWA-SHI
中津川市
Enakyō Land(A.P.)
Mino-Sakamoto
Nakatsugawa Bypass
Hatouchi Pass
Kirishi
Iida
飯田
Nentsūji
Seinaiji-mura
清内路村
Mt. Yogarasuyama
Enasan Tunnel
to Nagiso
to Tsumago
Ochiaigawa
to Ena
CHŪŌ EXPRESSWAY
中央自動車道
Chūō Line
Ena
恵那
Enakyō
恵那峡
Nakatsugawa
Sonohara
園原
Achi
阿智
Achi-mura
阿智村
Road closed when raining more than 100mm
Kaizenji
Tenryūkyō
Mizunami I.C.
Takenami
Ena
Higashino
Ishida 石田
Ena-jinja
Enasan-jinja
Mt. Enasan
恵那山
Mt. Hokoyama
Akechi Railway
ENA-SHI
恵那市
Enakyō
Akigawa Dam
Iinuma
Nakatsu River
Sanshū-kaidō
Achigawa River
Iida Line
Mt. Sangaimine
Iwamura
Agi
Mt. Yakeyama
Road closed when raining more than 100mm
Kanbara Pass
Shimojō-mura
下條村
Tenryūkyō(Gorge)
天竜峡
Karakasa
Tōei-chō
A
B
C
D
1
2
3
4
5
6

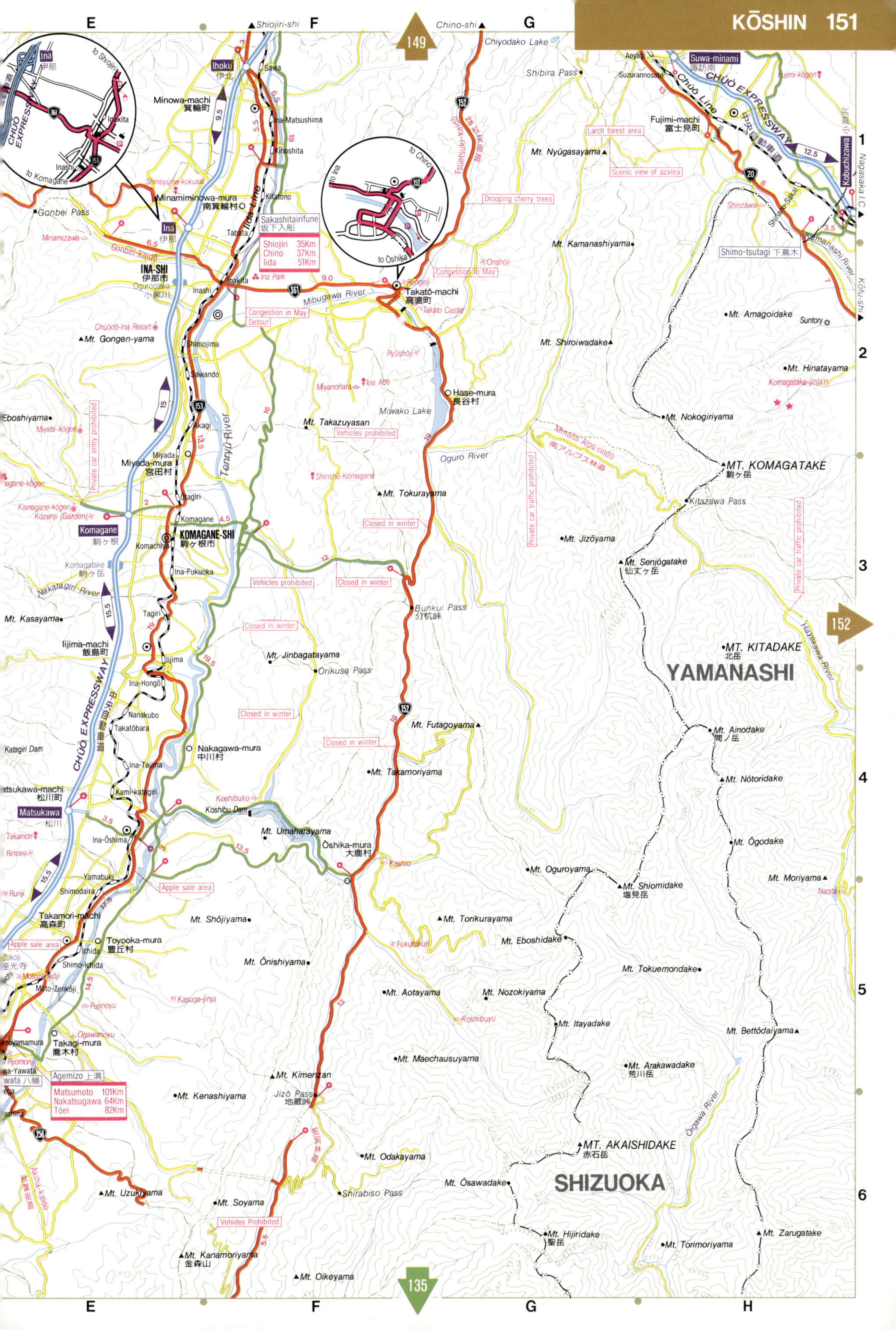
E
F
G
H
1
2
3
4
5
6
149
152
135
Shiojiri-shi
Chino-shi
Chiyodako Lake
Shibira Pass
Suwa-minami
CHŪŌ EXPRESSWAY
Chūō Line
Fujimi-machi
富士見町
Fujimi-kōgen
Aoyagi
Suzurannosato
Larch forest area
Scenic view of azalea
Mt. Nyūgasayama
Kobuchizawa
Nagasaka I.C.
Shiozawa
Shimo-tsutagi 下蔦木
Kamanashi River
Kōfu-shi
Mt. Kamanashiyama
Drooping cherry trees
Congestion in May
Onshōji
Rengeji
Takatō-machi
高遠町
Takato Castle
Mibugawa River
Congestion in May
Detour
Ina Park
Sakashitairifune
坂下入船
Shiojiri 35Km
Chino 37Km
Iida 51Km
Ina
伊那
Ihoku
伊北
Minowa-machi
箕輪町
Sawa
Ina-Matsushima
Kinoshita
Kitatono
Minamiminowa-mura
南箕輪村
Tabata
Iida Line
Inakita
Inashi
INA-SHI
伊那市
Ogurogawa
小黒川
Gonbei Pass
Gonbei-kaidō
Minamizawa
Shinsyūjin-kokusai
Chūōdō-Ina Resort
Mt. Gongen-yama
Shimojima
Sawando
Akagi
Miyada
Miyada-mura
宮田村
Tenryū River
Eboshiyama
Miyata-kōgen
Private car entry prohibited
Komagane-kōgen
Kōzenji (Garden)
Komagane
駒ケ根
Komagatake
駒ケ岳
Ōtagiri
Komagane
KOMAGANE-SHI
駒ケ根市
Komachiya
Ina-Fukuoka
Nakatagiri River
Mt. Kasayama
Tagiri
Iijima-machi
飯島町
Iijima
Ina-Hongō
Nanakubo
Takatōbara
Katagiri Dam
Ina-Tajima
Nakagawa-mura
中川村
Kami-katagiri
Matsukawa-machi
松川町
Matsukawa
松川
Takamori
Rinseiji
Ina-Ōshima
Yamabuki
Shimodaira
Runji
Takamori-machi
高森町
Apple sale area
Ichida
Shimo-Ichida
Toyooka-mura
豊丘村
Motozenkōji
Moto-Zenkōji
Fujinoyu
Takagi-mura
喬木村
Ogawanoyu
Ryomonji
Agemizo 上溝
Matsumoto 101Km
Nakatsugawa 64Km
Tōei 82Km
Akiha-kaidō
秋葉街道
Mt. Uzukiyama
Ryūshōji
Miyanohara
Ina Ace
Hase-mura
長谷村
Miwako Lake
Mt. Takazuyasan
Vehicles prohibited
Shinshū-Komagane
Mt. Tokurayama
Closed in winter
Vehicles prohibited
Closed in winter
Closed in winter
Bunkui Pass
分杭峠
Mt. Jinbagatayama
Ōrikusa Pass
Closed in winter
Closed in winter
Mt. Futagoyama
Mt. Takamoriyama
Koshibuko
Koshibu Dam
Mt. Umaharayama
Ōshika-mura
大鹿村
Kashio
Apple sale area
Mt. Shōjiyama
Mt. Ōnishiyama
Mt. Torikurayama
Fukutokuji
Kasuga-jinja
Mt. Aotayama
Mt. Nozokiyama
Koshibuyu
Mt. Maechausuyama
Mt. Kimenzan
Jizō Pass
地蔵峠
Mt. Kenashiyama
Mt. Odakayama
Shirabiso Pass
Mt. Soyama
Vehides Prohibited
Mt. Kanamoriyama
金森山
Mt. Oikeyama
Tsuetsuki-kaidō
Oguro River
Minami Alps-rindo
南アルプス林道
Private car traffic prohibited
Mt. Shiroiwadake
Mt. Amagoidake
Suntory
Mt. Hinatayama
Komagatake-jinja
Mt. Nokogiriyama
MT. KOMAGATAKE
駒ケ岳
Kitazawa Pass
Mt. Jizōyama
Mt. Senjōgatake
仙丈ケ岳
Private car traffic prohibited
MT. KITADAKE
北岳
YAMANASHI
Hayakawa River
Mt. Ainodake
間ノ岳
Mt. Nōtoridake
Mt. Ōgodake
Mt. Moriyama
Narata
Mt. Oguroyama
Mt. Shiomidake
塩見岳
Mt. Eboshidake
Mt. Tokuemondake
Mt. Itayadake
Mt. Bettōdaiyama
Mt. Arakawadake
荒川岳
Ōigawa River
MT. AKAISHIDAKE
赤石岳
SHIZUOKA
Mt. Ōsawadake
Mt. Hijiridake
聖岳
Mt. Torimoriyama
Mt. Zarugatake
to Shiojiri
Inakita
Inashi
to Komagane
CHŪŌ EXPRESSWAY
to Chino
to Ina
to Ōshika

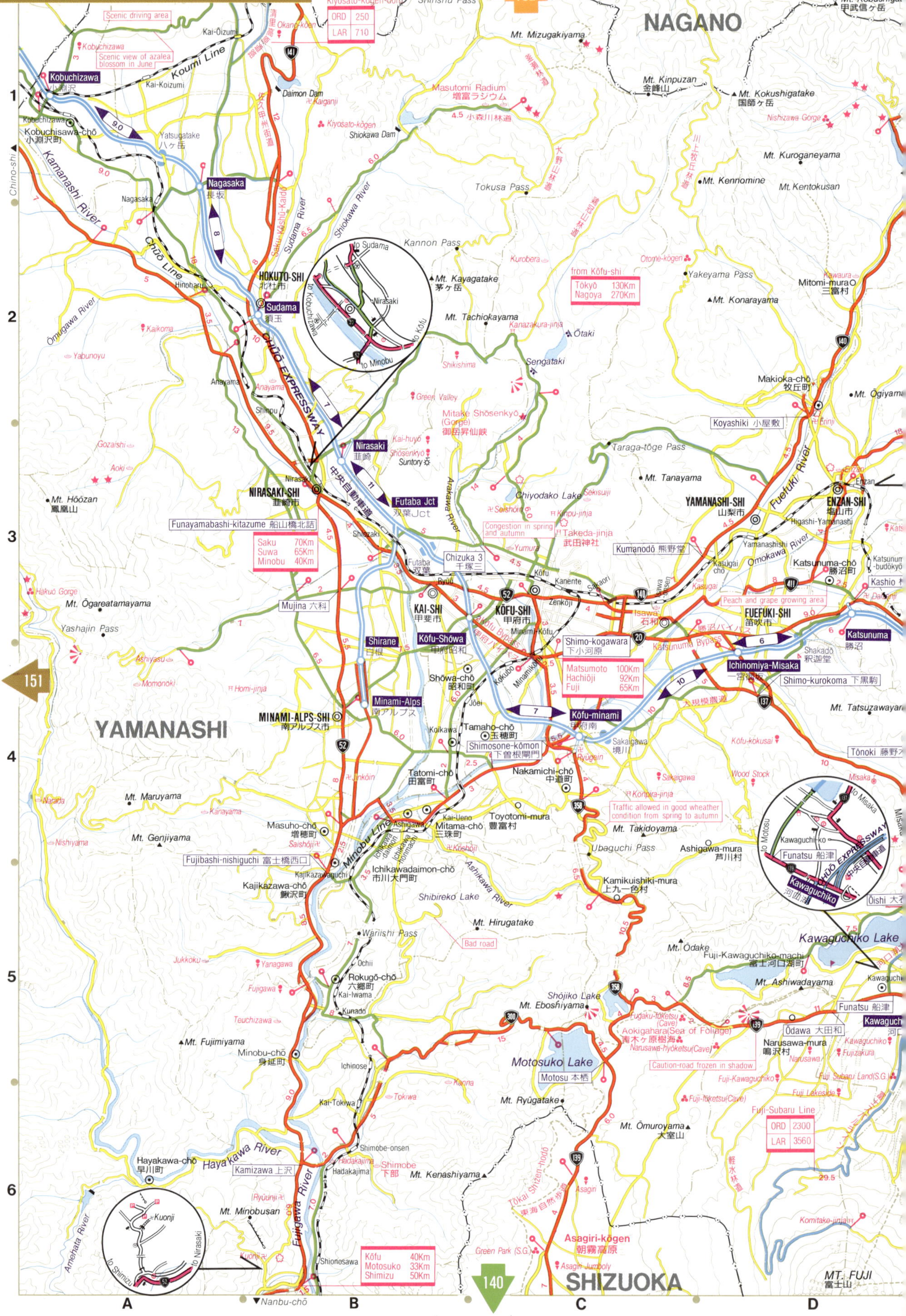

NAGANO
YAMANASHI
SHIZUOKA
162
151
140
B
C
D
A
1
2
3
4
5
6
Kobuchizawa 小淵沢
Kobuchisawa-chō 小淵沢町
Nagasaka 長坂
HOKUTO-SHI 北杜市
Sudama 須玉
Nirasaki 韮崎
NIRASAKI-SHI 韮崎市
Futaba Jct 双葉Jct
KAI-SHI 甲斐市
KŌFU-SHI 甲府市
Kōfu-Shōwa 甲府昭和
Shirane 白根
Minami-Alps 南アルプス
MINAMI-ALPS-SHI 南アルプス市
Kōfu-minami 甲府南
YAMANASHI-SHI 山梨市
ENZAN-SHI 塩山市
FUEFUKI-SHI 笛吹市
Ichinomiya-Misaka 一宮御坂
Katsunuma 勝沼
Kawaguchiko 河口湖
Kawaguchiko Lake
Motosuko Lake
Shōjiko Lake
Chūō Line
Koumi Line
Minobu Line
CHŪŌ EXPRESSWAY 中央自動車道
Kamanashi River
Fuefuki River
Fujigawa River
Hayakawa River
Mt. Mizugakiyama
Mt. Kinpuzan 金峰山
Mt. Kokushigatake 国師ヶ岳
Mt. Kobushigatake 甲武信ヶ岳
Mt. Kayagatake 茅ヶ岳
Mt. Hōōzan 鳳凰山
Mt. Ōgareatamayama
Mt. Maruyama
Mt. Genjiyama
Mt. Fujimiyama
Mt. Minobusan
Mt. Kenashiyama
Mt. Eboshiyama
Mt. Ryūgatake
Mt. Ōmuroyama 大室山
MT. FUJI 富士山
Shinshū Pass
Kannon Pass
Tokusa Pass
Yashajin Pass
Ubaguchi Pass
Warii Pass
Scenic driving area
Kiyosato-kōgen-dōro ORD 250 LAR 710
from Kōfu-shi Tōkyō 130Km Nagoya 270Km
Saku 70Km Suwa 65Km Minobu 40Km
Matsumoto 100Km Hachiōji 92Km Fuji 65Km
Kōfu 40Km Motosuko 33Km Shimizu 50Km
Fuji-Subaru Line ORD 2300 LAR 3560
Funayamabashi-kitazume 船山橋北詰
Fujibashi-nishiguchi 富士橋西口
Congestion in spring and autumn
Traffic allowed in good wheather condition from spring to autumn
Caution-road frozen in shadow
Bad road
Peach and grape growing area
Takeda-jinja 武田神社
Aokigahara(Sea of Foliage) 青木ヶ原樹海
Asagiri-kōgen 朝霧高原
Ichikawadaimon-chō 市川大門町
Kajikazawa-chō 鰍沢町
Minobu-chō 身延町
Hayakawa-chō 早川町
Nanbu-chō

SAITAMA
TŌKYŌ
KANAGAWA
SHIZUOKA
163
144
141
E
F
G
H
1
2
4
5
6
Chichibu-shi
Karisaka Pass
Karisaka Tunnel
雁坂トンネル道路
ORD 710
LAR 1980
Mt. Koreizan
Mt. Kasatoriyama
Mt. Mitsuminesan
三峰山
Mt. Kumotoriyama
雲取山
Mt. Tenmokusan
Takedera
Kurakake Pass
Mt. Bōnomine
Naguri
Naguri Gorge
Tōto-Hannō
Mt. Kawanoriyama
Ishiyama-jinja
Nippara Cave
Nippara River
Ozawa Pass
Mt. Ōborayama
Aoiwa Cave
Mt. Nanatsuishiyama
Jōfukuin
ŌME-SHI
青梅市
Ōme Line
Okutama-machi
奥多摩町
Tamagawa River
Mt. Fujioyama
Mt. Kurakakeyama
Mt. Iwadake
Tabayama-mura
丹波山村
Tabagawa River
Taba Valley
Scenic view of azalea blossom in April
Mt. Tosakayama
Ogōchi Dam
Okutama Tominnomori
Okutamako Lake
Mt. Gozenyama
Mitake-jinja
Yanagisawa Pass
柳沢峠
Closed in winter
Kosuge-mura
小菅村
Mt. Ōtakesan
大岳山
Ōtake Cave
Hinode-machi
日の出町
Mt. Daibosatsurei
大菩薩嶺
Daibosatsu Pass
Mt. Mitōzan
Hinohara Tominnomori
Tsuru Pass
Mt. Hazukariyama
AKIRUNO-SHI
あきる野市
Itsukaichi Line
Akikawa River
Hinohara-mura
檜原村
Akigawa Gorge
Musashi-Itsukaichi
Tōkyō Itsukaichi
Imakuma-jinja
Bad road
to Yanagisawa Pass
Kami-Ozo 上於曽
Enzan
to Katsunuma
Mt. Kariyoseyama
Sagashio
Kazuno River
Mt. Gongenyama
Mt. Shōtōsan
Jinba-kōgen
Lake Sagami
Higashi-Sagami
Tenmokuzan-Seiunji
Yamato-mura
大和村
Kanayama
Wada Pass
和田峠
Mt. Jinbasan
Tano
Uenohara-machi
上野原町
Mt. Kagenobuyama
Hachiōji I.C.
Keitokuin
Mt. Momokurayama
Mt. Ōgiyama
Mt. Takigoyama
Fukusenji
Dangōzaka
談合坂
Bijodani
Mt. Takaosan
高尾山
Hashikura
Magi
Ōtsuki Jct
Ōtsuki
大月
Ōtsuki
Nishi-Hachiōji
Olympic
Sagamiko
相模湖
Higashi off Ramp
東出口
CHŪŌ EXPRESSWAY
Fuzino
藤野
Uenohara
上野原
Sasago
Hatsukari
初狩
Saruhashi
ŌTSUKI-SHI
大月市
Katsura River
Sagamiko Lake
Sagamiko-machi
相模湖町
Sagamiko Picnic Land
Kōshū-kaidō
Chūō Line
Hatsukari
Tanokura
Otsukibashi-higashizume 大月橋東詰
Kōfu 40Km
Hachiōji 50Km
Yamanakako 34Km
Fujino-machi
藤野町
Sagamikoeki 相模湖駅
Mt. Tsurugadoyayama
Mt. Kuratakeyama
Aoyama 青山
Atsugi-shi
Kasei
Chūō-Tsuru
Akiyama River
Sagamiko
Makime Pass
牧馬峠
Tsukuiko
Tsuru
都留
Akasaka
Akiyama-mura
秋山村
Akiyama
Dōshigawa River
Mt. Mitsutōgeyama
三ツ峠山
Yamura
谷村
Tsurushi
TSURU-SHI
都留市
Mt. Akakuragatake
Tsukui-machi
津久井町
Mt. Yakeyama
Miyagase Dam
Yunosawa
Yamuramachi
Nishikatsura-machi
西桂町
Fujikyu Railway
Tsuru
Dōshi-mura
道志村
Kawaguchiko-ōhashi
ORD 200
LAR 730
Mitsutōge
Higashi-Katsura
Mt. Nabatakeyama
Dōshi
Mt. Ōmuroyama
Kotobuki
CHŪŌ EXPRESSWAY
中央自動車道
Nakatsu River
Gekkōji
FUJIYOSHIDA-SHI 富士吉田市
Kōfu 38Km
Motosuko 23Km
Gotenba 30Km
Fujiyoshida
Vehicles prohibited
Curves-used for detours
Mt. Mishōtaiyama
Mt. Hirugatake
Mt. Azegamaruyama
Mt. Hinokiboramaru
Mt. Tanzawayama
丹沢山
Kamiyoshida-kamimachi 上吉田上町
Oshino-hakkai
Oshino-mura
忍野村
Oshino
Mt. Komotsurushiyama
Mt. Tōgatake
Oshino-iriguchi 忍野入口
Mt. Ishiwariyama
Nakagawa
Mt. Ōyama
大山
Afuri-jinja
Yamanakako
Scenic view of cherry and wisteria blossom in May
Mt. Gongen-yama
Vehicles prohibited
Yabitsu Pass
ヤビツ峠
Ōyama-fudō
Yamanakako Lake
Tanzawako Lake
Yamanakako-mura
山中湖村
ORD 1040
LAR 3780
Fuji
Mikuni Pass
Ōhatano
Higashi-Fujigoko-dōro
Asahigaoka 旭ケ丘
Myōjin Pass
Mt. Furōzan
Hatano
Kagosaka Pass
籠坂峠
Drive-in area
Kouchi River
Taiheiyō Club Sagami
Odawara(Matsuda)
HADANO-SHI
秦野市
Kofuji
Fuji-kōgen
Fuji Greenhill
Fuji Health
Higasifuji
Shibusawa
Ōhatano
Odakyū Odawara Line
Gotenba-shi

C. Hajikizaki
弾崎
Mt. Tsurukiriyama
Large truck traffic prohibited
One-lane tunnel
Mt. Tategatairayama
Mt. Nakanooyama
C. Sabutozaki
C. Sekimisaki
Soto-Kaifu Coast
Uchi-Kaifu Coast
C. Akasaki
Mt. Utamiitadakisan
Hokakejima I.
C. Senbonohana
Mt. Dakeyama
C. Miyanosaki
Mt. Budōmine
Mt. Tsukaueyama
Mt. Kongōsan
Mt. Takazukōzan
C. Mourazaki
Ishige River
Mt. Dondenyama
Steep and narrow pass
Closed in winter
Risaian
C. Hiranezaki
Mt. Shorandōsan
Mt. Ōtsukayama
Mt. Kinpokusan
金北山
Senkaku-Wan Bay
(Scenic Rocky Coast)
尖閣湾
Mt. Myōkensan
Vehicles prohibited
Ryōtsu-wan
Sado-kisen Ferry (to Niigata)
Ryōtsu
Hajikizaki 36Km
Aikawa 27Km
Ogi 44Km
C. Himezaki
姫崎
Kamoko Lake
Sado
Shiizaki
Sumiyoshi
Uga-jinja
Ōsado Skyline
Closed in winter
Kobotoke Pass
Sado-kinzan (site of gold-mine)
Aono Pass
SADO-SHI
佐渡市
Yunosawa
Ushio-jinja
Katagami
Chōanji
One-lane curves
C. Bentenzaki
Mt. Ōsumiyama
C. Kasugazaki
Myōshōji
Jissōji
Konponji
SADOGASHIMA
佐渡島
Closed in winter
Honmachi-jūjiro
本町十字路
Kamo-jinja
Ōnogawa River
C. Nagatemisaki
Mano-wan
Kokubu River
One-lane
Katoshoten mae
加藤商店前
Myōsenji
Kokubunji
C. Daigahana
台ケ鼻
C. Shioyazaki
Mt. Ōjiyama
C. Ōsubana
Mt. Maruyama
Mt. Ogamiyama
C. Kōnosebana
C. Tagirisuzaki
Sairyūji
Mt. Hiruneyama
C. Takegahana
Mt. Bittsukeyama
Urazu 浦津
C. Uryūzaki
(to Niigata)
Sobama
Mt. Araisozan
Mt. Murasugeyama
(to Teradomari)
C. Nagatezaki
Rengebuji
Ogi-iriguchi 小木入口
Mt. Tsurusu
C. Sawasakibana 沢崎鼻
Ōishi-wan
Ogi
Sado-kisen Ferry
(to Naoetsu)
Ogi Coast
Oyashirazu
(Scenic Rocky Coast)
親不知
Oyashirazu
親不知
Ōmi
Denki Kagaku Kōgyō
Ōmi-machi
青海町
Suzawa
須沢
Caution-
high Waves
Yokomachi 横町
Kashiwazaki 81Km
Toyama 78Km
Omachi 75Km
Kajiyashiki
Itoigawa
ITOIGAWA-SHI
糸魚川市
Itoigawa
糸魚川
Rendaiji
蓮台寺
Ōito Line
Kubikiōno
Umikawa River
Hayakawa River
Hokuriku Line
Uramoto
Closed in winter
Sasakura
C. Gongenzaki
Nou-machi
能生町
Nou
能生
HOKURIKU EXPRESSWAY
北陸自動車道
Hokurikudō 北陸道
Tsutsuishi
Toyama-shi
to Senkaku-wan
Museum
to Skyline
to Skyline
to Ryōtsu
to Hajikizaki
to Aikawa
to Niigata
Shōbōsho mae
消防署前
Kamoko Lake
to Mano
to Jōetsu
Yokomachi
横町
Itoigawa
Terajima 寺島
to Toyama
to Hakuba
146
147
A
B
C
D
1
2
3
4
5
6

Kyūetsu Ferry (to Hakata)
Sado-kisen Ferry (to Ogi)
Higashi-Nihon Ferry (to Muroran)
Teradomari-machi
Niigata-shi
Kashiwazaki I.C.
Sabaishi River
KASHIWAZAKI-SHI
柏崎市
Higashi-Kashiwazaki
Banshindō
Kashiwazaki
Fukuura-hakkei
(Scenic Rocky Coast)
C. Kamomegahana
Kujiranami
Ōmigawa
Sekimachi 関町
Kasashima
Yoneyama
米山
Yoneyama
米山
Yoneyama
HOKURIKU EXPRESSWAY
北陸自動車道
Shin-etsu Line
Mt. Yoneyama
米山
Yoneyama-yakushi
Tochikubo
Kakizaki
Kakizaki
柿崎
Closed in winter
Mt. Jōyama
Jōgehama
Lake View
Asahiike Lake
Katamachi
Mt. Ogamidake
Dosokohama
Saigata
Ōgata
大潟
Closed in winter
Sakurasaka Pass
Kubiki
Ōike-ikoinomori
Mitsubishi Chemical Industries
Naoetsu
Kuroi
Arakawa River
Misoka Pass
Arasawa-fudō
Nikkōji
Closed in winter
Aono 青野
Closed in winter
Hokura River
Hokuetsu Express
Hokuhoku-Ōshima
Mt. Kingatake
Mt. Tōnosan
Mt. Shachiyama
Koguro River
Closed in winter
Closed in winter
Closed in winter
Closed in winter
Closed in winter
Mt. Shōmenkurayama
Mt. Nagakurayama
Mt. Hishigatake
Mt. Amamizuyama
Takaba
Kiyotaki Fall
Mt. Maeyama
Bōgaike Lake
Mt. Itayama
Closed in winter
Sekida Pass
NAGANO
Hirataki
Morimiya-Nahara
to Kashiwazaki
to Tōkamachi
Mitsuya
三ッ屋
to Ogi
Shimo-Gennyū
下源入
Naoetsu
to Jōetsu I.C.
to Itoigawa
to Nagano
Ishibashi
石橋
from Jōetsu-shi
Tōkyō 370Km
Kanazawa 190Km
Shimo-gennyu 下源入
Niigata 111Km
Matsunoyama 43Km
Nagano 80Km
Kuwadori River
Tanihama
Naoetsu
Arimagawa
Mt. Yudonosan
Mt. Kasugayama
Ishibashi 石橋
Rinsenji
Kasugayama
Kasugayama-jinja
Mitsuya
三ッ屋
Jōetsu
上越
Jōetsu-Jct
上越JCT
JŌETSU-SHI
上越市
Nadachi-Tanihama
名立谷浜
Takada
Kamiyudani
Kanayasan
Kamojima 鴨島
The site of the Takada Castle(Park)
Hokkoku-kaidō
北国街道
Minami Takada
Jōetsu-Takada
上越高田
Kushiike River
Iida River
Wakinoda
Shin-etsu Line
Bessho River
Mt. Aotananpasan
Teramachi 寺町
Kita-Arai
NIIGATA
Arai
新井
Arai
ARAI-SHI
新井市
Suwachō 諏訪町
Mt. Awadachiyama
Kyōzukayama-Park
Himegawara 姫川原
Nibongi
Iiyama-shi
147
160
158
E
F
G
H
1
2
3
5
6

from Niigata-shi
Tōkyō 340Km
Kanazawa 330Km
Sado-kisen Ferry (to Ryōtsu)
Shin-Nihonkai Ferry (to Otaru) (to Akita)
Shin-Nihonkai Ferry (to Tsuruga)
Sado-kisen Ferry (to Akadomari)
to Ryōtsu
Yoriichō 寄居町
Kurinoki 栗の木
Bandai Bridge
Shinano River
Niigata
to Shibata
to Maki
Shichikuyama Inter 紫竹山インター
to Nagaoka
to Aizu-Wakamatsu
Shichikuyama Inter 紫竹山インター
Murakami 66Km
Aizu-Wakamatsu 110Km
Nagaoka 62Km
Niigata
NIIGATA-SHI 新潟市
Hakusan
Sekiya
Aoyama
Nippon Light Metal
Igarashihama
Kobari
Niigata-chū 新潟中央
Terao
Niigata-nishi 新潟西
Niigata-daigaku-mae
Uchino
Otate
Kurosaki 黒崎
Shinkawa River
Sakata Lake
Echigo-Akatsuka
Nakanokuchi River
HOKURIKU EXPRESSWAY 北陸自動車道
to Maki
Iwamuro
Iwamuro 岩室
to Maze
Yahikosan Skyline
Hashimoto 橋本
to Teradomari
Myōkōji
Yunokoshi
C. Kakudamisaki
Echigo-Sone
Nishikawa-machi 西川町
Congestion in Jul. and Aug
Echigo Line
Ajikata-mura 味方村
Shirone
Mt. Kakudayama (Mt. Chōjaharayama)
Shirone 白根
Gōka Pass
Kinsenji
Niigata(Maki)
Maki-machi 巻町
Maki
Chūgakkō mae 中学校前
Katahigashi-mura 潟東村
SHIRONE-SHI 白根市
Kosudo
Maze 間瀬
Hashimoto 橋本
Maki-Katahigashi 巻潟東
Nishikawa River
Iwamuro 岩室
Nakanokuchi-mura 中之口村
Joetsu Shinkansen
Tsukigata-mura 月潟村
Yahiko-jinja
Yahiko
Kannonji
Yahiko
to Skyline
to Teradomari
Iwamuro-mura 岩室村
Iwamuro
Tominaga 富永
Shinano River
Tagami
Yahiko-jinja 弥彦神社
Mt. Yahikosan 弥彦山
Yahiko 弥彦
Kita-Yoshida
Yoshida-machi 吉田町
Yahiko Line
Yahagi
Tagami-machi 田上町
Hanyūda
Hinodechō 日之出町
Yoshida
Yahiko-mura 弥彦村
Minami-Yoshida
Kokujōji
Mt. Kugamiyama
TSUBAME-SHI 燕市
Tsubame
Ishigami 石上
KAMO-SHI 加茂市
Kamo
Shin-Shinano River
Aozu
Sanjō-Tsubame 三条燕
Tsubame-Sanjō
SANJŌ-SHI 三条市
Ōmi-jinja
Teradomari-machi 寺泊町
Teradomari
Congestion in Jul. and Aug
Honai
Bunsui
Kita-Sanjō
Kami-Sugoro 上須頃
Higashi-Sanjō
Teradomari
Bunsui-machi 分水町
Sanjō
Mt. Himenojōyama
Sakae 栄
Large truck traffic Pro
Kirihara
Hokkoku Kaidō
Igarashi River
Mt. Gomizawa
Kitano 北野
Sakae-machi 栄町
Tōkōji
Hie-jinja
Ushigakubi-yaku
Igarashi-jinja
Tsubame-ōhashi 燕大橋
Sanjō-Tsubame Inter 三条燕インター
to Yoshida
to Niigata
Ōjimaya
Myōhōji
Washima-mura 和島村
Koshinoyu
Obiori
Niigata Springs (Izumozaki)
Shionoiri Pass
Nakanoshima-machi 中之島町
Shin-etsu Line
Shitada-mura 下田村
Suidōchō 水道町
to Nagaoka
Congestion in Jul. and Aug
Izumozaki-machi 出雲崎町
Kōshōji
Yoita-machi 与板町
Mt. Kasanukiyama
Izumozaki
Nishihonganji-betsuin
Nakanoshima-Mitsuke 中之島見附
Imamachi 7 今町七
Mitsuke
MITSUKE-SHI 見附市
Kashiwazaki-shi
Nagaoka-shi
159

E
F
G
H
1
2
3
4
5
6
184
186
188
Mt. Tossakayama
Nakajō-machi
中条町
Nakajō
Ōzakura Pass
Kanazuka
Kaizuka
Shiun
Shiunji-machi
紫雲寺町
Shiunji
Niigata
Niigata Sunrise
Seirō-machi
聖籠町
Seirō-Shibata
Shinshin Bypass
Kajigawa-bunsui River
Kajikawa-mura
加治川村
Kaji
Shimagata 島潟
Shibata Castle
SHIBATA-SHI
新発田市
Shibata
Nishi-Shibata
Sasaki
Mitsubishi Gas Chemical
Niigata
Shibata River
Toyosaka-Niigata higashikō
豊栄新潟東港
Hayadōri
Kuroyama
Nizaki
Ōgata
Higashi-Niigata
Niigata-kūkō
新潟空港
TOYOSAKA-SHI
豊栄市
Toyosaka
Fukushimagata
Uetsu Line
Nakaura
Forest(Tsukioka)
Tsukioka
Tsukioka
Nakamine
Agano
Kameda
Kameda-machi
亀田町
Yokogoshi-machi
横越町
Jōsho Inter
城所インター
Cycling road
Kamiyama
Tokushōji
Koagano River
Suibara
AGANO-SHI
阿賀野市
Hyōko(Lake)
Mt. Shinkōjiyama
Tenjuji
Kehōji
Deyu
Sasagami-Gozu
Imaita
Murasugi
Mt. Toyagamine
Mt. Matsudairayama
Mt. Akayasuyama
Kyōgase
BAN-ETSU EXPRESSWAY
磐越自動車道
Satsukino
Niitsu
新津
Niitsu
Higashi-Niitsu
Niitsu
Shinseki
Noshiro
Haramachi 原町
Gosen
五泉
Yasuda
安田
Kita-Gosen
GOSEN-SHI
五泉市
Gosen
Hashiba 橋場
Murakami 65Km
Niigata 30Km
Aizu-wakamatsu 80Km
Kusōzu
Mt. Hōjusan
Mt. Hishigatake
Mt. Kasasugeyama
Sakihana
Sakihana
Aganogawa
阿賀野川
Maoroshi
Saruwada
Higashi-Gejō
Wakamatsu-kaidō
Igashima
Mikawa
Mikawa
三川
Mikawa-mura
三川村
Shirosaki 白崎
Mikawa-onsen
Mt. Shirahigeyama
Tsunogami
Kiyokawa-Kōgen
Tsunogami
Aganogawa Rhein
Mikawa
Yakushidō
Mt. Suganadake
Numakoe Pass
Muramatsu-machi
村松町
Hie-jinja
Haide River
NIIGATA
Mt. Fudōdoyama
Kanzewari
Large truck traffic Prohibited
Mt. Gongenyama
Sugawa River
Senmi River
Kawauchi Gorge
Mt. Ōmasutaniyama
Mt. Nihondairayama
Mt. Minowayama
Tsugawa
津川
Nikkōji
Mt. Futagurayama
Senic view of buckwheat bloom
Kamikawa
上川
Kamikawa-mura
上川村
Mt. Hakusan
Mt. Hōzōyama
Mt. Keishiyama
Mt. Kirokuyama
Mt. Nabekurayama
Nagase-jinja
Mt. Haigatake
Mt. Taihōyama
Mt. Goken-yadake
Mt. Hakamagoshiyama
Muroya River
Mt. Hakamagoshiyama
Mt. Mikaguradake
Mt. Kusahirayama
Mt. Kasakurayama
Mt. Mureyama
Tainai River
Jibiji
Sakai River
Mt. Kazekurayama
Tainaigawa Dam
Mt. Tossakamine
Shimagata 島潟
to Niigata
Nishi-Shibata
Shibata
to Murakami
to Gosen
Toyota-jinja
Ōdomo-inari
Ichinoji-jinja
Kajigawa River (Iide River)
Mt. Akibayama
Mt. Ninōjidake
Mt. Gakkōzan
Mt. Kōjōsan
Mt. Kōchiyama
Mt. Akatsuyama
Mt. Yakimineyama
Kajigawachisui Dam
Mt. Tanabashiyama
Mt. Hirubayama
Mt. Jinpentoyama
Araya River
Mt. Ōdanyama
Mt. Tsuchikurayama
Mikawa
Mt. Kurosakiyama
Hideya
Ban-etsu-Saisen Line
Kanose
Tsugawa
Kanose-machi
鹿瀬町
Kirinzan
Kanose
Mt. Usankurayama
Aizuwakamatsu-shi
若松街道
Sōza Pass
Torii Pass
Tsugawa-machi
津川町
Ibis
Mt. Tsuchiumeyama
Tsugawa
Mt. Toyayama
Shibakura River
Kashiwagi Pass
Mt. Kodōsan
Mt. Ōkurayama
Mt. Idogoyayama
Mt. Kanakoriyama

B
C
D
A
1
2
3
4
5
6
Mt. Yahiko
Kyuetsu Ferry (to Hakata)
Sado-kisen Ferry(to Ogi)
Higashi-Nihon Ferry(to Muroran)
Congestion in Jul. and Aug.
Kōshoji
Izumozaki-machi
出雲崎町
Oginojō
C. Kannonmisaki
Kannondō
Kashiwazaki
Raihai
Nishiyama-machi
西山町
Nishiyama
Echigo Line
Yakushi
Ishiji
Nishiyama
西山
Kariwa
Kariwa-mura
刈羽村
Kariwa
刈羽
Closed in winter
Tōfukuin
Arahama
Sochi Pass
曽地峠
Kashiwazaki Seaside
Nishi-Nakadōri
Hiyoshichō 日吉町
Niigata 70Km
Nagaoka 35Km
Tōkamachi 46Km
Kashiwazaki
Higashi-Kashiwazaki
Tatsuka
田塚
Banshindō
Kashiwazaki
Kashiwazaki
柏崎
Kashiwazaki Turkish Culture Village
Fukuura-hakkei(Scenic Rocky Coast)
Kujiranami
KASHIWAZAKI-SHI
柏崎市
Ibarame
Echigo-Hirota
Nagatori
Hirota
Tsukayama Pass
Ōmigawa
Caution-strong winds
北陸自動車道
Yasuda
Kitajō
Kasashima
Yoneyama
米山
Yoneyama
米山
Ukawa River
Takeishi Pass
Yoneyama
HOKURIKU EXPRESSWAY
Shin-etsu Line
Mt. Hakkokusan
Oguni-machi
小国町
Mt. Yoneyama
Yoneyama-yakushi
Tochikubo
Ishikawa Pass
Sabaishi River
Kakizaki
Komura Pass
NIIGATA
Closed in winter
Mt. Jōyama
Kakizaki
柿崎
Jōgehama
Mitsuzōin
Osawa Pass
Lake View
Asahiike Lake
Kaikizakigawa Dom
(Under construction)
Katamachi
Okanomachibashi
岡野町橋
Mt. Kurohimeyama
Takayanagi-machi
高柳町
Tsukiyume
Dosokohama
Mt. Ogamidake
Saigata
Ōgata
大潟
Sakurasaka Pass
Yamanaka
Mt. Yakushidake
Mt. Akatani
Kubiki
Mitsubishi Chemical Industries
Ōike-ikoinomori
Naoetsu
Kuroi
Misoka Pass
Nikkōji
Arasawa-fudō
Sabaishigawa Dam
Mt. Tennōzan
Naoetsu
Mitsuya
三屋
Ishibashi
石橋
Jōetsu
上越
Hokura River
Mt. Tōnosan
Hokuetsu Express
Mt. Kirigatake
Hokuhoku-Ōshima
Koguro River
Kawanishi
Mt. Gongen
JŌETSU-SHI
上越市
Kamo 蒲生
Ikejiri 池尻
Matsudai
Matsuno-jinja
Yakushi Pass
Matsudai-machi
松代町
Takada
Kamojima 鴨島
Minami-Takada
Kushiike River
Joshin Bypass
Arakawa River
Bessho River
Iida River
Mt. Shōmenkurayama
Matsunoyama-machi
松之山町
Kōshinnoyu
Shōinji
Mt. Shiroyama
Echigo-Mizusawa
Wakinoda
Mt. Nagakurayama
Matsunoyama
松之山
Bad road
Shikawatari
Echigo-Tazawa
Toyohara Pass
Kita-Arai
Teramachi
寺町
Shin-etsu Line
Tatsunoyu
Matsunoyama-onsen
Echigo-Shikawatari
Nakasato-mura
中里村
Suwachō 諏訪町
Mt. Koriyama
Bōgaike Lake
Takaba
Mt. Hishigatake
Mt. Amamizusan
Tsunan
Arai
ARAI-SHI
新井市
Kiyotaki
Mountain Park Tsunan
Kezukayama Park
Mt. Maeyama
NAGANO
Akinari-iriguchi 秋成入口
Tsunan-machi
津南町
Himegawara 姫川原
Mt. Itayama
Echigo-Tanaka
Ashidaki
Kosogari
Sekida Pass
Hirataki
Morinomiyahara
Scenic view of buckwheat bloom
Mitsuya
三ッ屋
to Kashiwazaki
to Tōkamachi
to Ogi
Shimo-Gennyū 下源入
Naoetsu
to Itoigawa
Ishibashi
石橋
to Jōetsu I.C.
Itoigawa-shi
Nagano-shi
Iiyama-shi
Nagano-shi
155
160

E
F
G
H
156
161
188
1
2
3
4
5
6
Sanjō-shi
Yoita-machi 与板町
Nakanoshima-chō 中之島町
Nakanoshima-Mitsuke
中之島見附
Mitsuke
MITSUKE-SHI 見附市
Mt. Kasanukiyama
Mishima-machi 三島町
Oshikiri
Kariyata River
Hitozura Pass 入面峠
Closed in winter
Niigata 62Km
Naoetsu 76Km
Tōkamachi 41Km
Kanda 3 神田三
Naginonoyu
Mitsuke
Kuwasagashi Pass
TOCHIO-SHI 栃尾市
Kitamachi 喜多町
Nagaoka Jct 長岡 Jct
Terajimamachi 寺島町
Kita-Nagaoka
Echigo-Higashiyama
Enoki Pass
Nigoro
Nagaoka Bypass
Nagaoka 長岡
Nagaoka
Nakazawamachi 中沢町
Moritate Pass
Joganji
Mt. Yūkyūzan
Yūkyūzan Park
Miyauchi
Nagaoka-Higashi Bypass
Jōetsu Line
Echigo kyūryō Park
Nagaoka-shiei
Maekawa
NAGAOKA-SHI 長岡市
Mt. Fūyasan
Mt. Nokogiriyama
from Nagaoka-shi
Tōkyō 280Km
Kanazawa 260Km
Raikōji
Koshiji-machi 越路町
Tōkamachi 十日町
Tōshōji
Shinpukuji
Echigo-Takiya
Yomogihira
Shinano River
KAN-ETSU EXPRESSWAY
関越自動車道
Tsukayama
Mt. Kanagurayama
Ojiya
Yamaya 山谷
OJIYA-SHI 小千谷市
Ojiya 小千谷
Jōetsu-Shinkansen
Yamakoshi-mura 山古志村
Mt. Toyagamine
Suhara
Jinpokudani
Uonuma-jinja
Mt. Mukōyama
Kawaguchi-machi 川口町
Echigo-Kawaguchi
Echigo-Kawaguchi 越後川口
Uchigamaki
Kita-Horinouchi
Echigo-Horinouchi
Koide
Wada 和田
Yokkamachi 四日町
Nagaoka 35Km
Tadami 65Km
Yuzawa 41Km
Horinouchi 堀之内
Echigo-Hirose
Yabukami
Uonuma-Tanaka
Yaburuma River
Echigo-Suhara
Kamijōeki-mae 上条駅前
Kamijō
Ishi Pass
Ōhira Pass
Mt. Yakushiyama
Sumon
Irihirose
Kakinoki
Ōshirakawa
Maburumagawa Dam
Tadami Line
Kuromatagawa-daiichi Dam
Rokujūri Pass
Tadami-machi
Mt. Ashizawayama
Mt. Maekemōyama
Kuromatagawa-daini Dam
Mt. Hyakujigatake
Mt. Kemōyama
FUKUSHIMA
Kuromata River
Mt. Eboshidake
Sumon River
Oyagawa River
Vehicles prohibited
Ōya Dam
Mt. Fukiyama
Amaoigaike Lake
Mt. Ban-yayama
Ōike Lake
Mt. Kuwadaiyama
Mt. Takamoriyama
Kurakake Pass
Mt. Sumondake 守門岳
Nunobikinotaki
Shin-etsu-kokusai ōhara
to Irihirose
to Nagaoka
to Okutadami
Hiwatashi 日渡
Iguchishinden 井口新田
to Muika-machi
Iguchishinden 井口新田
Chūshizawa
Hanegawa River
Sanashi River
Koide 小出
UONUMA-SHI 魚沼市
Mugurasawa
Imogawa
Oitate
Ōyu
Ōyu-onsen
Tochiomata
Silver Line
Mt. Tsuzumigakurayama
Mt. Mijōgatake
Mt. Kasakurayama
Mt. Hinatakurayama
Shiori Pass
Mizunashi River
Mt. Komagatake 駒ヶ岳
Kitanomata River
Ginzandaira-sansaro 銀山平三差路
Mt. Arasawadake
Mt. Nakanodake
Mt. Hakkaizan 八海山
Mt. Sarukurayama
Muikamachihakkaisan
Hakkaisanroku
Mt. Sakuramine
Shōjiyama
Kaebashi-iriguchi 栄橋入口
Gejō
Iiyama Line
Mushino 虫野
Urasa-kokusai
Yairo
Mt. Uenoyama
Hōzōji
Misaka Pass
Urasa
Urasa
Yamato 大和
Kitahara 北原
Senju-kannon
Uonuma-Nakajō
Jingūji
Bishamondō
Uono River
Niigata 110Km
Naoetsu 62Km
Nagano 81Km
Shinza
Tōkamachi
TŌKAMACHI-SHI 十日町市
Hokuetsu Express
Itsukamachi
Shimizu Pass
Muikamachi 六日町
Muikamachi
Mizawa River
Yawata 八幡
MINAMIUONUMA-SHI 南魚沼市
Jōetsu-kokusai Tōkamachi
Scenic view of Mt. Tanigawadake
Futatsuya
Muikamachi-minami
Mt. Taruyama
Tochikubo Pass
Echigotawarayama
Jōetsu Line
Jōetsu-kokusai
Jōetsu-kokusai-sukijō-mae
Ōsawa Pass
Ōsawa
Shiozawa
Shiozawa-machi 塩沢町
Caution-weak road shoulder
Mt. Atemayama
Ishiuchi 石打
Ishiuchi-korakuen
Ishiuchidaira
Shiozawa-Ishiuchi 塩沢石打
Mikuni Pass
to Koide
to Tōkamachi
to Yuzawa
Muikamachi
Yawata 八幡
Saguri River
Mt. Takakurayama
Mt. Usagidake
Mt. Ōsawayama
Mt. Ōwariyama
GUNMA
Mt. Hiragatake

B
C
D
158
159
1
2
4
5
6
147
162
A
B
C
D
NIIGATA
NIIGATA
NAGANO
Sekida Pass
Passage for small car only
Large truck traffic prohibited
Closed in winter
Road closed when raining more than 100mm
Vehicles prohibited
Ishiuchi 石打
Jūni Pass
Ashidaki
Echigo-Tanaka
Hirataki
Morimiyanohara
Nishi-Ōtaki
Shinano-Shiratori
Kuwanaga
Sakae-mura
栄村
Yokokura
Mt. Nabekurayama
Kami-Kuwanaga
Chikuma River
Iiyama Line
Nanatsugama Fall
Greenpia
Kiyotsukyō
Kiyotsukyō (Gorge)
Kiyotsu River
Mt. Idomine
Yuzawa
湯沢
GALA Yuzawa
Echigoyuzawa
Mt. Sasabamine
Mt. Takatsukurayama
Mt. Mitakoyama
Mt. Ōmine
Kumano
NASPA Sky Garden
Sakamaki
Kamisakai
Tokari
Nozawaonsen-mura
野沢温泉村
Nozawa
Nozawa-onsen
Kaminodaira
Kaminodaira-kōgen
Kamagawa River
Togarinozawa-onsen
Tokarikozakai
Shinanodaira
Hokuryuko
Hokuryūko Lake
Kosuge-jinja
Birch tree grove
Mt. Kenashiyama
Mt. Hōshiyama
Nakatsu River
Drive-in area
Naeba-Mitsumata-Kōgen
Mt. Mukaiyama
Mt. Shiraitayama
Shiraita-kōgen
IIYAMA-SHI
飯山市
Shinanotaira
Kagura
Kaikake
Sharp curves
Arai-shi
Iiyama-Kokusai
Kita-Iiyama
Iiyama
Kijimadaira-mura
木島平村
Mt. Jōkurayama
Mt. Kaguragamine
Tashiro
Mt. Nippakusan
Futai
Yashiki
Mt. Naebasan
苗場山
Mt. Torikabutoyama
Kijimadaira
Wayama
Akiyamagō
秋山郷
Kayanodaira
Mt. Takahyōyama
Beech tree forest
Zakogawa River
Kiriake
Gojūdaki
Akayu
Mt. Tairappyōyama
Hiuchi Pass
Nagano-shi
Hachiku
Mt. Takaitsuji
Shiga-kōgen
Mt. Akayuyama
Naeba Prince Hotel
Naeba
Naeba 苗場
Shirakaba
Mt. Komaruyama
Mt. Iimoriyama
Kitashiga-Ryūo
Mt. Takenokoyama
Uono River
Yomase
Yomase River
Mt. Saburyūyama
Asagai 浅貝
Okushiga
Mt. Eboshidake
Mikuni Tunnel
Mikuni
Shinano-Takehara
Mt. Yakebitaiyama
Yakebitaiyama
Kamijō
Yamanouchi-machi
山ノ内町
Mt. Gorinsan
Nakano-Matsukawa
Shinshū-Nakano
Yudanaka
Shibu
Yudanaka-Shibu Hot Springs
湯田中渋温泉
Mt. Iwasugeyama
若菅山
Fog
Jigokudani
Takamagahara
Entoku
NAKANO-SHI
中野市
Kanbayashi
Mt. Nishitateyama
Hoppo
Mt. Shirasunayama
Kakuma
Mt. Higashitateyama
Mt. Akazawayama
Sakurasawa
Birch tree grove
Shiga-Kōgen
Ōnumaike Lake
to Mt. Shiranesan
Nozoriko Lake
Mt. Hakkenzan
Ishinoyu
Mt. Shigayama
Mt. Misawayama
SHIGA HEIGHTS
志賀高原
Maeyama
Shirasuna River
Hinatami-Yakushidō
Oguranotaki
Koizuminotaki
Ōizuminotaki
Kumanoyu
Mt. Ainokurayama
Yamada-onsen
Kumanoyu
Yamada
Mt. Kasagatake
Yokoteyama
Shima
Takayama-mura
高山村
Closed in winter
Okuyamada-onsen
Yamada Farm (P.G.)
Shibu Pass
to Naganohara
Kusatsu dōro
Goshiki
Shichimi
Mt. Shinehagiyama
Yamada Pass
MT. SHIRANESAN
白根山
Mt. Manzayama
万座山
Manza
Manza-onsen
Shimyaki
Hanashiki
Mt. Matsuiwayama
Mt. Takadayama
Shimagawa River
Mt. Narayama
Fog
Aimomine
Honshirane
Kusatsu-kōgen
Kusatsu
草津
Kusatsu onsen
Sesshōgawara
Mt. Motoshiranesan
本白根山
Omotemanza
Sawatari
Kenashi Pass
Kusatsu-machi
草津町
Yunotaira
Kuresaka Pass
Mt. Arigasayama
Mt. Donabeyama
Kuni-mura
六合村
Mt. Kimyōsan
Manza Highway
ORD 1020
LAR 4080
Sukawa River
Kusatsu
Yonagodaki Fall
Matsunoyu-Kawanaka
Mt. Yakushidake
Minenohara
Manza River
Mt. Ōjoyama
Iwashima
Mt. Nekodake
Drive-in area
Haneo
Naganohara-Kusatsu-guchi
Agatsuma Line
Agatsuma Gorge
Kawarayu-onsen
Gobara
Sugadaira Green
Sugadaira-kōgen
to Kusatsu
Tsumagoi-kōgen
Gunma-Ōtsu
Kawarayu
Agatsuma River
Manza Highway
Fukurogura
Nihon-Dabos
Mt. Azumayasan
to Manza Spa
to Nakanojō
Manza-Kazawaguchi
Naganohara-machi
長野原町
Kumagawa River
to Ueda
Manza-Kazawaguchi
Tsumagoi-mura
嬬恋村
Sharp curves
Mt. Sugamine
Sugao Pass
鬼押ハイウェー
Omae
Onioshi Highway
ORD 610
LAR 2420
Nurukawa River
Mt. Kogarayama
Tashiroko Lake
Hatonoyu
Yakushi
Nurukawa
Torii Pass
鳥居峠
Shinkazawa
Prince-land
Kitakaruizawa
Palcall Tsumagoi
Rokurigahara
Mt. Murakamiyama
Ueda-shi

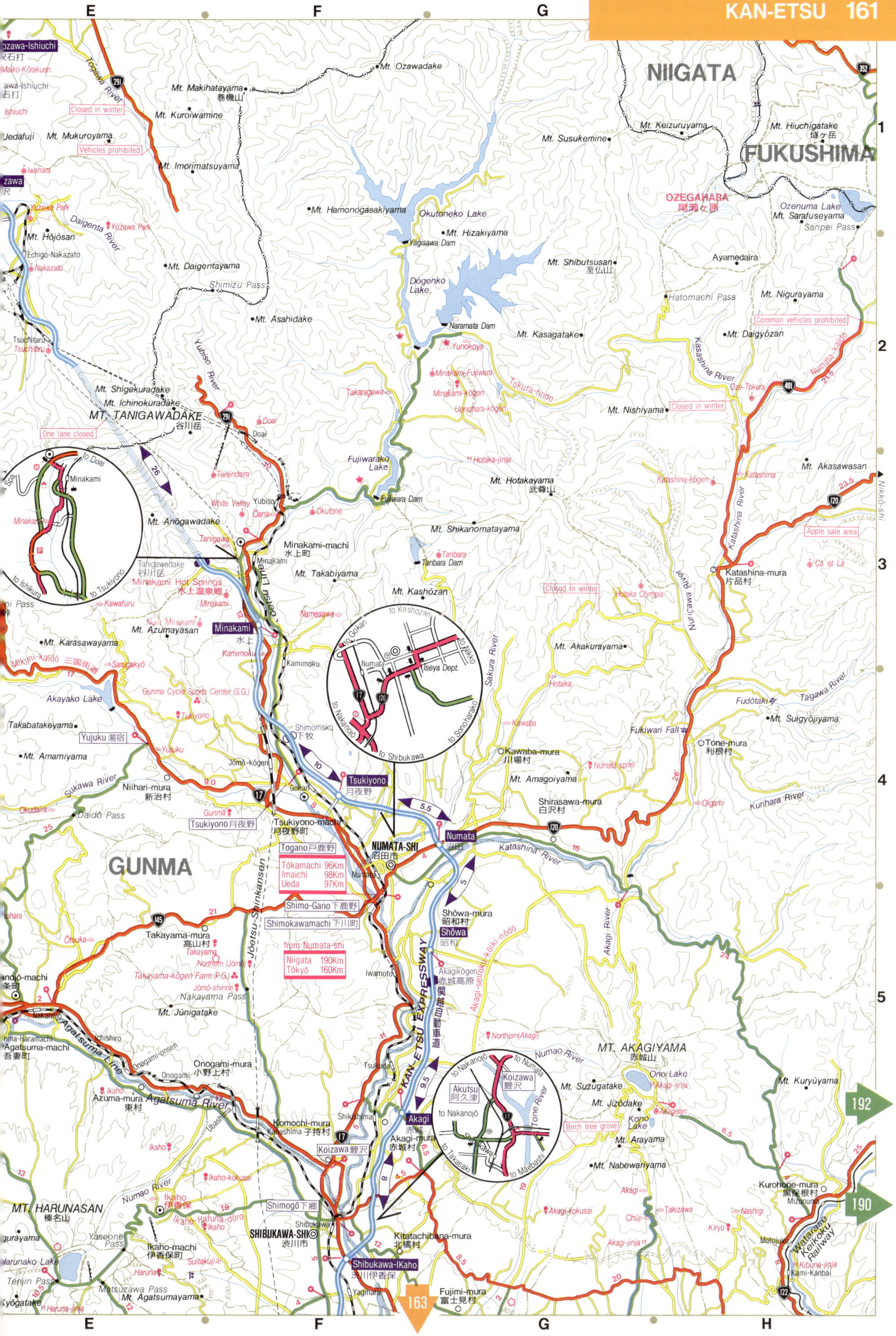
NIIGATA
FUKUSHIMA
GUNMA
OZEGAHARA
尾瀬ヶ原
Mt. Ozawadake
Mt. Makihatayama
巻機山
Mt. Kuroiwamine
Mt. Imorimatsuyama
Mt. Mukuroyama
Togawa River
Closed in winter
Vehicles prohibited
Mt. Hamonogasakiyama
Okutoneko Lake
Yagisawa Dam
Mt. Hizakiyama
Dōgenko Lake
Naramata Dam
Yunokoya
Mt. Keizuruyama
Mt. Susukemine
Mt. Hiuchigatake
燧ヶ岳
Ozenuma Lake
Mt. Sarafuseyama
Sanpei Pass
Ayamedaira
Mt. Shibutsusan
至仏山
Hatomachi Pass
Mt. Nigurayama
Common vehicles prohibited
Mt. Daigyōzan
Mt. Kasagatake
Kasashina River
Numata-kaidō
Oze-Tokura
Mt. Nishiyama
Tokura-rindō
Mt. Hōjōsan
Daigenta River
Yuzawa Park
Echigo-Nakazato
Nakazato
Mt. Daigentayama
Shimizu Pass
Mt. Asahidake
Yubiso River
Tsuchitaru
Mt. Shigekuradake
Mt. Ichinokuradake
MT. TANIGAWADAKE
谷川岳
One lane closed
Doai
Tenjindaira
Minakami-Fujiwara
Minakami-kōgen
Takaragawa
Fujiwarako Lake
Fujiwara Dam
Hotaka-jinja
Mt. Hotakayama
武尊山
Mt. Akasawasan
Katashina-kōgen
Katashina
Katashina River
Nikkō-shi
Apple sale area
Ça et Là
Katashina-mura
片品村
White Valley
Yubiso
Ōana
Okutone
Mt. Anōgawadake
Tanigawa
Minakami-machi
水上町
Mt. Shikanomatayama
Tanbara
Tanbara Dam
Mt. Takabiyama
Mt. Kashōzan
Closed in winter
Hotaka Olympia
Numata River
Minakami Hot Springs
水上温泉郷
Minakami
Kawafuru
Mt. Azumayasan
Mt. Karasawayama
Mikuni-kaidō 三国街道
Sarugakyō
Kamimoku
Kamimokku
Jōetsu Line
Numata
Iseya Dept.
to Kashōzan
to Nikkō
to Gokan
to Nakanojō
to Shibukawa
to Sonoharako
Sakura River
Mt. Akakurayama
Hotaka
Akayako Lake
Gunma Cycle Sports Center (S.G.)
Takabatakeyama
Tukiyono
Yujuku 湯宿
Shimomoku
下牧
Kawaba
Fukiwari Fall
Fudōtaki
Mt. Suigyōjiyama
Tagawa River
Tone-mura
利根村
Mt. Amamiyama
Sukawa River
Niihari-mura
新治村
Jōmō-kōgen
Tsukiyono
月夜野
Kawaba-mura
川場村
Numata spring
Mt. Amagoiyama
Okudaira
Daido Pass
Gunma
Tsukiyono 月夜野
Tsukiyono-machi
月夜野町
Shirasawa-mura
白沢村
Oigami
Kurihara River
NUMATA-SHI
沼田市
Togano 戸鹿野
Tōkamachi 96Km
Imaichi 98Km
Ueda 97Km
Katashina River
Shimo-Gano 下鹿野
Shimokawamachi 下川町
Jōetsu-Shinkansen
Takayama-mura
高山村
Takayama
Ōtsuka
from Numata-shi
Niigata 190Km
Tōkyō 160Km
Shōwa-mura
昭和村
Shōwa
昭和
KAN-ETSU EXPRESSWAY
関越自動車道
Akagikōgen
赤城高原
Akagi-seiroku-kōiki-nōdō
Akagi River
Iwamoto
Takayama-kōgen Farm (P.G.)
Jōmō-shinrin
Nakayama Pass
Mt. Jūnigatake
Nakanojō-machi
Agatsuma Line
Agatsuma-machi
吾妻町
Ichishiro
Onogami-onsen
Onogami
Onogami-mura
小野上村
Northern (Akagi)
MT. AKAGIYAMA
赤城山
Ono Lake
Akagi-jinja
Numao River
Mt. Suzugatake
Mt. Jizōdake
Kono Lake
Akagisan
Mt. Arayama
Birch tree grove
Mt. Kuryūyama
Ikaho
Azuma-mura
東村
Agatsuma River
Tsukuda
Komochi-mura
子持村
Shikishima
Koizawa 鯉沢
Akagi
赤城
Akagi-mura
赤城村
Akutsu 阿久津
to Nakanojō
to Numata
Tone River
to Takasaki
to Maebashi
Mt. Nabewariyama
Kurohone-mura
黒保根村
Mizunuma
Ikaho-kokusai
Numao River
MT. HARUNASAN
榛名山
Ikaho 伊香保
Ikaho-Haruna-dōro
Shimogō 下郷
Shibukawa
SHIBUKAWA-SHI
渋川市
Kitatachibana-mura
北橘村
Akagi
Akagi-kokusai
Chūji
Takizawa
Nashigi
Kiryū
Akagi-jinja
Motojuku
Watarase Keikoku Railway
Kibune-jinja
Kami-Kanbai
Yaseone Pass
Ikaho-machi
伊香保町
Suitakuji
Haruna
Harunako Lake
Tenjin Pass
Matsuzawa Pass
Mt. Agatsumayama
Shibukawa-Ikaho
渋川伊香保
Yagihara
Fujimi-mura
富士見村
Haruna-jinja
Kyōgatake
192
190
163
E
F
G
H
1
2
3
4
5

B
C
D
160
149
152
Sanada-machi
真田町
Mt. Yunomaruyama
湯ノ丸山
Mt. Sajikiyama
Mt. Eboshidake
Jizō Pass
Mt. Kagonotoyama
Mt. Sanpōgamine
Mt. Takamineyama
Kurumazaka Pass
MT. ASAMAYAMA
浅間山
Mt. Kurofuyama
Yunomaru-kōgen
Onioshidashi (Lava beds)
Onioshi Highway
ORD 610
LAR 2420
Mt. Takatsunagiyama
Mt. Asamakakushiyama
Taiheiyō Club Karuizawa
Vehicles prohibited
Shiraito Highland Way
ORD 300
LAR 1200
Asama Pass
浅間越
Kurabuchi-mura
倉渕村
Nishi-Matsuida
to Karuizawa
Matsuida
to Annaka
to Shimonita
Jizō Pass
Karasu River
Tōbu-Yunomaru
東部湯の丸
TŌMI-SHI
東御市
Mt. Kengamine
KARUIZAWA
軽井沢
Mt. Kirizumiyama
Mt. Sekisonzan
Kariyado 借宿
Numata 80Km
Ueda 34Km
Takasaki 50Km
Komoro-kōgen
Hishino-yakushi
Komoro
小諸
Karuizawa-machi
軽井沢町
Karuizawa 軽井沢
Naka-Karuizawa
中軽井沢
Minami-Karuizawa
南軽井沢
Usui Pass
碓氷峠
Yokokawa
横川
Yokokawa 横川
Usui River
Matsuida-machi
松井田町
Matsuida
Matsuida-Myōgi
松井田妙義
Ueda-shi
Shigeno
Chikuma River
KOMORO-SHI
小諸市
Miyota-machi
御代田町
Shinano-Oiwake
Drive-in area
Nakasendō
Shinano Line
Nagano Shinkansen
Miyota
Mimakigahara
Higashi-Komoro
Otome
Mitsuoka
Hirahara
Misato
Nakasato
Iwamurada
Kakuma River
NAGANO
Saku
佐久
Saku Ski Garden Parada
Mt. Hiraofuji
Kōsaka-kannon
Sakudaira Highway Oasis
佐久平ハイウェイオアシス
Wami Pass
JOSHIN-ETSU EXPRESSWAY
上信越自動車道
Usui-Karuizawa
碓氷軽井沢
Nakanotake-jinja
Mt. Yakyūzan
Mt. Myōgisan
妙義山
Myōgi-machi
妙義町
Myōgi-jinja
Tateshina-machi
Asashina-mura
浅科村
Mochizuki-machi
望月町
Kita-Nakagomi
SAKU-SHI
佐久市
Myōgi Arafunerindō
ORD 890
LAR 2200
Suginoki Pass
Mt. Midōsan
Mt. Ōgetayama
Sadayūmachi 佐太夫町
Namezu
Nakagomi
Kumanoyu
Shōanji
Nozawahonmachi
野沢本町
Ōtabe
Mt. Monomiyama
Uchiyama Pass
Shōya
Miyama
Arafune
Saimoku River
Sendaira
Shimonita
Shimonita-machi
下仁田町
to Komoro
to Karuizawa
Iwamurada
to Asashina
to Usuda
Nakagomi
to Tomioka
Tatsuokajō
Mt. Arafuneyama
荒船山
Mt. Kabutoiwayama
Mt. Yotsumatayama
Usuda
Usuda-machi
臼田町
Aonuma
Tatsuoka Castle
Taguchi Pass
Zenshōji
Fudōji
Nanmoku River
Mt. Fujisengen-yama
Haguroshita
Sobaranoyu
Takanomachi 高野町
Saku-machi
佐久町
Katsuze
Yoji Pass
Kannō
No thoroughfare
Nanmoku-mura
南牧村
Mt. Mitsuiwayama
Mikabo-rindō
Nukui River
Bushū-kaidō
Yachiho-mura
八千穂村
Shimizuchō 清水町
Yachiho
Shionosawa Pass
Shionosawa
Takaiwa
Mt. Moraiyama
Bad road
Jukkoku Pass
Managashi
Koumi-machi
小海町
Mt. Yomoharayama
Koumi
Mt. Atokurayama
Ameike Lake
Ikenotaira Farm (P.G.)
Koumi
Oinuana (Cave)
Ueno-mura
上野村
Hamadaira
Budō Pass
Koumi Resort City RE-EX
Mugikusa Pass
麦草峠
Closed in winter
Koumi RE-EX ski valley
Matsubarako Lake
Matsubarako
Koumi-Karuizawa Public
Kitaaiki-mura
北相木村
Shirakomaike Lake
Inagoyu
Aiki River
Mt. Maruyama
Umijiri
Minamiaiki-mura
南相木村
Mt. Ogurayama
Mt. Suwayama
Mt. Nakayama
Mt. Tengudake
天狗岳
Yatsugatake-kōgen
Saku-Uminokuchi
Uminokuchi
Minamimaki-mura
南牧村
Honzawa
Natsuzawa
Mt. Iōdake
Saku-Hirose
MT. YATSUGATAKE
八ヶ岳
Akadake
Mt. Yokodake
Mt. Amidadake
Mt. Akadake
赤岳
Saku-Kōshū-Kaidō
Mt. Otokoyama
Kawakami-mura
川上村
Mt. Mikuniyama
三国山
Mikuni Pass
Nakatsugawa-rindō
Bad
Shinano-Kawakami
Nobeyamahara
Chikuma River
Mt. Hakutaisan
Koumi Line
Nobeyama
Nobeyama-kōgen
Mt. Utsukushimoriyama
Mt. Amigasayama
編笠山
Scenic view
Mt. Onnayama
Mt. Gorōyama
Farm
Alpen
Nobeyama
Yatsugatake Sailer Valley
YAMANASHI
Kiyosato
Mt. Meshimoriyama
飯盛山
Mt. Yokooyama
Shinshū Pass
Mt. Kobushidake
Nirasaki-shi
A
B
C
D

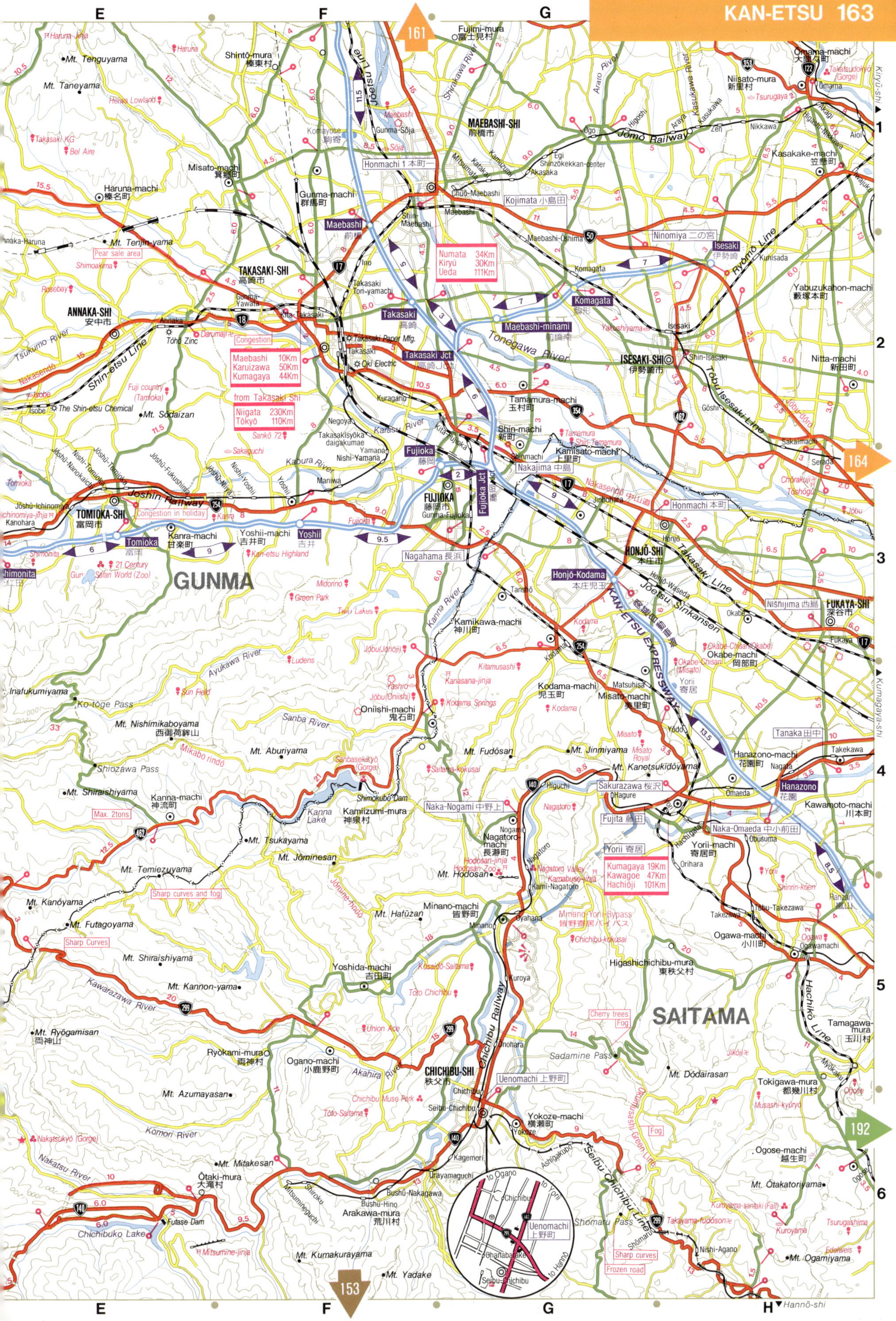
E
F
G
H
1
2
3
4
5
6
161
164
192
153
GUNMA
SAITAMA
MAEBASHI-SHI
前橋市
TAKASAKI-SHI
高崎市
ANNAKA-SHI
安中市
TOMIOKA-SHI
富岡市
FUJIOKA
藤岡市
HONJŌ-SHI
本庄市
ISESAKI-SHI
伊勢崎市
FUKAYA-SHI
深谷市
CHICHIBU-SHI
秩父市
Shintō-mura
榛東村
Fujimi-mura
富士見村
Ōmama-machi
大間々町
Niisato-mura
新里村
Haruna-machi
榛名町
Misato-machi
箕郷町
Gunma-machi
群馬町
Kasakake-machi
笠懸町
Yabuzukahon-machi
藪塚本町
Nitta-machi
新田町
Tamamura-machi
玉村町
Shin-machi
新町
Kamisato-machi
上里町
Kanra-machi
甘楽町
Yoshii-machi
吉井町
Kamikawa-machi
神川町
Kodama-machi
児玉町
Misato-machi
美里町
Okabe-machi
岡部町
Onishi-machi
鬼石町
Hanazono-machi
花園町
Kawamoto-machi
川本町
Kanna-machi
神流町
Kamiizumi-mura
神泉村
Yorii-machi
寄居町
Nagatoro-machi
長瀞町
Minano-machi
皆野町
Yoshida-machi
吉田町
Ogawa-machi
小川町
Higashichichibu-mura
東秩父村
Tamagawa-mura
玉川村
Ryōkami-mura
両神村
Ogano-machi
小鹿野町
Tokigawa-mura
都幾川村
Yokoze-machi
横瀬町
Ogose-machi
越生町
Ōtaki-mura
大滝村
Arakawa-mura
荒川村
Maebashi
前橋
Takasaki
高崎
Takasaki Jct
高崎JCT
Maebashi-minami
前橋南
Komagata
駒形
Isesaki
伊勢崎
Fujioka
藤岡
Fujioka Jct
Yoshii
吉井
Tomioka
富岡
Shimonita
下仁田
Honjō-Kodama
本庄児玉
Hanazono
花園
Honmachi 1 本町一
Kojimata 小島田
Ninomiya 二の宮
Nakajima 中島
Honmachi 本町
Nagahama 長浜
Nishijima 西島
Tanaka 田中
Naka-Nogami 中野上
Sakurazawa 桜沢
Fujita 藤田
Naka-Omaeda 中小前田
Yorii 寄居
Uenomachi 上野町
Numata 34Km
Kiryū 30Km
Ueda 111Km
Maebashi 10Km
Karuizawa 50Km
Kumagaya 44Km
from Takasaki Shi
Niigata 230Km
Tōkyō 110Km
Kumagaya 19Km
Kawagoe 47Km
Hachiōji 101Km
Congestion
Congestion in holiday
Pear sale area
Max. 2tons
Sharp curves and fog
Sharp Curves
Cherry trees
Fog
Sharp curves
Frozen road
Jōetsu Line
Jōmō Railway
Ryōmō Line
Tōbu Isesaki Line
Shin-etsu Line
Jōshin Railway
Takasaki Line
Jōetsu Shinkansen
Hachikō Line
Chichibu Railway
Seibu Chichibu Line
KAN-ETSU EXPRESSWAY
Tonegawa River
Karasu River
Kabura River
Kanna River
Ayukawa River
Sanba River
Kawarazawa River
Komori River
Nakatsu River
Akahira River
Usui River
Tsukumo River
Nakasendō
Mt. Tenguyama
Mt. Taneyama
Mt. Tenjin-yama
Mt. Sōdaizan
Mt. Nishimikaboyama
西御荷鉾山
Mt. Aburiyama
Mt. Shiraishiyama
Mt. Tsukayama
Mt. Jōminesan
Mt. Temiezuyama
Mt. Kanōyama
Mt. Futagoyama
Mt. Kannon-yama
Mt. Ryōgamisan
両神山
Mt. Azumayasan
Mt. Mitakesan
Mt. Kumakurayama
Mt. Yadake
Mt. Fudōsan
Mt. Jinmiyama
Mt. Kanetsukidōyama
Mt. Hafūzan
Mt. Hodosan
Mt. Dōdairasan
Mt. Ōtakatoriyama
Mt. Ogamiyama
Mt. Inafukumiyama
Ko-tōge Pass
Shiozawa Pass
Sadamine Pass
Shōmaru Pass
Kanna Lake
Shimokubo Dam
Chichibuko Lake
Futase Dam
21 Century Safari World (Zoo)
Kan-etsu Highland
The Shin-etsu Chemical
Tōhō Zinc
Takasaki Paper Mfg.
Oki Electric
Mikabo rindō
Minano-Yorii Bypass
皆野寄居バイパス
to Ogano
to Yorii
to Hannō
Uenomachi
上野町
Seibu-Chichibu
Kumagaya-shi
Kiryū-shi
Hannō-shi

GUNMA
SAITAMA
TŌKYŌ
HONJŌ-SHI 本庄市
FUKAYA-SHI 深谷市
KUMAGAYA-SHI 熊谷市
GYŌDA-SHI 行田市
TATEBAYASHI-SHI 館林市
HANYŪ-SHI 羽生市
KAZO-SHI 加須市
KŌNOSU-SHI 鴻巣市
KITAMOTO-SHI 北本市
OKEGAWA-SHI 桶川市
AGEO-SHI 上尾市
HIGASHIMATSUYAMA-SHI 東松山市
SAKADO-SHI 坂戸市
TSURUGASHIMA-SHI 鶴ヶ島市
KAWAGOE-SHI 川越市
KAMIFUKUOKA-SHI 上福岡市
FUJIMI-SHI 富士見市
SHIKI-SHI 志木市
ASAKA-SHI 朝霞市
NIIZA-SHI 新座市
WAKŌ-SHI 和光市
SAYAMA-SHI 狭山市
IRUMA-SHI 入間市
HANNŌ-SHI 飯能市
TOKOROZAWA-SHI 所沢市
ŌME-SHI 青梅市
HAMURA-SHI 羽村市
FUSSA-SHI 福生市
AKIRUNO-SHI あきる野市
MUSASHIMURAYAMA-SHI 武蔵村山市
HIGASHIYAMATO-SHI 東大和市
HIGASHIMURAYAMA-SHI 東村山市
KIYOSE-SHI 清瀬市
HIGASHIKURUME-SHI 東久留米市
NISHITŌKYŌ-SHI 西東京市
KODAIRA-SHI 小平市
KAN-ETSU EXPRESSWAY 関越自動車道
TŌHOKU EXPRESSWAY
Hanazono 花園
Ranzan-Ogawa
Higashimatsuyama
Tsurugashima
Tsurugashima Jct
Kawagoe
Tokorozawa
Ōizumi
Nerima
Wakō
Tatebayashi
Hanyu
Kazo
Kuki
Toda-higashi
Toda-nishi
Wakō-kita
Kumagaya 19Km
Ōmiya 47Km
Hachiōji 101Km
Niigata 320Km
Tōkyō 70Km
Takasaki 44Km
Yorii 19Km
Ōmiya 38Km
Yorii 47Km
Ōmiya 17Km
Tōkyō 43Km
Oyama 54Km
Kumagaya 38Km
Kashiwa 36Km
ORD 200
LAR 730
Arakawa River
Ichinokawa River
Oppegawa River
Tōbu Tōjō Line
Seibu Shinjuku Line
Chichibu Railway
Jō-etsu-shinkansen
Takasaki Line
Hachikō Line
Tōbu Ogose Line
Kawagoe Line
Musashino Line
Seibu Ikebukuro Line
Seibu Haijima Line
Itsukaichi Line
Ōme Line
Mt. Dōdairasan
Mt. Ogamiyama
Mt. Monomiyama
Sayamako Lake
Tamako Lake
A
B
C
D
1
2
3
4
5
6
192
144
163
153

TOCHIGI
IBARAKI
CHIBA
Oyama-shi
193
145
168
170
Akeno-machi 明野町
Sekijō-machi 関城町
Mt. Tsukubasan 筑波山
Tsukuba Skyline
ORD 400
LAR 1600
Kazekaeshi Pass
Ibukuro Pass
Fudō Pass
Nogi-machi 野木町
Misugimachi 三杉町
KOGA-SHI 古河市
Sanwa-machi 三和町
Yachiyo-machi 八千代町
SHIMOTSUMA-SHI 下妻市
Fudōjuku 不動宿
Sōwa-machi 総和町
Chiyogawa-mura 千代川村
Kinugawa River
Kokai River
Kurihashi 125gō 栗橋125号
Goka-machi 五霞町
Sashima-machi 猿島町
Sakai-machi 境町
Ishige-machi 石下町
Tonegawa River
Edogawa River
SATTE-SHI 幸手市
KUKI-SHI 久喜市
Shimousa-Tone-ōhashi
ORD 200
LAR 710
IWAI-SHI 岩井市
Mitsukaidō-dōro
ORD 200
LAR 560
TSUKUBA-SHI つくば市
Tsukuba-Ushiku
Yatabe 谷田部
MITSUKAIDŌ-SHI 水海道市
Sugoanuma Lake
Yawara-mura 谷和原村
JŌBAN EXPRESSWAY 常磐自動車道
Kanto Jōsō Line
Sugito-machi 杉戸町
Miyashiro-machi 宮代町
Shiraoka-machi 白岡町
HASUDA-SHI 蓮田市
Kobuchi 小淵
Shōwa-machi 庄和町
Nakazato 中里
KASUKABE-SHI 春日部市
IWATSUKI-SHI 岩槻市
Iwatsuki 岩槻
Yanagisawa 柳沢
NODA-SHI 野田市
Yawara 谷和原
Ina-machi 伊奈町
MORIYA-SHI 守谷市
Ushikunuma Lake
Fujishiro-machi 藤代町
Kokudō 294gō Iriguchi 国道294号入口
Matsubushi-machi 松伏町
Shimo-Makuri 下間久里
Matsudo-Noda-dōro
ORD 200
LAR 730
ORD 200
LAR 730
Shin-Ōtonebashi 新大利根橋
Yobatsuka 呼塚
Tsuchiura 34Km
Ōmiya 36Km
Sawara 54Km
Kashiwa 柏
ORD 150
LAR 560
Urawa 浦和
KOSHIGAYA-SHI 越谷市
YOSHIKAWA-SHI 吉川市
Musashino Line
Nagareyama
KASHIWA-SHI 柏市
NAGAREYAMA-SHI 流山市
ABIKO-SHI 我孫子市
Narita Line
Teganuma Lake
Kawaguchi-chūō
Kawaguchi-higashi
TŌKYŌ GAIKAN EXPRESSWAY
東京外環自動車道
Kawaguchi-nishi
Sōka 草加
Gaikan-Misato-nishi
Misato 三郷
MISATO-SHI 三郷市
Gaikan-Urawa
HATOGAYA-SHI 鳩ヶ谷市
WARABI-SHI 蕨市
TODA-SHI 戸田市
KAWAGUCHI-SHI 川口市
SŌKA-SHI 草加市
YASHIO-SHI 八潮市
Matsudo-Misato-dōro
ORD 250
LAR 940
Ōshimada 大島田
Shōnan-machi 沼南町
INZAI-SHI 印西市
SHIROI-SHI 白井市
Shiroi 白井
Hokusō Railway
MATSUDO-SHI 松戸市
KAMAGAYA-SHI 鎌ヶ谷市
Arakawa River
Kita-ku 北区
Adachi-ku 足立区
Arakawa-ku 荒川区
Itabashi-ku 板橋区
Toshima-ku 豊島区
Katsushika-ku 葛飾区
Yonamoto 米本
Chiba-shi
Tsuchiura-shi
Sakura-Tsuchiura I.C.
E
F
G
H
1
2
3
4
5
6

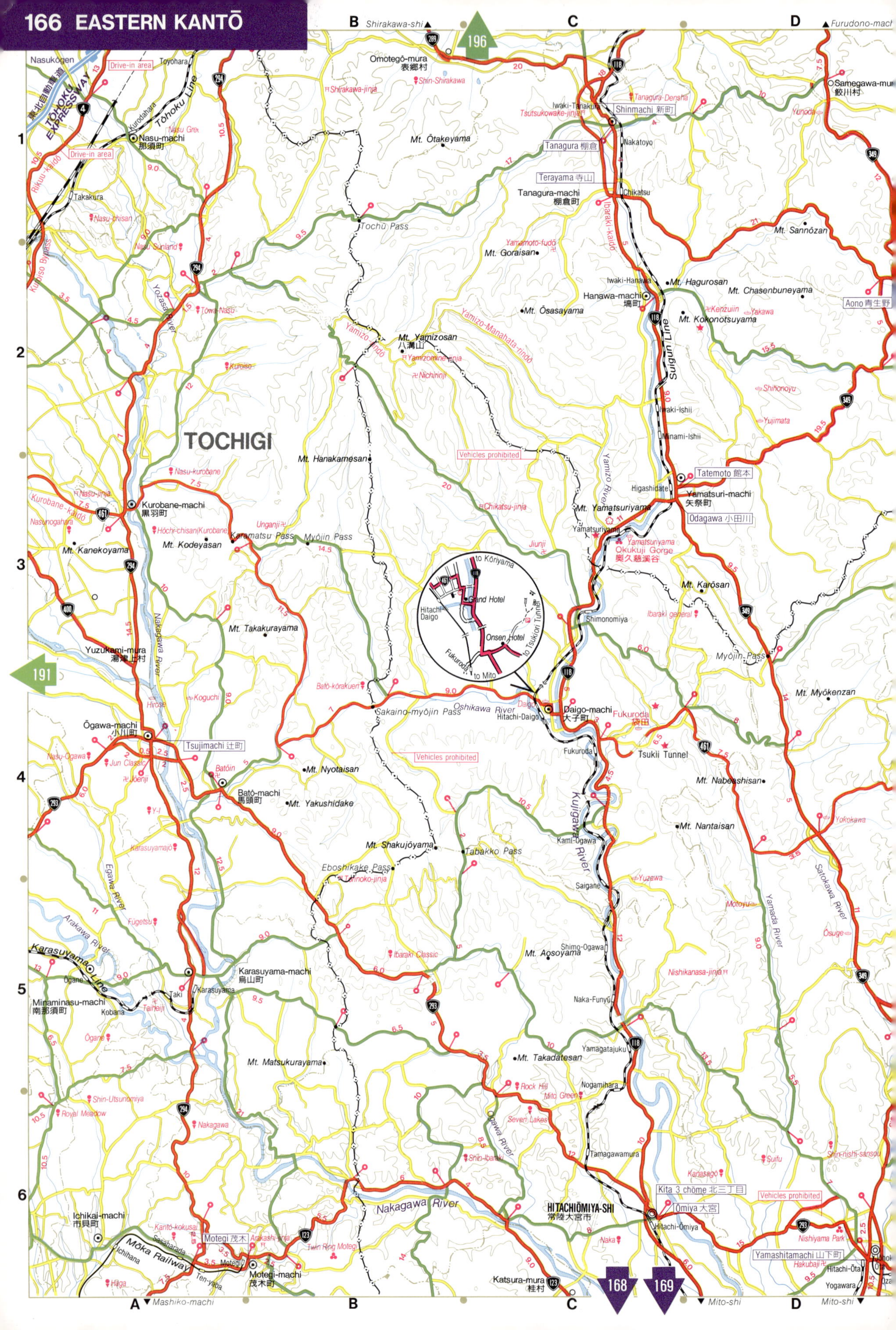
TOCHIGI
Nasu-machi 那須町
Kurobane-machi 黒羽町
Yuzukami-mura 湯津上村
Ōgawa-machi 小川町
Batō-machi 馬頭町
Karasuyama-machi 烏山町
Minaminasu-machi 南那須町
Ichikai-machi 市貝町
Motegi-machi 茂木町
Omotegō-mura 表郷村
Tanagura-machi 棚倉町
Hanawa-machi 塙町
Yamatsuri-machi 矢祭町
Daigo-machi 大子町
Katsura-mura 桂村
HITACHIŌMIYA-SHI 常陸大宮市
Samegawa-mura 鮫川村
Shinmachi 新町
Tanagura 棚倉
Terayama 寺山
Tatemoto 館本
Odagawa 小田川
Tsujimachi 辻町
Motegi 茂木
Kita 3 chōme 北三丁目
Ōmiya 大宮
Yamashitamachi 山下町
Aono 青生野
Fukuroda 袋田
Mt. Yamizosan 八溝山
Okukuji Gorge 奥久慈渓谷
Tōhoku Line
Suigun Line
Karasuyama Line
Mōka Railway
TOHOKU EXPRESSWAY 東北自動車道
Nakagawa River
Kujigawa River
Oshikawa River
Yamizo River
Yamada River
Satokawa River
Egawa River
Arakawa River
Yozasa River
Ogawa River
Tochū Pass
Karamatsu Pass
Myōjin Pass
Sakaino-myōjin Pass
Eboshikake Pass
Tabakko Pass
Tsukii Tunnel
Vehicles prohibited
Drive-in area
Grand Hotel
Onsen Hotel
to Kōriyama
to Tsukiori Tunnel
to Mito
Hitachi-Daigo
Shirakawa-shi
Furudono-machi
Mashiko-machi
Mito-shi
196
191
168
169

E
F
G
H
1
2
3
4
5
6
197
FUKUSHIMA
IBARAKI
PACIFIC OCEAN
太平洋
Natsui River
from Iwaki-shi
Sendai 150Km
Tōkyō 210Km
IWAKI-SHI
いわき市
Iwaki Jct.
いわきJct
Mt. Yunotake
Iwaki-Yumoto
いわき湯本
Yumotorittai 湯本立体
Yoshinoya
Shioyazaki
C. Shioyazaki
Onahama
C. Kassomisaki
Kajiro
C. Ryūgasaki
Takijiri 滝尻
Izumi
Nippon Kasei Chemical
Onahama
C. Misaki
Fujiwara River
Miyanoshita 宮ノ下
Ueda
Iwaki-Nakoso
いわき勿来
Jūjō Paper Mfg.
Nakoso
No. 289iriguchi 289号入口
C. Unokomisaki
Ōtsukōeki-iriguchi 大津港駅入口
Izura(Scenic Rocky Coast)
五浦
Kitaibaraki
北茨城
Isohara
Isoharamachi 磯原町
KITAIBARAKI-SHI
北茨城市
Takahagi
高萩
TAKAHAGI-SHI
高萩市
Sekine River
Hananuki 花貫
Hananuki River
C. Unomisaki
Jūō River
Hitachi-Kita
日立北
HITACHI-SHI
日立市
Hitachi Cable
Hitachi-chūō
日立中央
Shirakawa 120km
Iwaki 61km
Mito 36km
Kensetsushō mae 建設省前
Sukegawachō 助川町
Hitachi
to Daigo
to Taira
to Mito
Scenic view
Hitachi Harbor
JŌBAN EXPRESSWAY
常磐自動車道
Jōban Line
Hitachi Railway
Gozaisho-kaidō
Mt. Mikabuyama
Mt. Myōjin-yama
Mt. Takifuji
Samekawa River
Shitoki River
Shitokigawa Gorge
Mt. Butsuguyama
Mt. Oshōzan
Mt. Daimaruyama
Yatarōzaka Pass
Hanazono Gorge
花園渓谷
Mt. Hanazonosan
Hanazono-jinja
Mt. Takanosuyama
Hanazono River
Jorenji Gorge
Yunoami
Ibaraki Pacific
Saimyōji
Takahagi
Daishinenbōkai
Mt. Tsuchidake
Hananuki Gorge
花貫渓谷
Sunrise
Mt. Kaminesan
Kamine Park(R.A.)
Mt. Takasuzusan
Hitachi-dōro
日立道路
Hitachi-Takasuzu
Ayukawa
Sakuragawa
Kawarago
Ōnuma
Mizuki
Kawanakago
Hitachi-Taga
HIŌTA-SHI
太田市
Nakagō
中郷
Minami-Nakagō
Jūō
Ogitsu
Ōtsuko
Sekimoto
関本
Izura-teen
Iwaki Green Hills
Rikuzenhama-kaidō
Iwaki-Yumoto
Yumoto Springs
Spa Resort Hawaiians Center(R.A.)
Shiratori
Uchigō
Yunotake
湯ノ岳
Kōya
Motoyu
Shiramizu-amidadō
Iritōno River
Mt. Yunotake
Tabito
Nyūdō
to Taira
to Yunotake
Yumoto
to Mito
Spa Resort Hawaiians

166
191
193
170
Gozenyama-mu
Oyama-shi
Koga-shi
Toride-shi
Sakuragawa-mura
TOCHIGI
IBARAKI
MŌKA-SHI
真岡市
Mōka
Kita-Mōka
Mōka Bypass
Mashiko
Mashiko-machi
益子町
Tatara
Nanai
Ōsawa 大沢
Taiheiyō Club-Mashiko
Haga
Higashinomiya
Mt. Kakōgetsuyama
Katsura-mura
桂村
Aikawa
Ishizuka-yakushi
Jōhoku-machi
常北町
Fujii River
Southern yard
Komatsuji
Nanakai-mura
七会村
The Wings
Shin-Mito
Mt. Toriashiyama
Tsuna-jinja
Jizōin
Saimyōji
Nishidai
Kitayama
Ōsaki-jinja
Kinugawa River
Hotokenoyama Pass
Mt. Amamakisan
Mt. Butchōsan
Mt. Takamine
Ryōgonji
Mt. Isoyama
Terauchi
Ninomiya-jinja
Teito-Tochigi
Iwase-Sakuragawa
Mt. Tomiyasan
Ōte-zaka Pass
Senjuji
Ninomiya-machi
二宮町
Kugeta
Ninomiya
Spring Fields
Tsukuba-gakuen
Tomiya-kannon
Iwase-machi
岩瀬町
Iwase
Haguro
Osakata 長方
Mōka Railway
Higuchi
Kyōwa-machi
協和町
Asia Shimodate
Orimoto
Yamato
Yamato-mura
大和村
Kadoi 門井
Amabiki-kannon
Taihō
SHIMODATE-SHI
下館市
Nishiyagai 西谷貝
Niihari
Shimodatenikō-mae
congestion in Shimodate city
Tamado
Kawashima
Shimodate
Makabe
Mt. Kabasan
Kabayama-jinja
Makabe-machi
真壁町
Denshōji
Mt. Ashiozan
Ōtagō
KASAMA-SHI
笠間市
Kasama
Kasama-inari
笠間稲荷
Kasama chinaware sale area
Sangenya 三軒屋
Mito
Sakuranomiya
Uchihara
Uchihara-machi
内原町
Inada
Saineni
Fukuhara
Mito Line
Shishido
The lakes
Tomobe
友部
Tomobe-machi
友部町
Tomobe Jct
JŌBAN EXPRESSWAY
Ibaraki-machi
茨城町西
Mt. Wagakunisan
Bad road
Iwama-machi
岩間町
Iwama
岩間
Fudōdō
Hinuma River
Kashima Jingū
Kasama-tōyō
Hitachinoya
Shinrin-koen
Fujuji
Asami
Akeno-machi
明野町
Kurogo
Kantō Jōsō Line
Tobanoe
Ibukuro Pass
Tsukuba Skyline
ORD 400
LAR 1600
Mt. Tsukubasan
筑波山
Kazekaeshi Pass
Tsukubasan-jinja
Yasato-machi
八郷町
Higashi-Tsukuba
Mt. Fujiyama
Mt. Ryūjinsan
Koise River
Ishioka-dōro
ORD 100
LAR 370
Minori
美野里
Minori-machi
美野里町
Accident-prone area
Drive-in area
Sonobe River
Daihō
SHIMOTSUMA-SHI
下妻市
Fudōjuku 不動宿
Shimotsuma
Tsukubane
Scenic view of Kasumigaura and Kantō Plain
Sannōdai 山王台
ISHIOKA-SHI
石岡市
Ishioka
Higashi-Tanaka
Shin-Takahama
Shikamura
Ogawa-machi
小川町
Kuriyama 栗山
Tsukuba-tōkyū
Tsukuba-kokusai
Fudō Pass
Chiyoda-Ishioka
千代田石岡
Chiyoda
Fruit farming area
Shimō-Tsuchida
下土田
Takahama
Hitachi-Ogawa
Ogawakōkō-shita
Tamari-mura
玉里村
Yūmoa-mura(R.A.)
Sōdō
Chiyogawa-mura
千代川村
Sakura River
Niihari-mura
新治村
Chiyoda-machi
千代田町
Jōban Line
Momoura
Scenic
Yakima
Tamamura
Kokai River
Tsuchiurakita
土浦北
Nakanuki 中貫
Kandatsu
Ishige
Ishige-machi
石下町
Shitana 常名
Manabe
真鍋
Ichinose River
Fuji-country-Dejima
Minami-Ishige
Kinugawa River
Kokudō No.125gō iriguchi 国道125号入口
Mito 47Km
Oyama 64Km
Kashima 55Km
Kasumigaura-machi
霞ケ浦町
Clean Eight
Mitsukaidō-dōro
ORD 200
LAR 560
Mitsuma
Minami-Tsukuba
Sakura-Tsuchiura
桜土浦
Tsuchiura
TSUCHIURA-SHI
土浦市
to Mito
Senzokumachi
千束町
Shimo-Takatsu
下高津
to Tōkyō
to Sawara
Kasumigaura Lake
Scenic view
TSUKUBA-SHI
つくば市
Nakatsuma
水海道道路
Kasumigaura-kokusai
Yatabe-higashi
谷田部東
Arakawaoki
Ami-machi
阿見町
Tatenui-jinja
Kita-Mitsukaidō
Yatabe
谷田部
Tsukuba-Ushiku
Mitsukaidō
MITSUKAIDŌ-SHI
水海道市
Sugaonuma Lake
Jōyō
Hitachino-Ushiku
USHIKU-SHI
牛久市
Yawara-mura
谷和原村
Ibaraki Tsukuba
Toride-shinnihon
Takū 田宮
Kokinu
Mihō-mura
美浦村
A
B
C
D
1
2
3
4
5
6

166
167
171
Hitachi-shi
Hitachi-minami-Ōta
日立南太田
Tōkai
東海
Naka
那珂
NAKA-SHI
那珂市
Tōkai-mura
東海村
Kuji River
Suigun Line
Suigo Line
Jōban Line
Hitachi Railway
Minamimachi 1 chōme 南町1丁目
Hitachi 36Km
Utsunomiya 80Km
Oyama 69Km
Ichige 市毛
Edagawa 枝川
HITACHINAKA-SHI
ひたちなか市
Hitachinaka
Ibarakikōtsū Minato Line
Nakagawa River
MITO-SHI
水戸市
Kairakuen(Park)
偕楽園
Sakatsuraisozaki-jinja
Mito-minami
水戸南
Higashi-Mito-dōro
東水戸道路
Shiogasaki 塩ケ崎
Ibaraki-machi-higashi
茨城町東
ORD 350
LAR 950
Ōnuki 大貫
Drive-in area
Accident-prone area
Ōarai-machi
大洗町
Ibaraki-machi
茨城町
Okunoya 奥ノ谷
Hinuma Lake
Old Orchard
Asahi-mura
旭村
Kashimarinkai Ōarai Kashima Line
Takihama 滝浜
Hyakuri Airport
Tomoe River
Hokota-machi
鉾田町
Kashima Railway
Taiyōmura-yakuba-iriguchi
大洋村役場入口
Tamatsukuri-machi
玉造町
Taiyō-mura
大洋村
Kitaura-machi
北浦町
Royal Ocean
Scenic view of coast
Chōjagahama-shiosai hamanasu-kōenmae
Kitaura Lake
KASHIMA-SHI
鹿嶋市
Kashima Soccer Stadium
Asō-machi
麻生町
Scenic view
KASHIMA-NADA
鹿島灘
Higashi-Nihon Ferry・Shōsen-Mitsui Ferry(to Tomakomai)
to Utsunomiya
to Hitachiōta
to Kasama
Kairakuen
Mito
to Ōarai
to Hitachi
to Mito
Ōarai
to Ibaraki
to Kashima
E
F
G
H
1
2
3
4
5
6

IBARAKI
CHIBA
TŌKYŌ WAN
東京湾
168
145
172
173
USHIKU-SHI
牛久市
MORIYA-SHI
守谷市
TORIDE-SHI
取手市
RYŪGASAKI-SHI
龍ケ崎市
ABIKO-SHI
我孫子市
KASHIWA-SHI
柏市
INZAI-SHI
印西市
SHIROI-SHI
白井市
KAMAGAYA-SHI
鎌ケ谷市
ICHIKAWA-SHI
市川市
FUNABASHI-SHI
船橋市
NARASHINO-SHI
習志野市
YACHIYO-SHI
八千代市
SAKURA-SHI
佐倉市
NARITA-SHI
成田市
TOMISATO-SHI
富里市
YOTSUKAIDŌ-SHI
四街道市
YACHIMATA-SHI
八街市
CHIBA-SHI
千葉市
TŌGANE-SHI
東金市
ICHIHARA-SHI
市原市
Edosaki-machi
江戸崎町
Shintone-machi
新利根町
Kawachi-machi
河内町
Tone-machi
利根町
Sakae-machi
栄町
Shimofusa-machi
下総町
Motono-mura
本埜村
Inba-mura
印旛村
Shisui-machi
酒々井町
Shōnan-machi
沼南町
Ina-machi
伊奈町
Fujishiro-machi
藤代町
Ōamishirasato-machi
大網白里町
Shirako-machi
白子町
Sanbu-machi
山武町
Kōnoyama 高野山
Ōshimada 大島田
Nedo 根戸
Yobatsuka 呼塚
Tsuchiura 34Km
Ōmiya 36Km
Sawara 54Km
ORD 200
LAR 730
Kashiwa
Yawara
Shin-Ōtonebashi
Takū 田宮
Sanukimachi 佐貫町
Kokudō No. 294iriguchi 国道294号入口
Rokken-jūjiro 六軒十字路
Sakaemachi-yakuba-mae 栄町役場前
Tatsudai 竜台
Takaoka 高岡
Kichiokakaikon 吉岡開墾
Teradai 寺台
Ryūfukuji 竜腹寺
Shiroi 白井
Hatsutomi 初富
Kamagaya 鎌ケ谷
Nakanogi 中の木
Yotsukaidō
四街道
Chiba-kita
千葉北
Miyanogi Jct
宮野木Jct
Wangan-Narashino
湾岸習志野
Wangan-Chiba
湾岸千葉
Wangan-Ichikawa
Keiyō-dōro
ORD 150
LAR 300
Nobuto 登戸
Honchō 本町
Sawara 49Km
Kashiwa 36Km
Tōkyō 41Km
Shisui 酒々井
Sakura
佐倉
Narita
成田
Shin-kūkō
新空港
Narita International
Tomisato
富里
Sanrizuka 三里塚
Nihon-enoki
二本榎
Yachimata 八街
Sakado 坂戸
Yoshioka 吉岡
Nakatachō 仲田町
Yamadadai 山田台
Ono 小野
Daikata 台方
Chiba-Tōgane-dōro
ORD 1000
LAR 3500
Chiba-Sotobō-dōro
ORD 620
LAR 2100
Ōami Bypass-iriguchi
大網バイパス入口
Kyōden 経田
Horiage 堀上
Chōshi 55Km
Chiba 24Km
Katsuura 57Km
Tōgane-Kujūkuri-dōro
ORD 200
LAR 550
Hamano 浜野
Yawata-kaigan-dōri 八幡海岸通
Uruido 潤井戸
Ichihara
Nakayatsuhara
中谷原
Nagao 長尾
Congestion in summer
Drive-in area
Pear sale area
Pine trees
TATEYAMA EXPRESSWAY
館山自動車道
Jōban Line
Kantō Railway
Kantō-Jōsō Line
Narita Line
Sōbu Line
Keisei Line
Keiyō Line
Sotobō Line
Uchibō Line
Tōbu Noda Line
Musashino Line
Hokusō Railway
Tōyō-kōsoku Railway
Shin-Keisei Railway
Town Liner
Kominato Railway
Tonegawa River
Shin-Tonegawa River
Kinugawa River
Yōrō River
Ushikunuma Lake
Teganuma Lake
Inbanuma Lake
Seibu-chōseichi Lake
Mt. Gongenmori
Inage Seashore Park(R.A.)
Shōwa Denkō
Ube Industries
Mitsui Petrochemical Industries
Sumitomo Chemical
JFE
Tsuchiura-shi
Noda-shi
Misato I.C.
Matsudo-shi
Kisarazu-shi
Chiba
A
B
C
D
1
2
3
4
5
6

169
Mito-shi
Kasumigaura Lake
Kitaura Lake
Nagayama 永山
ITAKO-SHI
潮来市
KASHIMA-SHI
鹿嶋市
Kashima-jingū
Uwado 上戸
Tsuchi 辻
Umemachi 梅町
Mito 54Km
Tsuchiura 55Km
Sawara 21Km
Sumitomo Metal Industries
Kashima
SUIGO
水郷
Itako
潮来
Azuma-machi
東町
Nishishiro 西代
Tone
Congestion in spring
Scenic view
Suigō-dōro
ORD 150
LAR 580
Kashima Line
Tonegawa River
Takeda Chemical Industries
Dainippon Ink & Chemicals
Kanegafuchi Chemical Industries
Kamisu-machi
神栖町
SAWARA-SHI
佐原市
Sawara
佐原
Katori
Tsuchiura 41Km
Kashima 21Km
Kashiwa 54Km
Sawara-Katori
佐原香取
Narita Line
HIGASHI-KANTŌ EXPRESSWAY
東関東自動車道
Yōkaichiba 八日市場
Omigawa-machi
小見川町
Sasagawa
Taiei
大栄
Tōsō-dōro
ORD 200
LAR 730
Tōnoshō-machi
東庄町
Shimōsa-Tachibana
Kurimoto-machi
栗源町
Yamada-machi
山田町
Pine trees
Hasaki-machi
波崎町
Shimōsa-Toyosato
Tone-kamome-ōhashi
ORD 200
LAR 550
Nojiri 野尻
Wakamiya 若宮
Kashima 37Km
Sawara 38Km
Tōgane 55Km
Shiishiba
Taragai 田良貝
Iidaka 飯高
Hikata-machi
干潟町
Unakami-machi
海上町
Saruda
Kurahashi
Matsugishi
Somei 染井
Tako-machi
多古町
Hirōnuma 広沼
ASAHI-SHI
旭市
CHŌSHI-SHI
銚子市
Chōshi Railway
Inubōzaki
Kimigahama
Mt. Atagoyama
Naarai 名洗
C. Nagasakibana
YŌKAICHIBA-SHI
八日市場市
Sōbu Line
Higata
Iioka-machi
飯岡町
Yagi 八木
Byōbugaura (Scenic Rocky Coast)
Scenic view
Shibayama-machi
芝山町
No. 296-iriguchi 296号入口
Fukutomi 福富
Iigura 米倉
Hikari-machi
光町
Nosaka-machi
野栄町
Node 野手
Matsuo-Yokoshiba
Matsuoeki-iriguchi
松尾駅入口
Matsuo-machi
松尾町
Yokoshiba-machi
横芝町
Kito 木戸
Kujūkurihama
Narutō-machi
成東町
Hasunuma-mura
蓮沼村
Hasunuma-kaihinkōen (Swimming Pool Garden)
Minamihama 南浜
Congestion in summer
Tōgane
東金
Daikata 台方
to Chōshi
to Chiba
to Mobora
Horiage
堀上
Fudōdō
Shirasato
Kujūkuri-dōro
ORD 410
LAR 1680
PACIFIC OCEAN
太平洋
to Kashima
Tonegawa River
Wakamiya 若宮
Karakochō 唐子町
to Sawara
to Inubōzaki

TŌKYŌ-WAN
東京湾
KANAGAWA
170
145
143
Jōzai 請西
Chiba 39km
Katsuura 85km
Tateyama 53km
from Tateyama-shi
Tōkyō 130Km
Yokohama 70Km
TATEYAMA EXPRESSWAY
SODEGAURA-SHI
袖ケ浦市
Anesaki-Sodegaura
Kisarazu-kita
木更津北
Kisarazu Jct
木更津Jct
Kisarazu-minami Jct
木更津南Jct
Kisarazu-minami
木更津南
Kimitsu
君津
KISARAZU-SHI
木更津市
KIMITSU-SHI
君津市
FUTTSU-SHI
富津市
KAMOGAWA-SHI
鴨川市
TATEYAMA-SHI
館山市
C. Futtsumisaki
富津岬
Pine tree grove
Cherry trees
Congestion in Summer
Congestion in summer
Congestion between Shirahama-machi to Wada-machi in Summer
Pine trees
Sanuki 佐貫
Ichijuku 市宿
Awagura 粟倉
Sekijiri 関尻
Minato 湊
Obitsu 小櫃
Kururi 久留里
Miyayama 宮山
Hota 保田
Ichibu 市部
Funakata 船形
Anboya 安馬谷
Hōjō 北条
Ina 稲
Futomi 太海
Teraniwa 寺庭
Ainohama 相ノ浜
Takiguchi 滝口
Bōsō Skyline
ORD 410
LAR 1470
Nokogiriyama-tozandōro
ORD 700
LAR 3500
Kamogawa-dōro
ORD 200
LAR 730
Tōkyō-wan Ferry
C. Kannonzaki
C. Myōshōzaki
C. Kamegasaki
C. Nishigasaki
C. Daibusaki
C. Sunosaki
洲崎
C. Nojimazaki
野島崎
Ukishima I.
Okinoshima I.
Tateyama-wan
Mt. Mifuneyama
Mt. Ōtsukayama
Mt. Kanōzan
Mt. Fujisan
Mt. Daifukuzan
Mt. Takagoyama
Mt. Mitsuishiyama
Mt. Motokiyosumiyama
Mt. Nokogiri yama
Mt. Sengenyama
Mt. Iyogatake
Mt. Atagoyama
Mt. Tomisan
Mt. Goten-yama
Mt. Kyōzukayama
Mt. Shiroyama
Mt. Takatsukayama
Mt. Sekison
Mt. Kiyosumi
Kyonan-machi
鋸南町
Tomiyama-machi
富山町
Tomiura-machi
富浦町
Miyoshi-mura
三芳村
Maruyama-machi
丸山町
Wada-machi
和田町
Chikura-machi
千倉町
Shirahama-machi
白浜町
Amatsukominato-machi
天津小湊町
Yokone Pass
Koito River
Kamogawa River
Heguri River
Obitsu River
Yōrō River
Uchibō Line
Kururi Line
Kominato Railway
Daiichi Flowerline
to Kisarazu
to Kamogawa
to Tateyama
to Suzaki
to Shirahama
Nagasa-kō mae
長狭高前
Nagasa-kaidō-iriguchi
長狭街道入口
Awa-kamogawa
A
B
C
D
1
2
3
4
5
6

170
171
Tōgane-shi
Nagara-machi
長柄町
MOBARA-SHI
茂原市
Mobara
Mobara
arigaya 針ケ谷
Chōnan
Kasamori-kannon
Mobara
Congestion in spring
Chōsei-mura
長生村
Yatsumi
Kujūkuri-dōro
ORD 410
LAR 1680
Chōsei
Ichinomiya River
Chōnan-machi
長南町
Yasuragi-no-mori(R.A.)
Tamasaki-jinja
Kazusa-Ichinomiya
Ichinomiya-kaigan 一宮海岸
Ichinomiya-machi
一宮町
Minami-Mobara
Mutsuzawa-machi
睦沢町
Ichinomiya
Torami
Bōsō
Tōyō
Taitō
Yokoyama
横山
Ōtaki
Mangoji
C. Daitōzaki
太東崎
Misaki-machi
岬町
Chōjamachi
Isumi River
Sakuradai 桜台
Minami-Chiba
Ōtaki
Isumi Railway
Isumi-machi
夷隅町
Shimizuji
Ōtaki-machi
大多喜町
Kazusa-Nakagawa
Kuniyoshi
Nittano
Mikado
Koyamatsu
Higashi-Fusamoto
Kazusa-Azuma
Nishi-Ōhara
Ōhara-machi
大原町
Ōhara
Mt. Takatsuka
C. Hachimanmisaki
Daishōji
Kugahara
Fusamoto
Nishihata
Mimata 三叉
Kaisuka 貝須賀
Katsuura
Katsuura
Namihana
Ōhara-Onjuku
Sotobō Line
Mt. Nonozuka
Katsuura-dōro
ORD 200
LAR 730
勝浦道路
Onjuku
Onjuku-machi
御宿町
Ajiro-Wan
KATSUURA-SHI
勝浦市
Katsuura
Katsuura-tōkyū
Katsuura-wan
Chiba 67Km
Tōgane 57Km
Tateyama 52Km
Myōkakuji
Kazusa-Okitsu
Ubara
Katsuura-kaichū-kōen(Park)
Hachimanmisaki
Nichirenji
Namekawa-Island
C. Nyūdōgasaki
Katsuura-dōro
Katsuura
to Kamogawa
to Mobara
to Lighthouse
PACIFIC OCEAN
太平洋
E
F
G
H
1
2
3
4
5
6

C. Tappizaki
竜飛崎
Obijima I.
Caves
Tsugaru-kaikyō Line
Seikan Tunnel
339
Closed in winter
Minmaya-mura
三厩村
Minmaya
Masukawa River
Mt. Yakataishiyama
Closed in winter
Mt. Hamana
Mt. Masukawadake
Mt. Yotsutakiyama
四ッ滝山
Kyōmonjima I.
Kodomari-mura
小泊村
Mt. Ozakiyama
C. Kodomarimisaki
小泊岬
C. Shiraiwazaki
Scenic view of coast
Mt. Itawariyama
Mt. Kinashidake
Mt. Momoyama
Yotsudaki
Isomatsu River
Ōtagawa River
Sotome 五月女
Shiura-mura
市浦村
Pine trees
Scenic view of lake
Scenic view of lake
Drive-in area
Jūsanko Lake
Imaizumi
Toriya River
Pine trees
Nakasato
中里町
Tsugaru-Nakasato
Mt. Okonokinagare
Hakamagataike Lake
Iwaki River
Shariki-mura
車力村
Ushigataike Lake
Ōsawanai
Takayama-inari-jinja
Apple growing area
Kawakura
Mt. Byōbuzan
屏風山
Closed in winter
Fujieda tameike Lake
Tappinuma Lake
Yamada River
Ashinokōen
Inagaki-mura
稲垣村
Hiratakinuma Lake
Ōtakinuma Lake
Closed in winter
Scenic view of Mt. Iwaki
Jūsanmichi
Hiyamizunuma Lake
Kizukuri-machi
木造町
Kizukuri
Drive-in area
Motel area
Kita-Ukita 北浮田
Mt. Tennōzan
Congestion in Jul. and Aug.
Nanatsuishi 七ッ石
Koshimizu
101
Mutsu-Morita
Nakata
Kashiwa-mura
柏村
Narusawa
Ezogatate tameike Lake
Morita-mura
森田村
C. Ōtosezaki
Senjōjiki(Scenic Rocky Coast)
Ajigasawa
Ajigasawa-machi
鰺ヶ沢町
Mutsu-Akaishi
Broiled cuttlefish sale area
Mt. Takatsumoriyama
Closed in winter
Ōdose
Senjōjiki
Ōmagoshi-kaidō
39
Kita-Kanegasawa
Gonō Line
Mutsu-Yanagita
Tsuruta
Tsuruta-machi
鶴田町
Mutsu-
Todoshima I.
Kasose
Mt. Shirakusayama
Narusawa River
Tsugaru-Fujimiko
Gankisan-jinja
Mt. Otsukisan
Closed in winter
Noshiro-shi
176
177
A
B
C
D
1
2
3
4
5
6

E
F
G
H
218
216
218
214
177
1
2
4
5
6
Mt. Niiyama
C. Yakeyamazaki
Mt. Andoyama
Kaikyō Line
Mt. Akiyama
Mt. Tengumori
Mt. Yunosawadake
Mt. Tsukushimori
C. Takanozaki
C. Bentenzaki
Matsumae-Kaidō
280
Otoko River
C. Ōsaki
Wakinosawa River
Closed in winter
Imabetsu-machi
今別町
Imabetsu
Mt. Karasudake
Korokoro River
Mt. Togaridake
Mt. Hakamagoshidake
Mt. Shiriiwayama
Ōkawadai
Furōfushi
338
Mt. Anamayama
C. Amonamisaki
Mt. Maruyagatadake
TAIRADATE-KAIKYŌ
平舘海峡
Mt. Kinashidake
Tairadate-mura
平舘村
Tsugaru-Futamata
Tsugaru-Imabetsu
Wakinosawa-mura
脇野沢村
C. Hokkaimisaki
C. Ushinokubimisaki
Higashi-Nihon Ferry (to Tomakomai·Muroran)
Scenic view of coast
Mt. Shimizumatadake
Mt. Shinadake
MUTSU-WAN
陸奥湾
Mutsu-wan Ferry
Mt. Tengudake
Tsugaru Line
Ōdai
Mt. Kadohashizawayama
Kanita-machi
蟹田町
Naka-Oguni
Chūshi 中師
Kanita River
Kanita
Scenic view of coast
Mt. Tamashimizuyama
Hirose River
Rest house area
To scallop sale area
Ōshima I.
Congestion in summer
Congestion between Kominato and Natsudomarisaki Ist week in May
Tsugaru Pen.
津軽半島
Seheji
C. Natsudomarizaki
夏泊崎
Tsubaki-jinja
Taiheiyō Club
C. Hanakukurizaki
Mt. Kayadake
Mt. Hakamagoshiyama
Yomogita River
Gōsawa
Yomogita-mura
蓬田村
Yomogita
Mt. Ōguriyama
Mt. Hiyamizuyama
Mt. Maruyama
Natsudomari Pen.
夏泊半島
Mt. Mizugasawayama
to Nakasato
to Shariki
Kanagi
to Goshogawara
339
Nakasawa
Ushirogata River
Ushirogata
Aomori
to Kanita
Kami-Furukawa 上古川
to Hirosaki
Furukawa 古川
to kūkō
Mourajima I.
Mt. Namiuchiyama
AOMORI-WAN
青森湾
Kominato
Tōhoku Line
Kominato 小湊
Nishi-Hiranai
Mt. Ōsakayama
Mt. Chōbōzan
Uchimanpe River
Hidariseki
Mt. Yashikiyama
Mt. Nagareyama
Hiranai-machi
平内町
Mt. Takamoriyama
Mt. Hikinokoshiyama
AOMORI
Closed in winter
Okunai
Marine Park Asamushi(A.P.)
from Aomori-shi
Akita 200Km
Sendai 400Km
Yunoshima I.
Tsugaru-Miyata
Asamushi-onsen
Asamushi
浅虫
Scenic view of coast
Mt. Kōchiyama
Mt. Genpachimori
Mt. Asukayama
Aomori-chūō-ōhashi
ORD 100
LAR 370
C. Hanakurizaki
Road closed when raining more than 100mm
closed in winter
Bishamon
Ōbuchi River
Mt. Tazawamori
Aburakawa
C.Tappizaki 74Km
Goshogawara 32Km
Hirosaki 39Km
Nonai
Mayajiri 馬屋尻
Mt. Higashidake
Closed in winter
GOSHOGAWARA-SHI
五所川原市
Tsugaru-Iizume
to Jūsanko
Kanagi
Closed in winter
Shinjō 新城
Shinoda 2 篠田二
Aomori
Aomori-higashi
青森東
Teramachi 寺町
Apple growing area
Mt. Tsukushimoriyama
Tsugaru-Shinjō
Gappo Park
Closed in winter
Nonai River
Aomori
AOMORI-SHI
青森市
Tsukurimichi 造道
Michinoku-dōro
ORD 830
LAR 2940
Mt. Ōkenashiyama
Scenic view of Mt. Hakkōdasan
Aomori
青森
Aomori-chūō
Higashi-Aomori
Mt. Totoriyama
Tōō
Mt. Kamizutsumiyama
みちのく道路
Mt. Sankakudake
to Ajigasawa
Minato 湊
to Aomori
to Hirosaki
Ōu-Kaidō
Mt. Mejayama
Tsurugasaka
Aomori-kanjō Bypass
AOMORI EXPRESSWAY
青森自動車道
Drive-in area
Hamada 浜田
Mt. Naranokimoriyama
Aomori 32Km
Ōsaki 25Km
Noshiro 125Km
Mt. Kanetsukidōyama
EXPRESSWAY
Tsurugasaka
Drive-in area
Crab sale area
Mt. Sakaeyama
Aomori-kūkō-dōro
ORD 200
LAR 730
Sangaidaki
Mt. Origamiyama
Closed in winter
Apple growing area
TŌHOKU
Daishaka
Drive-in area
Daishaka 大釈迦
Komagome River
Yokouchi River
Closed in winter
Mt. Horikodake
Ko-tōge Pass
Namioka
浪岡
青森空港道路
Mt. Takazumoriyama
Aomori
Arakawa River
Aomori
Aomori-ken-Taikyou
Ō-toge Pass
Moya Pass
Moya
Closed in winter
Ōu-Line
Mt. Bōzuhatakeyama
Nyūnai Pass
Closed in winter
Mt. Shichijūmoriyama
Kuroishi I.C.

B
C
D
Goshogawara-shi
1
2
3
4
5
6
A
B
Noshiro-shi
C
D
Senjōjiki(Scenic Rocky Coast)
C. Ōtosezaki
Ōdose
Senjōjiki
Todoshima I.
39
Kasose
Mutsu-Akaishi
Ajigasawa-machi
鰺ヶ沢町
Kita-Kanegasawa
Gonō Line
Mutsu-Yanagita
Ko-dōji River
Ō-dōji River
Mt. Sasanagareyama
Mt. Takaniuyama
Mt. Masugatayama
Mt. Hakkeimori
Mt. Tsuchikurayama
24
Todoroki
C. Shiomizaki
101
Oirase
Hiroto
C. Yukiaizaki
Ōmagoshi-kaidō
Mt. Tangyōzan
Mt. Karakayama
Kumanoyu
Mt. Shikarigatake
Oirase River
C. Nyūmaezaki
Fukaura
Fukaura-machi
深浦町
Mt. Sudachisan
Akaishi River
Yokoiso
Koganezakifurōfushi
12
Nakayama Pass
8
Azuma River
C. Henashizaki
艫作橋
Henashi
Wespa-Tsubakiyama
Mutsu-Sawabe
Iwasaki-mura
岩崎村
Mutsu-Iwasaki
Iwasaki
Closed in winter
Mt. Sakasagawayama
AOMORI
Mt. Rangannomori
Sasanai River
Mt. Kobakomine
Jūniko Lake
Tengu Pass
Mt. Shiheimori
Nihon Canyon
3
Jūniko
Tsugaru Pass
Mt. Takakuramori
to Fukaura
to Noshiro
Matsukami
19
Mt. Mukaishirakamidake
Mt. Tengudake
Anmon Fall
Anmon River
Mt. Kushishiyama
Shirakamidake-tozanguchi
Closed in winter
Mt. Shiragamidake
白神岳
Ōmagoshi
Mt. Kabutonagareyama
Mt. Masedake
Mt. Daikokumori
Gonō Line
C. Sugōmisaki
Mt. Ōhachinagareyama
Mt. Futatsumori
Mt. Ganmoridake
Mt. Hiyamizu
Mt. Kodake
Ōtaki
大間越街道
Iwadate
Masegawa River
Mt. Ōusudake
Iwayanotaki
Akita-Shirakami
13.5
Takinoma
Mt. Osabanaidake
Hachimori
Hachimori-machi
八森町
Mt. Yakeyama
Mt. Shishibanadake
Shirataki-jinja
Mt. Kotakisan
Subari-jinja
Higashi-Hachimori
Shiohama
Mizusawa River
Mt. Komatsuzakiyama
Kasuge River
Ōgara Fall
Hanawa River
Mt. Takamineyama
Sawame
Minehama-mura
峰浜村
Taneume River
Noshiro
21.5
Torikata
Tokōgawa River
Kita-Noshiro
Tokiwa River
Noshiro
Mukai-Noshiro

178
179

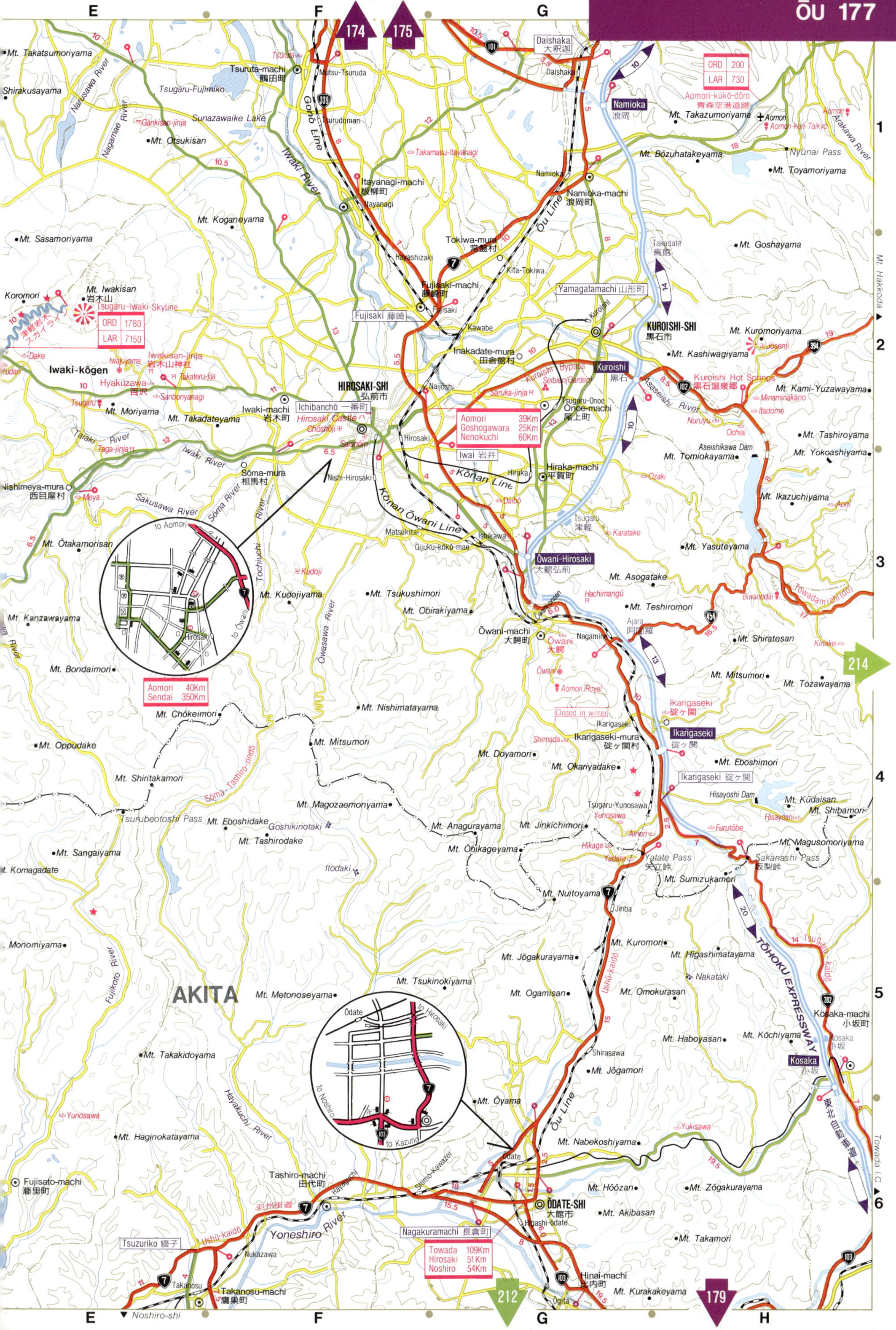

174
175
Tsuruta-machi
鶴田町
Tsugaru-Fujimiko
Sunazawaike Lake
Gonō Line
Iwaki River
Mt. Takatsumoriyama
Shirakusayama
Mt. Otsukisan
Mt. Koganeyama
Mt. Sasamoriyama
Itayanagi-machi
板柳町
Daishaka
大釈迦
Namioka
浪岡
ORD 200
LAR 730
Aomori-kūkō-dōro
青森空港道路
Mt. Takazumoriyama
Aomori-ken-Taikyō
Mt. Bōzuhatakeyama
Nyūnai Pass
Arakawa River
Mt. Toyamoriyama
Namioka-machi
浪岡町
Ōu Line
Tokiwa-mura
常盤村
Takadate
高館
Mt. Goshayama
Fujisaki-machi
藤崎町
Fujisaki 藤崎
Yamagatamachi 山形町
KUROISHI-SHI
黒石市
Mt. Kuromoriyama
Mt. Kashiwagiyama
Mt. Hakkoda
Koromori
Mt. Iwakisan
岩木山
Tsugaru-Iwaki Skyline
津軽岩木スカイライン
ORD 1780
LAR 7150
Iwakisan-jinja
岩木山神社
Iwaki-kōgen
Hyakuzawa
百沢
Inakadate-mura
田舎館村
Kuroishi Bypass
Kuroishi
黒石
Kuroishi Hot Springs
黒石温泉郷
Mt. Kami-Yuzawayama
HIROSAKI-SHI
弘前市
Ichibanchō 一番町
Hirosaki Castle
Iwaki-machi
岩木町
Mt. Moriyama
Mt. Takadateyama
Aomori 39Km
Goshogawara 25Km
Nenokuchi 60Km
Onoe-machi
尾上町
Iwai 岩井
Kōnan Line
Hiraka-machi
平賀町
Asaseishi River
Aseishikawa Dam
Mt. Tomiokayama
Mt. Tashiroyama
Mt. Yokoashiyama
Sōma-mura
相馬村
Nishimeya-mura
西目屋村
Sakusawa River
Kōnan Ōwani Line
Tsugaru
津軽
Mt. Ikazuchiyama
Mt. Ōtakamorisan
Matsukitai
Ōwani-Hirosaki
大鰐弘前
Mt. Yasuteyama
Mt. Asogatake
Mt. Kudojiyama
Mt. Tsukushimori
Mt. Obirakiyama
Tochiuchi River
Mt. Kanzawayama
Ōwani-machi
大鰐町
Mt. Teshiromori
Ajara
阿闍羅
Mt. Shiratesan
Towadamichi
214
Mt. Bondaimori
Ōwasawa River
Mt. Mitsumori
Mt. Tozawayama
Aomori 40Km
Sendai 350Km
Mt. Chōkeimori
Mt. Nishimatayama
Closed in winter
Ikarigaseki
碇ヶ関
Ikarigaseki-mura
碇ヶ関村
Mt. Oppudake
Mt. Mitsumori
Sōma-Tashiro-rindō
Mt. Doyamori
Mt. Okariyadake
Mt. Eboshimori
Mt. Shiritakamori
Ikarigaseki 碇ヶ関
Hisayoshi Dam
Mt. Kudaisan
Mt. Shibamori
Tsurubeotoshi Pass
Mt. Eboshidake
Goshikinotaki
Mt. Magozaemonyama
Tsugaru-Yunosawa
Mt. Tashirodake
Mt. Anagurayama
Mt. Jinkichimori
Mt. Magusomoriyama
Mt. Sangaiyama
Mt. Ōhikageyama
Yatate Pass
矢立峠
Sakanashi Pass
坂梨峠
Komagadate
Itodaki
Mt. Sumizukamori
Mt. Nuitoyama
Jinba
Monomiyama
Mt. Kuromori
Mt. Higashimatayama
Mt. Jōgakurayama
Nakataki
TŌHOKU EXPRESSWAY
東北自動車道
Fujikoto River
AKITA
Mt. Metonoseyama
Mt. Tsukinokiyama
Mt. Ogamisan
Mt. Omokurasan
Ushū-kaidō
Kosaka-machi
小坂町
Mt. Takakidoyama
Mt. Haboyasan
Mt. Kōchiyama
Kosaka
小坂
Hayakuchi River
Shirasawa
Mt. Jōgamori
Mt. Ōyama
Ōdate
to Hirosaki
to Noshiro
to Kazuno
Yukisawa
Mt. Haginokatayama
Mt. Nabekoshiyama
Towada I.C
Tashiro-machi
田代町
Mt. Hōōzan
Mt. Zōgakurayama
Fujisato-machi
藤里町
ŌDATE-SHI
大館市
Higashi-ōdate
Mt. Akibasan
Yoneshiro River
Nagakuramachi 長倉町
Tsuzuriko 綴子
Towada 109Km
Hirosaki 51Km
Noshiro 54Km
Mt. Takamori
Hinai-machi
比内町
Takanosu-machi
鷹巣町
Noshiro-shi
212
Mt. Kurakakeyama
179

Hachimori-machi
101
Mukai-Noshiro
NOSHIRO-SHI
能代市
Noshiro
Yoneshiro River
Gonō Line
Konpira-ji
Tsurugata
Higashi-Noshiro
Ushū-kaidō
Mt. Oriy
Shidō mori 芝童森
Goshogawara 125Km
Ōdate 54Km
Akita 60Km
Noshiro Bypass
6.5
to Hachimori
to Akita
to Ōdate
Noshiro-minami
Tahōin
Asanainuma Lake
Kita-Kanaoka
13.5
10
Hachiryū
Ōmagari 大曲
Moritake
Yamamoto-machi
山本町
Hachiryū-machi
八竜町
Mitane River
秋田自動車道
Moritake
12.5
ORD 450
LAR 1250
Akita-jidōshadō
Oga-kaidō
12
15
Kotooka-machi
琴丘町
Kado
7
Kotooka-Moritake
琴丘森岳
Ōshima I.
to C. Nyūdōzaki
Oga
to C. Nyūdōzaki
Ōgata-mura
大潟村
2.5
8
C. Nyūdōzaki
入道崎
Hachirōko
八郎湖
Koikawa
16
7.5
13
6.0
C. Daimyōjinzaki
Oga
男鹿
C. Hattozaki
Zuikōji
4.5
Mt. Takaokasan
Toga-wan
Ichinomegata(Maar)
Shiohama
5.5
Wakami-machi
若美町
Mt. Moriyama
Yūbinkyoku mae 郵便局前
Hachirōgata-machi
八郎潟町
Hachirōgata
Gojōme-machi
五城目町
Gojōme-Hachirōgata
五城目八郎潟
Mt. Kanpūzan
Oga Pen.
男鹿半島
Hachirōgata chōseiike Lake
Wakimoto
Oga Line
Funakoshi
Ikawa-Sakura
Ikawa-machi
井川町
Mt. Honzan
Hadachi
Chausu Pass
Funakawa-kaidō
Tennō
Tennō-machi
天王町
Ugo-Iizuka
Iizuka-Koseki 飯塚古関
C. Oibanazaki
OGA-SHI
男鹿市
Oga
Iitagawa-sansaro 飯田川三差路
Futada
Iitagawa-machi
飯田川町
Ōkubo
Kami-Futada
Shōwa-machi
昭和町
Sumiyoshi-jinja
Showa Bypass
Shōwa-Ogahantō
昭和男鹿半島
C. Kanegasaki
C. Tateyamazaki
C. Shiosezaki
C. Unosaki
Detohama
Kitano-jinja
Minami-Akita
Mt. Tateyama
Shin-Nihonkai Ferry(to Tomakomai)
Oiwake
Oiwake 追分
to Noshiro
Akita
Akita-kita
秋田北
Kami-Iijima
to Honjō
Nippon Oil
Akita
Tsuchizaki
AKITA EXPRESSWAY
Shin-Nihonkai Ferry(to Niigata,Tsuruga)
Kyū-Omono River
Ou Line
Taiheizan
太平山
Aomori 200Km
Sendai 250Km
from Akita
Akita Bypass
AKITA-SHI
秋田市
Barajima 茨島
Akita
Noshiro 60Km
Morioka 118Km
Yokote 72Km
Ugo-Ushijima
Omono River
Honjō-shi
Ōmagari-shi

180

176
177
Ōdate-shi
F
G
Caution-frozen road
Ōu Line
Takanosu
Takanosu-machi
鷹巣町
Tomine
Futatsui
Futatsui-machi
二ッ井町
Kirishi
Nanakura-jinja
Maeyama
Ōnodai
Ogata
Mt. Nanakurasan
Ōnodai
Ōdate-Noshiro
Mt. Matōyama
Hikake River
Hinai-machi
比内町
Hanawa Line
Ōdate
Ōtaki
大滝
Ōtaki-Onsen
Jūnisho
Saikawa River
Aikawa
Aikawa-machi
合川町
Kamisugi
Akita-nairiku Railway
Ani-kaidō
Yonaizawa
Nōkyō mae 農協前
Moriyoshi-machi
森吉町
Katsurase
Mt. Kuromoriyama
Mt. Ryūgamori
Mt. Ogurayama
Mt. Takaeboshi
Mt. Kotsunagimori
Sunakozawa Pass
Mt. Ishikurayama
Tashiro River
Gojōme-kaidō
Nanakura-jinja
Kamikoani-mura
上小阿仁村
Mt. Hōjūyama
Animaeda
Mt. Gengorōdake
Yunosawa
Shiraito Fall
Himegadake-rindō
Maeda-minami
Komata River
Kobuchi
Ko-ani River
Komatakyō(Gorge)
Mt. Takasugisan
Moriyoshiyama-moriyoshi
Mt. Himegatake
Aniai
Ani-machi
阿仁町
Mt. Kuryōyama
Mt. Akakurayama
Fudōtaki
Afase
Mt. Moriyoshiyama
森吉山
Moriyoshiyama-ani
Mt. Shibamori
Nametara
Mt. Bōshosan
Kayakusa
Mt. Warisawamori
212
Mt. Hōzukizan
Mt. Konretsudake
Okashinai
Anigawa River
Mt. Bunamori
Mt. Yakushizan
Mt. Karasumori
AKITA
Iwanome
Animatagi
Okuani
Uttō River
Babame River
Kase Pass
Babame-rindō
Hitachinai
Mt. Yatsupadake
Mt. Tōnaganemori
Tachimata Valley
Bunamori-rindō
Mt. Takashibamori
Kamidai
Mt. Gorōsan
Kazuno-shi
Hitachinai River
Mt. Bannaimori
Nakanotaki
Hinokinai River
Mt. Ogamiyama
Mt. Manaitayama
Mt. Tenjōgurayama
Mt. Yozaemon-yama
Tozawa
Mt. Nakamori
Mt. Shirasabakkimori
Shiritaka Pass
Mt. Sokkemori
Tomagawa Dam
Mt. Babamedake
Mt. Shirakomori
Mt. Daibutsudake
Mt. Futagamiyama
Kami-Hinokinnai
Mt. Naramori
Nibetsu-kokuminnomori(R.A.)
Ōtaki
Sadōri
Mt. Taiheizan
太平山
Taiheizan-jinja
Taiheizan
Mt. Bandorimori
Yoroihata Dam
Ōtakiyama
Kanayama Fall
Ugo-Nakazato
Mt. Tengumori
Mt. Hagurosan
Mt. Kabayama
Tazawako-machi
Mt. Tsukushimori
Gozanoishi-jinja
Matsuba
Mt. Takahatayama
Tazawa Super rindō
Ōtaki
Akita-nairiku Railway
Tazawako Lake
Akita-chūō
秋田中央
Akita-Taiheizan
Mt. Futatsumori
Mt. Tōshirōmori
Mt. Ōishidake
Ugo-Nagatoro
Mt. Kamabuchimori
Katano 潟野
Iwami River
Katajiri River
Mt. Bunamori
Mt. Zenkyōmori
Yatsu
Mt. Innaidake
181
E
F
G
Kakunodate-machi
H
1
2
3
4
5
6

178
Akita-shi
Araya
Ōmoriyama Park
Ōu Line
Katsurane
Mt. Kunimiyama
Shimohama
Uetsu Line
Michikawa
Iwaki-machi
岩城町
Iwaki
岩城
Iwaki-minato
Mt. Kannonmori
Fudōnotaki
Chisan Akita
Sakata-kaido
Kumano-jinja
Ugo-Kameda
Mt. Takagisan
Oriwatari
Mt. Gongenyama
Oriwatari Pass
Ōuchi-machi
大内町
Ugo-Iwaya
Tokusawa 徳沢
Hasedera
Shinzan-jinja
from Honjō-shi
Aomori 240Km
Niigata 230Km
Akita 36Km
Yokote 56Km
Sakata 59Km
Koyoshi River
Ugo-Honjō
HONJŌ-SHI
本荘市
Mizubayashi 水林
Ichibanzeki 一番堰
Honjō-kaido
Yashima-kaido
Yakushido
Koyoshi
Nishime-machi
西目町
Nishime
S-shaped curve
Ayukawa
Kurosawa
Magarisawa
Maegō
Mt. Kokuzōyama
Yuri-machi
由利町
Chōkaisanroku Line
Kubota
Mt. Shibakurayama
Nishi-Takisawa
Nishime River
Shirayuki River
C. Seritamisaki
Nikaho
Nikaho-machi
仁賀保町
Konoura-machi
金浦町
Konoura
Yoshizawa
Koyoshi River
Kawabe
Ōyachiike Lake
Yashima-machi
矢島町
Yashima
Tenjinnuma Lake
Kisakata
Kanmanji
Kisakata-machi
象潟町
Hamayama 浜山
Ōgata-tameike Lake
Chōkai-kōgen Yashima
Naso-no-shirataki(Falls)
Kamihama
Yunosawa
Sarukura
Chōkai-Okojo
Sakata-shi
182
183
A
B
C
D
1
2
3
4
5
6

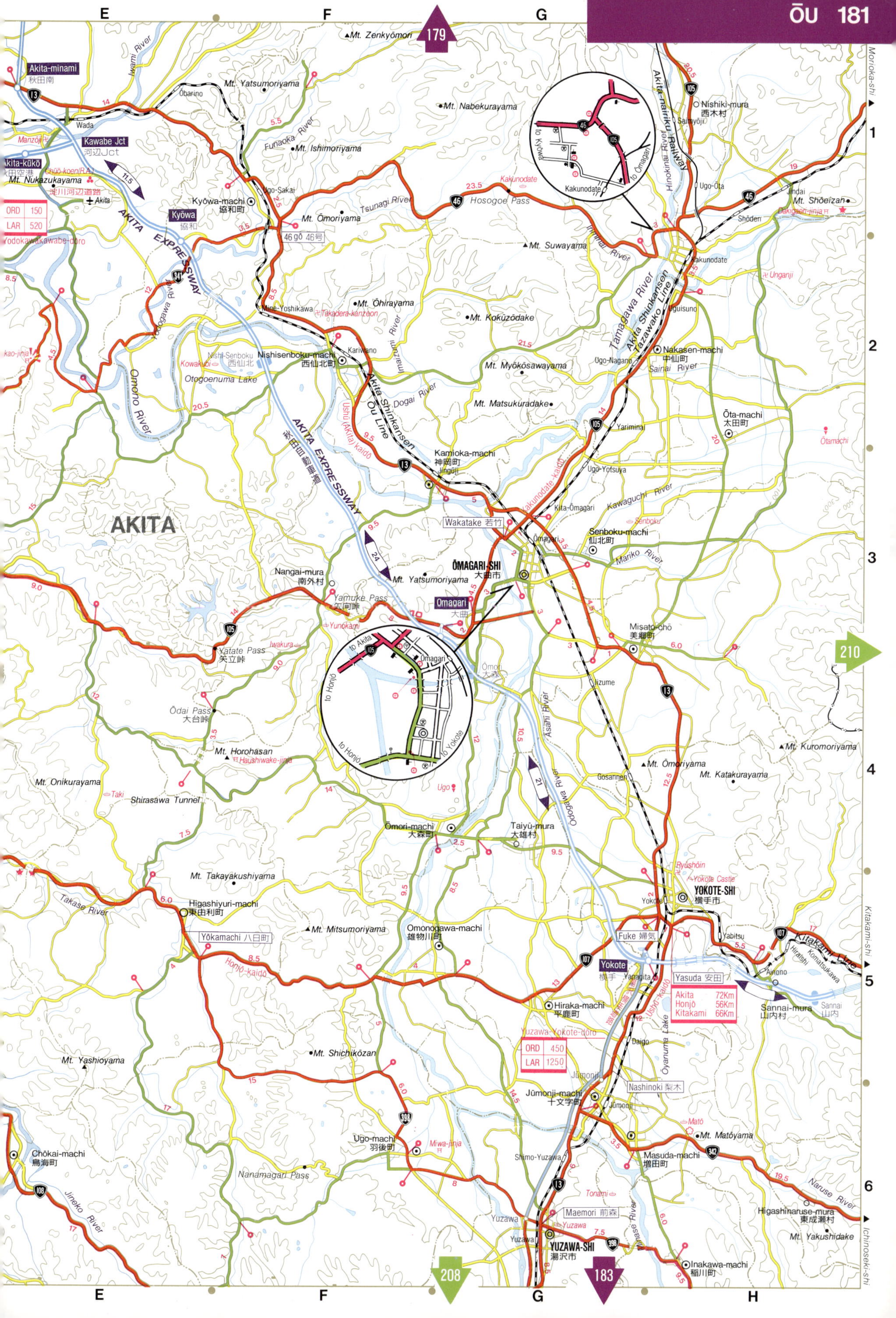

E
F
G
H
179
210
208
183
1
2
3
4
5
6
AKITA
AKITA EXPRESSWAY
秋田自動車道
Akita-minami
秋田南
Kawabe Jct
河辺Jct
Akita-kūkō
秋田空港
Kyōwa
協和
Omagari
大曲
Yokote
横手
Mt. Zenkyōmori
Mt. Yatsumoriyama
Mt. Nabekurayama
Mt. Ishimoriyama
Mt. Ōmoriyama
Mt. Suwayama
Mt. Ōhirayama
Mt. Kokuzōdake
Mt. Myōkōsawayama
Mt. Matsukuradake
Mt. Horohasan
Mt. Onikurayama
Mt. Takayakushiyama
Mt. Mitsumoriyama
Mt. Shichikōzan
Mt. Yashioyama
Mt. Kuromoriyama
Mt. Katakurayama
Mt. Matōyama
Mt. Yakushidake
Mt. Shōeizan
Mt. Nukazukayama
Kyōwa-machi
協和町
Nishisenboku-machi
西仙北町
Kamioka-machi
神岡町
ŌMAGARI-SHI
大曲市
Nangai-mura
南外村
Senboku-machi
仙北町
Misato-chō
美郷町
Nakasen-machi
中仙町
Ōta-machi
太田町
Nishiki-mura
西木村
Ōmori-machi
大森町
Taiyū-mura
大雄村
YOKOTE-SHI
横手市
Higashiyuri-machi
東由利町
Omonogawa-machi
雄物川町
Hiraka-machi
平鹿町
Jūmonji-machi
十文字町
Masuda-machi
増田町
Ugo-machi
羽後町
Chōkai-machi
鳥海町
YUZAWA-SHI
湯沢市
Inakawa-machi
稲川町
Sannai-mura
山内村
Higashinaruse-mura
東成瀬村
Kakunodate
Hosogoe Pass
Yamuke Pass
Yatate Pass
矢立峠
Ōdai Pass
大台峠
Nanamagari Pass
Shirasawa Tunnel
Omono River
Otogoenuma Lake
Tamagawa River
Asahi River
Kawaguchi River
Mariko River
Takase River
Jineko River
Naruse River
Akita Shinkansen
Ōu Line
Akita-nairiku Railway
Tazawako Line
Kitakami Line
Wakatake 若竹
Yōkamachi 八日町
Fuke 婦気
Yasuda 安田
Nashinoki 梨木
Maemori 前森
Akita 72Km
Honjō 56Km
Kitakami 66Km
ORD 150
LAR 520
ORD 450
LAR 1250
Yuzawa-Yokote-dōro
Honjō-kaidō
Morioka-shi
Kitakami-shi
Ichinoseki-shi

B
C
D
A
1
2
3
4
5
6
Kisakata-machi
C. Hachimanzaki
Tobishima I.
飛島
SAKATA-SHI
酒田市
Kosagawa
Mt. Inakurada
Mt. Kannonmori
Mt. Shōgatake
鳥海ブルーライン
Yunota
Jurokū-rakan 十六羅漢
Fukura
Fukura 吹浦
Eisenji
Ninotaki
Ichinotaki
Uetsu Line
Nishi-Kaigan-kaidō
Chōkaiyawat
Gekkō River
Yuza
Yuza-machi
遊佐町
Mt. Tengumori
Nikkō River
Minami-Chōkai
Shijō-teijiro 市条丁字路
Yawata-machi
八幡町
Mototate
Sakata-minato
酒田みなと
Sanzenbōyach
Yoshida-shinden 吉田新田
Honjō 59Km
Shinjō 57Km
Tsuruoka 22Km
Sakata
Mogami River
Sakata
SAKATA-SHI
酒田市
Miyanoura
Sakata Bypass
Higashi-Sakata
Sagoshi
Hirata-machi
平田町
Komonoimi-jinja
Ochinome 落野目
Asuka-jinja
Sakata
酒田
Kita-Amarume
Tatsugayu
Matsuyama-machi
松山町
Sōkōji
from Sakatashi
Sendai 160Km
Niigata 170Km
Amarume Bypass
Amarume-machi
余目町
Amarume
Rikuu-saisen Line
Shōnai-kūkō
庄内空港
Shōnai
Minamino
Nishibukuro
Naganuma
Karikawa 狩川
Karikawa
Karikawa 狩川
Tachikawa-machi
立川町
Yunohama
湯野浜
Yunohama
Zenpōji
Kamo
C. Arazaki
Mt. Takadateyama
Mikawa-machi
三川町
Fujishima
Fujishima-machi
藤島町
Tsuruoka Bypass
Uzen-Ōyama
Tsuruoka
鶴岡
Tsuruoka-ekimae 鶴岡駅前
Sakata 22Km
Shinjō 53Km
Yamagata 116Km
Yura
Yura 由良
Uzen-Mizusawa
TSURUOKA-SHI
鶴岡市
Haguro-machi
羽黒町
Takenokozawa
Closed in winter
Dewasanzan-jinja
出羽三山神社
Haguosan-dōro
ORD 400
LAR 1400
Closed in winter
Tsuruoka-shi-Akagawa-shimin
Sanze
C. Hatozaki
Kobato
Mt. Hachimoriyama
Yudagawa
湯田川
YAMAGATA EXPRESSWAY
山形自動車道
Mt. Kinpōzan
Akagawa River
Kushibiki-machi
櫛引町
Iragawa River
Iragawa
Mt. Fujikurayama
Mt. Hokariyama
Kushibiki
櫛引
Atsumi-machi
温海町
Atsumi-onsen
Mt. Atsumidake
Atsumi River
Atsumi
温海
Shōnai-Asahi
庄内あさひ
Mt. Kami-Ōtakiyama
Asahi-mura
朝日村
184
185
Shibata-shi
Nezugaseki
Yamagata-shi
to Honjō
to Yawata
to Hirata
to Matsuyama
to Tsuruoka
to Yunohama
Tsuruoka
to Sakata
to Tachikawa
to Haguro
to Sagae
to Yudagawa
to Atsumi

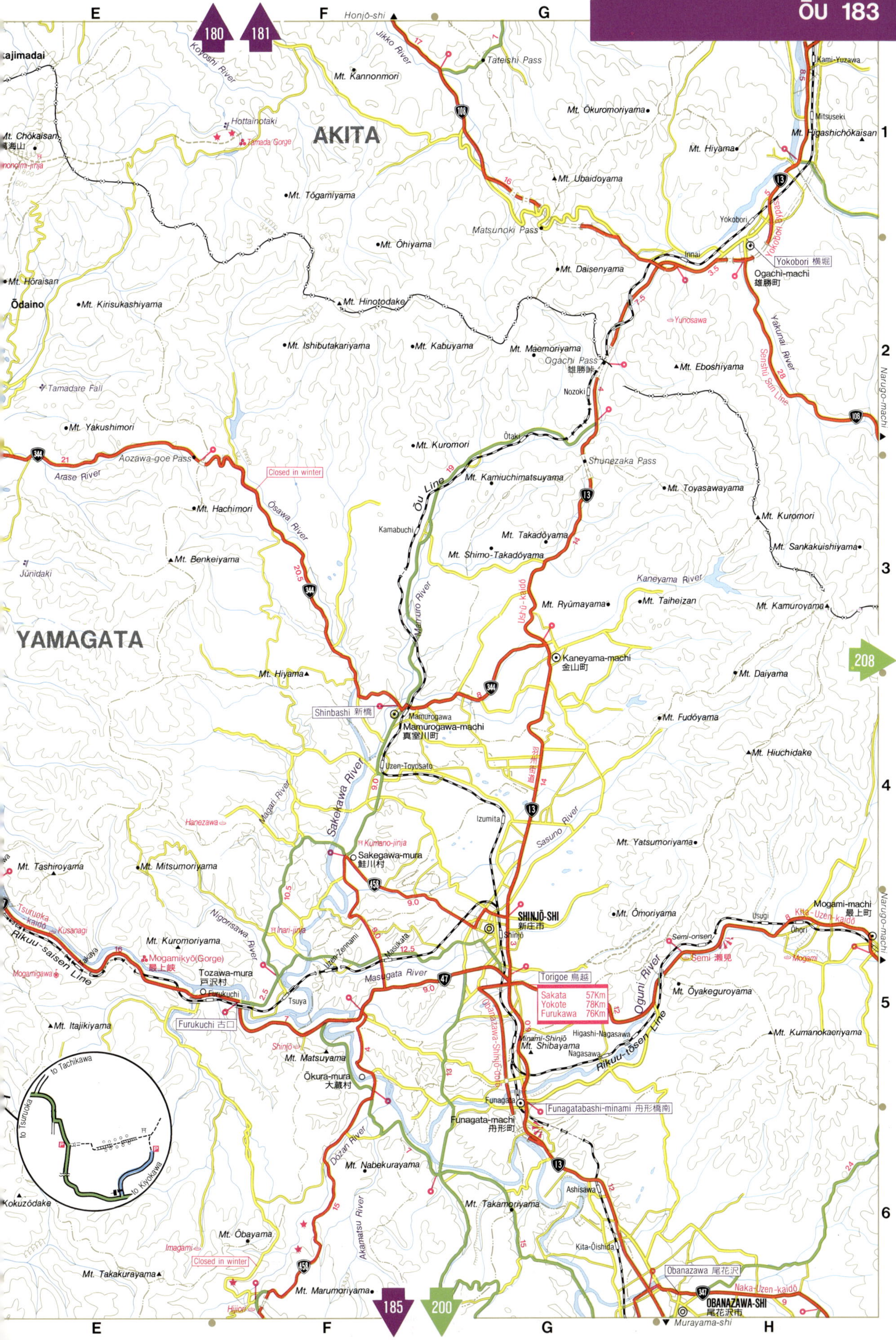
E
F
G
H
1
2
3
4
5
6
180
181
208
185
200
Honjō-shi
Narugo-machi
Murayama-shi
AKITA
YAMAGATA
Kajimadai
Koyoshi River
Jikko River
Tateishi Pass
Mt. Kannonmori
Hottainotaki
Tamada Gorge
Mt. Chōkaisan
鳥海山
Mt. Ōkuromoriyama
Kami-Yuzawa
Mitsuseki
Mt. Higashichōkaisan
Mt. Hiyama
Mt. Ubaidoyama
Mt. Tōgamiyama
Matsunoki Pass
Yokobori
Mt. Ōhiyama
Innai
Yokobori 横堀
Ogachi-machi
雄勝町
Mt. Daisenyama
Mt. Hōraisan
Ōdaino
Mt. Kirisukashiyama
Mt. Hinotodake
Yunosawa
Yakunai River
Senshū Sun Line
Mt. Ishibutakariyama
Mt. Kabuyama
Mt. Maemoriyama
Ogachi Pass
雄勝峠
Mt. Eboshiyama
Nozoki
Tamadare Fall
Mt. Yakushimori
Ōtaki
Mt. Kuromori
Aozawa-goe Pass
Closed in winter
Arase River
Shunezaka Pass
Mt. Kamiuchimatsuyama
Ōu Line
Mt. Toyasawayama
Mt. Hachimori
Ōsawa River
Kamabuchi
Mt. Kuromori
Mt. Takadōyama
Mt. Shimo-Takadōyama
Mt. Sankakuishiyama
Mt. Benkeiyama
Jūnidaki
Kaneyama River
Mamuro River
Ushū-kaidō
Mt. Ryūmayama
Mt. Taiheizan
Mt. Kamuroyama
Kaneyama-machi
金山町
Mt. Daiyama
Mt. Hiyama
Shinbashi 新橋
Mamurogawa
Mamurogawa-machi
真室川町
Mt. Fudōyama
Uzen-Toyosato
Mt. Hiuchidake
Sakekawa River
Magari River
Hanezawa
Izumita
Sasuno River
Kumano-jinja
Sakegawa-mura
鮭川村
Mt. Yatsumoriyama
Mt. Tashiroyama
Mt. Mitsumoriyama
Nigorisawa River
SHINJŌ-SHI
新庄市
Shinjō
Mt. Ōmoriyama
Mogami-machi
最上町
Usugi
Ohori
Kita-Uzen-kaidō
Tsuruoka-kaidō
Kusanagi
Inari-jinja
Mt. Kuromoriyama
Uzen-Zennami
Masukata
Semi-onsen
Semi 瀬見
Rikuu-saisen Line
Mogamikyō(Gorge)
最上峡
Mogamigawa
Tozawa-mura
戸沢村
Furukuchi
Masugata River
Torigoe 鳥越
Sakata 57Km
Yokote 78Km
Furukawa 76Km
Oguni River
Mogami
Mt. Ōyakeguroyama
Tsuya
Furukuchi 古口
Obanazawa-Shinjō-dōro
Higashi-Nagasawa
Mt. Itajikiyama
Shinjō
Mt. Matsuyama
Minami-Shinjō
Mt. Shibayama
Nagasawa
Rikuu-tōsen Line
Mt. Kumanokaeriyama
to Tachikawa
to Tsuruoka
to Kiyokawa
Ōkura-mura
大蔵村
Funagata
Funagatabashi-minami 舟形橋南
Funagata-machi
舟形町
Dōzan River
Mt. Nabekurayama
Kokuzōdake
Ashisawa
Mt. Takamoriyama
Akamatsu River
Mt. Ōbayama
Imagami
Closed in winter
Kita-Ōishida
Mt. Takakurayama
Obanazawa 尾花沢
Naka-Uzen-kaidō
Mt. Marumoriyama
OBANAZAWA-SHI
尾花沢市
Hijiori

B
C
D
A
1
2
3
4
5
6
Tsuruoka-shi
Nan-yō-shi
Awashima I.
粟島
C. Tossaki
C. Hatasaki
Awashimaura-mura
粟島浦村
C. Nagatehana
Oguni River
Mt. Genzōyama
Mt. Sanbōkurayama
Koiwagawa
Atsumigawa Dam
Mt. Yakushidake
Nezugaseki
Bentenjima I.
Okuda 奥田
Mt. Ōhatayama
Bad road
Closed in winter
Sekigawa Tunnel
Sekigawa Pass
関川峠
Mt. Nihonkoku
Mt. Imozawayama
Sanpoku-machi
山北町
Ōkawa River
Fuya
Mt. Mayazan
Nakatsugi River
Katsugi
Katsugi 勝木
Mt. Eboshidake
Amasaka Pass
Budōgawa River
Echigo-Kangawa
C. Kitsunesaki
Mt. Shiroyama
Mt. Jōgamine
Mt. Shirōdake
Imagawa
Mt. Budōyama
Mt. Kasatoriyama
Mt. Kitamatayama
Sasagawa-nagare
(Scenic Rocky Coast)
笹川流
Mt. Kareiyama
Budō
Mt. Shirodake
Kuwagawa
Mt. Tenjōyama
Mt. Shigekurayama
NIIGATA
Uetsu Line
Mt. Higurayama
Echigo-Hayakawa
Mt. Mitsubitaiyama
Komogawa River
Takane River
Mt. Nōkesan
Mt. Engoyama
Majima
Mt. Shikamoriyama
Mt. Takatoriyama
Asahi-mura
朝日村
Mt. Akamizoyama
Mt. Urehagiyama
Miomote River
C. Iwagasaki
Tsuruoka 83Km
Yonezawa 102Km
Niigata 60Km
Yaberi 山辺里
MURAKAMI-SHI
村上市
Murakami
Haguro-jinja
Senami
瀬波
Shōrinji
Iwafune-jinja
Iwafune
Kami-Sukebuchi 上助淵
Mt. Yatsuhashiyama
Mt. Washigasuyama
to Tsuruoka
to Shibata
Warabi Pass
蕨峠
Mt. Gakiyama
Monzen River
Iwafunemachi
Kamihayashi-mura
神林村
Mt. Ōtairayama
Sendai 200Km
Niigata 60Km
from Murakami-shi
Arakawa River
Hirabayashi
Momogawa Pass
Arakawa-machi
荒川町
Mt. Hōzakayama
Omna River
Nihonkai
Sakamachi
Mt. Yukurayama
Hitachi
Jūmonji 十文字
Tainai River
Hirakida
Echigo-Oshima
Yonezaka Line
Echigo-Shimoseki
Sekikawa-mura
関川村
Yusawa
Kira
Takase
Arakawa Hot Springs
荒川温泉郷
Takanosu
Okiniwa-jinja
Kaneme
Oguni-machi
小国町
Tōshiba Cer
Oguni
Kurokawa-mura
黒川村
Echigo-Katakake
Echigo-Kanamaru
Akashibakyō
Tarugahashi
157
186

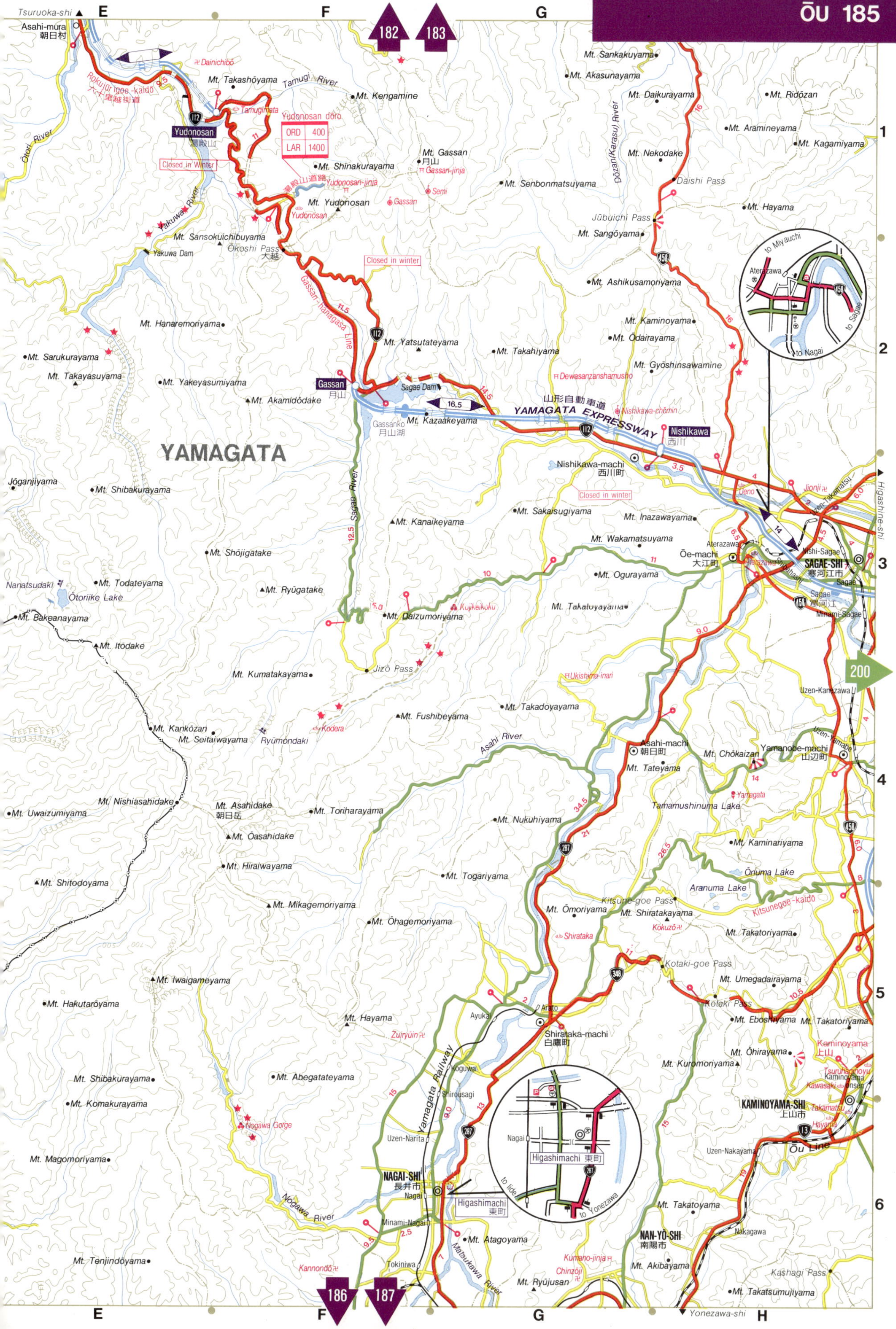
E
F
G
H
182
183
186
187
200
1
2
3
4
5
6
Tsuruoka-shi
Asahi-mura
朝日村
Rokujūrigoe-kaidō
六十里越街道
Dainichibō
Mt. Takashōyama
Tamugi River
Tamugimata
Mt. Kengamine
Yudonosan
湯殿山
Yudonosan dōro
ORD 400
LAR 1400
Closed in Winter
Ōtori River
Mt. Shinakurayama
Mt. Gassan
月山
Gassan-jinja
Yudonosan-jinja
Semi
Gassan
Mt. Yudonosan
Yudonosan
Yakuwa River
Mt. Sansokuichibuyama
Yakuwa Dam
Ōkoshi Pass
大越
Closed in winter
Gassan-hanagasa Line
Mt. Hanaremoriyama
Mt. Sarukurayama
Mt. Takayasuyama
Mt. Yatsutateyama
Mt. Yakeyasumiyama
Mt. Akamidōdake
Gassan
月山
Sagae Dam
16.5
Gassanko
月山湖
Mt. Kazaakeyama
YAMAGATA
Mt. Sankakuyama
Mt. Akasunayama
Mt. Daikurayama
Mt. Ridōzan
Mt. Aramineyama
Mt. Kagamiyama
Dōzan(Karasu) River
Mt. Nekodake
Daishi Pass
Mt. Senbonmatsuyama
Mt. Hayama
Jūbuichi Pass
Mt. Sangōyama
Mt. Ashikusamoriyama
Mt. Kaminoyama
Mt. Ōdaira yama
Mt. Takahiyama
Mt. Gyōshinsawamine
Dewasanzanshamusho
Nishikawa-chōmin
山形自動車道
YAMAGATA EXPRESSWAY
Nishikawa
西川
Nishikawa-machi
西川町
Closed in winter
Mt. Sakaisugiyama
Mt. Inazawayama
Mt. Wakamatsuyama
to Miyauchi
Aterazawa
to Sagae
to Nagai
Ueno
Jionji
Higashine-shi
Aterazawa
Ōe-machi
大江町
SAGAE-SHI
寒河江市
Nishi-Sagae
Sagae
寒河江
Minami-Sagae
Mt. Oguravama
Mt. Takatoyayama
Jōganjiyama
Mt. Shibakurayama
Sagae River
Mt. Kanaikeyama
Mt. Shōjigatake
Nanatsudaki
Mt. Todateyama
Ōtoriike Lake
Mt. Ryūgatake
Mt. Daizumoriyama
Mt. Bakeanayama
Mt. Itōdake
Jizō Pass
Mt. Kumatakayama
Ukishima-inari
Uzen-Kanezawa
Kodera
Mt. Fushibeyama
Mt. Takadoyayama
Mt. Kankōzan
Mt. Seitaiwayama
Ryūmondaki
Asahi River
Asahi-machi
朝日町
Mt. Chōkaizan
Yamanobe-machi
山辺町
Uzen-Yamabe
Mt. Tateyama
Yamagata
Mt. Uwaizumiyama
Mt. Nishiasahidake
Mt. Asahidake
朝日岳
Mt. Toriharayama
Mt. Nukuhiyama
Tamamushinuma Lake
Mt. Ōasahidake
Mt. Kaminariyama
Mt. Hiraiwayama
Mt. Shitodoyama
Mt. Togariyama
Ōnuma Lake
Aranuma Lake
Kitsune-goe Pass
Kitsunegoe-kaidō
Mt. Mikagemoriyama
Mt. Ōmoriyama
Mt. Shiratakayama
Mt. Ōhagemoriyama
Kokuzō
Shirataka
Mt. Takatoriyama
Kotaki-goe Pass
Mt. Umegadairayama
Mt. Iwaigameyama
Kotaki Pass
Mt. Hakutarōyama
Ayukai
Arato
Shirataka-machi
白鷹町
Mt. Hayama
Mt. Eboshiyama
Mt. Takatoriyama
Zuiryūin
Kaminoyama
上山
Mt. Ōhirayama
Mt. Kuromoriyama
Yamagata Railway
Koguwa
Tsuruhaginoyu
Kaminoyama Onsen
Kawasaki
Mt. Shibakurayama
Mt. Abegatateyama
Shirousagi
KAMINOYAMA-SHI
上山市
Takamatsu
Mt. Komakurayama
Nogawa Gorge
Nagai
Hayama
Uzen-Narita
Higashimachi 東町
to Iide
to Yonezawa
Uzen-Nakayama
Ōu Line
Mt. Magomoriyama
NAGAI-SHI
長井市
Nagai
Higashimachi
東町
Nogawa River
Mt. Takatoyama
Minami-Nagai
Mt. Atagoyama
NAN-YŌ-SHI
南陽市
Nakagawa
Mt. Tenjindōyama
Kannondō
Tokiniwa
Matsukawa River
Kumano-jinja
Chinzōji
Mt. Akibayama
Kashagi Pass
Mt. Ryūjusan
Mt. Takatsumujiyama
Yonezawa-shi

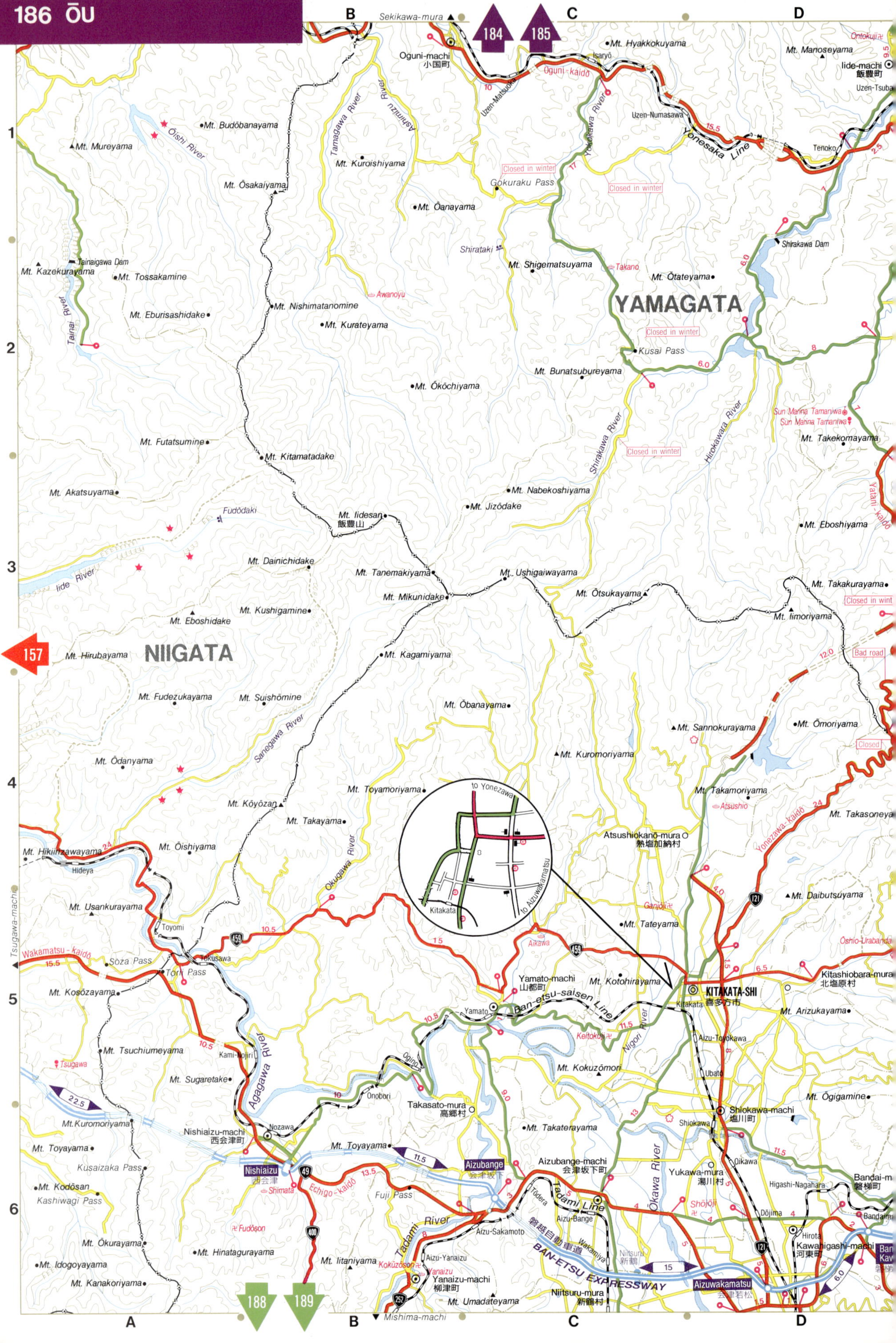

A
B
C
D
1
2
3
4
5
6
184
185
157
188
189
Sekikawa-mura
Oguni-machi
小国町
Isaryō
Mt. Hyakkokuyama
Mt. Manoseyama
Iide-machi
飯豊町
Uzen-Tsuba
Ontokuji
Oguni-kaidō
Uzen-Matsuoka
Uzen-Numasawa
Yonesaka Line
Tenoko
Mt. Budōbanayama
Mt. Mureyama
Ōishi River
Tamagawa River
Ashimizu River
Mt. Kuroishiyama
Mt. Ōsakaiyama
Closed in winter
Gokuraku Pass
Yokokawa River
Mt. Ōanayama
Shiratak Dam
Shirakawa Dam
Shirataki
Mt. Kazekurayama
Tainaigawa Dam
Mt. Tossakamine
Mt. Shigematsuyama
Takano
Mt. Ōtateyama
Awanoyu
YAMAGATA
Mt. Eburisashidake
Mt. Nishimatanomine
Tainai River
Mt. Kurateyama
Kusai Pass
Mt. Bunatsubureyama
Mt. Ōkōchiyama
Sun Marina Tamaniwa
Mt. Takekomayama
Mt. Futatsumine
Mt. Kitamatadake
Shirakawa River
Hirokawara River
Mt. Akatsuyama
Mt. Nabekoshiyama
Mt. Jizōdake
Fudōdaki
Mt. Iidesan
飯豊山
Yatani-kaidō
Mt. Eboshiyama
Iide River
Mt. Dainichidake
Mt. Tanemakiyama
Mt. Ushigaiwayama
Mt. Takakurayama
Mt. Ōtsukayama
Mt. Mikunidake
Mt. Kushigamine
Mt. Iimoriyama
Mt. Eboshidake
Bad road
Mt. Hirubayama
NIIGATA
Mt. Kagamiyama
Mt. Fudezukayama
Mt. Suishōmine
Mt. Ōbanayama
Mt. Sannokurayama
Mt. Ōmoriyama
Sanegawa River
Closed
Mt. Kuromoriyama
Mt. Ōdanyama
Mt. Toyamoriyama
to Yonezawa
Mt. Takamoriyama
Mt. Kōyōzan
Atsushio
Mt. Takayama
Mt. Takasoneyama
Yonezawa-kaidō
Mt. Hikiirizawayama
Hideya
Mt. Ōishiyama
Okugawa River
Atsushiokanō-mura
熱塩加納村
to Aizuwakamatsu
Kitakata
Mt. Usankurayama
Mt. Daibutsuyama
Ganjōji
Tsugawa-machi
Toyomi
Mt. Tateyama
Ōshio-Urabanda
Wakamatsu-kaidō
Sōza Pass
Tokusawa
Torii Pass
Aikawa
Yamato-machi
山都町
Mt. Kotohirayama
Kitashiobara-mura
北塩原村
Mt. Kosōzayama
KITAKATA-SHI
喜多方市
Ban-etsu-saisen Line
Yamato
Mt. Arizukayama
Keitokuji
Nigori River
Aizu-Toyokawa
Mt. Tsuchiumeyama
Kami-Nojiri
Tsugawa
Agagawa River
Mt. Kokuzōmori
Mt. Sugaretake
Ubato
Oginō
Onobori
Takasato-mura
高郷村
Mt. Ōgigamine
Shiokawa-machi
塩川町
Mt. Kuromoriyama
Nozawa
Shiokawa
Mt. Takaterayama
Nishiaizu-machi
西会津町
Mt. Toyayama
Mt. Toyoyama
Aizubange-machi
会津坂下町
Yukawa-mura
湯川村
Oikawa
Ōkawa River
Nishiaizu
西会津
Aizubange
会津坂下
Bandai-machi
磐梯町
Kusaizaka Pass
Shimata
Echigo-kaidō
Fuji Pass
Higashi-Nagahara
Mt. Kodōsan
Kashiwagi Pass
Tadami Line
Tōdera
Shōjōji
Dōjima
Aizu-Bange
Bandai
Fudōson
Tadami River
Aizu-Sakamoto
Hirota
Kawahigashi-machi
河東町
Mt. Ōkurayama
Mt. Hinataguraayama
Aizu-Yanaizu
Wakamiya
磐越自動車道
Niitsuru
新鶴
Mt. Idogoyayama
Mt. Iitaniyama
Kokūzōson
Yanaizu
BAN-ETSU EXPRESSWAY
Aizuwakamatsu
会津若松
Yanaizu-machi
柳津町
Mt. Kanakoriyama
Niitsuru-mura
新鶴村
Mt. Umadateyama
Mishima-machi

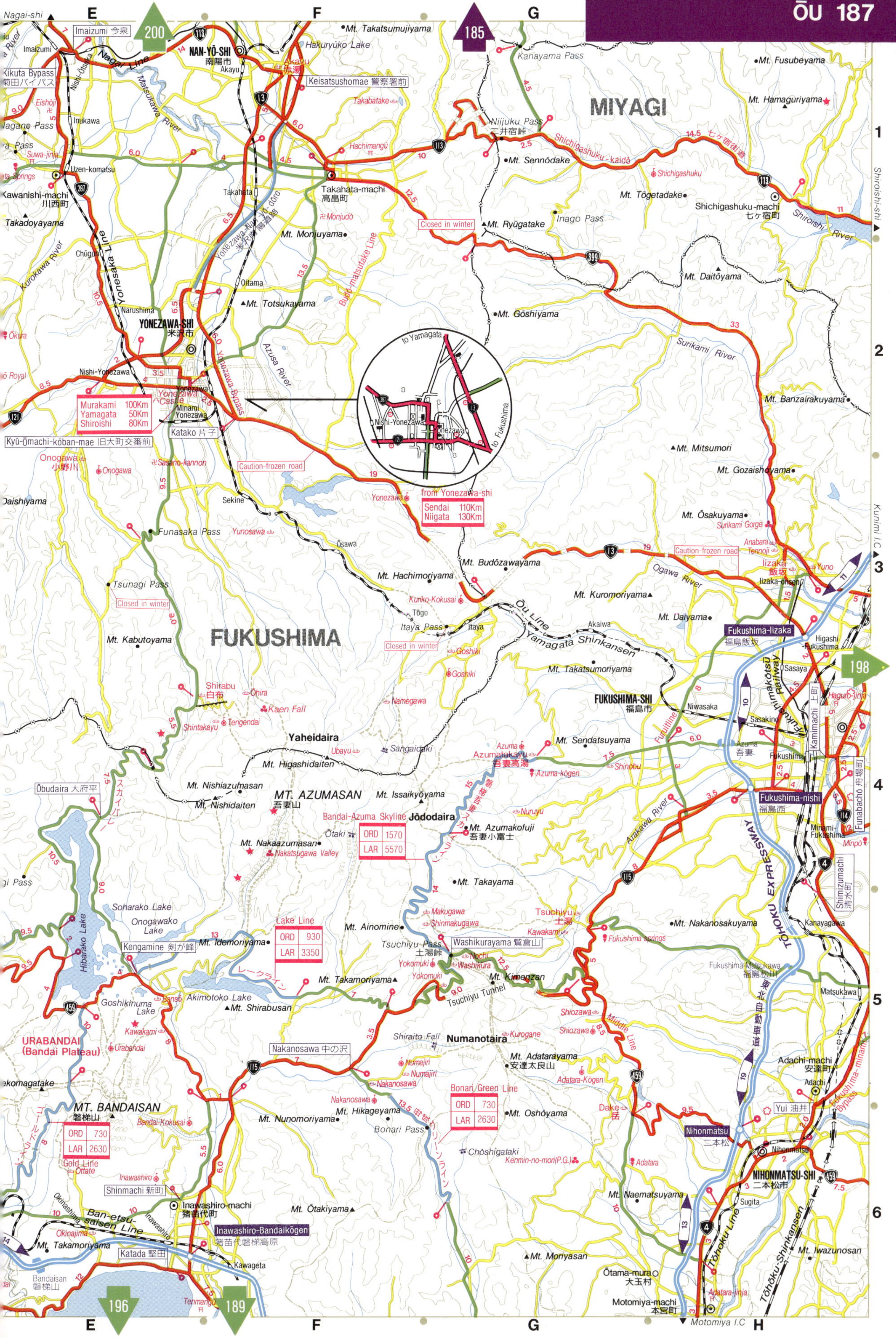
E
F
G
H
1
2
3
4
5
6
200
185
198
196
189
MIYAGI
FUKUSHIMA
Nagai-shi
Imaizumi 今泉
Imaizumi
Kikuta Bypass 菊田バイパス
Eishōji
Nagane Pass
Inukawa
Nagai Line
Nishi-Ōshio
Matsukawa River
NAN-YŌ-SHI 南陽市
Akayu
Akayu 赤湯
Keisatsushomae 警察署前
Hakuryūko Lake
Mt. Takatsumujiyama
Takabatake
Hachimangū
Suwa-jinja
Uzen-komatsu
Kawanishi-machi 川西町
Takadoyayama
Takahata
Takahata-machi 高畠町
Monjudō
Mt. Monjuyama
Yonezawa-Nan-yō-dōro 米沢南陽道路
Budō-matsutake Line
Chūgun
Kurokawa River
Yonesaka Line
Oitama
Mt. Totsukayama
Narushima
YONEZAWA-SHI 米沢市
Ōkura
Nishi-Yonezawa
Yonezawa
Yonezawa Castle
Minami Yonezawa
Yonezawa Bypass
Azusa River
Murakami 100Km
Yamagata 50Km
Shiroishi 80Km
Katako 片子
Kyū-Ōmachi-kōban-mae 旧大町交番前
Onogawa 小野川
Onogawa
Sasano-kannon
Caution-frozen road
to Yamagata
to Fukushima
Nishi-Yonezawa
Yonezawa
Yonezawa
from Yonezawa-shi
Sendai 110Km
Niigata 130Km
Daishiyama
Sekine
Funasaka Pass
Yunosawa
Ōsawa
Tsunagi Pass
Closed in winter
Mt. Hachimoriyama
Kuriko-Kokusai
Tōgo
Itaya Pass
Itaya
Closed in winter
Mt. Kabutoyama
Goshiki
Goshiki
Shirabu 白布
Ōhira
Kaen Fall
Namegawa
Shintakayu
Tengendai
Yaheidaira
Ubayu
Sangaidaki
Mt. Higashidaiten
Mt. Nishiazumasan
Mt. Nishidaiten
MT. AZUMASAN 吾妻山
Mt. Issaikyōyama
Ōbudaira 大府平
Bandai-Azuma Skyline
Jōdodaira
Ōtaki
ORD 1570
LAR 5570
Mt. Nakaazumasan
Nakatsugawa Valley
Mt. Azumakofuji 吾妻小富士
Soharako Lake
Onogawako Lake
Hibarako Lake
Lake Line
ORD 930
LAR 3350
Mt. Ainomine
Mt. Idemoriyama
Kengamine 剣が峰
Tsuchiyu Pass 土湯峠
Makugawa
Shinmakugawa
Washikurayama 鷲倉山
Nochi
Washikura
Yokomuki
Yokomuki
Mt. Takamoriyama
Mt. Kimenzan
Tsuchiyu Tunnel
Goshikinuma Lake
Banso
Akimotoko Lake
Mt. Shirabusan
Kawakami
URABANDAI (Bandai Plateau)
Urabandai
Nakanosawa 中の沢
Shiraito Fall
Numanotaira
Numajiri
Numajiri
Nakanosawa
Nakanosawa
Mt. Hikageyama
Mt. Nunomoriyama
Bonari Pass
Bonari Green Line
ORD 730
LAR 2630
Chōshigataki
Kenmin-no-mori(P.G.)
Mt. Adatarayama 安達太良山
Mt. Oshōyama
Kurogane
Shiozawa
Shiozawa
Middle Line
Adatara-Kōgen
Dake 岳
Adatara
Nekomagatake
MT. BANDAISAN 磐梯山
Bandai-Kokusai
ORD 730
LAR 2630
Gold Line
Ottate
Inawashiro
Shinmachi 新町
Inawashiro-machi 猪苗代町
Ban-etsu-saisen Line
Okinajima
Inawashiro-Bandaikōgen 猪苗代磐梯高原
Mt. Takamoriyama
Katada 堅田
Kawageta
Bandaisan 磐梯山
Tenmangū
Mt. Ōtakiyama
Mt. Moriyasan
Ōtama-mura 大玉村
Motomiya-machi 本宮町
Motomiya I.C
Mt. Naematsuyama
Kanayama Pass
Niijuku Pass 二井宿峠
Mt. Sennōdake
Shichigashuku-kaidō 七ヶ宿街道
Shichigashuku
Mt. Fusubeyama
Mt. Hamaguriyama
Mt. Tōgetadake
Shichigashuku-machi 七ヶ宿町
Shiroishi River
Shiroishi-shi
Closed in winter
Mt. Ryūgatake
Inago Pass
Mt. Daitōyama
Mt. Gōshiyama
Surikami River
Mt. Banzairakuyama
Mt. Mitsumori
Mt. Gozaishoyama
Mt. Ōsakuyama
Surikami Gorge
Kunimi I.C.
Mt. Budōzawayama
Caution-frozen road
Anabara
Tenjoji
Iizaka 飯坂
Iizaka-onsen
Yuno
Ogawa River
Mt. Kuromoriyama
Mt. Daiyama
Ōu Line
Akaiwa
Yamagata Shinkansen
Fukushima-Iizaka 福島飯坂
Higashi Fukushima
Mt. Takatsumoriyama
Fukushima-kōtsū Railway
Sasaya
FUKUSHIMA-SHI 福島市
Niwasaka
Furufuline
Sasakino
Kamimachi 上町
Haguro-jinja
Azuma
Azumatakayu 吾妻高湯
Mt. Sendatsuyama
Azuma 吾妻
Fukushima
Shinobu
Azuma-kōgen
Fukushima-nishi 福島西
Funabachō 舟場町
Nuruyu
Arakawa River
Minami-Fukushima
Minpo
TŌHOKU EXPRESSWAY
Mt. Takayama
Shimizumachi 清水町
Tsuchiyu 土湯
Kawakami
Fukushima springs
Mt. Nakanosakuyama
Kanayagawa
Fukushima-Matsukawa 福島松川
Matsukawa
東北自動車道
Adachi-machi 安達町
Adachi
Fukushima-minami Bypass
Yui 油井
Nihonmatsu 二本松
Nihonmatsu
NIHONMATSU-SHI 二本松市
Sugita
Tōhoku Line
Tōhoku-Shinkansen
Mt. Iwazunosan
Adatara-jinja
スカイバレー
レークライン
ゴールドライン
安達太良グリーンライン
磐梯吾妻スカイライン

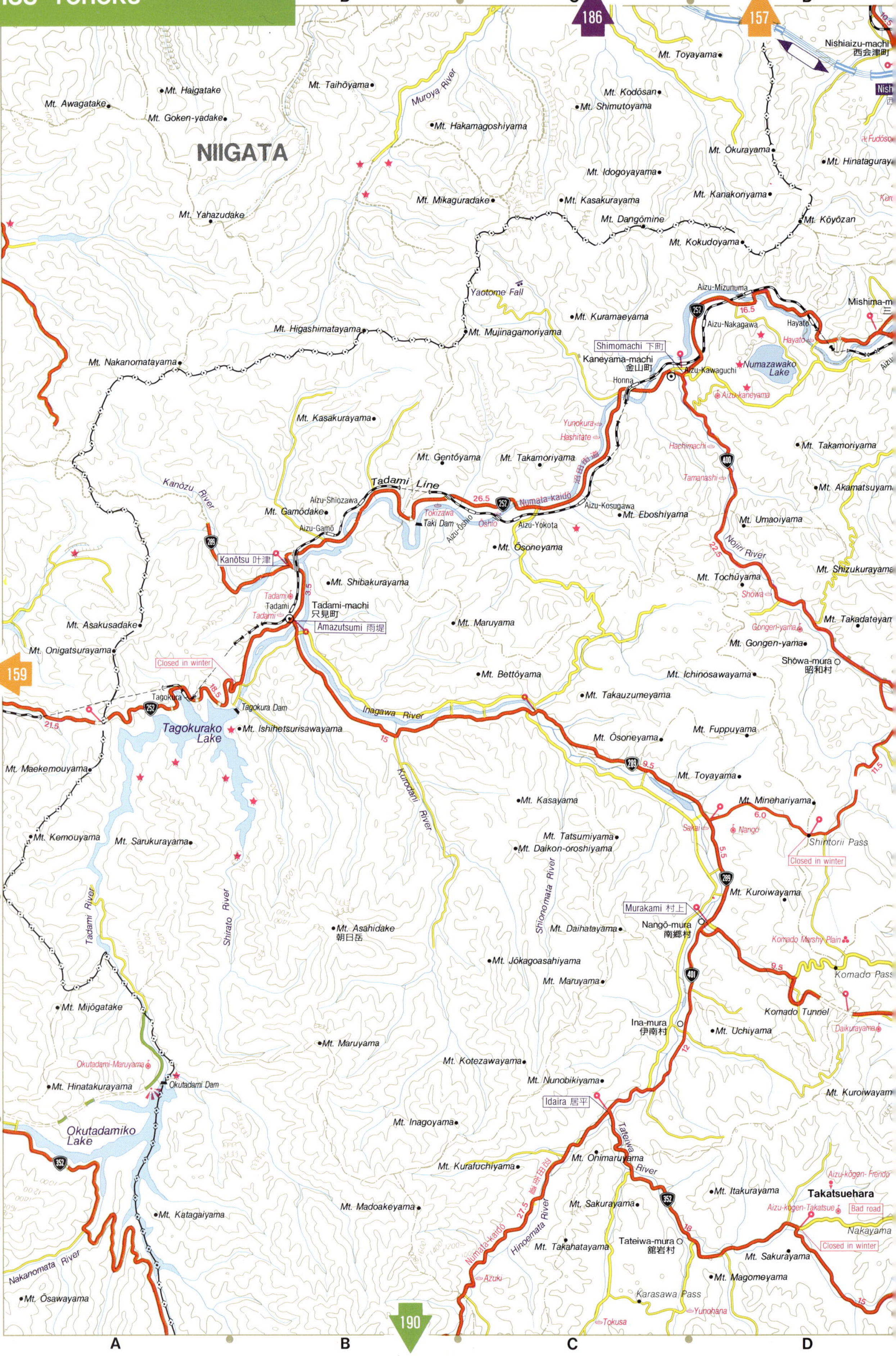
NIIGATA
Mt. Haigatake
Mt. Awagatake
Mt. Goken-yadake
Mt. Taihōyama
Muroya River
Mt. Hakamagoshiyama
Mt. Yahazudake
Mt. Mikaguradake
Mt. Toyayama
Mt. Kodōsan
Mt. Shimutoyama
Mt. Ōkurayama
Mt. Idogoyayama
Mt. Kasakurayama
Mt. Kanakoriyama
Mt. Dangōmine
Mt. Kokudoyama
Mt. Kōyōzan
Mt. Hinataguray
Fudōso
Nishiaizu-machi
西会津町
Yaotome Fall
Mt. Kuramaeyama
Mt. Higashimatayama
Mt. Mujinagamoriyama
Mt. Nakanomatayama
Aizu-Mizunuma
Aizu-Nakagawa
Hayato
Mishima-m
Shimomachi 下町
Kaneyama-machi
金山町
Honna
Aizu-Kawaguchi
Numazawako Lake
Aizu-kaneyama
Mt. Kasakurayama
Yunokura
Hashitate
Hachimachi
Mt. Gentōyama
Mt. Takamoriyama
Mt. Takamoriyama
Tamanashi
Mt. Akamatsuyam
Tadami Line
Kanōzu River
Aizu-Shiozawa
Tokizawa
Numata-kaidō
Aizu-Kosugawa
Mt. Gamōdake
Taki Dam
Aizu-Ōshio
Ōshio
Aizu-Yokota
Mt. Eboshiyama
Mt. Umaoiyama
Aizu-Gamō
Mt. Ōsoneyama
Nojiri River
Kanōtsu 叶津
Mt. Shibakurayama
Mt. Tochūyama
Mt. Shizukurayama
Tadami
Tadami-machi
只見町
Amazutsumi 雨堤
Showa
Mt. Asakusadake
Mt. Maruyama
Gongen-yama
Mt. Takadateyam
Mt. Onigatsurayama
Mt. Gongen-yama
Shōwa-mura
昭和村
Closed in winter
Mt. Bettōyama
Mt. Ichinosawayama
Tagokura
Mt. Takauzumeyama
Tagokura Dam
Inagawa River
Tagokurako Lake
Mt. Ishihetsurisawayama
Mt. Ōsoneyama
Mt. Fuppuyama
Mt. Maekemouyama
Kurodani River
Mt. Toyayama
Mt. Kasayama
Mt. Minehariyama
Sakai
Nango
Shintorii Pass
Closed in winter
Mt. Kemouyama
Mt. Sarukurayama
Mt. Tatsumiyama
Mt. Daikon-oroshiyama
Shionomata River
Mt. Kuroiwayama
Tadami River
Shirato River
Murakami 村上
Nangō-mura
南郷村
Mt. Asahidake
朝日岳
Mt. Daihatayama
Komado Marshy Plain
Mt. Jōkogoasahiyama
Komado Pass
Mt. Maruyama
Mt. Mijōgatake
Komado Tunnel
Ina-mura
伊南村
Mt. Uchiyama
Daikurayama
Mt. Maruyama
Okutadami-Maruyama
Mt. Kotezawayama
Mt. Nunobikiyama
Okutadami Dam
Mt. Hinatakurayama
Idaira 居平
Mt. Kuroiwayam
Okutadamiko Lake
Mt. Inagoyama
Tateiwa River
Mt. Onimaruyama
Mt. Kurafuchiyama
Aizu-kōgen-Frendo
Mt. Itakurayama
Takatsuehara
Mt. Katagaiyama
Mt. Madoakeyama
Mt. Sakurayama
Aizu-kōgen-Takatsue
Bad road
Nakayama
Closed in winter
Hinoemata River
Tateiwa-mura
舘岩村
Mt. Takahatayama
Mt. Sakurayama
Nakanomata River
Numata-kaidō
Azuki
Mt. Magomeyama
Mt. Ōsawayama
Karasawa Pass
Yunohana
Tokusa
A
B
C
D
1
2
3
4
5
6
186
157
159
190

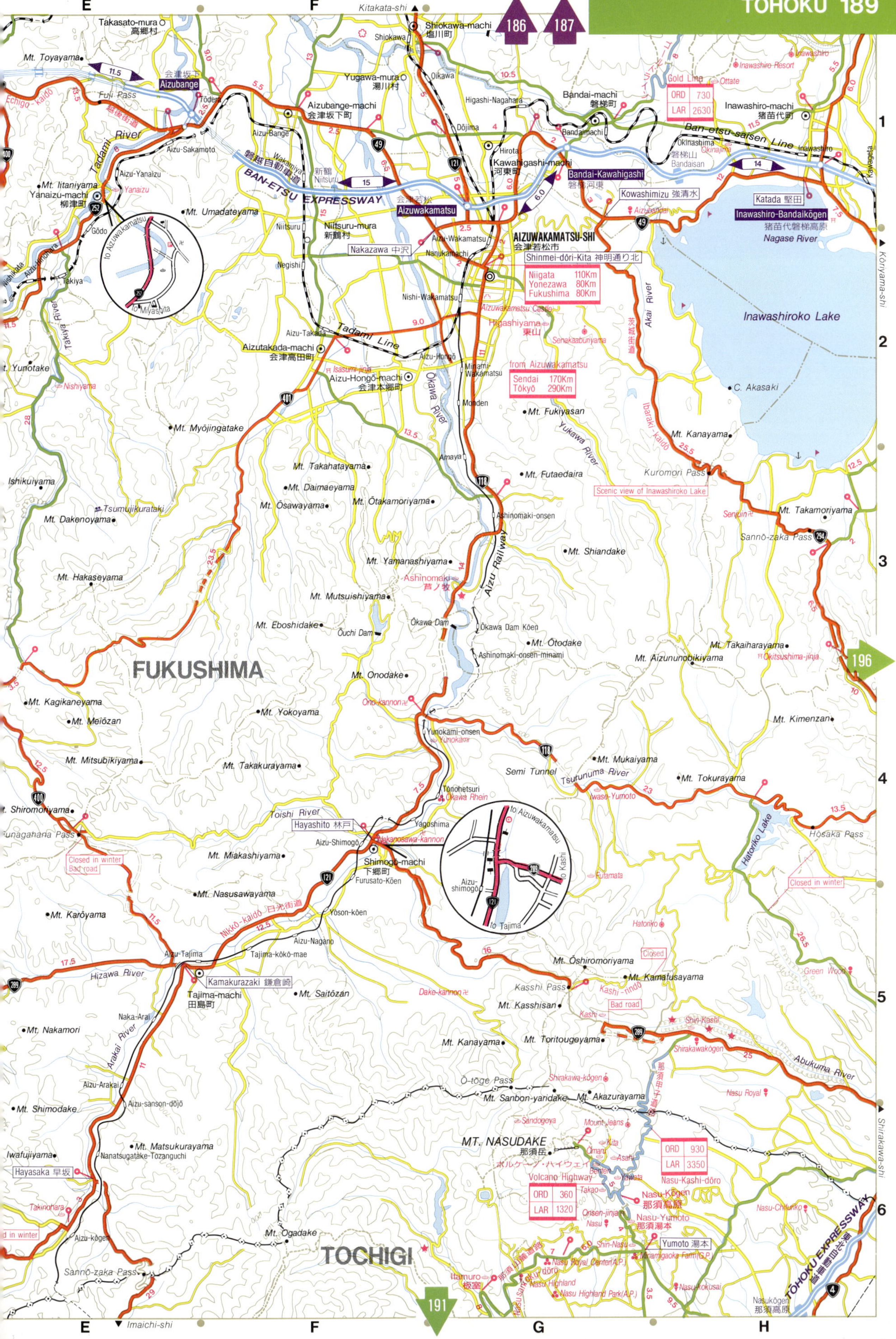

E
F
G
H
1
2
3
4
5
6
186
187
191
196
Kitakata-shi
Kōriyama-shi
Shirakawa-shi
Imaichi-shi
FUKUSHIMA
TOCHIGI
Takasato-mura 高郷村
Mt. Toyayama
Aizubange
Fuji Pass
Echigo-kaidō
Tadami River
Aizu-Sakamoto
Aizu-Yanaizu
Yanaizu-machi 柳津町
Mt. Iitaniyama
Mt. Umadateyama
Takiya
Takiya River
Shiokawa-machi 塩川町
Shiokawa
Oikawa
Yugawa-mura 湯川村
Aizubange-machi 会津坂下町
Higashi-Nagahara
Dōjima
Bandai-machi 磐梯町
Bandaimachi
Gold Line
ORD 730
LAR 2630
Inawashiro-machi 猪苗代町
Inawashiro
Inawashiro Resort
Ottate
Ban-etsu-saisen Line
Okinashima
Bandaisan
Kawagata
Kawahigashi-machi 河東町
Bandai-Kawahigashi
Hirota
Kowashimizu 強清水
Katada 堅田
Inawashiro-Bandaikōgen
Nagase River
BAN-ETSU EXPRESSWAY
Aizuwakamatsu
Niitsuru
Niitsuru-mura 新鶴村
Nakazawa 中沢
AIZUWAKAMATSU-SHI 会津若松市
Shinmei-dōri-Kita 神明通り北
Niigata 110Km
Yonezawa 80Km
Fukushima 80Km
Aizu-Wakamatsu
Nanukamachi
Nishi-Wakamatsu
Negishi
Aizu-Takada
Aizutakada-machi 会津高田町
Tadami Line
Aizu-Hongō
Aizu-Hongō-machi 会津本郷町
Isasumi-jinja
Aizuwakamatsu Castle
Higashiyama 東山
Senakaaburiyama
from Aizuwakamatsu
Sendai 170Km
Tōkyō 290Km
Minami-Wakamatsu
Monden
Ōkawa River
Akai River
Inawashiroko Lake
C. Akasaki
Mt. Fukiyasan
Yukawa River
Ibaraki-kaidō
Mt. Kanayama
Kuromori Pass
Mt. Myōjingatake
Mt. Takahatayama
Mt. Daimaeyama
Mt. Ōsawayama
Mt. Ōtakamoriyama
Amaya
Mt. Futaedaira
Scenic view of Inawashiroko Lake
Senjuin
Mt. Takamoriyama
Sannō-zaka Pass
Ishikuiyama
Tsumujikurataki
Mt. Dakenoyama
Ashinomaki-onsen
Mt. Shiandake
Mt. Hakaseyama
Mt. Yamanashiyama
Ashinomaki 芦ノ牧
Aizu Railway
Mt. Mutsuishiyama
Mt. Eboshidake
Ōuchi Dam
Ōkawa Dam
Ōkawa Dam Kōen
Mt. Otodake
Ashinomaki-onsen-minami
Mt. Takaiharayama
Mt. Aizununobikiyama
Okitsushima-jinja
Mt. Onodake
Ono-kannon
Mt. Kagikaneyama
Mt. Meiōzan
Mt. Yokoyama
Yunokami-onsen
Yunokami
Mt. Kimenzan
Mt. Mitsubikiyama
Mt. Takakurayama
Semi Tunnel
Tsurunuma River
Mt. Mukaiyama
Mt. Tokurayama
Iwase-Yumoto
Tōnohetsuri
Ōkawa Rhein
Shiromoriyama
Funagahana Pass
Toishi River
Hayashito 林戸
Yagoshima
Nakanosawa-kannon
Aizu-Shimogō
Shimogō-machi 下郷町
Furusato-Kōen
to Aizuwakamatsu
to Kashi
to Tajima
Hatoriko Lake
Hōsaka Pass
Closed in winter
Bad road
Mt. Miakashiyama
Futamata
Mt. Nasusawayama
Yoson-kōen
Mt. Karōyama
Nikkō-kaidō 日光街道
Aizu-Nagano
Tajima-kōkō-mae
Aizu-Tajima
Hatoriko
Closed
Mt. Ōshiromoriyama
Hizawa River
Kamakurazaki 鎌倉崎
Tajima-machi 田島町
Mt. Saitōzan
Dake-kannon
Kasshi Pass
Kashi-rindō
Mt. Kamafusayama
Mt. Kasshisan
Green Wood
Naka-Arai
Arakai River
Mt. Nakamori
Kashi
Shin-Kashi
Mt. Kanayama
Mt. Toritougeyama
Shirakawakōgen
Abukuma River
Aizu-Arakai
Ō-tōge Pass
Shirakawa-kōgen
Mt. Sanbon-yaridake
Mt. Akazurayama
Nasu Royal
Aizu-sanson-dōjō
Mt. Shimodake
Sandogoya
Mount Jeans
MT. NASUDAKE 那須岳
Kita
Ōmaru
Asahi
Mt. Matsukurayama
Nanatsugatake-Tozanguchi
Iwafujiyama
ORD 930
LAR 3350
Nasu-Kashi-dōro
Hayasaka 早坂
Volcano Highway
ORD 360
LAR 1320
Benten
Yawata
Takao
Nasu-Kōgen 那須高原
Onsen-jinja
Nasu
Nasu-Yumoto 那須湯本
Nasu-Chifuriko
Takinohara
Yumoto 湯本
Aizu-kōgen
Mt. Ogadake
Shin-Nasu
Nasu Royal Center(A.P.)
Minamigaoka Farm(G.P.)
Sannō-zaka Pass
Itamuro 板室
Nasu Highland
Nasu Highland Park(A.P.)
Nasu-Kokusai
TŌHOKU EXPRESSWAY
Nasukōgen 那須高原

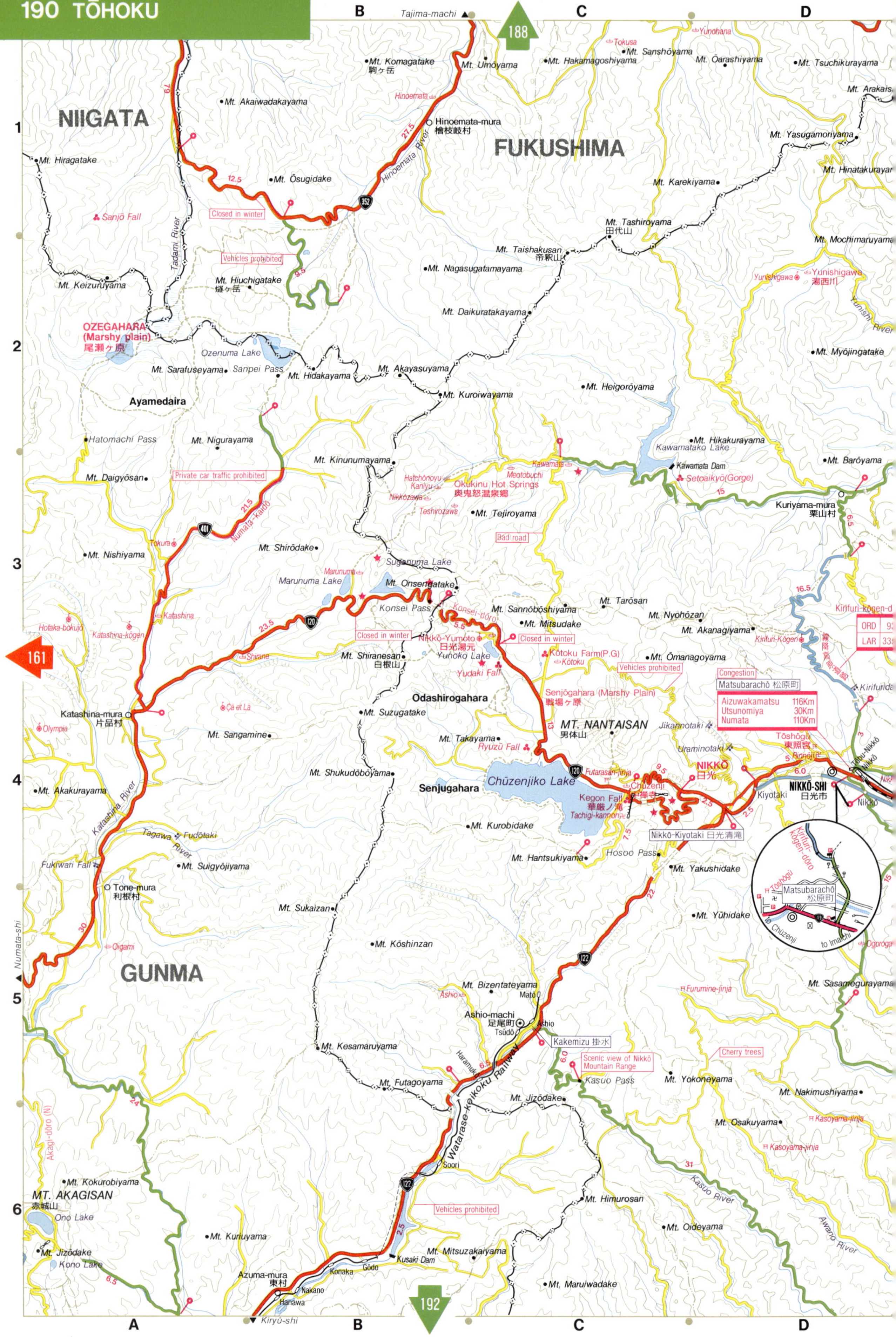
B
C
D
Tajima-machi
188
NIIGATA
FUKUSHIMA
GUNMA
Mt. Komagatake
駒ヶ岳
Mt. Umoyama
Mt. Hakamagoshiyama
Tokusa
Mt. Sanshōyama
Yunohana
Mt. Ōarashiyama
Mt. Tsuchikurayama
Mt. Arakais
Mt. Akaiwadakayama
Hinoemata
Hinoemata-mura
檜枝岐村
Hinoemata River
Mt. Yasugamoriyama
Mt. Hinatakurayar
Mt. Hiragatake
Mt. Ōsugidake
Mt. Karekiyama
Closed in winter
Sanjō Fall
Tadami River
Mt. Tashiroyama
田代山
Mt. Mochimaruyama
Vehicles prohibited
Mt. Taishakusan
帝釈山
Mt. Nagasugatamayama
Yunishigawa
Yunishigawa
湯西川
Mt. Keizuruyama
Mt. Hiuchigatake
燧ヶ岳
Mt. Daikuratakayama
Yunishi River
OZEGAHARA
(Marshy plain)
尾瀬ヶ原
Ozenuma Lake
Mt. Myōjingatake
Mt. Sarafuseyama
Sanpei Pass
Mt. Hidakayama
Mt. Akayasuyama
Mt. Kuroiwayama
Mt. Heigorōyama
Ayamedaira
Hatomachi Pass
Mt. Niguraya ma
Mt. Hikakurayama
Kawamatako Lake
Kawamata Dam
Mt. Barōyama
Mt. Kinunumayama
Private car traffic prohibited
Mt. Daigyōsan
Hatchōnoyu
Kaniyu
Meotobuchi
Kawamata
Okukinu Hot Springs
奥鬼怒温泉郷
Setoaikyō(Gorge)
Nikkozawa
Teshirozawa
Mt. Tejiroyama
Kuriyama-mura
栗山村
Numata-kaidō
Tokura
Bad road
Mt. Nishiyama
Mt. Shirōdake
Sugenuma Lake
Marunuma
Marunuma Lake
Mt. Onsengatake
Konsei Pass
Konsei-dōro
Mt. Sannōbōshiyama
Mt. Tarōsan
Mt. Nyohōzan
Kinfuri-kōgen-d
Katashina
Mt. Mitsudake
Mt. Akanagiyama
Hotaka-bokujo
Katashina-kōgen
Closed in winter
Nikkō-Yumoto
日光湯元
Yunoko Lake
Closed in winter
Kirifuri-kōgen
ORD
LAR
161
Shirane
Mt. Shiranesan
白根山
Yudaki Fall
Kōtoku Farm(P.G)
Kōtoku
Mt. Ōmanagoyama
Vehicles prohibited
Congestion
Matsubarachō 松原町
Kirifuri
Senjōgahara (Marshy Plain)
戦場ヶ原
Aizuwakamatsu 116Km
Utsunomiya 30Km
Numata 110Km
Katashina-mura
片品村
Ca et La
Odashirogahara
Mt. Suzugatake
Olympia
Mt. Sangamine
MT. NANTAISAN
男体山
Jikannotaki
Tōshōgū
東照宮
Mt. Takayama
Ryūzū Fall
Uraminotaki
Rinnōji
Tōbu-Nikkō
Mt. Shukudōbōyama
Futarasan-jinja
Chūzenji
NIKKŌ
日光
Mt. Akakurayama
Senjugahara
Chūzenjiko Lake
Kegon Fall
華厳ノ滝
Tachigi-kannon
Kiyotaki
NIKKŌ-SHI
日光市
Nikkō
Katashina River
Mt. Kurobidake
Nikkō-Kiyotaki 日光清滝
Tagawa River
Fudōtaki
Fukiwari Fall
Mt. Suigyōjiyama
Mt. Hantsukiyama
Hosoo Pass
Mt. Yakushidake
Tone-mura
利根村
Kirifuri-kōgen-dōro
Tōshōgū
Matsubarachō
松原町
to Chūzenji
to Imaichi
Mt. Sukaizan
Mt. Yūhidake
Numata-shi
Oigami
Mt. Kōshinzan
Ogprog
GUNMA
Mt. Bizentateyama
Matō
Furumine-jinja
Mt. Sasameguraya ma
Ashio
Ashio-machi
足尾町
Tsūdō
Ashio
Kakemizu 掛水
Mt. Kesamaruyama
Haramuki
Watarase-keikoku Railway
Scenic view of Nikkō Mountain Range
Kasuo Pass
Cherry trees
Mt. Futagoyama
Mt. Yokoneyama
Mt. Nakimushiyama
Mt. Jizōdake
Mt. Osakuyama
Kasoyama-jinja
Akagi-dōro (N)
Kasoyama-jinja
Soori
Kasuo River
Mt. Kokurobiyama
MT. AKAGISAN
赤城山
Mt. Himurosan
Ono Lake
Vehicles prohibited
Awano River
Mt. Oideyama
Mt. Kuruyama
Mt. Jizōdake
Mt. Mitsuzakaiyama
Kono Lake
Kusaki Dam
Azuma-mura
東村
Konaka
Gōdo
Nakano
Hanawa
Mt. Maruiwadake
192
Kiryū-shi
A
B
C
D
1
2
3
4
5
6

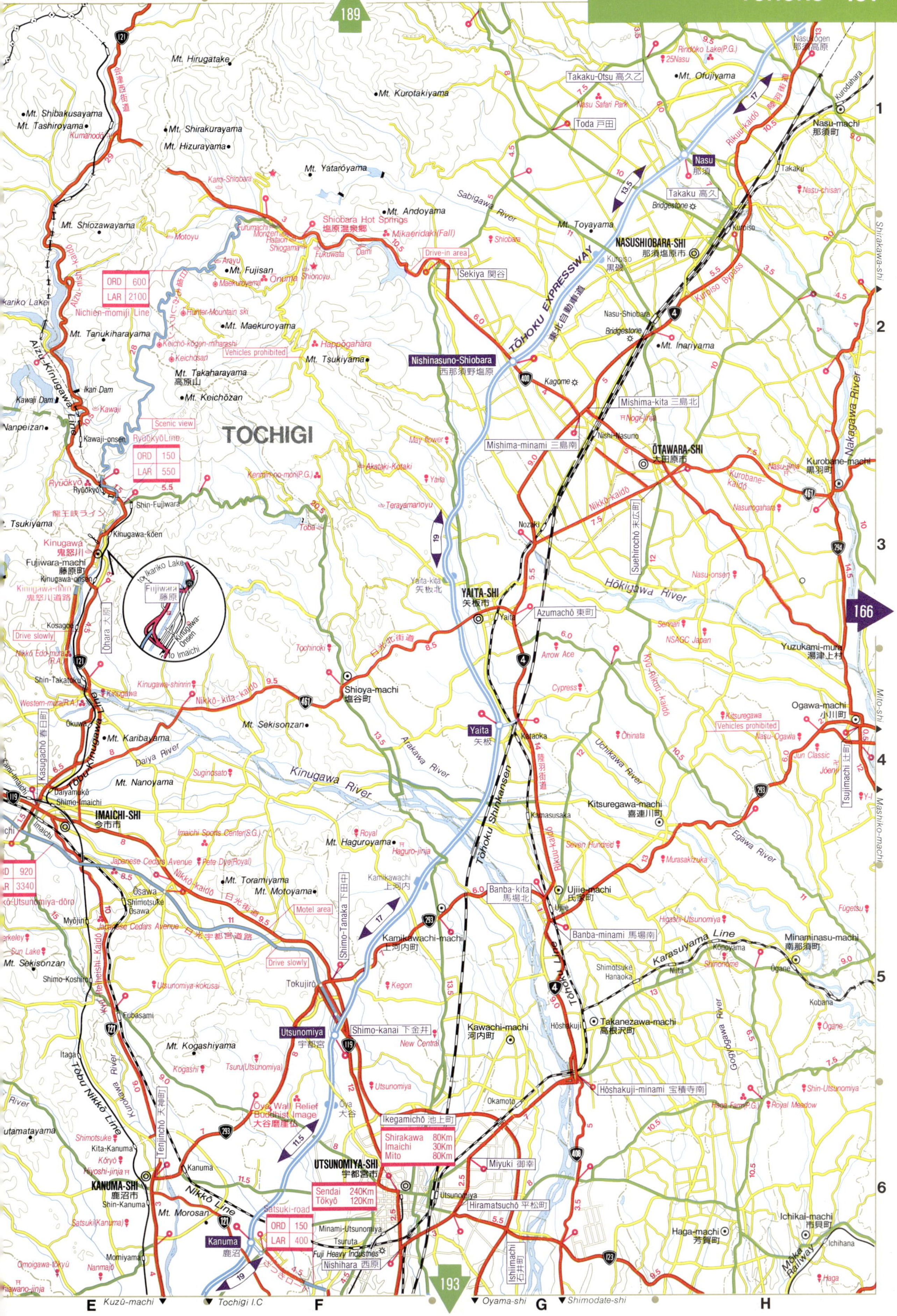
TOCHIGI
TŌHOKU EXPRESSWAY
東北自動車道
Tōhoku Shinkansen
Tōhoku Line
Nikkō Line
Tobu Nikkō Line
Karasuyama Line
Aizu-Kinugawa Line
NASUSHIOBARA-SHI
那須塩原市
ŌTAWARA-SHI
大田原市
YAITA-SHI
矢板市
IMAICHI-SHI
今市市
UTSUNOMIYA-SHI
宇都宮市
KANUMA-SHI
鹿沼市
Nasu-machi
那須町
Kurobane-machi
黒羽町
Yuzukami-mura
湯津上村
Ogawa-machi
小川町
Shioya-machi
塩谷町
Fujiwara-machi
藤原町
Kitsuregawa-machi
喜連川町
Ujiie-machi
氏家町
Kamikawachi-machi
上河内町
Kawachi-machi
河内町
Takanezawa-machi
高根沢町
Minaminasu-machi
南那須町
Haga-machi
芳賀町
Ichikai-machi
市貝町
Nishinasuno-Shiobara
西那須野塩原
Nasu
那須
Yaita
矢板
Utsunomiya
宇都宮
Kanuma
鹿沼
Takaku-Otsu 高久乙
Toda 戸田
Takaku 高久
Sekiya 関谷
Mishima-kita 三島北
Mishima-minami 三島南
Azumachō 東町
Banba-kita 馬場北
Banba-minami 馬場南
Shimo-kanai 下金井
Hōshakuji-minami 宝積寺南
Ikegamichō 池上町
Miyuki 御幸
Hiramatsuchō 平松町
Nishihara 西原
Shiobara Hot Springs
塩原温泉郷
Mt. Hirugatake
Mt. Kurotakiyama
Mt. Shibakusayama
Mt. Tashiroyama
Mt. Shirakurayama
Mt. Hizurayama
Mt. Yatarōyama
Mt. Andoyama
Mt. Shiozawayama
Mt. Fujisan
Mt. Tanukiharayama
Mt. Maekuroyama
Mt. Tsukiyama
Mt. Takaharayama
高原山
Mt. Keichōzan
Mt. Toyayama
Mt. Ofujiyama
Mt. Inariyama
Mt. Sekisonzan
Mt. Karibayama
Mt. Nanoyama
Mt. Haguroyama
Mt. Toramiyama
Mt. Motoyama
Mt. Kogashiyama
Mt. Morosan
Sabigawa River
Hōkigawa River
Nakagawa River
Kinugawa River
Daiya River
Arakawa River
Uchikawa River
Egawa River
Gogyōgawa River
Kurokawa River
ORD 600
LAR 2100
ORD 150
LAR 550
ORD 150
LAR 400
ORD 920
LAR 3340
Sendai 240Km
Tōkyō 120Km
Shirakawa 80Km
Imaichi 30Km
Mito 80Km
Drive-in area
Vehicles prohibited
Scenic view
Drive slowly
Motel area
189
166
193
E
F
G
H
1
2
3
4
5
6
Kuzū-machi
Tochigi I.C
Oyama-shi
Shimodate-shi
Shirakawa-shi
Mito-shi
Mashiko-machi

190
194
163
TOCHIGI
GUNMA
SAITAMA
Kurohone-mura 黒保根村
Watarase-keikoku Railway
Mt. Tadakayama
Mt. Takadoyayama
Mt. Ōdoyayama
Mt. Mitsumineyama
Ōkoshiji Pass 大越路峠
Oikoeji Pass 老越路峠
Ōmama-machi 大間々町
Niisato-mura 新里村
Mt. Azumasan
Jōmō Railway
KIRYŪ-SHI 桐生市
Fujisaka Pass 藤坂峠
Kasakake-machi 笠懸町
Kuzuu-machi 葛生町
Tanuma-machi 田沼町
Hirosawa 4 広沢4
Ryōmō Line
Tōbu Kiryū Line
Isesaki 伊勢崎
Yabuzukahon-machi 藪塚本町
ASHIKAGA-SHI 足利市
Tadakari 只上
Yasuraoka 安良岡
Minami-Ōmachi 南大町
Horigomechō 堀込町
ISESAKI-SHI 伊勢崎市
Nitta-machi 新田町
SANO-SHI 佐野市
Sano-Fujioka 佐野藤岡
ŌTA-SHI 太田市
Tōbu Isesaki Line
Takabayashi 高林
Ōra-machi 邑楽町
Fujioka-machi 藤岡町
HONJŌ-SHI 本庄市
Ojima-machi 尾島町
Ōizumi-machi 大泉町
TATEBAYASHI-SHI 館林市
Narushima 成島
Tatebayashi 館林
Itakura-machi 板倉町
Menuma-machi 妻沼町
Meiwa-machi 明和町
Chiyoda-machi 千代田町
Fukayachō 深谷町
FUKAYA-SHI 深谷市
Okabe-machi 岡部町
TOHOKU EXPRESSWAY
Kubojima 久保島
Dai 代
Minami-kawara-mura 南河原村
HANYŪ-SHI 羽生市
Hanyū 羽生
Keisatsusho mae 警察署前
Takasaki Line
Chichibu Railway
KUMAGAYA-SHI 熊谷市
Kamakurachō 鎌倉町
KAZO-SHI 加須市
Hanazono-machi 花園町
Kawamoto-machi 川本町
Hanazono 花園
Kōnan-machi 江南町
Sayada 佐谷田
Mochida 持田
GYŌDA-SHI 行田市
Shidami 志多見
Kazo 加須
KAN-ETSU EXPRESSWAY
Yorii-machi 寄居町
Ōsato-machi 大里町
Fukiage-machi 吹上町
Kawasato-machi 川里町
Kisai-machi 騎西町
Hachikō Line
Ranzan-Ogawa 嵐山小川
Namegawa-machi 滑川町
Arakawa River
KŌNOSU-SHI 鴻巣市
Higashichichibu-mura 東秩父村
Ogawa-machi 小川町
Higashidaira 東平
HIGASHIMATSUYAMA-SHI 東松山市
Tobu Tōjō Line
Shōbu-machi 菖蒲町
Kuki 久喜
Ōtsuka 大塚
Ranzan-machi 嵐山町
Higashimatsuyama 東松山
Yoshimi-machi 吉見町
Honchō 本町
KITAMOTO-SHI 北本市
Nakasendō 中山道
Mt. Dōdairasan
Tamagawa-mura 玉川村
Kuruwa 曲輪
Tokigawa-mura 都幾川村
Mt. Monomiyama
OKEGAWA-SHI 桶川市
Ina-machi 伊奈町
Hatoyama-machi 鳩山町
Takasaka 高坂
Kawajima-machi 川島町
AGEO-SHI 上尾市
Kawagoe-shi
Ōmiya-shi
A
B
C
D
1
2
3
4
5
6

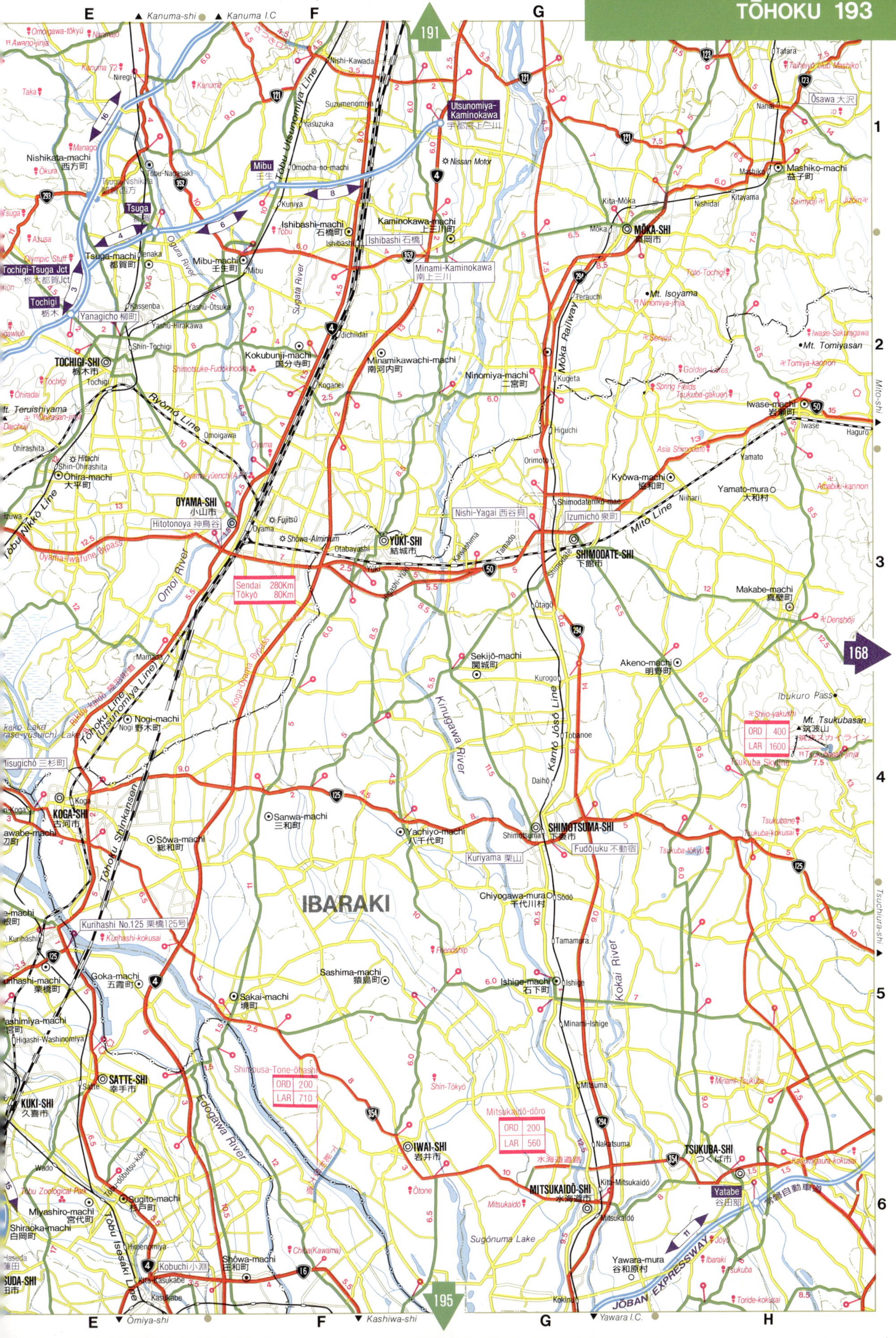

E
F
G
H
191
195
168
1
2
3
4
5
6
Kanuma-shi
Kanuma I.C
Ōmiya-shi
Kashiwa-shi
Yawara I.C.
Mito-shi
Tsuchiura-shi
Utsunomiya-Kaminokawa
宇都宮上三川
Nissan Motor
Mibu
壬生
Tsuga
Tochigi-Tsuga Jct
栃木都賀Jct
Tochigi
栃木
Yanagichō 柳町
Nishikata-machi
西方町
Tsuga-machi
都賀町
Mibu-machi
壬生町
Ishibashi-machi
石橋町
Ishibashi 石橋
Kaminokawa-machi
上三川町
Minami-Kaminokawa
南上三川
Tōbu Utsunomiya Line
Sugata River
Ogura River
TOCHIGI-SHI
栃木市
Kokubunji-machi
国分寺町
Minamikawachi-machi
南河内町
Ninomiya-machi
二宮町
MŌKA-SHI
真岡市
Mashiko-machi
益子町
Ōsawa 大沢
Mt. Isoyama
Mt. Tomiyasan
Iwase-machi
岩瀬町
Mōka Railway
Ryōmō Line
Tōbu Nikkō Line
Ōhira-machi
大平町
OYAMA-SHI
小山市
Hitotonoya 神鳥谷
Fujitsū
Shōwa-Aluminum
YŪKI-SHI
結城市
Nishi-Yagai 西谷貝
Izumichō 泉町
SHIMODATE-SHI
下館市
Mito Line
Kyōwa-machi
協和町
Yamato-mura
大和村
Makabe-machi
真壁町
Sendai 280Km
Tōkyō 80Km
Omoi River
Koga-Oyama Bypass
Sekijō-machi
関城町
Akeno-machi
明野町
Ibukuro Pass
Mt. Tsukubasan
筑波山
ORD 400
LAR 1600
Tsukuba Skyline
Kinugawa River
Kantō Jōsō Line
Nogi-machi
野木町
Tōhoku Line (Utsunomiya Line)
Tōhoku Shinkansen
KOGA-SHI
古河市
Sanwa-machi
三和町
Sōwa-machi
総和町
Yachiyo-machi
八千代町
SHIMOTSUMA-SHI
下妻市
Fudōjuku 不動宿
Kuriyama 栗山
IBARAKI
Chiyogawa-mura
千代川村
Kokai River
Kurihashi No.125 栗橋125号
Goka-machi
五霞町
Sashima-machi
猿島町
Ishige-machi
石下町
Sakai-machi
境町
SATTE-SHI
幸手市
KUKI-SHI
久喜市
Shimōsa-Tone-ōhashi
ORD 200
LAR 710
Edogawa River
IWAI-SHI
岩井市
Mitsukaidō-dōro
ORD 200
LAR 560
水海道道路
MITSUKAIDŌ-SHI
水海道市
TSUKUBA-SHI
つくば市
Yatabe
谷田部
常磐自動車道
JŌBAN EXPRESSWAY
Yawara-mura
谷和原村
Sugōnuma Lake
Sugito-machi
杉戸町
Miyashiro-machi
宮代町
Shiraoka-machi
白岡町
Shōwa-machi
庄和町
Kobuchi 小渕
Tōbu Isesaki Line
Tobu Zoological Park

SAITAMA
TŌKYŌ
KANAGAWA
KAN-ETSU EXPRESSWAY
CHŪŌ EXPRESSWAY
TŌMEI EXPRESSWAY
SAKADO-SHI 坂戸市
TSURUGASHIMA-SHI 鶴ヶ島市
Tsurugashima
Tsurugashima Jct
KAWAGOE-SHI 川越市
Kawagoe
AGEO-SHI 上尾市
Kawajima-machi 川島町
Ogose-machi 越生町
Moroyama-machi 毛呂山町
HIDAKA-SHI 日高市
HANNŌ-SHI 飯能市
SAYAMA-SHI 狭山市
IRUMA-SHI 入間市
KAMIFUKUOKA-SHI 上福岡市
FUJIMI-SHI 富士見市
SHIKI-SHI 志木市
Miyoshi-machi 三芳町
TOKOROZAWA-SHI 所沢市
Tokorozawa
NIIZA-SHI 新座市
ASAKA-SHI 朝霞市
WAKŌ-SHI 和光市
Wakō
Wakō-kita
Toda-higashi
Toda-nishi
Nerima
Ōizumi
KIYOSE-SHI 清瀬市
HIGASHIMURAYAMA-SHI 東村山市
HIGASHIKURUME-SHI 東久留米市
NISHITŌKYŌ-SHI 西東京市
ŌME-SHI 青梅市
HAMURA-SHI 羽村市
Mizuho-machi 瑞穂町
MUSASHIMURAYAMA-SHI 武蔵村山市
HIGASHIYAMATO-SHI 東大和市
FUSSA-SHI 福生市
AKIRUNO-SHI あきる野市
Hinode-machi 日の出町
KODAIRA-SHI 小平市
KOKUBUNJI-SHI 国分寺市
TACHIKAWA-SHI 立川市
AKISHIMA-SHI 昭島市
KUNITACHI-SHI 国立市
KOGANEI-SHI 小金井市
MUSASHINO-SHI 武蔵野市
MITAKA-SHI 三鷹市
FUCHŪ-SHI 府中市
CHŌFU-SHI 調布市
Chōfu
Takaido
HACHIŌJI-SHI 八王子市
Hachiōji
Kunitachi-Fuchū
Inagi
HINO-SHI 日野市
TAMA-SHI 多摩市
INAGI-SHI 稲城市
KOMAE-SHI 狛江市
Tōkyō
Sagamiko-higashi
Sagamiko-machi 相模湖町
Shiroyama-machi 城山町
Tsukui-machi 津久井町
Aikawa-machi 愛川町
Kiyokawa-mura 清川村
SAGAMIHARA-SHI 相模原市
MACHIDA-SHI 町田市
Tōmei-Kawasaki
Yokohama-Aoba
Yokohama-Machida
ZAMA-SHI 座間市
YAMATO-SHI 大和市
ATSUGI-SHI 厚木市
EBINA-SHI 海老名市
AYASE-SHI 綾瀬市
Sagami River
Arakawa River
Iruma River
Tamagawa River
Nakatsu River
ORD 200
LAR 730
ORD 250
LAR 940
19.5
9.0
7.5
7
2
9.5
12
15.5
6.5
5.5
Mt. Ōyama 大山
Atsugi-shi
Atsugi I.C
Kumagaya-shi
Chichibu-shi
Ōtsuki-shi
163
153
192
142
143
A
B
C
D
1
2
3
4
5
6

E
F
G
H
1
2
3
4
5
6
193
170
143
172
Sugito-machi
Kimitsu-shi
Sawara-shi
Tōgane-shi
IBARAKI
CHIBA
TŌKYŌ-WAN
東京湾
IWATSUKI-SHI
岩槻市
KASUKABE-SHI
春日部市
NODA-SHI
野田市
MORIYA-SHI
守谷市
Ina-machi
伊奈町
Yawara
谷和原
Ushikunuma Lake
Fujishiro-machi
藤代町
TORIDE-SHI
取手市
Kokudō No. 294iriguchi
国道294号入口
Yanagisawa 柳沢
Shimomakuri 下間久里
Matsubushi-machi
松伏町
KOSHIGAYA-SHI
越谷市
YOSHIKAWA-SHI
吉川市
Kashiwa
JŌBAN EXPRESSWAY
常磐自動車道
Nedo 根戸
KASHIWA-SHI
柏市
Yobatsuka 呼塚
Nagareyama
NAGAREYAMA-SHI
流山市
ABIKO-SHI
我孫子市
Narita Line
Teganuma Lake
Shōnan-machi
沼南町
Ōshimada 大島田
INZAI-SHI
印西市
SHIROI-SHI
白井市
Shiroi 白井
Hokusō Railway
Shimofusa Airport
TŌHOKU EXPRESSWAY
Urawa
Iwatsuki
Musashino Line
Kawaguchi-chūō
Kawaguchi-higashi
TOKYO GAIKAN EXPRESSWAY
東京外環自動車道
Kawaguchi-nishi
Gaikan-Urawa
HATOGAYA-SHI
鳩ケ谷市
Sōka
Gaikan-Misato-nishi
外環三郷西
Misato
MISATO-SHI
三郷市
SŌKA-SHI
草加市
YASHIO-SHI
八潮市
WARABI-SHI
蕨市
TODA-SHI
戸田市
KAWAGUCHI-SHI
川口市
MATSUDO-SHI
松戸市
KAMAGAYA-SHI
鎌ケ谷市
YACHIYO-SHI
八千代市
Adachi-ku
足立区
Kita-ku
北区
Arakawa-ku
荒川区
Katsushika-ku
葛飾区
Nishi-sugamo 西巣鴨
ICHIKAWA-SHI
市川市
Tōyō-kōsoku Railway
Shimoichiba
下市場
Toshima-ku
豊島区
Bunkyō-ku
文京区
Taitō-ku
台東区
Edogawa-ku
江戸川区
Shinjuku-ku
新宿区
Chiyoda-ku
千代田区
Sumida-ku
墨田区
Wangan-Ichikawa
湾岸市川
Higashi-Komatsugawa 東小松川
Keiyō Line
FUNABASHI-SHI
船橋市
NARASHINO-SHI
習志野市
HIGASHI-KANTŌ EXPRESSWAY
東関東自動車道
Miyanogi Jct
Chūō-ku
中央区
Kōtō-ku
江東区
Shibuya-ku
渋谷区
Minato-ku
港区
URAYASU-SHI
浦安市
Tōkyō Disneyresort(A.P.)
東京ディズニーリゾート
Wangan-Narashino
Wangan-Chiba
Chiba-kita
Meguro-ku
目黒区
Shinagawa-ku
品川区
International Exhibition Center
Museum of Maritime Science
Arakawa River
Mihama-ku
Inage Seashore Park(R.A.)
Nobuto 登戸
CHIBA-SHI
千葉市
Chūō-ku 中央区
Ōta-ku
大田区
Ōmori 大森
Tōkyō International(Haneda)
Ocean tōkyū(to Tokushima,Shin-Moji)
Shōsen-Mitsui Ferry(to Tomakomai)
Yōrōgawa River
Yawatakaigan-dōri 八幡海岸通
Kawasaki-ku
川崎区
KAWASAKI-SHI
川崎市
Tamagawa River
Ube Industries
Mitsui Petrochemical Industries
Idemitsu Kōsan
Sumitomo Chemical
Ichihara
ICHIHARA-SHI
市原市
TATEYAMA EXPRESSWAY
館山自動車道
Uchibo Line
Kominato Railway
Tōkyō-wan Aqua-Line
東京湾アクアライン
Umihotaru
海ほたる
Marine Express(to Miyazaki etc)
Nissan Motor
Mitsubishi Oil
YOKOHAMA-SHI

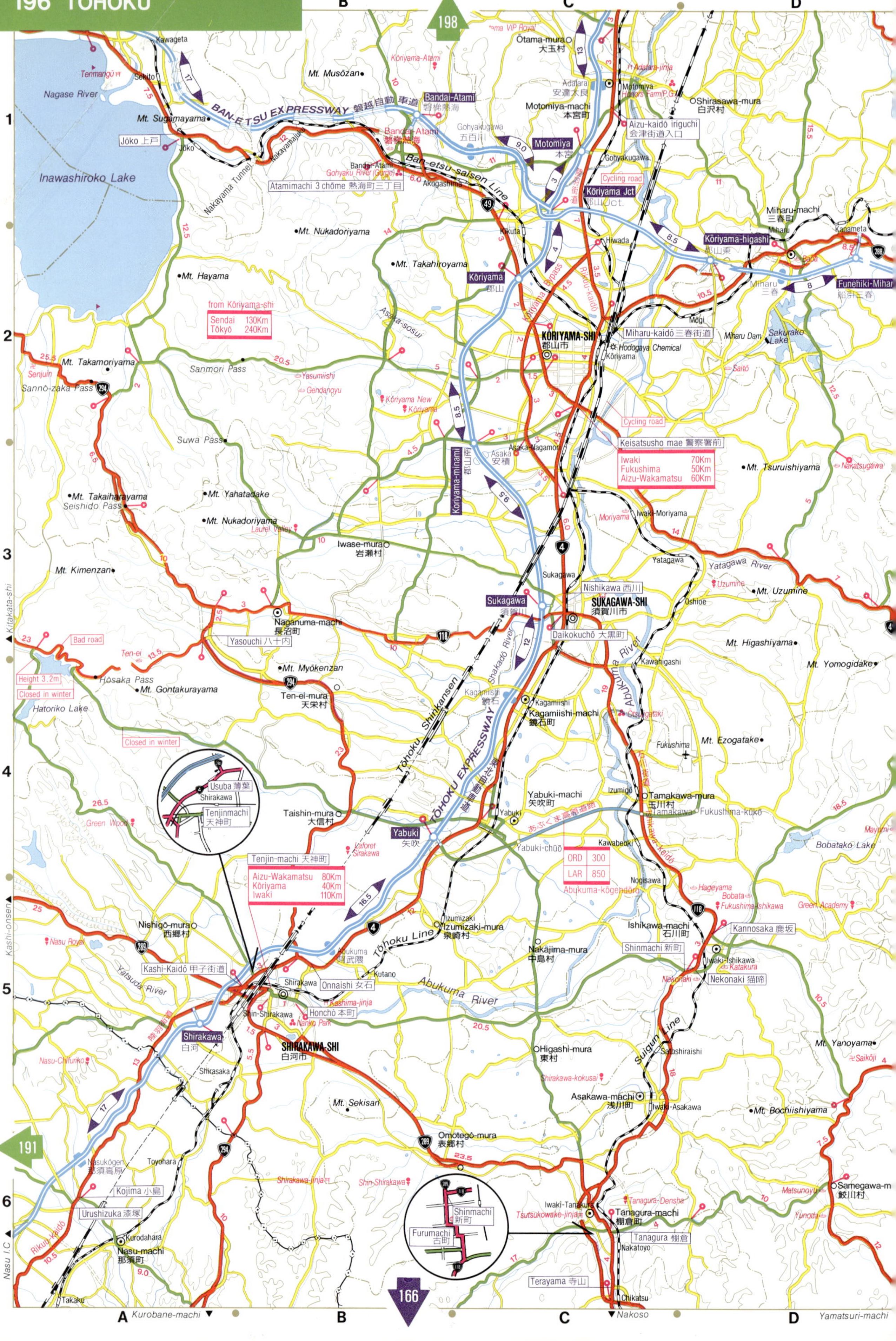
198
191
166
Inawashiroko Lake
Nagase River
Mt. Sugamayama
Jōko 上戸
BAN-ETSU EXPRESSWAY 磐越自動車道
Bandai-Atami
Mt. Musōzan
Ban-etsu-saisen Line
Atamimachi 3 chōme 熱海町三丁目
Mt. Nukadoriyama
Mt. Hayama
Mt. Takahiroyama
Kōriyama 郡山
from Kōriyama-shi
Sendai 130Km
Tōkyō 240Km
Ōtama-mura 大玉村
Motomiya-machi 本宮町
Motomiya 本宮
Aizu-kaidō iriguchi 会津街道入口
Shirasawa-mura 白沢村
Kōriyama Jct 郡山Jct.
Cycling road
Kōriyama-higashi 郡山東
Miharu-machi 三春町
Funehiki-Miharu 船引三春
KŌRIYAMA-SHI 郡山市
Miharu-kaidō 三春街道
Hodogaya Chemical
Miharu Dam
Sakurako Lake
Mt. Takamoriyama
Sannō-zaka Pass
Sanmori Pass
Suwa Pass
Kōriyama-minami 郡山南
Asaka 安積
Keisatsusho mae 警察署前
Iwaki 70Km
Fukushima 50Km
Aizu-Wakamatsu 60Km
Mt. Tsuruishiyama
Mt. Takaiharayama
Seishido Pass
Mt. Yahatadake
Mt. Nukadoriyama
Laurel Valley
Iwase-mura 岩瀬村
Mt. Kimenzan
Iwaki-Moriyama
Yatagawa River
Mt. Uzumine
Sukagawa 須賀川
Nishikawa 西川
SUKAGAWA-SHI 須賀川市
Daikokuchō 大黒町
Naganuma-machi 長沼町
Yasouchi 八十内
Bad road
Height 3.2m
Closed in winter
Hōsaka Pass
Mt. Gontakurayama
Hatoriko Lake
Mt. Myōkenzan
Ten-ei-mura 天栄村
Mt. Higashiyama
Mt. Yomogidake
Kagamiishi-machi 鏡石町
Abukuma River
Mt. Ezogatake
Tōhoku Shinkansen
TŌHOKU EXPRESSWAY
Usuba 薄葉
Tenjinmachi 天神町
Taishin-mura 大信村
Yabuki 矢吹
Yabuki-machi 矢吹町
Tamakawa-mura 玉川村
Fukushima-kūkō
Bobatako Lake
Tenjin-machi 天神町
Aizu-Wakamatsu 80Km
Kōriyama 40Km
Iwaki 110Km
ORD 300
LAR 850
Abukuma-kōgendōro
Nishigō-mura 西郷村
Izumizaki-mura 泉崎村
Tōhoku Line
Ishikawa-machi 石川町
Kannosaka 鹿坂
Shinmachi 新町
Nakajima-mura 中島村
Kashi-Kaidō 甲子街道
Yatsuda River
Onnaishi 女石
Honchō 本町
Nekonaki 猫啼
Shirakawa 白河
SHIRAKAWA-SHI 白河市
Higashi-mura 東村
Suigun Line
Mt. Yanoyama
Mt. Sekisan
Asakawa-machi 浅川町
Mt. Bochiishiyama
Omotegō-mura 表郷村
Nasukōgen 那須高原
Kojima 小島
Urushizuka 漆塚
Nasu-machi 那須町
Shinmachi 新町
Furumachi 古町
Tanagura-machi 棚倉町
Tanagura 棚倉
Samegawa-mura 鮫川村
Terayama 寺山
Kurobane-machi
Nakoso
Yamatsuri-machi
Kitakata-shi
Kashi-onsen
Nasu I.C.

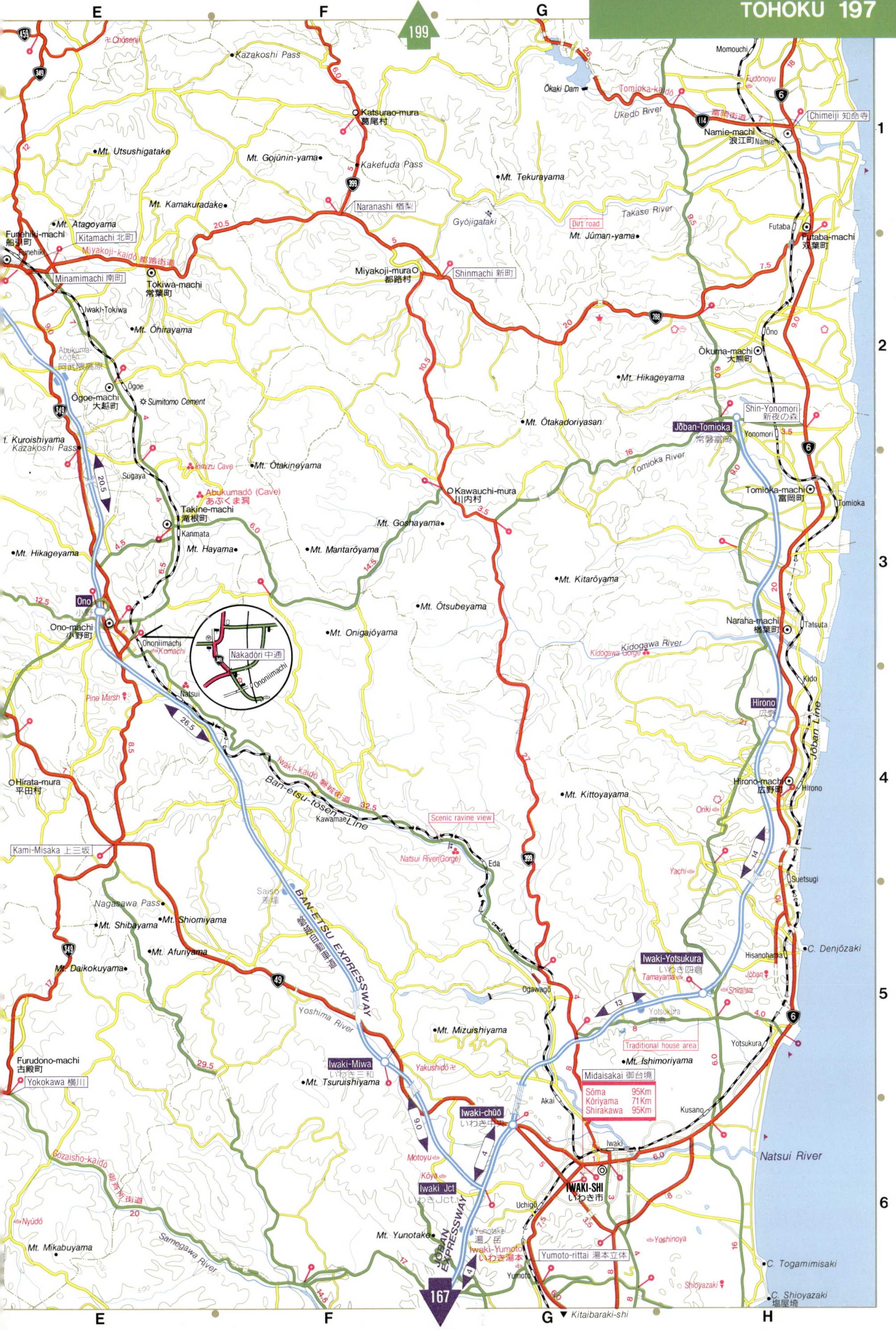
E
F
G
H
1
2
3
4
5
6
199
167
Kazakoshi Pass
Chōsenji
Katsurao-mura
葛尾村
Kakefuda Pass
Naranashi 楢梨
Mt. Utsushigatake
Mt. Gojūnin-yama
Mt. Kamakuradake
Mt. Atagoyama
Funehiki-machi
船引町
Funehiki
Kitamachi 北町
Miyakoji-kaidō 都路街道
Minamimachi 南町
Tokiwa-machi
常葉町
Iwaki-Tokiwa
Mt. Ōhirayama
Abukuma-kōgen
阿武隈高原
Ōgoe
Ōgoe-machi
大越町
Sumitomo Cement
Mt. Kuroishiyama
Kazakoshi Pass
Sugaya
Irimizu Cave
Mt. Ōtakineyama
Abukumadō (Cave)
あぶくま洞
Takine-machi
滝根町
Kanmata
Mt. Hayama
Mt. Mantarōyama
Mt. Hikageyama
Ono
小野
Ono-machi
小野町
Ononiimachi
Komachi
Nakadōri 中通
Ononiimachi
Natsui
Pine Marsh
Hirata-mura
平田村
Kami-Misaka 上三坂
Nagasawa Pass
Mt. Shibayama
Mt. Shiomiyama
Mt. Afuriyama
Mt. Daikokuyama
Furudono-machi
古殿町
Yokokawa 横川
Gozaisho-kaidō 御斎所街道
Nyūdō
Mt. Mikabuyama
Samegawa River
Ōkaki Dam
Tomioka-kaidō
富岡街道
Ukedo River
Momouchi
Fudōnoyu
Chimeiji 知命寺
Namie-machi
浪江町
Namie
Mt. Tekurayama
Gyōjigataki
Dirt road
Takase River
Mt. Jūman-yama
Futaba
Futaba-machi
双葉町
Miyakoji-mura
都路村
Shinmachi 新町
Ōno
Ōkuma-machi
大熊町
Mt. Hikageyama
Mt. Ōtakadoriyasan
Shin-Yonomori
新夜の森
Jōban-Tomioka
常磐富岡
Yonomori
Tomioka River
Kawauchi-mura
川内村
Tomioka-machi
富岡町
Tomioka
Mt. Goshayama
Mt. Kitarōyama
Mt. Ōtsubeyama
Mt. Onigajōyama
Naraha-machi
楢葉町
Tatsuta
Kidogawa River
Kidogawa Gorge
Kido
Hirono
広野
Jōban Line
Iwaki-kaidō 磐城街道
Ban-etsu-tōsen Line
Kawamae
Mt. Kittoyayama
Hirono-machi
広野町
Hirono
Oriki
Scenic ravine view
Natsui River (Gorge)
Eda
Yachi
Suetsugi
Saiso
差塩
BAN-ETSU EXPRESSWAY
磐越自動車道
C. Denjōzaki
Hisanohama
Jōban
Iwaki-Yotsukura
いわき四倉
Tamayama
Shiraiwa
Ogawagō
Yotsukura
四倉
Yoshima River
Mt. Mizuishiyama
Traditional house area
Mt. Ishimoriyama
Yotsukura
Iwaki-Miwa
いわき三和
Yakushidō
Mt. Tsuruishiyama
Midaisakai 御台境
Sōma 95Km
Kōriyama 71Km
Shirakawa 95Km
Akai
Kusano
Iwaki-chūō
いわき中央
Iwaki
IWAKI-SHI
いわき市
Natsui River
Motoyu
Kōya
Iwaki Jct
いわきJct.
Uchigō
Mt. Yunotake
JŌBAN EXPRESSWAY
Yunotake
湯ノ岳
Iwaki-Yumoto
いわき湯本
Yumoto-rittai 湯本立体
Yoshinoya
Yumoto
C. Togamimisaki
Shioyazaki
C. Shioyazaki
塩屋埼
Kitaibaraki-shi

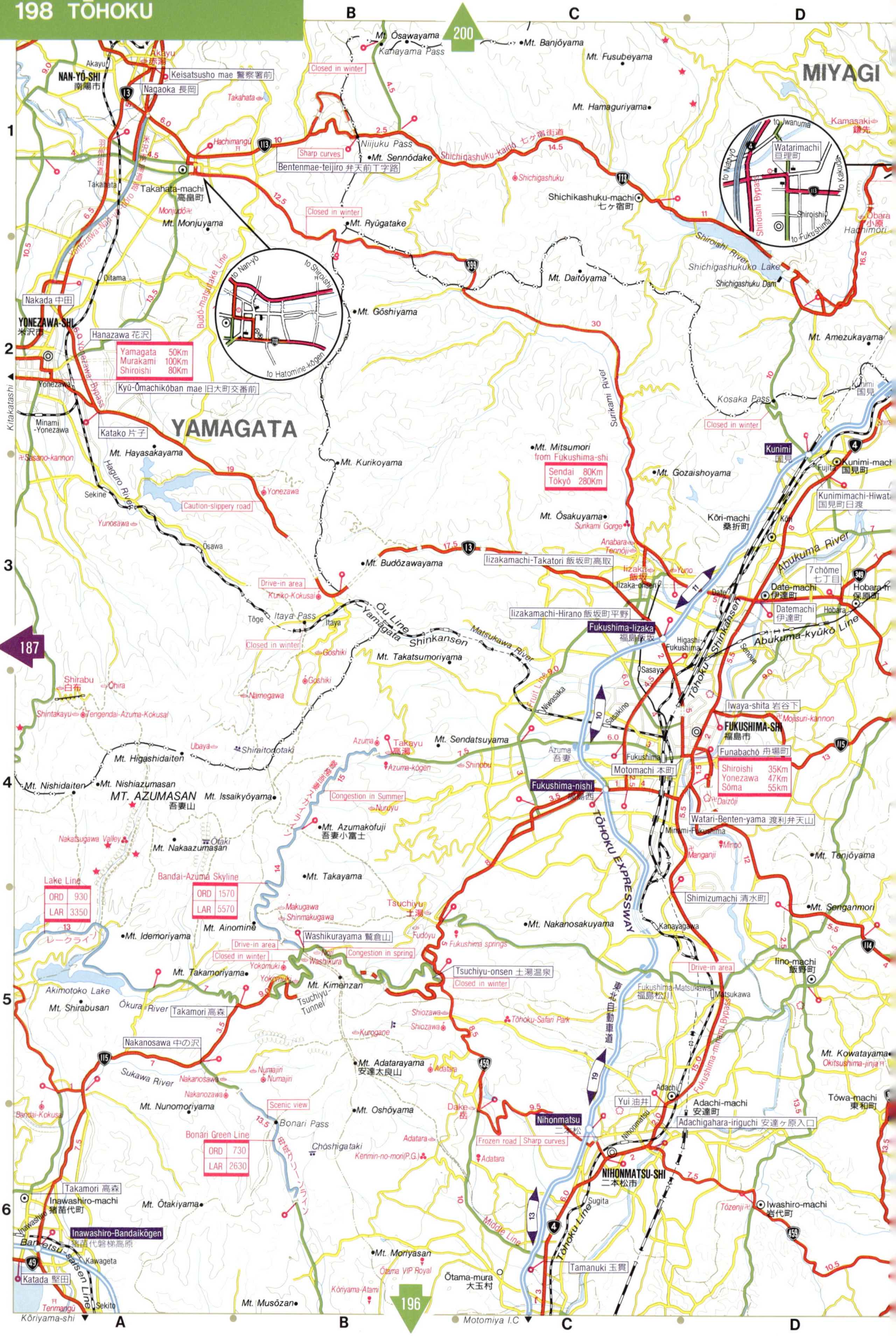

B
C
D
200
187
196
A
B
C
D
1
2
3
4
5
6
MIYAGI
YAMAGATA
NAN-YŌ-SHI
南陽市
Akayu
赤湯
Keisatsusho mae 警察署前
Nagaoka 長岡
Takahata
Hachimangū
Takahata-machi
高畠町
Monjudō
Mt. Monjuyama
Oitama
Nakada 中田
YONEZAWA-SHI
米沢市
Hanazawa 花沢
Yamagata 50Km
Murakami 100Km
Shiroishi 80Km
Kyū-Ōmachikōban mae 旧大町交番前
Yonezawa
Minami -Yonezawa
Kitakatashi
Katako 片子
Sasano-kannon
Mt. Hayasakayama
Haguro River
Sekine
Yonezawa
Caution-slippery road
Yunosawa
Ōsawa
Yonezawa-Nan-yō Bypass
Yonezawa Bypass
Budō-matsukake Line
Mt. Ōsawayama
Kanayama Pass
Closed in winter
Sharp curves
Niijuku Pass
Mt. Sennōdake
Bentenmae-teijiro 弁天前丁字路
Closed in winter
Mt. Ryūgatake
to Nan-yō
to Shiroishi
to Hatomine-kōgen
Mt. Gōshiyama
Mt. Kurikoyama
Mt. Budōzawayama
Drive-in area
Kuriko-Kokusai
Tōge
Itaya Pass
Itaya
Closed in winter
Ōu Line
Yamagata Shinkansen
Matsukawa River
Goshiki
Goshiki
Mt. Takatsumoriyama
Mt. Banjōyama
Mt. Fusubeyama
Mt. Hamaguriyama
Shichigashuku-kaidō 七ヶ宿街道
Shichigashuku
Shichikashuku-machi
七ヶ宿町
Mt. Daitōyama
Surikami River
Mt. Mitsumori
from Fukushima-shi
Sendai 80Km
Tōkyō 280Km
Mt. Gozaishoyama
Mt. Ōsakuyama
Surikami Gorge
Anabara
Tennōji
Iizaka
飯坂
Yuno
Iizaka-onsen
Iizakamachi-Takatori 飯坂町高取
Iizakamachi-Hirano 飯坂町平野
Fukushima-Iizaka
福島飯坂
Kamasaki
鎌先
to Iwanuma
Watarimachi
亘理町
to Nan-yō
Shiroishi Bypass
to Kakuda
Shiroishi
to Fukushima
Obara
小原
Hachimori
Shiroishi River
Shichigashukuko Lake
Shichigashuku Dam
Mt. Amezukayama
Kosaka Pass
Closed in winter
Kunimi
国見
Kunimi
国見
Kunimi-machi
国見町
Fujita
Kunimimachi-Hiwata
国見町日渡
Kōri-machi
桑折町
Kōri
Abukuma River
7 chōme
七丁目
Date-machi
伊達町
Hobara-machi
保原町
Date
Datemachi
伊達町
Hobara
Abukuma-kyūkō Line
Higashi-Fukushima
Tōhoku Shinkansen
Sasaya
Fruit Line
Niwasaka
Sasakino
Iwaya-shita 岩谷下
Mojisuri-kannon
FUKUSHIMA-SHI
福島市
Funabachō 舟場町
Shiroishi 35Km
Yonezawa 47Km
Sōma 55Km
Daizōji
Azuma
吾妻
Fukushima
Motomachi 本町
Fukushima-nishi
福島西
Watari-Benten-yama 渡利弁天山
Minami-Fukushima
Manganji
Miripō
Mt. Tenjōyama
TŌHOKU EXPRESSWAY
Shimizumachi 清水町
Mt. Senganmori
Mt. Nakanosakuyama
Kanayagawa
Drive-in area
Iino-machi
飯野町
Fukushima-Matsukawa
福島松川
Matsukawa
東北自動車道
Fukushima-minami Bypass
Mt. Kowatayama
Okitsushima-jinja
Tōwa-machi
東和町
Adachi
Yui 油井
Adachi-machi
安達町
Adachigahara-iriguchi 安達ヶ原入口
Nihonmatsu
二本松
NIHONMATSU-SHI
二本松市
Sugita
Iwashiro-machi
岩代町
Tōzenji
Tamanuki 玉貫
Tōhoku Line
Middle Line
Ōtama-mura
大玉村
Motomiya I.C
Shirabu
白布
Ōhira
Shintakayu
Tengendai-Azuma-Kokusai
Namegawa
Ubaya
Shiraitonotaki
Mt. Higashidaiten
Mt. Nishidaiten
Mt. Nishiazumasan
MT. AZUMASAN
吾妻山
Mt. Issaikyōyama
Azuma
Takayu
高湯
Azuma-kōgen
Shinobu
Mt. Sendatsuyama
Congestion in Summer
Nuruyu
Mt. Azumakofuji
吾妻小富士
Nakatsugawa Valley
Ōtaki
Mt. Nakaazumasan
Lake Line
ORD 930
LAR 3350
Bandai-Azuma Skyline
ORD 1570
LAR 5570
Mt. Takayama
Makugawa
Shinmakugawa
Tsuchiyu
土湯
Fudōyu
Mt. Ainomine
レークライン
Mt. Idemoriyama
Washikurayama 鷲倉山
Drive-in area
Closed in winter
Noji
Washikura
Congestion in spring
Fukushima springs
Yokomuki
Yokomuki
Mt. Takamoriyama
Mt. Kimenzan
Tsuchiyu-onsen 土湯温泉
Closed in winter
Tsuchiyu Tunnel
Akimotoko Lake
Mt. Shirabusan
Ōkura River
Takamori 高森
Shiozawa
Shiozawa
Tōhoku-Safari Park
Kurogane
Nakanosawa 中の沢
Sukawa River
Nakanosawa
Nakanozawa
Numajiri
Numajiri
Mt. Adatarayama
安達太良山
Adatara
Bandai-Kokusai
Mt. Nunomoriyama
Scenic view
Bonari Pass
Mt. Oshōyama
Dake
岳
Bonari Green Line
ORD 730
LAR 2630
Chōshigataki
Adatara
Kenmin-no-mori(P.G.)
Frozen road
Sharp curves
Adatara
Takamori 高森
Inawashiro-machi
猪苗代町
Mt. Ōtakiyama
Inawashiro
Inawashiro-Bandaikōgen
猪苗代磐梯高原
Bandaisu-saisen Line
Kawageta
Katada 堅田
Tenmangū
Sekito
Kōriyama-shi
Mt. Moriyasan
Ōtama VIP Royal
Kōriyama-Atami
Mt. Musōzan

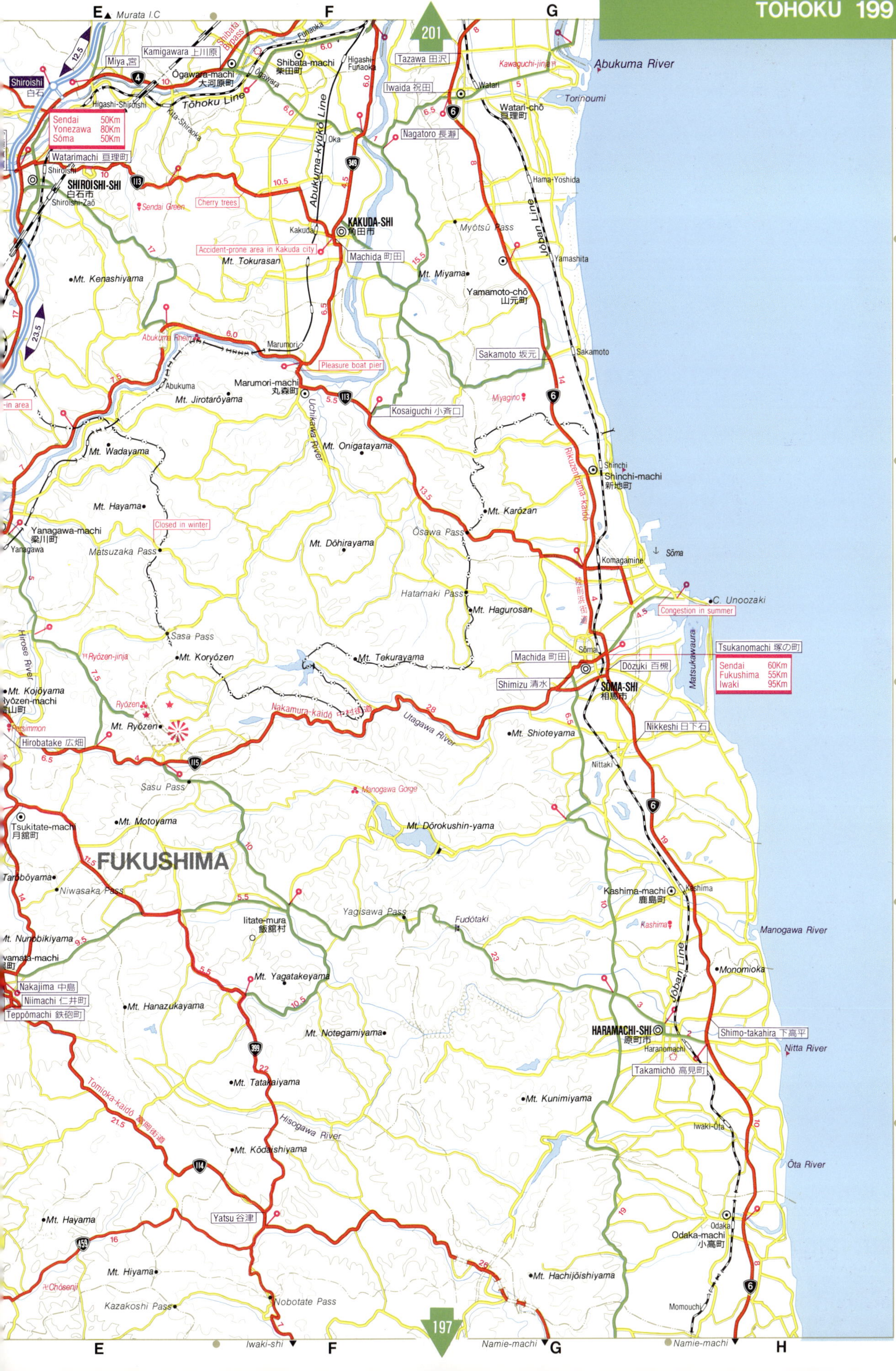

E
F
G
H
Murata I.C
201
197
1
2
3
4
5
6
Shiroishi 白石
Kamigawara 上川原
Miya 宮
Shibata Bypass
Funaoka
Ōgawara-machi 大河原町
Shibata-machi 柴田町
Higashi-Funaoka
Ōgawara
Tōhoku Line
Higashi-Shiroishi
Kita-Shiraoka
Sendai 50Km
Yonezawa 80Km
Sōma 50Km
Watarimachi 亘理町
Shiroishi
SHIROISHI-SHI 白石市
Shiroishi-Zaō
Sendai Green
Cherry trees
Abukuma-kyūkō Line
Oka
Tazawa 田沢
Iwaida 祝田
Nagatoro 長瀞
Kawaguchi-jinja
Abukuma River
Watari
Watari-chō 亘理町
Torinoumi
Hama-Yoshida
Jōban Line
KAKUDA-SHI 角田市
Kakuda
Accident-prone area in Kakuda city
Machida 町田
Mt. Tokurasan
Mt. Kenashiyama
Myōtsū Pass
Mt. Miyama
Yamashita
Yamamoto-chō 山元町
Abukuma Rhein
Marumori
Pleasure boat pier
Sakamoto 坂元
Sakamoto
Abukuma
Marumori-machi 丸森町
Mt. Jirotarōyama
Uchikawa River
Kosaiguchi 小斉口
Miyagino
Mt. Wadayama
Mt. Onigatayama
Rikuzenhama-kaidō
Shinchi
Shinchi-machi 新地町
Mt. Hayama
Mt. Karōzan
Yanagawa-machi 梁川町
Yanagawa
Closed in winter
Matsuzaka Pass
Ōsawa Pass
Mt. Dōhirayama
Komagamine
Sōma
陸前浜街道
Hatamaki Pass
Mt. Hagurosan
C. Unoozaki
Congestion in summer
Hirose River
Sasa Pass
Ryōzen-jinja
Mt. Koryōzen
Mt. Tekurayama
Machida 町田
Sōma
Tsukanomachi 塚の町
Matsukawaura
Dōzuki 百槻
Sendai 60Km
Fukushima 55Km
Iwaki 95Km
Shimizu 清水
SŌMA-SHI 相馬市
Mt. Kojōyama
Ryōzen
Nakamura-kaidō 中村街道
Utagawa River
Mt. Ryōzen
Persimmon
Nikkeshi 日下石
Mt. Shioteyama
Hirobatake 広畑
Nittaki
Sasu Pass
Manogawa Gorge
Tsukitate-machi 月舘町
Mt. Motoyama
Mt. Dōrokushin-yama
FUKUSHIMA
Niwasaka Pass
Kashima-machi 鹿島町
Kashima
Yagisawa Pass
Iitate-mura 飯舘村
Fudōtaki
Manogawa River
Mt. Nunobikiyama
Monomioka
Mt. Yagatakeyama
Nakajima 中島
Niimachi 仁井町
Teppōmachi 鉄砲町
Mt. Hanazukayama
HARAMACHI-SHI 原町市
Haranomachi
Shimo-takahira 下高平
Mt. Notegamiyama
Nitta River
Takamichō 高見町
Mt. Tatakaiyama
Tomioka-kaidō 富岡街道
Mt. Kunimiyama
Hisogawa River
Mt. Kōdaishiyama
Iwaki-Ōta
Ōta River
Yatsu 谷津
Mt. Hayama
Odaka
Odaka-machi 小高町
Mt. Hiyama
Chōsenji
Mt. Hachijōishiyama
Nobotate Pass
Kazakoshi Pass
Momouchi
Iwaki-shi
Namie-machi
Namie-machi

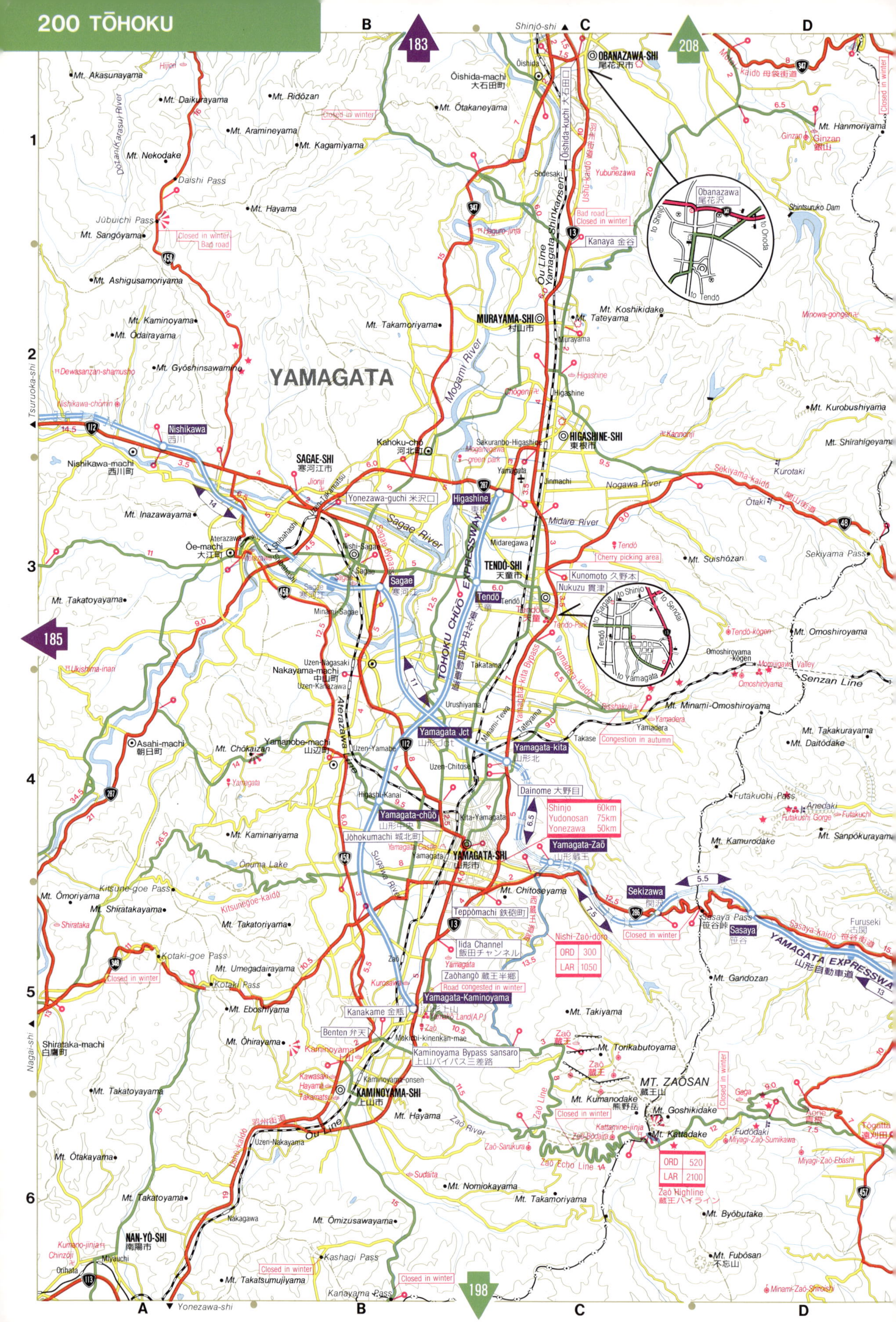

183
208
185
198
Shinjō-shi
Tsuruoka-shi
Nagai-shi
Yonezawa-shi
YAMAGATA
OBANAZAWA-SHI
尾花沢市
Ōishida
Ōishida-machi
大石田町
Mt. Akasunayama
Mt. Daikurayama
Mt. Ridōzan
Mt. Ōtakaneyama
Mt. Aramineyama
Mt. Kagamiyama
Mt. Nekodake
Daishi Pass
Jūbuichi Pass
Mt. Sangōyama
Mt. Hayama
Mt. Ashigusamoriyama
Mt. Kaminoyama
Mt. Ōdairayama
Mt. Gyōshinsawamine
Dewasanzan-shamusho
Nishikawa-chōmin
Closed in winter
Bad road
Hijiori
Haguro-jinja
Yubunezawa
Ōishida-kuchi 大石田口
Sodesaki
Kanaya 金谷
Ou Line
Yamagata Shinkansen
Ushū-kaidō
Obanazawa
尾花沢
to Shinjō
to Onoda
to Tendō
Mt. Hanmoriyama
Ginzan
銀山
Mōgami-kaidō 母袋街道
Shintsuruko Dam
Mt. Koshikidake
Mt. Tateyama
Minowa-gongen
MURAYAMA-SHI
村山市
Murayama
Mt. Takamoriyama
Mogami River
Higashine
Chōgenji
Higashine
HIGASHINE-SHI
東根市
Kannonji
Mt. Kurobushiyama
Mt. Shirahigeyama
Nishikawa
西川
Nishikawa-machi
西川町
SAGAE-SHI
寒河江市
Kahoku-chō
河北町
Sakuranbo-Higashine
Mogamigawa green park
Yamagata
Jinmachi
Nogawa River
Sekiyama-kaidō
関山街道
Kurotaki
Ōtaki
Jionji
Yonezawa-guchi 米沢口
Higashine
東根
Midare River
Mt. Inazawayama
Aterazawa
Ōe-machi
大江町
Sagae River
Nishi-Sagae
Sagae
Midaregawa
TENDŌ-SHI
天童市
Tendō
Cherry picking area
Mt. Suishōzan
Sekiyama Pass
Kunomoto 久野本
Nukuzu 貫津
Sagae
寒河江
Tendō
天童
Tendō-Park
to Shinjo
to Sendai
to Yamagata
Mt. Takatoyayama
Minami-Sagae
TŌHOKU CHŪŌ EXPRESSWAY
東北中央自動車道
Tendō-kōgen
Mt. Omoshiroyama
Omoshiroyama-kōgen
Momijigawa Valley
Omoshiroyama
Senzan Line
Ukishima-inari
Uzen-Nagasaki
Nakayama-machi
中山町
Uzen-Kanazawa
Takatama
Yamahara-kaidō
Yamagata-kita Bypass
Urushiyama
Risshakuji
Yamadera
Mt. Minami-Omoshiroyama
Asahi-machi
朝日町
Mt. Chōkaizan
Yamanobe-machi
山辺町
Aterazawa Line
Uzen-Yamabe
Yamagata Jct
山形Jct
Minami-Tewa
Tateyama
Takase
Congestion in autumn
Yamagata-kita
山形北
Mt. Takakurayama
Mt. Daitōdake
Yamagata
Uzen-Chitose
Dainome 大野目
Futakuchi Pass
Anedaki
Futakuchi Gorge
Higashi-Kanai
Yamagata-chūō
山形中央
Kita-Yamagata
Shinjo 60km
Yudonosan 75km
Yonezawa 50km
Mt. Kaminariyama
Jōhokumachi 城北町
Yamagata Castle
Yamagata
YAMAGATA-SHI
山形市
Yamagata-Zaō
山形蔵王
Mt. Kamurodake
Mt. Sanpōkurayama
Ōnuma Lake
Sugawa River
Kitsune-goe Pass
Mt. Ōmoriyama
Mt. Shiratakayama
Kitsunegoe-kaidō
Mt. Chitoseyama
Sekizawa
関沢
Sasaya Pass
笹谷峠
Sasaya
笹谷
Furuseki
古関
Sasaya-kaidō
YAMAGATA EXPRESSWAY
山形自動車道
Shirataka
Mt. Takatoriyama
Teppōmachi 鉄砲町
Iida Channel
飯田チャンネル
Nishi-Zaō-dōro
ORD 300
LAR 1050
Kotaki-goe Pass
Mt. Umegadairayama
Zaō
Zaōhangō 蔵王半郷
Road congested in winter
Kotaki Pass
Kurosawa
Yamagata-Kaminoyama
Mt. Gandozan
Mt. Eboshiyama
Kanakame 金瓶
Mt. Takiyama
Shirataka-machi
白鷹町
Benten 弁天
Mokichi-kinenkan-mae
Mt. Ōhirayama
Kaminoyama
Kaminoyama Bypass sansaro
上山バイパス三差路
Mt. Torikabutoyama
Zaō
蔵王
Kawasaki
Hayama
Takamatsu
Kaminoyama-onsen
KAMINOYAMA-SHI
上山市
MT. ZAŌSAN
蔵王山
Mt. Kumanodake
熊野岳
Mt. Goshikidake
Mt. Takatoyayama
Mt. Hayama
Zaō River
Zaō Line
Kattamine-jinja
Zaō-Bodaira
Mt. Kattadake
Fudōdaki
Miyagi-Zaō-Sumikawa
Gaga
Aone
青根
Togatta
遠刈田
Uzen-Nakayama
Ou Line
Zaō-Sarukura
Zaō Echo Line
ORD 520
LAR 2100
Zaō Highline
蔵王ハイライン
Miyagi-Zaō-Ebashi
Mt. Ōtakayama
Sudaira
Mt. Nomiokayama
Mt. Takamoriyama
Mt. Takatoyama
Mt. Byōbutake
Nakagawa
Mt. Ōmizusawayama
NAN-YŌ-SHI
南陽市
Kumano-jinja
Chinzōji
Miyauchi
Orihata
Kashagi Pass
Mt. Fubōsan
不忘山
Mt. Takatsumujiyama
Kanayama Pass
Minami-Zaō-Shiroishi

E
F
G
H
1
2
3
4
5
6
208
202
199
Ishinomaki-shi
Wakuya-chō
Shiroishi-shi
Sōma-shi
MIYAGI
Furukawa
FURUKAWA-SHI
古川市
Kitamachi 北町
Kami-Furukawa 上古川
Shinjō 80Km
Ichinoseki 50Km
Ishinomaki 40Km
Okamachi 岡町
Kami-machi
加美町
Shikama-cho
色麻町
Higashi-Ōsaki
Naka-uzen-kaidō 中羽前街道
Tagawa River
Naruse River
Mt. Yakuraisan
Mt. Kuromori
Mt. Amagaoka
Hanakawa River
Ōjōjihara
Sanbongi-chō
三本木町
Sanbongi
三本木
Inaba
Furukawa Bypass
Rikuu-tōsen Line
Tōhoku Line
Tajiri-chō
田尻町
Kogota-chō
小牛田町
Kogota
Matsuyama-machi
松山町
Kashimadai-machi
鹿島台町
to Ichinoseki
to Naruko
to Ishinomaki
to Obanazawa
to Taiwa
TŌHOKU EXPRESSWAY
東北自動車道
Mt. Tatsuimori
Ōhira-mura
大衡村
Taiwa-chō
大和町
Taiwa
大和
Takada 高田
Iwagamiyamazumi-jinja
Mt. Funagatayama
Mt. Togakurayama
Mt. Akakuzureyama
Mt. Ushiroshirahigeyama
Mt. Izumigatake
Mt. Araragiyama
Mt. Nanatsumori-Sasakurayama
Izumigadake
Mt. Kurohanayama
Jōgi
Jōgi-nyorai
Mt. Byōbudake
Mt. Zazendōyama
Eianji
Izumi
Izumi-kokusai
Tomiya
Tomiya-machi
富谷町
Tsurusu
鶴巣
Yoshida River
Shinainuma
Sanriku-jidōshadō
ORD 1300
LAR 3550
Ōsato-chō
大郷町
Matsushima-kokusai
Matsushima-chisan(Sendai)
Matsushima-Ōsato
Matsushima-chisan(Matsushima)
Atago
Matsushima-machi
松島町
Matsushima
Konashiya
Matsushima-kaigan
Hamada
浜田
Rikuzen-Hamada
Matsushima
松島
Tōhoku Shinkansen
Mt. Kameyama
Rifu-Shirakashidai
Rifu-chō
利府町
Rifu-naka
Sen-en
Izumi Parktown
Izumi
泉
Izumi-ku
泉区
Nanakita 七北田
Kenmin-no-mori(P.G.)
Mt. Takamoriyama
Tsubamezawa
燕沢
Kenchō mae 県庁前
Furukawa 40Km
Yamagata 70Km
Ishinomaki 50Km
Shiogama-wan
Nakajima 中島
SHIOGAMA-SHI
塩竈市
Shiogama-jinja
塩釜神社
Shin-Rifu
Rifu Jct
Shichigahama-machi
七ヶ浜町
TAGAJŌ-SHI
多賀城市
Tagajō
Sendaikō-kita
Taiheiyō Ferry
Sendai
Rikuzen-Sannō
Miyagino-ku
宮城野区
Senseki Line
Nakano-Sakae
Fukudamachi
Kozurushinden
Nigatake Inter 苦竹インター
Sendai-higashi
Nanakita River
Sakunami
作並
Nikkawa
Sakunami-kaidō
Yatsumori
Nikka
Fudōdaki
Kumagane
Nishisendai Highland
Nishi-Sendai Highland(A.P.)
Shirasawa 白沢
Ōkura River
Mt. Gongenmori
Hirose River
Ayashi
Rikuzen-Shirasawa
Akiu Ōtaki(Fall)
Futakuchi-kaidō 二口街道
Takanosuyama
New world
Nishisendai
Aoba-ku
青葉区
Kitayama
Kita-Sendai
Tōshōgū
Higashi-Sendai
Kunimi
Kuzuoka
SENDAI-SHI
仙台市
Sendai
Sendai-Miyagi
仙台宮城
Great Sendai
Kōnosu Kankane
Shinrin Sports Kōen(S.G.)
Akiu
Mt. Ōkurayama
Akiu
秋保
Futakuchi Gorge
Magnolia
Akaishi 赤石
Yagiyama Zoological Park
Taihaku-ku
太白区
Wakabayashi-ku
若林区
Kasuminome Airport
Minami-Koizumi 南小泉
Sendai Bypass
Yamada
Shikano 鹿野
仙台南部道路
Sendai-minami
仙台南
Nagamachi
Imaizumi
Sendai-tōbu-dōro
Nojō 野上
Higashi-Zaō
Kamafusa Dam
Goishi River
Mt. Kamafusayama
Kawasaki-machi
川崎町
Miyagi-Kawasaki
宮城川崎
Misawa-Morinokōen
ORD 500
LAR 1350
Sendai-nanbu-dōro
Minami-Sendai
Sendai-Wakabayashi Jct
Natori
NATORI-SHI
名取市
Natori River
from Sendai
Tōkyō 350Km
Aomori 390Km
Sugō
菅生
Taniyama-ikoi-no-hiroba(P.G.)
Mt. Toyama
Iinozaka 飯野坂
Tatekoshi
Sendai
Sendai-kūkō
Miyagi-Zaō
Chestnut picking area
Taniyama
Sugō Sports Land(S.G.)
Murata Jct.
村田JCT
Shiratori-jinja
Murata-machi
村田町
Murata
村田
Nagano 永野
Matsukawa River
Zaō-machi
蔵王町
Mt. Aosoyama
Tohoku Shinkansen
IWANUMA-SHI
岩沼市
Iwanuma
Takekoma-jinja
Fujinami 藤浪
Tōhoku Line
Shibata-machi
柴田町
Shirahata 白幡
Hayama-jinja
Omotezao-kokusai
Shibata Bypass
Tsukinoki
Abukuma
Abukuma River
Watari
Ōkuma
Funaoka
Yamagishi 山岸
Zaō
蔵王

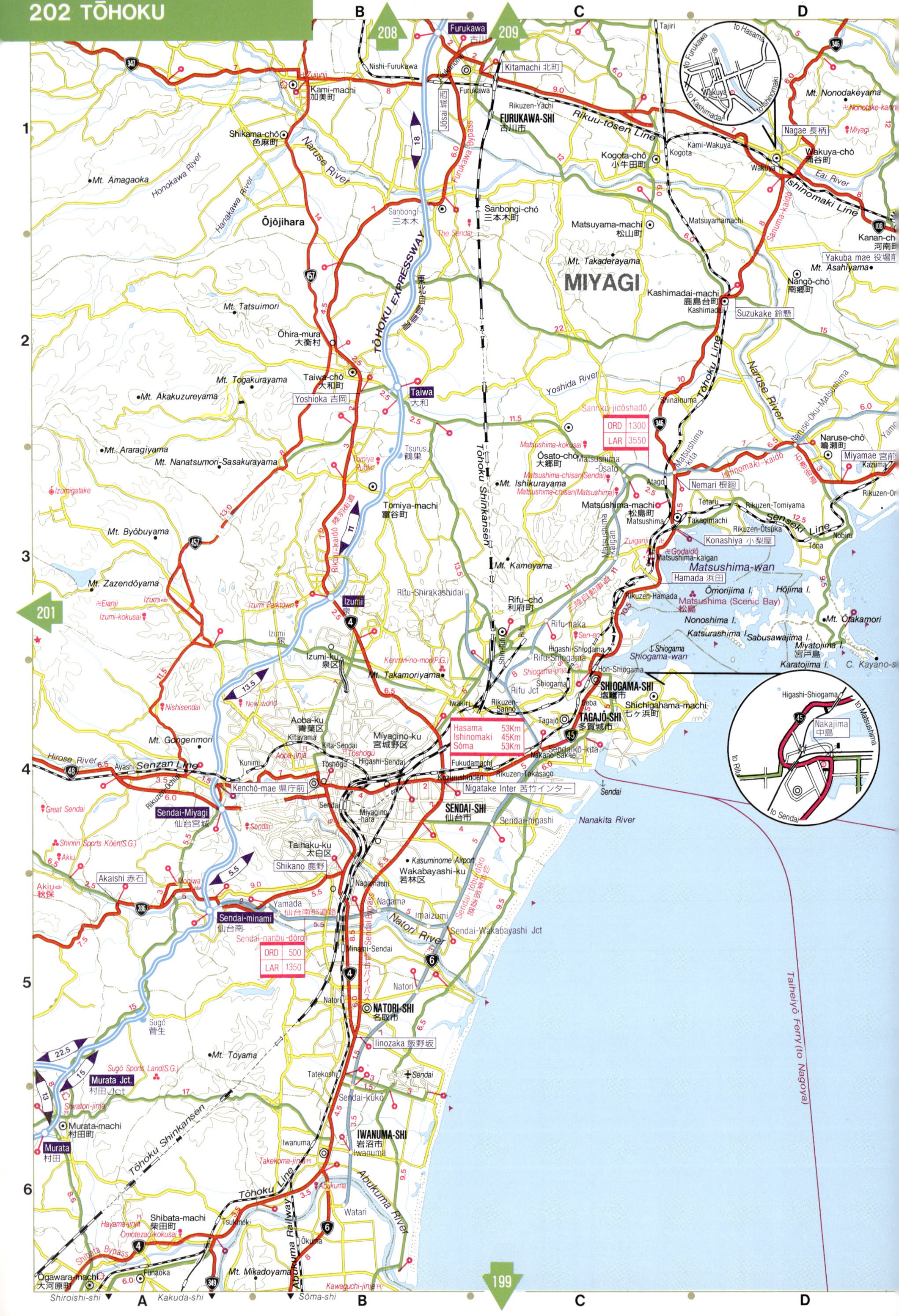
MIYAGI
FURUKAWA-SHI 古川市
Furukawa 古川
Kitamachi 北町
Kami-machi 加美町
Shikama-chō 色麻町
Ōjōjihara
Mt. Amagaoka
Naruse River
Honokawa River
Hanakawa River
Rikuu-tōsen Line
Kogota-chō 小牛田町
Wakuya-chō 涌谷町
Nagae 長柄
Mt. Nonodakeyama
Eai River
Ishinomaki Line
Sanbongi-chō 三本木町
Matsuyama-machi 松山町
Mt. Takaderayama
Kanan-chō 河南町
Yakuba mae 役場前
Mt. Asahiyama
Nangō-chō 南郷町
Kashimadai-machi 鹿島台町
Suzukake 鈴懸
TŌHOKU EXPRESSWAY
Mt. Tatsuimori
Ōhira-mura 大衡村
Taiwa-chō 大和町
Mt. Togakurayama
Mt. Akakuzureyama
Yoshioka 吉岡
Taiwa 大和
Yoshida River
Tōhoku Line
Naruse River
Sannku-jidōshadō
ORD 1300
LAR 3550
Mt. Araragiyama
Mt. Nanatsumori-Sasakurayama
Tsurusu 鶴巣
Ōsato-chō 大郷町
Mt. Ishikurayama
Tomiya-machi 富谷町
Naruse-chō 鳴瀬町
Miyamae 宮前
Nemari 根廻
Matsushima-machi 松島町
Senseki Line
Konashiya 小梨屋
Mt. Byōbuyama
Tōhoku Shinkansen
Mt. Kameyama
Matsushima-wan
Hamada 浜田
Mt. Zazendōyama
Rifu-Shirakashidai
Rifu-chō 利府町
Ōmorijima I.
Hōjima I.
Matsushima (Scenic Bay) 松島
Nonoshima I.
Mt. Ōtakamori
Izumi 泉
Katsurashima I.
Sabusawajima I.
Miyatojima I. 宮戸島
Izumi-ku 泉区
Shiogama-wan
Karatojima I.
C. Kayano-s
Mt. Takamoriyama
SHIOGAMA-SHI 塩竈市
Rifu Jct
Shichigahama-machi 七ヶ浜町
TAGAJŌ-SHI 多賀城市
Aoba-ku 青葉区
Miyagino-ku 宮城野区
Hasama 53Km
Ishinomaki 45Km
Sōma 53Km
Higashi-Shiogama
Nakajima 中島
to Matsushima
to Rifu
to Sendai
Mt. Gongenmori
Hirose River
Senzan Line
Kenchō-mae 県庁前
Nigatake Inter 苦竹インター
SENDAI-SHI 仙台市
Sendai-Miyagi 仙台宮城
Nanakita River
Taihaku-ku 太白区
Shikano 鹿野
Kasuminome Airport
Wakabayashi-ku 若林区
Akaishi 赤石
Akiu 秋保
Sendai-minami 仙台南
Natori River
Sendai-Wakabayashi Jct
Sendai-nanbu-dōro
ORD 500
LAR 1350
NATORI-SHI 名取市
Taiheiyō Ferry (to Nagoya)
Sugō 菅生
Mt. Toyama
Iinozaka 飯野坂
Murata Jct. 村田Jct
Murata-machi 村田町
Murata 村田
Tōhoku Shinkansen
IWANUMA-SHI 岩沼市
Tōhoku Line
Abukuma River
Abukuma Railway
Shibata-machi 柴田町
Mt. Mikadoyama
Ogawara-machi 大河原町
Shiroishi-shi
Kakuda-shi
Sōma-shi
201
208
209
199
A
B
C
D
1
2
3
4
5
6

E
F
G
H
1
2
3
4
5
6
209
204
Kesennuma-shi
Toyosato-chō
豊里町
Rikuzen-Toyosato
Monou-chō
桃生町
Wabuchi
Scenic road along Kitakami river
Ichinoseki Kaidō
Mt. Kyōyama
Kahoku-chō
河北町
Kitakami-machi
北上町
Oppa-wan
C. Hashirigasaki
Yakeishima I.
C. Tōgesaki
Nagatsura-ura
Ogatsu-shōgakkō mae 雄勝小学校前
Mt. Myōzin-yama
Ogatsu-chō
雄勝町
Mt. Ishimine
Mt. Fujisan
Fujinuma Lake
Kitakami River (Oppa River)
Kyū-Kitakami River
Kakeyama
Kanomata
Mt. Jōbōsan
Onagawa
to Ishinomaki
to Kitakami
to Oshika
Oyster cultivation area
Rias Blue Line
Okachi-wan
C. Shiroganesaki
Refined and elaborate shore line
Maruido 丸井戸
Kesennuma 85Km
Ichinoseki 70Km
Naruko 70Km
Sobanokami
Ishinomaki-Betsu-kaidō
Ishinomaki Kanal
Detour
Ishinomaki Ocean
Rikuzen-Inai
Onagawa-chō
女川町
Izushima I.
出島
Onagawa-wan
Hebita
Rikuzen-Yamashita
Rikuzen-Akai
ISHINOMAKI-SHI
石巻市
Daikaidō 大街道
Jūjō Paper Mfg.
Urashuku
Sawada
Mangoku-ura
Watanoha
Watanoha-ekimae 渡波駅前
Kasagaijima I.
Matsushima Airport
Ishinomaki
from Ishinomaki-shi
Aomori 390Km
Tōkyō 420Km
Mt. Dairokutenzan
Mikuni-jinja
Kazakoshi Pass
Hirashima I.
Enoshima I.
Mt. Hakamagatake
C. Yoriisozaki
Ashijima I.
C. Ozaki
Oshika Cobalt Line
牡鹿コバルトライン
C. Ōmurozaki
ISHINOMAKI-WAN
石巻湾
Oshika Pen.
牡鹿半島
Mt. Okusayama
C. Atsuisaki
Jūichimen-kannon
C. Nikishirozaki
Kinkazan-seto
Oshika-chō
牡鹿町
Koganeyama-jinja
C. Ōhakozaki
Senjōjiki (Scenic Rocky Coast)
Tashirojima I.
田代島
Kinkasan I.
金華山
C. Kamagasaki
C. Awabiarasaki
C. Kurosaki
Ajishima I.
網地島
Taiheiyō Ferry (to Tomakomai)

211
205
209
203
B
C
D
A
1
2
3
4
5
6
Sumita-chō
Senmaya-chō
Tōwa-chō
IWATE
MIYAGI
Mt. Haradaiyama
Mt. Tochizawayama
Mt. Jingamori
Mt. Raijin-yama
Kesen River
Takada-kaidō
Mawaridate 廻館
Mt. Kuromoriyama
Mt. Takaborayayama
Sasanoda Pass
Imaizumi-kaidō
Yahagi River
Mt. Hiraneyama
Closed in winter
Mt. Hachimoridairayama
Jimori Pass
Mt. Sasanaganeyama
Mt. Muroneyama
Murone-jinja
Mt. Kimigahanayama
Kamishishiori
Ōfunato Line
Yatsuse River
Mt. Kuromoriyama
Orikabe
Murone-mura
室根村
Mt. Atagoyama
Mt. Fuchūyama
Mt. Nabekoshiyama
Shishiori 鹿折
Marumori 丸森
Mt. Kiridachiyama
Nittsuki
KESENNUMA-SHI
気仙沼市
Kesennuma
Shishiori
Karakuwa
Fudōnosawa
Minami-Kesennuma
Mikkamachi 三日町
Kamaishi 75Km
Ichinoseki 48Km
Ishinomaki 80Km
Kesennuma Bypass
Ōshima Ferry
Matsuiwa
Kesennuma -wan
Saichi
Mt. Ōmoriyama
Hada-jinja
Mt. Iwakurayama
Mt. Tokusenjōyama
Kesennuma
Rikuzen-Hashikami
Mt. Nagamoriyama
C. Tatsumaizaki
C. Asahizaki
C. Tatehanazaki
Ōya-kaigan
Motoyoshi-chō
本吉町
Mt. Takaganeyama
Koganezawa
Tsuya 津谷
Motoyoshi
Rikuzen-Koizumi
Kesennuma Line
Kurauchi
Mt. Tatsukanesan
Rikuzen-minato
Utatsu-chō
歌津町
Utatsu
Isatomae-wan
C. Utatsusaki
Shizugawa-chō
志津川町
Shizuhama
C. Biwazaki
C. Aratozaki
Nojima I.
Arashima I.
Nanokamachi 七日町
Shizukawa-wan
C. Bentenzaki
Tsubakijima I.
Oritate 折立
C. Konpirasaki
Takekoma
Hinokami-jinja
Rikuzen-Yahagi
RIKUZENTAKATA-SHI
陸前高田市
Numata 沼田
Rikuzen-Takata
Wakinosawa
Takata-matsubara (Beautiful Beach)
Kayooka Pass
Hirota-wan
C. Mazaki
C. Myōjinzaki
Dairiseki-kaigan (Scenic Rocky Coast)
C. Ōirizaki
C. Hirotazaki
Aomatsushima I.
C. Matsugahana
Ishiwari Pass
Karakuwa-chō
唐桑町
Ōshima I (Scenic View Point)
大島
Takami-jinja
C. Osakimisaki
Mt. Nitayama
Otomo
C. Jagasaki
Kurosaki-jinja
C. Kurosaki
Goishi-kaigan (Scenic Rocky Coast)
Hosoura
C. Nagaiso
Ōfunato-wan
Mt. Hijōchiyama
Shimofunato
Gongendō 権現堂
ŌFUNATO-SHI
大船渡市
Sakari
Ōfunato
Onoda Cement
Rikuzen-Akasaki
Minami Rias Line
Mt. Imadeyama
Ō-tōge Pass
Maeda 前田
Sanriku
Okkirai-wan
Horei
Koishihama
Ryōri
Ryōri-wan
Mt. Tateishiyama
C. Ryōrizaki
綾里崎
C. Kōjimisaki
Kesennuma
to Ōfunato
to Ichinoseki
Mikkamachi 三日町
to Motoyoshi

E
F
G
H
1
2
3
4
5
6
206
211
204
IWATE
MIYAKO-SHI
宮古市
Miyako -wan
Jōdogahama(Scenic Rocky Coast)
浄土ヶ浜
C. Heizaki
閉伊(尾)崎
Mt. Gassan
Shirahama Pass
C. Todogasaki
Mt. Netakiyama
Samukaze Pass
C. Tategasaki
C. Konegasaki
C. Myōjinzaki
Mt. Karogatake
Hakamada 袴田
Yamada-wan
Yamada-machi
山田町
Rikuchū-Yamada
C. Ōurazaki
Funakoshi-kaigan (Scenic Rocky Coast)
Iwate-Funakoshi
Ushikorobashi Pass
C. Ōkamasaki
Tabuno-Ōshima I.
Funakoshi-wan
Higashihama-kaido
Yamada Line
Fudōtaki
Namiita
Kirikiri
Ōtsuchi-chō
大槌町
Ōtsuchi
C. Nanamodorizaki
C. Ohakozaki
C. Nagasaki
Ōtsuchi-wan
Unosumai 鵜の住居
Unosumai
Mt. Kamomemoriyama
Mt. Gozaishoyama
Ryōishi
C. Kurosaki
Ozaki-jinja
C. Shirozaki
KAMAISHI-SHI
釜石市
C. Washinosuzaki
Kamaishi-wan
Mt. Mainemoriyama
C. Kamasaki
C. Kurozaki
C. Ozaki
尾崎
Ozaki-jinja
Sanriku
Mt. Takanosuyama
C. Ōnezaki
Tōni
Tōni-wan
Mt. Monomiyama
C. Shikotsuzaki
Minami Rias Line
Yoshihama
Yoshihama-wan
Rashō Pass
C. Nagamozaki
Kuji 94Km
Morioka 109Km
Kamaishi 51Km
Atago 愛宕
Heigawa River
Mt. Sarukabeyama
Moichi 茂市
Kebaraichi
Sentoku
Miyako
Sokei
Tsugaruishi
Tsugaruishi River
Nagasawa River
Mt. Ōsasayama
Mt. Tanesashiyama
Mt. Sanbotojigashira
Mt. Nagaiwamori
Arakawa River
Shimada
Toyomane
Toyomane River
Mt. Horiaigatake
Sainokami Pass
to Tarō
to Morioka
to Kamaishi
Orikasa River
Orikasa
Mt. Kujirayama
Miyazawa Pass
Ōzuchi River
Kozuchi River
Mt. Torikonomori
Mt. Takasakimori
Mt. Nenekomori
Mt. Shiromiyama
Nakasato
Kariya River
Iwate-Kariya
Iwaizumi Line
Mt. Takatoriyama
Niisato-mura
新里村
Hikime
Mt. Maekariyama
Haratai
Yamada Line
Kawauchi
Hakoishi
Kawai-mura
川井村
Kami-Kawai 上川井
Rikuchū-Kawai
Mt. Shiwasumori
Oguni River
Mt. Myōsawayama
Mt. Hitotsuishiyama
Mt. Ōkuromori
Closed in winter
Mt. Ōzudake
Narrow road
Tachimaru Pass
Mt. Mimikiriyama
Kogarasa River
Mt. Gorosakuyama
Three Greenline
Mt. Oinegamori
Hashino River
Fuefuki Pass
Aonoki
Mt. Odake
Mt. Rokkoushisan
Mt. Iwakurayama
Caution-frozen road
Shiromizu
Ōzasa
Kamigō 上郷
Mt. Ōbirakiyama
Mt. Karakasamoriyama
Rikuchū-Ōhashi
Iwate-Kamigō
Hirakura
Ashigase
Kamaishi Line
Kami-Arisu
Akabane Pass
Sekemai-kaido
Dōsen
Matsukura
Kamaishi-kaido
Kosano
Kasshi River
Ekimae 駅前
to Miyako
to Tōno-shi
to Ōfunato
Aomori 310Km
Sendai 220Km
from Kamaishi-shi
Miyako 51Km
Kitakami 88Km
Kesennuma 75Km
Closed in winter
Mt. Aizen-yama
Mt. Hatonomine
Naranokidaira
Mt. Horoshiyama
Mt. Goyōzan
Amidadō
Goyōzan-jinja
Hachiman-jinja
Closed in winter
Kumano River
Closed in winter
Mt. Takamoriyama
Akasaka Pass
Mt. Azumanesan
Rokurō Pass
Yoshihama River
Sumita-chō
住田町
Sakari-kaido
Mt. Kenashimoriyama
Ō-tōge Pass
Ōfunato-shi

A
B
C
D
1
2
3
4
5
6
Hachinohe-shi
207
205
213
Niisato-mura
Miyako-shi
Rikuchū-Natsui
KUJI-SHI
久慈市
Kuji
Mt. Imoyayama
Kujigawa River
Kuji-keiryū(Gorge)
Ginza 銀座
Hachinohe 54Km
Morioka 123Km
MiyaKo 94Km
Shimo-Kawai 下川井
Yamagata-mura
山形村
Hosogoe Pass
Mt. Fukadakanayama
Mt. Manedokoyama
Rikuchū-Ube
Hama-kaidō 浜街道
Rikuchū-Noda
Noda-mura
野田村
Tsunokake Pass
Yamane
Noda-Tamagawa
Usaka Pass
Mt. Owasarabiyama
Horinai
Akka River
Shiraikaigan
Mt. Yomogimori
Mt. Tōjimayama
Ōtsuki Pass
Mt. Unetoriyama
Fudai 普代
Fudai-mura
普代村
Fudai
C. Kurosaki
Fudai River
Kitayamazaki(Cape)
Akkadō(Cave)
Mt. Kōneyama
Mt. Ōminesan
Closed in winter
C. Bentenzaki
Mt. Anamegatake
Tanohata
RIKUCHŪ KAIGAN COAST
陸中海岸
Kunizakai Pass
Tanohata-mura
田野畑村
Shimanokoshi
Mt. Kuromoriyama
Ishi Pass
Sanriku Kita-Rias Line
C. Mizujirizaki
Mt. Myōjin-yama
Nameiri 名目入
Mt. Tsuzukuishiyama
Vehicles prohibited
Shin-Omoto-kaidō 新小本街道
Mt. Iwakurayama
Ryūsendō (Cave)
龍泉洞
Iwaizumi
Matsuzaka Pass
Mt. Kameyama
Nakano 中野
Nishōishi
Iwaizumi-chō
岩泉町
Omoto River
Omoto
Ochiai 落合
Asanai
Ōkawa River
to Kuji
Ryusendo
to Hayasaka-kogen
to Omoto
Mt. Ōmori
Mt. Sashigaradake
Settai
Mt. Budōmori
Iwate-Ōkawa
Ōtaki
Nanataki
Iwaizumi Line
Greenpia Tarō
Settai River
Ushikorobashi Pass
Mt. Menzumeyama
C. Myōjinzaki
Mt. Takamine
Hama-kaidō 浜街道
Mt. Sakainokamidake
Narrow road
C. Masaki
Tarō-chō
田老町
Tarō
Oshikado
Mt. Tōgenokamiyama
Tarō River
to Kuji
to Miyako
Mt. Gaitakamori
Sharp curve
Mt. Kamegamori
Sabane
Wainai
Atenosawa
Miyako
Kō-tōge Pass
Ichinowatari
C. Anegasaki
Mt. Sarumaiyama
Omata Pass
Iwate-Wainai
Shiofukiana(Rocks)
Kariya River
to Hachinohe
to Yamagata
to Miyako

E F G

1 2 3 4 5 6

E F G H

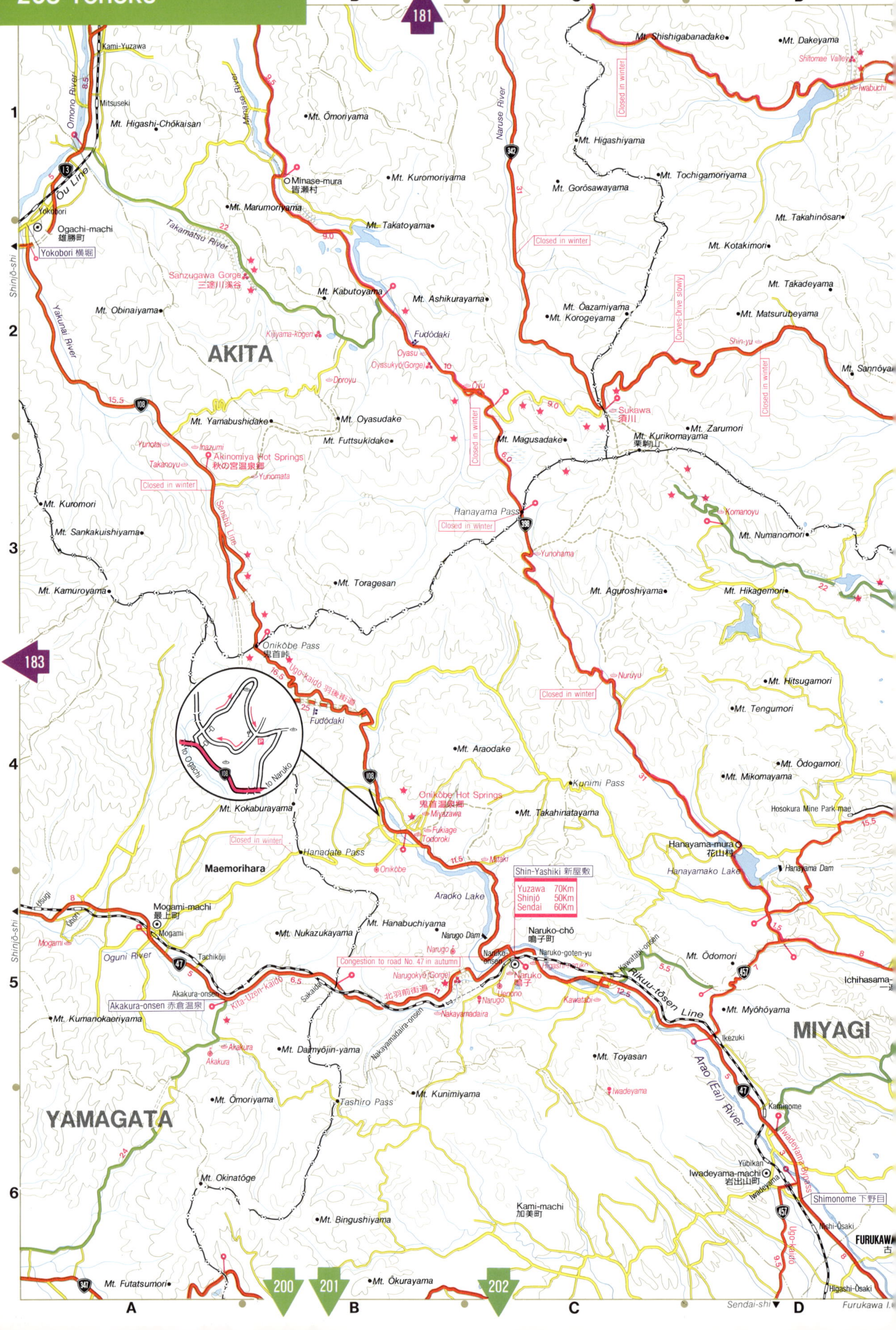

181
183
200
201
202
AKITA
YAMAGATA
MIYAGI
Kami-Yuzawa
Mitsuseki
Omono River
Mt. Higashi-Chōkaisan
Ōu Line
Yokobori
Ogachi-machi
雄勝町
Yokobori 横堀
Shinjō-shi
Yakunai River
Mt. Obinaiyama
Takamatsu River
Sanzugawa Gorge
三途川渓谷
Kijiyama-kogen
Minase River
Minase-mura
皆瀬村
Mt. Marumoriyama
Mt. Ōmoriyama
Mt. Kuromoriyama
Mt. Takatoyama
Mt. Kabutoyama
Mt. Ashikurayama
Fudōdaki
Oyasu
Oyasukyō (Gorge)
Doroyu
Ōyu
Naruse River
Closed in winter
Mt. Shishigabanadake
Mt. Dakeyama
Shitomae Valley
Iwabuchi
Mt. Higashiyama
Mt. Tochigamoriyama
Mt. Gorōsawayama
Mt. Takahinōsan
Mt. Kotakimori
Mt. Takadeyama
Mt. Ōazamiyama
Mt. Korogeyama
Mt. Matsurubeyama
Curves-Drive slowly
Shin-yu
Mt. Sannōyama
Sukawa
須川
Mt. Zarumori
Mt. Kurikomayama
栗駒山
Mt. Magusadake
Mt. Yamabushidake
Mt. Oyasudake
Mt. Futtsukidake
Yunotai
Inazumi
Akinomiya Hot Springs
秋の宮温泉郷
Takanoyu
Yunomata
Senshū Line
Mt. Kuromori
Mt. Sankakuishiyama
Hanayama Pass
Komanoyu
Mt. Numanomori
Yunohama
Mt. Toragesan
Mt. Kamuroyama
Mt. Aguroshiyama
Mt. Hikagemori
Onikōbe Pass
鬼首峠
Ugo-kaidō 羽後街道
Fudōdaki
Nuruyu
Mt. Hitsugamori
Mt. Tengumori
to Ogachi
to Naruko
Mt. Araodake
Kunimi Pass
Mt. Ōdogamori
Mt. Mikomayama
Hosokura Mine Park mae
Mt. Kokaburayama
Onikōbe Hot Springs
鬼首温泉郷
Miyazawa
Fukiage
Todoroki
Mt. Takahinatayama
Hanadate Pass
Maemorihara
Onikōbe
Mitaki
Shin-Yashiki 新屋敷
Yuzawa 70Km
Shinjō 50Km
Sendai 60Km
Araoko Lake
Hanayama-mura
花山村
Hanayamako Lake
Hanayama Dam
Usugi
Mogami-machi
最上町
Mogami
Mt. Nukazukayama
Mt. Hanabuchiyama
Narugo Dam
Naruko-chō
鳴子町
Oguni River
Tachikōji
Narugo
Naruko-onsen
Naruko
鳴子
Naruko-goten-yu
Higashi-naruko
Kawatabi-onsen
Congestion to road No. 47 in autumn
Narugokyō (Gorge)
Kita-Uzen-kaidō
北羽前街道
Sakaida
Akakura-onsen
Akakura-onsen 赤倉温泉
Nakayamadaira-onsen
Nakayamadaira
Narugo
Uenono
Kawatabi
Rikuu-tōsen Line
Mt. Ōdomori
Ichihasama-
Mt. Kumanokaeriyama
Akakura
Mt. Daimyōjin-yama
Mt. Myōhōyama
Ikezuki
Mt. Toyasan
Iwadeyama
Arao (Eai) River
Mt. Ōmoriyama
Mt. Kunimiyama
Tashiro Pass
Kaminome
Iwadeyama Bypass
Yūbikan
Iwadeyama-machi
岩出山町
Shimonome 下野目
Mt. Okinatōge
Kami-machi
加美町
Mt. Bingushiyama
Nishi-Ōsaki
FURUKAWA
Ugo-kaidō
Mt. Futatsumori
Mt. Ōkurayama
Higashi-Ōsaki
Sendai-shi
Furukawa I.C.

IWATE
Tainichidōri 太日通り
Nakadachō 中田町
MIZUSAWA-SHI 水沢市
Mizusawa
Mizusawa-Esashi
Isawa River
Isawa-chō 胆沢町
Mt. Miwakemori
東北自動車道
TŌHOKU EXPRESSWAY
Tōhoku Line
Rikuchū-Orii
Kitakami River
Mt. Daishimori
Mt. Abarayama
Arakamisha
Mt. Takanosuyama
Mt. Ōhachimoriyama
Mt. Hagigasakiyama
Kitamata River
Maesawa 前沢
Maesawa-chō 前沢町
t. Kunimiyama
Koromogawa-mura 衣川村
Hiraizumi-Maesawa 平泉前沢
Minamimata River
Gassan-jinja
Kanpukuji 観福寺
Okita River
Jizō Pass
Mt. Ōmoriyama
Daitō-chō 大東町
Chōsenji
Rikuzentakata-shi
to Kitakami
Hiraizumi
to Ichinoseki
Chūsonji 中尊寺
Hiraizumi
Hiraizumi-chō 平泉町
Higashidake Pass
Higashiyama-chō 東山町
Yugendō (Cave)
Shibajuku
Surisawa
Yotsukado 四角
Kōkenji
Geibikei
Geibikei (Gorge) 猊鼻渓
Rikuchū-Matsukawa
Mt. Hachirōmine
Mt. Tateishiyama
Iwai River
Takkoku-no-iwaya (Cave)
Chūsonji 中尊寺
Ōtsuki 大槻
Kitakami 47Km
Kesennuma 48Km
Furukawa 45Km
Satetsu River
Iwanoshita
Ichinoseki Bypass
ICHINOSEKI-SHI 一関市
Genbikei (Gorge) 厳美渓
Ichinoseki 一関
Jūnishin 十二神
Ichinoseki
from Ichinoseki-shi
Aomori 200Km
Sendai 90Km
Mt. Ishikurayama
Yokoiguchi 横井口
Senmaya
Konashi
Yagoshi
Senmaya-chō 千厩町
Mt. Yagoshiyama
Shin-Ōmachi 新大町
Ōfunato Line
Rikuchū-Kanzaki
Mataki
Hachiman 八幡
Kawasaki-mura 川崎村
Kesennuma-kaidō
Ichinoseki
Arikabe
Minami-Iwate
Mt. Koganeyama
Fujisawa-chō 藤沢町
Shimizuhara
Kurikoma-machi 栗駒町
Kurikoma
Kannari 金成
Hanaizumi-machi 花泉町
Hanaizumi
Rikuu-kaidō
Kurihara-den-en Railway
Sanhasama River
Kannari-chō 金成町
Mt. Mitsumineyama
Nanamagari Pass
Closed in winter
Mt. Ōminesan
Mt. Nagasakiyama
Kinryu River
Ichinoseki-kaidō 一関街道
Kitakami River
Mt. Kogaisan
isuzawa-chō
Kanbayashi 神林
Sawabe
Wakayanagi-Kannari 若柳金成
Yushima
Nihasama River
Ōdan
Yachihata
Wakayanagi
Mt. Ōmineyama
Yonekawa 米川
Motoyoshi-chō
Wakayanagi-chō 若柳町
Ishikoshi
Mt. Takakurayama
Futamata River
Mt. Gongenmori
Shiwahime 志波姫
Shiwahime-chō 志波姫町
Kurikoma-kōgen
Ishikoshi-machi 石越町
Tomeba 留場
Tōwa-chō 東和町
Ichihasama River
Tsukidate-chō 築館町
Hasama River
Horigome 堀米
Mt. Sugiyama
Tsukidate 築館
Izunuma Lake
Nitta
Nakada-chō 中田町
Mt. Dōjiyama
Suikai Pass
Uchinuma Lake
Tōhoku Shinkansen
Tōhoku Line
Toyoma-kaidō
Naganuma Lake
Hasama-chō 迫町
Haseyama-sansaro 長谷山三差路
to Wakayanagi
to Takashimizu
to Nakada
to Wakuya
Shizugawa
Kesennuma-shi
Umegasawa
Takashimizu Bypass
Semine-chō 瀬峰町
Semine
Minamikata-machi 南方町
Mt. Horobayama
Rikuzen-Togura
Takashimizu-machi 高清水町
Toyoma-machi 登米町
Higashihama-kaidō
Yokoyama-fudō
Kesennuma Line
Onagawa-chō
Chōjahara 長者原
Yoneyama-chō 米山町
Mt. Kusudayama
Hiradonuma Lake
Honchō 本町
Tsuyama-chō 津山町
Rikuzen-Yokoyama
Yanaizu
Mitakedō
Mt. Okinakurayama
Tajiri-chō 田尻町
kawa-shi
Ishinomaki-shi

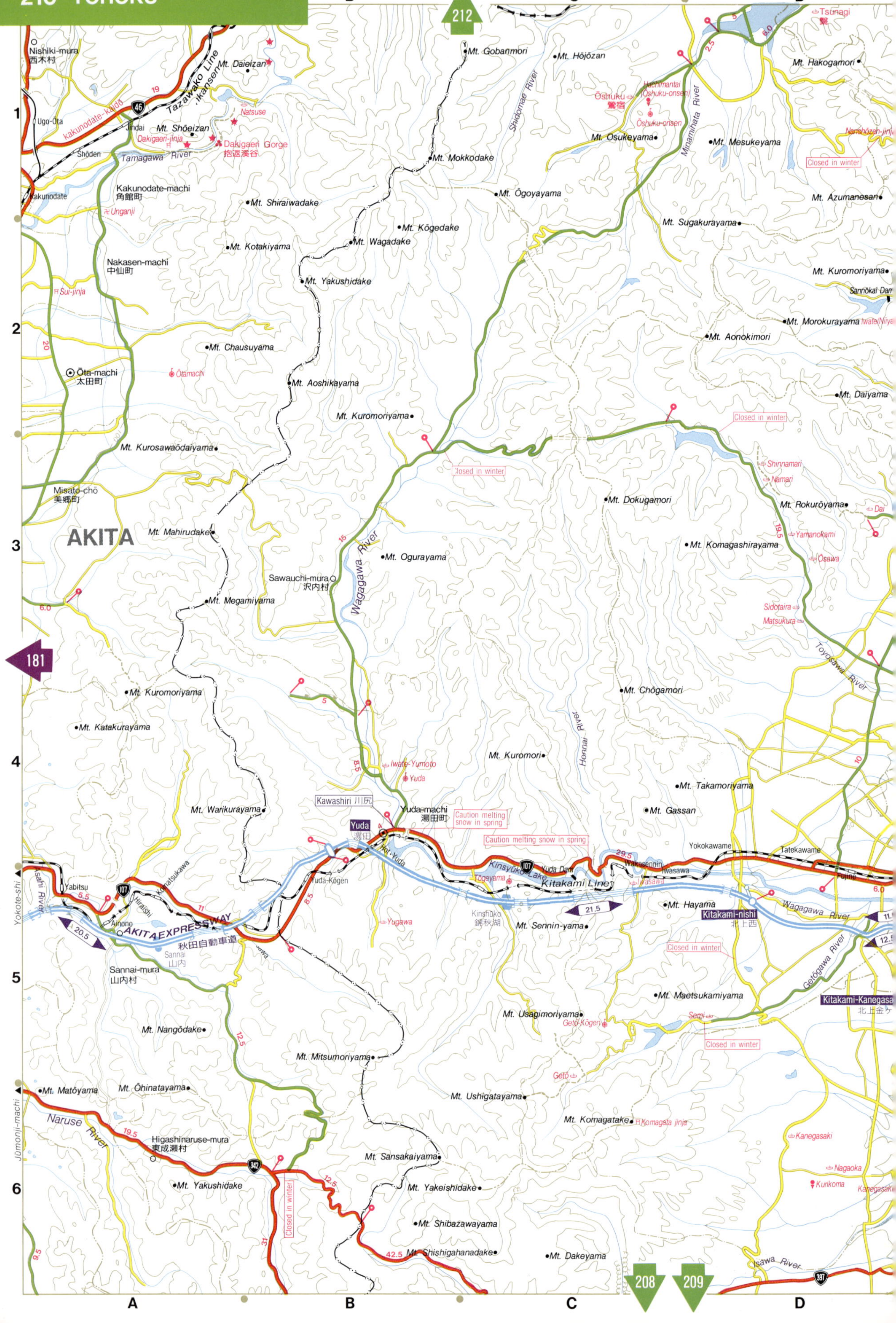

212
181
208
209
A
B
C
D
1
2
3
4
5
6
AKITA
Nishiki-mura
西木村
Ugo-Ōta
Tazawako Line
Akita-Shinkansen
Kakunodate-kaidō
46
19
Jindai
Shōden
Tamagawa River
Kakunodate
Kakunodate-machi
角館町
Unganji
Mt. Daieizan
Natsuse
Mt. Shōeizan
Dakigaeri-jinja
Dakigaeri Gorge
抱返渓谷
Mt. Shiraiwadake
Mt. Kotakiyama
Nakasen-machi
中仙町
Sui-jinja
20
Ōta-machi
太田町
Ōtamachi
Mt. Chausuyama
Mt. Kurosawaōdaiyama
Misato-chō
美郷町
Mt. Mahirudake
6.0
Mt. Megamiyama
Mt. Kuromoriyama
Mt. Katakurayama
Mt. Warikurayama
Mt. Gobanmori
Mt. Mokkodake
Mt. Kōgedake
Mt. Wagadake
Mt. Yakushidake
Mt. Aoshikayama
Mt. Kuromoriyama
Closed in winter
15
Wagagawa River
Mt. Ogurayama
Sawauchi-mura
沢内村
5
8.5
Iwate-Yumoto
Yuda
Kawashiri 川尻
Yuda-machi
湯田町
Yuda
湯田
Caution melting snow in spring
Caution melting snow in spring
Hot-Yuda
Yuda-Kōgen
Mt. Hōjōzan
Shidomae River
Hachimantai (Ōshuku-onsen)
Ōshuku
鶯宿
Ōshuku-onsen
Mt. Osukeyama
Mt. Ōgoyayama
Minamihata River
2.5
5
6.0
Tsunagi
繋
Mt. Hakogamori
Mt. Mesukeyama
Nanshōzan-jinja
Closed in winter
Mt. Azumanesan
Mt. Sugakurayama
Mt. Kuromoriyama
Sannōkai Dam
Mt. Morokurayama
Iwate(Niiya)
Mt. Aonokimori
Mt. Daiyama
Closed in winter
Shinnamari
Namari
Mt. Dokugamori
Mt. Rokurōyama
Dai
19.5
Yamanokami
Mt. Komagashirayama
Ōsawa
Sidotaira
Matsukura
Toyosawa River
Mt. Chōgamori
Mt. Kuromori
Honnai River
10
Mt. Takamoriyama
Mt. Gassan
Yokokawame
Tatekawame
Fujine
6.0
29.5
Kinsyuko Lake
107
Yuda Dam
Wakasennin
Iwasawa
Kitakami Line
Iwasawa
Togeyama
Kinshūko
錦秋湖
21.5
Mt. Hayama
Kitakami-nishi
北上西
Wagagawa River
11.5
12.5
Mt. Sennin-yama
Closed in winter
Getōgawa River
Kitakami-Kanegasaki
北上金ケ
Mt. Maetsukamiyama
Mt. Usagimoriyama
Getō-Kōgen
Semi
Closed in winter
Getō
Mt. Ushigatayama
Mt. Komagatake
Komagata jinja
Kanegasaki
Nagaoka
Kurikoma
Kanegasaki
Mt. Dakeyama
Isawa River
397
Yokote-shi
Asahi River
Yabitsu
5.5
107
Kōmatsukawa
Hiraishi
11
Aimono
20.5
AKITA EXPRESSWAY
秋田自動車道
Sannai
山内
Sannai-mura
山内村
8.5
Yugawa
Mt. Nangōdake
12.5
Mt. Mitsumoriyama
Jūmonji-machi
Mt. Matōyama
Mt. Ōhinatayama
Naruse River
19.5
Higashinaruse-mura
東成瀬村
342
Closed in winter
Mt. Yakushidake
12.5
Mt. Sansakaiyama
Mt. Yakeishidake
Mt. Shibazawayama
31
42.5
Mt. Shishigahanadake
9.5

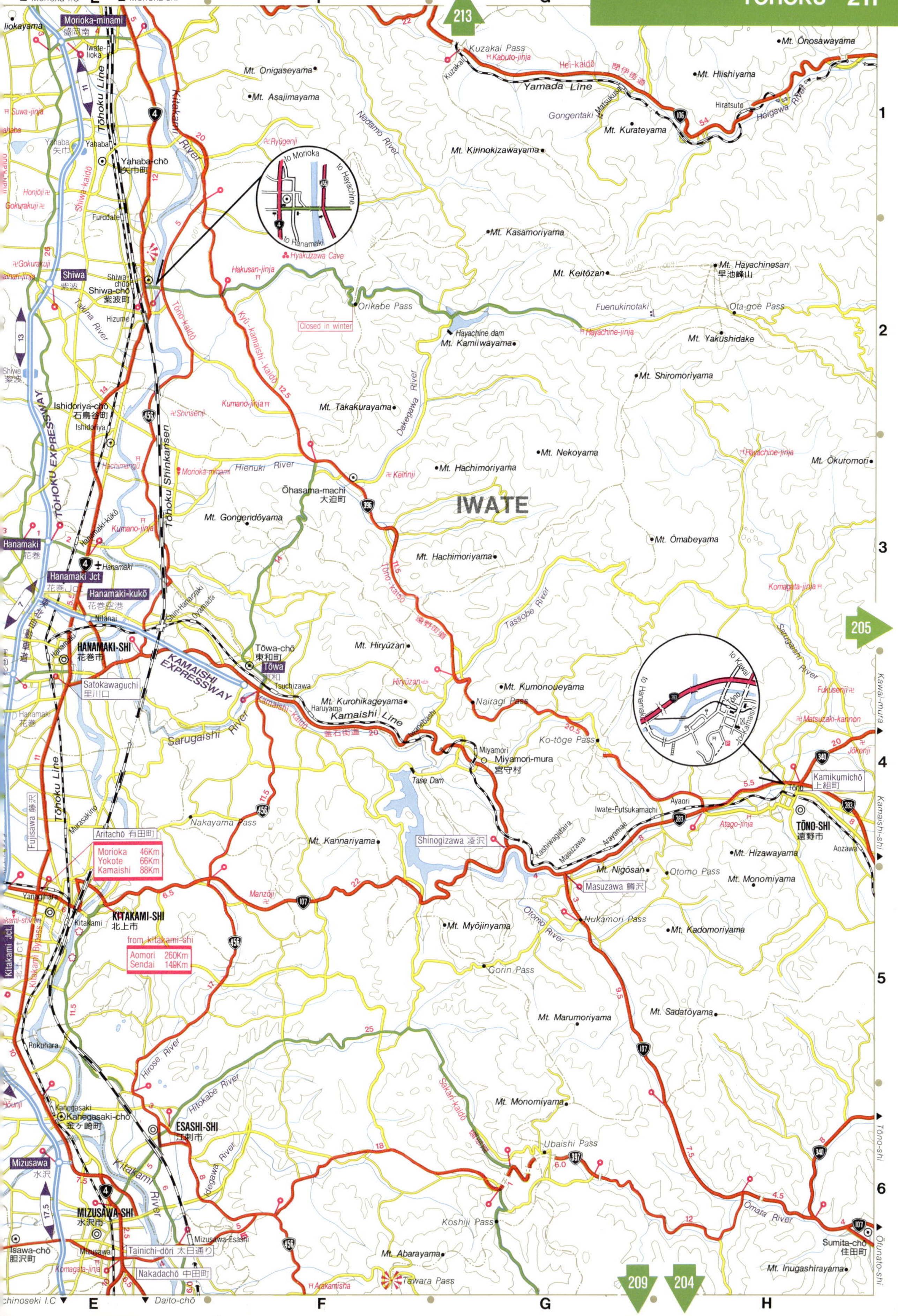

▲ Morioka I.C
E
▲ Morioka-shi
F
G
213
Morioka-minami
盛岡南
Iwate-iioka
Suwa-jinja
Yahaba
矢巾
Yahaba-chō
矢巾町
Tōhoku Line
Kitakami River
Shiwa-kaidō
Honjōji
Gokurakuji
Furudate
Gokurakuji
Shiwa
紫波
Shiwa-chō
紫波町
Hizume
Takina River
Tōno-kaidō
Shiwa
紫波
TŌHOKU EXPRESSWAY
Ishidoriya-chō
石鳥谷町
Ishidoriya
Hachimangū
Hanamaki-kūkō
Hanamaki
花巻
Hanamaki Jct
花巻Jct
Hanamaki-kukō
花巻空港
Nitanai
Shin-Hanamaki
HANAMAKI-SHI
花巻市
Satokawaguchi
里川口
Hanamaki
花巻
Tōhoku Line
Fujisawa 藤沢
Murasakino
Aritachō 有田町
Morioka 46Km
Yokote 66Km
Kamaishi 88Km
Yanagihara
KITAKAMI-SHI
北上市
Kitakami
Kitakami Jct
北上Jct
Kitakami Bypass
from kitakami-shi
Aomori 260Km
Sendai 140Km
Rokuhara
Kanegasaki
Kanegasaki-chō
金ケ崎町
Mizusawa
水沢
MIZUSAWA-SHI
水沢市
Isawa-chō
胆沢町
Mizusawa
Mizusawa-Esashi
Tainichi-dōri 太日通り
Nakadachō 中田町
Komagata-jinja
Ichinoseki I.C ▼
▼ Daito-chō
Mt. Onigaseyama
Mt. Asajimayama
Ryūgenji
Nedamo River
to Morioka
to Hayachine
to Hanamaki
Hyakuzawa Cave
Hakusan-jinja
Kyū-kamaishi-kaidō
Orikabe Pass
Closed in winter
Tōhoku Shinkansen
Shinsenji
Kumano-jinja
Morioka-minami
Hienuki River
Ōhasama-machi
大迫町
Mt. Gongendōyama
Kumano-jinja
Mt. Takakurayama
Dakegawa River
Keirinji
Mt. Hachimoriyama
Tōno-kaidō
遠野街道
Mt. Hiryūzan
Tōwa-chō
東和町
Tōwa
東和
Tsuchizawa
KAMAISHI EXPRESSWAY
Kamaishi-kaidō
釜石街道
Haruyama
Mt. Kurohikageyama
Kamaishi Line
Hiryūzan
Sarugaishi River
Nakayama Pass
Mt. Kannariyama
Tase Dam
Manzōji
Kuzakai Pass
Kabuto-jinja
Kuzakai
Yamada Line
Hei-kaidō
閉伊街道
Gongentaki
Matsukusa
Mt. Kurateyama
Mt. Kirinokizawayama
Mt. Kasamoriyama
Mt. Keitōzan
Hayachine dam
Mt. Kamiiwayama
Hayachine-jinja
Mt. Nekoyama
Mt. Hachimoriyama
IWATE
Tassobe River
Mt. Kumonoueyama
Nairagi Pass
Ko-tōge Pass
Miyamori
Miyamori-mura
宮守村
Shinogizawa 凌沢
Kashiwagidaira
Masuzawa
Masuzawa 鱒沢
Mt. Myōjinyama
Otomo River
Gorin Pass
Mt. Marumoriyama
Sakari-kaidō
Mt. Monomiyama
Ubaishi Pass
Koshiji Pass
Mt. Abarayama
Arakamisha
Tawara Pass
209
204
Mt. Ōnosawayama
Mt. Hiishiyama
Hiratsuto
Heigawa River
Mt. Hayachinesan
早池峰山
Fuenukinotaki
Ota-goe Pass
Mt. Yakushidake
Mt. Shiromoriyama
Hayachine-jinja
Mt. Ōkuromori
Mt. Ōmabeyama
Komagata-jinja
205
Sarugaishi River
to Kamaishi
to Hanamaki
to Kawai
Fukusenji
Matsuzaki-kannon
Kawai-mura
Jōkenji
Kamikumichō
上組町
Tōno
TŌNO-SHI
遠野市
Ayaori
Iwate-Futsukamachi
Arayamae
Atago-jinja
Aozawa
Kamaishi-shi
Mt. Hizawayama
Mt. Nigōsan
Otomo Pass
Mt. Monomiyama
Nukamori Pass
Mt. Kadomoriyama
Mt. Sadatōyama
Tōno-shi
Ōmata River
Sumita-chō
住田町
Ōfunato-shi
Mt. Inugashirayama
1
2
3
4
5
6
H

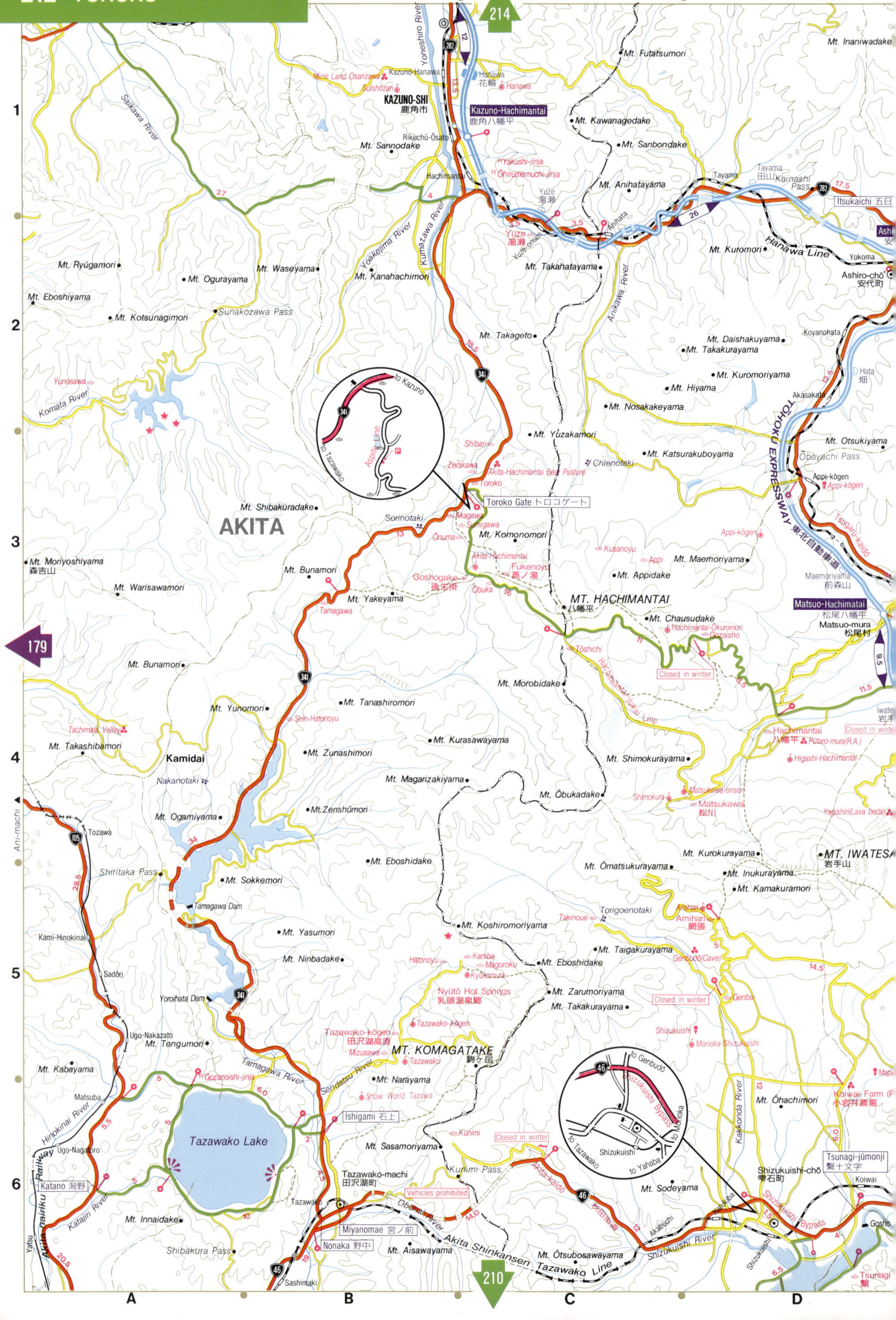

214
179
210
AKITA
KAZUNO-SHI
鹿角市
Kazuno-Hachimantai
鹿角八幡平
Ōdate-shi
Yoneshiro River
Kazuno-Hanawa
Hanawa
花輪
Mine Land Osarizawa
Suishōzan
Rikuchū-Ōsato
Mt. Sannodake
Hachimantai
Yakushi-jinja
Ōhirumamuchi-jinja
Yuze
湯瀬
Yuze-onsen
Anihata
Tayama
田山
Kainashi Pass
Itsukaichi 五日
Hanawa Line
Yokoma
Ashiro-chō
安代町
Mt. Futatsumori
Mt. Kawanagedake
Mt. Sanbondake
Mt. Anihatayama
Mt. Inaniwadake
Mt. Kuromori
Mt. Takahatayama
Sakkawa River
Kumazawa River
Yoakejima River
Mt. Ryūgamori
Mt. Oguraуama
Mt. Waseyama
Mt. Kanahachimori
Mt. Eboshiyama
Mt. Kotsunagimori
Sunakozawa Pass
Anikawa River
Mt. Takageto
Mt. Daishakuyama
Mt. Takakurayama
Mt. Kuromoriyama
Koyanohata
Hata
畑
Akasakata
Mt. Hiyama
Mt. Nosakakeyama
Mt. Yuzakamori
Mt. Katsurakuboyama
Mt. Otsukiyama
Ōbayachi Pass
Appi-kōgen
TŌHOKU EXPRESSWAY
東北自動車道
Yunosawa
Komata River
to Kazuno
to Tazawako
Aspite Line
Shibari
Zenikawa
Akita-Hachimantai Bear Pasture
Toroko
Toroko Gate トロコゲート
Chienotaki
Mt. Shibakuradake
Sorinotaki
Akagawa
Sumigawa
Ōnuma
Mt. Komonomori
Kusanoyu
Appi
Appi-kōgen
Tsugaru-kaidō
Mt. Moriyoshiyama
森吉山
Mt. Bunamori
Akita-Hachimantai
Goshogake
後生掛
Fukenoyu
蒸ノ湯
Ōbuka
Mt. Maemoriyama
Mt. Appidake
Maemoriyama
前森山
Mt. Warisawamori
Mt. Yakeyama
Tamagawa
MT. HACHIMANTAI
八幡平
Mt. Chausudake
Matsuo-Hachimatai
松尾八幡平
Matsuo-mura
松尾村
Hachimantai-Ōkuromori
Gozaisho
Tōshichi
Closed in winter
Mt. Bunamori
Mt. Morobidake
Hachimantai Jukai Line
Mt. Tanashiromori
Mt. Yunomori
Shin-Hatonoyu
Tachimata Valley
Hachimantai
八幡平
Pūtaro-mura(R.A.)
Higashi-Hachimantai
Iwate
岩手
Closed in winter
Mt. Takashibamori
Kamidai
Mt. Zunashimori
Mt. Kurasawayama
Mt. Shimokurayama
Nakanotaki
Mt. Magarizakiyama
Mt. Ōbukadake
Shimokura
Matsukawa-onsen
Matsukawa
松川
Yagishiri(Lava beds)
Ani-machi
Mt. Ogamiyama
Mt. Zenshūmori
Tozawa
Shiritaka Pass
Mt. Sokkemori
Mt. Eboshidake
Mt. Kurokurayama
MT. IWATESAN
岩手山
Mt. Ōmatsukurayama
Mt. Inukurayama
Mt. Kamakuramori
Tamagawa Dam
Kami-Hinokinai
Mt. Yasumori
Mt. Koshiromoriyama
Takinoue
Torigoenotaki
Amihari
網張
Mt. Taigakurayama
Genbudō(Cave)
Sadōri
Mt. Ninbadake
Hatonoyu
Kaniba
Magoroku
Kyūkamura
Mt. Eboshidake
Nyūtō Hot Springs
乳頭温泉郷
Mt. Zarumoriyama
Mt. Takakurayama
Closed in winter
Genbu
Yoroihata Dam
Tazawako-kōgen
Ugo-Nakazato
Mt. Tengumori
Tazawako-kōgen
田沢湖高原
Mizusawa
MT. KOMAGATAKE
駒ケ岳
Tazawako
Shizukuishi
Morioka-Shizukuishi
Mt. Kabayama
Gozanoishi-jinja
Tamagawa River
Sendatsu River
Mt. Narayama
Snow World Tazawa
Matsuba
Hinokinai River
Ishigami 石上
to Genbudō
Shizukuishi Bypass
to Morioka
Koiwai Farm
小岩井農場
Kakkonda River
Mt. Ōhachimori
Tazawako Lake
Kunimi
Closed in winter
Ugo-Nagatoro
Mt. Sasamoriyama
Kunimi Pass
Akita-kaidō
to Tazawako
Shizukuishi
to Yahaba
Tsunagi-jūmonji
繋十文字
Katano 潟野
Tazawako-machi
田沢湖町
Vehicles prohibited
Mt. Sodeyama
Shizukuishi-chō
雫石町
Koiwai
Akita Dairiku Railway
Kataji River
Tazawako
Ōbonai River
Akabuchi
Shizukuishi River
Shizukuishi Bypass
Gosho
Mt. Innaidake
Miyanomae 宮ノ前
Nonaka 野中
Akita Shinkansen Tazawako Line
Mt. Aisawayama
Mt. Ōtsubosawayama
Tsunagi
繋
Shibakura Pass
Yatsu
Sashimaki
A
B
C
D
1
2
3
4
5
6

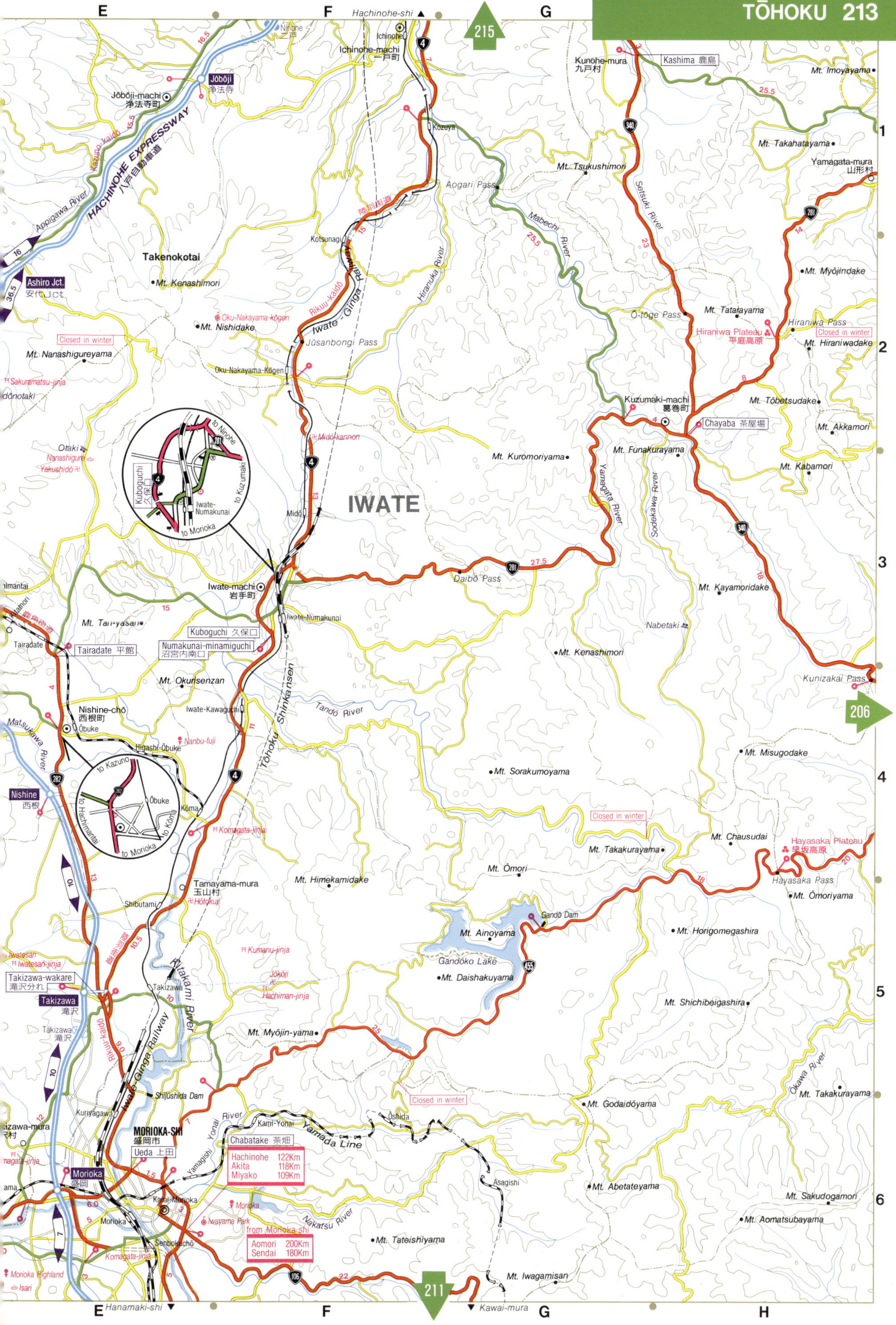
E
F
G
H
Hachinohe-shi
215
206
211
1
2
3
4
5
6
Hanamaki-shi
Kawai-mura
IWATE
HACHINOHE EXPRESSWAY
八戸自動車道
Jōbōji
浄法寺
Jōbōji-machi
浄法寺町
Appigawa River
Ashiro Jct.
安代Jct
Takenokotai
Mt. Kenashimori
Mt. Nishidake
Oku-Nakayama-kōgen
Closed in winter
Mt. Nanashigureyama
Sakuramatsu-jinja
Ninohe
Ichinohe
Ichinohe-machi
一戸町
Kozuya
Aogari Pass
Mabechi River
Hiranuka River
Kotsunagi
Rikuu-kaidō
Iwate-Ginga Railway
Jūsanbongi Pass
Oku-Nakayama-Kōgen
Midō-kannon
Midō
Kuboguchi
久保口
to Ninohe
to Kuzumaki
Iwate-Numakunai
to Morioka
Otaki
Nanashigure
Yakushidō
Iwate-machi
岩手町
Mt. Tan-yasan
Kuboguchi 久保口
Numakunai-minamiguchi
沼宮内南口
Tairadate
Tairadate 平館
Mt. Okurisenzan
Iwate-Kawaguchi
Nishine-chō
西根町
Ōbuke
Higashi-Ōbuke
Nanbu-fuji
Matsukawa River
Nishine
西根
to Kazuno
to Hachimantai
to Morioka
to Kōma
Kōma
Komagata-jinja
Tōhoku Shinkansen
Tandō River
Tamayama-mura
玉山村
Hōtokuji
Shibutami
Kumanu-jinja
Jōkōji
Hachiman-jinja
Iwatesan-jinja
Takizawa-wakare
滝沢分れ
Takizawa
滝沢
Takizawa
Kitakami River
Iwate-Ginga Railway
Mt. Myōjin-yama
Shijūshida Dam
Kuriyagawa
MORIOKA-SHI
盛岡市
Ueda 上田
Morioka
盛岡
Kami-Morioka
Morioka
Senbokuchō
Komagata-jinja
Morioka Highland
Isari
Yonai River
Kami-Yonai
Yamada Line
Chabatake 茶畑
Hachinohe 122Km
Akita 118Km
Miyako 109Km
Morioka
Iwayama Park
from Morioka-shi
Aomori 200Km
Sendai 180Km
Nakatsu River
Yamagishi
Ōshida
Asagishi
Mt. Tateishiyama
Mt. Iwagamisan
Closed in winter
Kunohe-mura
九戸村
Kashima 鹿島
Mt. Imoyayama
Mt. Takahatayama
Yamagata-mura
山形村
Mt. Tsukushimori
Setsuki River
Mt. Myōjindake
Ō-tōge Pass
Mt. Tatarayama
Hiraniwa Plateau
平庭高原
Hiraniwa Pass
Closed in winter
Mt. Hiraniwadake
Kuzumaki-machi
葛巻町
Chayaba 茶屋場
Mt. Tōbetsudake
Mt. Akkamori
Mt. Funakurayama
Mt. Kabamori
Mt. Kuromoriyama
Yamagata River
Sodekawa River
Daibō Pass
Mt. Kayamoridake
Nabetaki
Mt. Kenashimori
Kunizakai Pass
Mt. Misugodake
Mt. Sorakumoyama
Closed in winter
Mt. Chausudai
Mt. Takakurayama
Hayasaka Plateau
早坂高原
Hayasaka Pass
Mt. Ōmori
Mt. Ōmoriyama
Mt. Himekamidake
Gandō Dam
Mt. Ainoyama
Gandōko Lake
Mt. Daishakuyama
Mt. Horigomegashira
Mt. Shichibeigashira
Ōkawa River
Mt. Takakurayama
Mt. Godaidōyama
Mt. Abetateyama
Mt. Sakudogamori
Mt. Aomatsubayama
Kawai-mura

216
212
177
AOMORI
AKITA
TŌHOKU EXPRESSWAY
Namioka
浪岡
Namioka-machi
浪岡町
Aomori-kūkō-dōro
青森空港道路
Mt. Takazumoriyama
Mt. Bōzuhatakeyama
Mt. Toyamoriyama
Nyūnai Pass
Only authorized vehicles in winter
Moya Pass
Moya
Closed in winter
Mt. Horikodake
Ko-tōge Pass
Ō-tōge Pass
Komagome River
Mt. Shichijūmoriyama
Mt. Shibamoriyama
Sankaidaki
Tashiromotoyu
Hakkōda
Congestion in summer and autumn
Mt. Maedake
Mt. Hachimandake
Mt. Ishikurayama
Gankake Pass
Mt. Tsukamoriyama
Mt. Goshayama
Takadate
高館
Kita-Tokiwa
Hakkōdasan
Mt. Tamoyachiyama
Mt. Minamimatayama
Mt. Ōdake
Mt. Hakkōdasan
八甲田山
Mt. Hinadake
Mt. Takadaōdake
Mt. Kuromori
Sukayu
Jōgakura
Mt. Ishikuradake
Yachi
Yachi 谷地
Sarukura
Tsutagawa River
KUROISHI-SHI
黒石市
Inakadate-mura
田舎館村
Mt. Kuromoriyama
Mt. Kashiwagiyama
Kuroishi
黒石
Kuroishi Bypass
Seibien(Garden)
Saruga-jinja
Onoe-machi
尾上町
Kuroishi Hot Springs
黒石温泉郷
Nakano River
Minaminakano
Itadome
Nuruyu
Ochiai
Aseishikawa Dam
Aseishi River
Mt. Kamiyuzawayama
Mt. Minamizawadake
Mt. Yokodake
Mt. Komagamine
Mt. Kushigamine
Akanuma Lake
Mt. Akakuradake
Tsutanuma
Tsuta
Mt. Norikuradake
Mt. Tashiroyama
Mt. Yokoashiyama
Mt. Tomiokayama
Ozaki
Hiraka
Hiraka-machi
平賀町
Karadake
Tsugaru
津軽
Mt. Ikazuchiyama
Mt. Kenashiyama
Hakkoda View
Towadako
Towadako onsen
Yakeyama 焼山
Towadako
十和田湖
Mt. Tassobeyama
Matsuminotaki
Mt. Tokusamori
Ōse River
Owani-Hirosaki
大鰐弘前
Mt. Yasuteyama
Mt. Asogatake
Tsugaru-kōgen
Biwanodai
Towadami(chi(dō)
十和田道
Mt. Fujisawamori
Narrow road-Congestion 1st week of May
Oirase Valley
奥入瀬渓流
Mt. Umanoka
Hachimangū
Mt. Teshiromori
Closed in winter
Ajara
阿闍羅
Ōwani-onsen
Ōwani
Nagamine
Nagamine 長峰
Mt. Shiratesan
Nurukawa
Hyakko River
Mt. Ohanabeyama
Kumoinotaki
Mt. Ajarayama
Aomori Royal
Mt. Mitsumori
Mt. Tozawayama
Kirigake
Mt. Shibamori
Choshiotaki
Bakufu-kaidō
Sobe River
Ikarigaseki
碇ケ関
Ikarigaseki-mura
碇ケ関村
Mt. Iwadake
Towadako Lake
Nenokuchi 子ノ口
Shimada
Mt. Doyamori
Mt. Okariyadake
Mt. Eboshimori
Wainai-jinja
Mt. Kurayama
Mt. Towadayama
Higashinoumi Lake
Mt. Heiraidake
Utarube 宇樽部
Ikarigaseki 碇ケ関
Mt. Kūdaisan
Mt. Shirojiyama
Nakanoumi Lake
Towada-jinja
Tsugaru-Yunosawa
Yunosawa
Tsukari River
Hisayoshi
Mt. Shibamori
Mt. Takayama
Mt. Jinkichimori
Ainori
Mt. Towariyama
Hikage
Yatate
Yatate Pass 矢立峠
Sakanashi Pass
Mt. Magusomoriyama
Mt. Nagabikiyama
Nishinoumi Lake
Sharp curves
Mt. Ohikageyama
Mt. Sumizukamori
Caution-slippery road
Wainai 和井内
Hakka Pass
発荷峠
Mt. Tairamori
Mt. Nuitoyama
Jinba
Mt. Sasamori
Mt. Kuromori
Mt. Dokonomori
Mt. Kuromori
Mt. Aosabayama
Mt. Jōgakurayama
Mt. Higashimatayama
Nakataki 中滝
Chōshidaki
Nakataki
Mt. Aoiwayama
Nakataki
Mt. Nishinomori
Mt. Ogamisan
Mt. Omokurasan
Mt. Sugisawasan
Ōtaki
Nanataki
Ōyu River
Mt. Sasamoriyama
Oguni River
Ushū-kaidō
Shimonai River
Shirasawa
Mt. Haboyasan
Mt. Kōchiyama
Kosaka-machi
小坂町
Kosaka
小坂
Mt. Tsukushimori
Mt. Jōgamori
Mt. Yahazuyama
Ōshimizu River
Mt. Asahinadake
Mt. Kuromoriyama
Mt. Yosugedōmori
Tsugaru-kaidō
Yukizawa
Mt. Nabekoshiyama
Ōyu
Mt. Inuhoemori
Mirokunotaki
Akuya River
Ōdate
Nagaki River
Ariura 1 有浦一
Mt. Hōōzan
Mt. Zōgakurayama
Mt. Morosukeyama
Raiman Pass
Nagakuramachi 長倉町
Higashi-Ōdate
Mt. Akibasan
Ōyu Stone Circle
Furokura Pass
to Kosaka
to Towadako Lake
Towada-minami
to Ōdate
Saruga-jinja
ŌDATE-SHI
大館市
Mt. Takamori
Towada
十和田
Towada-minami
Mt. Shikakudake
Mt. Nakadake
Mt. Kurakakeyama
Sawajiri
Matsunoki
松ノ木
Ōgita
Suehiro
Shibahira
Hinai-machi
比内町
Ōtaki
大滝
Dobukai
Hanawa Line
Ōdate (Yokozawa)
KAZUNO-SHI
鹿角市
Hachimantai
Mt. Ōkuramori
Ōu Line
東北自動車道
Hirosaki-shi
to Namioka
to Hirosaki
to Towada
to Ōwani
to Sukayu
to Nenokuchi
to Towadako Lake
A
B
C
D
1
2
3
4
5
6

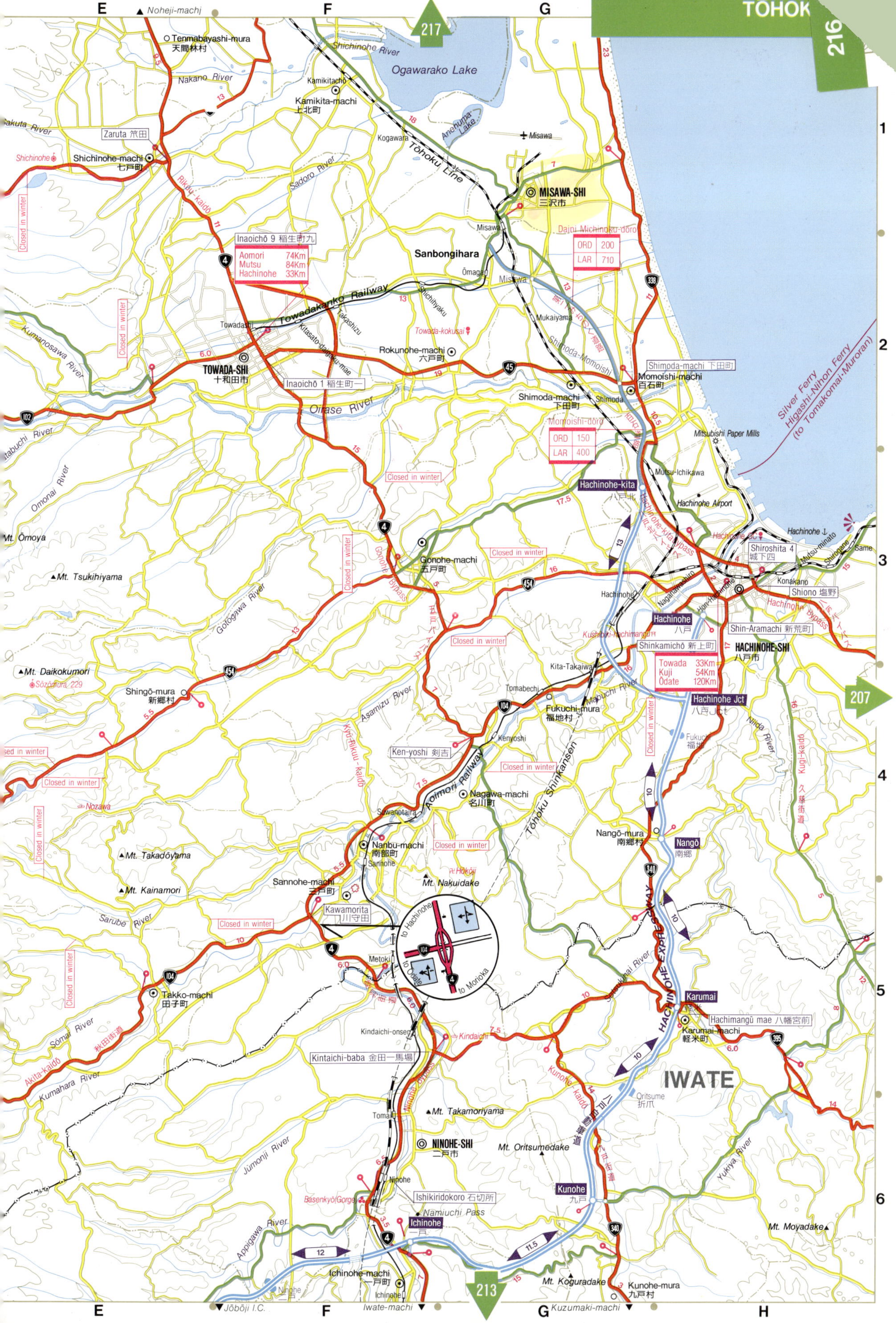
E
F
G
H
1
2
3
4
5
6
217
207
213
Noheji-machi
Tenmabayashi-mura
天間林村
Nakano River
Shichinohe River
Ogawarako Lake
Kamikitachō
Kamikita-machi
上北町
Sakuta River
Zaruta 笊田
Shichinohe
Shichinohe-machi
七戸町
Kogawara
Anenuma Lake
Tōhoku Line
Misawa
Sadoro River
Rikuu-kaidō
MISAWA-SHI
三沢市
Misawa
Dajni Michinoku-dōro
ORD 200
LAR 710
Closed in winter
Inaoichō 9 稲生町九
Aomori 74Km
Mutsu 84Km
Hachinohe 33Km
Sanbongihara
Ōmagari
Misawa
Towadakanko Railway
Shichihyaku
Takashizu
Kitasato-daigaku-mae
Towadashi
Kumanosawa River
TOWADA-SHI
十和田市
Towada-kokusai
Mukaiyama
Shimoda-Momoishi
Rokunohe-machi
六戸町
Inaoichō 1 稲生町一
Shimoda-machi 下田町
Momoishi-machi
百石町
Shimoda-machi
下田町
Shimoda
Oirase River
Momoishi-dōro
ORD 150
LAR 400
Silver Ferry
Higashi-Nihon Ferry
(to Tomakomai·Muroran)
Mitsubishi Paper Mills
Mutsu-Ichikawa
Hachinohe-kita
八戸北
Hachinohe Airport
Hachinohe-Kita Bypass
Hachinohe ↓
Omonai River
Mt. Ōmoya
Mt. Tsukihiyama
Gonohe Bypass
Gonohe-machi
五戸町
Shiroshita 4
城下四
Mutsu-minato
Shirogane
Same
Gorogawa River
Hachinohe
Naganawashiro
Hon-Hachinohe
Konakano
Shiono 塩野
Hachinohe
八戸
Hachinohe Bypass
Kushibiki-hachimangū
Shin-Aramachi 新荒町
Shinkamichō 新上町
HACHINOHE-SHI
八戸市
Mt. Daikokumori
Sōzōmura 229
Kita-Takaiwa
Towada 33Km
Kuji 54Km
Ōdate 120Km
Tomabechi
Mabuchi River
Shingō-mura
新郷村
Asamizu River
Fukuchi-mura
福地村
Hachinohe Jct
八戸Jct
Kenyoshi
Fukuchi
福地
Niida River
Kyū-Rikuu-kaidō
Ken-yoshi 剣吉
Closed in winter
Kugi-kaidō
Aoimori Railway
Nagawa-machi
名川町
Tōhoku Shinkansen
Nozawa
Suwanotaira
Mt. Takadōyama
Nanbu-machi
南部町
Sannohe
Closed in winter
Nangō-mura
南郷村
Nangō
南郷
Mt. Kainamori
Sannohe-machi
三戸町
Hōkōji
Mt. Nakuidake
Kawamorita
川守田
Sarube River
to Hachinohe
to Ōdate
to Morioka
Metoki
HACHINOHE EXPRESSWAY
Takko-machi
田子町
Sōmai River
Kindaichi-onsen
Kindaichi
Karumai
Hachimangū mae 八幡宮前
Karumai-machi
軽米町
Akita-kaidō
Kintaichi-baba 金田一馬場
Kumahara River
IWATE
Kunohe-kaidō
Oritsume
折爪
Tomai
Mt. Takamoriyama
Jūmonji River
NINOHE-SHI
二戸市
Mt. Oritsumedake
Yukiya River
Ninohe
Basenkyō Gorge
Ishikiridokoro 石切所
Kunohe
九戸
Namiuchi Pass
Ichinohe
一戸
Mt. Moyadake
Appigawa River
Ichinohe-machi
一戸町
Ichinohe
Mt. Koguradake
Kunohe-mura
九戸村
Jōbōji I.C.
Iwate-machi
Kuzumaki-machi

218
214
175
177
AOMORI-WAN
青森湾
AOMORI
AOMORI-SHI
青森市
AOMORI EXPRESSWAY
青森自動車道
TŌHOKU EXPRESSWAY
東北自動車道
KUROISHI-SHI
黒石市
Mutsu-wan Ferry (to Wakinosawa)
Higashi-Nihon Ferry (to Tomakomai-Muroran)
Mt. Kadohashizawayama
Tsugaru Line
Kanita-machi
蟹田町
Chūshi 中師
Kanita River
Kanita
Naka-Oguni
Hirose River
Matsumae-kaidō
Sehejī
Gōsawa
Yomogita River
Yomogita-mura
蓬田村
Yomogita
Mt. Ōkuradake
Nakasawa
Ushiro-jinja
Ushirogata River
Ushirogata
Hidariseki
Mt. Ōsakayama
Mt. Chōbōzan
Uchimanpe River
Okunai
Closed in winter
Tsugaru-Miyata
Mt. Genpachimori
Mt. Asukayama
Aomori-chūō-ōhashi
ORD 100
LAR 370
Minmaya 61Km
Hirosaki 40Km
Nenokuchi 55Km
Aburakawa
Mt. Tazawamori
Shinoda 2
篠田二
Aomori
Tsukurimichi
造道
to Kanita
to Hirosaki
to Noheji
Mt. Manokamiyama
Mt. Tsukushimoriyama
Aomori-nishi Bypass
Tsugaru-Shinjō
Shin-Aomori
Aomori 青森
青森中央大橋
Gappo Park
Yatamae
Koyanagi
Higashi-Aomori
Mt. Totoriyama
Aomori-higashi
青森東
Shinjō River
Mt. Bonjusan
Ushū-kaidō
Mt. Mejayama
Tsurugasaka
Aomori-Kanjō Bypass
Aomori-chūō
青森中央
Hamada 浜田
Mt. Kanetsukidōyama
Daishaka 大釈迦
Tsurugasaka
Mt. Sakaeyama
Komagome River
Yokouchi River
ORD 200
LAR 730
Aomori-kūkō-dōro
青森空港道路
Daishaka
Namioka
浪岡
Mt. Takazumoriyama
Aomori
Aomori-ken-Taikyō
Arakawa River
Moya Pass
Moya
Ōu Line
Mt. Bōzuhatakeyama
Nyūnai Pass
Namioka
Mt. Toyamoriyama
Namioka-machi
浪岡町
Gankake Pass
Mt. Tsukamoriyama
Takadate
高舘
Mt. Goshayama
Tokiwa-mura
常盤村
Kita-Tokiwa
Hirosaki-shi
Kōnan-Kuroishi
Mt. Kuromoriyama
Josenji
Inakadate-mura
田舎館村
Kuroishi
黒石
Kuroishi Bypass
Kuroishi Hot Springs
黒石温泉郷
Saruga-jinja
Saruga
Tsugaru-Onoe
Onoe-machi
尾上町
Nakano River
Minaminakano
Itadome
Nuruyu
Ochiai
Aseishi Dam
Aseishikawa
Mt. Tashiroyama
Mt. Tomiokayama
Hiraka-machi
平賀町
Hiraka
Ozaki
Mt. Ikazuchiyama
Aoni
Mt. Kenashiyama
Tsugaru
津軽
Karadake
Towada Lake
C. Natsudomarizaki
夏泊崎
Ōshima I.
Pine trees
Resthouse area
Tsubaki-jinja
Aomori Seaside
Kujinohama
Mt. Kayadake
C. Hanakukurizaki
Mt. Ōguriyama
To scallop sale area
Mt. Hiyamizuyama
Mt. Maruyama
Natsudomari Pen
C. Yasuizaki
Mt. Mizugasawayama
Mourajima I.
Mt. Namiuchiyama
Nishi-Hiranai
Kominato
Tōhoku Line
Shimizugawa
Road closed when raining more than 100mm
Hiranai-machi
平内町
Kominato 小湊
Mt. Yashikiyama
Mt. Nagareyama
Mt. Nabemoriyama
Marine Park Asamushi
Yunoshima I.
Mt. Takamoriyama
Mt. Hikinokoshiyama
Asamushi-onsen
Asamushi
浅虫
Mt. Kōchiyama
Mt. Naruyama
Asamushi
C. Hanakurizaki
Shimizu River
Mt. Matsukurayama
Nonai
Aomori-higashi Bypass
Mt. Higashidake
Mt. Eboshidake
Tōō
Michinoku-dōro
ORD 830
LAR 2940
Mt. Ōkenashiyama
Mt. Sankakudake
Mt. Hanbeitakamori
Mt. Naranokimoriyama
Mt. Yaseyama
Sankaidaki
Mt. Shihonkatsurayama
Mt. Origamiyama
Mt. Horikodake
Kotsubo River
Otsubo River
Ko-tōge Pass
Ō-tōge Pass
Mt. Shichijūmoriyama
Mt. Shibamoriyama
Sankaidaki
Tashiromotoyu
Hakkōda
Tashirotai
Sankaidaki
Mt. Hachimandake
Congestion in summer and autumn
Mt. Ishikurayama
Mt. Maedake
Hakkōdasan
Mt. Tamoyachiyama
Mt. Minamimatayama
Mt. Hakkōdasan
八甲田山
Mt. Ōdake
Mt. Hinadake
Mt. Takadaodake
Jōgakura
Sukayu
Mt. Kuromori
Mt. Ishikurayama
Yachi
Sarukura
Skunk cabbage area
Farming area
Mt. Yokodake
Mt. Kamiyuzawayama
Mt. Minamizawadake
Akameshidai
Mt. Komagamine
Akanuma Lake
Tsutagawa River
Hakkōda View
Mt. Kushigamine
Mt. Norikuradake
Mt. Akakuradake
Tsuta
Towadako
Yakeyama 焼山
Towadako-onsen
Towadako
十和田湖
Mt. Yokoashiyama
Matsuminotaki
Kazuno-shi
Mt. Tassobeyama
A
B
C
D
1
2
3
4
5
6

219
215
C. Nakayamazaki
Closed in winter
Mutsu-Yokohama
Yokohama-machi
横浜町
Mt. Hachirōeboshi
Mt. Ōtsukushiyama
Mt. Fukkoshieboshi
Myōjindaira
Fukkoshi
NOHEJI-WAN
野辺地湾
Bad road
Oippe River
Rokkasho-mura
六ヶ所村
Itakonuma Lake
Obuchinuma Lake
Takahokonuma Lake
Ōminato Line
to Mutsu
to Aomori
to Towada
Ichiyanaginuma Lake
Takase River
Arito
Karibasawa
Makado 馬門
Noheji River
Kita-Noheji
Noheji
Noheji-machi
野辺地町
Closed in winter
Tamoginuma Lake
Amagamori 天ヶ森
Uchinuma Lake
Closed in winter
Matsunokitaira 松ノ木平
Mutsu 54Km
Aomori 44Km
Hachinohe 52Km
Shimizume River
Chibiki
Chibiki-onsen
Ogawarako Lake
Tsubokawa River
Ottomo
Tōhoku-machi
東北町
Mt. Sogamori
Akagawa River
Tenmabayashi-mura
天間林村
Shichinohe River
Nakano River
Kamikitachō
Kamikita-machi
上北町
Sakuta River
Zaruta 荒田
Shichinohe
Shichinohe-machi
七戸町
Kogawara
Anenuma Lake
Misawa
Tōhoku Line
Wadagawa River
to Aomori
Inaoichō 9
稲生町九
to Hachinohe
to Gonohe
MISAWA-SHI
三沢市
Rikuu-kaidō
Inaoichō 9
稲生町九
Aomori 74Km
Nenokuchi 38Km
Sannohe 41Km
Misawa
Sanbongihara
Daini Michinoku-dōro
ORD 200
LAR 710
Ōmagari
Shichihyaku
Misawa
Towadakankō Railway
Takashizu
Towadashi
Kitasatodaigakumae
Towada-kokusai
Mukaiyama
Shimoda-Momoishi
Shimodamachi 下田町
Kumanosawa River
TOWADA-SHI
十和田市
Inaoichō 1 稲生町一
Rokunohe-machi
六戸町
Momoishi-machi
百石町
Shimoda-machi
下田町
Shimoda
Oirase River
Momoishi-dōro
ORD 150
LAR 400
Mitsubishi Paper Mills
Higashi-Nihon Ferry
Silver Ferry
Mutsu-Ichikawa
Hachinohe-shi
E
F
G
H
1
2
3
4
5
6

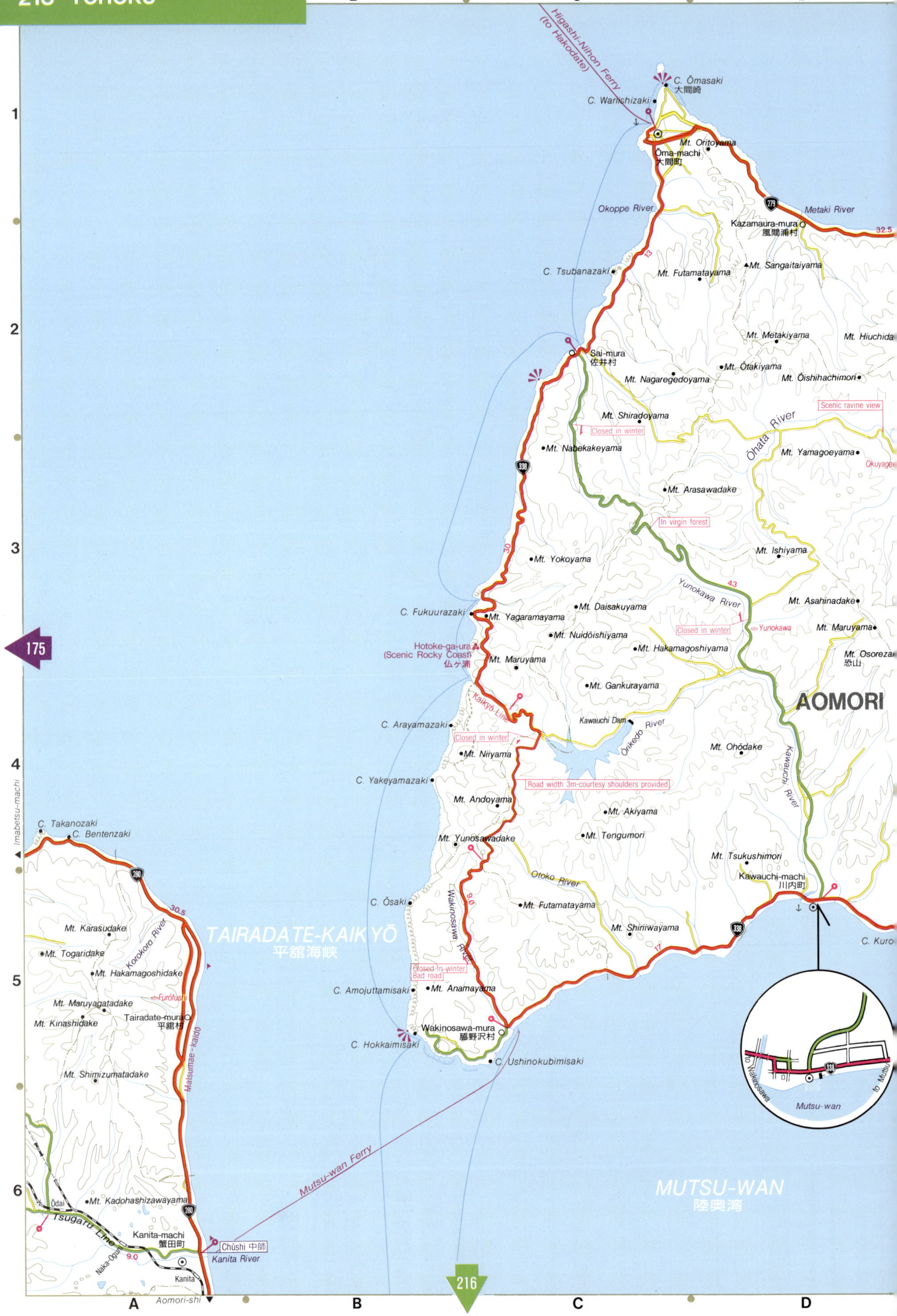

B
C
D
1
2
3
4
5
6
A
Higashi-Nihon Ferry (to Hakodate)
C. Ōmasaki 大間崎
C. Warishizaki
Mt. Oritoyama
Ōma-machi 大間町
Okoppe River
Metaki River
Kazamaura-mura 風間浦村
32.5
279
13
C. Tsubanazaki
Mt. Futamatayama
Mt. Sangaitaiyama
Mt. Metakiyama
Mt. Hiuchida
Sai-mura 佐井村
Mt. Ōtakiyama
Mt. Nagaregedoyama
Mt. Ōishihachimori
Scenic ravine view
Mt. Shiradoyama
Closed in winter
Ōhata River
Mt. Nabekakeyama
Mt. Yamagoeyama
Okuyage
338
Mt. Arasawadake
In virgin forest
30
Mt. Ishiyama
Mt. Yokoyama
43
Yunokawa River
Mt. Asahinadake
C. Fukuurazaki
Mt. Yagaramayama
Mt. Daisakuyama
Mt. Nuidōishiyama
Yunokawa
Mt. Maruyama
Hotoke-ga-ura (Scenic Rocky Coast) 仏ヶ浦
Mt. Hakamagoshiyama
Mt. Osorezan 恐山
175
Mt. Maruyama
Mt. Gankurayama
AOMORI
Kaikyō Line
Kawauchi Dam
C. Arayamazaki
Orikedo River
Closed in winter
Mt. Niiyama
Mt. Ohōdake
Kawauchi River
C. Yakeyamazaki
Road width 3m-courtesy shoulders provided
Mt. Andoyama
Mt. Akiyama
Imabetsu-machi
C. Takanozaki
C. Bentenzaki
Mt. Yunosawadake
Mt. Tengumori
Mt. Tsukushimori
Kawauchi-machi 川内町
280
Otoko River
9.0
Wakinosawa River
C. Ōsaki
Mt. Futamatayama
30.5
Mt. Karasudake
Mt. Shiriiwayama
C. Kuro
TAIRADATE-KAIKYŌ 平舘海峡
Korokoro River
Mt. Togaridake
Mt. Hakamagoshidake
Closed in winter Bad road
C. Amojuttamisaki
Mt. Anamayama
Furōfushi
Mt. Maruyagatadake
Tairadate-mura 平舘村
Mt. Kinashidake
Matsumae-kaidō
Wakinosawa-mura 脇野沢村
C. Hokkaimisaki
C. Ushinokubimisaki
to Wakinosawa
to Mutsu
Mutsu-wan
Mt. Shimizumatadake
Mutsu-wan Ferry
MUTSU-WAN 陸奥湾
Ōdai
Mt. Kadohashizawayama
Tsugaru Line
Kanita-machi 蟹田町
Chūshi 中師
Kanita River
Naka-Oguni
Kanita
216
Aomori-shi

E
F
G
H
1
2
3
4
5
6
from Mutsu-shi
Akita 300Km
Morioka 210Km
C. Yakeyamazaki
C. Hiyorizaki
Mt. Sankakuyama
to Ōma
to Yagen
to Mutsu
Ōhata-machi
大畑町
Dainji
9.5
Mt. Sokobeyama
Closed in winter
Ōtaki
Asunaro Line
3.5
4
Dedogawa River
Hachitaki
9.5
Jizōdō
Congestion about the end of July
Closed in winter
Usorisanko Lake
Mt. Byōbuyama
MUTSU-SHI
むつ市
Shōjiyama
Mt. Kamabuseyama
Ōminato
Shimokita
Ōminato
Kamabuseyama
Ōminato-wan
C. Ashisaki
26.5
Nagashita River
Ōkawame River
Akagawa
Ōminato Line
Kanayasawa
to Ōhata
to Ōhata
Honmachi 本町
Kamikawachō 上川町
to Hachinohe
Kogawamachi 小川町
to Kawauchi
to Noheji
to Noheji
Japanese red pine trees
Closed in winter
Tanabe River
Mt. Ishigamiyama
Yokomukai 1 横迎一
Ōma 50Km
Aomori 98Km
Towada 84Km
Kanamagari 金曲
Aohira River
Yokonagare Pass
Higashidōri-mura
東通村
Mutsu-hamanasu Line
To scallop sale area
Shimokita Pen.
下北半島
Okunai River
Chikagawa
Chikagawa River
31.5
Mt. Issaiyama
Mt. Ishikawadai
Arihata
C. Shiriyazaki
尻屋崎
C. Fujiishizaki
Mt. Kuwahatayama
C. Kukidōnosaki
27
Mt. Katasakiyama
Naganuma Lake
Ōnuma Lake
Sakyōnuma Lake
Kooibe River
Oippe River
C. Monomisaki
51.5
Mt. Gassan
C. Nakayamazaki
Hinoki River
Mt. Kanatsuyama
Closed in winter
Mutsu-Yokohama
Sanpō River
Yokohama Bypass
Yokohama-machi
横浜町
Mt. Hachirōeboshi
Noushi River
Mt. Ōtsukushiyama
338
279
217

222
A
B
C
D
1
2
3
4
5
6
Rankoshi-chō
Kuromatsunai
Kuromatsunai-chō
黒松内町
Mt. Ōbirayama
Chiwase
Warabitai
34
39.5
5
Oshamanbe 長万部
Kutchan 79Km
Muroran 90Km
Hakodate 106Km
30
Shizukari
Kohoro
C. Mottamisaki
茂津多岬
229
Mt. Karibayama
Mt. Oshamanbedake
Futamata
Futamata
15
Asahihama
Shishiiwa
Mt. Kasubedake
Mt. Meppudake
Pirika
Oshamanbe
長万部
Shizukari-kokudō
Oshamanbe
Oshamanbe-chō
長万部町
11
10.5
Pirika Pass
美利河峠
Setana-chō
瀬棚町
Nagabuchi 長渕
230
Imakane-chō
今金町
Kunnui 国縫
Kunnui
国縫
43
Kitahiyama-chō
北檜山町
Toshibetsu River
Imagane-kokudō
Kita-Toyotsu
Kuroiwa
21
UCHIURA-WAN
内浦湾
Higashi-Nihon Ferry
C. Obanasaki
尾花岬
Yamasaki
C. Inahomisaki
稲穂岬
Yakumo-chō
八雲町
Washinosu
Honchō 本町
Taisei-chō
大成町
Mt. Maruyama
47.5
Yakumo
Hakodate Line
277
Mt. Yūrappudake
33.5
Yamakoshi
Nodaoi
Okushiritō I.
奥尻島
Okushiri-chō
奥尻町
Mt. Kamuiyama
Mt. Shiromizudake
16
Otoshibe
Otoshibe 落部
Ishikura
Scenic view of coast
Kumaishi-chō
熊石町
C. Nagaisomisaki
Hon-Ishikura
17.5
Mori-machi
森町
Nigorigawa
Ginkon-yu
Ishiya
Katsura gawa
Ayukawa 鮎川
Ainumako Lake
Okushiri
229
Morikawachō 森川町
C. Aonaemisaki
Closed in winter
Ōnuma Lake
48.5
Hiyama-kokudō
to Mori
Ōnuma-kōen
C. Shibinomisaki
Mt. Otobedake
Ōnuma
Scenic view of coast
Closed in winter
29
5
Higashi-Nihon Ferry
Otobe-chō
乙部町
to Hakodate
Keiki
227
41.5
Yanagisawa 柳沢
Ōno-kokudō
Assabu River
6.5
Assabu-chō
厚沢部町
Gamushi 俄虫
Oshamanbe 138Km
Hakodate 65Km
Matsumae 771Km
227
Esashi-chō
江差町
Esashi
14.5
Closed in winter
Ōtome 大留
Umezuke Pass
Kamiiso
Kaminokuni-chō
上ノ国町
Kaminokuni
Mt. Hashigodake
Closed in winter
Nakasuda
Mt. Katsuradake
Katsuraoka
Miyakoshi
Oshima-Tōbetsu
Yunotai
Shinmei
Esashi Line
Satsukari
Izumisawa
Kamaya
228
28.5
39.5
228
Matsumae Pen.
松前半島
Kikonai-chō
木古内町
Honchō 本町
Kikonai
Yoshibori
Oshima-Tsuruoka
Kikonai River
C. Hikatadomarisaki
Mt. Hakamagoshidake
62.5
Mt. Nanatsudake
9.0
Shiriuchi
Shiriuchi
Fukuyama-kaidō
Mt. Daisengendake
Matsumae-kokudō
Tsugaru-kaikyō Railway
Shiriuchi-chō
知内町
25.5
C. Kitsunegoshimisaki
Vehicles Prohibited
Fukushima Pass
C. Yagoshimisaki
Fukushima-chō
福島町
Ōshima I.
White sand beach
Closed in winter
C. Tonomamisaki
Matsumae Castle
Seikan Tunnel
TSUGARU-KAIKYŌ
津軽海峡
Matsumae-chō
松前町
19
C. Shiragamimisaki
Kojima I.
A
B
C
D

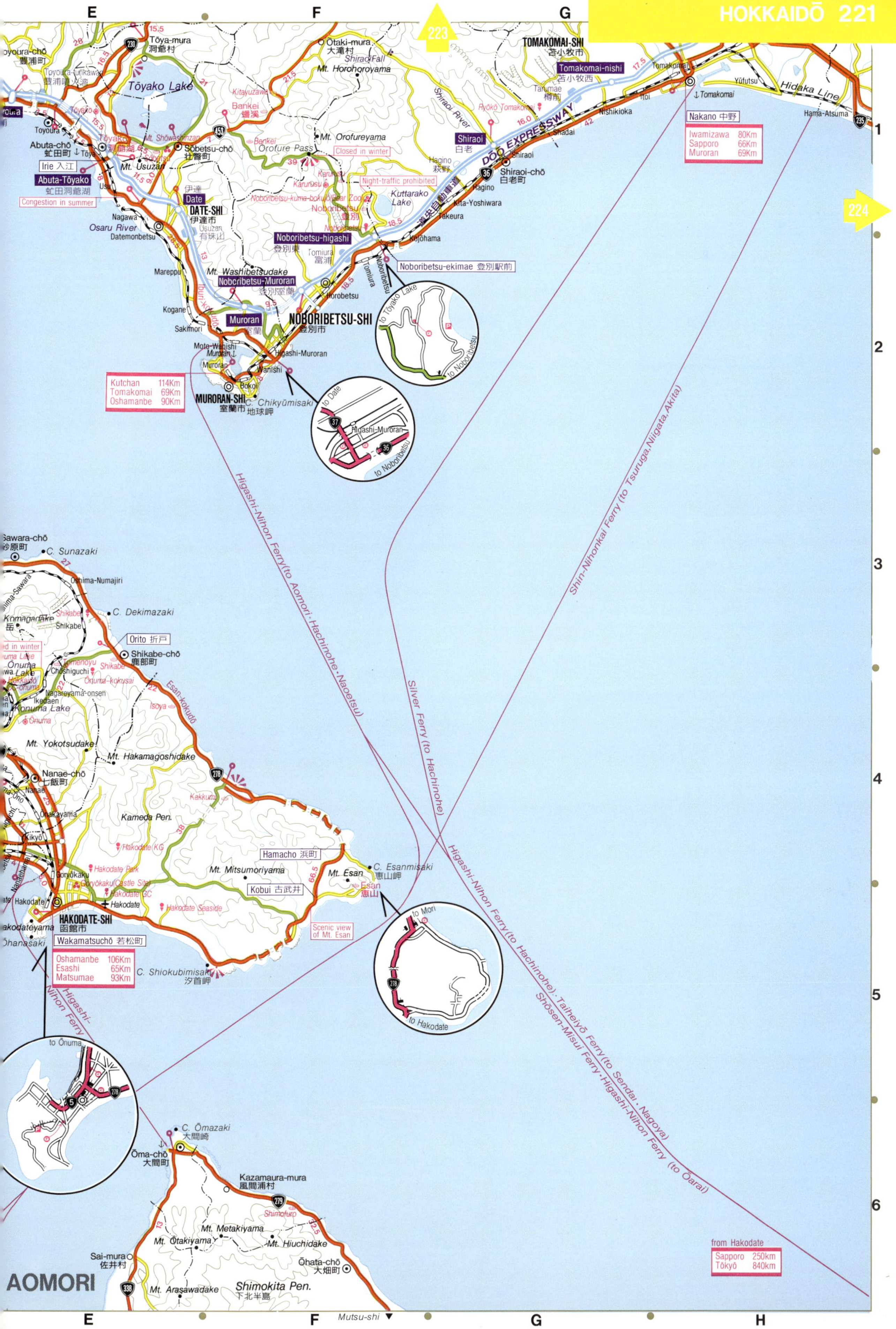
E
F
G
H
223
224
1
2
3
4
5
6
Tōya-mura
洞爺村
Tōyako Lake
Toyoura
Abuta-chō
虻田町
Irie 入江
Abuta-Tōyako
虻田洞爺湖
Congestion in summer
Sobetsu-chō
壮瞥町
Mt. Usuzan
Mt. Shōwashinzan
Date
DATE-SHI
伊達市
Usuzan
有珠山
Osaru River
Datemonbetsu
Nagawa
Mareppu
Kogane
Sakimori
Mote-Wanishi
Muroran
Bokoi
MURORAN-SHI
室蘭市
C. Chikyūmisaki
地球岬
Kutchan 114Km
Tomakomai 69Km
Oshamanbe 90Km
Mt. Washibetsudake
Noboribetsu-Muroran
登別室蘭
Higashi-Muroran
Wanishi
NOBORIBETSU-SHI
登別市
Horobetsu
Noboribetsu-higashi
登別東
Tomiura
富浦
Noboribetsu-ekimae 登別駅前
Otaki-mura
大滝村
Shiraoi Fall
Mt. Horohoroyama
Kitayuzawa
Bankei
蟠渓
Orofure Pass
Mt. Orofureyama
Closed in winter
Night-traffic prohibited
Noboribetsu-kuma-bokujō(Bear Zoo)
Kuttarako Lake
Noboribetsu
登別
Karurusu
TOMAKOMAI-SHI
苫小牧市
Tomakomai-nishi
苫小牧西
Tarumae
樽前
Shiraoi River
Shiraoi
白老
Hagino
萩野
Shiraoi-chō
白老町
DŌŌ EXPRESSWAY
道央自動車道
Kita-Yoshiwara
Takeura
Kojohama
Shadai
Nishikioka
Itoi
Tomakomai
Yūfutsu
Hidaka Line
Hama-Atsuma
Nakano 中野
Iwamizawa 80Km
Sapporo 66Km
Muroran 69Km
to Tōyako Lake
to Noboribetsu
to Date
Higashi-Muroran
Higashi-Nihon Ferry(to Aomori・Hachinohe・Naoetsu)
Silver Ferry (to Hachinohe)
Shin-Nihonkai Ferry (to Tsuruga, Niigata, Akita)
Higashi-Nihon Ferry(to Hachinohe): Taiheiyō Ferry(to Sendai・Nagoya)
Shōsen-Mitsui Ferry・Higashi-Nihon Ferry (to Ōarai)
Sawara-chō
砂原町
C. Sunazaki
Oshima-Numajiri
C. Dekimazaki
Shikabe
Orito 折戸
Shikabe-chō
鹿部町
Chōshiguchi
Ōnuma-kokusai
Nagareyama-onsen
Ikedaen
Konuma Lake
Esan-kokudō
Isoya
Mt. Yokotsudake
Mt. Hakamagoshidake
Nanae-chō
七飯町
Nanae
Onakayama
Kameda Pen.
Kakkumi
Hakodate KG
Hakodate Park
Goryōkaku
Goryōkaku(Castle Site)
Hakodate GC
Hakodate Seaside
Hakodate
HAKODATE-SHI
函館市
Hakodateyama
Ōhanasaki
Wakamatsuchō 若松町
Oshamanbe 106Km
Esashi 65Km
Matsumae 93Km
Mt. Mitsumoriyama
Hamacho 浜町
Kobui 古武井
Mt. Esan
C. Esanmisaki
恵山岬
Esan
恵山
Scenic view of Mt. Esan
C. Shiokubimisaki
汐首岬
to Mori
to Hakodate
to Ōnuma
Higashi-Nihon Ferry
C. Ōmazaki
大間崎
Ōma-chō
大間町
Kazamaura-mura
風間浦村
Shimofuro
Mt. Metakiyama
Mt. Ōtakiyama
Mt. Hiuchidake
Sai-mura
佐井村
Ōhata-chō
大畑町
AOMORI
Mt. Arasawadake
Shimokita Pen.
下北半島
Mutsu-shi
from Hakodate
Sapporo 250km
Tōkyō 840km

B
C
D
1
2
3
4
5
6
C. Shakotanmis
積丹岬
C. Kamuimisaki
神威岬
229
21.5
Shakotan-c
積丹
Mt. Yobetsudake
余別岳
Mt. Shakota
Mt. Daitenguyama
Mt. Doronoki
Mt. Sannaidake
Tōmaru Pass
Shakotan Pen.
積丹半島
34
Closed in winter
Kamoenai-mura
神恵内村
Kamoenai-mura-s
神恵内村市街
Mt. Kumaoiyama
Moiwa Sakazuki
Scenic view of coast
25
Tomari-mura
泊村
to Kutchan
to Oshamanbe
Konbu
5
to Kutchan
Iwanai-chō
岩内町
C. Raidenmisaki
Scenic view of coast
Raiden
雷電
Mt. Raiden-yama
Closed in winter
Niimi
34.5
Raiden-kokudō
Shiribetsu River
229
C. Benkeimisaki
弁慶岬
Suttsu-wan
Suttsu-chō
寿都町
Rankoshi-chō
蘭越町
Niseko resort
Rankoshi
Mt. Horonaisan
Otani 大
Closed in win
Yubetsu 湯別
Mena
Yōtei-kokudō
15
Shimamaki-mura
島牧村
Gūnai
84
Neppu
39.5
Mena Pass
Mt. Horonaisan
Closed in winter
Scenic view of coast
Chiwase
Kuromatsunai
Kuromatsunai-chō
黒松内町
34
Mt. Ōbirayama
Warabitai
C. Mottamisaki
茂津多岬
Mt. Karibayama
Oshamanbe 長万部
Kutchan 79Km
Muroran 90Km
Hakodate 106Km
30
Shizukari
Kohoro
Mt. Oshamanbedake
Futamata
Futamata
15
Asahihama
Mt. Kasubedake
Mt. Meppudake
Pirika
Oshamanbe
長万部
Shizukari-kokudō
Scenic view of coast
Oshamanbe-chō
長万部町
11
10.5
Setana-chō
瀬棚町
Pirika Pass
Osabuchi 長淵
Imakane-chō
今金町
Kunnui 国縫
Kunnui
国縫
Kunnui
230
43
Yoshibetsu River
Imagane-kokudō
5
Kitahiyama-chō
北檜山町
Kita-Toyotsu
Shin-Nihonkai Ferry (to Niigata)
Higashi-Nihonkai Ferry (to Okushiri)
Kuroiwa
Uchiura-wan
229
C. Obanasaki
尾花岬
31
Hakodate Line
Yamasaki
47.5
220
Washinosu
Okushiritō I.
A
B
Kumaishi-chō
C
Yakumo-chō
D

E
F
G
H
1
2
3
4
5
6
226
224
221
from Sapporo-shi
Obihiro 240Km
Hakodate 250Km
Hamamasu-mura
浜益村
Sōshi Pass
Naka-Toppu
Shimo-Toppu
Mt. Pinneshiri
Minami-shimo-Toppu
Osatsunai
Tsurunuma
Urausu-chō
浦臼町
Satteki
Mt. Betsukaridake
Closed in winter
Ishikari-kokudō
Atsuta-mura
厚田村
Tsukigata-chō
月形町
Tōbetsu River
BIBAI-SHI
美唄市
Nae-chō
Atsutomamisaki
Furubira-chō
古平町
Furubirachō-shigai
古平町市街
Congestion between Yoichi and Zenibako in summer
C. Takashimamisaki
高島岬
C. Shiripamisaki
Yoichi-wan
Ishikari-wan
Congestion in Ishikari-chō in summer
Ishikari River
Tōbetsu-chō
当別町
Shinshinotsu-mura
新篠津村
Kita-mura
北村
MIKASA-SHI
三笠市
IWAMIZAWA-SHI
岩見沢市
Namikichō 3 ban
並木町3番
Tengudake
Yoichi-chō
余市町
OTARU-SHI
小樽市
Bannaguro 花畔
Irifune 入船
ISHIKARI-SHI
石狩市
Teine-ku
手稲区
Kita-ku
北区
Asahikawa 119Km
Otaru 38Km
Kutchan 92Km
EBETSU-SHI
江別市
Iwamizawa
岩見沢
Kurisawa-chō
栗沢町
Niki-chō
仁木町
Mt. Ōnoboriyama
Hiyamizu Pass
Cherry sale area
Zenibako
Teine
Sapporo-nishi
Sapporo
Ebetsu-nishi
Ebetsu-higashi
Nanporo-chō
南幌町
Kuriyama-chō
栗山町
Akaigawa-mura
赤井川村
Mt. Asaridake
Mt. Teineyama
手稲山
SAPPORO-SHI
札幌市
Sapporo-minami
Atsubetsu-ku
厚別区
Naganuma-chō
長沼町
13ku 13区
Mt. Ginzan
Takasago 高砂
Mt. Yoichidake
Nishi-ku
西区
Chūō-ku
中央区
Mt. Eboshidake
Toyohira-ku
豊平区
Minami-ku
南区
Sapporo 92Km
Tomakomai 103Km
Muroran 114Km
Jōzankei Nishikibashi
定山渓錦橋
Jōzankei
定山渓
ORD 660
LAR 2000
Kitahiroshima
KITAHIROSHIMA-SHI
北広島市
Kiyota-ku
清田区
Yuni-chō
由仁町
18ku 18区
Mikawa
三川
Kutchan Pass
Mt. Muineyama
Hōheikyō Dam
Mt. Sapporodake
Kutchan
Kutchan-chō
倶知安町
Mt. Kimobetsudake
Mt. Sausuyama
Closed in winter
ENIWA-SHI
恵庭市
Eniwa
Chitose-higashi
Oiwake-chō
追分町
Mt. Soranumadake
Nakayama Pass
中山峠
Kyōgoku-chō
京極町
Mt. Yōteizan
羊蹄山
Niseko-chō
ニセコ町
Motomachi 元町
Fujimidai 富士見台
Kimobetsu-chō
喜茂別町
Mt. Izaridake
Chitose-Eniwa Jct
Chitose
CHITOSE-SHI
千歳市
Konbu 昆布
Makkari-mura
真狩村
Mt. Shiribetsudake
Mt. Eniwadake
恵庭岳
Bad road
Shikotsuko Lake
Closed in winter
Hayakita-chō
早来町
Rusutsu-mura
留寿都村
Mt. Nukkibetsuyama
Mt. Fuppushidake
Tomakomai-higashi
TOMAKOMAI-SHI
苫小牧市
Atsuma-chō
厚真町
Tōya-mura
洞爺村
Bifue Pass
美笛峠
Mt. Shiraoidake
Ōtaki-mura
大滝村
Mt. Horohoroyama
Tōyako Lake
Hidaka Line
Nakano 中野
Iwamizawa 80Km
Sapporo 66Km
Muroran 69Km
Tōyako
洞爺湖
Bankei
Mt. Orofureyama
Shiraoi
白老
DŌŌ EXPRESSWAY
道央自動車道
Shiraoi-chō
白老町
Abuta-chō
虻田町
Irie 入江
Abuta-Tōyako
Mt. Usuzan
Sōbetsu-chō
壮瞥町
Orofure Pass
Night-traffic prohibited
Kuttarako Lake
Congestion in summer
DATE-SHI
伊達市
Date
Noboribetsu-higashi
Date-Monbetsu
Kita-Funaoka
Mt. Washibetsudake
Noboribetsu-ekimae 登別駅前
Noboribetsu-Muroran
Muroran
NOBORIBETSU-SHI
登別市
Kutchan 114Km
Tomakomai 69Km
Oshamanbe 90Km
MURORAN-SHI
室蘭市
C. Chikyūmisaki
地球岬
Higashi-Nihon Ferry
Shōsen-Mitsui Ferry
Taiheiyō Ferry
Nihon-enkai-Ferry
Silver Ferry
Shin-Nihonkai Ferry (to Tsuruga,Niigata,Akita)
Mukawa-chō

Mikasa I.C
226
Furano-shi
Katsurazawako Lake
Shimokanayama 下金山
IWAMIZAWA-SHI
岩見沢市
Iwamizawa
岩見沢
Namikichō 3 ban 並木町3番
Takigawa 43Km
Sapporo 43Km
Tomakomai 80Km
Sasshō Line
Ebetsu-shi
江別市
Ebetsu-higashi
Ebetsu-nishi
Sapporo
札幌
SAPPORO-SHI
札幌市
Sapporo-minami
Mt. Moiwayama
Kitahiroshima
KITAHIROSHIMA-SHI
北広島市
Chitose Line
Kuriyama-chō
栗山町
Naganuma-chō
長沼町
Yūbari-shi
夕張市
Historical Village of Coal(R.A.)
Mt. Yūbaridake
夕張岳
Mt. Kikkyōdake
Mt. Rōnebetsuyama
Mt. Byōbuyama
Shimukappu-mura
占冠村
Sekishō Line
Hidaka Pass
日高峠
Hidaka 日高
Hidaka-chō
日高町
to Furano
Mt. Hattaomanaidake
ハッタオマナイ岳
Mikawa 三川
Minami 6gō
南6号
18ku 18区
13ku 13区
Closed in winter
223
Oiwake-chō
追分町
Yūbari
夕張
ENIWA-SHI
恵庭市
Eniwa
恵庭
Chitose-higashi
千歳東
to Eniwa
to Ebetsu
to Tomakomai
Chitose
千歳
CHITOSE-SHI
千歳市
Shikotsuko Lake
Mt. Fuppushidake
Mt. Tarumaeyama
樽前山
Hayakita-chō
早来町
Crab sale area
Drive-in area
Tomakomai-higashi
苫小牧東
Utonaitonuma Lake
TOMAKOMAI-SHI
苫小牧市
Tomakomai-nishi
苫小牧西
DŌŌ EXPRESSWAY
道央自動車道
Nakano 中野
Iwamizawa 80Km
Sappro 66Km
Muroran 69Km
Yūfutsu 勇払
Atsuma-chō
厚真町
Hobetsu-chō
穂別町
Horokeshi
幌毛志
Nioi 荷負
Mukawa River
Biratori-chō
平取町
Yoshitsune Pass
Mt. Nukkibetsuyama
Mt. Ribirayama
Mt. Piudake
Shiraoi
白老
Shiraoi-chō
白老町
Noboribetsu-shi
to Shikotsu Lake
to Chitose
to Noboribetsu
Tomakomai
Mukawa-chō
鵡川町
Miyato 宮戸
Mukawa 鵡川
Farming area of thoroughbred
Hidaka Kentucky Farm(P.G.)
Sarugawa River
Monbetsu-chō
門別町
Hidaka Line
Niikappu River
Niikappu-chō
新冠町
Shizunai-chō
静内町
Miyuki 御幸
Shizunai River
Shōsen-Mitsui Ferry (to Ōarai)
Taiheiyō Ferry(to Sendai·Nagoya)
Higashi-Nihon Ferry(to Hachinohe)
Silver Ferry (to Hachinohe)
Higashi-Nihon Ferry(to Ōarai)
Shin-Nihonkai Ferry (to Tsuruga, Niigata, Akita)

E
F
G
H
1
2
3
4
5
6
227
230
Shihoro-chō 士幌町
Shihoro 士幌
Honbetsu-chō 本別町
Honbetsu 本別
Honbetsu Jct 本別Jct
Minami-Honbetsu
Okamedo
Senbiri
Mt. Sahorodake
Sahoro
Karikachi Pass 狩勝峠
Kita-Shintoku 北新得
Shintoku-chō 新得町
Shikaoi-chō 鹿追町
Mt. Odasshuyama
Tomamu
Mt. Karifuridake
Shimizu 清水
Shimizu-chō 清水町
Tokachi-Shimizu 十勝清水
Tokachi-Heigen 十勝平原
Memuro 芽室
Otofuke-Obihiro 音更帯広
Otofuke-chō 音更町
Otofuke River
Obihiro-Shiraka
Ikeda 池田
Takashima
Toshibetsu River
Urahoro River
DŌTŌ EXPRESSWAY 道東自動車道
Hokkaidō Maple
Mikage 御影
Tokachi-Kokudō
十勝国道
Haobi
Nishi-Obihiro
Obihiro
Satsunaigawa
Tokachigawa 十勝川
Toshibetsu
Ikeda-chō 池田町
Samamai
Akeno 明野
Satsunai
Makubetsu
Memuro-chō 芽室町
OBIHIRO-SHI 帯広市
Inashibetsu
Makubetsu-chō 幕別町
Teshikaga 159Km
Furano 121Km
Kushiro 122Km
Obihiro-kokusai (Satsunai)
Obihiro (Shin-Arashiyama)
Mt. Tsurugisan
Obihiro River
Satsunai River
Sarubetsu River
Tofutsu
Nemuro Line
Urahoro-chō 浦幌町
Urahoro
Urahoro 浦幌
Toyokoro
Toyokoro-chō 豊頃町
Shin-Yoshino
Yoshino 吉野
Kami-Atsunai
Atsunai
Kushiro-shi
Urahoro-Tokachi River
to Shimizu
to Shihoro
to Makubetsu
to Sarabetsu
Utamatayama
Mt. Myōshikiyama
Mt. Obihirodake
Mt. Tottabetsudake
Tottabetsu River
Mt. Poroshiridake 幌尻岳
Mt. Poroshiridake
Nakasatsunai 中札内
Nakasatsunai-mura 中札内村
Mt. Namewakkadake
Mt. Idonnappudake
Mt. Kamuiekuuchikaushiyama
Sarabetsu-mura 更別村
Mt. Koikakushusatsunaidake
Mt. Yaoromappudake ヤオロマップ岳
Mt. Rubetsuneyama
Mt. Petegaridake
Chūrui-mura 忠類村
Taiki-chō 大樹町
Mt. Nakanodake
Mt. Pirigaiyama
Mt. Kamuidake
Mt. Soematsudake
Mt. Pisenaiyama
Mt. Pirikanupuri
Rekifune River
Toyoni 豊似
Hiroo-Kokudō
Tokachi
Hiroo-chō 広尾町
広尾国道
Mt. Tokachidake 十勝岳
Mt. Rakkodake 楽古岳
Hōei
Honkiri
Hidaka Line
Ogifushi
Efue
Urakawa
Urakawa-chō 浦河町
Urakawa
Higashi-chō
Hidaka-Horobetsu
Utoma
Nishi-Samani
Samani-chō 様似町
Samani
C. Enrumumisaki
Mt. Apoidake
Scenic view of fall and coast
Mt. Toyonidake
Shoya 庶野
Erimo-Kokudō
襟裳国道
Precipious criff coast
Oiwake Pass
Erimo-chō えりも町
Erimo
Utabetsu 歌別
Kushiro 188Km
Obihiro 131Km
Tomakomai 159Km
C. Erimomisaki 襟裳岬
to Hiroo
to Urakawa
from Obihiro-shi
Abashiri 230Km
Sapporo 240Km

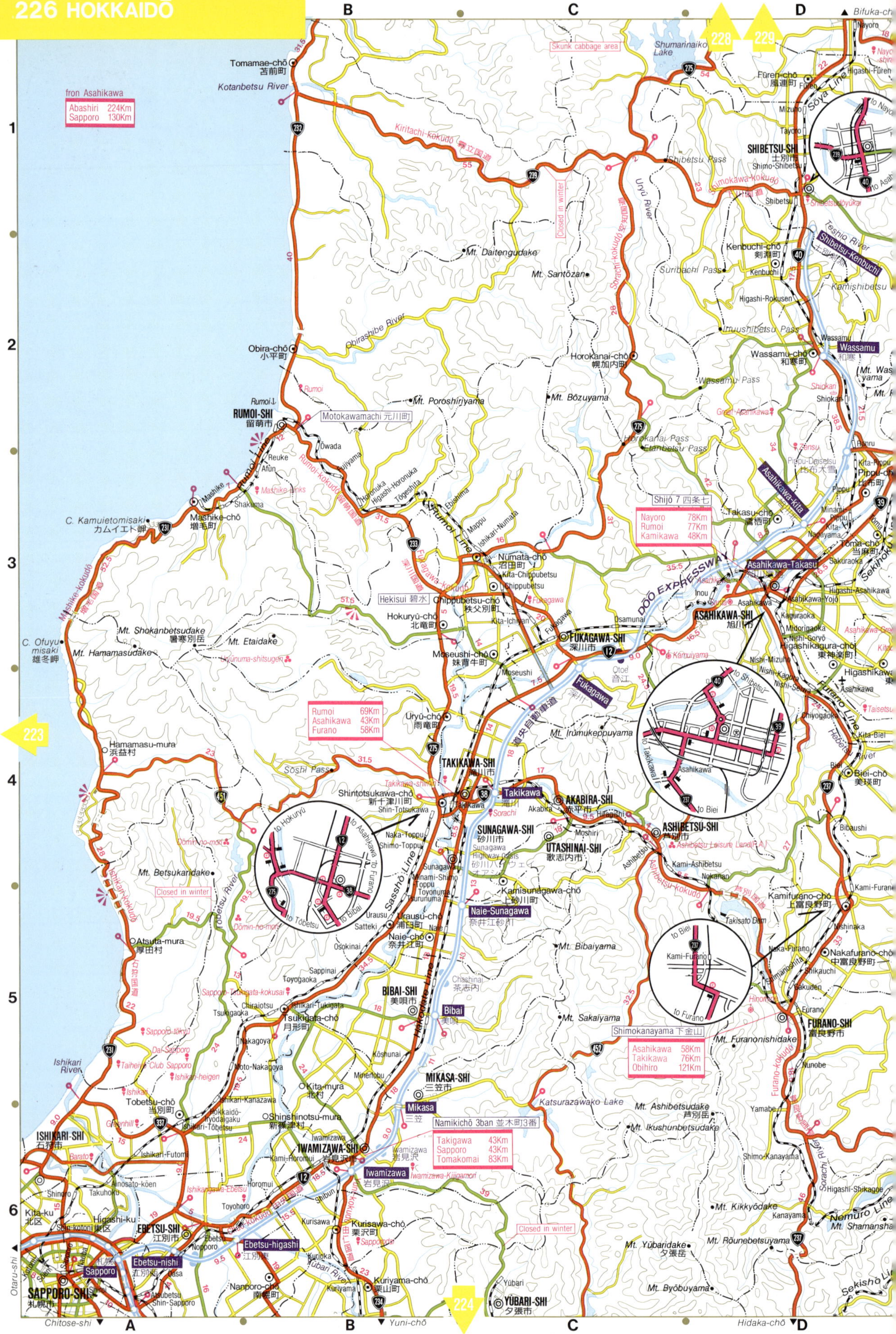
A
B
C
D
1
2
3
4
5
6
228
229
223
224
fron Asahikawa
Abashiri 224Km
Sapporo 130Km
Tomamae-chō 苫前町
Kotanbetsu River
Kiritachi-kokudō 霧立国道
Skunk cabbage area
Shumarinaiko Lake
Shibetsu Pass
Closed in winter
Uryū River
Sorachi-kokudō
Bifuka-chō
Nayoro
Fūren-chō 風連町
Soya Line
SHIBETSU-SHI 士別市
Shimo-Shibetsu
Shimokawa-kokudō
Shibetsu
Kenbuchi-chō 剣淵町
Kenbuchi
Teshio River
Shibetsu-Kenbuchi
Kamishibetsu
Higashi-Rokusen
Mt. Daitengudake
Mt. Santōzan
Suribachi Pass
Obiashibe River
Ituushibetsu Pass
Obira-chō 小平町
Horokanai-chō 幌加内町
Wassamu-chō 和寒町
Wassamu
Wassamu Pass
Rumoi
Mt. Poroshiriyama
Mt. Bōzuyama
Rumoi
RUMOI-SHI 留萌市
Motokawamachi 元川町
Owada
Reuke
Afun
Rumoi Line
Rumoi-kokudō
Horokanai Pass
Etanbetsu Pass
Asahikawa-kita
Pippu-chō 比布町
Mashike
Shakuma
Mashike links
Mashike-chō 増毛町
C. Kamuietomisaki カムイエト岬
Shijō 7 四条七
Nayoro 78Km
Rumoi 77Km
Kamikawa 48Km
Takasu-chō 鷹栖町
Numata-chō 沼田町
Kita-Chippubetsu
Chippubetsu
Fukagawa-kokudō
Mashike-kokudō
Hekisui 碧水
Chippubetsu-chō 秩父別町
Hokuryū-chō 北竜町
DŌŌ EXPRESSWAY
Asahikawa-Takasu
ASAHIKAWA-SHI 旭川市
C. Ofuyu misaki 雄冬岬
Mt. Shokanbetsudake 暑寒別岳
Mt. Hamamasudake
Mt. Etaidake
Uryūnuma-shitsugen
Moseushi-chō 妹背牛町
FUKAGAWA-SHI 深川市
Fukagawa
Kamuiyama
Higashikagura-chō 東神楽町
Higashikawa
Rumoi 69Km
Asahikawa 43Km
Furano 58Km
Uryū-chō 雨竜町
Mt. Irumukeppuyama
Furano Line
Hamamasu-mura 浜益村
Sōshi Pass
TAKIKAWA-SHI 滝川市
Takikawa
AKABIRA-SHI 赤平市
Shintotsukawa-chō 新十津川町
Shin-Totsukawa
ASHIBETSU-SHI 芦別市
Biei-chō 美瑛町
SUNAGAWA-SHI 砂川市
UTASHINAI-SHI 歌志内市
Ashibetsu Leisure Land
Mt. Betsukaridake
Closed in winter
Ishikari-kokudō
Kamisunagawa-chō 上砂川町
Naie-Sunagawa
Kamifurano-chō 上富良野町
Sasshō Line
Hakodate Line
Urausu-chō 浦臼町
Naie-chō 奈井江町
Atsuta-mura 厚田村
Mt. Bibaiyama
Nakafurano-chō 中富良野町
Takisato Dam
BIBAI-SHI 美唄市
Bibai
Mt. Sakaiyama
Shimokanayama 下金山
Asahikawa 58Km
Takikawa 76Km
Obihiro 121Km
FURANO-SHI 富良野市
Mt. Furanonishidake
Tsukigata-chō 月形町
Ishikari River
Kita-mura 北村
MIKASA-SHI 三笠市
Mikasa
Katsurazawako Lake
Mt. Ashibetsudake 芦別岳
Furano-kokudō
Tobetsu-chō 当別町
Shinshinotsu-mura 新篠津村
Namikichō 3ban 並木町3番
Takigawa 43Km
Sapporo 43Km
Tomakomai 83Km
Mt. Ikushunbetsudake
ISHIKARI-SHI 石狩市
IWAMIZAWA-SHI 岩見沢市
Iwamizawa
Mt. Kikkyōdake
Nemuro Line
Mt. Shamanshadake
Kita-ku 北区
Higashi-ku 東区
EBETSU-SHI 江別市
Ebetsu-higashi
Kurisawa-chō 栗沢町
Closed in winter
Mt. Yūbaridake 夕張岳
Mt. Rōunebetsuyama
Ebetsu-nishi
Sapporo
SAPPORO-SHI 札幌市
Nanporo-chō 南幌町
Kuriyama-chō 栗山町
YŪBARI-SHI 夕張市
Mt. Byōbuyama
Sekishō Line
Otaru-shi
Chitose-shi
Yuni-chō
Hidaka-chō

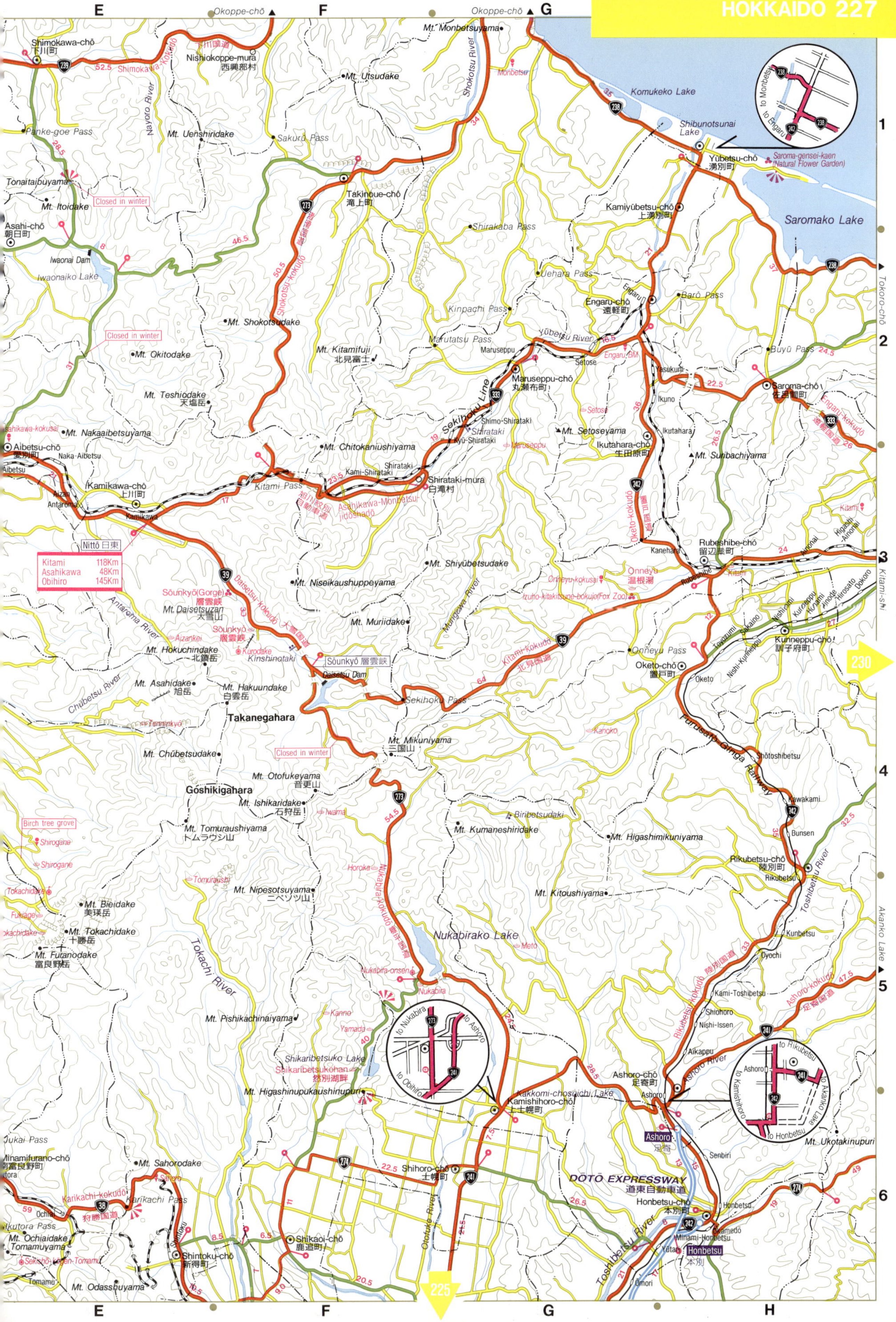
E
F
G
H
Okoppe-chō
Mt. Monbetsuyama
Shimokawa-chō
下川町
Shimokawa-kokudō
Nishiokoppe-mura
西興部村
Mt. Utsudake
Shokotsu River
Monbetsu
Komukeko Lake
Shibunotsunai Lake
Yūbetsu-chō
湧別町
Saroma-gensei-kaen (Natural Flower Garden)
Saromako Lake
to Monbetsu
to Engaru
Panke-goe Pass
Nayoro River
Mt. Uenshiridake
Sakuru Pass
Tonaitaibuyama
Mt. Itoidake
Closed in winter
Takinoue-chō
滝上町
Asahi-chō
朝日町
Kamiyūbetsu-chō
上湧別町
Shirakaba Pass
Iwaonai Dam
Iwaonaiko Lake
Shokotsu-kokudō
Uehara Pass
Baro Pass
Kinpachi Pass
Engaru-chō
遠軽町
Tokoro-chō
Mt. Shokotsudake
Mt. Kitamifuji
北見富士
Marutatsu Pass
Yūbetsu River
Maruseppu
Setose
Engaru
Buyū Pass
Mt. Okitodake
Maruseppu-chō
丸瀬布町
Yasukuni
Saroma-chō
佐呂間町
Mt. Teshiodake
天塩岳
Sekihoku Line
Shimo-Shirataki
Shirataki
Kyū-Shirataki
Ikuno
Engaru-kokudō
Asahikawa-kokudō
Mt. Nakaaibetsuyama
Mt. Setoseyama
Ikutahara-chō
生田原町
Ikutahara
Aibetsu-chō
愛別町
Naka-Aibetsu
Mt. Chitokaniushiyama
Maruseppu
Mt. Suribachiyama
Aibetsu
Kamikawa-chō
上川町
Kami-Shirataki
Shirataki-mura
白滝村
Kitami Pass
Aizan
Antaroma
Kamikawa
Asahikawa-Monbetsu-jidōshadō
Oketo-kokudō
Kitami
Higashi-Ainonai
Ainonai
Nittō 日東
Kitami 118Km
Asahikawa 48Km
Obihiro 145Km
Rubeshibe-chō
留辺蘂町
Kanehana
Rubeshibe
Mt. Shiyūbetsudake
Onneyu
温根湯
Onneyu-kokusai
Izumo-kitakitsune-bokujo (Fox Zoo)
Sōunkyō (Gorge)
層雲峡
Mt. Niseikaushuppeyama
Daisetsu-kokudō
Mt. Daisetsuzan
大雪山
Mugawa River
Kitami-shi
Antaroma River
Sōunkyō
層雲峡
Mt. Muriidake
Aizankei
Kurodake
Kinshinotaki
Kitami-kokudō
Onneyu Pass
Kunneppu-chō
訓子府町
Mt. Hokuchindake
北鎮岳
Sōunkyō 層雲峡
Daisetsu Dam
Oketo-chō
置戸町
Oketo
Mt. Asahidake
旭岳
Mt. Hakuundake
白雲岳
Chūbetsu River
Sekihoku Pass
Tenninkyō
Takanegahara
Kanoko
Furusato-Ginga Railway
Mt. Chūbetsudake
Mt. Mikuniyama
三国山
Closed in winter
Shōtoshibetsu
Mt. Otofukeyama
音更山
Goshikigahara
Mt. Ishikaridake
石狩岳
Iwama
Kawakami
Birch tree grove
Shirogane
Mt. Tomuraushiyama
トムラウシ山
Biribetsudake
Mt. Kumaneshiridake
Mt. Higashimikuniyama
Bunsen
Horoka
Rikubetsu-chō
陸別町
Rikubetsu
Toshibetsu River
Tomuraushi
Nukabira-kokudō
Mt. Nipesotsuyama
ニペソツ山
Mt. Kitoushiyama
Tokachidake
Mt. Bieidake
美瑛岳
Fukiage
Mt. Tokachidake
十勝岳
Nukabirako Lake
Meto
Kunbetsu
Akanko Lake
Mt. Furanodake
富良野岳
Oyochi
Tokachi River
Nukabira-onsen
Nukabira
Kami-Toshibetsu
Rikubetsu-kokudō
Ashoro-kokudō
Shiohoro
Nishi-Issen
Mt. Pishikachinaiyama
Kanno
Yamada
to Nukabira
to Ashoro
to Obihiro
Aikappu
Ashoro River
to Rikubetsu
Shikaribetsuko Lake
Shikaribetsukohan
然別湖畔
Ashoro-chō
足寄町
Ashoro
to Kamishihoro
to Akanko Lake
to Honbetsu
Mt. Higashinupukaushinupuri
Kakkomi-chosuichi Lake
Kamishihoro-chō
上士幌町
Ashoro
足寄
Yukai Pass
Senbiri
Mt. Ukotakinupuri
Minamifurano-chō
南富良野町
Mt. Sahorodake
Shihoro-chō
士幌町
DŌTŌ EXPRESSWAY
道東自動車道
Karikachi-kokudō
狩勝国道
Karikachi Pass
Otofuke River
Honbetsu-chō
本別町
Honbetsu
Ochiai
Kutora Pass
Mt. Ochiaidake
Tomamuyama
Shintoku-chō
新得町
Shikaoi-chō
鹿追町
Toshibetsu River
Minami-Honbetsu
Okamedo
Yūtari
Honbetsu
本別
Sekishō-kōgen-Tomamu
Tomamu
Mt. Odassbuyama
Omori
230
225

B
C
D
1
2
3
4
5
6
A
B
C
D
C. Sōyamisaki
宗谷岬
Shiomi 5 chōme 潮見5丁目
Hamatonbetsu 88Km
Nayoro 170Km
Rumoi 183Km
C. Sukotonmisaki
C. Kanedanomisaki
Rebun
Higashi-Nihonkai Ferry
C. Noshappumisaki
野寒布岬
WAKKANAI-SHI
稚内市
Wakkanai
Minami-Wakkanai
Masuboro River
Sōya-wan
Wakkanai
Wakkanai
Ōnuma Lake
Rebuntō I.
礼文島
Mt. Rebundake
Higashi-Nihonkai Ferry
Higashi-Nihonkai Ferry
to Toyotomi
to Hamatonbetsu
Rebun-chō
礼文町
Sarufutsu-mura
猿払村
C. Bakkaimisaki
Bakkai
Makubetsu River
Scenic view of
Rishiri I. and Rebun I.
Yūchi
Rebun-suidō
Rishiri
Rishirifuji-chō
利尻富士町
Kabutonuma
Kabutonuma Lake
Wakkanai-kokudō 稚内国道
Closed in winter
Rishiri-chō
利尻町
Mt. Rishirizan
利尻山
Rishiritō I.
利尻島
Sarobetsugenya
Tokumitsu
Mt. Horoshiriyama
Kutcharo Lake
Rishiri-suidō
Toyotomi-chō
豊富町
Toyotomi
Toyotomi
Sarobetsu-gensei-kaen
(Natural Flower Garden)
Sarufutsu River
Penketō Lake
Panketō Lake
Shimonuma
Minami-Shimonuma
Horonobe-chō
幌延町
Horonobe
Mt. Isosannupuriyama
Kami-Horonobe
Minami-Horonobe
Yasuushi
Mt. Shirikomadake
Teshio-chō
天塩町
Onoppunai
Nukanan
Toikanbetsu
Teshio River
Utanai
Rokushinai Pass
Mt. Pinneshiridake
Teshio-kokudō 天塩国道
Mt. Penkeyama
Teshio-Nakagawa
Nakagawa-chō
中川町
Sōya Line
Saku
Osashima
Enbetsu-chō
遠別町
Enbetsu River
Otoineppu-mura
音威子府
Sakku
Mt. Onizashibeyama
Teshiogawa-onsen
Abeshinai River
Toyoshim
Oguruma Pass
Shosanbetsu-mura
初山別村
Teuri-kokudō
Teuritō I.
天売島
Yagishiritō I.
焼尻島
Haboro-Ororon
Closed in winter
Haboro-chō
羽幌町
Chikubetsu River
Mt. Pisshiriyama
Shumarinaiko Lake
Tomamae-chō
苫前町
Haboro River
Skunk cabbage area
Skunk cabbage area and Birch tree grove
Bifuka-kokudō
Kotanbetsu River
Uehira 上平
Kiritachi-kokudō
Uryūdoentei Dam
Closed in winter
Rumoi-shi
Shibetsu-shi
Horokanai-chō

E
F
G
1
2
3
4
5
6
SEA OF OKHOTSK
オホーツク海
okeuninuma Lake
Beniya-gensei-kaen
(Natural Flower Garden)
Tonbetsu River
Hamatonbetsu-chō
浜頓別町
Hamatonbetsuchō-shigai 浜頓別町市街
Wakkanai 88Km
Nayoro 78Km
Monbetsu 122Km
C. Kamuimisaki
Mt. Shubundake
to Hamatonbetsu
to Okoppe
Nakatonbetsu-chō
中頓別町
C. Usutaibemisaki
Esashi-chō
枝幸町
Moutsu モウツ
Utanobori-chō
歌登町
Tokushibetsu River
enboku Pass
ineppu
Sakkuru Pass
Mt. Bōzuyama
C. Otoshibemisaki
Mt. Hakodake
Horonai River
Mt. Ochifuneyama
Mt. Kuroiwayama
Closed in winter
Okhotsk-kokudō
Onnenai
Mt. Shiasshiriyama
Ōmu-chō
雄武町
to Okoppe
to Yūbetsu
Monbonai
C. Hinodemisaki
Biuka Pass
Hatsuno
Bifuka-chō
美深町
Bifuka
to Bifuka
to Shimokawa
to Shibetsu
Okoppe River
Minami-Bifuka
Chiebun
Mt. Keganeshiriyama
Motomachi 本町
Okoppe-chō
興部町
Sōya Line
Hokusei
C. Sarumisaki
Shokotsu 渚滑
Nayoro 90Km
Abashiri 117Km
Kamikawa 102Km
Chito
天北国道
Bifuka Pass
美深峠
Piyashiri
Mt. Poronupuridake
Tenpoku-kokudō
Nisshin
NAYORO-SHI
名寄市
Wakkanai 170km
Monbetsu 90km
Asahikawa 78km
Monbetsu
MONBETSU-SHI
紋別市
Sapporo 210km
Kushiro 380km
Mt. Monbetsuyama
Shimokawa-chō
下川町
下川国道
Nishiokoppe-mura
西興部村
Fūren-chō
風連町
Nayoroshirakaba
Higashi-Fūren
Shimokawa-kokudō
Mt. Utsutsudake
Monbetsu
Okhotsk-Monbetsu
Shokotsu River
Komukeko Lake
Fūren
Mizuho
Tayoro
Nayoro-kokudō
226
227
Sakuru Pass
Shibetsu-shi
Takinoue-chō
H

A
B
C
D
1
2
3
4
5
6
Saromako Lake
Tokoro-chō
常呂町
Tokoro River
Notoroko Lake
C. Notoromisaki
能取岬
Monbetsu 117Km
Kitami 58Km
Nemuro 188Km
Ōmagari 大曲
ABASHIRI-SHI
網走市
Abashiri
to C.Notoromisaki
to Memanbetsu
to Shari
to Kitami
to Abashiri
to Akankolake
to Teshikaga
Closed in winter
Nikura Pass
Abashiriko Lake
Abashirikohan
Masuura
Yobito
Mokoto
Kitahama
Mokotoko Lake
Koshimizu-gensei-kaen (Natural Flower Garden)
Hama-Koshimizu
Memanbetsu
Memanbetsu-chō
女満別町
Okhotsk
Abashiri-kokusai
Tōfutsuko Lake
Yamubetsu
Shari-chō
斜里町
Shiretoko-Shari
Sharigawa River
Toyokura 豊倉
Shin-Memanbetsu
Nishi-Memanbetsu
Hushinai
Sekihoku Line
Tanno
Tanno-chō
端野町
Hakuyō
Kitami
KITAMI-SHI
北見市
Bihoro
Bihoro-chō
美幌町
Higashimokoto-mura
東藻琴村
Koshimizu-chō
小清水町
Naka-Shari
Minami-Shari
Kiyosatochō
Kiyosato-chō
清里町
Sattsuru
Wakamatsu
Abashiri River
Bihoro-kokudō
Urashibetsu River
Tsubetsu-chō
津別町
Mt. Mokotoyama
Closed in winter
Nogami Pass
Midori
Mt. Sharidake
斜里岳
Mt. Mataochidake
Mt. Samakkenupuriyama
Mt. Shibetsudake
Mt. Musadake
Bihoro Pass
美幌峠
Nakajima I.
Nibushi
Kawayu
川湯
Sunayu
Mt. Atosanupuri
Ikenoyu
Kussharoko Lake
Wakoto
Kawayu
Closed in winter
Kiyosato Pass
Mashūko Lake
Mt. Kamuinupuri
Mt. Nishibetsudake
Yōroushi
Tsubetsu Pass
Closed in winter
Senpoku-kokudō
Biruwa
Teshikaga
Mashū farm
from Teshikaga-chō
Asahikawa 320Km
Sapporo 400Km
Teshikaga-chō
弟子屈町
Mashū
Tobetsu
Satsutomonai 札友内
Abashiri 91Km
Obihiro 159Km
Nemuro 116Km
Panketō Lake
Akanko Lake
Mt. Oakandake
雄阿寒岳
Senpoku Pass
Shirikomabetsu
シリコマベツ
Akankohan
阿寒湖畔
Odan-kokudō
Okurushibe
オクルシベ
Scenic view of Mt. Oakandake
to Bihoro
Teshikaga
to Akanko Lake
to Bekkai
Minami-Teshikaga
Isobunnai
Senmō Line
Meakan
Onneto Lake
Mt. Meakandake
雌阿寒岳
Mt. Akanfuji
Dub (Mashūko)
Shibecha-chō
標茶町
Shibecha
Akanko Lake
to Bihoro
to Teshikaga
to Kushiro
Marimo-kokudō
Kuchoro River
Tsurui-mura
鶴居村
Gojikkoku
Kayanuma
225
Tōroko Lake
Tōro
Kushiro CC
Kushiro-Fūrin
Kushiro Marshy Plains
釧路湿原
Akan-chō
阿寒町
Akan
Hosooka
Kushiro-shitsugen
Karikan Pass
Akangawa River
KUSHIRO-SHI
釧路市
Tōya
Kami-Oboro
Kushiro
Kushiro-kūkō
Otanoshige 大楽毛
Otanoshike
Shin-Fuji
Kushiro-chō
釧路町
Beppo
Kushiro River
Kushiro
Higashi-Kushiro
Kushiro
Kamibetsuho 上別保
Akkeshi
Shorogawa River
Shoro
Kushiro-kokudō
Shiranuka-chō
白糠町
Shiranuka
Nemuro Line
Furuse
Charogawa River
Onbetsu-chō
音別町
Onbetsu
Shakubetsu
Chokubetsu
to Akkeshi
to Shiranuka
Abashiri 161Km
Nemuro 120Km
Obihiro 122Km
227
Iwaobetsu
Mt. Rausudake
羅臼岳
C. Utorozaki
Utoro
Shiretoko Pass
Rausu
C. Oshinkoshinzaki
Mt. Onnebetsudake
SHIRETOKO PEN.
知床半島
Shiretoko-kokudō
Kunashiri-kokudō
Mt. Unabetsudake
Distant view of Kunashiri I.
Shari-kokudō
Kawakita
Ichani 伊茶仁
Shibetsu-chō
標津町
Shibetsu River
Nakashibetsu
Nakashibetsu-Gōdō
Nakashibetsu-chō
中標津町
Birch tree grove and posture continue
Bekkai-chō
別海町
Pilot-kokudō
Hamanaka
Chanai
Bekanbeushi River
Konsen-kokudō
Akkeshi-chō
厚岸町
Akkeshi
Itoizawa
Akkeshiko Lake
Hamanaka-chō
浜中町
Monshizu
Oboro
Akkeshi-wan
Daikokujima I.
Yūbetsu-chō
Engaru-chō
Rubeshibe-chō
Urahoro-chō

E
F
G
H
1
2
3
4
5
6
C. Shiretokomisaki
知床岬
Rausu-chō
羅臼町
Mt. Shiretokodake
SHIRETOKO PEN.
知床半島
Mt. Iōzan
C. Kinakaisaki
C. Ōmisaki
Kunashiritō I.
国後島
C. Rausuzaki
C. Hatchasuzaki
NEMURO-KAIKYŌ
根室海峡
Notsuke-suidō
C. Keramuisaki
ケラムイ崎
Tarakutō I.
多楽島
Taraku-suidō
Notsuke-wan
C. Ryūjinzaki
C. Notsukesaki
野付崎
Notsuke-kokudō
C. Aidomarisaki
Shibotsutō I.
志発島
C. Sankakusaki
Shibotsu-suidō
Suishōtō I.
水晶島
Yuritō I.
勇留島
Harukarimoshiritō I.
Goyōmai-suidō
Abashiri 188Km
Teshikaga 116Km
kushiro 120Km
to C.Nosappumisaki
to Atsutoko
Nemuro
Kaigarajima I.
C. Nosappumisaki
納沙布岬
Habomaishotō I.
歯舞諸島
Akiyuritō I.
Nemuro-wan
Nemuro Pen.
NEMURO-SHI
根室市
Higashi-Nemuro
Okuyukiusu 奥行臼
Fūrenko Lake
Hanasaki
Nishi-Wada
Onnetō Lake
Moeyururijima I.
Konbumori
Yururijima I.
Atsutoko
Bettoga
Nemuro Line
Hattaushi
Ochiishi
Anebetsu
C. Ochiishimisaki
落石岬
manaka-wan
C. Tōbutsumisaki
湯沸岬
Mt. Kamuidake
C. Ōmisaki
Sea of Okhotsk
Mt. Odamoeyama
Etorofutō I.
択捉(エトロフ)島
Kunashiri-suidō
C. Mekkarisaki
C. Ruruimisaki
C. Atoiyamisaki
Mt. Chachadake
C. Shiretokomisaki
Kunashiritō I.
国後(クナシリ)島
Mt. Rausudake
Mt. Rausuyama
Shikotantō I.
Shikotan-suidō
Habomaishotō Is.
歯舞諸島
Nemuro-kaikyō
C. Keramuisaki
Tarakutō I.
Shibotsutō I.
Yuritō I.
C. Nosappumisaki
Pacific Ocean

B
C
D
1
2
3
4
5
6
A
FUKUOKA
N
1 : 125,000
0 500 1000 1500m
GENKAI-NADA
玄界灘
Hanami
Nishitetsu-Koga
Koga
KOGA-SHI
古賀市
Koga
Koga-Golf-jō-mae
Koga
古賀
Shingū-machi
新宮町
C.Isozakibana
Nishitetsu-Shingū
Nishitetsu Miyajidake Line
Kagoshima Line
Mitoma
Chikuzen-Shingū
Wajiro
Fukuoka
Gannosu
Nata
Shikanoshima I.
志賀島
Shikaumi-jinja
Mt.Tachibanayama
KYŪSHŪ-ŌDAN EXPRESSWAY
九州横断自動車道
Mikazuki
Uminonakamichi
Uminonakamichi
Kashii-kaenmae
Kashii
Kashii
Saitozaki-seaside
Uminonakamichi
Seashore Park
Saitozaki
C.Saitozaki
Kashiihama
Kashii-jingū
Kashiigū
Chihaya
Mai-Matsubara
Hisayama
Hisayama-machi
久山町
Kyūshū-yūsen Ferry (to Gōnoura-Izuhara) (to Hitakatsu)
Kyūetsu Ferry (to Naoetsu)
HAKATA-WAN
博多湾
Higashi-ku
東区
Takasuma 高須磨
Doi
Fukuoka
福岡
Matsushima
Tōkaidō Sanyō Shinkansen
Kasuya
Nokonoshima I.
能古島
Hakozaki
Fukuoka-higashi Bypass
Hakata Bypass
Uga
Kasuya-machi
粕屋町
Iizuka-shi
Hakozaki
Hakozakigū
Sasaguri Line
Hakata
Higashihama
Harumachi
Higashi Park
Chikukō
Sakado
Nishi-kōen
Gofukumachi 呉服町
Katakasu
Kūkō-dōri
Futamatase 二股瀬
Sue
Chūō-ku
中央区
Momochi
Fukuoka Dome
Nishi Park
Tenjin 天神
Akasakamon 赤坂門
Kushida-jinja
Fukuoka Tower
Hakata
Hakata-ku
博多区
Enokida
Shime-machi
志免町
Atago
Nishijin 西新
Ōhori Park
Fukuoka-jō Castle
Kego 警固
Hakataeki-higashi
Hanmichibashi
Fukuoka
Sue
須恵
Sue-machi
須恵町
Meinohama
Muromibashi
Nishi-ku
西区
Yakuin
Meinohama
Jōnan-ku
城南区
Watanabe-dōri.1 渡辺通一
Fukuoka-minami Bypass
Shinbaru
Ishimaru
Minami Park
Nishitetsu-Hirao
Karatsu-shi
Jūrokucho
Fukushige
Imajuku Bypass
Tsukikuma
Itazuke 板付
Umi-hachimangū
Takamiya
Takeshita
Umi
Umi-machi
宇美町
Kanenokuma
Sawara-ku
早良区
Hiikawa River
Minami-ku
南区
Kagoshima Line
Nishi-Tsukikuma
Ōhashi
Ijiri
Itazuke
Ōnojō
ŌNOJŌ-SHI
大野城市
Zasshonokuma
Nakagawa River
Notame
Minami-Fukuoka
Yamada 山田
Nishitetsu Ōmuta Line
春日市
KASUGA-SHI
Mizuki
Dazaifu
太宰府
Ōnojō
Shimo-Ōri
Muromi River
Hakata-minami
Mizuki
DAZAIFU-SHI
太宰府市
Kanzeonji
Rokutan 六反
Saga-shi
Chikushigaoka
Nakagawa-machi
那珂川町
Kyūshū
Futsukaichi
CHIKUSHINO-SHI
筑紫野市
Futsukaichi
Tosu-shi
Sevenmillion
Chikushino
筑紫野
Tosu I.C

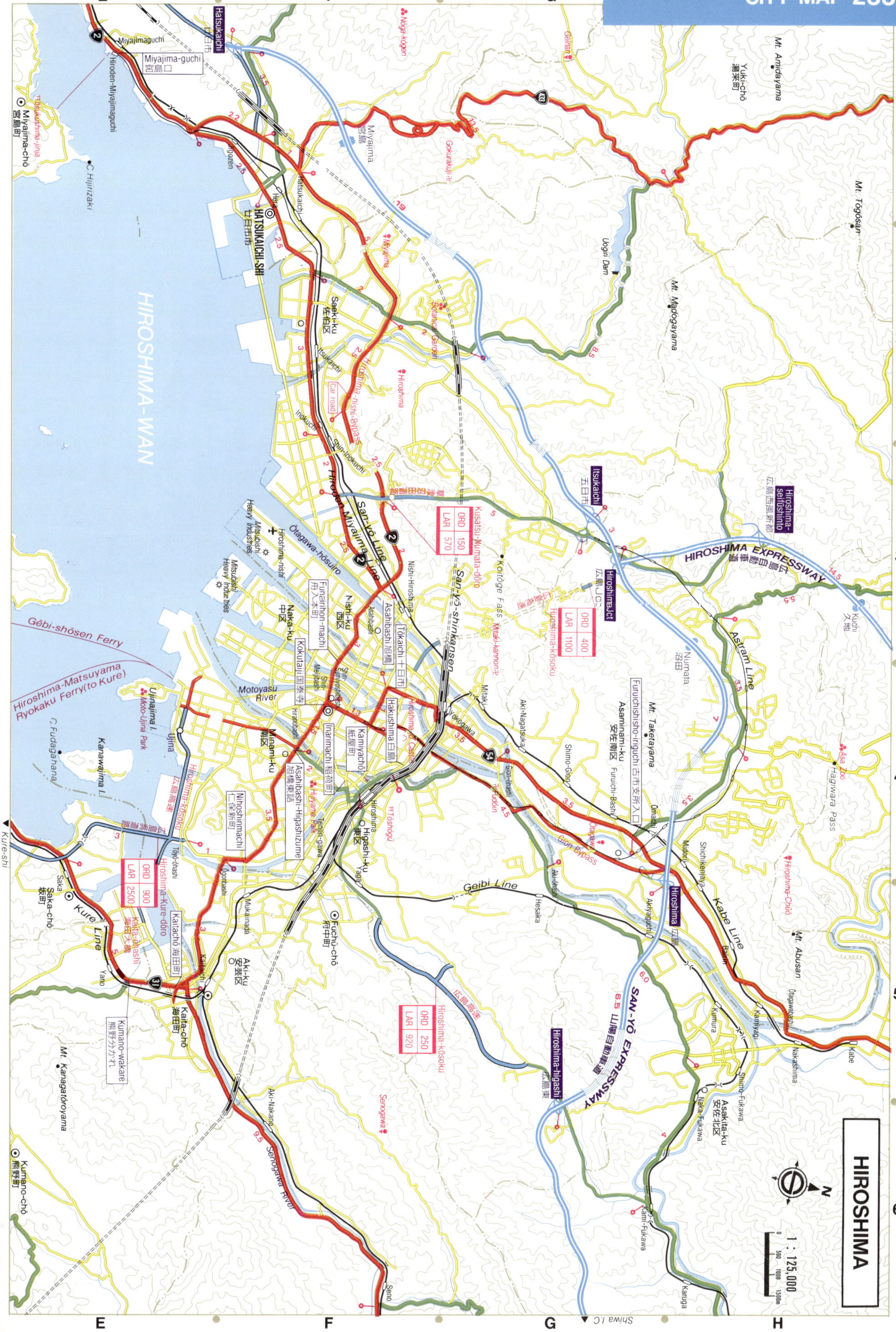
HIROSHIMA
1 : 125,000
HIROSHIMA-WAN
HIROSHIMA EXPRESSWAY
SAN-YŌ EXPRESSWAY
San-yō-shinkansen
San-yō Line
Geibi Line
Kabe Line
Kure Line
Astram Line
Hatsukaichi
Miyajima-guchi
宮島口
HATSUKAICHI-SHI
廿日市市
Saeki-ku
佐伯区
Nishi-ku
西区
Naka-ku
中区
Minami-ku
南区
Higashi-ku
東区
Aki-ku
安芸区
Asaminami-ku
安佐南区
Asakita-ku
安佐北区
Itsukaichi
五日市
Hiroshima J.C.
広島J.C.
Hiroshima-nishi-fūshinto
広島西風新都
Hiroshima
広島
Hiroshima-higashi
広島東
Hiroshima-Matsuyama
Ryokaku Ferry (to Kure)
Gēbi-shōsen Ferry
Ōtagawa-hōsuiro
Motoyasu River
Ujinajima I.
Kanawajima I.
Mitsubishi Heavy Industries
Hiroshima-nishi-Bypass
Hirodori Miyajima Line
Kusatsu-Numata-dōro
Hiroshima-kōsoku
Hiroshima-Kure-dōro
Gion Bypass
Funairihon-machi
舟入本町
Tōkaichi
十日市
Asahibashi
旭橋
Kokutaiji
国泰寺
Hakushima
白島
Inarimachi
稲荷町
Kamiyachō
紙屋町
Asahibashi-Higashizume
旭橋東詰
Nihoshinmachi
仁保新町
Kaitachō
海田町
Kumano-wakare
熊野分れ
Furuichishisho-iriguchi
古市支所入口
ORD 150 LAR 570
ORD 400 LAR 1100
ORD 900 LAR 2500
ORD 250 LAR 920
Mt. Amidayama
Mt. Tōgōsan
Mt. Madogayama
Mt. Taketayama
Mt. Abusan
Mt. Kanagatōroyama
Yuki-chō
湯来町
Miyajima-chō
宮島町
Kumano-chō
熊野町
Saka-chō
坂町
Kaita-chō
海田町
Fuchū-chō
府中町
Kuchi
久地
Numata
沼田
Kurse-shi
Shiwa I.C.
Senogawa River
E
F
G
H
1
2
3
4
5
6

ŌSAKA·KŌBE
1 : 125,000
0 500 1000 1500m
N
ŌSAKA-WAN
大阪湾
CHŪGOKU EXPRESSWAY
中国自動車道
Hanshin Railway
Hankyū Kōbe Line
Hankyū Imazu Line
Tōkaidō Line
Shintetsu Sanda Line
Mukogawa River
Rokkō Tunnel
Expressway Kobe-Nishinomiya Line
Harbor Highway
ORD 200
LAR 200
Maya-ōhashi
ORD 100
LAR 100
Rokkō-kita-dōro
ORD 400
LAR 1510
Nishinomiya-kita-dōro
ORD 250
LAR 900
Dōyū Driveway
ORD 800
LAR 3200
Rokkō-dōro
ORD 200
LAR 730
Shin-kōbe tunnel
ORD 600
LAR 2200
Higashi-Rokkō Driveway
Bellevue-Arima-road
Nishi-Rokkō Driveway
Oku-Maya Driveway
Mt. Rokkōsan
Mt. Shakunageyama
Mt. Mayasan
KŌBE-SHI
神戸市
NISHINOMIYA-SHI
西宮市
TAKARAZUKA-SHI
宝塚市
ASHIYA-SHI
芦屋市
ITAMI-SHI
伊丹市
AMAGASAKI-SHI
尼崎市
Nada-ku
灘区
Higashinada-ku
東灘区
Chūō-ku
中央区
Takarazuka
宝塚
Nishinomiya
Iwaya 岩屋
Hamada 浜田
Hon machi
Rokkō Island kita
Rokkō I.
Port I.
Kōbe
C. Wadamisaki
Yanagihara
Kōbe Steel
Kansai-Kisen(to Beppu)
Diamond Ferry (to Matsuyama-Ōita)· Jumbo Ferry(to Takamatsu)
Meimontaiyō Ferry (to Moji) Shikokukaihatsu Ferry· Hiroshima green Ferry (to Hiroshima)· Taiyō Ferry
Ōsaka-Kōchi tokkyū Ferry (to Kannoura·Kōchi)
Ube Industrie
Shinyū
Okaba
Nakano
Gosha
Arimaguchi
Arima-onsen
Arima
Karatodai
Rokkō-tozanguchi
Oike
Hanayama
Karato-nishi
Nishinomiya-kōgen
Namaze
Takarazuka-minamiguchi
Kiyoshi-kōjin
Takarazuka-ōhashi
Mefu-jinja
Nakayamadera
Hankyū-Nakayama
Hankyū-Yamamoto
Kawanishi-Ikeda
Sakasegawa
Obayashi
Nigawa
Hankyū-Nigawa
Kōtōen
Kōyōen
Mondoyakujin
Kurakuenguchi
Shukugawa
Nishinomiya
Koroen
Ashiyagawa
Ashiya
Okamoto
Mikage
Settsu-Motoyama
Fukae
Sumiyoshi
Uozaki
Rokkō
Ōji-kōen
Maya
Sannomiya
Motomachi
Kōbe-ōhashi
Kyōbashi
Sumiyoshihama
Uozakihama
Fukaehama
Minami-Ashiyahama
Nishinomiyahama
Kōshienhama
Mukogawa-danchimae
Naruohama
Kōshienguchi
Kōshien
Kusugawa
Naruo
Mukogawa
Mukogawabashi
Higashi-Naruo
Suzaki
Amagasaki-nishi
Amagasaki-Suehiro
Muko-ōhashi
Mukonosō
Tachibana
Imazu
Shin-Itami
Itami
Himeji-shi
Rokkōsan Farm
Ōji Zoo
Ashiya
A
B
C
D
1
2
3
4
5
6

Nose-chō
Takatsuki-shi
Kyōto-minami I.C
Kyōto-shi
Kizu-chō
Kōriyama I.C
Sennan-shi
Kawachinagano-shi
E
F
G
H
1
2
3
4
5
6
IKEDA-SHI 池田市
MINOO-SHI 箕面市
TOYONAKA-SHI 豊中市
SUITA-SHI 吹田市
IBARAKI-SHI 茨木市
SETTSU-SHI 摂津市
NEYAGAWA-SHI 寝屋川市
HIRAKATA-SHI 枚方市
MORIGUCHI-SHI 守口市
KADOMA-SHI 門真市
SHIJŌNAWATE-SHI 四條畷市
DAITŌ-SHI 大東市
HIGASHIŌSAKA-SHI 東大阪市
YAO-SHI 八尾市
MATSUBARA-SHI 松原市
FUJIIDERA-SHI 藤井寺市
KASHIWARA-SHI 柏原市
HABIKINO-SHI 羽曳野市
SAKAI-SHI 堺市
Chūgoku-Ikeda
Chūgoku-Toyonaka 中国豊中
Suita Jct 吹田JCT
Suita 吹田
Ibaraki 茨木
Settsu-kita 摂津北
Settsu-minami 摂津南
Kadoma 門真
Daitō-Tsurumi 大東鶴見
Higashiōsaka-kita 東大阪北
Higashiōsaka Jct 東大阪JCT
Higashiōsaka-minami 東大阪南
Yao 八尾
Nagahara 長原
Matsubara 松原
Fujiidera 藤井寺
Mihara-kita 美原北
Kashiwabara 柏原
Toyonaka 豊中
Senri-Inter 千里インター
Sakurazuka 桜塚
Shitomiya 蔀屋
Sumoto 巣本
Akai 赤井
Furuichi-ōdōri-5 古市大通五
Imaichi 今市
Imafuku-5 今福五
Gamō-4 蒲生四
Fukaebashi 深江橋
Imazato 今里
Shinfukae 新深江
Kita-Hagusa 北蛇草
Kumatachō 杭全町
Kanaoka-kodōkyō 金岡跨道橋
Hiranobaba 平野馬場
Kamei-kodōkyō 亀井跨道橋
Nagayoshi 長吉
Yūge 弓削
Ōdōri-3 大通三
Tamade 玉出
Suminoekōenmae 住之江公園前
Sentaichō 千躰町
Nagai 長居
Abiko 我孫子
Ebisujima-1 戎島一
Nagayamaen 永山園
Tannan 丹南
Osaka International(Itami)
MEISHIN EXPRESSWAY 名神高速道路
KINKI EXPRESSWAY 近畿自動車道
NISHI-MEIHAN EXPRESSWAY 西名阪自動車道
Tōkaidō-Sanyō-shinkansen
Tōkaidō Line
Hankyu Senri Line
Hankyu Kyōto Line
Hankyu Takarazuka Line
Keihan Railway
Katamachi Line
Kintetsu Nara Line
Kintetsu Railway
Kintetsu Ōsaka Line
Kintetsu Minami Ōsaka Line
Kansai Line
Ōsaka Kanjō Line
Osaka Subway
Sakurajima Line
Hankai Railway
Nankai Kōya Line
Nankai Railway
Hanwa Line
Yodogawa-ku 淀川区
Nishiyodogawa-ku 西淀川区
Higashiyodogawa-ku 東淀川区
Asahi-ku 旭区
Miyakojima-ku 都島区
Jōtō-ku 城東区
Tsurumi-ku 鶴見区
Kita-ku 北区
Fukushima-ku 福島区
Konohana-ku 此花区
Minato-ku 港区
Nishi-ku 西区
Chūō-ku 中央区
Higashinari-ku 東成区
Naniwa-ku 浪速区
Tennōji-ku 天王寺区
Ikuno-ku 生野区
Taishō-ku 大正区
Nishinari-ku 西成区
Abeno-ku 阿倍野区
Higashisumiyoshi-ku 東住吉区
Hirano-ku 平野区
Suminoe-ku 住之江区
Sumiyoshi-ku 住吉区
Ōsaka Castle
Jōhoku Park
Tsurumi Park
Hattori Park
Nagai Park
Sumiyoshi-taisha
Nintoku Imperial Old Mound
Nippon Steel
Hitachi Shipbuilding & Engineering
Yamato River
Inagawa River
Aikawa River
Neyagawa River
Shin-Yodogawa River
Umeda
Namba
Tennōji
Kyōbashi
Shin-Ōsaka
Tsuruhashi

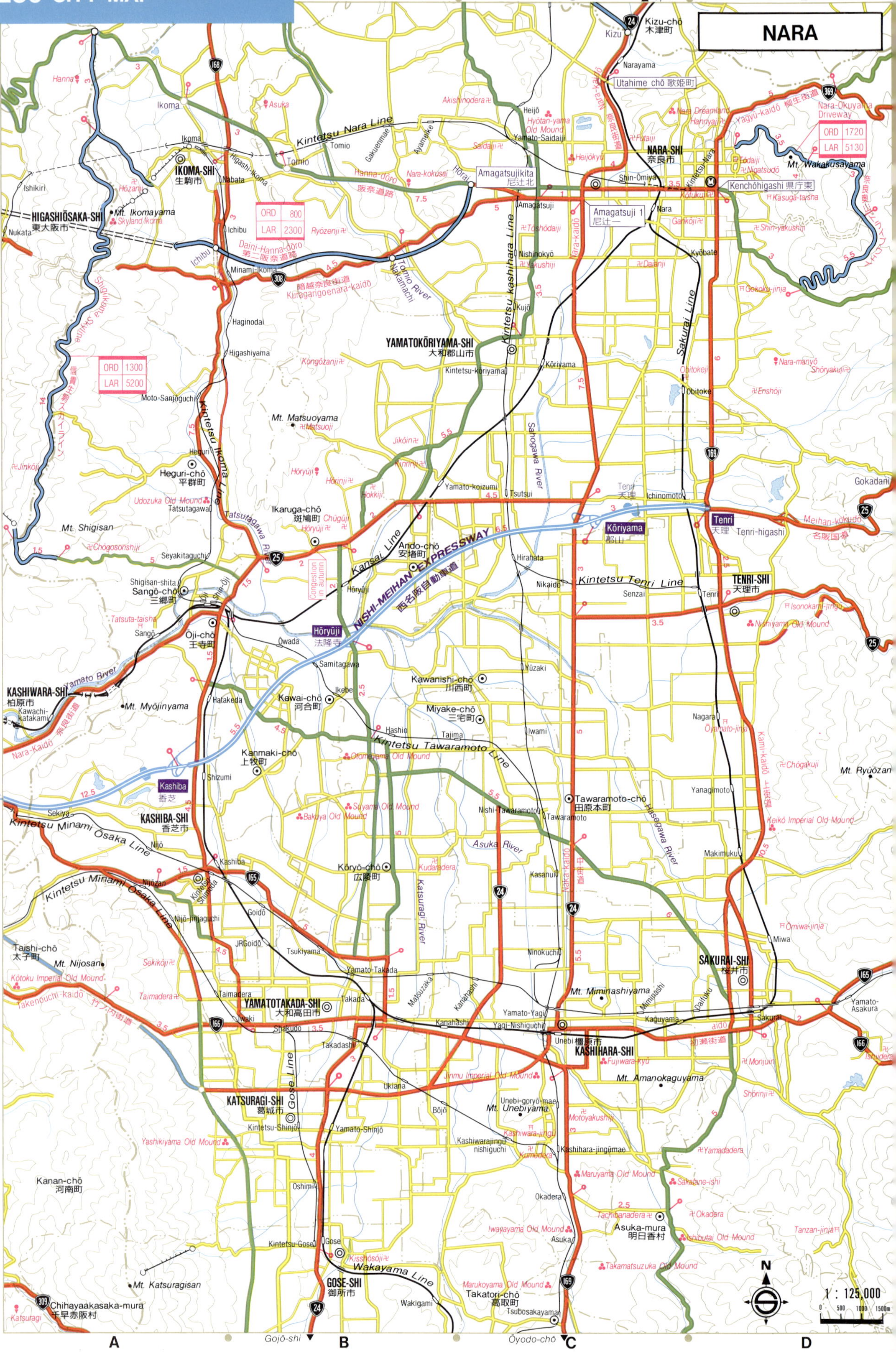
NARA
B
C
D
A
1
2
3
4
5
6
Uji-shi
Kizu-chō
木津町
Kizu
Narayama
Utahime chō 歌姫町
Nara Dreamland
Hannyaji
Futaiji
NARA-SHI
奈良市
Nara-Okuyama Driveway
Yagyū-kaidō 柳生街道
ORD 1720
LAR 5130
Mt. Wakakusayama
Tōdaiji
Nigatsudō
Kenchōhigashi 県庁東
Kōfukuji
Kasuga-taisha
Gankōji
Nara
Shin-Ōmiya
Kintetsu Nara
Shin-yakushiji
Kyōbate
Gokoku-jinja
Amagatsujikita
尼辻北
Amagatsuji 1
尼辻一
Amagatsuji
Heijō
Hyōtan-yama Old Mound
Yamato-Saidaiji
Saidaiji
Heijōkyū
Tōshōdaiji
Nishinokyō
Yakushiji
Daianji
Akishinodera
Kintetsu Nara Line
Tomio
Gakuenmae
Ayameike
Hannya-dōro
阪奈道路
Nara-kokusai
Hōrai
Ikoma
IKOMA-SHI
生駒市
Hanna
Asuka
Ishikiri
HIGASHIŌSAKA-SHI
東大阪市
Nukata
Mt. Ikomayama
Skyland Ikoma
Hōzanji
Higashi-Ikoma
Nabata
Ichibu
ORD 800
LAR 2300
Ryōzenji
Daini-Hanna-dōro
第二阪奈道路
Minami-Ikoma
Kuragarigoenara-kaidō
暗越奈良街道
Tomio River
Nakamachi
Haginodai
Higashiyama
Shigiikoma Skyline
信貴生駒スカイライン
ORD 1300
LAR 5200
Moto-Sanjōguchi
Kongōzanji
YAMATOKŌRIYAMA-SHI
大和郡山市
Kintetsu-kōriyama
Kōriyama
Kujō
Kintetsu Kashihara Line
Sakurai Line
Obitoke
Nara-man'yō
Shōryakuji
Enshōji
Mt. Matsuoyama
Matsuoji
Jikōin
Hōryūji
Hōrinji
Hokkiji
Kinrinji
Heguri
Heguri-chō
平群町
Kintetsu Ikoma Line
Jinkōji
Udozuka Old Mound
Tatsutagawa
Mt. Shigisan
Chōgosonshiji
Ikaruga-chō
斑鳩町
Chūgūji
Tatsutagawa River
Yamato-koizumi
Tsutsui
Sahogawa River
Tenri
天理
Ichinomoto
Gokadani
Kōriyama
郡山
Meihan-kokudō
名阪国道
Tenri-higashi
TENRI-SHI
天理市
Isonokami-jingū
Nishiyama Old Mound
Seyakitaguchi
Shigisan-shita
Sangō-chō
三郷町
Ōji
Shin-Ōji
Tatsuta-taisha
Sangō
Ōji-chō
王寺町
Congestion in autumn
Kansai Line
Ando-chō
安堵町
NISHI-MEIHAN EXPRESSWAY
西名阪自動車道
Hirahata
Nikaidō
Kintetsu Tenri Line
Senzai
Hōryūji
法隆寺
Ōwada
Samitagawa
Kawanishi-chō
川西町
Yūzaki
KASHIWARA-SHI
柏原市
Yamato River
Kawachi-Katakami
Mt. Myōjinyama
Hatakeda
Kawai-chō
河合町
Ikebe
Miyake-chō
三宅町
Hashio
Tajima
Iwami
Kintetsu Tawaramoto Line
Nara-Kaidō
奈良街道
Nagara
Ōyamato-jinja
Kashiba
香芝
Kanmaki-chō
上牧町
Otomeyama Old Mound
Shizumi
Chōgakuji
Mt. Ryūōzan
Kami-kaidō
上街道
Tawaramoto-chō
田原本町
Yanagimoto
Sekiya
KASHIBA-SHI
香芝市
Kintetsu Minami Ōsaka Line
Nijō
Suyama Old Mound
Bakuya Old Mound
Nishi-Tawaramoto
Tawaramoto
Asuka River
Hasegawa River
Keikō Imperial Old Mound
Matsubara I.C
Kashiba
Kōryō-chō
広陵町
Kudaradera
Kasanui
Naka-kaidō
中街道
Makimuku
Nijōzan
Kintetsu Shimoda
Goidō
Katsuragi River
Ōmiwa-jinja
Miwa
Nijō-jinjaguchi
Taishi-chō
太子町
Mt. Nijosan
JRGoidō
Tsukiyama
Ninokuchi
SAKURAI-SHI
桜井市
Habikino-shi
Sekikōji
Kōtoku Imperial Old Mound
Taimadera
Yamato-Takada
Takenouchi-kaidō
竹内街道
Taimadera
YAMATOTAKADA-SHI
大和高田市
Takada
Matsuzuka
Kanahashi
Mt. Miminashiyama
Miminashi
Daifuku
Yamato-Yagi
Yagi-Nishiguchi
Kaguyama
Sakurai
Yamato-Asakura
Iwaki
Shakudo
Takadashi
Unebi
KASHIHARA-SHI
橿原市
Fujiwara-kyū
Hase-kaidō
初瀬街道
Ishidera
Monjuin
Mt. Amanokaguyama
Shōrinji
Jinmu Imperial Old Mound
Ukiana
KATSURAGI-SHI
葛城市
Gose Line
Unebi-goryō-mae
Mt. Unebiyama
Bōjō
Kintetsu-Shinjō
Yamato-Shinjō
Motoyakushiji
Yashikiyama Old Mound
Kashiwarajingu nishiguchi
Kashihara-jingū
Kashihara-jingūmae
Kumedera
Yamadadera
Kanan-chō
河南町
Oshimi
Maruyama Old Mound
Sakafune-ishi
Okadera
Tachibanadera
Okadera
Asuka-mura
明日香村
Iwayayama Old Mound
Asuka
Kintetsu-Gose
Gose
Kisshōji
Ishibutai Old Mound
Tanzan-jinja
Takamatsuzuka Old Mound
GOSE-SHI
御所市
Wakayama Line
Mt. Katsuragisan
Marukoyama Old Mound
Takatori-chō
高取町
Chihayaakasaka-mura
千早赤阪村
Katsuragi
Wakigami
Tsubosakayama
Gojō-shi
Ōyodo-chō
N
1 : 125,000
0
500
1000
1500m

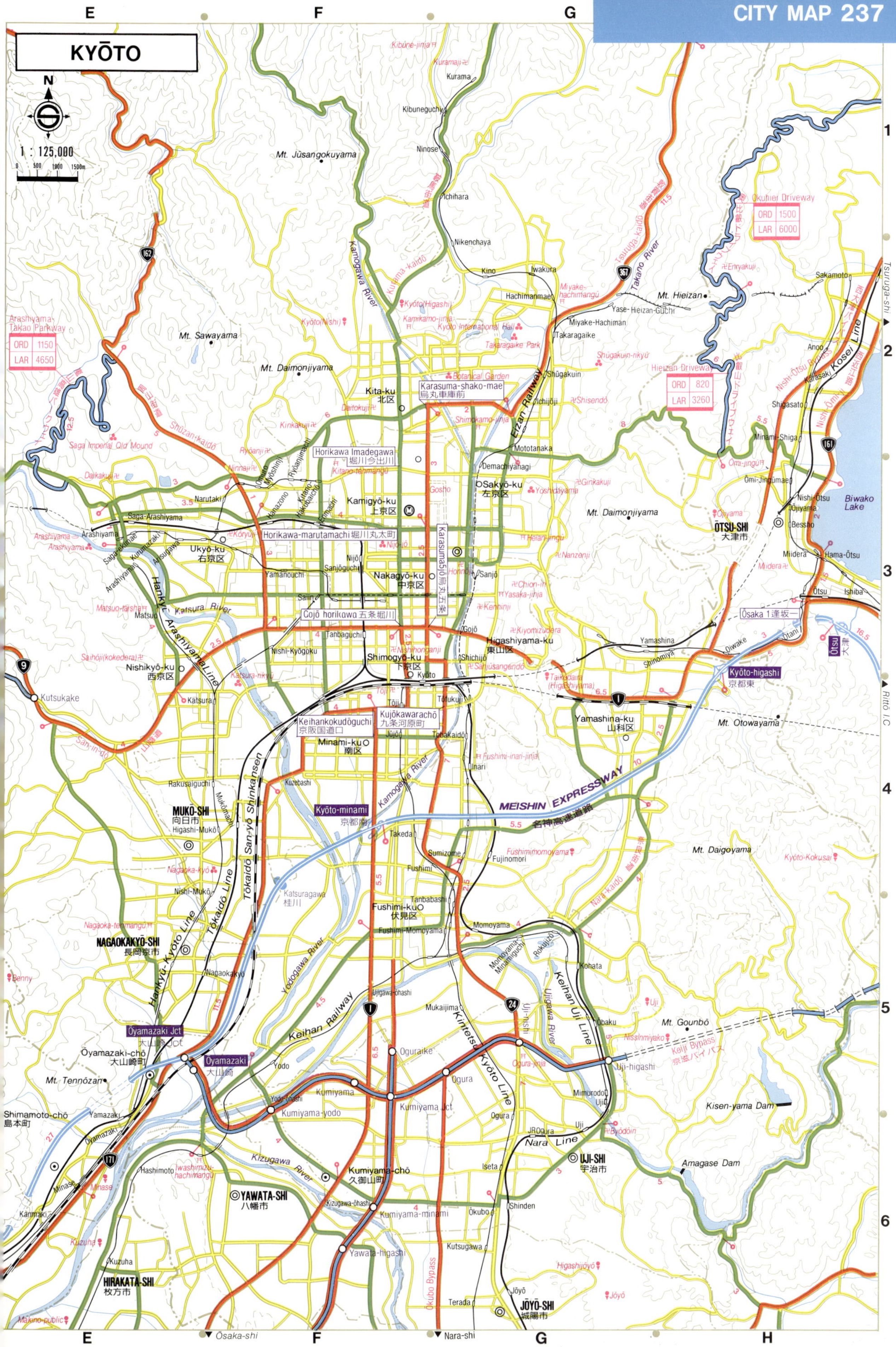
KYŌTO
N
1 : 125,000
0 500 1000 1500m
E
F
G
H
1
2
3
4
5
6
Mt. Jūsangokuyama
Mt. Sawayama
Mt. Daimonjiyama
Mt. Hieizan
Mt. Daimonjiyama
Mt. Otowayama
Mt. Daigoyama
Mt. Gounbō
Mt. Tennōzan
Arashiyama-Takao Parkway
ORD 1150
LAR 4650
Okuhiei Driveway
ORD 1500
LAR 6000
Hieizan Driveway
ORD 820
LAR 3260
Kibune-jinja
Kuramadera
Kurama
Kibuneguchi
Ninose
Ichihara
Nikenchaya
Kino
Iwakura
Hachimanmae
Miyake-Hachiman
Takaragaike
Shūgakuin
Ichijōji
Mototanaka
Demachiyanagi
Kita-ku
北区
Karasuma-shako-mae
烏丸車庫前
Horikawa Imadegawa
堀川今出川
Kamigyō-ku
上京区
Sakyō-ku
左京区
Horikawa-marutamachi 堀川丸太町
Karasuma Gojō 烏丸五条
Nakagyō-ku
中京区
Gojō horikawa 五条堀川
Ukyō-ku
右京区
Shimogyō-ku
下京区
Higashiyama-ku
東山区
Nishikyō-ku
西京区
Kyōto
Keihankokudōguchi
京阪国道口
Kujōkawarachō
九条河原町
Minami-ku
南区
Yamashina-ku
山科区
Kyōto-higashi
京都東
Kyōto-minami
京都南
MEISHIN EXPRESSWAY
名神高速道路
Fushimi-ku
伏見区
MUKŌ-SHI
向日市
NAGAOKAKYŌ-SHI
長岡京市
ŌTSU-SHI
大津市
UJI-SHI
宇治市
YAWATA-SHI
八幡市
HIRAKATA-SHI
枚方市
JŌYŌ-SHI
城陽市
Ōyamazaki Jct
大山崎Jct
Ōyamazaki
大山崎
Ōyamazaki-chō
大山崎町
Shimamoto-chō
島本町
Kumiyama-chō
久御山町
Kumiyama Jct
Ōsaka 1 逢坂一
Ōtsu
大津
Biwako Lake
Sakamoto
Tsuruga-shi
Rittō I.C
Ōsaka-shi
Nara-shi
Kamogawa River
Takano River
Katsura River
Kamogawa River
Yodogawa River
Uji River
Kizugawa River
Eizan Railway
Hankyū Arashiyama Line
Hankyū-Kyōto Line
Tōkaidō Line
Tōkaidō San-yō Shinkansen
Keihan Railway
Kintetsu Kyōto Line
Keihan Uji Line
Nara Line
Kosei Line
Ōkubo Bypass
Keiji Bypass
京滋バイパス
Kisen-yama Dam
Amagase Dam
Kutsukake
Saga Imperial Old Mound
Daikakuji
Ninnaji
Ryōanji
Kinkakuji
Daitokuji
Kitano-tenmangū
Gosho
Ginkakuji
Yoshidayama
Shisendō
Shūgakuin-rikyū
Botanical Garden
Kyōto International Hall
Takaragaike Park
Enryakuji
Hiyoshi-taisha
Ōmi-jingū
Miidera
Heian-jingū
Nanzenji
Chion-in
Yasaka-jinja
Kenninji
Kiyomizudera
Sanjūsangendō
Nishihonganji
Tōji
Kōryūji
Matsuo-taisha
Saihōji(kokedera)
Katsura-rikyū
Fushimi-inari-jinja
Fushimimomoyama
Nagaoka-tenmangū
Iwashimizu-hachimangū
Byōdōin
Mimurodo
Uji
Ōbaku
Kohata
Rokujizō
Momoyama
Tanbabashi
Fushimi
Sumizome
Fujinomori
Takeda
Kuzebashi
Rakusaiguchi
Higashi-Mukō
Nishi-Mukō
Nagaokakyō
Yodo
Kumiyama
Kumiyama-yodo
Ogura
Iseta
Ōkubo
Shinden
Kutsugawa
Terada
Jōyō
Kuzuha
Hashimoto
Yamazaki
Kyōto-Kokusai
Higashijōyō

NAGOYA
B
C
D
A
1
2
3
4
5
6
Inuyama-shi
Tokoname-shi
Handa I.C
Toyohashi-shi
Maibara I.C
Yokkaichi-shi
Komaki 小牧
Komaki-kita
KOMAKI-SHI 小牧市
Horinouchi
Komaki-minami
Machiya 町屋
Ishibotoke
Mama 間々
MEISHIN EXPRESSWAY 名神高速
IWAKURA-SHI 岩倉市
Iwakura
Owari-Ichinomiya
Ichinomiya 一宮
Tōkaidō Line
Meitetsu Inuyama Line
Taisanji
Tokushige
Kōnomiya
Inazawa
Nakanogō 中之郷
Kunotsubo 九之坪
Nishiharu
Nishiharu-chō 西春町
Shikatsu-chō 師勝町
Aoyama 青山
Toyoyama-chō 豊山町
Toyotama-kita
Nagoya
Toyoba 豊場
Toyotama-minami
Shimozue 下末
Kamitaraga 上田楽
Komakiguchi
Manai
Ushiyama
Kasugai
Meitetsu Komaki Line
Mizuhodōri 5chōme 瑞穂通5丁目
KASUGAI-SHI 春日井市
Komaki Jct 小牧Jct
Sakashitabashi-Kita 坂下橋北
CHŪŌ EXPRESSWAY 中央自動車道
Daisenji 大泉寺
Degawa 出川
Kasugai 春日井
Chūō Line
Okuda
Haruhi-chō 春日町
Ōsato
Kiyosu
Kiyosu-higashi 清洲東
Hirata
Yamada-higashi
Kusunoki Jct
Kusunoki
Kamiotai
Hira
Shōnaibashi
Yamada-nishi
Ajiyoshi
Ajima
Kachigawa
Kachigawa 勝川
Kachikawaguchi 勝川口
19 gō B.P iriguchi 19号B・P入口
Matsukawado 松河戸
Midorigaoka
OWARIASAHI-SHI 尾張旭市
Kiyosu-nishi 清洲西
Kiyosu-chō 清洲町
Shin-Kiyosu
Owari-Hoshinomiya
Nakaotai
Shōnairyokuchi-kōen
Kōshin 幸心
Moriyama-ku 守山区
Obata 小幡
Asahimae
Inba
Jinmokuji-kita 甚目寺北
Jimokuji-chō 甚目寺町
Shinkawa-chō 新川町
Nishibiwajima-chō 西枇杷島町
Kurokawahontōri 黒川本通
Higashi-Ōzone 東大曽根
Heian-dōri
Kami-iida
Shin-Moriyama
Kitayama
Obata 小幡
Ōmorikinjō-gakuenmae
Meitetsu Tsushima Line
Biwajima
Chichibutōri 秩父通
Kurokawa
Hyōtanyama
Yatagawa River
TŌMEI EXPRESSWAY 東名高速道路
Jinmokuji-minami 甚目寺南
Kamisara 上更
Kita-ku 北区
Nagoya-jō Castle
Ōzone
Kodeki machi 古出来町
Hikiyama 引山
Nishi-ku 西区
Ōharu-kita 大治北
Higashi-Katahashi
Higashi-ku 東区
Heiwa Park
Kamiyashiro 上社
Hongō 本郷
Ōharu-chō 大治町
Marunouchi
Takatake 高岳
Higashi-Shimmachi
Nagoya 名古屋
Meitō-ku 名東区
Nakamura-ku 中村区
Nagoya
Meieki
Nichigin 日銀
Chikusa
Chikusa-ku 千種区
Ōharu-minami 大治南
Naka-ku 中区
Imaike 今池
Taikōtōri 3 大閤通三
Nagoya Jct. 名古屋Jct
HIGASHI-MEIHAN EXPRESSWAY
Komeno
Chikusatōri 7 千種通り七
Fukiage
Kasumori
Kogane
Tsurumai
Tsurumai Park
Yotsuya
Higashiyama Zoo
Nagoya-nishi 名古屋西
Expressway No.5 Manba Line
Expressway Intercircular Line
Kintetsu-Hatta
Hatta
Komoto
Shōwa-ku 昭和区
Yamanaka 山中
Takabari
Kansai Line
Nakagawa-ku 中川区
Otoubashi
Kanayama
Takatsuji 高辻
Aichi
Fushiya
Arako
Sakurayama 桜山
Nishi Takakura 西高蔵
ORD 750
LAR 1500
Minami-araka
Daimon 大門
Shōwabashitōri 3 昭和橋通三
Atsuta-ku 熱田区
Atsuta-jingū
Mizuho-ku 瑞穂区
Ueda 植田
Nakajima
Jingumae
Akaike 赤池
Nakase 中瀬
Hotta
Shimada 島田
Tenpaku-ku 天白区
Hirabari Kita 平針北
Nagoya (Wago)
Nagoya-keibajō-mae
Aonami Line
Toyoda-Honmachi
Yobetsugu
Tenpaku River
Chitose 千年
Minato-ku 港区
Yobitsugi
Sakura
Meishi chō 名四町
Dōtoku
Expressway No.3 Ōdaka Line
Nonami 野並
名四国道
Ryūgū chō 竜宮町
Ōe
Kasadera
Minami-ku 南区
Kasadera
Shōnai-shinbashi
Shōnai River
Meishi Kokudō
Inaei
Mitsubishi Heavy Industries
Nagoya
Higashi-Nagoyakō
Kōtōtōri 港東通
Tōkaidō Line
Moto-Hoshizaki
Kyōten 京田
Narumi
Daidōchō
Hoshizaki
Noseki
Tōkaidō San-yō Shinkansen
Tobishima-mura 飛島村
Shibata
Midori-ku 緑区
Sakyōyama
Arimatsu
Chidoribashi
Chūkyōkeibajō
Chūkyō-Keibajō-mae
Nippon Steel
Nawakita 名和北
Ōdaka
Meitetsu Nagoya Line
Nawa
Ōdaka
Ōdaka-Kita
TOYOAKE-SHI 豊明市
Tōkai 東海
Zengo
Tobishima
伊勢湾岸自動車道
Meikō-chūō
Kinjo-futō
Meikō-Shiomi
ISEWANGAN EXPRESSWAY
Ōbu 大府
Nagoya-minami 名古屋南
Toyoake 豊明
Ikeshita 池下
Toyoake
Ōbu-nishi
Nippon Steel
Urakuen
知多半島道路 Chitahantō-dōro
ORD 450
LAR 1250
TŌKAI-SHI 東海市
Shin-Nittetsu-mae
Kyōwa
Toyoake inter 豊明インター
N
1 : 125,000

YOKOHAMA·KAWASAKI
TŌMEI EXPRESSWAY
東名高速道路
Aoba-ku
Daisan-keihin-dōro
ORD 250
LAR 700
Tsuzuki
Tsunashima
Keihin-Kawasaki I.C
Endōmachi 遠藤町
Nambu Line
Yakō
Kawasaki
Keikyū-Kawasaki
Shiohama 塩浜
Kawasaki-ku 川崎区
Miyamae 宮前
Hamakawasaki
Hamachō 浜町
Tsurumi River
Sueyoshi 末吉
都筑区
Tōkaichiba
Kōhoku
Ōkurayama
Kōhoku-ku 港北区
Midori-ku 緑区
Nakayama
Yokohama Line
Kamoi
Kozukue
Shin-Yokohama
Kikuna
Keikyū Railway
Kawasaki-Shimmachi
Tsurumi
Sōjiji
Tsurumi-ku 鶴見区
Shiohi
Asada
Shōwa
Ōgimachi
Musashi-Shiraishi
Kokudō
Tsurumiono
Daikokuchō 大黒町
Namamugi
Bentenbashi
Shin-Shibaura
Nishi-Kishine 西岸根
Kōhokushō 港北小
Myorenji
Tōkyū Tōyoko Line
Tatemachi 立町
Oguchi
Kishine 岸根
Hakuraku
Shimokawaichō 下川井町
Asahi-ku 旭区
Tōkaidō Shinkansen
Mitsuzawa Nishichō 三ツ沢西町
Higashi-Hakuraku
Kanagawa-ku 神奈川区
Higashi-Kanagawa
Shin-koyasu
Koyasu-Moriyachō
ORD 600
LAR 1200
JFE
Imajuku 今宿
Tsurugamine
Mitsuzawa Jct
Congestion
Mitsuzawa
Nishiguchi
Kanagawa
Mitsuzawa Park
Yokohama
Tsurumi-Tsubasabashi
Honmurachō 本村町
Futamatagawa
Sagami Railway
Kami-Hoshikawa
Wadamachi
Hodogaya-ku 保土ヶ谷区
Hoshikawa
Higashiguchi
Daikoku-futō
Kibōgaoka
Hodogaya Bypass
Hodogaya Park
Tennōchō
Nishi-Yokohama
Tobe
Nishi-ku 西区
Yokohama Bay Bridge
Minami-Makigahara
Fujitsuka
Shin-Hodogaya
Hodogayachō 保土ヶ谷町
Sakuragichō
Yamashita Park
Yokohama
Totsuka
Imai
Hodogaya
Kariba
Hodogayabashi 保土ヶ谷橋
Hamamatsuchō 浜松町
Kannai
Yokohama Park
Minatomirai
Koganechō
Ishikawachō
Shin-yamashita
Ryokuentoshi
Idogaya
Yoshinochō 吉野町
Naka-ku 中区
Kawakami
Higashi-Totsuka
Minami-ku 南区
Yamate
Honmoku-futō
Izumi-ku 泉区
Gumyōji
Yokohama-shindō
ORD 200
LAR 550
Tōkaidō Line
Tōkaidō
Shinrin Park
Bessho
Negishi
Sankeien
Sankeien Garden
Kami-Ōoka
Sumitomo Metal Industries
Isogo-ku 磯子区
Tōkyō Gas
Totsukachō 戸塚町
Totsuka-ku 戸塚区
Kōnan-ku 港南区
Isogo
Byōbugaura
Ishikawajima-Harima
TŌKYŌ-WAN
東京湾
Hino
Shin-Sugita
Sugita
Nakahara 中原
Kōnandai
Yōkōdai
Negishi Line
Hongōdai
Kōnandai
Keikyū-Tomioka
Sakae-ku 栄区
Yokohama-Yokosuka-dōro
ORD 1200
LAR 3350
Nōkendai
Namiki
Sachiura
Ōfuna-kannon
Ōfuna
Kamakura Cinema World
Kanazawa-shizenkōen
Shōmyōji
Kanazawa-bunko
Kamakura Public
Kamakura C.C
Yokosuka Line
Kanazawa-Bunko
Kita-Kamakura
Engakuji
Kanazawa-ku 金沢区
Hakkeijima Sea Paradise
Jōchiji
Kenchōji
Asahina
Kanazawa-Hakkei
KAMAKURA-SHI 鎌倉市
Tsurugaoka-hachimangū
Zuisenji
Jufukuji
Jōmyōji
Mutsuura 六浦
Daibutsu
Kamakura
Oppama
Gokurakuji
Inamuragasaki
Enoshima Railway
Yokosuka
ZUSHI-SHI 逗子市
C. Inamuragasaki
Jinmuji
Higashi-Zushi
Funakoshi 船越
Honchō-Yamanaka-dōro
ORD 200
LAR 700
Zushi Marina
Shin-Zushi
逗葉新道
Zushi
Taura
Zuyō-shindō
ORD 100
LAR 300
Anjinzuka
Yokosuka
Ōdakichō 大滝町
Sarujima I.
Yokosuka-Chūō
YOKOSUKA-SHI 横須賀市
Hemi
Shioiri
N
1 : 125,000
0 500 1000 1500m
E
F
G
H
1
2
3
4
5
6
Miura-shi

Ōmiya-shi
Urawa I.C
Atsugi-shi
Yokohama-shi
A
B
C
D
1
2
3
4
5
6
Tokorozawa 所沢
TOKOROZAWA-SHI 所沢市
Musashino Line
Nobidome 野火止
ASAKA-SHI 朝霞市
Toda-nishi 戸田西
Wako-kita 和光北
TODA-SHI 戸田市
Tōhoku Shinkansen
Saikyō Line
Honchō 本町
Kawagishi 川岸
KAWAGUCHI-SHI 川口市
NIIZA-SHI 新座市
WAKŌ-SHI 和光市
Wakō 和光
Toda-minami
Takashimadaira
Shimura-sakashita 志村坂下
Akabane 赤羽
KIYOSE-SHI 清瀬市
KAN-ETU EXPRESSWAY
関越自動車道
Shimura-sakaue 志村坂上
Wakō-rikkyō 和光陸橋
Ōizumi 大泉
Tōbu Tōjō Line
Yamatochō 大和町
Kitamachi 1chōme 北町一丁目
HIGASHIKURUME-SHI 東久留米市
Nerima 練馬
Maesawa 前沢
Itabashi-chūōrikkyō 板橋中央陸橋
Yahara 谷原
Itabashi-ku 板橋区
Kita-ku 北区
Seibu Ikebukuro Line
Shakujii Park
Kita-Ikebukuro
Nerima-ku 練馬区
Yamanote Line
Toshima-ku 豊島区
NISHITŌKYŌ-SHI 西東京市
Seibu Shinjuku Line
Koganei Park
MUSASHINO-SHI 武蔵野市
Zenpukuji 善福寺
Hon-Amanuma 本天沼二丁目
Yamato-rikkyō 大和陸橋
KOGANEI-SHI 小金井市
Chūō Line
Nakano-ku 中野区
Suginami-ku 杉並区
Kōenji-rikkyō 高円寺陸橋
Shinjuku-ku 新宿区
Nozaki 野崎
FUCHŪ-SHI 府中市
MITAKA-SHI 三鷹市
Keiō Inokashira Line
Takaido 高井戸
CHŪŌ EXPRESSWAY
中央自動車道
Inagi 稲城
Chōfu 調布
Chōfushomae 調布署前
Keiō Line
Shibuya-ku 渋谷区
CHOFU-SHI 調布市
Kanpachi-Funabashi 環八船橋
Odakyū Line
Setagaya-ku 世田谷区
Meguro-ku 目黒区
KOMAE-SHI 狛江市
INAGI-SHI 稲城市
Komae-sansaro 狛江三差路
Tōkyō 東京
Yomiuri Land
Tama-ku 多摩区
Tamagawa River
Tōkyū Tōyoko Line
Meguro Line
Shinagawa-ku 品川区
Ōimachi Line
TŌMEI EXPRESSWAY
東名高速道路
Ikegami Line
Takatsu-ku 高津区
Asao-ku 麻生区
Miyamae-ku 宮前区
KAWASAKI-SHI 川崎市
Tōkaidō-San'yō Shinkansen
Yokosuka Line
Tōkaidō Line
Tomei-kawasaki 東名川崎
Tōkyū Den-entoshi Line
Nanbu Line
Maginu 馬絹
Ōta-ku 大田区
Nakahara-ku 中原区
Edachō 荏田町
Daisankeihin dōro
ORD 250
LAR 700
YOKOHAMA-SHI 横浜市
Aoba-ku 青葉区
Yokohama-Aoba 横浜青葉
Kōhoku-ku 港北区
Saiwai-ku 幸区

Urawa I.C
Misato I.C
E
F
G
H
1
2
3
4
5
6
SŌKA-SHI
草加市
YASHIO-SHI
八潮市
MISATO-SHI
三郷市
Matsudo-Misato-dōro
ORD 250
LAR 940
MATSUDO-SHI
松戸市
Shin-Keisei Railway
Tokiwadaira
Mabashi
Kita-Matsudo
Matsudoshinden
Yabashira
Shin-Yahashira
Kami-Hongō
Matsudo
Motoyama
Kunugiyama
Ōmachi
Hokusō Railway
Higashi-Matsudo
Kamagaya
Musashino Line
Ichikawaōno
Shingō
Yatsuka
Adachi-Iriya
Yashio-minami
Kaga
Takenotsuka
Tōbu Isesaki Line
Nikkō Kaidō
日光街道
Higashi-Ryōke
Nishiaraidaishi
Daishimae
Ōyata 大谷田
Kahei
Nishi-Arai
Umejima-rikkyō
梅島陸橋
Kita-Ayase
Kanamachi
Umejima
Gotanno
Senju-Shinbashi
Kameari
Ōgi-Ōhashi
Ayase
Jōban Line
Aoto 8 chōme 青戸八丁目
Matsudo
Taishakuten
Nishi-Araibashi
Adachi-ku
足立区
Katsushika-ku
葛飾区
Ohanajaya
Shibamata
Keisei-Takasago
Kita-Senju
Kosuge
Ushida
Aoto
Mito Kaidō
Shibamata Kaidō
Keisei Railway
Edogawa River
Keisei-Koiwa
Kōnodai
Machiya
Arakawa-ku
荒川区
Tabata
Tsutsumidōri
Minami-Senju
Keisei-Tateishi
Nishi-Nippori
Yotsugi
Nippori
Mukōjima
Tōbu Isesaki Line
Yahiro
Funabori Kaidō
Koiwa
Ichikawamama
Sōbu Line
Sugano
ICHIKAWA-SHI
市川市
Keisei-Yawata
Funabashihōten
Uguisudani
Iriya
Sumida River
Tatsumibashi たつみ橋
Hikifune
Keisei-Hikifune
Hirai-Ōhashi
Shin-Koiwa
Shikamotochūmae
鹿本中前
Onigoe
Keisei-Nakayama
Higashi-Nakayama
Tsukada
Ueno Park
Ueno
Taitō-ku
台東区
Asakusa
Komagata
Oshiage
Omurai
Higashi-Azuma
Chiba Kaidō
FUNABASHI-SHI
船橋市
Shin-Funabashi
Shimōsa-Nakayama
Edogawa-ku
江戸川区
Edogawa-Funabashi
Edogawa
Motoyawata
Ichikawa
Nishi-Funabashi
Okachimachi
Hirai
Komatsugawabashi
Shin-Nakagawa River
Barakinakayama
Baraki
Kuramaebashi dōri
Sumida-ku
墨田区
Kinshichō
Kameido
Keiyō dōri
Ichinoe
Komatsugawa
Shin-Gyōtokubashi
Funabashi
Chiba-shi
Nishi-Kanda
Chiyoda-ku
千代田区
Kanda
Kinshichō
Expressway Route7
Funaboribashi
Funaboribashi
Kyū-Edogawa River
Tōzai Line
Wangan-Ichikawa
Akebashi
Honchō
Edobashi
Higashi-Ōjima
Tōkyō
Hakozaki
Fukuzumi
Mitsume dōri
Minamisuna4chōme
南砂四丁目
Nagashimachō
長島町
Kannana dōri
Gyōtoku
Muromachi
Kyobashi
Chūō-ku
中央区
Kōtō-ku
江東区
Kiba
Meiji dōri
Kasaibashi
Gyōtoku Kaidō
Minami-Gyōtoku
Chidorichō
HIGASHI-KANTŌ EXPRESSWAY
Keiyō Line
Shintomichō
Shinbashi
Ginza
Kiba 5 chōme
木場五丁目
Ichikawa-Shiohama
Urayasu
Shiodome
Shiohama
Expressway Route9
Nishi-Kasai
Kasai
URAYASU-SHI
浦安市
Shin-Urayasu
Shin-Kiba
Shinkiba
Kasai-rinkai-Kōen
Kasai-rinkaikōen
Kasai
Expressway
Bayshore Line
Urayasu
Shibaura
Rainbow Bridge
レインボーブリッジ
Shinonome
東雲
Ariake
有明
Ariake
Tōkyō International Exhibition Center
Maihama
Tōkyō Disneyland
Tōkyō Disneysea
Tōkyō Port
13gōchi
Yurikamome
Telecom Center
Ōi
Ōi-minami
N
TŌKYŌ-WAN
東京湾
1 : 125,000
0 500 1000 1500m
Metropolitan Expressway
ORD 700
LAR 1400
Tōkyō International Airport
Kūkō-chūō
Kūkō-nishi
TŌKYŌ

Nishiochiaiitchōme 西落合一丁目
Mejiro-dōri 目白通り
Naka-Ochiai
Nakaochiainichōme 中落合二丁目
Shimo-Ochiai
Nakai
Yakuōin Temple
Otomeyama Park
Yamanote Line
Mejiro
Gakushūin Univ.
Toden Arakawa Line
Zōshigaya Cemetery
Zōshigaya
Toshima-ku
豊島区
Toshimagaoka Imperial Cemetery
Gokokuji
Shinobazu-dōri
Ōtsuka
Ochanomizu Women's Univ.
Atomi Gakuen High School
Ward Sports Center
Teisei Gakuen High School
Takushoku Univ.
Nihon Women's Univ.
Mejirodai
Seibu Shinjuku Line
Shimo-Ochiai
Shin-mejiro-dōri 新目白通り
Takada
Kami-Ochiai
Ochiai Chūō Park
Yamate-dōri
Takadanobaba
Big Box
Sekiguchi
Chin-Zan-Sō
Dokkyō Gakuen
Kohinata
Mejirozakashita 目白坂下
Babaguchi 馬場口
Waseda-dōri 早稲田通り
Takadanobaba
Totsuka
Nishi-Waseda
Edogawabashi 江戸川橋
Expressway Route
Kamiochiainichōme 上落合二丁目
Waseda Univ.
Waseda
Yamabukichō
Higashi Nakano
Hyakuninchō
Saikyō Line
Shinjuku Sports Center
Gakushūin Girl's College
Waseda High School
Higashi-Nakano
Chūō Line
Toyama High School
Waseda Univ. (Science & Engineering)
Shinjuku ward Gymnasium
Kaijō Gakuen High School
Toyama
Waseda-dōri 早稲田通り
Bentenchō 弁天町
Kagurazaka
Kikuichō
National Medical Center
Kagurazakaue 神楽坂上
Hotel Kaiyō
Ōkubo-dōri 大久保通り
Shin-Ōkubo
Ōkubo-dōri 大久保通り
Ushigome-Yanagichō 牛込柳町
Ushigome-Kagurazaka
Kita-Shinjuku
Ōkubo
Meiji-dōri
Shinjuku-ku
新宿区
Wakamatsuchō
Ushigome Post Office
Ushigome Police Station
Wakamatsu-Kawada
Yodobashi Taxation Office
Higashi-Shinjuku
Toei Oedo Line
Tōkyō Women's Medical College
Kabukichō
Tōkyō Women's Medical College Hospital
Kawadachō
Ichigaya-Yakuōjimachi
Ichigaya-Kagachō
Narukotenjin Shrine
Shinjuku Koma Stadium
Dai Nippon Printing
Shinjuku Prince Hotel
Shinjuku Bunka Center Hall
Sumiyoshi-chō
Ichigaya-Nakanochō
Ichigaya-Honmurachō
Nishi-shinjuku
Star Hotel
Shinjuku-ku Ward Office
Tōkyō Medical College
Tōkyō Medical College Hospital
Hilton Tōkyō
I-Land Tower
Tomihisachō
Kappazaka 合羽坂
Sony Records
Defence Agency
Yasukuni-dōri 靖国通り
Nomura Bldg.
Sompo Japan
Studio Alta
Shinjukugochōme 新宿五丁目
Kōsei Nenkin Kaikan
Green Tower Bldg.
Mitsui Bldg.
Daiichi Seimei Bldg.
Sumitomo Bldg.
Hotel Century Hyatt
Keiō Plaza Hotel
Odakyū Dept.
Isetan Dept.
Mitsukoshi Dept.
My city
Shinjuku
Toei Shinjuku Line
Ichigaya
Kudan-Minami
Shinjuku Central Park
Keiō Dept.
Lumine
Shinjuku Sanchōme
Shinjuku-dōri 新宿通り
Yotsuya
Aisumi-chō
Sakamachi
Metropolitan Government Office
Nishi-Shinjuku
Shinjukugyoenmae
Yotsuyasanchōme
San-eichō
Goban-chō
Sophia Univ. (Ichigaya)
Shinjuku New City Hotel
N.S Bldg.
KDDI Bldg.
Marunouchi Line
Tōa Bldg.
Nippon TV
Washington Hotel
Takashimaya Dept.
Rokuban-chō
Embassy of Luxembourg
Embassy of Israel
Southern Century Hotel
Samonchō
Yotsuyamitsuke 四谷見附
Embassy of Kingdom of Belgium
Kōjimachi
Keiō Line
Shinjuku Park Hotel
Daikyōchō
Sotobori-dōri
St. Ignatius Church
Tokyo Gas
Bunka Women's College
Shinjuku Gyoen Garden
Naitōchō
Sugachō
Wakaba
Sophia Univ.
Nishisandōguchi 西参道口
Yoyogi
Minami-Shinjuku
Hideyo Noguchi Memorial Hall
Shinanomachi
Hotel New Otani
Keiō Hospital
Sendagaya
Kioichō
Akasaka Prince Hotel
Hatsudai
Expressway Route4
Shinjuku Line
Shinanomachi
State Guest House (Akasaka Palace)
Yoyogi
Treasure Museum
Sendagaya
Metropolitan Gymnasium
Gaien
Sangūbashi
Meiji Jingū Shrine
National Stadium
Akasaka Imperial Palace
Suntory Museum of Art
Hatsudai
Yoyogi
Jingū-mae
Kasumigaokamachi
Motoakasaka
Toyokawa Inari
Akasaka Tōkyū Hotel
Olympic Memorial Youngmen's Center
Nihon Seinen Kan
Victor Studio
Jingū Stadium
Gaien-higashi-dōri
Hanzōmon Line
Ginza Line
Odakyū Odawara Line
Renown
Embassy of Republic of Turkey
Akasaka
Moto-Yoyogichō
Yoyogi Park
Tōgō Jinja Shrine
Chichibunomiya Rugby Stadium
Aoyamaitchōme
Embassy of Iraq
Embassy of Canada
Nippon Columbia
TBS
Shibuya-ku
渋谷区
Harajuku
Kita-Aoyama
Aoyama-dōri 青山通り
Honda Motor Head Office
Kokusai Akasaka Bldg.
Gaien-nishi-dōri
Gaienmae
Nihon Unisys
Yoyogihachiman
La Foret Harajuku
Aoyama Metro Kaikan
Nogi Jinja Shrine
Hotel Yōkō Akasaka
Yoyogi-Kōen
Marroad Inn Akasaka
Hotel Tōkyū Kankō
Jingūmae 神宮前
Embassy of Portugal
Yoyogi National Stadium
Tomigaya 富ケ谷
Tomigaya
NHK Hall
Jinnan
Chiyoda Line
Minami-Aoyama
Aoyama Cemetery
Toei Oedo Line
Nogizaka
NHK Broadcasting Center
Omotesandō 表参道
Omotesandō
Kamiyamachō
Roppongi Prince Hotel
Shibuya-ku Ward Office
Tōbu Hotel
Parco
Aoyama Hospital
Roppongi 六本木
Roppongi-dōri 六本木通り
Iikura
Komaba
Shibuya
Aoyama Gakuin Univ.
Nishi-Azabu
Tōkyō Nissan Bldg.
WAVE
Minato-ku
港区
Tōkyū Bunka Mura
Tōkyū Dept.
Seibu Dept.
Shibuya Tōkyū Inn
Aoyama Shanpia Hotel
Shibuya Line
TV Asahi
Roppongi Center
Roppongi
Azabu
Dōgenzaka
Shibuya
Expressway Route3
Takagicho
Kōwa International Bldg.

Bunkyō-ku
文京区
Taitō-ku
台東区
Chiyoda-ku
千代田区
Chūō-ku
中央区
Hakusan
Yanaka
Negishi
Iriya
Nezu
Yayoi
Nishikata
Koishikawa
Kasuga
Kita-Ueno
Matsugaya
Higashi-ueno
Kotobuki
Hongō
Taitō
Kojima
Misuji
Kōraku
Iidabashi
Misakichō
Soto-Kanda
Yokoami
Yanagibashi
Fujimi
Nishi-Kanda
Sarugakuchō
Kanda Surugadai
Higashi-Kanda
Kanda-Jinbōchō
Iwamotochō
Hyogoku
Kanda-Nishikichō
Uchikanda
Higashi -Nihonbashi
Chitose
Sanbanchō
Ōte-machi
Shin-Ōhashi
Ichibancho
Chiyoda
Nihonbashi -Hamachō
Nihonbashi -Ningyochō
Tokiwa
Kiyosumi
Nihonbashi
Yaesu
Saga
Fukagawa
Marunouchi
Kasumigaseki
Hatchōbori
Shinkawa
Monzen-nakachō
Eitai
Shintomi
Irifune
Botan
Tsukuda
Etchūjima
Nishi-Shinbashi
Shinbashi
Tsukiji
Tukishima
Kachidoki
Kokyo Chūō
Kasuga-dori
Kototoi-dori
Hongo-dori
Kuramaebashi-dori
Chūō-dori
Showa-dori
Harumi-dori
Kiyosumi-dori
Sakurada-dori
Expressway Route1
Expressway Route6 Mukōjima Line
Expressway Route7
Expressway Route9
Chūō Line
Sōbu Line
Sumida River
Ueno Park
Tōkyō National Museum
Tokyo Univ. of Art
Ueno Zoological Garden
The University of Tokyo
Tōkyō Dome
Kōrakuen Amusement Park
Koishikawa Botanical Park
Kitanomaru-Park
Nippon Budokan Hall
Yasukuni Jinja Shrine
Imperial Household Agency
New Palace Bldg
East Imperial Palace Garden
National Theatre
National Diet Library
Tokyo Station Hotel
Tokyo Central Post Office
Tōkyō Stock Exchange
Tokyo City Air Terminal
Sensō-ji Temple
Hama Detached Palace Garden
Tōkyō Central Wholesale Market
National Cancer Center
Tsukiji Hongan-ji Temple
Tokyo Tower
Nezuitchōme 根津一丁目
Kasugachō 春日町
Hongōsanchōme 本郷三丁目
Nishiasakusasanchōme 西浅草三丁目
1 : 30,000
N
CENTRAL TŌKYŌ

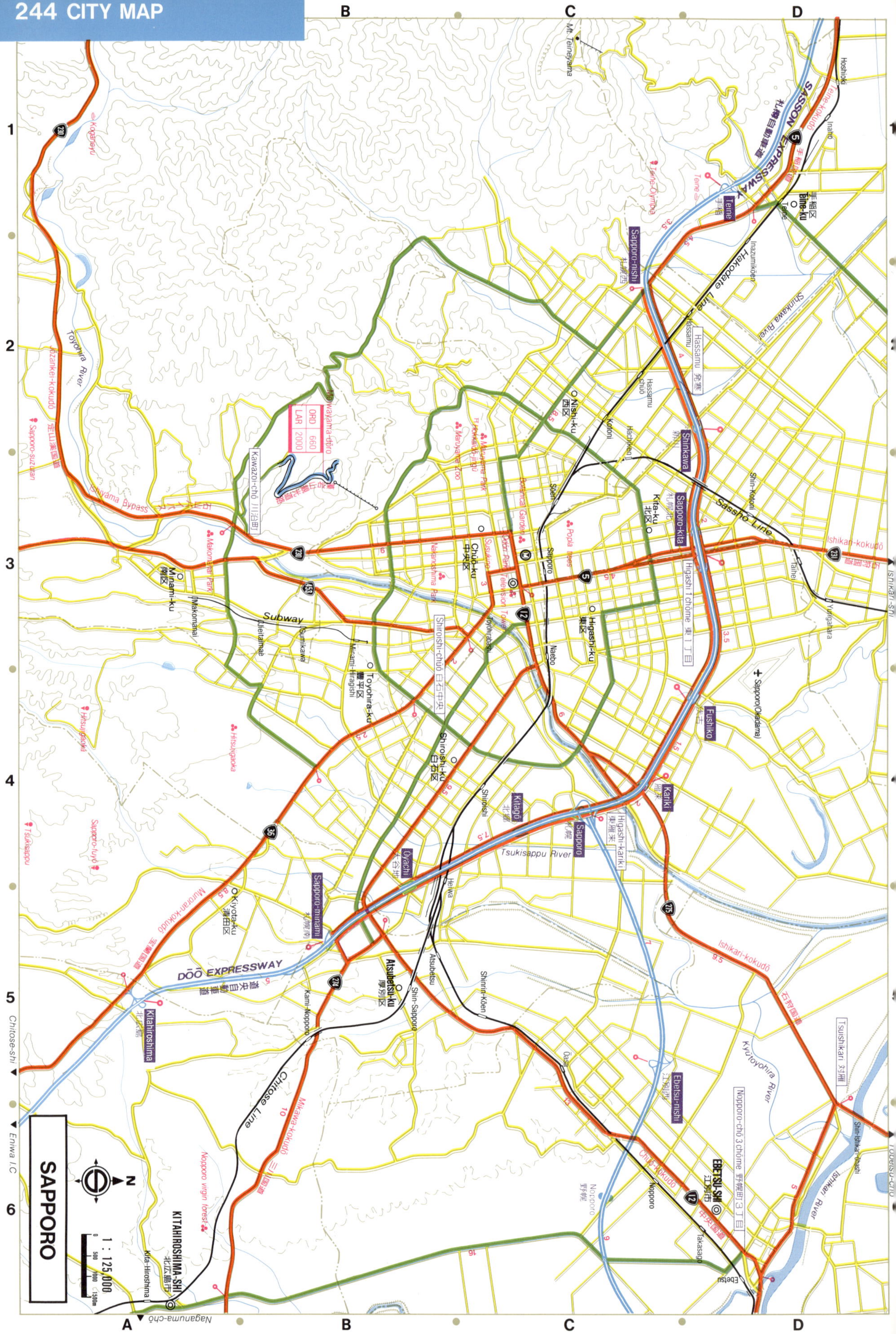
SAPPORO
1 : 125,000
N
Mt. Teineyama
SASSON EXPRESSWAY
札樽自動車道
Teine-ku
手稲区
Teine
手稲
Hoshioki
Inaho
Teine-Olympia
Sapporo-nishi
Hakodate Line
Inazumikōen
Shinkawa River
Hassamu
Hassamu-chūō
Nishi-ku
西区
Kotoni
Hachiken
Shinkawa
Shin-Kotoni
Sasshō Line
Sapporo-kita
Kita-ku
北区
Sōen
Botanical Garden
Popla trees
Ishikari-kokudō
Maruyama Park
Hokkaidō-jingū
Maruyama Zoo
Moiwayama-dōro
ORD 660
LAR 2000
Kawazoi-chō 川沿町
Ishiyama Bypass
Makomanai Park
Chūō-ku
中区
Susukino
Ōdōri Park
Television Tower
Sapporo
Nakanoshima Park
Higashi 1chōme 東1丁目
Higashi-ku
東区
Naebo
Minami-ku
南区
Makomanai
Subway
Jieitaimae
Sumikawa
Minami-Hiragishi
Toyohira-ku
豊平区
Toyohira River
Shiroishi-chūō 白石中央
Shiroishi-ku
白石区
Shiroishi
Hitsujigaoka
Sapporo (Okadama)
Fushiko
Kariki
Kitagō
Sapporo
Higashi-kariki 東雁来
Tsukisappu River
Tsukisappu
Sapporo-fuyō
Ōyachi
Heiwa
Kiyota-ku
清田区
Sapporo-minami
Muroran-kokudō
DŌŌ EXPRESSWAY
道央自動車道
Kitahiroshima
Atsubetsu-ku
厚別区
Atsubetsu
Shin-Sapporo
Kami-Nopporo
Shinrin-Kōen
Ishikari-kokudō
Tsushikari 対雁
Kyūtoyohira River
Ebetsu-nishi
Nopporo-chō 3chōme 野幌町3丁目
EBETSU-SHI
江別市
Chūō-kokudō
Nopporo
Takasago
Ebetsu
Chitose Line
Mikawa-kokudō
Nopporo virgin forest
KITAHIROSHIMA-SHI
北広島市
Kita-Hiroshima
Nagarruma-chō
Shin-Ishikari-hashi
Ishikari River
Jōzankei-kokudō
Sapporo-suzuran
Koganeyu
Chitose-shi
Eniwa I.C.
Ishikari-shi
Tōbetsu-chō
Taihei
Yurigahara

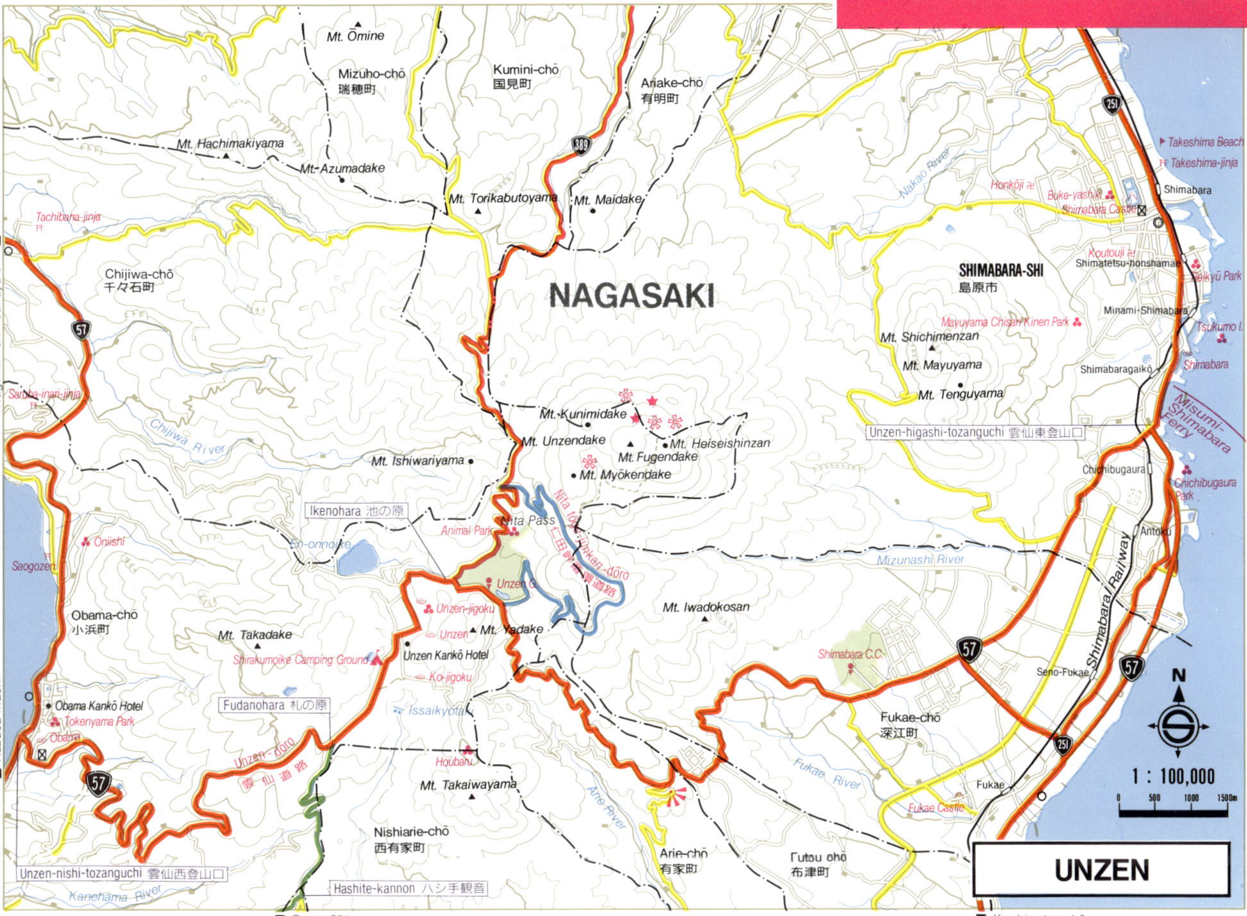
UNZEN
1 : 100,000
NAGASAKI
Mt. Ōmine
Mizuho-chō
瑞穂町
Kumini-chō
国見町
Ariake-chō
有明町
Mt. Hachimakiyama
Mt. Azumadake
Mt. Torikabutoyama
Mt. Maidake
Tachibana-jinja
Chijiwa-chō
千々石町
Saruba-inari-jinja
Chijiwa River
Mt. Kunimidake
Mt. Unzendake
Mt. Heiseishinzan
Mt. Fugendake
Mt. Myōkendake
Mt. Ishiwariyama
Ikenohara 池の原
Nita Pass
Animal Park
Unzen G.
Unzen-jigoku
Unzen
Mt. Yadake
Unzen Kankō Hotel
Ko-jigoku
Issaikyōtaki
Houbaru
Mt. Takaiwayama
Mt. Iwadokosan
Onishi
Saogozen
Obama-chō
小浜町
Mt. Takadake
Shirakumoike Camping Ground
Fudanohara 札の原
Obama Kankō Hotel
Tokenyama Park
Obama
Unzen-dōro
雲仙道路
Unzen-nishi-tozanguchi 雲仙西登山口
Kanehama River
Hashite-kannon ハシ手観音
Nishiarie-chō
西有家町
Arie-chō
有家町
Futsu-chō
布津町
Ane River
Fukae River
Fukae Castle
Fukae
Fukae-chō
深江町
Shimabara C.C.
Seno-Fukae
Shimabara Railway
Mizunashi River
Antoku
Chichibugaura
Chichibugaura Park
Misumi-Shimabara Ferry
Unzen-higashi-tozanguchi 雲仙東登山口
Mt. Tenguyama
Mt. Mayuyama
Mt. Shichimenzan
Mayuyama Chisan Kinen Park
SHIMABARA-SHI
島原市
Nakao River
Honkōji
Buke-yashiki
Shimabara Castle
Shimabara
Takeshima Beach
Takeshima-jinja
Koutouji
Shimatetsu-honshamae
Reikyū Park
Minami-Shimabara
Tsukumo I.
Shimabaragaikō
Shimabara
▼ Route 251
▼ Kuchinotsu-chō

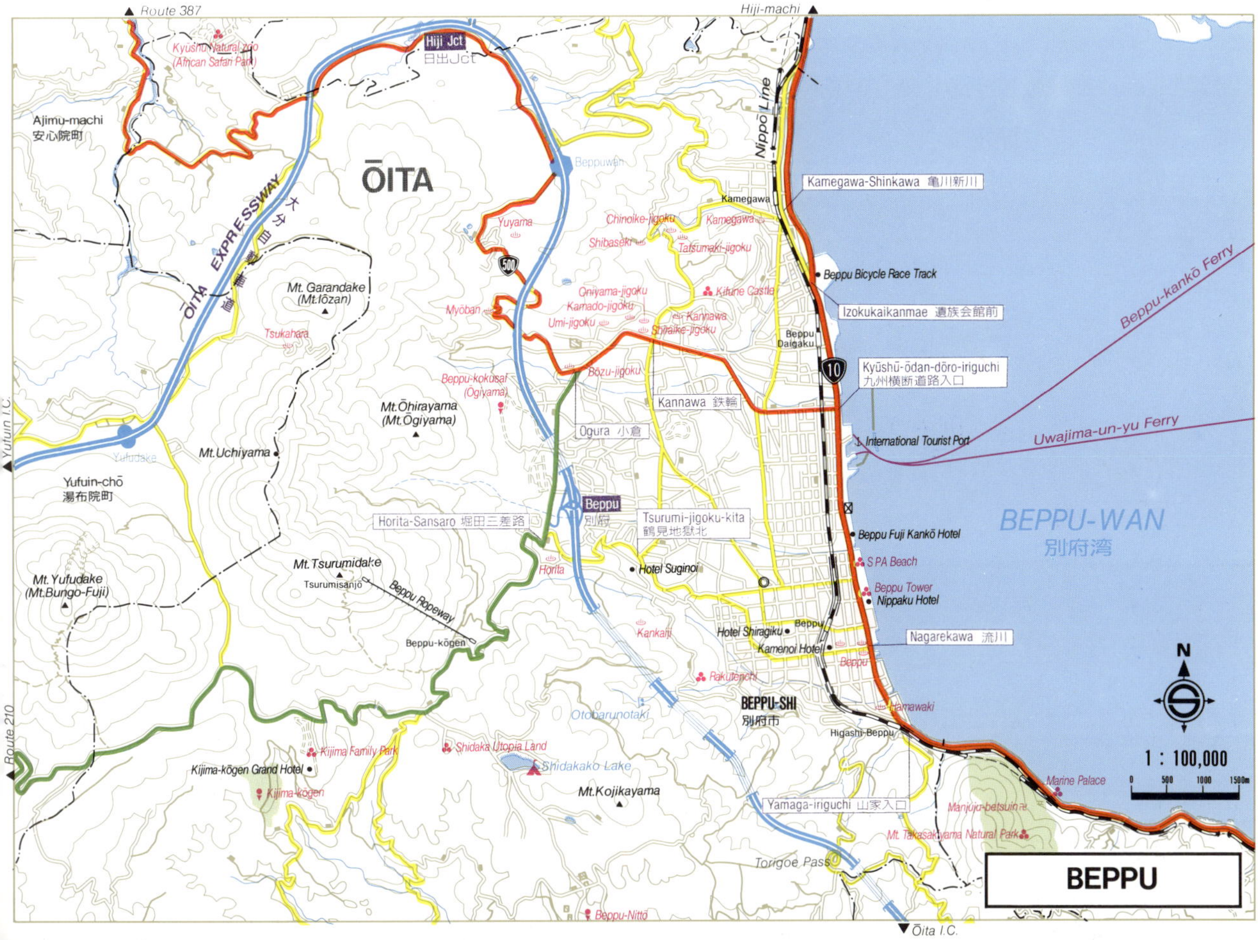
BEPPU
1 : 100,000
ŌITA
▲ Route 387
▲ Hiji-machi
Kyūshū Natural Zoo (African Safari Park)
Hiji Jct
日出Jct
Ajimu-machi
安心院町
ŌITA EXPRESSWAY
大分自動車道
Beppuwan
Nippō Line
Kamegawa-Shinkawa 亀川新川
Kamegawa
Chinoike-jigoku
Kamegawa
Yuyama
Shibaseki
Tatsumaki-jigoku
Beppu Bicycle Race Track
Izokukaikanmae 遺族会館前
Mt. Garandake (Mt. Iōzan)
Tsukahara
Myōban
Oniyama-jigoku
Kamado-jigoku
Kifune Castle
Umi-jigoku
Kannawa
Shiraike-jigoku
Beppu Daigaku
Bōzu-jigoku
Beppu-kokusai (Ogiyama)
Kyūshū-ōdan-dōro-iriguchi
九州横断道路入口
Kannawa 鉄輪
Mt. Ōhirayama (Mt. Ogiyama)
Ogura 小倉
International Tourist Port
Uwajima-un-yu Ferry
Beppu-kankō Ferry
Mt. Uchiyama
Yufuindake
Yufuin-chō
湯布院町
Beppu
別府
Horita-Sansaro 堀田三差路
Tsurumi-jigoku-kita
鶴見地獄北
BEPPU-WAN
別府湾
Beppu Fuji Kankō Hotel
S.P.A Beach
Hotel Suginoi
Horita
Mt. Tsurumidake
Tsurumisanjō
Beppu Ropeway
Beppu Tower
Nippaku Hotel
Mt. Yufudake (Mt. Bungo-Fuji)
Beppu-kōgen
Kankaiji
Hotel Shiragiku
Kamenoi Hotel
Beppu
Nagarekawa 流川
Rakutenchi
BEPPU-SHI
別府市
Hamawaki
Otobarunotaki
Higashi-Beppu
Kijima Family Park
Shidaka Utopia Land
Shidakako Lake
Kijima-kōgen Grand Hotel
Kijima-kōgen
Mt. Kojikayama
Yamaga-iriguchi 山家入口
Marine Palace
Manjuji-betsuin
Mt. Takasakiyama Natural Park
Torigoe Pass
Beppu-Nitto
Route 210
Yufuin I.C.
Center of Ōita-shi
▼ Ōita I.C.

ISE-WAN
伊勢湾
ISE-SHI
伊勢市
Matsusaka-shi
Obata
Kintetsu Yamada Line
Miyagawa-ohashi Brid.
Misono-mura
御薗村
Miyamachi
Yamadakamiguchi
Ise International Hotel
Iseshi
Uji-Yamada
Ise-jingū-gegū
Gegū-chō 外宮町
Yamatohimenomiya
Kōgakukan Univ.
Isuzugaoka
Tōri I.C. 通インター
Ise
伊勢
Isuzugawa
Ise-nishi
伊勢西
Route 260
Tamaki I.C.
ISE EXPRESSWAY
伊勢自動車道
Sarutahiko-jinja
Urata 浦田
Isuzu Tunnel
Ise-jingu-naigu
1 : 100,000
ISE·TOBA
Futami Hotel Urashima
Okitama-jinja
Futamigaura
Meotoiwa
Meoto Paradise
Futaminoura
Taiko-ji
Sangū Line
Ise-azuchimomoyamamura
Futami-chō
二見町
Matsushita
Ise-Futami-Toba Line 伊勢二見鳥羽ライン
MIE
Fuji Excellent C.
Asama
Asama River
Kintetsu Toba Line
Ise-Shima Skyline
伊勢志摩スカイライン
Kongōshōji
Hikogatake
Toba Rest Park
Mt. Maruyama
C. Kōzakimisaki
C. Kamenoshimahana
Tobishima I.
Ukishima I.
Ushijima I.
Hinatajima I.
(Irukajima I.)
Toshijima I.
C. Shimazaki
Ise-wan Ferry
Toba
Toba Grand Hotel
Hotel Shōtō
Toba International Hotel
Sakatejima I.
Toba Aquarium
Toba Castle
Mikimoto Kinenkan
Shokubutsu Jido Park
Kotohiragū
Nakanogō
Ikenoura
Arashima 安楽島
Arashima-ohashi Brid.
Shimaakasaki
TOBA-SHI
鳥羽市
Kintetsu Shima Line
Funato
Toba Seaside Hotel
Toba Royal Hotel
Kamo
Pearl Road
Nansei-chō
Shima-shi

Toba-shi
Nansei-chō
南勢町
MIE
Kintetsu Shima Line
Shima-Yokoyama
Pearl Road
パールロード
Ugata
Kokufu-Shirahama
Riding Club
Mt. Yokoyama
Shinmei 神明
Kashikojima C.C.
Sports Land
SHIMA-SHI
志摩市
Shima-Shinmei
Kiinagashima-chō
Hamajima C.C.
(Shin-Kashikojima)
Shima Marine Land
Kashikojima-ohashi Brid.
Shima Kankō Hotel
Kashikojima
Hotel Shima Sekitei
Hamajima
Hamajima 浜島
Hotel Nemu
Nemunosato
Doigaharajima I.
Yatorijima I.
Tendōjima I.
Ago-wan
Tomoyama Park
Tomoyama Kankō Hotel
Daiōjima I.
Sakiyama Park
Asekaki-jizō
C. Daiōzaki
Goza-jinja
Shirahama Beach
Shirahama Camping Ground
Zagajima I.
Mt. Konpirasan
Shima Bypass
志摩バイパス
Funakoshihama Beach
Funakoshi
C. Gozamisaki
C. Taijizaki
Azurihama Camping Ground
Yakumo-jinja
Fukaya 深谷
KUMANO-NADA
熊野灘
1 : 100,000
C. Mugisaki
SHIMA

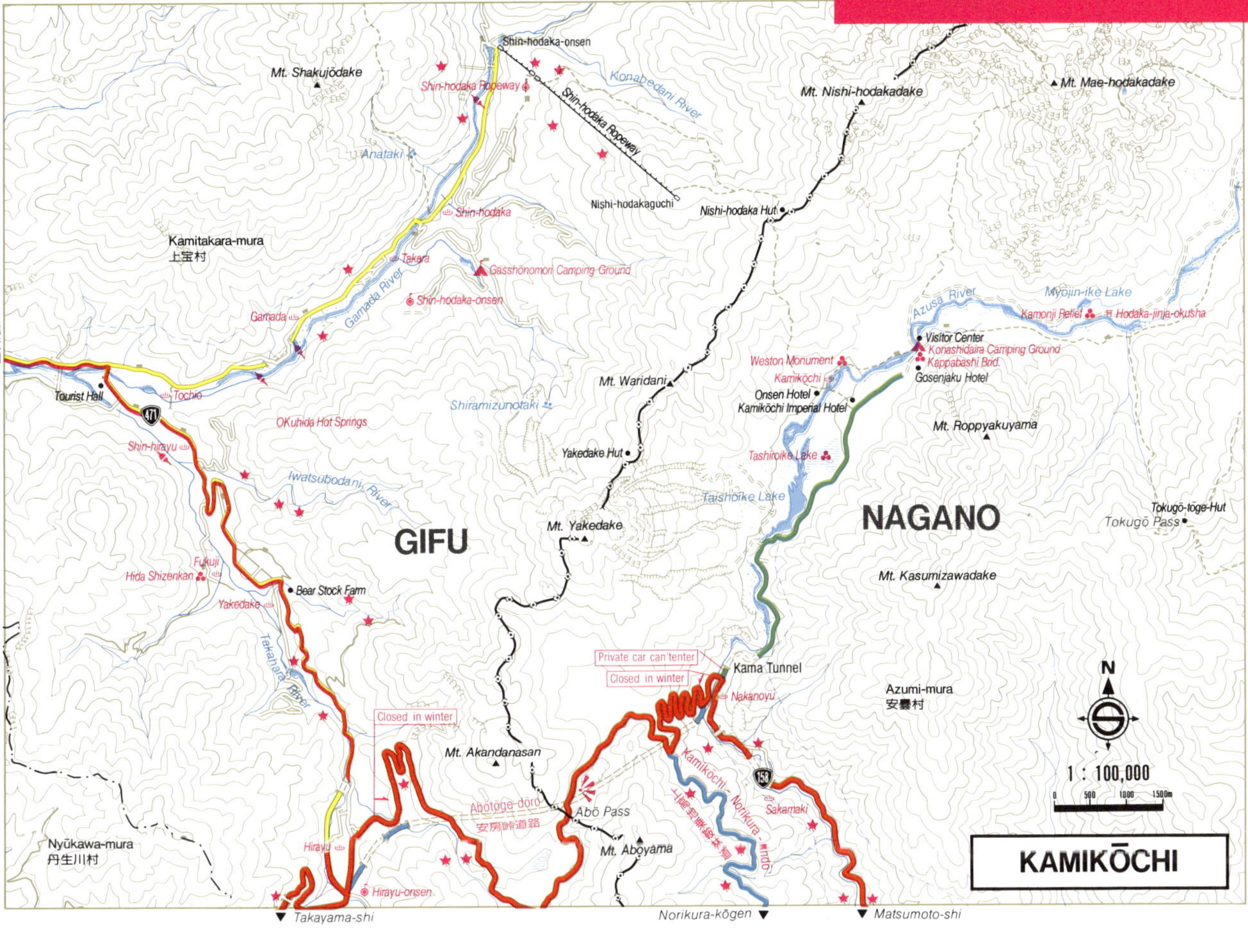
KAMIKŌCHI
1 : 100,000
0 500 1000 1500m
N
GIFU
NAGANO
Shin-hodaka-onsen
Mt. Shakujōdake
Shin-hodaka Ropeway
Shin-hodaka Ropeway
Konabedani River
Mt. Nishi-hodakadake
Mt. Mae-hodakadake
Anataki
Nishi-hodakaguchi
Nishi-hodaka Hut
Shin-hodaka
Kamitakara-mura
上宝村
Takara
Gasshōnomori Camping Ground
Shin-hodaka-onsen
Gamada
Gamada River
Azusa River
Myojin-ike Lake
Kamonji Refiel
Hodaka-jinja-okusha
Visitor Center
Konashidaira Camping Ground
Kappabashi Brid.
Gosenjaku Hotel
Weston Monument
Kamikōchi
Onsen Hotel
Kamikōchi Imperial Hotel
Tourist Hall
Tochio
471
Shiramizunotaki
Mt. Waridani
OKuhida Hot Springs
Shin-hirayu
Yakedake Hut
Tashiroike Lake
Mt. Roppyakuyama
Iwatsubodani River
Taishoike Lake
Tokugō-tōge-Hut
Tokugō Pass
Mt. Yakedake
Mt. Kasumizawadake
Fukuji
Hida Shizenkan
Bear Stock Farm
Yakedake
Takahara River
Private car can'tenter
Closed in winter
Kama Tunnel
Nakanoyu
Azumi-mura
安曇村
Closed in winter
Mt. Akandanasan
Kamikōchi Norikura rindo
158
Sakamaki
Abōtoge-dōro
安房峠道路
Abō Pass
Mt. Aboyama
Nyūkawa-mura
丹生川村
Hirayu
Hirayu-onsen
Takayama-shi
Norikura-kōgen
Matsumoto-shi
Hida-shi

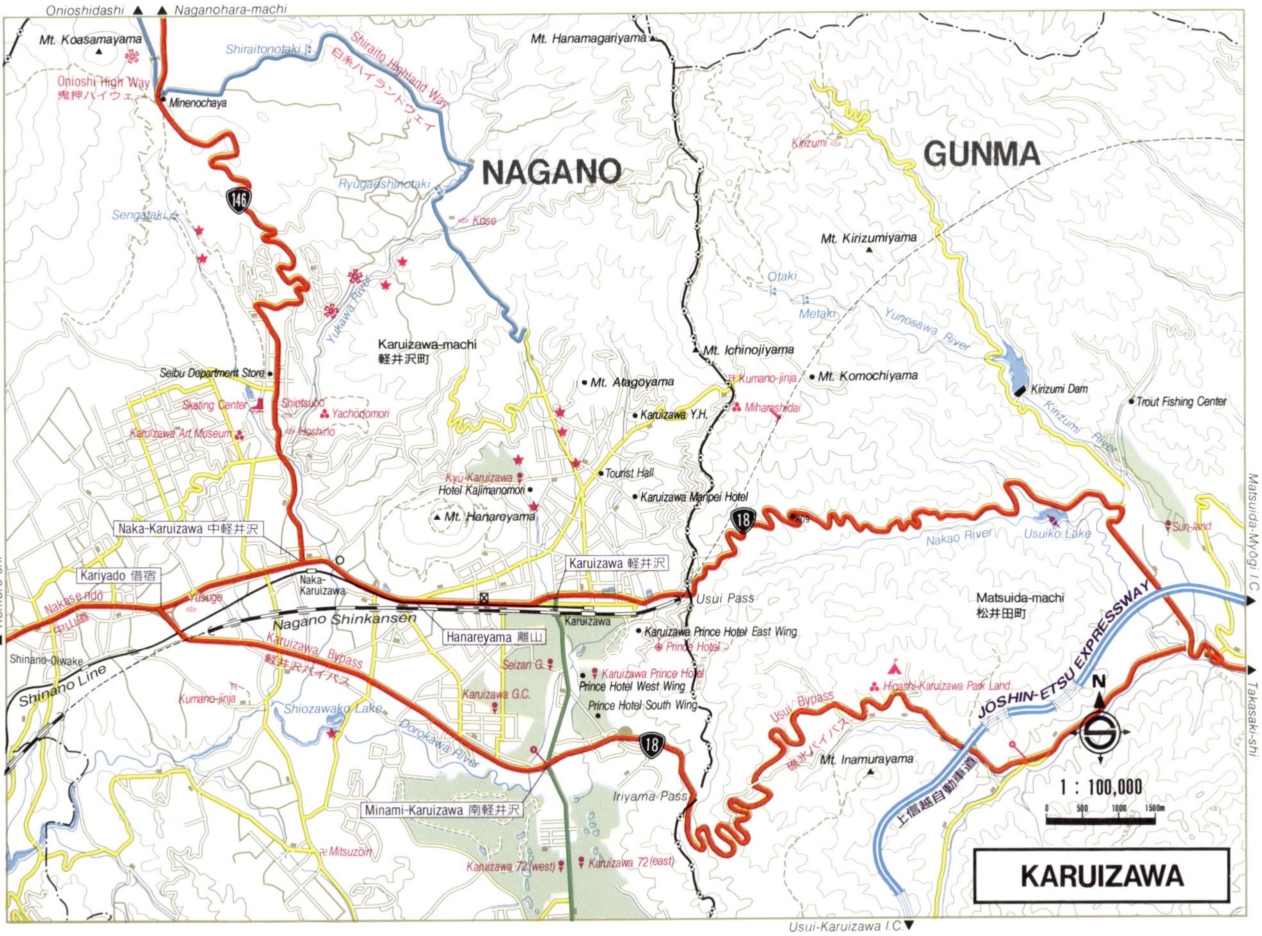
KARUIZAWA
1 : 100,000
0 500 1000 1500m
N
Onioshidashi
Naganohara-machi
Mt. Koasamayama
Shiraitonotaki
Shiraito Highland Way
白糸ハイランドウェイ
Mt. Hanamagariyama
Onioshi High Way
鬼押ハイウェー
Minenochaya
NAGANO
GUNMA
Kirizumi
146
Ryugaeshinotaki
Sengataki
Kose
Mt. Kirizumiyama
Otaki
Metaki
Yukawa River
Yunosawa River
Karuizawa-machi
軽井沢町
Mt. Ichinojiyama
Seibu Department Store
Mt. Atagoyama
Kumano-jinja
Mt. Komochiyama
Kirizumi Dam
Trout Fishing Center
Skating Center
Shiotsubo
Yachōnomori
Karuizawa Y.H.
Miharashidai
Kirizumi River
Karuizawa Art Museum
Hoshino
Tourist Hall
Kyū-Karuizawa
Hotel Kajimanomori
Karuizawa Manpei Hotel
Mt. Hanareyama
18
Nakao River
Usuiko Lake
Sun-land
Naka-Karuizawa 中軽井沢
Kariyado 借宿
Naka-Karuizawa
Karuizawa 軽井沢
Yusuge
Nagano Shinkansen
Usui Pass
Matsuida-machi
松井田町
Nakase-rindo
Karuizawa
Hanareyama 離山
Karuizawa Prince Hotel East Wing
Prince Hotel
Shinano-Oiwake
Karuizawa Bypass
軽井沢バイパス
Seizan G.
Karuizawa Prince Hotel
Prince Hotel West Wing
Higashi-Karuizawa Park Land
JŌSHIN-ETSU EXPRESSWAY
Shinano Line
Kumano-jinja
Karuizawa G.C.
Prince Hotel South Wing
Usui Bypass
碓氷バイパス
Shiozawako Lake
Dorokawa River
18
Mt. Inamurayama
上信越自動車道
Iriyama Pass
Minami-Karuizawa 南軽井沢
Mitsuzōri
Karuizawa 72 (west)
Karuizawa 72 (east)
Komoro-shi
Matsuida-Myōgi I.C.
Takasaki-shi
Usui-Karuizawa I.C.

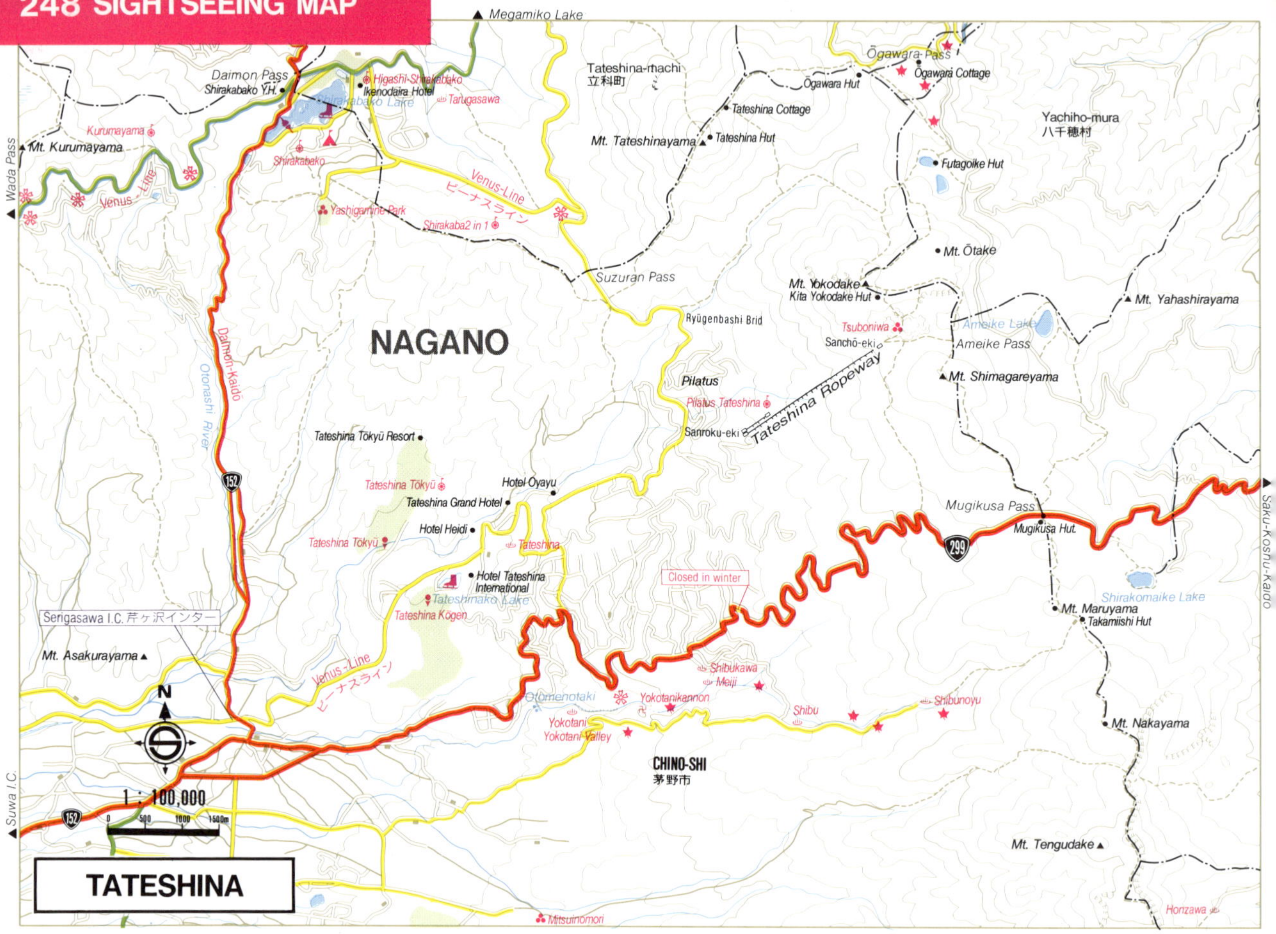
TATESHINA
1 : 100,000
N
NAGANO
Megamiko Lake
Daimon Pass
Shirakabako Y.H.
Higashi-Shirakabako
Ikenodaira Hotel
Shirakabako Lake
Tarugasawa
Kurumayama
Mt. Kurumayama
Wada Pass
Venus-Line
Shirakabako
Yashigamine Park
Shirakaba2 in 1
Venus-Line
ビーナスライン
Tateshina-machi
立科町
Tateshina Cottage
Mt. Tateshinayama
Tateshina Hut
Ōgawara Pass
Ogawara Hut
Ogawara Cottage
Yachiho-mura
八千穂村
Futagoike Hut
Mt. Ōtake
Suzuran Pass
Mt. Yokodake
Kita Yokodake Hut
Mt. Yahashirayama
Ryūgenbashi Brid
Tsuboniwa
Sanchō-eki
Ameike Lake
Ameike Pass
Mt. Shimagareyama
Pilatus
Pilatus Tateshina
Sanroku-eki
Tateshina Ropeway
Daimon-Kaidō
Otonashi River
Tateshina Tōkyū Resort
Tateshina Tōkyū
Hotel Oyayu
Tateshina Grand Hotel
Hotel Heidi
Tateshina Tōkyū
Tateshina
Hotel Tateshina International
Tateshinako Lake
Tateshina Kōgen
Mugikusa Pass
Mugikusa Hut
Saku-Koshu-Kaido
Closed in winter
Shirakomaike Lake
Mt. Maruyama
Takamiishi Hut
Serigasawa I.C. 芹ヶ沢インター
Mt. Asakurayama
Venus-Line
ビーナスライン
Shibukawa
Meiji
Otomenotaki
Yokotanikannon
Shibu
Shibunoyu
Yokotani
Yokotani Valley
Mt. Nakayama
CHINO-SHI
茅野市
Suwa I.C.
Mt. Tengudake
Mitsuinomori
Honzawa
152
299

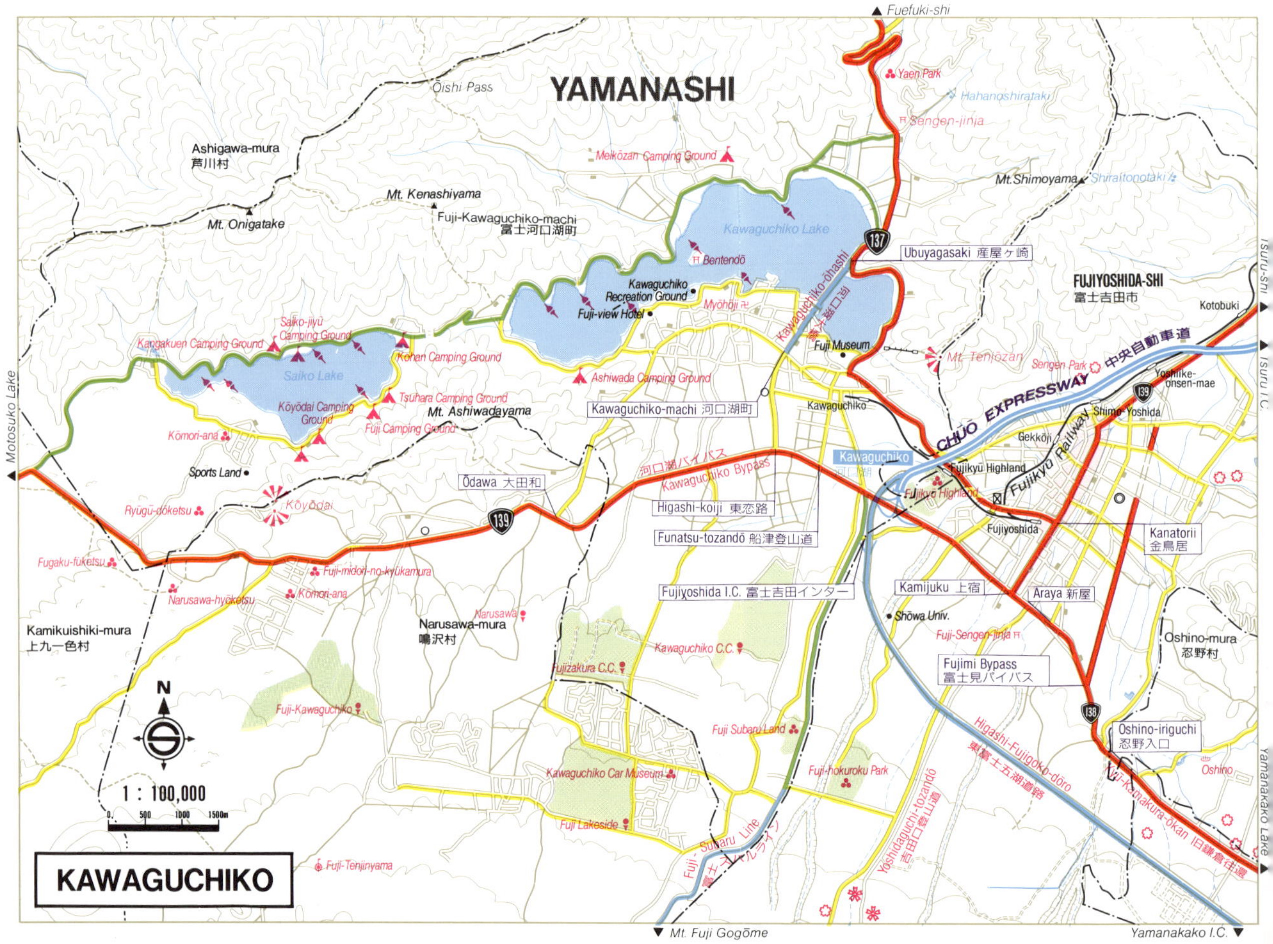
KAWAGUCHIKO
1 : 100,000
N
Fuefuki-shi
YAMANASHI
Oishi Pass
Yaen Park
Hahanoshirataki
Sengen-jinja
Ashigawa-mura
芦川村
Meikōzan Camping Ground
Mt. Kenashiyama
Mt. Shimoyama
Shiraitonotaki
Fuji-Kawaguchiko-machi
富士河口湖町
Mt. Onigatake
Kawaguchiko Lake
Bentendō
Ubuyagasaki 産屋ヶ崎
FUJIYOSHIDA-SHI
富士吉田市
Kawaguchiko Recreation Ground
Fuji-view Hotel
Myōhōji
Kawaguchiko-ōhashi
河口湖大橋
Kotobuki
Saiko-jiyū Camping Ground
Kanpakuen Camping Ground
Saiko Lake
Kohan Camping Ground
Fuji Museum
Mt. Tenjozan
Sengen Park
CHŪŌ EXPRESSWAY
中央自動車道
Yoshike-onsen-mae
Ashiwada Camping Ground
Tsuhara Camping Ground
Kōyōdai Camping Ground
Mt. Ashiwadayama
Kawaguchiko-machi 河口湖町
Kawaguchiko
Shimo-Yoshida
Fuji Camping Ground
Kōmori-ana
Motosuko Lake
Fujikyū Railway
Gekkōji
Kawaguchiko
Fujikyū Highland
Sports Land
Ōdawa 大田和
河口湖バイパス
Kawaguchiko Bypass
Higashi-koiji 東恋路
Fujiyoshida
Kanatorii
金鳥居
Ryūgū-dōketsu
Kōyōdai
Funatsu-tozandō 船津登山道
Fugaku-fūketsu
Fuji-midori-no-kyūkamura
Fujiyoshida I.C. 富士吉田インター
Kamijuku 上宿
Araya 新屋
Narusawa-hyōketsu
Kōmori-ana
Shōwa Univ.
Kamikuishiki-mura
上九一色村
Narusawa-mura
鳴沢村
Narusawa
Fuji-Sengen-jinja
Oshino-mura
忍野村
Fujizakura C.C.
Kawaguchiko C.C.
Fujimi Bypass
富士見バイパス
Fuji-Kawaguchiko
Fuji Subaru Land
Higashi-Fujigoko-dōro
東富士五湖道路
Oshino-iriguchi
忍野入口
Kawaguchiko Car Museum
Fuji-hokuroku Park
Oshino
Fuji Lakeside
Yoshidaguchi-tozandō
吉田口登山道
Kamakura-ōkan 旧鎌倉往還
Fuji-Subaru Line
富士スバルライン
Fuji-Tenjinyama
Isuru-Shi
Tsuru I.C.
Yamanakako Lake
Mt. Fuji Gogōme
Yamanakako I.C.
137
139
138

Ōi-Matsuda I.C.
Susono I.C.
Numazu-shi
Shimoda-kaidō
Amagi-kōgen
Itō-shi
Route 1
Odawara-Atsugi-dōro • Seisho Bypass
Seishō Bypass
KANAGAWA
SHIZUOKA
GOTENBA-SHI
御殿場市
SUSONO-SHI
裾野市
MISHIMA-SHI
三島市
MINAMIASHIGARA-SHI
南足柄市
ODAWARA-SHI
小田原市
ATAMI-SHI
熱海市
Oyama-chō
小山町
Kannami-chō
函南町
Hakone-machi
箱根町
Yugawara-machi
湯河原町
Gotenba
御殿場
Fukazawa 深沢
Higashi-Tanaka 東田中
Sengokubara 仙石原
Miyanoshita 宮の下
Ōshiba 大芝
Moto-Hakone 元箱根
Hakone-tōge 箱根峠
Hakoneguchi I.C.
箱根口インター
Yamazaki I.C.
山崎インター
Sukumogawa I.C.
須雲川インター
Ashinoko-daikan I.C.
芦ノ湖大観インター
Atami-tōge I.C. 熱海峠インター
TŌMEI EXPRESSWAY
Gotenba Line
Izu Hakone Railway
Hakone Tozan Railway
Tōkaidō-shinkansen
Tōkaidō Line
Hakone Ropeway
Komagatake Ropeway
Ashigara Pass
Ashigara-sekishoato
Seitendō
Tōmei-Oyama
Dajun-in
Hōjiin
Ashigara-shinrin
Ninnsha Museum
Fuji C.C.
YMCA Tōzansō
Otome Tunnel
Otome Pass
Mt. Kintokiyama
Yagurazawa Pass
Mt. Myojingatake
Mt. Myōjōgatake
Mt. Marudake
Yūhinotaki
Ashigara Shinrin Park
Saijōji
Dōryōson
Chōsen-in
Konpradō
Tsukahara
Daiyūzan
Fuji-Film-mae
Minamiashigara-kōiki nōdō
Sōseiji
Sengoku G.
Hakone Shisseikaen
Sengokuhara
Odakyū Hakone Highland Hotel
Hayakawa River
Hakone-urakaidō
138
箱根裏街道
Miyagino
Mt. Kozukayama
Mt. Daigatake
Dai-Hakone
Belle View-Nagao
Gotenba G.C.
Nagao Pass
Hakone Sengokuhara Prince Hotel
Hakone C.C.
Hakone Skyline
Hakone Kankō Hotel
Hotel Kagetsuen
Hakone-kohan
Ubako
Ōwakudani
Shitayu
Uwayu
Hakone Art Museum
Sōunzan
Gōra
Gōra Park
Kiga
Ninodaira
Chōkokunomori
Fujiya Hotel
Dōgashima
Miyanoshita
Ohiradai
Kowakudani
Hotel Kowakien
Sokokura
Mt. Sōunzan
Tōgendai
Tōmei-Gotenba
Kojiri Pass
Mt. Kamiyama
Mt. Maruyama
Mt. Hakoneyama
Mt. Komagatake
Yunohana
Yunohanasawa
Yunohana Onsen Hotel
Ashinoyu
Mt. Tōnomine
Amidaji
Hakone-Yumoto
Tōnosawa
Yumoto Fujiya Hotel
Yumoto
Odawara-Yumoto
Kyū-Tōkaidō
旧東海道
Hakone-shindō
箱根新道
Iriuda
Picnic Garden
Ashinoko Skyline
芦ノ湖スカイライン
Mt. Mikuniyama
Hakoneen
Hakone Prince Hotel
Ryūgūden
Tōkaidō
東海道
Mt. Futagoyama
Odakyū Yamano Hotel
Hakone-jinja
Ashinoko
Ashinoko Lake
Bentenyama-Seiryū Park
Mt. Shiroganesan
箱根ターンパイク
Hakone Park
Sekishoato
Hakone Hotel
Hakone Turnpike
Odawarajō C.C.
Mt. Hoshigayama
Hakone Pass
Ashinoko C.C.
Hakone-Kurakake
Mt. Kurakakeyama
Turnpike
ターンパイク
Tsubaki Line
椿ライン
Yugawara Parkway
湯河原パークウェイ
Oku-Yugawara
Fuji-Hakone Land
Mishima C.C.
Yugawara C.C.
Shinsaki River
Fujiki River
Fudōnotaki
Man'yō Park
Jōganji
Yugawara
Yugawara Beach
Orange Center
Hama-Yugawara
Chitose River
Tenjuin
908
Kodomonomori Park
Kannami G.C.
Raiko River
Mt. Iwatosan
Myōhokkeji
Kannami Springs
Kōgenji
Atami Pass
Izu Skyline
伊豆スカイライン
Himenosawa Park
Nishi-Atami
Izusan-jinja
Atami G.C.
MOA Art Museum
熱海街道
Atami-kaidō
Takakura
Kannami
135
N
1 : 100,000
0 500 1000 1500m
HAKONE

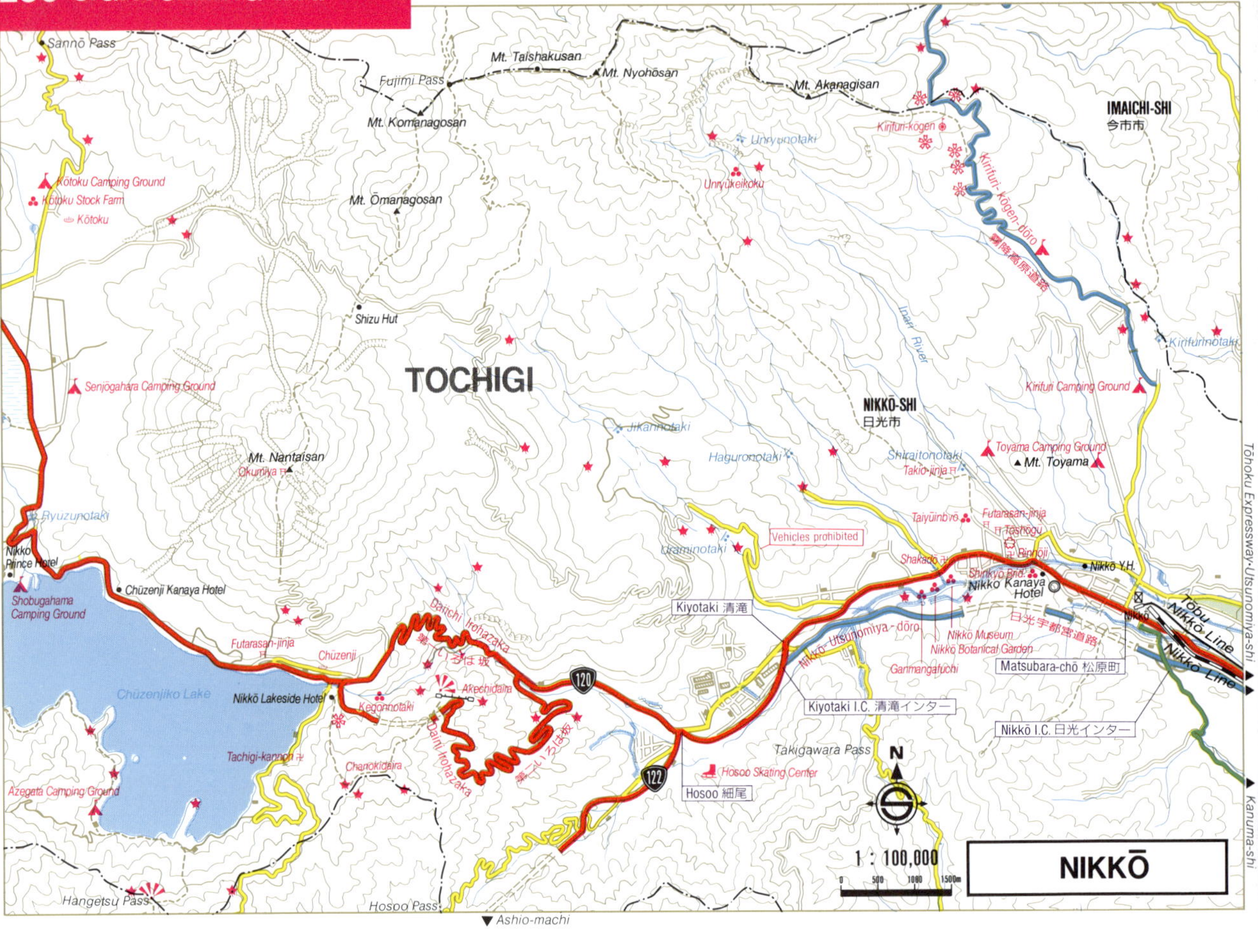
Sannō Pass
Mt. Taishakusan
Fujimi Pass
Mt. Nyohōsan
Mt. Akanagisan
Mt. Komanagosan
IMAICHI-SHI
今市市
Kinfuri-kōgen
Unryunotaki
Kōtoku Camping Ground
Kōtoku Stock Farm
Kōtoku
Unryukeikoku
Mt. Ōmanagosan
Kinfuri-kōgen-dōro
Konsei Pass
Shizu Hut
Inari River
Kinfurinotaki
Senjōgahara Camping Ground
TOCHIGI
Kinfuri Camping Ground
NIKKŌ-SHI
日光市
Jikannotaki
Toyama Camping Ground
Mt. Nantaisan
Haguronotaki
Shiraitonotaki
Mt. Toyama
Okumiya
Takio-jinja
Tōhoku Expressway-Utsunomiya-shi
Ryuzunotaki
Nikkō Prince Hotel
Taiyūinbyō
Futarasan-jinja
Vehicles prohibited
Tōshōgū
Rinnōji
Uraminotaki
Shakadō
Shinkyō Brid.
Nikkō Y.H.
Shobugahama Camping Ground
Chūzenji Kanaya Hotel
Nikkō Kanaya Hotel
Kiyotaki 清滝
Dainichi Irohazaka
Tōbu Nikkō Line
Nikkō
Futarasan-jinja
Chūzenji
Nikkō Museum
Nikkō-Utsunomiya-dōro
日光宇都宮道路
Nikkō Botanical Garden
Ganmangafuchi
Matsubara-chō 松原町
Nikkō Line
Chūzenjiko Lake
Nikkō Lakeside Hotel
Akechidaira
Kegonnotaki
120
Kiyotaki I.C. 清滝インター
Nikkō I.C. 日光インター
Daini Irohazaka
Tachigi-kannon
Takigawara Pass
Chanokidaira
Hosoo Skating Center
N
122
Azegata Camping Ground
Hosoo 細尾
Kanuma-shi
1 : 100,000
0 500 1000 1500m
NIKKŌ
Hangetsu Pass
Hosoo Pass
Ashio-machi

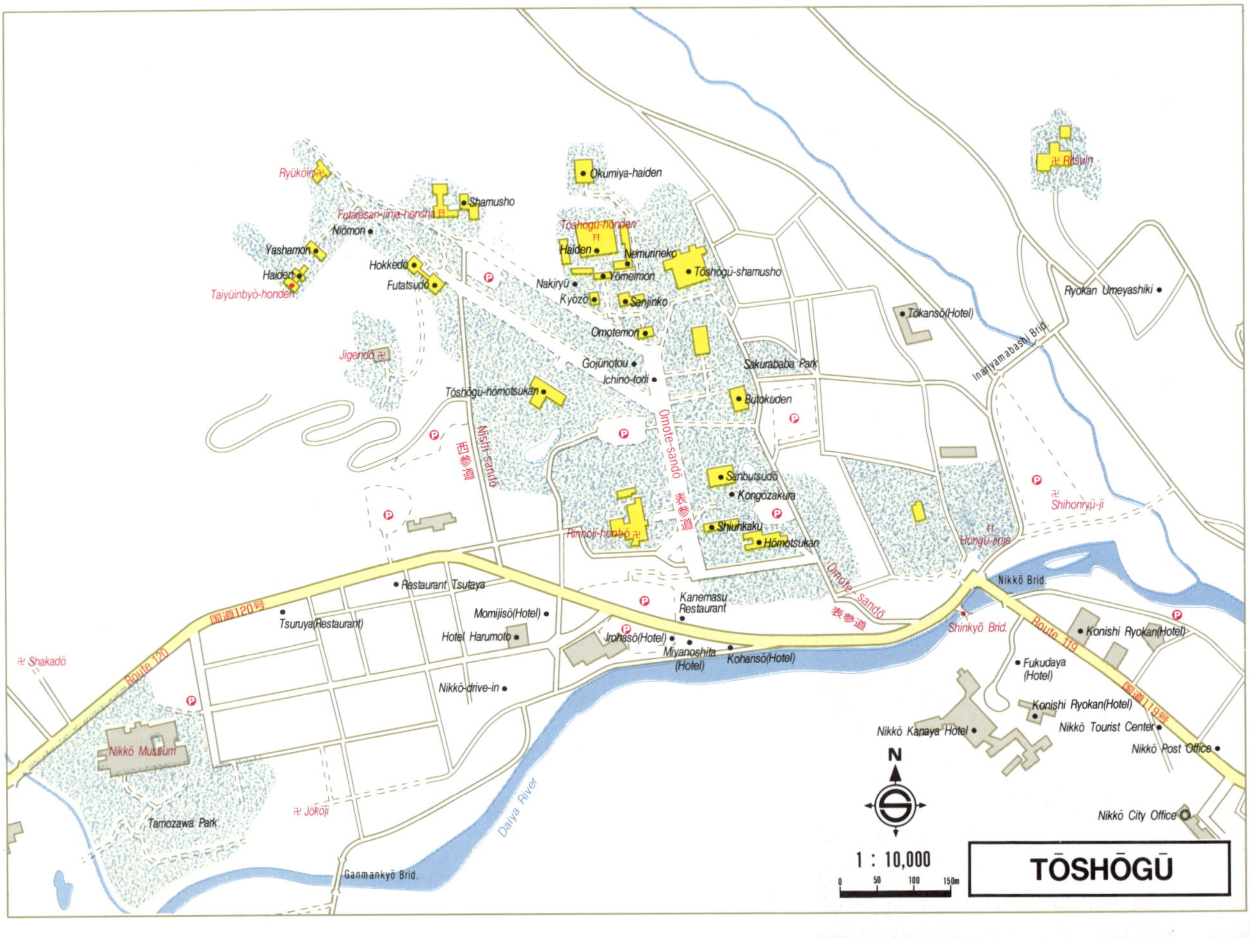
Ritsuin
Ryūkōin
Okumiya-haiden
Shamusho
Futarasan-jinja-honden
Niōmon
Tōshōgū-honden
Yashamon
Haiden
Nemurineko
Tōshōgū-shamusho
Hokkedō
Haiden
Yōmeimon
Futatsudō
Nakiryū
Taiyūinbyō-honden
Kyōzō
Sanjinko
Ryokan Umeyashiki
Tokansō(Hotel)
Omotemon
Jigendō
Gojūnotou
Sakurababa Park
Ichino-torii
Inariyamabashi Brid.
Tōshōgū-hōmotsukan
Butokuden
Nishi-sandō
西参道
Omote-sandō
表参道
Sanbutsudō
Kongōzakura
Shihonryū-ji
Rinnōji-hondō
Shiunkaku
Hōmotsukan
Hongū-jinja
Restaurant Tsutaya
Nikkō Brid.
Kanemasu Restaurant
国道120号
Momijisō(Hotel)
Tsuruya(Restaurant)
Hotel Harumoto
Irohasō(Hotel)
Miyanoshita (Hotel)
Kohansō(Hotel)
Omote-sandō
表参道
Shinkyō Brid.
Konishi Ryokan(Hotel)
Route 119
Shakadō
Route 120
Fukudaya (Hotel)
Nikkō-drive-in
Konishi Ryokan(Hotel)
国道119号
Nikkō Kanaya Hotel
Nikkō Tourist Center
Nikkō Museum
Nikkō Post Office
N
Daiya River
Jōkōji
Tamozawa Park
Nikkō City Office
1 : 10,000
0 50 100 150m
TŌSHŌGŪ
Ganmankyō Brid.

GENERAL INFORMATION OF JAPAN NATIONAL EXPRESSWAYS

Motorcycles with a gross exhaust volume of 125cc or less and motorized bicycles (mopeds) are not allowed to enter Japan National Expressways. Other vehicles or equipment such as farm machinery which, due to its mechanical limitations, can not reach a speed of 50km/h, or other combinations of vehicles which, due to being hitched-up or towed together, can not safely reach a speed of 50km/h, are prohibited to drive on Japan National Expressways. Japan National Expressways have a toll system, so called distance-proportional toll system. You will be charged a fee proportional to the distance you travel. The toll road fee list for TYPE II (Regular Vehicles) begins on the next page.

VEHICLE TYPE CATEGORY ON NATIONAL EXPRESSWAYS IN JAPAN

VEHICLE TYPE CATEGORY	TYPE OF VEHICLES	TOLL[¥/km]
TYPE I Light Vehicles & Motor Cycles	■ **Light vehicles** ■ **Motor cycles** [including combinations]	**19.68yen**
TYPE II Regular Vehicles	■ **Small vehicles** ■ **Regular passenger vehicles** ■ **Trailers** [Light vehicle tractor coupled on by a vehicle (with 1 axle shaft)]	**24.6yen**
TYPE III Middle Vehicles	■ **Regular trucks** [gross weight less than 8t, maximum carrying capacity less than 5t and 3 or less than 3 axle shafts] [tractor with 2 axle shafts for semitrailer] ■ **Buses** [passenger capacity 11 or more than 11 persons and 29 or less than 29 persons as well as gross weight less than 8t] ■ **Trailers** [light vehicle tractor couled on by a vehicle (with 2 or more than 2 axle shafts)] [regular vehicle tractor coupled on by a vehicle with 1 axle shaft]	**27.798yen**
TYPE IV Large Vehicles	■ **Regular trucks** [gross weight 8t or more than 8t and 3 or less than 3 axle shafts] [maximum carrying capacity 5t or more than 5t and 3 or less than 3 axle shafts] [gross weigt 25t or less than 25t and 4 axle shafts for semitrailer] ■ **Buses** [fixed route bus of which passenger capacity 30 or more than 30 persons or gross weigt 8t or more than 8t] [gross weigt 8t or more than 8t, passenger capacity 29 or less than 29 persons and body length less than 9 meters] ■ **Trailers** [regular vehicle tractor couped on by a vehicle(with 2 or more than 2 axle shafts)] [middle vehicle tractor coupled on by a vehicle (with 1 axle shaft)] [large vehicle tractor (with 2 axle shafts) coupled on by a vehicle (with 1 axle shaft)]	**39.36yen**
TYPE V Extra Large Vehicles	■ **Regular trucks** [regular truck with 4 or more than 4 axle shafts except for that categorized in large vehicles] ■ **Trailers** [middle vehicle tractor coupled on by a vehicle with 2 or more than 2 axle shafts] [large vehicle tractor coupled on by a vehicle with 4 or more than 4 axle shafts as a whole] [extra large vehicle tractor coupled on by a vehicle] ■ **Large special vehicles** ■ **Buses** [passenger capacity 30 or more than 30 persons except for fixed route bus] [gross weigt 8t or more than 8t and body length 9 or more than 9 meters except for fixed route bus]	**67.65yen**

HAMADA EXPRESSWAY / SAN-IN-DŌ

	GŌTSU	GŌTSU-NISHI	HAMADA-HIGASHI	HAMADA	ASAHI	MIZUHO	ŌASA	CHŪGOKU-SUITA	TSUYAMA	MIYOSHI	CHIYODA	HIROSHIMA-KITA	TOGŌCHI	YAMAGUCHI
GŌTSU-NISHI	200													
HAMADA-HIGASHI	400	200												
HAMADA	550	350	300											
ASAHI	1050	850	650	600										
MIZUHO	1450	1250	1050	1000	550									
ŌASA	1750	1550	1350	1300	850	450								
CHŪGOKU-SUITA	8650	8450	8250	8200	7850	7600	7400							
TSUYAMA	5800	5600	5400	5350	5000	4750	4550	3850						
MIYOSHI	3050	2850	2650	2600	2150	1750	1450	6500	3550					
CHIYODA	2150	1950	1750	1650	1200	850	500	7150	4250	1050				
HIROSHIMA-KITA	2450	2250	2050	2000	1550	1150	850	7300	4600	1500	600			
TOGŌCHI	2850	2650	2450	2400	1950	1550	1250	7700	4850	1900	950	700		
YAMAGUCHI	5000	4800	4600	4550	4200	3900	3700	9600	6800	4150	3500	3250	2900	
SHIMONOSEKI	6350	6150	5950	5850	5550	5300	5050	10900	8100	5500	4900	4700	4300	2050

	NAGOYA	KYŌTO-MINAMI	CHŪGOKU-SUITA	CHŪGOKU-TOYONAKA · IKEDA	TAKARAZUKA	NISHINOMIYA-KITA JCT	NISHINOMIYA-KITA	KŌBE-SANDA	YOKAWA	HYŌGO-TŌJŌ	TAKINO-YASHIRO	KASAI	FUKUZAKI	YAMASAKI	SAYŌ
TŌKYŌ	7100	10050	/	10850	11000	11250	11300	11450	11550	11650	11850	12000	12200	12550	12900
NAGOYA		4000	/	4850	5050	5250	5300	5450	5550	5650	5850	6000	6200	6550	6900
KYŌTO-MINAMI			/	1250	1500	1850	1900	2100	2250	2350	2650	2900	3150	3500	3900
CHŪGOKU-SUITA				450	650	1000	1100	1250	1450	1550	1850	2100	2350	2900	3250
CHŪGOKU-TOYONAKA · IKEDA					350	700	800	950	1150	1250	1550	1800	2050	2600	3050
TAKARAZUKA						500	550	750	950	1050	1350	1600	1850	2350	2850
NISHINOMIYA-KITA JCT								/	/	/	/	/	/	/	/
NISHINOMIYA-KITA								300	500	600	900	1150	1450	1950	2450
KŌBE-SANDA									350	450	750	1000	1250	1800	2300
YOKAWA										250	550	800	1050	1600	2100
HYŌGO-TŌJŌ											450	700	950	1500	2000
TAKINO-YASHIRO												400	650	1200	1700
KASAI													400	950	1450
FUKUZAKI														700	1200
YAMASAKI															650
SAYŌ															
SAKUTŌ															
MIMASAK															

YONAGO·OKAYAMA EXPRESSWAY

	TSUYAMA	INNOSHŌ	YONAGO	MIZOKUCHI	KŌFU	HIRUZEN	YUBARA	KUSE	OCHIAI	UKAN	KAYŌ	OKAYAMA-SŌJA	OKAYAMA	KURASHIKI	MIYOSHI	HIROSHIMA-KITA	YAMAGUCHI	SHIMONOSEKI
CHŪGOKU-SUITA	3850	4050	5550	5400	5250	4950	4650	4400	4450	4800	5050	5400	5550	5600	6500	7450	9650	10950
TSUYAMA		400	2500	2250	2050	1650	1200	850	950	1400	1750	2250	2500	2550	3550	4600	6800	8100
INNOSHŌ			2250	2000	1800	1400	900	600	700	1150	1450	2000	2250	2300	3350	4400	6600	7900
YONAGO				400	600	1000	1450	1800	2050	2500	2800	3200	3400	3400	4400	5350	7550	8850
MIZOKUCHI					350	750	1250	1550	1800	2250	2600	3000	3200	3250	4200	5200	7400	8700
KŌFU						550	1000	1350	1600	2050	2400	2850	3050	3050	4050	5050	7250	8550
HIRUZEN							600	950	1200	1650	2000	2500	2750	2800	3750	4750	6950	8250
YUBARA								450	750	1200	1500	2050	2300	2300	3400	4400	6650	7950
KUSE									400	850	1200	1700	1950	2000	3150	4150	6400	7700
OCHIAI										600	950	1450	1700	1750	2950	4000	6250	7550
UKAN											500	1000	1250	1300	2950	3950	6200	7550
KAYŌ												650	900	950	3200	4200	6450	7750
OKAYAMA-SŌJA													400	450	3600	4000	6350	7700
OKAYAMA														550	3800	4100	6450	7750
KURASHIKI															3800	3800	6150	7500
MIYOSHI																1500	4150	5500
HIROSHIMA-KITA																	3250	4700
YAMAGUCHI																		2050
SHIMONOSEKI																		

KYŪSHŪ EXPRESSWAY

	HIROSHIMA	MOJI-KŌ	MOJI	SHIN-MOJI	KOKURA-HIGASHI	KOKURA-MINAMI	YAHATA	WAKAMIYA	KOGA	FUKUOKA	DAZAIFU	CHIKUSHINO	TOSU	SASEBO-MINATO	NAGASAKI	BEPPU	ŌITA	KURUME	HIROKAWA	YAME	NANKAN	KIKUSUI	UEKI	KUMAMOTO	MASHIKI-KUMAMOTO-KŪKŌ	MIFUNE	MATSUBASE	YATSUSHIRO	YATSUSHIRO-MINAMI	HINAGU	HITOYOS
MOJI-KŌ	5300
MOJI	5400	/
SHIN-MOJI	/	/	/
KOKURA-HIGASHI	5650	/	500	400
KOKURA-MINAMI	5750	/	700	550	300
YAHATA	5950	/	950	850	600	450
WAKAMIYA	6200	/	1350	1200	1000	800	500
KOGA	6450	/	1650	1550	1300	1150	850	450
FUKUOKA	6600	/	1900	1800	1600	1400	1100	750	400
DAZAIFU	6850	/	2200	2100	1900	1700	1400	1050	750	450
CHIKUSHINO	6950	/	2400	2300	2050	1900	1600	1250	900	650	350
TOSU	7150	/	2650	2550	2300	2150	1850	1500	1200	900	600	400
SASEBO-MINATO	9260	/	4860	4760	4610	4460	4260	4010	3760	3510	3210	3010	2760
NAGASAKI	9300	/	4950	4900	4750	4600	4400	4100	3850	3650	3450	3300	3100	2560
BEPPU	9150	/	4800	4750	4550	4450	4200	3950	3700	3500	3300	3150	3000	5160	5250
ŌITA	9400	/	5100	5000	4850	4700	4500	4250	4000	3800	3550	3450	3300	5460	5550	550
KURUME	7300	/	2850	2750	2550	2350	2050	1700	1400	1100	800	650	400	3010	3300	3150	3450
HIROKAWA	7450	/	3000	2900	2750	2550	2250	1900	1600	1300	1000	850	650	3210	3450	3300	3600	350
YAME	7550	/	3100	3000	2850	2700	2400	2050	1750	1450	1150	950	750	3360	3550	3400	3700	500	300
NANKAN	7800	/	3400	3350	3150	3050	2800	2500	2150	1900	1600	1400	1200	3760	3900	3750	4000	900	700	600
KIKUSUI	8050	/	3650	3550	3400	3250	3050	2750	2450	2200	1900	1700	1500	4010	4100	3950	4250	1200	1000	900	450
UEKI	8250	/	3850	3750	3600	3450	3250	2950	2750	2450	2150	2000	1750	4210	4300	4150	4450	1500	1300	1150	750	450
KUMAMOTO	8500	/	4100	4050	3850	3750	3500	3250	3000	2800	2500	2350	2150	4460	4600	4450	4700	1850	1650	1500	1100	800	500
MASHIKI-KUMAMOTO-KŪKŌ	8550	/	4200	4150	3950	3850	3600	3350	3100	2900	2650	2450	2250	4560	4700	4550	4800	2000	1800	1650	1250	950	650	300
MIFUNE	8700	/	4350	4250	4100	3950	3750	3450	3250	3050	2800	2650	2450	4710	4800	4650	4950	2150	1950	1850	1400	1100	800	450	350
MATSUBASE	8900	/	4600	4500	4350	4200	4000	3700	3450	3250	3050	2900	2750	4910	5050	4900	5150	2450	2250	2150	1700	1400	1150	750	650	450
YATSUSHIRO	9250	/	4900	4850	4700	4550	4350	4050	3800	3600	3400	3250	3100	5260	5350	5200	5500	2900	2750	2600	2200	1900	1600	1250	1100	950	650
YATSUSHIRO-MINAMI	9450	/	5150	5050	4900	4750	4550	4250	4050	3850	3600	3450	3300	5510	5550	5400	5700	3100	2950	2850	2400	2100	1800	1450	1350	1150	850	350
HINAGU	9650	/	5350	5250	5100	4950	4750	4450	4250	4050	3800	3650	3500	5710	5750	5600	5900	3300	3150	3050	2600	2300	2000	1650	1550	1350	1050	550	200
HITOYOS	9950	/	5600	5550	5400	5250	5050	4800	4550	4350	4150	4000	3850	6010	6050	5900	6150	3650	3500	3400	3050	2850	2600	2250	2100	1950	1650	1150	/	/
	10350	/	6000	5950	5800	5650	5450	5200	5000	4800	4550	4450	4300	6410	6450	6300	6600	4100	3900	3800	3500	3300	3050	2800	2700	2500	2200	1750	/	/	750
	10600	/	6300	6250	6050	5950	5750	5500	5250	5050	4850	4750	4600	6710	6750	6600	6850	4400	4250	4150	3800	3600	3350	3100	3000	2850	2600	2150	/	/	1150
	10750	/	6400	6350	6150	6050	5850	5600	5350	5200	4950	4850	4700	6810	6850	6700	6950	4500	4350	4250	3900	3700	3500	3200	3100	3000	2750	2300	/	/	1300
	11000	/	6650	6600	6400	6300	6100	5850	5600	5450	5200	5100	4950	7060	7100	6950	7200	4750	4600	4500	4200	3950	3750	3500	3400	3250	3050	2650	/	/	1650
	11100	/	6800	6700	6550	6450	6250	6000	5750	5550	5350	5250	5100	7210	7250	7100	7350	4900	4750	4650	4350	4100	3900	3650	3550	3400	3150	2800	/	/	1850
	11250	/	6950	6850	6700	6600	6400	6150	5900	5700	5500	5400	5250	7360	7400	7250	7500	5050	4900	4800	4500	4250	4050	3800	3700	3550	3300	2950	/	/	2000
	11350	/	7050	6950	6800	6700	6500	6250	6000	5800	5600	5500	5350	7460	7500	7350	7600	5150	5000	4900	4600	4350	4150	3900	3800	3650	3400	3050	/	/	2100
	11450	/	7150	7050	6900	6750	6550	6300	6100	5900	5700	5550	5400	7510	7600	7450	7700	5250	5100	5000	4700	4450	4250	4000	3900	3750	3500	3150	/	/	2200
	11850	/	7550	7450	7300	7200	7000	6750	6500	6300	6100	5950	5850	7910	8000	7850	8100	5650	5500	5400	5100	4900	4700	4400	4300	4200	3950	3600	/	/	2800
	11300	/	6950	6900	6700	6600	6400	6150	5900	5700	5500	5400	5250	7360	7400	7250	7500	5050	4900	4800	4500	4300	4100	3800	3700	3600	3350	3000	/	/	2050
	11450	/	7100	7050	6850	6750	6550	6300	6050	5900	5650	5550	5400	7510	7550	7400	7650	5200	5050	4950	4650	4450	4250	3950	3850	3750	3500	3150	/	/	2300
	11600	/	7300	7200	7050	6900	6700	6450	6250	6050	5850	5700	5550	7660	7700	7550	7850	5350	5250	5150	4850	4650	4400	4150	4050	3900	3700	3350	/	/	2550
	11600	/	7300	7200	7050	6900	6700	6450	6250	6050	5850	5700	5550	7660	7700	7550	7850	5350	5250	5150	4850	4650	4400	4150	4050	3900	3700	3350	/	/	2550
	—	/	—	—	—	—	—	—	—	—	—	—	—	—	—	—	—	—	—	—	—	—	—	—	—	—	—	—	/	/	—
	11800	/	7500	7400	7250	7100	6900	6650	6450	6250	6050	5900	5750	7860	7900	7750	8050	5550	5450	5350	5050	4850	4600	4350	4250	4100	3900	3550	/	/	2750
	11950	/	7650	7550	7400	7250	7050	6800	6600	6400	6200	6050	5900	8010	8050	7900	8200	5700	5600	5500	5200	5000	4750	4500	4400	4250	4050	3700	/	/	2900
	12200	/	7900	7800	7650	7500	7300	7050	6850	6650	6450	6300	6150	8260	8300	8150	8450	5950	5850	5750	5450	5250	5000	4750	4650	4500	4300	3950	/	/	3150

ŌITA EXPRESSWAY/USA-BEPPU DŌRO

	KOKURA-MINAMI	FUKUOKA	KURUME	KUMAMOTO	KAGOSHIMA	CHIKUGO-OGŌRI	AMAGI	ASAKURA	HAKI	HITA	AMAGASE-TAKATSUKA	KUSU	KOKONOE	YUFUIN	USA	INNAI	AJIMU	ŌITA-NŌGYŌ-BUNKA-KŌEN	HIJI	HAYAMI	BEPPU	ŌITA	ŌITA-MITSUYOSHI	ŌITA-MERA	ŌITA-MIYAGAWAUCHI	USUKI	TSUKUMI
HIROSHIMA	5750	6600	7300	8500	11600	7200	7300	7450	7600	7850	8100	8300	8500	8700	9750	9600	9450	9250	9350	9050	9150	9400	9500	9550	9650	9900	10050
KOKURA-MINAMI		1400	2350	3750	6900	2250	2400	2600	2800	3100	3350	3550	3750	4000	5050	4900	4750	4550	4650	4350	4450	4700	4800	4850	5000	5250	5350
FUKUOKA			1100	2800	6050	1000	1150	1350	1600	1950	2300	2600	2800	3050	4150	4000	3850	3650	3750	3450	3500	3800	3900	3950	4050	4350	4450
KURUME				1850	5350	500	700	900	1100	1450	1800	2100	2350	2650	3800	3650	3500	3300	3400	3100	3150	3450	3550	3600	3700	4000	4100
KUMAMOTO					4150	2250	2400	2600	2800	3050	3300	3550	3750	3950	5050	4900	4750	4550	4650	4350	4450	4700	4800	4850	4950	5200	5350
KAGOSHIMA						5650	5750	5900	6050	6300	6550	6750	6900	7150	8200	8050	7900	7700	7800	7500	7550	7850	7900	8000	8100	8350	8450
CHIKUGO-OGŌRI							300	500	750	1100	1450	1750	2000	2300	3500	3350	3200	3000	3100	2800	2900	3150	3250	3300	3450	3700	3850
AMAGI								350	600	950	1300	1600	1850	2150	3350	3200	3050	2850	2950	2650	2750	3050	3150	3200	3300	3600	3700
ASAKURA									350	750	1100	1400	1600	1950	3150	3000	2850	2650	2750	2450	2550	2900	2950	3050	3150	3450	3550
HAKI										500	850	1150	1400	1700	2950	2800	2650	2450	2550	2250	2350	2700	2800	2900	3000	3250	3400
HITA											500	800	1050	1350	2600	2450	2300	2100	2200	1900	2000	2350	2450	2550	2700	3000	3150
AMAGASE-TAKATSUKA												450	700	1000	2250	2100	1950	1750	1850	1550	1650	2000	2150	2200	2350	2750	2850
KUSU													400	700	1950	1800	1650	1450	1550	1250	1350	1700	1850	1900	2100	2450	2600
KOKONOE														450	1700	1550	1400	1200	1300	1000	1100	1450	1600	1700	1850	2200	2400
YUFUIN															1350	1200	1050	850	950	650	750	1150	1250	1350	1500	1900	2050
USA																/	300	500	1000	700	1100	1500	1600	1700	1850	2250	2400
INNAI																	150	350	850	550	950	1350	1450	1550	1700	2100	2250
AJIMU																		200	700	400	800	1200	1300	1400	1550	1950	2100
ŌITA-NŌGYŌ-BUNKA-KŌEN																			500	200	600	1000	1100	1200	1350	1750	1900
HIJI																				300	700	1100	1200	1300	1450	1850	2000
HAYAMI																					400	800	900	1000	1150	1550	1700
BEPPU																						550	650	750	900	1250	1450
ŌITA																							250	350	500	900	1050
ŌITA-MITSUYOSHI																								/	/	/	/
ŌITA-MERA																									300	700	850
ŌITA-MIYAGAWAUCHI																										500	700
USUKI																											350
TSUKUMI																											

NAGASAKI EXPRESSWAY

	KOKURA-MINAMI	FUKUOKA	DAZAIFU	TOSU	HIGASHI-SEFURI	SAGA-YAMATO	TAKU	TAKEO-KITAGATA	TAKEO-MINAMI	URESHINO	HIGASHI-SONOGI	ŌMURA	ISAHAYA	NAGASAKI-TARAMI	NAGASAKI-SUSUKIZUKA	NAGASAKI	KUMAMOTO	HITOYOSHI
FUKUOKA	1400																	
DAZAIFU	1700	450																
TOSU	2150	900	600															
HIGASHI-SEFURI	2500	1250	950	500														
SAGA-YAMATO	2800	1550	1250	800	450													
TAKU	3100	1950	1650	1200	850	550												
TAKEO-KITAGATA	3300	2250	1950	1500	1150	850	450											
TAKEO-MINAMI	/	/	/	/	/	/	/	/										
URESHINO	3600	2650	2350	1900	1550	1250	850	550	/									
HIGASHI-SONOGI	3800	2850	2600	2150	1800	1500	1100	800	/	400								
ŌMURA	4050	3100	2900	2500	2150	1850	1450	1150	/	750	500							
ISAHAYA	4300	3350	3150	2800	2450	2150	1750	1500	/	1050	800	450						
NAGASAKI-TARAMI	4400	3450	3200	2900	2600	2300	1900	1600	/	1200	950	600	250					
NAGASAKI-SUSUKIZUKA	4550	3600	3400	3050	2800	2500	2100	1800	/	1400	1150	800	500	350				
NAGASAKI	4600	3650	3450	3100	2850	2600	2200	1900	/	1500	1250	900	600	450	/			
KUMAMOTO	3750	2800	2500	2150	2500	2800	3050	3300	/	3600	3800	4050	4250	4350	4550	4600		
HITOYOSHI	5250	4350	4150	3850	4100	4350	4650	4850	/	5100	5300	5550	5750	5850	6000	6050	2250	
KAGOSHIMA	6900	6050	5850	5550	5800	6000	6300	6500	/	6800	6950	7200	7400	7500	7650	7700	4150	2550

CHŪGOKU • HIROSHIMA EXPRESSWAY

	13500	13700	15150	14050	13800	14250	14750	15200	15750	16050	16450	16700	16900	16700	16500	17250	17550	18050	18500	18800	19200	19400	19750	20000	20200	20500	20700	20800	21050	22050
	7500	7650	9100	8050	7800	8250	8750	9200	9750	10050	10400	10700	10900	10700	10500	11250	11550	12000	12500	12800	13150	13400	13750	13950	14200	14500	14700	14800	15050	16000
	4500	4700	6150	5100	4850	5300	5800	6250	6800	7100	7450	7700	7900	7700	7500	8250	8550	9050	9550	9850	10200	10450	10750	11000	11250	11500	11700	11800	12050	13050
	3850	4050	5550	4450	4200	4700	5200	5650	6200	6500	6850	7150	7300	7150	6900	7700	7950	8450	8950	9250	9600	9850	10150	10400	10650	10900	11150	11250	11450	12450
	3650	3850	5350	4250	4000	4450	5000	5450	6000	6300	6650	6900	7100	6900	6700	7450	7750	8250	8750	9050	9400	9650	9950	10200	10450	10700	10950	11000	11250	12250
	3450	3650	5200	4050	3800	4300	4850	5250	5800	6150	6500	6750	6950	6750	6550	7300	7600	8100	8600	8900	9250	9450	9800	10050	10300	10550	10750	10850	11100	12100
	/	/	/	/	/	/	/	/	/	/	/	/	/	/	/	/	/	/	/	/	/	/	/	/	/	/	/	/	/	/
	3150	3350	4900	3750	3500	3950	4500	5000	5500	5850	6200	6450	6650	6450	6250	7000	7300	7800	8300	8600	8950	9200	9500	9750	10000	10250	10500	10550	10800	11800
	3000	3200	4750	3600	3550	3850	4400	4850	5400	5700	6050	6350	6650	6500	6300	6900	7200	7700	8200	8500	8850	9100	9400	9650	9900	10150	10350	10450	10700	11700
	2900	3100	4650	3450	3700	3700	4250	4750	5250	5600	5950	6200	6500	6650	6450	6800	7100	7550	8050	8350	8700	8950	9300	9500	9750	10050	10250	10350	10600	11550
	2800	3000	4550	3400	3750	3650	4150	4650	5200	5500	5850	6150	6450	6650	6500	6700	7000	7500	8000	8300	8650	8900	9200	9450	9700	9950	10200	10250	10500	11500
	2500	2750	4350	3150	4000	3400	3950	4450	5000	5300	5650	5950	6250	6400	6650	6500	6800	7300	7750	8050	8450	8650	9000	9250	9450	9750	9950	10050	10300	11300
	2250	2550	4150	3000	4150	3200	3750	4250	4800	5100	5500	5750	6050	6250	6450	6300	6600	7100	7600	7900	8250	8500	8800	9050	9300	9550	9800	9900	10100	11100
	2000	2250	3950	2800	3950	3000	3550	4050	4650	4950	5300	5550	5900	6050	6250	6150	6450	6900	7400	7700	8100	8300	8650	8900	9100	9400	9600	9700	9950	10950
	1500	1750	3550	2300	3550	2600	3150	3650	4250	4550	4950	5200	5500	5700	5900	5750	6050	6550	7050	7350	7700	7950	8250	8500	8750	9000	9250	9350	9550	10550
	950	1250	3150	1750	3200	2050	2800	3250	3850	4200	4550	4850	5150	5350	5550	5400	5700	6200	6700	7000	7350	7600	7900	8150	8400	8650	8900	9000	9200	10200
	UNDER CONSTRUCTION																													
	450	700	2800	1250	2800	1550	2300	2900	3450	3800	4200	4450	4800	5000	5200	5050	5350	5850	6300	6650	7000	7200	7550	7800	8000	8300	8500	8600	8850	9850
YAMA		400	2500	950	2500	1250	2000	2650	3250	3550	3950	4250	4600	4750	5000	4850	5150	5650	6100	6400	6800	7000	7350	7600	7800	8100	8300	8400	8650	9650
INNOSHŌ			2250	700	2250	1000	1700	2350	3050	3350	3750	4050	4400	4600	4800	4650	4950	5450	5950	6250	6600	6850	7150	7400	7650	7900	8150	8200	8450	9450
YONAGO				2050	3400	2350	3000	3500	4050	4400	4750	5050	5350	5550	5750	5600	5900	6400	6900	7200	7550	7800	8100	8350	8600	8850	9100	9150	9400	10400
OCHIAI					1700	450	1200	1850	2600	2950	3350	3650	4000	4200	4400	4250	4600	5050	5550	5850	6250	6450	6800	7050	7250	7550	7750	7850	8100	9100
OKAYAMA						1550	2250	2850	3450	3800	4150	4450	4100	3900	3700	4500	4800	5300	5800	6100	6450	6700	7000	7250	7500	7750	8000	8050	8300	9300
HOKUBŌ							900	1550	2300	2750	3150	3400	3750	3950	4200	4050	4350	4850	5350	5650	6000	6250	6550	6800	7050	7350	7550	7650	7900	8850
NIIMI								800	1600	2000	2550	2900	3200	3400	3650	3500	3800	4350	4850	5150	5500	5750	6050	6300	6550	6800	7050	7150	7350	8350
TŌJŌ									950	1400	1900	2300	2700	2950	3150	3000	3300	3850	4350	4700	5050	5300	5600	5850	6100	6350	6600	6700	6900	7900
SHŌBARA										600	1100	1500	1950	2200	2500	2300	2750	3250	3800	4100	4500	4750	5050	5300	5550	5800	6050	6150	6400	7350
MIYOSHI											700	1050	1500	1750	2050	1900	2300	2950	3450	3800	4150	4400	4750	5000	5250	5500	5750	5850	6050	7050
TAKATA												550	1000	1250	1550	1350	1800	2450	3050	3400	3800	4000	4350	4650	4850	5150	5400	5450	5700	6700
CHIYODA													600	850	1150	950	1400	2100	2750	3100	3500	3750	4100	4350	4600	4900	5100	5200	5450	6450
HIROSHIMA-KITA														450	700	700	1100	1800	2500	2900	3250	3500	3850	4150	4400	4700	4900	5000	5250	6250
HIROSHIMA-SEIFŪSHINTO															450	950	1350	2050	2750	3100	3450	3700	4050	4350	4600	4850	5100	5200	5450	6400
HIROSHIMA																1250	1650	2350	3000	3300	3700	3950	4300	4550	4800	5050	5300	5400	5650	6600
TOGŌCHI																	600	1250	1950	2400	2900	3100	3450	3750	4000	4300	4550	4600	4900	5850
YOSHIWA																		850	1550	2000	2500	2800	3150	3400	3650	3950	4200	4300	4550	5550
MUIKAICHI																			850	1300	1800	2150	2600	2900	3150	3450	3700	3800	4050	5100
KANO																				600	1100	1450	1900	2250	2600	2900	3200	3300	3550	4600
TOKUJI																					650	1000	1450	1800	2150	2550	2850	2950	3200	4250
YAMAGUCHI																						500	950	1300	1650	2050	2300	2450	2800	3900
OGŌRI																							650	950	1300	1700	2000	2150	2450	3650
MINE																								500	850	1250	1550	1650	2000	3300
MINE-NISHI																									500	900	1200	1300	1650	3050
OZUKI																										550	850	1000	1300	2750
SHIMONOSEKI																											350	600	900	2350
MIJI-KŌ																												/	/	/
MOJI																													500	1900
KOKURA-HIGASHI																														1600
FUKUOKA																														

OBAMA-NISHI															
Ō I-TAKAHAMA	450														
MAIZURU-HIGASHI	800	500													
MAIZURU-NISHI	1050	750	450												
MIYAZU-AMANOHASHIDATE	2000	1750	1400	1100											
MAIZURU-ŌE	1650	1400	1050	750	350										
AYABE-ANKOKUJI	1250	1000	650	350	750	400									
AYABE	1400	1100	750	450	1000	650	250								
FUKUCHIYAMA	1650	1350	1000	750	1300	950	550	400							
KASUGA	2100	1800	1450	1200	1750	1400	1000	850	600						
TANNAN-SASAYAMAGUCHI	2450	2150	1800	1550	2100	1750	1350	1250	950	500					
SANDA-NISHI	2900	2650	2300	2000	2550	2200	1800	1700	1450	1000	650				
KYŌTO-MINAMI	4500	4300	4050	3850	4450	4100	3700	3600	3400	3100	2750	2300			
CHŪGOKU-SUITA	3900	3650	3400	3200	3800	3450	3050	3000	2750	2300	1950	1450	/		
KŌBE-SANDA	3050	2800	2500	2200	2750	2400	2000	1900	1650	1200	850	350	2100	1250	
OKAYAMA	5700	5500	5250	5050	5700	5350	4950	4850	4650	4350	4050	3700	4850	4200	3550

MAIZURU-WAKASA • KYŌTŌ-JŪKAN EXPRESSWAY

MIYAZAKI•HIGASHI-KYŪSHŪ EXPRESSWAY

KOKURA-MINAMI	1400	3750	5650	6900	6000	6150	6550	6900	7150	7100	7200	7500
FUKUOKA		2800	4800	6050	5100	5300	5650	6050	6300	6200	6350	6650
KUMAMOTO			2800	4150	3150	3350	3750	4150	4400	4300	4450	4800
EBINO				1950	600	900	1400	1950	2300	2200	2400	2800
KAGOSHIMA					2300	2600	3000	3450	3650	3600	3750	4050
KOBAYASHI						350	950	1500	1850	1700	1950	2350
TAKAHARU							700	1250	1550	1450	1650	2100
MIYAKONOJŌ								700	1050	900	1150	1550
TANO									450	400	600	1000
MIYAZAKI										350	600	1000
KIYOTAKE											350	800
MIYAZAKI-NISHI												600
SAITO												

EBINO														
KURINO														
YOKOGAWA														
MIZOBE-KAGOSHIMA-KŪKŌ	500													
KAJIKI	700	350												
HAYATO-NISHI	850	500	150											
HAYATO-HIGASHI	950	600	250	150										
KOKUBU	1100	750	550	450	300									
SUEYOSHI-TAKARABE	1650	1300	1100	1000	850	750								
AIRA	950	600	350	500	600	750	1350							
SATSUMA-YOSHIDA	1150	800	600	750	850	1000	1550	350						
KAGOSHIMA-KITA	1400	1050	850	1000	1100	1200	1800	600	300					
KAGOSHIMA	1400	1050	850	1000	1100	1200	1800	600	300	250				
KAGOSHIMA-NISHI	—	—	—	—	—	—	—	—	—	—	—			
MATSUMOTO	1600	1250	1050	1200	1300	1400	2000	800	500	450	—	200		
IJŪIN	1750	1400	1200	1350	1450	1550	2150	950	650	600	—	350	150	
ICHIKI	2000	1650	1450	1600	1700	1800	2400	1200	900	850	—	600	450	300

ISE-WANGAN EXPRESSWAY

TOYOTA-MINAMI	350	500	550	600	850	1150	1300	1450	/	1550	1600	1650	/	2450	2350	2200	2100	2000	1900	1900	2050	2300	2600
TOYOAKE		300	350	450	700	1000	1150	1250	/	1350	1450	1450	/	2250	2150	2000	1900	1800	1700	1700	1850	2100	2400
NAGOYA-MINAMI			200	300	550	850	1000	1100	/	1200	1300	1350	/	2100	2000	1850	1750	1700	1600	1550	1750	1950	2250
ŌBU				250	500	800	950	1100	/	1200	1250	1300	/	2050	1950	1850	1750	1650	1550	1500	1700	1950	2250
TŌKAI					250	550	850	1000	/	1100	1150	1200	/	1950	1850	1750	1650	1550	1450	1450	1600	1850	2150
MEIKŌ-SHIOMI						350	600	900	/	1000	1050	1100	/	1850	1750	1650	1550	1450	1350	1350	1500	1750	2050
MEIKŌ-CHŪŌ							300	600	/	700	750	800	/	1550	1450	1350	1250	1150	1050	1050	1200	1450	1750
TOBISHIMA								300	/	400	450	500	/	1250	1150	1050	950	850	750	750	900	1150	1450
WANGAN-YATOMI									/	/	/	/	/	/	/	/	/	/	/	/	/	/	/
YATOMI-KISOSAKI										250	350	350	/	1150	1050	900	800	700	600	600	750	1000	1300
WANGAN-NAGASHIMA											200	250	/	1050	950	800	700	600	500	500	650	900	1200
WANGAN-KUWANA												200	/	950	850	750	650	550	450	450	600	850	1150
MIE-KAWAGOE													/	900	800	700	600	500	400	400	550	800	1100
MIE-ASAHI														800	700	600	500	400	300	300	450	700	1000
NAGOYA-NISHI JCT															250	350	500	550	650	800	1000	1250	1550
KANIE																300	350	450	600	750	900	1150	1450
YATOMI																	250	350	450	600	750	1000	1300
NAGASHIMA																		250	350	500	650	900	1200
KUWANA-HIGASHI																			250	400	600	800	1100
KUWANA																				300	450	700	1000
YOKKAICHI-HIGASHI																					300	550	850
YOKKAICHI																						400	700
SUZUKA																							450
KAMEYAMA																							

SEKI								
GEINŌ	300							
TSU	550	350						
HISAI	700	550	300					
ICHISHI-URESHINO	850	700	450	300				
MATSUSAKA	1000	850	650	450	300			
SEIWA-TAKI	1400	1200	1000	850	700	500		
TAMAKI	1650	1500	1250	1100	950	800	400	
ISE・ISE-NISHI	1900	1750	1500	1350	1200	1050	650	400

ISE EXPRESSWAY

KYODA									
GINOZA	150								
KIN	300	150							
YAKA	/	/	/						
ISHIKAWA	450	300	150	150					
OKINAWA-KITA	600	500	350	300	250				
OKINAWA-MINAMI	700	600	450	350	300	200			
KITANAKAGUSUKU	800	700	550	450	400	300	200		
NISHIHARA	900	750	650	600	500	400	300	200	
NAHA	1000	850	750	700	600	500	400	300	200

OKINAWA EXPRESSWAY

SUITA																																
	SETTSU-KITA				NAKAJŌ			450	650	850	1050	1150	1200	1600	1850	2250	2550	2850	3050	3300	3500	3850	5250	4150	4400	4700	4950	5250	5400	5550	5750	5900
500	500	SETTSU-MINAMI				SEIRŌ-SHIBATA			350	600	750	850	900	1300	1550	1950	2300	2600	2850	3050	3300	3650	5050	3900	4200	4500	4700	5050	5200	5350	5550	5700
500	500		KADOMA				TOYOSAKA-NIIGATA-HIGASHIKŌ			400	550	650	700	1100	1400	1750	2100	2400	2700	2900	3150	3500	4900	3750	4050	4350	4600	4900	5050	5250	5400	5550
				DAITŌ-TSURUMI				NIIGATA-KŪKŌ			300	400	500	900	1150	1550	1850	2150	2450	2750	2950	3300	4750	3600	3900	4150	4400	4750	4900	5050	5250	5400
500	500			500	HIGASHI-ŌSAKA-KITA				NIIGATA-KAMEDA			250	300	700	1000	1400	1700	2000	2300	2600	2850	3200	4650	3450	3750	4050	4300	4650	4800	4950	5150	5300
500	500			500		HIGASHI-ŌSAKA JCT				NIIGATA-CHŪŌ			250	650	950	1300	1650	1950	2250	2550	2800	3150	4600	3450	3700	4000	4250	4600	4750	4900	5100	5250
							HIGASHI-ŌSAKA-MINAMI				NIIGATA-HISHI			550	800	1200	1550	1850	2100	2400	2700	3050	4500	3350	3650	3900	4150	4500	4650	4850	5000	5150
500	500			500		500	500	YAO				MAKIKATA-HIGASHI			400	800	1150	1450	1700	2050	2300	2800	4200	3050	3350	3650	3850	4200	4350	4550	4750	4900
									NAGAHARA				SANJŌ-TSUBAME			550	850	1200	1450	1750	2050	2500	4000	2850	3150	3450	3650	4000	4150	4350	4550	4700
										MATSUBARA JCT				NAKANOSHIMA-MITSUKE			450	800	1050	1350	1650	2150	3700	2500	2850	3150	3350	3700	3900	4050	4250	4400
900	900			900		900	900		400	400	FUJIIDERA				NAGAOKA			550	850	1150	1450	1900	3550	2250	2650	2950	3200	3550	3700	3900	4050	4200
900	900			900		900	900		400	400	400	KASHIWABARA				NISHIYAMA			450	750	1050	1500	3250	1850	2250	2650	2900	3250	3400	3600	3750	3950
900	900			900		900	900		400	400	400		KASHIBA				KASHIWAZAKI			450	750	1200	3050	1600	2000	2350	2700	3050	3200	3400	3550	3700
1300	1300			1300		1300	1300		800	800	800		400	HŌRYŪJI				YONEYAMA			450	900	2800	1300	1650	2050	2350	2800	2950	3150	3350	3500
1300	1300			1300		1300	1300		800	800	800		400	400	KŌRIYAMA				KAKIZAKI			600	2550	1000	1400	1750	2100	2500	2750	2950	3100	3250
1300	1300			1300		1300	1300		800	800	800		400	400	400	TENRI				JŌETSU			2100	500	900	1300	1600	2050	2300	2550	2750	2900
500	500			500		500	500		400	400	400	400	400	800	800	800	MATSUBARA				SUZAKA-NAGANO-HIGASHI			2200	2600	2900	3150	3500	3650	3850	4050	4200
1000	1000			1000		1000	1000		500	500	900	900	900	1300	1300	1300		MIHARA-KITA				NADACHI-TANIHAMA			550	900	1250	1700	1900	2150	2400	2600
																			MIHARA				NOU			500	850	1300	1550	1800	2000	2250
1200	1200			1200		1200	1200		700	700	1100	1100	1100	1500	1500	1500			200	MIHARA-HIGASHI				ITOIGAWA			450	950	1150	1400	1650	1850
1200	1200			1200		1200	1200		700	700	1100	1100	1100	1500	1500	1500			200		HABIKINO				OYASHIRAZU			600	850	1100	1300	1550
1300	1300			1300		1300	1300		800	800	1200	1200	1200	1600	1600	1600			300		100	HABIKINO-HIGASHI				ASAHI			350	650	850	1100
1400	1400			1400		1400	1400		900	900	1300	1300	1300	1700	1700	1700			400		200		TAISHI				KUROBE			400	650	850
1650	1650			1650		1650	1650		1150	1150	1550	1550	1550	1950	1950	1950			650		450		250	KATSURAGI				UOZU			400	600
																									MIHARA-MINAMI				NAMERIKAWA			350
1000	1000			1000		1000	1000		500	500	900	900	900	1300	1300	1300				700	700	800	900	1150	500	SAKAI JCT				TATEYAMA		
1000	1000			1000		1000	1000		500	500	900	900	900	1300	1300	1300				700	700	800	900	1150	500		SAKAI				TOYAMA	
1000	1000			1000		1000	1000		500	500	900	900	900	1300	1300	1300				700	700	800	900	1150	500		500	KISHIWADA-IZUMI				TOYAMA-
1400	1400			1400		1400	1400		900	900	1300	1300	1300	1700	1700	1700				1100	1100	1200	1300	1550	900		900	400	KAIZUKA			
1550	1550			1550		1550	1550		1050	1050	1450	1450	1450	1850	1850	1850				1250	1250	1350	1450	1700	1050		1050	550	350	KAMINOGŌ		
1750	1750			1750		1750	1750		1250	1250	1650	1650	1650	2050	2050	2050				1450	1450	1550	1650	1900	1250		1250	750	500		IZUMISANO-RI	
1750	1750			1750		1750	1750		1250	1250	1650	1650	1650	2050	2050	2050				1450	1450	1550	1650	1900	1250		1250	750	500	350	500	SENNAN-HA
2100	2100			2100		2100	2100		1600	1600	2000	2000	2000	2400	2400	2400				1800	1800	1900	2000	2250	1600		1600	1100	900	750	900	550
2450	2450			2450		2450	2450		1950	1950	2350	2350	2350	2750	2750	2750				2150	2150	2250	2350	2600	1950		1950	1450	1200	1050	1250	900
2710	2710			2710		2710	2710		2210	2210	2610	2610	2610	3010	3010	3010				2410	2410	2510	2610	2860	2210		2210	1710	1460	1310	1510	1160
3380	3380			3380		3380	3380		2880	2880	3280	3280	3280	3680	3680	3680				3080	3080	3180	3280	3530	2880		2880	2380	2130	1980	2180	1830
3530	3530			3530		3530	3530		3030	3030	3430	3430	3430	3830	3830	3830				3230	3230	3330	3430	3680	3030		3030	2530	2280	2130	2330	1980
3580	3580			3580		3580	3580		3080	3080	3480	3480	3480	3880	3880	3880				3280	3280	3380	3480	3730	3080		3080	2580	2330	2180	2380	2030
3730	3730			3730		3730	3730		3230	3230	3630	3630	3630	4030	4030	4030				3430	3430	3530	3630	3880	3230		3230	2730	2480	2330	2530	2180
3880	3880			3880		3880	3880		3380	3380	3780	3780	3780	4180	4180	4180				3580	3580	3680	3780	4030	3380		3380	2880	2630	2480	2680	2330
4030	4030			4030		4030	4030		3530	3530	3930	3930	3930	4330	4330	4330				3730	3730	3830	3930	4180	3530		3530	3030	2780	2630	2830	2480
4280	4280			4280		4280	4280		3780	3780	4180	4180	4180	4580	4580	4580				3980	3980	4080	4180	4430	3780		3780	3280	3030	2930	3080	2730
4580	4580			4580		4580	4580		4080	4080	4480	4480	4480	4880	4880	4880				4280	4280	4380	4480	4730	4080		4080	3580	3330	3230	3380	3030

KINKI • NISHIMEIHAN • KANSAI-KŪKŌ EXPRESSWAY

TŌKYŌ																																		
7100	NAGOYA																																	
10050	4000	KYŌTO-MINAMI																																
			CHŪGOKU-SUITA																															
11400	5400	2000	1200	KŌBE-KITA																														
11800	5800	2600	1750	750	KŌBE-NISHI																													
11650	5650	2400	1600	550	450	MIKI-HIGASHI																												
11850	5850	2650	1850	800	700	400	MIKI-ONO																											
12100	6100	3000	2200	1150	1050	750	500	KAKOGAWA-KITA																										
12250	6250	3200	2400	1400	1300	1000	750	400	SAN-YŌ-HIMEJI-HIGASHI																									
12450	6450	3400	2750	1700	1650	1300	1050	700	500	SAN-YŌ-HIMEJI-NISHI																								
12600	6600	3550	2900	1900	1800	1500	1250	900	650	300	TATSUNO																							
12650	6650	3650	3000	2000	1900	1600	1350	1000	750	450	250	TATSUNO-NISHI																						
12950	6950	3900	3250	2350	2300	1950	1700	1350	1150	800	650	500	AKŌ																					
13100	7100	4100	3450	2650	2550	2250	2000	1650	1400	1100	900	800	400	BIZEN																				
13300	7300	4300	3650	2850	2800	2500	2250	1900	1700	1350	1200	1050	700	400	WAKE										NARUTO			450	750	900	1100	1300	1400	1550
13550	7550	4600	3950	3150	3100	2850	2600	2300	2050	1700	1550	1450	1050	800	500	SAN-YŌ										ITANO			500	600	800	1000	1100	1250
13800	7800	4850	4200	3400	3350	3100	2900	2650	2400	2050	1900	1800	1400	1150	850	500	OKAYAMA										HIKETA			300	500	700	800	950
14100	8100	5150	4550	3750	3650	3450	3250	3000	2800	2500	2350	2200	1850	1600	1300	950	600	HAYASHIMA										SHIROTORI-ŌCHI			350	550	650	800
14100	8100	5100	4500	3700	3650	3400	3200	2950	2800	2450	2300	2200	1800	1550	1300	900	550	300	KURASHIKI										TSUDA-HIGASHI			200	300	450
14250	8250	5300	4700	3900	3850	3600	3400	3150	2950	2700	2550	2450	2050	1800	1500	1150	800	550	400	TAMASHIMA										TSUDA-SANGAWA			150	300
14450	8450	5450	4900	4100	4000	3800	3600	3350	3150	2900	2800	2700	2300	2050	1800	1400	1050	800	650	400	KAMOGATA										SHIDO			150
14600	8600	5600	5000	4250	4200	3950	3750	3500	3350	3100	2950	2850	2550	2250	2000	1650	1300	1000	850	650	350	KASAOKA										SANUKI-MIKI		
14800	8800	5800	5250	4450	4400	4150	4000	3700	3550	3300	3150	3100	2800	2550	2300	1950	1600	1300	1150	950	650	450	FUKUYAMA-HIGASHI										TAKAMATSU-HIG	
15100	9100	6150	5550	4800	4750	4500	4300	4050	3900	3650	3500	3400	3150	2950	2750	2350	2000	1750	1600	1350	1100	900	600	FUKUYAMA-NISHI										TAKAMATSU
15200	9200	6250	5650	4900	4850	4600	4400	4150	4000	3750	3600	3550	3250	3050	2850	2500	2150	1900	1750	1500	1250	1050	750	300	ONOMICHI									
15450	9450	6450	5850	5100	5050	4850	4650	4400	4250	4000	3850	3750	3500	3300	3100	2800	2500	2250	2100	1850	1600	1350	1050	650	500	MIHARA-KUI								
15650	9650	6650	6050	5350	5250	5050	4850	4600	4450	4200	4100	4000	3700	3500	3300	3050	2750	2500	2400	2150	1900	1650	1350	950	800	450	HONGŌ							
15800	9800	6800	6200	5450	5400	5200	5000	4800	4600	4350	4250	4150	3850	3650	3450	3200	2950	2750	2600	2350	2100	1900	1600	1150	1000	650	350	KŌCHI						
16000	10000	7000	6400	5650	5600	5400	5200	5000	4800	4600	4450	4350	4100	3900	3700	3400	3150	2950	2850	2650	2350	2150	1850	1450	1300	950	650	450	SAIJŌ					
16200	10200	7200	6600	5850	5800	5600	5400	5150	5000	4800	4650	4600	4300	4100	3900	3600	3350	3150	3050	2850	2650	2450	2150	1700	1550	1250	950	750	450	SHIWA				
16400	10350	7400	6800	6050	6000	5800	5600	5350	5200	4950	4850	4800	4500	4300	4100	3800	3550	3350	3250	3050	2900	2700	2400	2000	1850	1500	1200	1000	700	400	HIROSHIMA-HIGASHI			
16500	10500	7500	6900	6200	6100	5900	5700	5500	5300	5100	4950	4900	4600	4400	4200	3950	3700	3500	3400	3200	3000	2850	2600	2150	2000	1650	1350	1150	900	600	300	HIROSHIMA		
16700	10650	7700	7100	6350	6300	6100	5900	5650	5500	5300	5150	5100	4800	4600	4400	4150	3900	3700	3600	3400	3200	3050	2800	2400	2250	1950	1650	1450	1150	850	600	400	ITSUKAICH	
17050	11050	8050	7450	6750	6650	6450	6250	6050	5850	5650	5500	5450	5200	5000	4800	4550	4250	4050	3950	3800	3600	3450	3200	2850	2750	2400	2100	1900	1600	1350	1050	900	600	HATSUK
17300	11300	8300	7700	7000	6900	6700	6500	6300	6100	5900	5750	5700	5450	5250	5050	4800	4500	4300	4200	4050	3850	3700	3450	3100	3000	2650	2350	2150	1850	1600	1300	1150	850	350
17650	11650	8650	8050	7350	7250	7050	6850	6650	6450	6250	6100	6050	5800	5600	5400	5150	4850	4650	4550	4400	4200	4050	3800	3450	3350	3000	2700	2500	2200	1950	1650	1500	1200	700
17850	11850	8850	8250	7550	7450	7250	7050	6850	6700	6450	6300	6250	6000	5800	5600	5350	5100	4900	4800	4600	4400	4250	4000	3700	3600	3300	3000	2750	2500	2200	1950	1750	1500	1100
18100	12100	9100	8500	7800	7750	7500	7350	7100	6950	6700	6600	6500	6250	6050	5850	5600	5350	5150	5050	4850	4650	4500	4300	3950	3850	3600	3350	3150	2850	2550	2300	2150	1850	1500
18300	12300	9350	8750	8000	7950	7750	7550	7300	7150	6900	6800	6700	6450	6250	6100	5800	5600	5400	5300	5100	4900	4750	4500	4200	4100	3850	3600	3450	3150	2900	2600	2450	2200	1800
18550	12500	9550	8950	8200	8150	7950	7750	7500	7350	7150	7000	6950	6650	6500	6300	6050	5800	5600	5500	5350	5150	5000	4750	4450	4300	4050	3850	3700	3450	3200	2900	2750	2500	2100
18850	12850	9850	9300	8550	8500	8250	8100	7850	7700	7450	7350	7250	7000	6800	6600	6350	6100	5950	5850	5650	5500	5350	5100	4750	4650	4400	4200	4050	3800	3600	3400	3200	2950	2600
19100	13100	10150	9550	8800	8750	8500	8350	8100	7950	7700	7600	7500	7250	7050	6850	6600	6350	6200	6100	5900	5750	5600	5400	5050	4950	4700	4450	4300	4100	3900	3700	3550	3300	2950
19300	13300	10300	9700	9000	8950	8700	8550	8300	8150	7900	7800	7700	7450	7250	7050	6800	6550	6400	6300	6100	5900	5800	5550	5250	5150	4900	4650	4500	4300	4100	3900	3750	3550	3200
19400	13400	10450	9850	9100	9050	8800	8650	8400	8250	8000	7900	7800	7550	7350	7200	6900	6700	6500	6400	6200	6050	5900	5700	5400	5250	5050	4850	4700	4500	4250	4050	3950	3800	3500
19750	13750	10750	10150	9450	9350	9150	9000	8750	8600	8350	8200	8150	7900	7700	7500	7250	7000	6800	6700	6550	6350	6200	6000	5700	5600	5350	5150	5000	4800	4600	4400	4300	4150	3850
20000	13950	11000	10400	9650	9600	9400	9200	9000	8800	8600	8450	8400	8100	7950	7750	7500	7250	7050	6950	6800	6600	6450	6250	5950	5850	5600	5400	5250	5050	4850	4650	4550	4400	4100
20900	14850	11900	11300	10550	10500	10300	10100	9850	9700	9500	9350	9300	9000	8850	8650	8400	8150	7950	7850	7700	7500	7350	7150	6850	6750	6500	6300	6150	5950	5750	5550	5450	5350	5050
20900	14850	11900	11300	10550	10500	10300	10100	9850	9700	9500	9350	9300	9000	8850	8650	8400	8150	7950	7850	7700	7500	7350	7150	6850	6750	6500	6300	6150	5950	5750	5550	5450	5350	5050
20750	14700	11750	11150	10400	10350	10150	9950	9700	9550	9350	9200	9150	8850	8700	8500	8250	8000	7800	7700	7550	7350	7200	7000	6700	6600	6350	6150	6000	5800	5600	5400	5300	5200	4900
20650	14600	11650	11050	10300	10250	10050	9850	9600	9450	9250	9100	9050	8750	8600	8400	8150	7900	7700	7600	7450	7250	7100	6900	6600	6500	6250	6050	5900	5700	5500	5300	5200	5100	4800
20800	14750	11800	11200	10450	10400	10200	10000	9750	9600	9400	9250	9200	8900	8750	8550	8300	8050	7850	7750	7600	7400	7250	7050	6750	6650	6400	6200	6050	5850	5650	5450	5350	5250	4950
20550	14550	11600	11000	10250	10200	10000	9800	9550	9400	9150	9050	8950	8700	8500	8350	8100	7850	7650	7550	7400	7200	7050	6850	6550	6450	6200	6000	5850	5650	5450	5250	5150	5000	4750
20400	14350	11400	10800	10100	10000	9800	9600	9400	9200	9000	8850	8800	8550	8350	8150	7900	7650	7450	7350	7200	7000	6850	6650	6350	6250	6000	5800	5650	5450	5250	5100	4950	4800	4550
20200	14200	11250	10650	9900	9850	9650	9450	9200	9050	8800	8700	8600	8350	8150	8000	7700	7500	7300	7200	7000	6850	6700	6500	6200	6100	5850	5650	5500	5300	5100	4900	4800	4650	4350
20200	14200	11250	10650	9900	9850	9650	9450	9200	9050	8800	8700	8600	8350	8150	8000	7750	7500	7300	7200	7050	6850	6700	6500	6200	6100	5850	5650	5500	5300	5100	4900	4800	4650	4350
20500	14500	11500	10900	10200	10150	9900	9750	9500	9350	9100	9000	8900	8650	8450	8250	8000	7750	7600	7500	7300	7150	7000	6750	6450	6350	6150	5900	5800	5550	5400	5200	5050	4950	4650
20800	14800	11800	11250	10500	10450	10200	10050	9800	9650	9400	9300	9200	8950	8750	8550	8300	8050	7900	7800	7600	7450	7300	7100	6800	6650	6450	6250	6100	5900	5700	5500	5400	5300	5000
21050	15050	12050	11450	10750	10700	10450	10300	10050	9900	9650	9550	9450	9200	9000	8800	8550	8300	8150	8050	7850	7700	7550	7300	7000	6900	6700	6500	6350	6150	5950	5750	5650	5550	5250
22050	16000	13050	12450	11750	11650	11450	11250	11050	10850	10650	10500	10450	10200	10000	9800	9550	9300	9100	9000	8850	8650	8500	8300	8000	7900	7650	7450	7300	7100	6900	6750	6600	6550	6250

SAN-YŌ- EXPRESSWAY

HOKURIKU • NIHONKAI-TŌHOKU • TŌKAI-HOKURIKU EXPRESSWAY

	6350	6600	7050	6850	6850	6850	7150	7450	6750	7000	7100	7200	7450	7650	7800	8000	8150	8350	8450	8600	8800	8900	9100	9500	9900	10150	10350	10350	11900	12500
	6150	6400	6850	6650	6650	6650	6950	7250	6550	6800	6900	7000	7250	7450	7600	7800	7950	8150	8250	8400	8600	8700	8900	9300	9700	9950	10150	10150	11700	12300
	6000	6250	6750	6550	6550	6550	6800	7100	6450	6700	6750	6900	7100	7300	7450	7700	7800	8000	8150	8250	8450	8550	8750	9150	9600	9850	10000	10050	11550	12150
	5850	6100	6550	6350	6350	6350	6650	6950	6250	6500	6600	6700	6950	7150	7300	7500	7650	7850	7950	8100	8300	8400	8600	9000	9400	9650	9850	9850	11400	12000
	5750	6000	6450	6250	6250	6250	6550	6850	6150	6400	6450	6600	6850	7050	7200	7400	7550	7750	7850	7950	8200	8250	8500	8900	9300	9550	9700	9750	11250	11850
	5700	5950	6400	6200	6200	6200	6500	6800	6100	6350	6450	6550	6800	7000	7150	7350	7500	7700	7800	7950	8150	8250	8450	8850	9250	9500	9700	9700	11250	11850
	5600	5850	6350	6150	6150	6150	6450	6700	6050	6300	6350	6500	6700	6900	7050	7300	7400	7600	7750	7850	8050	8150	8400	8750	9200	9450	9600	9650	11150	11750
	5350	5600	6050	5850	5850	5850	6150	6450	5750	6000	6100	6200	6450	6650	6800	7000	7150	7350	7450	7600	7800	7900	8100	8500	8900	9150	9300	9350	10900	11450
	5150	5400	5850	5650	5650	5650	5950	6250	5550	5850	5900	6050	6250	6450	6600	6850	6950	7150	7300	7400	7600	7700	7900	8300	8750	9000	9150	9150	10700	11300
	4850	5150	5600	5400	5400	5400	5700	5950	5300	5550	5600	5750	5950	6150	6350	6550	6700	6900	7000	7100	7300	7400	7650	8050	8450	8700	8850	8900	10400	11000
	4700	4950	5450	5250	5250	5250	5550	5800	5150	5400	5450	5600	5800	6000	6150	6400	6500	6700	6850	6950	7150	7250	7500	7850	8300	8550	8700	8750	10250	10850
	4400	4700	5150	4950	4950	4950	5250	5550	4850	5100	5150	5300	5550	5750	5900	6100	6250	6450	6550	6700	6900	7000	7200	7600	8000	8250	8400	8450	10000	10550
	4200	4500	4950	4750	4750	4750	5050	5350	4650	4900	5000	5100	5350	5550	5700	5900	6050	6250	6350	6500	6700	6800	7000	7400	7800	8050	8250	8250	9800	10400
	3950	4250	4750	4550	4550	4550	4850	5100	4450	4700	4750	4900	5150	5350	5500	5700	5850	6050	6150	6250	6450	6550	6800	7200	7600	7850	8000	8050	9550	10150
	3750	4050	4500	4300	4300	4300	4650	4900	4200	4500	4550	4700	4900	5100	5250	5500	5650	5800	5950	6050	6250	6350	6600	7000	7400	7650	7800	7850	9350	9950
	3400	3700	4150	3950	3950	3950	4300	4600	3850	4150	4200	4350	4600	4800	4950	5200	5300	5500	5600	5750	5950	6050	6250	6650	7050	7300	7500	7550	9050	9650
	4650	4950	5400	5200	5200	5200	5500	5750	5100	5350	5400	5550	5800	6000	6150	6350	6500	6700	6800	6900	7100	7200	7450	7850	7550	7300	7100	6200	8650	9250
	3150	3400	3900	3700	3700	3700	4000	4300	3600	3850	3950	4100	4300	4550	4700	4900	5050	5250	5350	5500	5700	5800	6000	6400	6800	7050	7250	7600	8800	9400
	2850	3100	3600	3400	3400	3400	3700	4000	3300	3600	3650	3800	4000	4250	4400	4650	4800	4950	5100	5200	5400	5500	5750	6100	6550	6800	6950	7900	8500	9100
	2500	2850	3300	3100	3100	3100	3450	3750	3000	3300	3350	3500	3750	3950	4100	4350	4500	4700	4850	4950	5150	5250	5450	5850	6300	6550	6700	8150	8250	8850
	2150	2550	3050	2850	2850	2900	3200	3500	2750	3050	3100	3250	3500	3700	3900	4100	4250	4450	4600	4700	4900	5000	5250	5650	6050	6300	6450	7900	8000	8600
	1700	2100	2600	2400	2400	2500	2850	3150	2350	2700	2800	2950	3150	3400	3550	3800	3950	4150	4250	4400	4600	4700	4950	5300	5750	6000	6150	7600	7700	8300
	1500	1850	2350	2150	2150	2250	2700	3000	2100	2500	2550	2750	3000	3200	3350	3600	3750	3950	4100	4200	4450	4550	4750	5150	5600	5850	6000	7450	7550	8150
	1250	1600	2100	1900	1900	2000	2450	2800	1850	2250	2300	2500	2800	3000	3200	3450	3550	3750	3900	4050	4250	4350	4600	5000	5400	5650	5800	7250	7400	8000
	1000	1400	1900	1700	1700	1750	2200	2600	1600	2000	2100	2300	2600	2850	3000	3250	3400	3600	3750	3850	4050	4150	4400	4800	5250	5500	5650	7100	7200	7800
	800	1150	1650	1450	1450	1550	2000	2350	1400	1800	1850	2050	2400	2650	2850	3100	3250	3450	3550	3700	3900	4000	4250	4650	5100	5350	5500	6950	7050	7650
	450	850	1350	1150	1150	1250	1650	2050	1100	1450	1550	1750	2050	2350	2550	2850	3000	3200	3350	3450	3650	3800	4000	4450	4850	5100	5300	6750	6850	7450
	300	650	1150	950	950	1050	1450	1850	900	1300	1350	1550	1850	2150	2400	2700	2850	3050	3200	3300	3550	3650	3900	4300	4750	5000	5150	6600	6700	7300
SUGI		500	1050	850	850	900	1350	1750	750	1150	1200	1400	1750	2000	2250	2550	2750	2950	3100	3200	3450	3550	3750	4200	4650	4900	5050	6500	6600	7200
TONAMI			650	450	450	550	950	1350	400	750	850	1050	1350	1650	1900	2200	2400	2650	2800	2950	3150	3250	3500	3900	4350	4650	4800	6250	6350	6950
TAKAOKA				200	200	850	1250	1650	700	1050	1150	1350	1650	1950	2150	2500	2700	2950	3150	3250	3500	3600	3800	4250	4700	4950	5100	6600	6700	7300
FUKUOKA					0	650	1050	1450	500	850	950	1150	1450	1750	1950	2300	2500	2750	2950	3050	3300	3400	3600	4050	4500	4750	4900	6400	6500	7100
OYABE-HIGASHI						650	1050	1450	500	850	950	1150	1450	1750	1950	2300	2500	2750	2950	3050	3300	3400	3600	4050	4500	4750	4900	6400	6500	7100
FUKUMITSU							600	950	600	950	1050	1250	1550	1850	2050	2400	2550	2800	2950	3050	3300	3400	3650	4050	4500	4750	4950	6400	6500	7100
GOKAYAMA								550	1000	1400	1450	1650	2000	2250	2500	2800	2950	3150	3250	3400	3600	3700	3950	4350	4800	5050	5200	6650	6800	7400
SHIRAKAWAGŌ									1400	1750	1850	2050	2350	2650	2850	3100	3200	3450	3550	3700	3900	4000	4250	4650	5100	5350	5500	6950	7050	7650
OYABE										550	600	800	1150	1400	1650	1950	2150	2400	2600	2750	2950	3050	3300	3750	4200	4450	4600	6100	6200	6800
KANAZAWA-MORIMOTO											250	450	750	1050	1250	1600	1750	2050	2200	2400	2650	2800	3050	3450	3900	4150	4350	5800	5900	6550
KANAZAWA-HIGASHI												350	650	950	1200	1500	1700	1950	2150	2300	2600	2750	2950	3400	3850	4100	4300	5750	5850	6450
KANAZAWA-NISHI													450	750	1000	1300	1500	1750	1950	2100	2400	2550	2850	3250	3700	3950	4150	5600	5750	6350
MIKAWA														450	650	1000	1200	1450	1600	1800	2100	2200	2550	3000	3450	3700	3900	5400	5500	6100
KOMATSU															350	700	900	1150	1350	1500	1800	1950	2250	2800	3250	3500	3700	5200	5300	5900
KATAYAMATSU																450	650	950	1100	1300	1550	1700	2050	2600	3100	3350	3500	5000	5150	5750
KAGA																	350	600	800	950	1250	1400	1700	2250	2850	3100	3250	4800	4950	5550
KANATSU																		400	600	750	1050	1200	1500	2100	2700	2950	3150	4700	4800	5400
MARUOKA																			300	500	800	950	1250	1800	2400	2750	2950	4500	4600	5200
FUKUI-KITA																				300	600	750	1050	1650	2250	2600	2800	4350	4450	5100
FUKUI																					450	600	900	1450	2050	2400	2650	4250	4350	5000
SABAE																						300	600	1200	1750	2150	2350	4000	4150	4750
TAKEFU																							450	1050	1650	2000	2200	3900	4000	4650
IMAJŌ																								700	1300	1650	1900	3650	3800	4450
TSURUGA																									750	1100	1350	3250	3350	4000
KINOMOTO																										500	750	2800	2900	3550
NAGAHAMA																											350	2450	2600	3300
MAIHARA																												2250	2350	3150
NAGOYA																													4000	4650
KYŌTO-MINAMI																														1000
SUITA																														

YAMA										
KAINAN-HIGASHI										
SHIMOTSU										
KIBI										
KIBI-MINAMI										
YUASA			100							
HIROKAWA			150							
HIROKAWA-MINAMI			300		150					
KAWABE			450		300					
GOBŌ			600		450					
GOBŌ-MINAMI										
INAMI			1000		850			400	400	
MINABE			1300		1150			700	700	450

TAKAMATSU•TOKUSHIMA•KŌCHI•MATSUYAMA EXPRESSWAY

	1950		2400	2550	2950	3150	3900	4300	4500	4850	5150	5300	3650	4000	4400	4550	4750	4900	5200	3500	3700	3950	4100	4400		4500	4800	4850	5050	5250	5700	5850
	1650		2150	2300	2650	2900	3650	4100	4300	4650	4950	5100	3400	3800	4200	4350	4550	4700	5000	3250	3500	3750	3900	4200		4300	4600	4650	4850	5050	5500	5650
	1300		1800	1950	2350	2550	3450	3850	4050	4400	4700	4850	3150	3550	3950	4100	4300	4450	4750	2950	3250	3500	3650	3950		4050	4350	4400	4600	4800	5250	5400
	1200		1650	1800	2200	2450	3350	3750	3950	4300	4600	4750	3000	3450	3850	4000	4200	4350	4650	2800	3100	3400	3550	3850		3950	4250	4300	4500	4700	5150	5300
	1000		1450	1600	2000	2250	3150	3600	3800	4150	4450	4600	2800	3300	3700	3850	4050	4200	4500	2600	2900	3250	3400	3700		3800	4100	4150	4350	4550	5000	5200
	800		1250	1400	1800	2050	2950	3400	3600	3950	4250	4400	2600	3100	3500	3650	3850	4000	4300	2400	2700	3050	3200	3500		3600	3900	3950	4150	4350	4800	5000
	700		1150	1300	1700	1950	2850	3300	3500	3850	4150	4300	2500	3000	3400	3550	3750	3900	4200	2300	2600	2950	3100	3400		3500	3800	3850	4050	4250	4700	4900
	450		900	1050	1450	1700	2600	3050	3250	3600	3900	4050	2250	2750	3150	3300	3500	3650	3950	2050	2350	2700	2850	3150		3250	3550	3600	3800	4000	4450	4650
	350		800	950	1350	1550	2450	2950	3150	3550	3800	3950	2150	2600	3050	3200	3400	3550	3850	1950	2250	2550	2800	3100		3200	3500	3500	3750	3900	4400	4550
U-DANSHI																																
MATSU-NISHI			550	700	1100	1350	2250	2750	3000	3350	3600	3800	1900	2400	2900	3000	3200	3400	3700	1700	2000	2350	2550	2900		3000	3300	3300	3550	3750	4200	4350
SAKAIDE				400	800	1000	1950	2450	2750	3150	3400	3550	1600	2050	2600	2800	3000	3150	3450	1400	1700	2050	2250	2650		2750	3050	3100	3300	3500	4000	4150
ZENTSŪJI					500	750	1700	2200	2500	2950	3200	3350	1350	1800	2350	2550	2800	3000	3250	1150	1450	1800	2000	2400		2500	2800	2900	3150	3350	3800	3950
SANUKI-TOYONAKA						350	1300	1850	2150	2650	2900	3100	950	1450	2000	2200	2450	2700	3000	750	1050	1400	1650	2050		2150	2450	2600	2850	3050	3500	3650
ŌNOHARA							1050	1600	1900	2400	2750	2900	750	1200	1750	1950	2200	2450	2800	550	800	1150	1400	1800		1900	2200	2350	2650	2850	3350	3500
IKAWA-IKEDA								700	1000	1500	1850	2050	950	1400	1950	2150	2400	2650	2950	850	1150	1500	1700	2100		2200	2500	2650	2900	3100	3550	3750
MIMA									450	950	1300	1500	1500	1950	2500	2700	2900	3100	3350	1400	1700	2050	2250	2650		2750	3050	3100	3300	3500	4000	4150
WAKIMACHI										650	1000	1200	1800	2250	2800	2950	3150	3300	3600	1700	2000	2300	2550	2900		3000	3300	3300	3550	3750	4200	4350
DONARI											500	750	2250	2750	3150	3300	3500	3650	3950	2200	2450	2800	2950	3250		3350	3650	3700	3900	4100	4550	4700
AIZUMI												400	2600	3000	3400	3550	3750	3900	4200	2500	2800	3050	3200	3500		3600	3900	3950	4150	4350	4800	4950
TOKUSHIMA													2800	3150	3600	3700	3900	4100	4400	2750	2950	3200	3400	3700		3800	4100	4100	4350	4550	5000	5100
SHINGŪ														650	1150	1350	1650	1850	2250	500	800	1150	1400	1750		1850	2150	2350	2650	2850	3300	3500
ŌTOYO															700	900	1150	1400	1800	1000	1300	1600	1850	2250		2350	2650	2800	3000	3200	3650	3850
NANKOKU																350	600	850	1250	1550	1800	2150	2400	2800		2900	3200	3200	3400	3600	4100	4250
KŌCHI																	400	650	1050	1750	2000	2350	2600	2900		3000	3300	3350	3550	3750	4250	4400
INO																		400	750	2000	2300	2600	2850	3100		3200	3500	3550	3750	3950	4450	4600
TOSA																			550	2250	2500	2850	3000	3300		3400	3700	3700	3950	4150	4600	4750
SUSAKI-HIGASHI																				2600	2850	3100	3300	3600		3700	4000	4000	4250	4450	4900	5000
MISHIMA-KAWANOE																					350	800	1000	1400		1500	1800	1950	2300	2550	3050	3200
DOI																						500	750	1150		1250	1550	1700	2000	2250	2850	3000
NIIHAMA																							400	800		900	1200	1350	1650	1900	2500	2750
IYO-SAIJŌ																								550		650	950	1100	1400	1650	2300	2500
IYO-KOMATSU																												700	1000	1300	1900	2100
IYO-KOMATSU-KITA																										100	350					
TŌYO-TANBARA																											300	800	1100	1400	2000	2200
IMABARI-YUNOURA																												1100	1400	1700	2300	2500
KAWAUCHI																													450	700	1350	1550
MATSUYAMA																														400	1050	1250
IYO																															800	1000
UCHIKO-IKAZAKI																																350
OZU																																

ŌTAKE																						
IWAKUNI																						
KUGA	500																					
KUMAGE	850	450																				
TOKUYAMA-HIGASHI	1150	800	450																			
TOKUYAMA-NISHI	1600	1250	950	600																		
HŌFU-HIGASHI · HŌFU-NISHI	1950	1600	1300	1000	500																	
YAMAGUCHI-MINAMI	2250	1900	1550	1250	800	400																
OGŌRI	2550	2150	1850	1550	1100	700	450															
MINE	2950	2650	2300	2000	1550	1200	900	650														
MINE-NISHI	3200	2900	2650	2350	1900	1550	1250	950	500													
KAGAWA	4150	3850	3650	3400	3050	2700	2450	2150	1650	1300												
YURA	4150	3850	3650	3400	3050	2700	2450	2150	1650	1300												
AJISU	4000	3700	3500	3250	2900	2550	2300	2000	1500	1150	150	150										
UBE-HIGASHI	3900	3600	3400	3150	2800	2450	2200	1900	1400	1050	250	250	100									
UBE-MINAMI	4050	3750	3550	3300	2950	2600	2350	2050	1550	1200	400	400	250	150								
UBE	3850	3550	3300	3100	2750	2350	2100	1800	1350	1000	500	500	350	250	400							
ONODA	3650	3350	3100	2900	2500	2100	1850	1550	1100	750	750	750	600	500	650	400						
HABU	3450	3150	2950	2700	2250	1850	1600	1300	850	500	1000	1000	850	750	900	650	400					
OZUKI	3450	3150	2950	2700	2250	1850	1600	1300	850	500	1300	1300	1150	1050	1200	950	700	450				
SHIMONOSEKI	3750	3450	3250	3000	2650	2250	2000	1700	1250	900	1700	1700	1550	1450	1600	1350	1100	850	550			
MOJI	4100	3800	3600	3350	3000	2700	2400	2150	1650	1300	2100	2100	1950	1850	2000	1750	1500	1250	1000	600		
KOKURA-HIGASHI	4350	4100	3850	3600	3250	3000	2750	2450	2000	1650	2450	2450	2300	2200	2350	2100	1850	1600	1300	900	500	
FUKUOKA	5350	5100	4900	4650	4350	4050	3850	3650	3300	3050	3700	3700	3550	3450	3600	3350	3200	3000	2750	2350	1900	1600

ŌZU-KITATADA	550
SEIYO-UWA	

MATSUYAMA EXPRESSWAY

NIIGATA-NISHI	800	3050	1550	1950
SANJŌ-TSUBAME		2500	850	1300
JŌETSU			1900	2300
NAGAOKA				550
OJIYA				
ECHIGO-KAWAGU				
HORINOU				

NIIGATA-NISHI
3050	JŌETSU
5400	3150	TOYAMA
3250	400	3200	JŌETSU-TAKADA
3550	800	3450	550	NAKAGŌ
3800	1100	3700	850	450	MYŌKŌ-KŌGEN
3900	1250	3800	950	600	300	SHINANO-MACHI
4150	1600	4050	1300	950	650	500	TOYOTA-IIYAMA
4300	1800	4200	1500	1150	850	700	350	SHINSHŪ-NAKANO
4500	2100	4450	1800	1450	1150	1000	650	450	SUZAKA-NAGANO-HIGASHI
4700	2350	4600	2050	1700	1400	1250	900	700	400	NAGANO
4800	2500	4750	2250	1850	1550	1450	1100	900	600	350	KŌSHOKU
5700	3500	5650	3300	3050	2800	2700	2350	2150	1850	1600	1450	MATSUMOTO
5050	2800	5000	2600	2200	1900	1750	1450	1250	950	700	550	1800	SAKAKI
5200	3000	5150	2800	2400	2100	1950	1650	1450	1150	900	750	2000	350	UEDA-SUGADAIRA
5350	3150	5300	2950	2650	2300	2200	1850	1650	1350	1100	950	2250	600	350	TŌBU-YUNOMARU
5450	3250	5400	3050	2800	2500	2350	2000	1800	1500	1250	1150	2400	750	550	300	KOMORO
5650	3450	5600	3250	3000	2750	2650	2300	2100	1800	1550	1400	2700	1000	800	600	450	SAKU
6000	3850	5950	3650	3350	3100	3050	2750	2600	2300	2050	1900	3050	1500	1300	1100	900	650	USUI-KARUIZAWA
6050	4150	6200	3950	3650	3400	3300	3050	2900	2650	2400	2300	3350	1900	1700	1500	1300	1050	550	MATSUIDA-MYŌGI
5850	4350	6400	4150	3850	3600	3500	3250	3100	2900	2700	2550	3550	2150	1950	1750	1600	1300	800	450	SHIMONITA
5750	4450	6500	4250	4000	3750	3650	3400	3250	3050	2850	2750	3700	2350	2150	1950	1750	1500	1000	600	300	TOMIOKA
5550	4650	6700	4450	4150	3900	3850	3550	3400	3200	3000	2900	3850	2600	2350	2150	2000	1700	1200	850	550	400	YOSHII
5400	4800	6850	4600	4350	4100	4000	3750	3600	3400	3200	3100	4050	2800	2600	2400	2250	1950	1450	1100	800	650	400	FUJIOKA
5500	5200	7250	5050	4750	4550	4450	4200	4050	3800	3600	3500	4450	3250	3100	2900	2800	2550	2050	1650	1400	1200	1000	750	ISESAKI
5400	5100	7150	4900	4650	4400	4300	4050	3900	3700	3500	3400	4350	3100	2950	2800	2650	2350	1850	1450	1200	1050	800	550	350	KOMAGATA
5300	5000	7050	4800	4550	4300	4200	3950	3800	3600	3400	3300	4250	3000	2850	2700	2500	2250	1750	1350	1100	900	700	450	450	250	MAEBASHI-MINAMI
5150	5100	7150	4900	4650	4400	4300	4050	3900	3700	3500	3400	4350	3100	2950	2800	2650	2350	1850	1450	1200	1050	800	550	750	550	450	MAEBASHI
5200	5000	7050	4800	4550	4300	4200	3950	3800	3600	3400	3300	4250	3000	2850	2650	2500	2200	1750	1350	1050	900	650	400	600	400	300	300	TAKASAKI
5550	5000	7050	4800	4550	4300	4200	3950	3800	3600	3400	3300	4250	3000	2850	2700	2500	2250	1750	1350	1100	900	700	450	900	750	600	750	600	HONJŌ-KODA
5750	5250	7300	5050	4800	4600	4500	4200	4050	3850	3650	3550	4500	3250	3100	2950	2850	2600	2100	1700	1450	1250	1050	800	1250	1100	950	1100	950	500	HANAZ
5900	5400	7450	5200	4950	4750	4650	4400	4250	4000	3850	3750	4700	3450	3300	3100	3000	2800	2300	1950	1650	1500	1250	1000	1500	1300	1200	1300	1200	750	400	
6050	5550	7600	5350	5100	4900	4800	4550	4400	4150	4000	3900	4800	3600	3450	3300	3150	2950	2550	2150	1850	1700	1450	1200	1700	1500	1400	1500	1400	950	600	
6300	5750	7800	5600	5300	5100	5000	4800	4650	4400	4200	4100	5050	3850	3700	3500	3400	3200	2800	2450	2150	2000	1750	1500	2000	1800	1700	1800	1700	1250	900	
6450	5950	8000	5750	5500	5300	5200	4950	4850	4600	4400	4300	5250	4050	3900	3700	3600	3400	3000	2700	2450	2250	2000	1800	2250	2100	1950	2100	1950	1500	1150	
6750	6200	8250	6050	5750	5550	5450	5250	5100	4900	4700	4600	5500	4300	4150	4000	3900	3650	3300	3000	2800	2600	2400	2150	2650	2450	2350	2450	2300	1850	1500	
6950	6450	8450	6250	6000	5750	5700	5450	5300	5100	4900	4850	5700	4550	4400	4250	4100	3900	3550	3250	3050	2900	2700	2450	2900	2750	2600	2750	2600	2150	1800	

JŌSHINETSU • KANETSU EXPRESSWAY

FUTTSU-TATEYAMA DŌRO

FUTTSU-CHŪŌ	UNDER CONSTRUCTION			
FUTTSU-TAKEOKA	150	250	350	650
FUTTSU-KANAYA		150	250	500
KYONAN-HOTA			100	400
KYONAN-TOMIYAMA				300
TOMIURA				

TŌKYŌ	350	550	750	1250	1650	1850	2500	2750	3000	3350	3850	4100	4350	4550	4750	4850	5000	5200	5250	5350
TŌMEI-KAWASAKI		350	500	1000	1400	1600	2250	2550	2750	3150	3650	3900	4150	4400	4600	4700	4800	5000	5100	5200
YOKOHAMA-AOBA			350	850	1200	1400	2100	2350	2600	3000	3500	3800	4000	4250	4450	4550	4650	4900	4950	5100
YOKOHAMA-MACHIDA				650	1000	1200	1900	2150	2400	2850	3350	3650	3850	4100	4300	4400	4500	4750	4800	4950
ATSUGI					550	750	1400	1700	1900	2400	3000	3250	3500	3700	3950	4050	4150	4400	4450	4600
HADANO-NAKAI						350	1050	1300	1550	2000	2700	2950	3200	3450	3650	3750	3850	4100	4150	4300
ŌI-MATSUDA							800	1100	1350	1800	2500	2800	3050	3300	3500	3600	3700	3950	4000	4150
GOTENBA								400	650	1150	1800	2150	2500	2800	3000	3100	3200	3450	3500	3650
SUSONO									400	850	1550	1900	2200	2550	2800	2900	3000	3250	3300	3450
NUMAZU										650	1300	1650	1950	2300	2550	2700	2850	3050	3150	3250
FUJI											850	1200	1500	1800	2100	2250	2400	2700	2800	2900
SHIMIZU												500	800	1150	1400	1550	1700	2000	2100	2300
SHIZUOKA													450	750	1050	1200	1350	1650	1750	1900
YAIZU														450	750	900	1050	1350	1450	1600
YOSHIDA															450	600	750	1050	1150	1300
SAGARA-MAKINOHARA																300	450	750	850	1000
KIKUGAWA																	300	600	700	900
KAKEGAWA																		450	550	750
FUKUROI																			250	400
IWATA																				350
HAMAMATSU																				
HAMAMATSU-N																				
MIKKA																				

TAKAIDO
600	CHŌFU
600	600	INAGI
600	600	/	KUNITACHI-FUCHŪ
600	600	/	600	HACHIŌJI
1250	1250	/	1250	650	SAGAMI-KO
1400	1400	/	1400	800	300	UENOHARA
1900	1900	/	1900	1300	800	700	ŌTSUKI
2100	2100	/	2100	1500	1000	850	350	TSURU
2500	2500	/	2500	1900	1400	1300	750	/	KAWAGUCHI-KO
2400	2400	/	2400	1800	1300	1200	650	800	1200	KATSUNUMA
2600	2600	/	2600	2000	1450	1350	850	950	1400	300	ICHINOMIYA-MISAKA
2800	2800	/	2800	2200	1700	1600	1050	1200	1600	550	400	KŌFU-MINAMI
3000	3000	/	3000	2400	1900	1800	1250	1400	1800	750	600	350	KŌFU-SHŌWA
3400	3400	/	3400	2800	2350	2200	1700	1800	2250	1200	1000	800	600	MINAMI-ALPS
3300	3300	/	3300	2700	2200	2050	1550	1700	2100	1050	900	650	450	550	NIRASAKI
3450	3450	/	3450	2850	2400	2250	1750	1850	2300	1200	1050	800	650	700	350	SUTAMA
3600	3600	/	3600	3000	2600	2500	1950	2100	2500	1450	1300	1050	850	950	550	350	NAGASAKA
3800	3800	/	3800	3200	2800	2700	2150	2300	2750	1650	1500	1250	1050	1150	750	600	350	KOBUCHIZAWA
4000	4000	/	4000	3400	3050	2950	2500	2650	2950	2000	1850	1600	1400	1450	1100	900	700	450	SUWA-MINAMI
4250	4250	/	4250	3650	3250	3150	2750	2850	3200	2250	2100	1850	1700	1750	1400	1200	1000	750	450	SUWA
4500	4500	/	4500	3900	3500	3450	3050	3150	3450	2650	2450	2250	2050	2100	1750	1550	1350	1150	800	500	OKAYA
4650	4650	/	4650	4050	3650	3550	3200	3300	3600	2800	2650	2400	2200	2300	1950	1750	1500	1300	1000	700	350	SHIOJIRI
4750	4750	/	4750	4150	3800	3700	3300	3400	3700	2950	2800	2600	2400	2450	2100	1900	1700	1500	1150	850	500	300	SHIOJIRI-KITA
4950	4950	/	4950	4350	3950	3850	3450	3550	3900	3100	2950	2800	2600	2700	2300	2150	1900	1700	1350	1100	750	550	350	MATSUMOTO
5050	5050	/	5050	4450	4100	4000	3600	3700	4000	3250	3100	2950	2800	2850	2500	2300	2100	1900	1550	1250	900	750	550	350	TOYOSHINA
5500	5500	/	5500	4900	4550	4450	4050	4150	4450	3700	3550	3400	3250	3300	3000	2900	2700	2500	2150	1850	1500	1350	1150	950	750	OMI
5850	5850	/	5850	5250	4900	4800	4400	4500	4800	4050	3900	3750	3600	3650	3350	3250	3050	2900	2650	2350	2000	1800	1650	1450	1250	650	KŌSHOKU
5950	5950	/	5950	5350	5000	4900	4550	4650	4950	4150	4050	3850	3700	3800	3500	3350	3200	3050	2800	2550	2150	2000	1800	1600	1400	800	350	NAGANO
7500	7500	/	7500	6900	6550	6450	6100	6200	6450	5750	5600	5450	5300	5350	5100	5000	4800	4650	4450	4200	3950	3800	3700	3500	3400	2950	2500	2350	JŌET
4700	4700	/	4700	4100	3700	3650	3250	3350	3650	2850	2750	2500	2300	2400	2000	1850	1600	1400	1050	800	600	800	950	1200	1350	1950	2450	2650	4300	
4900	4900	/	4900	4300	3900	3800	3400	3500	3850	3050	2900	2750	2550	2600	2250	2050	1850	1650	1300	1000	850	1050	1200	1450	1600	2200	2700	2850	4450	
5200	5200	/	5200	4600	4200	4100	3700	3800	4150	3350	3200	3050	2900	2950	2650	2450	2250	2050	1700	1400	1250	1450	1600	1800	2000	2600	3000	3150	4750	
5450	5450	/	5450	4850	4500	4400	4000	4100	4450	3650	3500	3350	3200	3250	2950	2850	2650	2400	2100	1800	1650	1850	2000	2200	2400	2950	3300	3450	5050	
5750	5750	/	5750	5150	4800	4700	4300	4400	4700	3950	3800	3650	3500	3550	3250	3150	2950	2800	2500	2200	2050	2250	2400	2600	2800	3250	3600	3750	5300	
/	/	/	/	/	/	/	/	/	/	/	/	/	/	/	/	/	/	/	/	/	/	/	/	/	/	/	/	/	/	
6700	6700	/	6700	6100	5750	5650	5300	5400	5700	4950	4800	4650	4500	4550	4300	4150	4000	3850	3600	3400	3250	3400	3550	3700	3800	4250	4600	4750	6250	
6850	6850	/	6850	6250	5900	5800	5450	5550	5850	5100	5000	4800	4700	4750	4450	4350	4150	4000	3750	3550	3450	3600	3700	3850	4000	4450	4800	4950	6450	
7200	7200	/	7200	6600	6250	6150	5800	5900	6150	5450	5300	5150	5000	5100	4800	4700	4500	4350	4100	3900	3800	3900	4050	4200	4350	4800	5150	5250	6750	
7250	7250	/	7250	6650	6300	6250	5850	5950	6250	5500	5400	5250	5100	5150	4900	4750	4600	4450	4200	4000	3850	4000	4150	4300	4450	4850	5200	5350	6850	
7400	7400	/	7400	6800	6450	6400	6000	6100	6400	5650	5550	5400	5250	5300	5050	4950	4750	4600	4350	4150	4050	4150	4300	4450	4600	5050	5350	5500	7000	
7550	7550	/	7550	6950	6600	6550	6150	6250	6550	5800	5700	5550	5400	5450	5200	5100	4900	4750	4500	4300	4200	4350	4450	4600	4750	5200	5500	5650	7150	
7950	7950	/	7950	7350	7000	6900	6550	6650	6950	6200	6100	5900	5800	5850	5600	5450	5300	5150	4950	4700	4600	4750	4850	5000	5150	5550	5900	6000	7550	
10400	10400	/	10400	9800	9450	9350	9000	9100	9400	8650	8550	8350	8250	8300	8050	7900	7750	7600	7400	7200	7050	7200	7300	7450	7600	8000	8350	8450	9050	
11000	11000	/	11000	10400	10050	9950	9600	9700	10000	9250	9150	8950	8850	8900	8650	8500	8350	8200	8000	7800	7650	7800	7900	8050	8200	8600	8950	9050	9650	
16850	16850	/	16850	16250	15850	15800	15400	15500	15800	15050	14950	14800	14650	14700	14450	14300	14150	14000	13800	13600	13450	13600	13700	13850	14000	14400	14750	14900	15450	
22350	22350	/	22350	21750	21400	21300	20950	21050	21350	20600	20500	20300	20200	20250	20000	19850	19700	19550	19300	19100	19000	19150	19250	19400	19550	19950	20300	20400	21000	

CHŪŌ•NAGANO EXPRESSWAY

KAN-ETSU • KITA-KANTŌ EXPRESSWAY / KEN-Ō-DŌ

50	2550	2950	3150	3350	4200	4400	4500	4600	4750	4900	5150	5200	5500	5400	5300	4700	5650	5550	5750	5900	6050	6300	6400	6650	6900	7100	7450		6450	6750	6950
00	1900	2350	2650	2850	3700	3900	4000	4100	4300	4450	4650	4750	5050	4950	4850	4200	5200	5050	5300	5450	5600	5850	5950	6200	6450	6650	7000		6000	6300	6500
50	2900	3200	3450	3600	4450	4650	4750	4850	5050	5200	5100	5000	5200	5100	5000	2350	3450	5000	5250	5400	5550	5750	5900	6150	6400	6600	6950		5950	6200	6450
00	1200	1650	1950	2150	3200	3400	3500	3600	3750	3900	4100	4200	4550	4400	4300	3750	4750	4550	4800	4950	5100	5350	5500	5750	6000	6200	6550		5500	5800	6000
00	800	1250	1550	1750	2850	3100	3200	3300	3450	3600	3850	3900	4250	4100	4050	4050	5050	4250	4500	4700	4850	5050	5200	5450	5700	5900	6250		5250	5500	5700
00	600	1050	1350	1550	2600	2900	3000	3150	3300	3450	3700	3750	4100	3950	3900	4200	5200	4100	4350	4500	4700	4900	5050	5300	5550	5750	6100		5100	5350	5600
	350	800	1100	1300	2400	2650	2800	2900	3150	3300	3500	3600	3950	3800	3700	4350	5100	3950	4200	4350	4500	4750	4900	5150	5400	5600	5950		4950	5200	5400
	OIDE	600	900	1100	2200	2450	2600	2750	2950	3150	3350	3450	3800	3650	3550	4500	4950	3800	4050	4200	4350	4600	4750	5000	5250	5450	5800		4800	5050	5300
		UIKAMACHI	450	650	1750	2000	2150	2250	2500	2700	3000	3150	3450	3300	3250	4850	4650	3450	3700	3900	4050	4250	4400	4650	4900	5100	5450		4450	4750	4950
			SHIOZAWA-ISHIUCHI	350	1450	1700	1850	2000	2200	2400	2700	2850	3250	3100	3000	5050	4400	3250	3500	3650	3800	4050	4200	4450	4700	4900	5250		4250	4500	4750
				YUZAWA	1250	1500	1600	1750	2000	2200	2500	2650	3050	2900	2750	5200	4250	3100	3350	3500	3650	3900	4050	4300	4550	4750	5100		4100	4350	4600
					MINAKAMI	400	550	700	950	1150	1400	1550	2000	1800	1700	4450	3400	2000	2350	2600	2750	3000	3150	3400	3650	3850	4200		3200	3500	3700
						TSUKIYONO	300	450	650	850	1150	1300	1750	1550	1450	4250	3200	1750	2100	2300	2550	2800	2950	3200	3450	3650	4000		3000	3300	3550
							NUMATA	300	500	750	1050	1150	1600	1400	1300	4150	3100	1600	1950	2200	2400	2700	2850	3100	3350	3550	3900		2900	3200	3450
								SHŌWA	400	600	900	1050	1450	1300	1150	4050	3000	1450	1800	2050	2250	2550	2700	2950	3200	3400	3750		2800	3100	3350
									AKAGI	350	650	800	1200	1050	900	3850	2800	1250	1600	1800	2000	2300	2450	2700	2950	3150	3500		2600	2950	3150
										SHIBUKAWA-IKAHO	450	600	1000	850	700	3700	2650	1050	1400	1600	1800	2100	2250	2500	2750	2950	3300		2350	2750	3000
											MAEBASHI	300	750	550	450	3500	2350	750	1100	1300	1500	1800	2000	2250	2500	2700	3050		2100	2450	2750
												TAKASAKI	600	400	300	3400	2200	600	950	1200	1400	1700	1850	2100	2350	2550	2900		1950	2300	2600
													ISESAKI	350	450	3600	2550	900	1250	1500	1700	2000	2150	2400	2650	2850	3200		2250	2650	2900
														KOMAGATA	250	3500	2350	750	1100	1300	1500	1800	2000	2250	2500	2700	3050		2100	2450	2750
															MAEBASHI-MINAMI	3400	2250	600	950	1200	1400	1700	1850	2100	2350	2550	2900		1950	2350	2600
																NAGANO	1550	3400	3650	3850	4000	4200	4350	4600	4850	5050	5400		4400	4700	4900
																	SAKU	2250	2600	2800	2950	3200	3350	3600	3850	4050	4400		3400	3650	3900
																		HONJŌ-KODAMA	500	750	950	1250	1400	1650	1900	2100	2450		1500	1850	2150
																			HANAZONO	400	600	900	1050	1300	1550	1750	2100		1150	1500	1800
																				RANZAN-OGAWA	350	650	800	1050	1300	1500	1850		950	1300	1600
																					HIGASHI-MATSUYAMA	450	600	850	1100	1300	1650		700	1100	1400
																						TSURUGASHIMA	300	550	800	1000	1350		400	800	1050
																							KEN-Ō-TSURUGASHIMA	250	500	700	1050		450	850	1100
																								SAYAMA-HIDAKA	250	450	800		700	1100	1350
																									IRUMA	200	550		950	1350	1600
																										ŌME	350		1150	1550	1800
																											HINODE		1500	1900	2150
																												AKIRUNO	UNDER CONSTRUCTION		
																													KAWAGOE	500	800
																														TOKOROZAWA	450
																															NERIMA·ŌIZUMI

HIDA-KIYOMI																
650	SHOKAWA															
1000	500	TAKASU														
1200	700	350	SHIROTORI													
1500	1000	650	450	GIFUYAMATO												
1650	1150	800	600	300	GUJŌHACHIMAN											
1900	1400	1050	850	600	400	MINAMI										
2350	1850	1500	1300	1050	850	600	MINO									
2550	2050	1700	1450	1200	1050	800	300	SEKI								
2800	2350	2000	1800	1500	1350	1100	650	450	GIFU-KAKAMIGAHARA							
2950	2500	2150	1950	1650	1500	1250	800	600	300	ICHINOMIYA-KISOGAWA						
3000	2600	2250	2050	1750	1600	1350	900	700	400	250	BISAI					
/	/	/	/	/	/	/	/	/	/	/	/	ICHINOMIYA-NISHI				
3150	2800	2450	2250	2000	1800	1550	1100	950	600	500	/	300	ICHINOMIYA			
4550	4200	3900	3750	3550	3450	3250	2900	2750	2450	2300	/	2150	2000	NAKATSUGAWA		
3750	3350	3100	2950	2750	2600	2300	1900	1700	1400	1250	/	1050	900	1950	NAGOYA	
5550	5200	4950	4800	4600	4500	4300	3950	3850	3600	3500	/	3350	3450	4800	4000	KYŌTO-MINAMI

ZAN-OGAWA				
ASHI-MATSUYAMA				
50	TSURUGASHIMA			
00	400	KAWAGOE		
00	800	500	TOKOROZAWA	
00	1050	800	450	NERIMA·ŌIZUMI

TŌKAI-HOKURIKU EXPRESSWAY

TŌMEI • MEISHIN EXPRESSWAY

50	6100	6300	6500	6750	6850	6900	7150	7100	7300	7500	7600	7850	8000	8250	8650	9050	9300	9500		9650	9800	9850	10050	10250	10600	10650	10900	11000	11150	16500	22050
00	5900	6100	6350	6550	6650	6750	6950	6900	7150	7300	7450	7700	7800	8100	8500	8900	9100	9300		9500	9600	9700	9900	10050	10450	10500	10700	10800	10950	16350	21850
50	5800	6000	6200	6450	6550	6600	6850	6800	7000	7200	7350	7550	7700	7950	8400	8750	9000	9200		9350	9500	9550	9800	9950	10300	10350	10600	10700	10850	16200	21750
00	5650	5850	6100	6300	6400	6500	6700	6650	6850	7050	7200	7400	7550	7800	8250	8600	8850	9050		9250	9350	9400	9650	9800	10150	10250	10450	10550	10700	16050	21600
50	5300	5500	5750	5950	6050	6150	6350	6300	6550	6700	6850	7100	7200	7450	7900	8300	8500	8700		8900	9000	9100	9300	9450	9800	9900	10100	10200	10350	15750	21250
00	5000	5200	5450	5700	5800	5850	6100	6050	6250	6400	6550	6800	6950	7200	7600	8000	8250	8450		8600	8750	8800	9000	9200	9550	9600	9850	9950	10100	15450	21000
50	4900	5100	5300	5550	5650	5700	5950	5900	6100	6300	6450	6650	6800	7050	7500	7850	8100	8300		8500	8600	8650	8900	9050	9400	9500	9700	9800	9950	15300	20850
50	4400	4600	4850	5100	5150	5250	5500	5450	5650	5800	5950	6200	6350	6600	7000	7400	7650	7850		8000	8100	8200	8400	8600	8950	9000	9250	9350	9500	14850	20400
50	4200	4400	4650	4900	5000	5100	5300	5250	5450	5650	5800	6000	6150	6400	6850	7200	7450	7650		7850	7950	8000	8250	8400	8750	8850	9050	9150	9300	14650	20200
50	4000	4250	4500	4750	4800	4900	5100	5100	5300	5450	5600	5850	5950	6250	6650	7050	7250	7450		7650	7750	7850	8050	8250	8600	8650	8850	9000	9150	14500	20050
00	3650	3900	4150	4400	4450	4550	4800	4750	4950	5150	5300	5500	5650	5900	6350	6700	6950	7150		7350	7450	7500	7750	7900	8250	8350	8550	8650	8800	14150	19700
00	3150	3350	3600	3850	3950	4050	4300	4250	4500	4650	4800	5050	5150	5450	5850	6250	6450	6650		6850	6950	7050	7250	7450	7800	7850	8050	8200	8350	13700	19250
50	2900	3100	3350	3600	3700	3800	4000	3950	4200	4400	4550	4800	4900	5200	5600	6000	6200	6400		6600	6700	6800	7000	7200	7550	7600	7800	7950	8100	13450	19000
50	2600	2850	3100	3350	3450	3550	3800	3750	4000	4150	4300	4550	4700	4950	5400	5750	6000	6200		6400	6500	6550	6800	6950	7300	7400	7600	7700	7850	13200	18750
50	2300	2600	2900	3150	3250	3350	3550	3500	3750	3900	4100	4350	4450	4750	5150	5550	5800	6000		6150	6300	6350	6600	6750	7100	7200	7400	7500	7650	13000	18550
50	2050	2300	2650	2900	3000	3100	3350	3300	3550	3700	3850	4150	4250	4550	4950	5350	5600	5800		5950	6100	6150	6400	6550	6900	7000	7200	7300	7450	12800	18350
50	1900	2200	2500	2800	2900	3000	3250	3200	3450	3600	3750	4000	4150	4450	4900	5250	5500	5700		5850	6000	6050	6300	6450	6800	6900	7100	7200	7350	12700	18250
00	1750	2050	2350	2700	2800	2900	3100	3100	3300	3500	3650	3900	4050	4300	4750	5150	5400	5600		5750	5900	5950	6200	6350	6700	6800	7000	7100	7250	12600	18150
00	1450	1750	2050	2400	2500	2650	2900	2850	3100	3250	3450	3700	3800	4100	4550	4950	5150	5350		5550	5650	5750	5950	6150	6500	6550	6800	6900	7050	12400	17950
50	1350	1600	1950	2300	2400	2550	2800	2800	3000	3200	3350	3600	3750	4000	4450	4850	5100	5300		5500	5600	5650	5900	6050	6450	6500	6700	6800	6950	12300	17850
00	1150	1450	1800	2100	2250	2350	2650	2600	2900	3050	3200	3500	3600	3900	4350	4750	5000	5200		5350	5500	5550	5750	5950	6300	6400	6600	6700	6850	12200	17750
00	900	1200	1500	1850	1950	2100	2350	2350	2650	2850	3000	3300	3400	3700	4150	4550	4800	5000		5150	5300	5350	5600	5750	6100	6200	6400	6500	6650	12000	17550
	600	900	1250	1600	1700	1850	2100	2100	2400	2650	2800	3050	3200	3500	3950	4350	4600	4800		5000	5100	5150	5400	5550	5950	6000	6200	6300	6500	11800	17350
	OKAWA	450	800	1100	1250	1350	1650	1600	1950	2150	2400	2700	2850	3150	3600	4000	4250	4450		4650	4750	4850	5050	5250	5600	5700	5900	6000	6150	11500	17050
		OWA-GAMAGŌRI	500	800	950	1100	1350	1350	1650	1900	2100	2450	2600	2900	3350	3800	4050	4250		4450	4550	4650	4850	5050	5400	5500	5700	5800	5950	11300	16850
			OKAZAKI	500	600	750	1000	1000	1300	1550	1750	2100	2250	2650	3100	3550	3800	4000		4200	4300	4400	4600	4800	5150	5250	5450	5550	5700	11050	16600
				TOYOTA-HIGASHI	400	500	800	750	1050	1300	1500	1850	2050	2400	2950	3350	3600	3800		4000	4150	4200	4450	4650	5000	5100	5300	5400	5550	10900	16450
					TOYOTA	300	550	550	850	1100	1300	1650	1800	2200	2800	3200	3450	3650		3850	3950	4050	4300	4450	4850	4950	5150	5250	5400	10750	16300
						TŌMEI-MIYOSHI	450	400	700	950	1150	1500	1700	2050	2650	3100	3350	3550		3750	3850	3950	4200	4400	4750	4850	5050	5150	5300	10650	16200
							NAGAKUTE	350	650	900	1100	1450	1600	2000	2600	3050	3300	3550		3750	3850	3950	4150	4350	4750	4800	5050	5150	5300	10650	16200
								NAGOYA	450	700	900	1250	1450	1800	2400	2900	3150	3350		3550	3700	3750	4000	4200	4550	4650	4900	5000	5150	10500	16000
									KASUGAI	350	600	950	1100	1500	2100	2650	2900	3150		3350	3450	3550	3750	3950	4350	4400	4650	4750	4950	10250	15800
										KOMAKI	350	700	900	1250	1850	2400	2750	2950		3150	3300	3350	3600	3800	4150	4250	4450	4600	4750	10100	15650
											ICHINOMIYA	500	650	1050	1650	2200	2550	2800		3000	3100	3200	3450	3600	4000	4100	4300	4450	4600	9950	15500
												GIFU-HASHIMA	300	700	1300	1850	2200	2500		2750	2850	2950	3200	3350	3750	3850	4050	4200	4350	9700	15250
													ŌGAKI	500	1150	1700	2000	2300		2550	2750	2800	3050	3250	3650	3700	3950	4050	4200	9600	15150
														SEKIGAHARA	750	1300	1650	1950		2200	2350	2450	2750	2950	3350	3450	3650	3750	3950	9350	14850
															HIKONE	700	1050	1300		1600	1750	1850	2150	2400	2900	3000	3200	3350	3500	8900	14450
																YŌKAICHI	500	750		1050	1200	1300	1600	1850	2350	2450	2750	2900	3100	8500	14050
																	RYŪŌ	450		700	850	950	1250	1500	2000	2100	2400	2550	2800	8300	13850
																		RITTŌ		350	600	700	1000	1250	1750	1850	2150	2300	2500	8100	13650
																			KUSATSU-TANAKAMI	UNDER CONSTRUCTION											
																				SETA-HIGASHI·SETA-NISHI	300	400	750	950	1450	1550	1850	2000	2250	7900	13450
																					ŌTSU	250	550	800	1300	1400	1700	1850	2050	7800	13350
																						KYŌTO-HIGASHI	450	700	1200	1300	1600	1750	1950	7750	13250
																							KYŌTO-MINAMI	400	900	1000	1300	1450	1650	7500	13050
																								ŌYAMAZAKI	650	750	1050	1200	1400	7350	12850
																									IBARAKI	250	550	700	900	7000	12500
																										SUITA	450	600	800	/	/
																											TOYONAKA	300	500	/	/
																												AMAGASAKI	350	/	/
																													NISHINOMIYA	/	/
																														HIROSHIMA	6600
																															FUKUOKA

HOKU															
INA															
50	KOMAGANE														
50	550	MATSUKAWA													
50	950	550	ĪDA												
/	/	/	/	SONOHARA											
50	2250	1850	1450	1050	NAKATSUGAWA										
00	2500	2100	1700	1300	400	ENA									
50	2950	2550	2150	1800	850	650	MIZUNAMI								
50	3050	2700	2300	1900	1000	750	250	TOKI							
00	3250	2900	2500	2100	1200	950	500	350	TAJIMI						
00	3400	3100	2700	2350	1400	1200	700	600	350	KOMAKI-HIGASHI					
00	3800	3500	3200	2900	1950	1750	1250	1150	900	700	NAGOYA				
0	6300	6050	5750	5500	4800	4650	4300	4200	4000	3850	4000	KYŌTO-MINAMI			
00	6900	6650	6350	6100	5400	5250	4900	4850	4650	4500	4650	1000	SUITA		
00	12700	12450	12150	11900	11250	11050	10750	10650	10500	10350	10500	7500	/	HIROSHIMA	
00	18250	17950	17700	17400	16750	16600	16300	16200	16050	15900	16000	13050	/	6600	FUKUOKA

YAMAGATA · TŌHOKU-CHŪŌ · EXPRESSWAY

	SAKATA	SHŌNAI-KŪKŌ	TSURUOKA	SHŌNAI-ASAHI	YUDONOSAN	GASSAN	NISHIKAWA	SAGAE	YAMAGATA-KITA	YAMAGATA-ZAŌ	SEKISAWA	SASAYA	MIYAGI-KAWASAKI	HIGASHINE	TENDŌ	YAMAGATA-CHŪŌ	YAMAGATA-KAMINOYAMA	MORIOKA	SENDAI-MIYAGI	KAWAGUCHI JCT
SAKATA-MINATO	250	450	700	1050	1250	—	1850	2200	2500	2650	/	3050	3350	2650	2550	2500	2750	7500	4100	9750
SAKATA		200	450	800	1000	—	1600	1950	2250	2400	/	2800	3100	2400	2300	2250	2500	7250	3850	9500
SHŌNAI-KŪKŌ			250	600	800	—	1400	1750	2050	2200	/	2600	2900	2200	2100	2050	2300	7050	3650	9300
TSURUOKA				350	550	—	1150	1500	1800	1950	/	2350	2650	1950	1850	1800	2050	6800	3400	9050
SHŌNAI-ASAHI					200	—	800	1150	1450	1600	/	2000	2300	1600	1500	1450	1700	6450	3050	8700
YUDONOSAN						—	—	—	—	—	/	—	—	1400	1300	1250	1500	—	—	—
GASSAN							600	950	1250	1400	/	1800	2100	1400	1300	1250	1500	6250	2850	8500
NISHIKAWA								500	800	950	/	1350	1650	1000	850	800	1100	5950	2400	8200
SAGAE									450	600	/	1000	1300	650	500	450	750	5700	2050	7950
YAMAGATA-KITA										300	/	700	1000	600	450	400	700	5500	1750	7750
YAMAGATA-ZAŌ											/	550	850	750	600	550	850	5350	1600	7650
SEKISAWA												200	650	/	/	/	/	5250	1400	7500
SASAYA													450	1150	1000	950	1250	5050	1200	7300
MIYAGI-KAWASAKI														1450	1300	1250	1550	4800	900	7100
HIGASHINE															300	600	850	5800	2150	8050
TENDŌ																450	750	5700	2050	7950
YAMAGATA-CHŪŌ																	450	5650	2000	7900
YAMAGATA-KAMINOYAMA																		5850	2250	8100
MORIOKA																			4300	10450
SENDAI-MIYAGI																				7200
KAWAGUCHI JCT																				

TŌHOKU EXPRESSWAY

	AOMORI-HIGASHI	AOMORI-CHUŌ	AOMORI	NAMIOKA	KUROISHI	ŌWANI-HIROSAKI	IKARIGASEKI	KOSAKA	TOWADA	KAZUNO-HACHIMANTAI	ASHIRO	HACHINOHE	ICHINOHE	MATSUO-HACHIMANTAI	NISHINE	TAKIZAWA	MORIOKA	MORIOKA-MINAMI	SHIWA	HANAMAKI	HANAMAKI-MINAMI	KITAKAMI-EZURIKO	KITAKAMI-KANEGASAKI	MIZUSAWA	HIRAIZUMI-MAESAWA	ICHINOSEKI	WAKAYANAGI-KANNARI	TSUKIDATE	FURUKAWA	TAIWA	IZUMI	SENDAI-MIYAGI	SENDAI-MINAMI	MURATA	SHIROISHI
AOMORI-HIGASHI																																			
AOMORI-CHUŌ	400																																		
AOMORI	/	/																																	
NAMIOKA	800	550	450																																
KUROISHI	1200	950	850	450																															
ŌWANI-HIROSAKI	1450	1200	1100	750	350																														
IKARIGASEKI	1750	1500	1400	1100	750	450																													
KOSAKA	2300	2050	1950	1650	1250	1000	650																												
TOWADA	2500	2250	2150	1850	1450	1200	900	350																											
KAZUNO-HACHIMANTAI	2800	2550	2450	2150	1800	1550	1200	650	450																										
ASHIRO	3300	3100	3050	2800	2450	2200	1850	1350	1150	850																									
HACHINOHE	4650	4450	4350	4150	3850	3700	3450	3050	2900	2600	1950																								
ICHINOHE	3850	3650	3550	3350	3050	2900	2600	2050	1850	1550	900	1200																							
MATSUO-HACHIMANTAI	3750	3550	3450	3250	2950	2800	2450	1950	1750	1400	750	2450	1400																						
NISHINE	3900	3750	3650	3450	3150	2950	2700	2200	2000	1650	1000	2700	1650	400																					
TAKIZAWA	4100	3950	3850	3600	3350	3150	2900	2450	2250	1950	1250	2900	1900	650	400																				
MORIOKA	4300	4100	4050	3800	3550	3350	3100	2700	2500	2200	1500	3100	2150	900	700	400																			
MORIOKA-MINAMI	4450	4250	4200	3950	3700	3500	3250	2850	2700	2350	1700	3250	2350	1100	850	600	350																		
SHIWA	4650	4450	4400	4150	3900	3700	3450	3050	2900	2650	2000	3450	2650	1400	1150	900	600	450																	
HANAMAKI	4900	4700	4650	4400	4150	3950	3700	3300	3150	2900	2300	3700	2900	1700	1450	1200	950	750	500																
HANAMAKI-MINAMI	5000	4850	4750	4550	4250	4100	3850	3450	3300	3050	2500	3850	3050	1900	1650	1400	1150	950	650	300															
KITAKAMI-EZURIKO	5200	5000	4950	4750	4450	4250	4000	3650	3450	3250	2750	4050	3250	2150	1900	1650	1400	1200	900	600	400														
KITAKAMI-KANEGASAKI	5300	5150	5050	4850	4600	4400	4150	3750	3600	3350	2850	4150	3350	2300	2050	1800	1550	1350	1100	750	600	300													
MIZUSAWA	5450	5300	5200	5000	4750	4550	4300	3950	3750	3550	3050	4350	3550	2550	2300	2050	1800	1600	1300	1000	800	550	350												
HIRAIZUMI-MAESAWA	5800	5600	5550	5350	5050	4900	4650	4250	4100	3900	3400	4650	3850	2950	2750	2500	2250	2050	1750	1450	1250	1000	850	600											
ICHINOSEKI	6000	5800	5750	5550	5300	5100	4850	4500	4350	4100	3600	4900	4100	3150	2950	2800	2550	2350	2050	1750	1550	1300	1150	900	450										
WAKAYANAGI-KANNARI	6300	6150	6050	5850	5600	5400	5200	4800	4650	4450	3950	5200	4450	3500	3300	3100	2900	2800	2500	2200	2000	1750	1600	1350	900	600									
TSUKIDATE	6500	6350	6250	6050	5800	5650	5400	5050	4900	4650	4150	5400	4650	3700	3550	3350	3150	3000	2800	2500	2300	2050	1900	1650	1200	900	450								
FURUKAWA	6800	6650	6550	6350	6100	5900	5700	5300	5150	4950	4450	5700	4950	4050	3850	3650	3450	3300	3100	2850	2750	2450	2300	2050	1600	1350	900	550							
TAIWA	7150	6950	6900	6700	6400	6250	6000	5650	5500	5300	4800	6000	5250	4400	4200	4000	3800	3650	3450	3200	3100	2900	2750	2550	2100	1800	1350	1050	600						
IZUMI	7350	7150	7100	6850	6600	6450	6200	5850	5700	5500	5000	6200	5450	4600	4400	4200	4000	3900	3650	3400	3300	3100	2950	2800	2350	2050	1650	1300	900	450					
SENDAI-MIYAGI	7600	7400	7350	7100	6850	6700	6450	6100	5950	5750	5250	6450	5700	4850	4650	4500	4300	4150	3950	3700	3550	3350	3250	3050	2750	2450	2000	1700	1250	800	500				
SENDAI-MINAMI	7700	7500	7450	7200	6950	6800	6550	6200	6050	5850	5350	6550	5800	4950	4800	4600	4400	4250	4050	3800	3650	3450	3350	3200	2850	2550	2150	1800	1400	950	650	300			
MURATA	7950	7800	7700	7500	7250	7050	6850	6450	6300	6100	5650	6850	6100	5200	5050	4850	4700	4550	4350	4100	3950	3750	3650	3450	3150	2900	2500	2200	1800	1350	1050	700	550		
SHIROISHI	8200	8000	7950	7700	7450	7300	7050	6700	6550	6350	5850	7050	6300	5450	5250	5100	4900	4800	4550	4350	4200	4000	3850	3700	3350	3150	2800	2550	2100	1650	1350	1000	850	450	
	8600	8450	8350	8150	7900	7700	7450	7100	6950	6750	6300	7500	6750	5850	5700	5500	5350	5200	5000	4750	4650	4450	4350	4150	3800	3600	3250	3050	2700	2250	1950	1600	1450	1100	750
	8800	8650	8550	8350	8100	7900	7700	7300	7150	6950	6500	7700	6950	6050	5900	5700	5550	5400	5200	4950	4850	4650	4550	4400	4050	3800	3500	3250	2950	2550	2250	1900	1750	1350	1050
	9000	8800	8750	8500	8250	8100	7850	7500	7350	7150	6650	7850	7100	6250	6100	5900	5700	5600	5400	5150	5050	4850	4750	4550	4250	4000	3650	3450	3150	2800	2500	2150	2000	1650	1300
	9300	9150	9100	8850	8600	8450	8200	7850	7700	7450	7000	8200	7450	6600	6400	6250	6050	5950	5750	5500	5350	5200	5100	4900	4600	4350	4050	3800	3500	3150	2950	2650	2500	2100	1800
	9550	9400	9300	9100	8850	8650	8450	8050	7900	7700	7250	8450	7700	6800	6650	6450	6300	6150	5950	5750	5600	5450	5300	5150	4850	4600	4300	4050	3750	3400	3200	2900	2800	2450	2150
	9700	9500	9450	9200	8950	8800	8550	8200	8050	7850	7350	8550	7800	6950	6750	6600	6400	6300	6100	5850	5750	5550	5450	5250	4950	4750	4400	4200	3900	3550	3300	3050	2950	2600	2300
	9850	9650	9600	9400	9100	8950	8700	8350	8200	8000	7500	8700	8000	7100	6950	6750	6550	6450	6250	6000	5900	5700	5600	5450	5100	4900	4600	4350	4050	3700	3500	3200	3100	2800	2550
	10000	9850	9750	9550	9300	9100	8900	8500	8350	8150	7700	8900	8150	7250	7100	6900	6750	6600	6400	6200	6050	5900	5750	5600	5300	5100	4750	4550	4250	3900	3650	3400	3300	3000	2750
	10200	10050	10000	9750	9500	9350	9100	8750	8600	8350	7900	9100	8350	7500	7300	7150	6950	6850	6650	6400	6250	6100	5950	5800	5500	5300	5000	4750	4450	4100	3900	3650	3550	3250	3000
	10500	10350	10300	10050	9800	9650	9400	9050	8900	8650	8200	9400	8650	7800	7600	7450	7250	7150	6950	6700	6550	6400	6250	6100	5800	5600	5300	5050	4800	4450	4200	3950	3850	3550	3300
	10850	10650	10600	10400	10100	9950	9700	9350	9200	9000	8500	9700	8950	8100	7950	7750	7550	7450	7250	7000	6900	6700	6600	6450	6100	5900	5600	5400	5100	4750	4550	4300	4200	3900	3650
	11100	10900	10850	10600	10350	10200	9950	9600	9450	9250	8750	9950	9200	8350	8150	8000	7800	7700	7500	7250	7150	6950	6850	6650	6350	6150	5850	5600	5350	5000	4800	4550	4450	4150	3900
	11400	11250	11150	10950	10700	10550	10300	9950	9800	9550	9100	10300	9550	8700	8500	8350	8150	8000	7800	7600	7450	7300	7150	7000	6700	6500	6150	5950	5650	5350	5150	4900	4800	4500	4300
	11750	11550	11500	11250	11000	10850	10600	10250	10100	9900	9400	10600	9850	9000	8800	8650	8450	8350	8150	7900	7800	7600	7500	7300	7000	6800	6500	6250	6000	5650	5450	5200	5100	4850	4600
	11950	11750	11700	11500	11200	11050	10800	10450	10300	10100	9600	10800	10100	9200	9050	8850	8650	8550	8350	8100	8000	7800	7700	7550	7200	7000	6700	6500	6200	5850	5650	5400	5300	5050	4800
	12300	12100	12050	11800	11550	11400	11150	10800	10650	10450	9950	11150	10400	9550	9350	9200	9000	8900	8700	8450	8350	8150	8050	7850	7550	7350	7050	6800	6550	6200	6000	5750	5650	5400	5150
	12600	12450	12350	12150	11900	11700	11450	11100	10950	10750	10300	11500	10750	9850	9700	9500	9350	9200	9000	8750	8650	8450	8350	8200	7850	7650	7350	7150	6850	6500	6300	6100	6000	5700	5500
	12750	12600	12500	12300	12050	11850	11650	11250	11150	10900	10450	11650	10900	10000	9850	9650	9500	9350	9150	8950	8800	8650	8500	8350	8050	7850	7500	7300	7000	6700	6500	6250	6150	5850	5650
	12900	12700	12650	12400	12150	12000	11750	11400	11250	11050	10550	11750	11000	10150	9950	9800	9600	9500	9300	9050	8950	8750	8650	8450	8150	7950	7650	7400	7150	6800	6600	6350	6250	6000	5750
	13000	12800	12750	12550	12300	12100	11850	11500	11350	11150	10650	11850	11150	10250	10100	9900	9700	9600	9400	9150	9050	8850	8750	8600	8250	8050	7750	7550	7250	6900	6700	6450	6350	6100	5850
	13150	13000	12900	12700	12450	12250	12050	11650	11550	11300	10850	12050	11300	10450	10250	10050	9900	9750	9550	9350	9200	9050	8900	8750	8450	8250	7900	7700	7400	7100	6900	6650	6550	6250	6050
	13500	13300	13250	13050	12800	12600	12350	12000	11850	11650	11150	12400	11650	10750	10600	10400	10200	10100	9900	9650	9550	9350	9250	9100	8750	8550	8250	8050	7750	7400	7200	7000	6900	6600	6400
	13600	13450	13350	13150	12900	12750	12500	12150	12000	11750	11300	12500	11750	10900	10700	10550	10350	10200	10000	9800	9650	9500	9350	9200	8900	8700	8400	8150	7850	7550	7350	7100	7000	6750	6500
	13700	13550	13500	13250	13000	12850	12600	12250	12100	11850	11400	12600	11850	11000	10800	10650	10450	10350	10150	9900	9750	9600	9500	9300	9000	8800	8500	8250	8000	7650	7450	7200	7100	6850	6600

DŌTŌ EXPRESSWAY

	HONBETSU	IKEDA	OTOFUKE-OBIHIRO	OBIHIRO JCT	MEMURO	TOKACHI-SHIMIZU
ASHORO	/	600	1100	1350	1550	1700
HONBETSU		600	1100	1350	1550	1700
IKEDA			500	750	950	1100
OTOFUKE-OBIHIRO				250	450	600
OBIHIRO JCT					250	600
MEMURO						600
TOKACHI-SHIMIZU						

HACHINOHE EXPRESSWAY

	HACHINOHE	NANGŌ	KARUMAI	KUNOHE	ICHINOHE	JŌHŌJI	ŌWANI-HIROSAKI	TOWADA	MORIOKA	SENDAI-MIYAGI	FUKUSHIMA-ĪZAKA	KAWAGUCHI JCT
HACHINOHE-KITA	/	650	900	1150	1450	1750	3850	3050	3300	6650	7850	[illegible]
HACHINOHE		400	650	950	1200	1550	3700	2900	3100	6450	7700	[illegible]
NANGŌ			400	650	950	1250	3500	2650	2900	6300	7500	[illegible]
KARUMAI				400	700	1000	3300	2400	2750	6100	7350	[illegible]
KUNOHE					450	750	3100	2150	2450	5950	7150	[illegible]
ICHINOHE						450	2900	1850	2150	5700	6950	[illegible]
JŌHŌJI							2600	1550	1850	5500	6750	[illegible]
ŌWANI-HIROSAKI								1200	3350	6700	7900	[illegible]
TOWADA									2500	5950	7150	[illegible]
MORIOKA										4300	5550	[illegible]
SENDAI-MIYAGI											1900	[illegible]
FUKUSHIMA-ĪZAKA												[illegible]
KAWAGUCHI JCT												

DŌŌ · SASSON · DŌTŌ EXPRESSWAY

	SHIBETSU-KENBUCHI	WASSAMU	ASAHIKAWA-KITA	ASAHIKAWA-TAKASU	FUKAGAWA	FUKAGAWA-NISHI	TAKIGAWA	SUNAGAWA-OASIS	NAIE-SUNAGAWA	BIBAI	MIKASA	IWAMIZAWA	EBETSU-HIGASHI	EBETSU-NISHI	SAPPORO	OTARU	ASARI	ZENIBAKO	TEINE	SAPPORO-NISHI	SHINKAWA	SAPPORO-KITA	FUSHIKO	KARIKI	KITAGŌ	ŌYACHI	SAPPORO-MINAMI	KITA-HIROSHIMA	ENIWA	CHITOSE-HIGASHI	OIWAKECHŌ	YŪBARI	CHITOSE	TOMAKOMAI-HIGASHI	NUMANOHATA-NISHI	TOMAKOMAI-NISHI	SHIRAOI	NOBORIBETSU-HI	NOBORIBETSU-
SHIBETSU-KENBUCHI																																						
WASSAMU	550																																					
ASAHIKAWA-KITA	1100	700																																				
ASAHIKAWA-TAKASU	1350	950	400																																			
FUKAGAWA	2050	1600	1050	850																																		
FUKAGAWA-NISHI	2300	1900	1350	1150	450																																	
TAKIGAWA	2500	2100	1550	1300	600	650																																
SUNAGAWA-OASIS	2550	2150	1600	1350	650	700	200																															
NAIE-SUNAGAWA	2850	2450	1900	1650	1000	1000	500	300																														
BIBAI	3100	2800	2250	2000	1350	1350	850	650	500																													
MIKASA	3300	3000	2550	2300	1600	1650	1150	950	800	450																												
IWAMIZAWA	3500	3200	2800	2550	1900	1900	1400	1200	1050	700	400																											
EBETSU-HIGASHI	3800	3500	3100	2900	2300	2300	1800	1600	1450	1100	800	550																										
EBETSU-NISHI	4000	3700	3250	3100	2550	2550	2050	1850	1700	1350	1050	800	400																									
SAPPORO	4100	3800	3400	3250	2700	2700	2250	2050	1900	1550	1250	1000	600	300																								
OTARU	5300	5000	4600	4450	3900	3900	3450	3250	3100	2750	2450	2200	1800	1500	/																							
ASARI	5200	4900	4500	4350	3800	3800	3350	3150	3000	2650	2350	2100	1700	1400	/	250																						
ZENIBAKO	4900	4600	4200	4050	3500	3500	3050	2850	2700	2350	2050	1800	1400	1100	/	550	450																					
TEINE	4750	4450	4050	3900	3350	3350	2900	2700	2550	2200	1900	1650	1250	950	/	/	/	/																				
SAPPORO-NISHI	/	/	/	/	/	/	/	/	/	/	/	/	/	/	/	800	700	400	250																			
SHINKAWA	4500	4200	3800	3650	3100	3100	2650	2450	2300	1950	1650	1400	1000	700	/	/	/	/	/	/																		
SAPPORO-KITA	4500	4200	3800	3650	3100	3100	2650	2450	2300	1950	1650	1400	1000	700	/	1200	1100	800	650	/	400																	
FUSHIKO	4500	4200	3800	3650	3100	3100	2650	2450	2300	1950	1650	1400	1000	700	/	/	/	/	/	/	/	/																
KARIKI	/	/	/	/	/	/	/	/	/	/	/	/	/	/	/	1200	1100	800	650	/	400	400	400															
KITAGŌ	/	/	/	/	/	/	/	/	/	/	/	/	/	/	/	/	/	/	/	/	/	/	/	/														
ŌYACHI	4500	4200	3800	3650	3100	3100	2650	2450	2300	1950	1650	1400	1000	700	/	1200	1100	800	650	/	400	400	400	/	400													
SAPPORO-MINAMI	4500	4200	3800	3650	3100	3100	2650	2450	2300	1950	1650	1400	1000	700	/	1200	1100	800	650	/	400	400	400	/	400	/												
KITA-HIROSHIMA	4750	4450	4050	3900	3350	3350	2900	2700	2550	2200	1900	1650	1250	950	/	1450	1350	1050	900	/	650	650	650	/	650	/	250											
ENIWA	5150	4850	4450	4300	3750	3750	3300	3100	2950	2600	2300	2050	1650	1350	/	1850	1750	1450	1300	/	1050	1050	1050	/	1050	/	650	500										
CHITOSE-HIGASHI	5550	5250	4850	4700	4150	4150	3700	3500	3350	3000	2700	2450	2050	1750	/	2250	2150	1850	1700	/	1450	1450	1450	/	1450	/	1050	950	600									
OIWAKECHŌ	5800	5500	5100	4950	4400	4400	3950	3750	3600	3250	2950	2700	2300	2000	/	2500	2400	2100	1950	/	1700	1700	1700	/	1700	/	1300	1200	850	400								
YŪBARI	6300	6000	5600	5450	4900	4900	4450	4250	4100	3750	3450	3200	2800	2500	/	3000	2900	2600	2450	/	2200	2200	2200	/	2200	/	1800	1700	1350	900	700							
CHITOSE	5350	5050	4650	4500	3950	3950	3500	3300	3150	2800	2500	2250	1850	1550	/	2050	1950	1650	1500	/	1250	1250	1250	/	1250	/	850	750	350	600	850	1350						
TOMAKOMAI-HIGASHI	5650	5350	4950	4800	4250	4250	3800	3600	3450	3100	2800	2550	2150	1850	/	2350	2250	1950	1800	/	1550	1550	1550	/	1550	/	1150	1050	700	900	1150	1700	450					
NUMANOHATA-NISHI	5800	5500	5100	4950	4400	4400	3950	3750	3600	3250	2950	2700	2300	2000	/	2500	2400	2100	1950	/	1700	1700	1700	/	1700	/	1300	1200	850	1050	1300	1850	600	150				
TOMAKOMAI-NISHI	6150	5850	5450	5300	4750	4750	4300	4100	3950	3600	3300	3050	2650	2350	/	2850	2750	2450	2300	/	2050	2050	2050	/	2050	/	1650	1500	1150	1350	1600	2150	900	600	750			
SHIRAOI	6550	6250	5850	5700	5150	5150	4700	4500	4350	4000	3700	3450	3050	2750	/	3250	3150	2850	2700	/	2450	2450	2450	/	2450	/	2050	1900	1550	1800	2000	2550	1350	1000	1150	550		
NOBORIBETSU-HI	7000	6700	6300	6150	5600	5600	5150	4950	4800	4450	4150	3900	3500	3200	/	3700	3600	3300	3150	/	2900	2900	2900	/	2900	/	2500	2400	2050	2250	2500	2950	1800	1500	1650	1050	650	
NOBORIBETSU-	7300	7000	6600	6450	5900	5900	5450	5250	5100	4750	4450	4200	3800	3500	/	4000	3900	3600	3450	/	3200	3200	3200	/	3200	/	2800	2700	2350	2550	2800	3150	2100	1800	1950	1350	950	450
	7500	7200	6800	6650	6100	6100	5650	5450	5300	4950	4650	4400	4000	3700	/	4200	4100	3800	3650	/	3400	3400	3400	/	3400	/	3000	2900	2600	2800	2950	3350	2350	2050	2200	1600	1200	700	400
	7750	7450	7050	6900	6350	6350	5900	5700	5550	5200	4900	4650	4250	3950	/	4450	4350	4050	3900	/	3650	3650	3650	/	3650	/	3250	3150	2850	3050	3200	3600	2700	2400	2550	1900	1500	1050	750
	7950	7650	7250	7100	6550	6550	6100	5900	5750	5400	5100	4850	4450	4150	/	4650	4550	4250	4100	/	3850	3850	3850	/	3850	/	3450	3350	3100	3250	3450	3850	2900	2650	2800	2200	1800	1350	1050
	8250	7950	7550	7400	6850	6850	6400	6200	6050	5700	5400	5150	4750	4450	/	4950	4850	4550	4400	/	4150	4150	4150	/	4150	/	3750	3650	3400	3550	3750	4150	3200	3000	3150	2600	2200	1750	1450
	8900	8600	8200	8050	7500	7500	7050	6850	6700	6350	6050	5800	5400	5100	/	5600	5500	5200	5050	/	4800	4800	4800	/	4800	/	4400	4300	4050	4200	4400	4800	3850	3650	3800	3300	3000	2600	2300
	9100	8800	8400	8250	7700	7700	7250	7050	6900	6550	6250	6000	5600	5300	/	5800	5700	5400	5250	/	5000	5000	5000	/	5000	/	4600	4550	4250	4450	4600	5000	4100	3850	4000	3500	3200	2850	2600

HIGASHI-KANTŌ • SHIN-KŪKŌ • TATEYAMA EXPRESSWAY/AQUA-LINE

MATSUO-YOKOSHIBA	300	600	/	700	800	900	1000	5300	2300	2150	2150	2150	1900	1700	1450	1100	1100	/	1100	1300	3000	2750	2550	2350	2250	2050	1750	1600	1400	/	1500	/	1700
	SANBU-NARUTŌ	300	/	400	500	600	700	5000	2000	1850	1850	1850	1600	1400	1150	800	800	/	800	1000	2700	2450	2250	2050	1950	1750	1450	1300	1100	/	1200	/	1400
		TŌGANE	/	100	200	300	400	4700	1700	1550	1550	1550	1300	1100	850	500	500	/	500	700	2400	2150	1950	1750	1650	1450	1150	1000	800	/	900	/	1100
			YAMADA	100	200	300	400	4700	1700	1550	1550	1550	1300	1100	850	500	500	/	500	700	2400	2150	1950	1750	1650	1450	1150	1000	800	/	900	/	1100
				NAKANO	100	200	300	4600	1600	1450	1450	1450	1200	1000	750	400	400	/	400	600	2300	2050	1850	1650	1550	1350	1050	900	700	/	800	/	1000
					TAKADA	100	200	4500	1500	1350	1350	1350	1100	900	650	300	300	/	300	500	2200	1950	1750	1550	1450	1250	950	800	600	/	700	/	900
						ŌMIYA	100	4400	1400	1250	1250	1250	1000	800	550	200	200	/	200	400	2100	1850	1650	1450	1350	1150	850	700	500	/	600	/	800
							CHIBA-HIGASHI	/	/	/	/	/	/	/	/	/	/	/	/	/	/	/	/	/	/	/	/	/	/	/	/	/	/
								UKISHIMA	3000	3150	3700	3700	3550	3700	4000	/	4300	/	4400	4600	6150	5900	5650	5500	5350	5200	4900	4750	4550	/	4650	/	5000
									KISARAZU-KANEDA	150	700	700	550	700	1000	/	1300	/	1400	1600	3150	2900	2650	2500	2350	2200	1900	1750	1550	/	1650	/	2000
										SODEGAURA	550	550	400	550	850	/	1150	/	1250	1450	3000	2750	2500	2350	2200	2050	1750	1600	1400	/	1500	/	1850
											KISARAZU-MINAMI	350	400	600	850	/	1150	/	1250	1450	3000	2800	2550	2350	2250	2050	1750	1600	1450	/	1500	/	1900
												KIMITSU	400	600	850	/	1150	/	1250	1450	3000	2750	2550	2350	2250	2050	1750	1600	1400	/	1500	/	1850
													KISARAZU-KITA	350	600	/	900	/	1000	1200	2750	2500	2300	2100	2000	1800	1500	1350	1150	/	1250	/	1600
														ANESAKI-SODEGAURA	400	/	700	/	800	1000	2550	2350	2100	1900	1800	1650	1350	1150	1000	/	1100	/	1450
															ICHIHARA	/	450	/	550	750	2300	2100	1850	1650	1550	1350	1100	900	700	/	800	/	1200
																SOGA	100	/	200	400	2100	1850	1650	1450	1350	1150	850	700	500	/	600	/	800
																	MATSUGAOKA	/	200	400	2100	1850	1650	1450	1350	1150	850	700	500	/	600	/	800
																		KAIZUKA	100	300	2000	1750	1550	1350	1250	1050	750	600	400	/	500	/	700
																			ANAGAWA	200	1900	1650	1450	1250	1150	950	650	500	300	/	400	/	600
																				CHIBA-NISHI	/	/	/	/	/	/	/	/	/	/	/	/	/
																					ITAKO	350	600	1050	900	1100	1400	1550	1750	1900	1950	/	2300
																						SAWARA-KATORI	400	800	700	850	1150	1350	1500	1650	1750	/	2100
																							TAIĒ	600	450	650	900	1100	1250	1450	1500	/	1850
																								SHIN-KŪKŌ	/	450	750	900	1100	1250	1300	/	1650
																									NARITA	300	600	800	950	1150	1200	/	1550
																										TOMISATO	450	600	800	950	1000	/	1400
																											SAKURA	300	500	650	750	/	1100
																												YOTSUKAIDŌ	350	500	550	/	900
																													CHIBA-KITA	300	350	/	750
																														MIYANOGI	/	/	/
																															WANGAN-CHIBA	/	/
																																WANGAN-NARASHINO	400
																																	WANGAN-ICHIKAWA

UTSUNOMIYA-KAMINOKAWA							
350	MIBU						
550	300	TSUGA					
1050	850	650	KANUMA				
700	500	350	650	TOCHIGI			
1150	950	800	1100	600	SANO-FUJIOKA		
2450	2200	2050	2350	1900	1450	IWATSUKI	
2750	2550	2400	2700	2200	1750	450	KAWAGUCHI JCT

KITA-KANTŌ EXPRESSWAY

KUNIMI																						
KUSHIMA-ĪZAKA																						
400	FUKUSHIMA-NISHI																					
900	650	NIHONMATSU																				
250	1000	500	MOTOMIYA																			
400	1150	650	300	KORIYAMA																		
650	1400	900	550	350	KORIYAMA-MINAMI																	
900	1600	1150	800	650	400	SUKAGAWA																
200	1950	1450	1100	950	700	450	YABUKI															
600	2350	1850	1550	1350	1150	900	600	SHIRAKAWA														
000	2800	2300	2000	1800	1600	1350	1050	600	NASU													
250	3050	2650	2350	2150	1950	1700	1400	950	500	NISHI-NASUNO-SHIOBARA												
600	3400	3050	2800	2650	2400	2150	1850	1450	1000	650	YAITA											
950	3750	3400	3150	3000	2850	2600	2300	1900	1450	1100	600	UTSUNOMIYA										
150	3950	3600	3350	3200	3050	2850	2600	2200	1750	1400	900	450	KANUMA									
550	4350	3950	3700	3600	3400	3250	3000	2650	2200	1850	1400	950	650	TOCHIGI								
850	4700	4300	4050	3950	3750	3600	3350	3050	2700	2350	1850	1400	1100	600	SANO-FUJIOKA							
000	4850	4500	4250	4100	3950	3750	3500	3200	2850	2550	2050	1650	1350	850	350	TATEBAYASHI						
150	4950	4600	4350	4250	4050	3900	3650	3350	3000	2750	2250	1800	1500	1000	550	300	HANYŪ					
250	5050	4700	4500	4350	4200	4000	3750	3450	3100	2850	2400	1950	1650	1150	700	450	300	KAZO				
400	5250	4900	4650	4550	4350	4200	3950	3650	3300	3050	2650	2200	1900	1400	950	750	550	400	KUKI			
750	5600	5250	5000	4900	4750	4550	4300	4000	3650	3400	3050	2650	2350	1900	1450	1200	1000	850	600	IWATSUKI		
900	5700	5350	5150	5000	4850	4700	4450	4150	3800	3550	3200	2850	2550	2050	1600	1350	1200	1050	800	300	URAWA	
000	5800	5500	5250	5100	4950	4800	4550	4250	3900	3650	3300	2950	2700	2200	1750	1500	1350	1200	950	450	250	KAWAGUCHI JCT

AKITA EXPRESSWAY

NOSHIRO-MINAMI	0	450	850	1150	1500	1750	1900	2050	2400	2200	2400	2800	3350	3550	3800	3800	4200	8400	5350	6800	12950
	HACHIRYŪ	450	850	1150	1500	1750	1900	2050	2400	2200	2400	2800	3350	3550	3800	3800	4200	8400	5350	6800	12950
		KOTOOKA-MORITAKE	400	700	1050	1300	1450	1600	1950	1750	1950	2350	2900	3100	3350	3350	3750	7950	4900	6350	12500
			GOJŌME-HACHIRŌGATA	450	800	1050	1200	1350	1700	1500	1700	2100	2650	2850	3100	3150	3600	7750	4700	6150	12300
				SHŌWA-OGAHANTŌ	350	750	950	1050	1450	1200	1400	1850	2400	2600	2850	2900	3350	7550	4500	5950	12100
					AKITA-KITA	400	600	700	1100	850	1050	1500	2050	2250	2500	2550	3000	7200	4150	5600	11750
						AKITA-CHŪŌ	350	500	850	650	850	1250	1800	2000	2250	2300	2850	7050	4000	5450	11600
							AKITA-MINAMI	300	650	450	650	1050	1600	1800	2050	2150	2700	6950	3850	5350	11450
								AKITA-KŪKŌ	550	450	650	1050	1600	1800	2050	2100	2700	6900	3850	5300	11450
									IWAKI	800	1000	1400	1950	2150	2400	2500	2950	7200	4100	5600	11700
										KYŌWA	350	750	1300	1600	1750	1850	2100	6700	3650	5150	11250
											NISHI-SENBOKU	600	1100	1300	1550	1650	2200	6600	3500	5000	11150
												ŌMAGARI	700	900	1150	1200	1800	6300	3150	4700	10850
													YOKOTE	200	450	700	1250	5900	2750	4300	10450
														JŪMONJI	250	900	1450	6100	2950	4500	10650
															YUZAWA	1150	1700	6350	3200	4750	10900
																YUDA	700	5550	2250	3900	10100
																	KITAKAMI-NISHI	5150	1700	3500	9700
																		AOMORI	4050	7350	13500
																			MORIOKA	4300	10450
																				SENDAI-MIYAGI	7200
																					KAWAGUCHI JCT

JŌBAN • KITA-KANTŌ EXPRESSWAY

SENDAI-MIYAGI	5650	3050	5250	4950	4700	4450	4450	4700	4900	5050	5250	5350	5550	5800	6000	6400	6350	6200	6250	6250	6500	6650	6800	6900	6950	7200	7350	7450	7600
	NIIGATA-CHŪŌ	3600	5750	5450	5200	5000	5000	5200	5450	5550	5750	5900	6100	6300	6500	6950	6850	6750	6800	6750	7000	7150	7300	7450	7450	7700	7900	8000	8150
		KŌRIYAMA	3200	2850	2550	2200	2200	2550	2800	2950	3150	3300	3550	3750	4000	4400	4350	4200	4300	4250	4500	4650	4800	4950	4950	5200	5400	5500	5650
			JŌBAN-TOMIOKA	600	950	1250	1500	1800	2100	2300	2600	2750	3000	3200	3450	3900	3800	3700	3750	3700	4000	4150	4300	4400	4450	4700	4900	5000	5150
				HIRONO	500	850	1050	1400	1700	1900	2150	2350	2650	2900	3150	3550	3500	3350	3450	3400	3650	3800	3950	4100	4150	4400	4600	4700	4850
					IWAKI-YOTSUKURA	500	700	1050	1350	1550	1800	2000	2300	2600	2850	3300	3250	3100	3150	3100	3400	3550	3700	3850	3850	4150	4350	4450	4600
						IWAKI-CHŪŌ	350	700	1000	1200	1500	1650	1950	2250	2550	3050	3000	2850	2900	2850	3150	3300	3450	3600	3600	3900	4100	4200	4350
							IWAKI-YUMOTO	450	800	1000	1250	1450	1750	2050	2350	2900	2800	2650	2750	2700	3000	3150	3300	3400	3450	3700	3900	4050	4200
								IWAKI-NAKOSO	450	650	950	1100	1450	1750	2050	2600	2500	2350	2450	2350	2750	2900	3050	3200	3200	3500	3700	3800	3950
									KITA-IBARAKI	350	650	800	1100	1400	1700	2300	2200	2050	2100	2050	2400	2650	2800	2950	2950	3250	3450	3550	3700
										TAKAHAGI	450	600	950	1250	1550	2100	2000	1850	1950	1850	2250	2450	2650	2800	2850	3100	3300	3400	3550
											HITACHI-KITA	350	650	950	1250	1850	1750	1550	1650	1600	1950	2150	2350	2500	2600	2900	3100	3200	3350
												HITACHI-CHŪŌ	450	750	1050	1650	1550	1400	1450	1400	1800	2000	2200	2350	2400	2750	2950	3100	3250
													HITACHI-MINAMI-ŌTA	450	750	1350	1250	1050	1150	1100	1450	1650	1900	2050	2100	2450	2700	2850	3000
														NAKA	450	1050	950	800	850	800	1150	1400	1600	1750	1800	2150	2400	2550	2750
															MITO	750	650	450	550	500	850	1050	1300	1450	1500	1850	2100	2250	2450
																MITO-MINAMI	250	400	700	650	1000	1250	1450	1600	1650	2000	2250	2400	2600
																	IBARAKI-MACHI-HIGASHI	350	650	550	950	1150	1350	1500	1550	1900	2150	2300	2500
																		IBARAKI-MACHI-NISHI	450	400	750	950	1150	1350	1400	1750	2000	2150	2350
																			TOMOBE	450	850	1050	1250	1400	1450	1800	2100	2200	2400
																				IWAMA	500	750	950	1100	1150	1500	1750	1900	2100
																					CHIYODA-ISHIOKA	350	550	750	800	1150	1400	1550	1750
																						TSUCHIURA-KITA	350	500	600	950	1200	1350	1500
																							SAKURA-TSUCHIURA	300	350	700	1000	1100	1300
																								TSUKUBA-USHIKU	300	650	900	1050	1250
																									YATABE	500	750	900	1100
																										YAWARA	400	550	750
																											KASHIWA	300	500
																												NAGAREYAMA	350
																													MISATO

NAGAOKA																						
1850	NIIGATA-KŪKŌ																					
1650	400	NIIGATA-CHŪŌ																				
1950	750	500	NIITSU																			
2200	1000	750	400	YASUDA																		
2600	1350	1150	800	550	MIKAWA																	
2800	1600	1350	1000	750	350	TSUGAWA																
3200	2150	1950	1550	1300	950	750	NISHI-AIZU															
3450	2450	2250	1850	1600	1250	1050	450	AIZU-BANGE														
3750	2800	2600	2250	2000	1600	1400	850	550	AIZU-WAKAMATSU													
3850	2950	2750	2400	2150	1750	1550	1000	700	300	BANDAI-KAWAHIGASHI												
4100	3200	3050	2750	2500	2150	1950	1350	1050	650	500	INAWASHIRO-BANDAIKŌGEN											
4450	3550	3400	3100	2900	2600	2400	1800	1500	1150	1000	600	BANDAI-ATAMI										
6650	5800	5650	5400	5200	4950	4800	4400	4150	3850	3750	3500	3150	SENDAI-MIYAGI									
4700	3800	3600	3350	3150	2850	2700	2150	1850	1450	1300	950	450	3050	KŌRIYAMA								
8750	7900	7750	7500	7300	7050	6900	6500	6300	6000	5900	5650	5350	7200	5100	KAWAGUCHI JCT							
4750	3850	3700	3400	3250	2950	2800	2250	1950	1550	1400	1050	550	3150	450	5350	KŌRIYAMA-HIGASHI						
4900	4000	3850	3550	3400	3100	2950	2450	2150	1750	1600	1250	750	3300	650	5450	350	FUNEHIKI-MIHARU					
5300	4400	4250	3950	3800	3500	3350	2900	2650	2300	2150	1750	1300	3700	1200	5850	900	700	ONO				
5750	4900	4750	4500	4300	4000	3850	3400	3200	2900	2800	2450	2000	4200	1850	6300	1600	1350	850	IWAKI-MIWA			
6000	5150	5000	4750	4550	4250	4100	3650	3450	3150	3050	2800	2300	4450	2200	6550	1900	1700	1200	500	IWAKI-CHŪŌ		
7550	6650	6500	6250	6100	5800	5700	5250	5050	4800	4700	4400	4050	6000	4000	8100	3750	3600	3200	2700	2550	MITO	
9150	8300	8150	7850	7700	7450	7300	6900	6700	6400	6300	6050	5750	7600	5650	9700	5450	5300	4950	4450	4350	2450	MISATO

BAN-ETSU EXPRESSWAY

URORAN				
DATE				
450	ABUTA-TŌYAKO			
350	550	TOYOURA		
700	1450	1050	OSHAMANBE	
000	1700	1300	450	KUNNUI

CITY NAME INDEX

CITY NAME INDEX

I

CITY NAME INDEX

J

K

CITY NAME INDEX

CITY NAME INDEX

CITY NAME INDEX

CITY NAME INDEX

INDEX

INDEX

INDEX

INDEX

INDEX

INDEX

INDEX

INDEX

M

INDEX

INDEX

N

INDEX

O

INDEX

INDEX

INDEX

INDEX

T

INDEX

U

W

Y

INDEX

INDEX

Z

ROAD ATLAS JAPAN

Art Direction: ATELIER DESKA

SHOBUNSHA
3-1 Koji-machi Chiyoda-Ku
Tokyo 102-8238
Phone: 03-3556-8111

Thirtieth Published Jan. 2005

ISBN4-398-20104-1

1:1,000,000 Japan map, 1:200,000 regional map and 1:50,000 & 1:25,000 topographical map published by Geographical Survey Institute.
(Approval number SOU-SHI No.439 2004)

Printed in Japan

SHOBUNSHA